Mathematical Methods in the Applied Sciences

Mathematical Methods in the Applied Sciences

Editors

Nuno Bastos
Touria Karite
Amir Khan

Basel • Beijing • Wuhan • Barcelona • Belgrade • Novi Sad • Cluj • Manchester

Editors

Nuno Bastos
Polytechnic Institute of Viseu
Viseu
Portugal

Touria Karite
Sidi Mohamed Ben Abdellah University
Fez
Morocco

Amir Khan
Swat University
Khyber Pakhtunkhwa
Pakistan

Editorial Office
MDPI AG
Grosspeteranlage 5
4052 Basel, Switzerland

This is a reprint of articles from the Special Issue published online in the open access journal *Axioms* (ISSN 2075-1680) (available at: https://www.mdpi.com/journal/axioms/special_issues/PQM23H1A3C).

For citation purposes, cite each article independently as indicated on the article page online and as indicated below:

Lastname, A.A.; Lastname, B.B. Article Title. *Journal Name* **Year**, *Volume Number*, Page Range.

ISBN 978-3-7258-1467-1 (Hbk)
ISBN 978-3-7258-1468-8 (PDF)
doi.org/10.3390/books978-3-7258-1468-8

© 2024 by the authors. Articles in this book are Open Access and distributed under the Creative Commons Attribution (CC BY) license. The book as a whole is distributed by MDPI under the terms and conditions of the Creative Commons Attribution-NonCommercial-NoDerivs (CC BY-NC-ND) license.

Contents

About the Editors vii

Preface ix

Nuno R. O. Bastos and Touria Karite
Mathematical Methods in Applied Sciences
Reprinted from: *Axioms* **2024**, *13*, 327, doi:10.3390/axioms13050327 1

Abida Hussain, Ibrahima Faye, Mohana Sundaram Muthuvalu, Tong Boon Tang and Mudasar Zafar
Advancements in Numerical Methods for Forward and Inverse Problems in Functional near Infra-Red Spectroscopy: A Review
Reprinted from: *Axioms* **2023**, *12*, 326, doi:10.3390/axioms12040326 6

Miguel S. Concha-Aracena, Leonardo Barrios-Blanco, David Elal-Olivero, Paulo Henrique Ferreira da Silva and Diego Carvalho do Nascimento
Extending Normality: A Case of Unit Distribution Generated from the Moments of the Standard Normal Distribution
Reprinted from: *Axioms* **2022**, *11*, 666, doi:10.3390/axioms11120666 28

Sajjad Pakzad, Siamak Pedrammehr and Mahsa Hejazian
A Study on the Beech Wood Machining Parameters Optimization Using Response Surface Methodology
Reprinted from: *Axioms* **2023**, *12*, 39, doi:10.3390/axioms12010039 46

D. Karaoulanis, A. K. Lazopoulos, N. Lazopoulou and K. Lazopoulos
On Λ-Fractional Derivative and Human Neural Network
Reprinted from: *Axioms* **2023**, *12*, 136, doi:10.3390/axioms12020136 58

Adelaide Freitas, Helena Sofia Rodrigues, Natália Martins, Adela Iutis, Michael A. Robert, Demian Herrera and Manuel Colomé-Hidalgo
Multiplicative Mixed-Effects Modelling of Dengue Incidence: An Analysis of the 2019 Outbreak in the Dominican Republic
Reprinted from: *Axioms* **2023**, *12*, 150, doi:10.3390/axioms12020150 68

Luyang Han, Yongjun He, Bolin Liao and Cheng Hua
An Accelerated Double-Integral ZNN with Resisting Linear Noise for Dynamic Sylvester Equation Solving and Its Application to the Control of the SFM Chaotic System
Reprinted from: *Axioms* **2023**, *12*, 287, doi:10.3390/axioms12030287 90

Arturo J. Fernández
Tolerance Limits and Sample-Size Determination Using Weibull Trimmed Data
Reprinted from: *Axioms* **2023**, *12*, 351, doi:10.3390/axioms12040351 108

Refah Alotaibi, Mazen Nassar and Ahmed Elshahhat
Reliability Estimation under Normal Operating Conditions for Progressively Type-II XLindley Censored Data
Reprinted from: *Axioms* **2023**, *12*, 352, doi:10.3390/axioms12040352 124

Ali Fareed Jameel, Dulfikar Jawad Hashim, Nidal Anakira, Osama Ababneh, Ahmad Qazza, Abedel-Karrem Alomari and Khamis S. Al Kalbani
Application of the Optimal Homotopy Asymptotic Approach for Solving Two-Point Fuzzy Ordinary Differential Equations of Fractional Order Arising in Physics
Reprinted from: *Axioms* **2023**, *12*, 387, doi:10.3390/axioms12040387 147

Fahad Al Basir, Jahangir Chowdhury and Delfim F. M. Torres
Dynamics of a Double-Impulsive Control Model of Integrated Pest Management Using Perturbation Methods and Floquet Theory
Reprinted from: *Axioms* 2023, 12, 391, doi:10.3390/axioms12040391 165

Gurpreet Singh, Inderdeep Singh, Afrah M. AlDerea, Agaeb Mahal Alanzi and Hamiden Abd El-Wahed Khalifa
Solutions of (2+1)-D & (3+1)-D Burgers Equations by New Laplace Variational Iteration Technique
Reprinted from: *Axioms* 2023, 12, 647, doi:10.3390/axioms12070647 179

Liang-Ching Chen and Kuei-Hu Chang
An Extended AHP-Based Corpus Assessment Approach for Handling Keyword Ranking of NLP: An Example of COVID-19 Corpus Data
Reprinted from: *Axioms* 2023, 12, 740, doi:10.3390/axioms12080740 192

Hassan S. Bakouch, Christophe Chesneau, Radhakumari Maya, Muhammed Rasheed Irshad, Sreedeviamma Aswathy and Najla Qarmalah
A Flexible Dispersed Count Model Based on Bernoulli Poisson–Lindley Convolution and Its Regression Model
Reprinted from: *Axioms* 2023, 12, 813, doi:10.3390/axioms12090813 207

Xue Hu and Haiping Ren
Reliability Estimation of Inverse Weibull Distribution Based on Intuitionistic Fuzzy Lifetime Data
Reprinted from: *Axioms* 2023, 12, 838, doi:10.3390/axioms12090838 227

Mohamed A. Zaitri, Cristiana J. Silva and Delfim F. M. Torres
An Analytic Method to Determine the Optimal Time for the Induction Phase of Anesthesia
Reprinted from: *Axioms* 2023, 12, 867, doi:10.3390/axioms12090867 244

Khalaf S. Sultan and Nashmiah R. AL-Shamari
Some Axioms and Identities of L-Moments from Logistic Distribution with Generalizations
Reprinted from: *Axioms* 2023, 12, 928, doi:10.3390/axioms12100928 259

Ammar Khanfer, Lazhar Bougoffa and Smail Bougouffa
A Nonclassical Stefan Problem with Nonlinear Thermal Parameters of General Order and Heat Source Term
Reprinted from: *Axioms* 2024, 13, 14, doi:10.3390/axioms13010014 281

About the Editors

Nuno Bastos

Nuno Bastos is Adjunct Professor at the Polytechnic Institute of Viseu, where he teaches mathematics and informatics to undergraduate students and is also an integrated member of the Research Unit CIDMA (Center for Research & Development in Mathematics and Applications) held at the University of Aveiro. He holds a PhD in Mathematics (2012) from the University of Aveiro. His research interests include fractional calculus, variational calculus, mathematical education, educational technology, and the popularization of mathematics. He has attended and presented his research outcomes at several international conferences. In 2015, he received the EURASIP Best Paper Award for the Signal Processing journal at the "EUSIPCO 2015: 23rd European Signal Processing Conference" for his joint work with Delfim F.M.Torres and Rui A.C.Ferreira, entitled "Discrete-time fractional variational problems".

Touria Karite

Touria Karite is an Associate Professor of Applied Mathematics at the National School of Applied Sciences of Fez, Sidi Mohamed Ben Abdellah University. She holds a Habilitation to conduct research from Sidi Mohamed Ben Abdellah University (2022). She is a member of the Engineering, Systems and Applications Laboratory, and the Department of Applied Mathematics Engineering. She holds a Master's degree in Theoretical Systems and Informatics (2014) and a PhD in Optimization and Optimal Control (2018) from the Faculty of Sciences of Meknes, Moulay Ismail University. Her research interests include optimization, optimal control, fractional calculus, bio-mathematics, automation, and machine learning.

Amir Khan

Amir Khan is an assistant professor of Applied Mathematics at the University of Swat, Pakistan. Amir Khan's academic journey indeed showcases a commendable evolution. Starting with his M.Phil thesis on the "Study of Jordan Loops" from Quaid-i-Azam University, Islamabad, in 2010, he laid the foundation in theoretical mathematics. His subsequent pursuit of a Ph.D. with a focus on "Fractional Order Generalized Fluid Flow Models: An Analytical Approach" from the University of Malakand in 2016 signifies a shift towards the practical applications of mathematics, particularly in the realm of fluid dynamics. His post-doctoral research at King Mongkut's University, Bangkok, on the "Mathematical Modeling of Epidemic Diseases: Stochastic and Deterministic Approaches" in 2022 reflects his deepening involvement in addressing real-world challenges, especially in the critical domain of epidemiology.

Preface

We are pleased to present the "Mathematical Methods in Applied Sciences" Special Issue of Axioms, which includes 17 meticulously selected articles and an editorial. This collection explores a wide range of topics in applied mathematics, encompassing both pure mathematical methods and their applications across various scientific disciplines.

The articles featured in this Special Issue cover several pivotal fields, including mathematical methods and analysis, statistical methods, natural language processing, neural networks, numerical methods, and fuzzy systems. Each contribution offers unique insights and advancements, reflecting the dynamic and interdisciplinary nature of contemporary mathematical research.

The primary objective of this Special Issue is to provide a platform for scholars to publish their recent work, enabling them to delve deeper into a variety of complex problems and propose innovative solutions through mathematical approaches. By bringing together diverse perspectives and cutting-edge research, we aim to enhance our collective understanding of these critical areas and stimulate further developments in applied mathematics.

We extend our gratitude to the authors for their exceptional contributions and to the reviewers for their diligent efforts in ensuring the high quality of this Special Issue. We hope that readers will find these articles both informative and inspiring and that they will serve as a valuable resource for researchers and practitioners alike, sparking new ideas and collaborations in the field of applied mathematics.

Nuno Bastos, Touria Karite, and Amir Khan
Editors

Editorial

Mathematical Methods in Applied Sciences

Nuno R. O. Bastos [1,2,*] and Touria Karite [3]

1 School of Technology and Management of Viseu, Polytechnic Institute of Viseu, Campus Politécnico, 3504-510 Viseu, Portugal
2 Center for Research and Development in Mathematics and Applications, Department of Mathematics, University of Aveiro, 3810-193 Aveiro, Portugal
3 National School of Applied Sciences, Sidi Mohamed Ben Abdellah University, Avenue My Abdallah Km 5 Route d'Imouzzer, Fez BP 72, Morocco; touria.karite@usmba.ac.ma
* Correspondence: nbastos@estgv.ipv.pt

1. Introduction

In this editorial, we introduce "Mathematical Methods in Applied Sciences", a Special Issue of *Axioms* comprising 17 articles. These articles delve into various mathematical methods and emerging trends in applied sciences, spanning from theoretical explorations to practical applications. While covering diverse topics, particular emphasis is placed on fields such as mathematical methods and analysis, statistical modeling, natural language processing, neural networks, inverse problems, numerical methods, and fuzzy systems. The primary objective of this Special Issue is to provide a platform for scientists and researchers to showcase their work in optimization, optimal control theory, biomathematical studies, population dynamics, network problems, and reinforcement learning, as well as machine learning and deep learning, thereby enhancing our understanding of the world.

2. Overview of the Published Papers

This Special Issue contains 17 papers that were accepted for publication after a rigorous review process.

In contribution 1, A. Khanfar et al. present an analytic solution to the Stefan problem, a mathematical model describing the phase change of a material with a moving boundary, considering nonlinear temperature-dependent thermal parameters and a heat source term. The authors establish the existence and uniqueness of the solution in scenarios both with and without a heat source. They then determine lower and upper bounds for solutions of the problem under different conditions. Remarkably, the lower bounds closely align with numerical solutions, suggesting their utility as approximate analytic solutions.

In contribution 2, K. S. Sultan et al. present the derivation of L-moments for several distributions, including logistic, generalized logistic, doubly truncated logistic, and doubly truncated generalized logistic distributions. They introduce new axioms and identities, including recurrence relations specific to L-moments derived from these distributions. They also establish general recurrence relations applicable to L-moments derived from any distribution.

In contribution 3, M. A. Zaitri et al. introduce an analytical solution for the time-optimal control problem during the induction phase of anesthesia, aligning closely with results obtained via the shooting method. The authors employ a pharmacokinetic/pharmacodynamic (PK/PD) model for propofol infusion, proposed by Bailey and Haddad in 2005. The study evaluates this solution by comparing it with the existing literature using the Pontryagin minimum principle and numerical simulations in MATLAB. The results indicate a similarity between the newly proposed analytical method and the shooting method, with the advantage of the former being independence from unknown initial conditions for the adjoint variables.

In contribution 4, X. Hu and H. Ren address reliability estimation using the inverse Weibull distribution with intuitionistic fuzzy lifetime data. They extend fuzzy set theory concepts to derive intuitionistic fuzzy conditional density, likelihood function, and conditional expectation. Both maximum likelihood and Bayesian estimations, employing the EM algorithm and gamma priors, respectively, are explored. Monte Carlo simulations favor Bayesian estimation, validated by real data, offering precise reliability estimates for intuitionistic fuzzy lifetime data in scientific analysis.

In contribution 5, H. S. Bakouch et al. explore count data analysis using the two-parameter Bernoulli–Poisson–Lindley distribution, obtained through convolution of Bernoulli and Poisson–Lindley distributions. Statistical properties such as moments, survival functions, and parameter inference via maximum likelihood are investigated. Simulation exercises assess estimation effectiveness, followed by application to real datasets. Additionally, a flexible count data regression model is constructed based on the proposed distribution, illustrated with practical examples.

In contribution 6, L. C. Chen and K. H. Chang introduce a corpus assessment method crucial for Natural Language Processing (NLP), especially pertinent in contexts like COVID-19 information retrieval. Traditional approaches based on single parameters, such as keyness value, are deemed inadequate. To address this limitation, the authors propose an extended Analytic Hierarchy Process (AHP)-based approach, considering multiple parameters (keyness, frequency, and range) simultaneously. Empirical validation using COVID-19 research articles confirms the effectiveness of this approach, offering improvements in refining corpus data, multi-parameter consideration, and integration of expert evaluation.

In contribution 7, G. Singh et al. propose a new Laplace variational iterative method for solving (2+1)-D and (3+1)-D Burgers equations, employing a combination of modified variational iteration method and Laplace transform. This method transforms the differential problem into algebraic equations via Laplace transform, and iteratively solves them using the modified variational iterative approach. The technique enables both numerical and analytical solutions for the Burgers equations, validated through three specific examples, demonstrating its effectiveness.

In contribution 8, F. Al Basir et al. devise an integrated pest management model for crop pest control, utilizing periodic application of biopesticide and chemical pesticides. Theoretical analysis yields a periodic solution for pest eradication, ensuring boundedness of system variables. Optimization aims to find the most effective pesticide concentration and application frequency. Employing Floquet theory and small amplitude perturbation method, the study establishes local and global stability of pest eradication periodic solution. Numerical comparisons validate integrated pest management's superiority over single controls, with analytical results illustrated through simulations.

In contribution 9, A. F. Jameel et al. propose a novel approach to solve and analyze two-point fuzzy boundary value problems in fractional ordinary differential equations (FFOBVPs). FFOBVPs describe complex phenomena with uncertainty, making exact or close analytical solutions challenging, particularly for nonlinear problems. The study extends the optimal homotopy asymptotic method (OHAM) to handle FFOBVPs, incorporating fuzzy sets theory and fractional calculus principles. Fuzzification and defuzzification transform fuzzy problems into solvable crisp ones. The method's efficiency and accuracy are demonstrated through solving and analyzing linear and nonlinear FFOBVPs at various fractional derivatives, showcasing its viability for fuzzy analysis.

In contribution 10, R. Alotaibi et al. investigate constant-stress accelerated life tests with test units following the XLindley distribution, employing maximum likelihood and Bayesian estimation methods based on progressively Type-II censored samples. They derive point and interval estimations of model parameters and reliability indices under normal operating conditions. Bayesian estimates are calculated using the Markov chain Monte Carlo algorithm with the squared error loss function. A performance simulation illustrates the proposed methodology, with application to two real-life accelerated life test cases. Numerical outcomes suggest the superiority of the Bayesian estimation method, particularly in evaluating XLindley parameters and reliability measures, under constant-stress accelerated life tests with progressively Type-II censoring.

In contribution 11, A. J. Fernández presents guaranteed-coverage and expected-coverage tolerance limits for Weibull models, addressing situations where extreme sample values are censored or disregarded due to data collection restrictions or outliers. Both unconditional and conditional tolerance bounds are discussed, particularly when the smallest observations are discarded. The paper also explores determining the minimum sample sizes for setting Weibull tolerance limits from trimmed data with fixed numbers or proportions of trimmed observations. Step-by-step procedures for optimal sampling plans are outlined, with numerical examples provided for illustration.

In contribution 12, L. Han et al. address the challenge of solving the dynamic Sylvester equation (DSE) in noisy environments using neural networks. While the original zeroing neural network (OZNN) performs well in noise-free settings, it struggles in noisy conditions. An integral-enhanced zeroing neural network (IEZNN) improves noise handling, but lacks speed. To overcome these limitations, an accelerated double-integral zeroing neural network (ADIZNN) is proposed, designed to resist linear noise and accelerate convergence. Theoretical proofs confirm the convergence and robustness of the ADIZNN, while simulation experiments demonstrate its superior convergence rate and noise resistance compared to OZNN and IEZNN. Additionally, chaos control experiments with a sine function memristor chaotic system highlight the ADIZNN's superior performance in terms of accuracy and error reduction.

In contribution 13, A. Freitas et al. investigate the relationship between meteorological variables and dengue transmission during the 2019 outbreak in the Dominican Republic. Using generalized linear mixed modeling, they analyze weekly dengue incidence rates, finding that temperature and rainfall impact outbreaks with a delay of 2–5 weeks, conducive to mosquito breeding conditions. The study employs a backward-type selection method to identify influential variables, noting variations in lag correlations across provinces. These findings provide critical insights for healthcare authorities to prepare and manage dengue outbreaks effectively.

In contribution 14, D. Karaoulanis et al. highlight the significance of fractional derivatives in modeling anomalous diffusion in brain tissue, linked to diseases like Alzheimer's, multiple sclerosis, and Parkinson's. The accumulation of proteins in axons and discrete swellings contribute to neurodiseases. To model voltage propagation in axons, a fractional cable geometry is adopted, although the absence of a fractional differential geometry based on well-known fractional derivatives poses questions. The Λ-fractional derivative (Λ-FD) is introduced as the unique fractional derivative generating differential geometry for modeling the human neural system's intricate parts. Examples are provided to draw meaningful conclusions, aiding medical and bioengineering scientists in combating brain diseases.

In contribution 15, S. Pakzad et al. emphasize the significance of surface quality in wooden product manufacturing, necessitating a comprehensive understanding of cutting parameters' impacts on wood. Response surface methodology is employed to design experiments and analyze the effects of feed rate, spindle speed, step over, and depth of cut on beech wood surface quality. Mathematical models are derived for the parameters and surface roughness. Optimal machining parameters are determined to enhance surface quality, reducing roughness by up to 4.2 μm. Notably, the feed rate exhibits the most significant impact on surface quality among the machining parameters.

In contribution 16, M. S. Concha-Aracena et al. introduce a theorem demonstrating the generation of density functions from moments of the standard normal distribution, leading to a family of models. Different random variable domains are achieved through transformations, exemplified by transforming the second-order moment to create the Alpha-Unit (AU) distribution, characterized by a single parameter α (AU(α)$\in$[0, 1]). Properties of the AU distribution are presented, along with estimation methods for the α parameter. Monte Carlo simulations confirm the statistical consistency and robustness of the estimators. Real-world applications demonstrate the competitiveness of the AU model, especially for data with a range greater than 0.4 and extremely heavy asymmetric tail, compared to other commonly used unit models.

In contribution 17, A. Hussain et al. delve into biomedical image reconstruction, particularly focusing on functional near infra-red spectroscopy (fNIRs), a non-invasive imaging technology using near infra-red light. Image reconstruction involves solving both forward and backward problems to deduce the image's optical properties from measured boundary data. Researchers employ various numerical methods to tackle these challenges. This study highlights the latest advancements in numerical methods for solving forward and backward problems in fNIRs, offering insights into physical interpretations, state-of-the-art numerical techniques, and toolbox descriptions. A comprehensive discussion on numerical solution approaches for the inverse problem in fNIRs is provided, shedding light on this evolving field.

Funding: This work was supported by CIDMA (Center for Research and Development in Mathematics and Applications) and is funded by the Fundação para a Ciência e a Tecnologia, I.P. (FCT, Funder ID = 50110000187) under Grants https://doi.org/10.54499/UIDB/04106/2020 and https://doi.org/10.54499/UIDP/04106/2020.

Acknowledgments: The authors deeply thank Axioms (ISSN 2075-1680) and the Section Managing Editor, for all the support given to the Special Issue "Mathematical Methods in the Applied Sciences". The authors of this editorial are also deeply grateful to all authors for submitting high-quality articles to this Special Issue.

Conflicts of Interest: The authors declare no conflict of interest.

List of Contributions

1. Khanfer, A.; Bougoffa, L.; Bougouffa, S. A Nonclassical Stefan Problem with Nonlinear Thermal Parameters of General Order and Heat Source Term. *Axioms* **2024**, *13*, 14. https://doi.org/10.3390/axioms13010014.
2. Sultan, K.S.; AL-Shamari, N.R. Some Axioms and Identities of L-Moments from Logistic Distribution with Generalizations. *Axioms* **2023**, *12*, 928. https://doi.org/10.3390/axioms12100928.
3. Zaitri, M.A.; Silva, C.J.; Torres, D.F.M. An Analytic Method to Determine the Optimal Time for the Induction Phase of Anesthesia. *Axioms* **2023**, *12*, 867. https://doi.org/10.3390/axioms12090867.
4. Hu, X.; Ren, H. Reliability Estimation of Inverse Weibull Distribution Based on Intuitionistic Fuzzy Lifetime Data. *Axioms* **2023**, *12*, 838. https://doi.org/10.3390/axioms12090838.
5. Bakouch, H.S.; Chesneau, C.; Maya, R.; Irshad, M.R.; Aswathy, S.; Qarmalah, N. A Flexible Dispersed Count Model Based on Bernoulli Poisson–Lindley Convolution and Its Regression Model. *Axioms* **2023**, *12*, 813. https://doi.org/10.3390/axioms12090813.
6. Chen, L.-C.; Chang, K.-H. An Extended AHP-Based Corpus Assessment Approach for Handling Keyword Ranking of NLP: An Example of COVID-19 Corpus Data. *Axioms* **2023**, *12*, 740. https://doi.org/10.3390/axioms12080740.
7. Singh, G.; Singh, I.; AlDerea, A.M.; Alanzi, A.M.; Khalifa, H.A.E.-W. Solutions of (2+1)-D & (3+1)-D Burgers Equations by New Laplace Variational Iteration Technique. *Axioms* **2023**, *12*, 647. https://doi.org/10.3390/axioms12070647.
8. Al Basir, F.; Chowdhury, J.; Torres, D.F.M. Dynamics of a Double-Impulsive Control Model of Integrated Pest Management Using Perturbation Methods and Floquet Theory. *Axioms* **2023**, *12*, 391. https://doi.org/10.3390/axioms12040391.
9. Jameel, A.F.; Jawad Hashim, D.; Anakira, N.; Ababneh, O.; Qazza, A.; Alomari, A.-K.; Al Kalbani, K.S. Application of the Optimal Homotopy Asymptotic Approach for Solving Two-Point Fuzzy Ordinary Differential Equations of Fractional Order Arising in Physics. *Axioms* **2023**, *12*, 387. https://doi.org/10.3390/axioms12040387.

10. Alotaibi, R.; Nassar, M.; Elshahhat, A. Reliability Estimation under Normal Operating Conditions for Progressively Type-II XLindley Censored Data. *Axioms* **2023**, *12*, 352. https://doi.org/10.3390/axioms12040352.
11. Fernández, A.J. Tolerance Limits and Sample-Size Determination Using Weibull Trimmed Data. *Axioms* **2023**, *12*, 351. https://doi.org/10.3390/axioms12040351.
12. Han, L.; He, Y.; Liao, B.; Hua, C. An Accelerated Double-Integral ZNN with Resisting Linear Noise for Dynamic Sylvester Equation Solving and Its Application to the Control of the SFM Chaotic System. *Axioms* **2023**, *12*, 287. https://doi.org/10.3390/axioms12030287.
13. Freitas, A.; Rodrigues, H.S.; Martins, N.; Iutis, A.; Robert, M.A.; Herrera, D.; Colomé-Hidalgo, M. Multiplicative Mixed-Effects Modelling of Dengue Incidence: An Analysis of the 2019 Outbreak in the Dominican Republic. *Axioms* **2023**, *12*, 150. https://doi.org/10.3390/axioms12020150.
14. Karaoulanis, D.; Lazopoulos, A.K.; Lazopoulou, N.; Lazopoulos, K. On Λ-Fractional Derivative and Human Neural Network. *Axioms* **2023**, *12*, 136. https://doi.org/10.3390/axioms12020136.
15. Pakzad, S.; Pedrammehr, S.; Hejazian, M. A Study on the Beech Wood Machining Parameters Optimization Using Response Surface Methodology. *Axioms* **2023**, *12*, 39. https://doi.org/10.3390/axioms12010039.
16. Concha-Aracena, M.S.; Barrios-Blanco, L.; Elal-Olivero, D.; Ferreira da Silva, P.H.; Nascimento, D.C.d. Extending Normality: A Case of Unit Distribution Generated from the Moments of the Standard Normal Distribution. *Axioms* **2022**, *11*, 666. https://doi.org/10.3390/axioms11120666.
17. Hussain, A.; Faye, I.; Muthuvalu, M.S.; Tang, T.B.; Zafar, M. Advancements in Numerical Methods for Forward and Inverse Problems in Functional near Infra-Red Spectroscopy:
A Review. *Axioms* **2023**, *12*, 326. https://doi.org/10.3390/axioms12040326.

Disclaimer/Publisher's Note: The statements, opinions and data contained in all publications are solely those of the individual author(s) and contributor(s) and not of MDPI and/or the editor(s). MDPI and/or the editor(s) disclaim responsibility for any injury to people or property resulting from any ideas, methods, instructions or products referred to in the content.

Review

Advancements in Numerical Methods for Forward and Inverse Problems in Functional near Infra-Red Spectroscopy: A Review

Abida Hussain [1,2], Ibrahima Faye [1,2,*], Mohana Sundaram Muthuvalu [1], Tong Boon Tang [2] and Mudasar Zafar [1,3]

1. Department of Fundamental and Applied Sciences, Universiti Teknologi PETRONAS, Seri Iskandar 32610, Perak, Malaysia
2. Centre for Intelligent Signal and Imaging Research, Department of Electrical and Electronic Engineering, Universiti Teknologi PETRONAS, Seri Iskandar 32610, Perak, Malaysia
3. Centre of Research in Enhanced Oil Recovery, Universiti Teknologi PETRONAS, Seri Iskandar 32610, Perak, Malaysia
* Correspondence: ibrahima_faye@utp.edu.my

Abstract: In the field of biomedical image reconstruction, functional near infra-red spectroscopy (fNIRs) is a promising technology that uses near infra-red light for non-invasive imaging and reconstruction. Reconstructing an image requires both forward and backward problem-solving in order to figure out what the image's optical properties are from the boundary data that has been measured. Researchers are using a variety of numerical methods to solve both the forward and backward problems in depth. This study will show the latest improvements in numerical methods for solving forward and backward problems in fNIRs. The physical interpretation of the forward problem is described, followed by the explanation of the state-of-the-art numerical methods and the description of the toolboxes. A more in-depth discussion of the numerical solution approaches for the inverse problem for fNIRs is also provided.

Keywords: image reconstruction; functional near infra-red spectroscopy; forward problem; inverse problem; numerical methods

MSC: 81-10; 65L03

1. Introduction

Neuroscientists have proposed several imaging modalities to comprehend and study the anatomical and functional aspects of the human brain. Magnetic resonance imaging (MRI), computerized tomography (CT), magnetoencephalography (MEG), electroencephalography (EEG), functional magnetic resonance imaging (fMRI), and Fourier-domain near-infrared spectroscopy (fNIRs) are some of the most well-known imaging methods. fNIRs is a relatively recent non-invasive neuroimaging technology that uses near infrared light with frequency ranges between 650 and 900 nanometers to evaluate the optical characteristics of the brain tissues. In the near-infrared part of the electromagnetic spectrum, the most important optical absorbers are the oxygenated (HbO) and deoxygenated (HbR) hemoglobin's found in brain tissue.

The location of the source and detector, as well as the equipment used, affect NIR light measurements. In the context of source or detector probes, the measurement of NIR light is regarded as a measurement of transmission or reflectance. It is possible to measure the transmission by positioning the source and detector in the opposite direction if the NIR light is bright enough. However, only biological tissues like hands and arms can be used with this technique. The source and detector probes are typically arranged on the same side of the measuring instrument when measuring reflectance. Currently, three techniques can

be used to simulate how light moves through tissue: time-domain (TD), frequency-domain (FD), and continuous wave (CW) (Figure 1) [1–5].

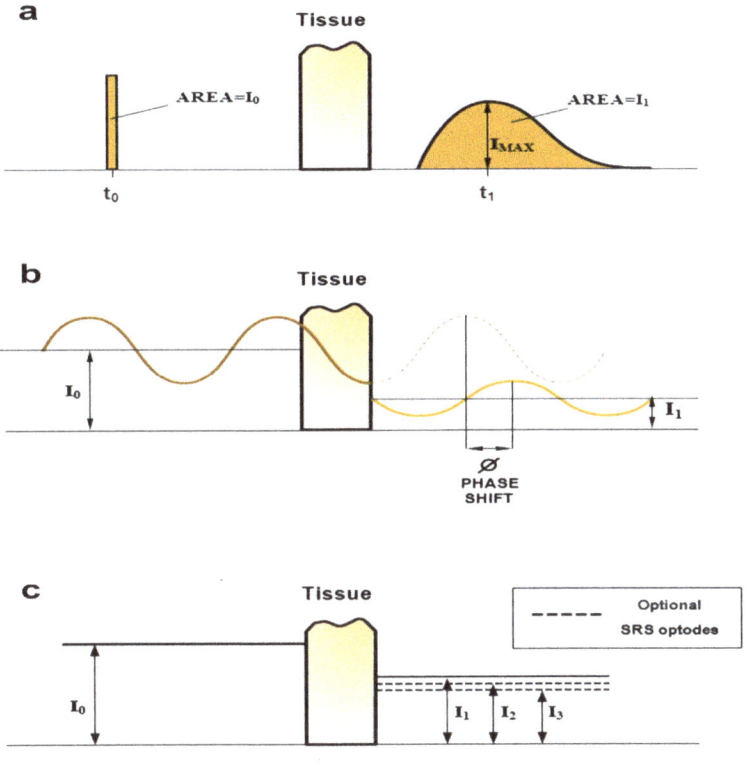

Figure 1. Visual representation of the case (**c**) continuous wave, case (**b**) frequency domain, and case (**a**) (adapted from Ref. [6]).

TD systems illuminate tissues with incredibly brief light pulses, which are widened and attenuated as they travel through the tissue. Detectors in time-resolved devices capture the temporal distribution of photons as they leave the tissue. The optical properties of the tissue can be figured out by looking at the shape and size of this distribution [3]. In FD systems, the light that comes in is changed in amplitude at a frequency between tens and hundreds of megahertz. Both the change in amplitude and the change in phase with respect to the signal that came in are measured. By using both data formats, it is possible to get unique information about the optical properties of tissues, such as the absorption and scattering coefficients [4]. The simplest and least expensive approach is CW mode. It makes use of a light source that is modulated at a frequency lower than a few tens of hertz or one that has a constant amplitude. It only examines the light's amplitude attenuation after it has contacted biological tissues. Therefore, attenuation effects due to light scattering and absorption cannot be separated. It, however, has the highest signal-to-noise ratio. The most common modality is this one [5].

In fNIRs, the scalp is covered with an Optode montage, a spatially distributed arrangement of sources and detectors that emit and detect near-infrared light. The HbO and HbR hemoglobin found in brain tissue are the two most prominent optical absorbers in the near-infrared range of the electromagnetic spectrum, respectively. The result of this conversion is that variations in hemoglobin concentration ([HbO] and [HbR]) at a single location can be derived from differences in optical density (OD) detected at two or more wavelengths. It is common practice to use a modified version of the Beer-Lambert Law (mBLL) when calculating these changes.

Mathematically, the procedure of image reconstruction entails reconstructing the optical properties using the experimentally measured boundary data and can be thought of as consisting of two parts: developing a forward model of light propagation and obtaining an inverse solution to the forward problem (Figure 2). The forward problem tries to estimate the boundary data at the position of the detector based on the distribution of the optical properties inside the object. This means making an estimate of the sensitivity matrix as absorption changes at each location in the head or trying to predict the optical flux density at the detectors based on a geometric model with optical parameters like source-detector location and functionality. The inverse problem is based on the same general equation as the forward problem. However, the goal is to dissect the vector of intracranial phenomena that can explain the vector of observed scalp values, given a specific sensitivity matrix.

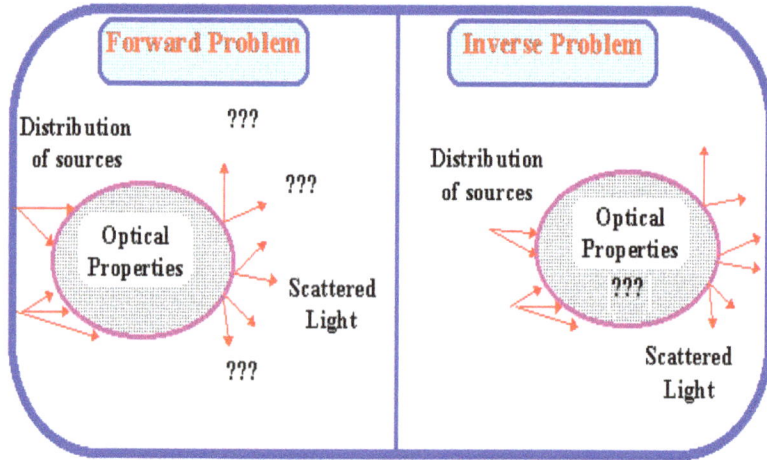

Figure 2. A graphical representation of the forward and inverse problems (adapted from Ref. [7]).

This review is being done to learn more about the basic ideas behind the forward and inverse problems in fNIRs. For researchers who are new to the subject, it is designed to provide insight into the most up-to-date methods for tackling the problem and the types of toolboxes currently being used. It is also meant to give the reader a good idea of the best ways to solve the inverse problem in fNIRs so that the reader can understand these methods thoroughly.

The following is the flow of the paper; it begins with the fundamental concepts of modeling light transport through biological tissue as a forward problem, which are discussed in detail. The available methods and toolboxes that were applied to simulate the forward problem were thoroughly investigated. The review also includes an in-depth discussion of the inverse problem and a detailed explanation of various available image reconstruction methods. Aside from that, the paper offers a comparison of several algorithms as well as conclusions and recommendations.

2. Mathematical Modeling of Light Transport in Biological Tissue as Forward Problem

The radiative transport equation (RTE), which is based on the idea that energy stays the same as light moves through a volume element of a medium with an absorber and scattered light, accurately describes how light moves through biological tissue. The RTE in the TD is expressed as [8,9],

$$\left\{ \frac{\partial}{c(r)\partial t} + \Omega \cdot V + \mu_a(r) + \mu(r) \right\} I(r,\Omega,t) = \mu_s(r) \int_{4\pi} d\hat{\Omega} P(r,\Omega \cdot \hat{\Omega}) I(r,\Omega,t) + q(r,\Omega,t) \qquad (1)$$

here $I(r,\Omega,t)$ described as the energy radiance or light intensity as a function of position $r(x,y,z)$, Ω is defined as angular direction with zenith and azimuth angles, and time t. The absorption and scattering coefficients are represented by $\mu_a(r)$ and $\mu_s(r)$, respectively. The velocity of light in a turbid medium is denoted by $c(r)$, and the light source is denoted by $q(r, \Omega, t)$. Moreover, $P(r, \Omega \cdot \hat{\Omega})$ is the scattering phase function, which determines the probability that a photon travelling in a direction $\hat{\Omega}$ will be scattered in that direction Ω during a scattering event. And P is normalised to the value of 1.

$$\int_{4\pi} d\hat{\Omega} P(r, \Omega \cdot \hat{\Omega}) = \int_{-1}^{1} P(\cos\theta) d\cos\theta = 1 \qquad (2)$$

As the sprinkling phase function, the Henyey–Greenstein function is widely used as follows:

$$P(r, \Omega \cdot \hat{\Omega}) = \frac{1}{4\pi} \frac{1 - g(r)^2}{\left\{1 + g(r)^2 - 2g\Omega \cdot \hat{\Omega}\right\}^{\frac{3}{2}}} \qquad (3)$$

where $g(r)$ denotes the anisotropy factor, which ranges from -1 (full backscattering) to $+1$ (full forward scattering) and anything between 0 (isotropic scattering).

A numerical solution to the RTE is challenging since it is an integrodifferential equation, and the computational complexity for numerical solutions is exceedingly high. On the other hand, the diffusion equation (DE) assumes that radiance in a medium that is optically thick and has multiple scattering is almost entirely isotropic. The DE can be calculated using the diffusion approximation to the RTE. The following equation shows the TD and DE:

$$\frac{\partial}{c(r)\partial t} \Phi(r,t) - \nabla \cdot \kappa(r) \nabla \Phi(r,t) + \mu_a(r)\Phi(r,t) = q(r,t) \qquad (4)$$

where $\Phi(r,t)$ denotes the fluence rate as estimated by $\int_{4\pi} d\Omega I(r, \Omega, t)$, $\kappa(r)$ is denoted as diffusion coefficient as determined by $1/3(\mu_a(r) + (1-g)\mu_s(r))$, and $q(r,t)$ signifies the light source as calculated by $\int_{4\pi} d\Omega q(r, \Omega, t)$ and the reduced scattering coefficient is defined as $(1-g)\mu_s = \mu'_s$.

Similarly, RTE in terms of FD and CW is given as follow [10]:

$$\frac{\partial}{c(r)\partial t} \Phi(r,\omega) - \nabla \cdot \kappa(r) \nabla \Phi(r,\omega) + \mu_a(r)\Phi(r,\omega) = q(r,\omega) \qquad (5)$$

The fluence rate with modulated frequency ω from the light source $q(r,\omega)$ in a medium at the same frequency is denoted by $\Phi(r,\omega)$. In an FD, the frequency $\omega \neq 0$, whereas in a CW instrument, the frequency is equal to zero. In the fNIRs context, the DA equation is generally nonlinear, so it can be linearized as given in [11] and then used to perform the Rytov approximation [12]. When performing functional brain imaging, the absorption coefficient is assumed to be proportional to hemoglobin change, whereas the scattering coefficient is supposed to be constant. So, under these assumptions, the Rytov approximation can be formulated as [13]

$$y = Ax \qquad (6)$$

where A denotes the sensitivity matrix as determined by the absorption proportion within the brain, y is the difference in log-ratio between the optical density recorded before and after blood flow, x denotes the change in absorption coefficient.

3. Methods for Forward Model Simulation

The methods used to solve the forward problem are discussed in this section. The forward problem, in general, considers the modeling of light propagation from sources to sensors across the head. The solutions to this problem can be divided into three categories. (i) Analytical techniques (ii) Numerical techniques (iii) Stochastic techniques.

3.1. Analytical Methods

The term "Green's function approach" generally refers to the analytical method. The solution can be visualized using Green's function, which is defined as follows when the source is represented as a spatial and temporal delta function: First and foremost, one must ascertain their own GI functions. Following that, Green's functions can be used to create more general solutions. In homogeneous media, the convolution of these Green's functions with the source term yields the full fluence rate solution, which is simple to compute.

Equation gives the most basic analytical solution for TD-DE for an infinitely homogeneous medium [14],

$$\phi(r,t) = \frac{c}{(4\pi Dct)^{\frac{3}{2}}} exp\left(-\frac{r^2}{4Dct} - \mu_a ct\right) \tag{7}$$

where r is the distance from the origin to a point impulse source. The authors [15] first used the mirror image source method to find analytical solutions for TD-DE for semi-infinite and slab media with a zero-boundary condition. The pulsed laser source systems (TD systems) are close enough to the source that they can be calculated with convolution methods [16].

Even in modern times, Green's function approach is most commonly used to find solutions to the DE in regular geometries [15,17]. For instance, researchers [17] came up with ways to solve an endless cylinder by putting in a source line that goes on forever. Also, they used Green's function method to solve the DE for a point source in several regular geometries. In addition, authors [18] Using a series expansion method, solved the DE for concentric spheres. In a separate piece of work, authors [19] solved the DE in the CW, frequency, and time domains using the Green's function approach with extended boundary conditions for a multiple-layered finite cylinder. These solutions were obtained by solving the equation for a multiple-layered finite cylinder. In addition, researchers [20] provided a CW solution for a point source that made use of the extrapolated boundary conditions in cylindrical coordinates. Finally, by employing a number of different integral transformations, Liemert and Kienle were able to derive specific solutions for the DE [21] when it was applied to a homogeneous and turbid medium with a point source.

In recent research, Erkol et al. [22] have derived analytical solutions to the DE in two and three dimensions for the steady state CW case in a cylindrical media. In this case, a Dirac function with different strengths is used to model the light source. To get the Green's function for the Robin boundary condition, an integral method is used. This method is extremely adaptable, allowing the implementation of any boundary condition (i.e., not limited to the Robin boundary condition). This is also applicable to other regular geometries, like spherical. Because finding solutions to the DE at the boundary is the primary focus of their study, this method is perfectly suited for determining the DOI in homogeneous or nearly homogeneous environments.

Theoretically, analytical solutions could be a direct and accurate way to get light to travel, but the complexity of biological tissue makes it hard to make analytical solutions. The analytical solutions of the RTE and the DA are faster to calculate, but they can only be used for certain specific geometries with values that are almost all the same inside. Therefore, numerical methods are usually used to solve the RTE and the DA models. The critical constraint in its applicability is that the solutions are only available for simple homogeneous geometries [17], which induces severe modeling errors by providing a poor approximation [23]. In some cases, it has been possible to get these solutions for time-domain DE, like slab media [24].

3.2. Numerical Methods

In diffuse optical imaging, numerical methods are often used because they are good at simulating how light moves through realistic, complex geometries as well as different types of media. Numerical solutions for the forward model can be found using the partial differential equation, which can be solved in a variety of ways. The finite difference method

(FDM), the finite volume method (FVM), the boundary element method (BEM), and the finite-element method (FEM) are all examples of this.

3.2.1. Finite Difference Method

In the finite difference method, the medium is broken up into small pieces using a regular grid, and complex shapes are made around the points inside the grid. Points with absorption values in the thousands are assigned outside of the required form. It has been demonstrated that this method produces more accurate results than other methods such as Monte Carlo and analytic solutions [25]. However, because the FEM is so simple to use when dealing with complex geometries, the FDM is rarely used in DOT applications. However, it has been used to determine the dispersion of light in the human brain and the cranium of a rat [26,27]. This method has been employed in the literature: for additional details, read the following studies [28–30].

3.2.2. Finite Volume Method

In a way like the finite element and finite difference methods, the FVM calculates values at discrete points within a meshing geometry. In this way, both approaches compute values. The element (in a cell center formulation) is known as a volume of control, or VC for short, in FVM. This is a distinct region of space in which the PDEs will be integrated. During this step of the process, you will be evaluating the volumetric sources as well as the surface fluxes that flow into and out of VC. In order to convert the surface integral into volume integrals, it will be necessary to make use of Gauss' theorem. Interpolation functions that are the same, like the FDM method, or almost the same, like the Laplace equation, are used to get close to surface derivatives. The name of the method comes from the fact that each node in the mesh takes up a relatively small amount of space.

The primary advantage of this method over FDM is that it does not require the use of structured grids. Additionally, the effort that would have been required to transform the provided mesh into a structured numerical grid internally may be completely avoided. In the same way as with FDM, the approximation that is reached results in a discrete solution; however, the variables are often positioned at the centres of the cells rather than at the nodal points. This is not always the case, however, as there are also approaches that centre on the face of the volume. Interpolation is used to determine the values of field variables at locations other than storage locations (such as vertices). This is the case regardless.

The finite volume technique is used a lot in optical tomography reconstructions [31,32], because it uses less energy than other methods. It takes a long time to run [33], despite the fact that it has a high level of mesh flexibility, which is necessary for modelling complex shapes.

3.2.3. Boundary Element Method

The BEM has evolved as a viable alternative mathematical technique over the last twenty years. Because it just necessitates surface discretisation and hence is less computationally expensive. BEM is like FDM and FEM in that it calculates values at discrete points for solving PDEs. The simplicity of this method is derived from the fact that it meshes only the boundary of the body rather than the full domainIn DOT, the BEM uses Green's second identity to describe the field via its integral on the surface, i.e., photon density and fluxes. In large-scale geometries [34–39], it outperforms FEM in terms of performance, but it cannot predict light propagation in complicated heterogeneous domains accurately. This is attributed to the complex nature of the boundaries encountered between the tissue interfaces. The hybrid or coupled BEM-FEM method has also been employed. It shows that, compared to analytical solutions, the meshing task can be made easier and the size of the problem can be reduced while the model's correctness is kept.

The BEM is better than the FEM because you don't have to break up the area you're looking at into smaller pieces. Instead, you only need to know the area's edges. As a result, meshing effort is reduced, and system matrices are smaller. However, the BEM has some disadvantages over the FEM; the BEM matrices are fully populated with complex and frequency-dependent coefficients, which reduces the solution's efficiency. Furthermore, singularities may occur in the solution, which must be avoided [6].

3.2.4. Finite Element Method

In optical imaging applications [40–46] with irregular boundaries, FEM is one of the most common ways to solve the DE. FEM is a mathematical method for approximating boundary values and making absorption spectra and optical flux for a given distribution of absorption and diffusion coefficients. The method employs a collection of basis functions on a mesh, also known as interpolation functions, to convert the PDE into a system of differential equations in finite-dimensional space [41]. As a result of its ability to handle irregular geometries [47], it has been utilized to solve both the RTE and DE models [41,48,49]. As a result, numerical solutions are required. Because of its ease in handling complex geometries and modeling boundary effects, the FEM is more versatile than other methods, including the finite difference method. The FEM is a variational method that uses a family of finite-dimensional basis functions to approximate the solution.

Researchers like the FEM because it uses a piecewise representation of the solution in terms of certain basis functions. The computational domain is broken up into smaller areas called "finite elements", and the solution for each element is built from the basis functions. The typical method for obtaining the actual equations is to restate the conservation equation in weak form, write the field variables in terms of the basis functions, multiply the equation by the appropriate test functions, and then integrate over an element. Because the FEM solution is expressed in terms of specific basis functions, it is much better known than the FDM or FVM solutions. This can be a double-edged sword because the selection of basis functions is critical, and boundary conditions may be more difficult to formulate. Again, a system of equations (usually for nodal values) is obtained and must be solved in order to obtain a solution.

3.3. Stochastic Methods

The Monte-Carlo (MC) simulation is the most widely used stochastic approach for modeling photon transport through tissue. It is used with random-walk or Markov-chain models to provide the best results. A photon's or a photon packet's propagation across a medium can be simulated using MC models, which helps make the process more efficient. This process is accomplished by tracing the photon's passage through the medium and modeling each event the photon meets sequentially. More than two decades ago, it became a standard method for simulating light transport in tissues because of its versatility and rigorousness in dealing with turbid fluids with complicated structures.

The MC method entails the following steps: In the first step, voxels representing various types of tissues are first divided into three-dimensional tissue geometry. In the second step, the optical properties of each voxel, such as scattering and absorption, are allocated to each voxel in the second step. The third step is to "inject" a photon at a specific location on the surface of this shape. The photon's movement is accomplished in the fourth step through probabilistic scattering and absorption as it travels through tissue. Repeat steps 3–4 hundred or even millions of times to figure out how much fluence (photon weight) and how far each tissue type has travelled through it [50].

Interest in using MC to calculate the forward model for optical tomography has resurfaced in recent years, thanks to the combination of efficient MC formulations with improved processing capacity and geometrical complexity [51,52].

4. Types of Toolboxes for Forward Model Simulation

There is a wide variety of software/toolboxes available to simulate forward problems that are currently in use. Some of them are listed and explained in greater detail below.

4.1. MCML

Due to its user-friendliness, Researchers [50] first introduced the programming tool known as MC simulation for light propagation in multi-layered tissue (MCML) in planner geometry, which is still widely used today. The multilayer model was greatly simplified. The simulation geometry was set by the number of layers and the thickness of each layer. Each layer represented a homogeneous part of the simulated medium. The MCML simulation code is written in ANSI C, which is a standard programming language. Figure 3 shows the main steps of the MCML simulation process, which are explained and shown in [53].

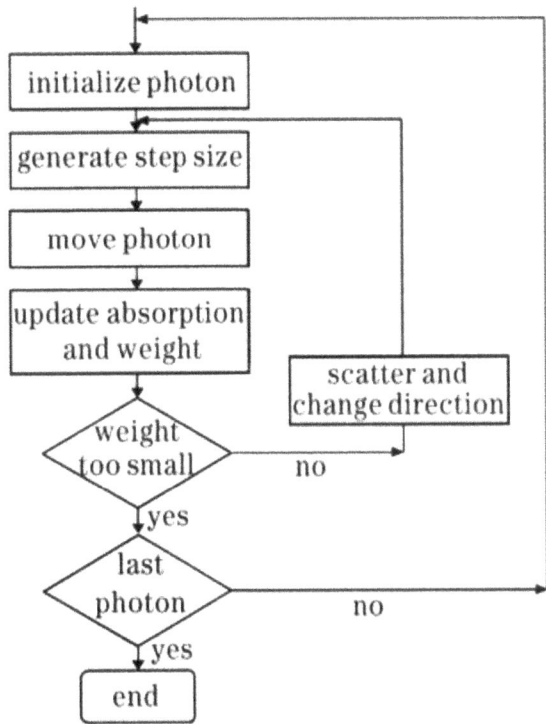

Figure 3. Fundamental steps of MCML technique (adapted from Ref. [53]).

4.2. NIRFAST

The Near-infrared Frequency-domain Absorption and Scattering Tomography (NIRFAST) program is a FEM-based technique developed by the National Institute of Standards and Technology in 2009 [54], and this software is offered free of charge. In this package, many MATLAB.m files are produced and executables are included, which the user can customise to incorporate the programme into their measurement apparatus (Figure 4, for details, see [54]). NIRFAST requires that a finite element mesh be provided before any simulation can be started. The user's responsibility is to provide this mesh, which can be in either 2D or 3D format. NIRFAST cannot produce a mesh on its own. The DE is changed into a set of linear equations that can be solved on a finite element grid. A finite element mesh represents the flux rate at each node.

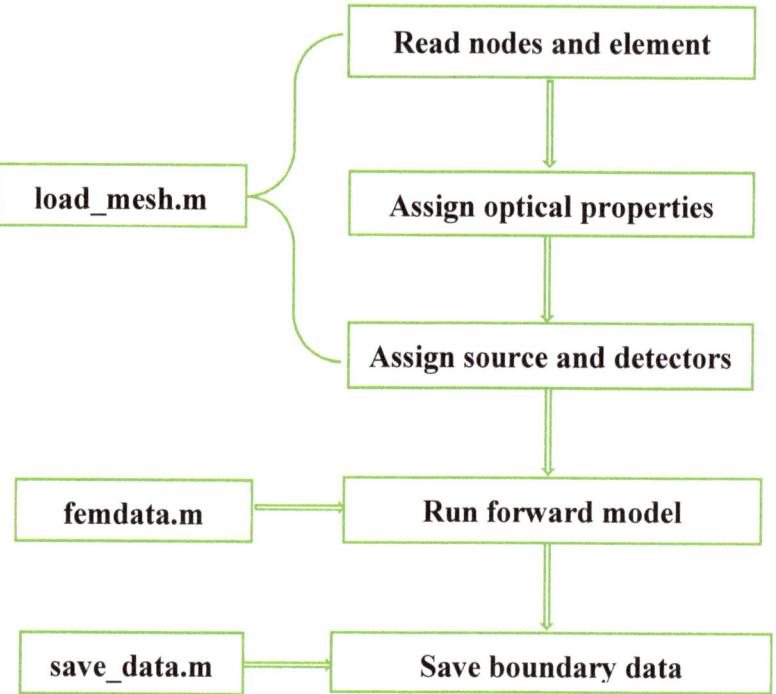

Figure 4. Fundamental steps of the NIRFAST technique for the forward problem (adapted from Ref. [54]).

NIRFAST has been shown to work well for geometries with a single boundary condition, especially when the boundary condition is a modified Robin (or Type III) in which air is assumed to surround the simulation region (as implemented in NIRFAST), also known as a Neumann boundary condition. NIRFAST has been developed for 2D and 3D and is widely used for FEM analysis in forward models with image reconstruction. It is available for free via the following URL link: http://newton.ex.ac.uk/research/biomedical/hd/NIRFAST.html (accessed on 5 October 2022).

4.3. TOAST++

To tackle DOT's forward and inverse problems, Martin Schweiger and Simon R. Arridge [55] developed an efficient open-source software framework that some researchers are using. Originally built in C++, it was later rewritten as a toolbox that includes a set of MATLAB routines and PYTHON code, which is now available. This software suite contains libraries for computation of sparse matrices, finite-element, alternative numerical modeling, nonlinear inverse, MATLAB and, python bindings, and visualization tools (see Figure 5). This toolbox offers parallel matrix assembly and solver capabilities for distributed and shared memory architectures and graphics processor platforms, which enable scalability on distributed and collective memory architectures. In this way, researchers can quickly design analysis tools without worrying about developing the low-level sparsity matrix and finite-element subroutines beforehand.

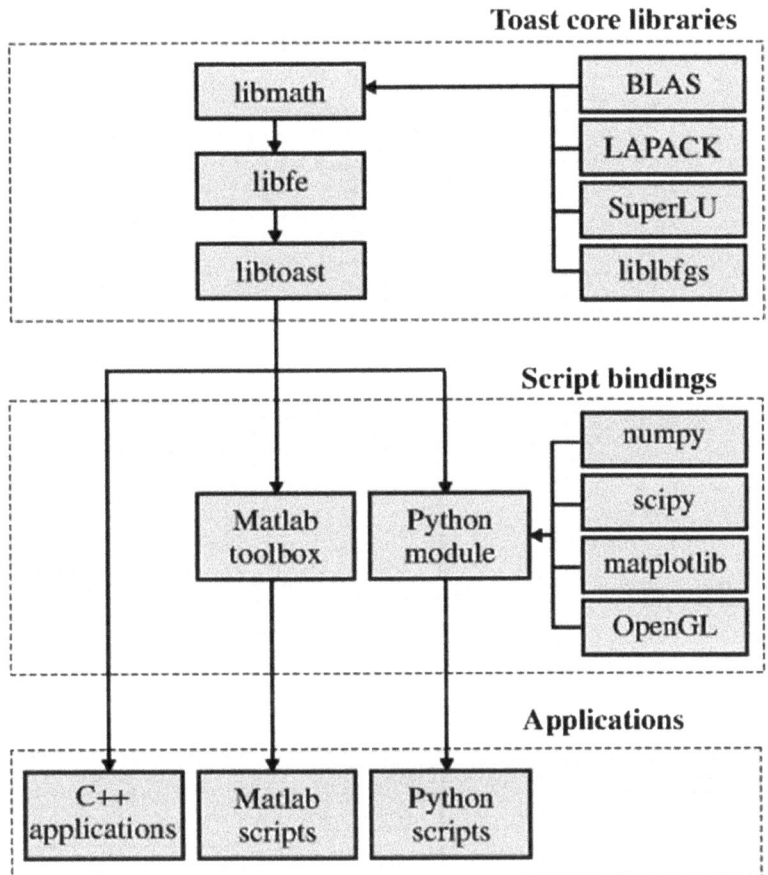

Figure 5. Libraries for Toast++ technique for forward model simulation (adapted from Ref [55]).

4.4. MCX/MMC

Qianqian Fang created open-source MC simulators called Monte Carlo eXtreme (MCX) and Mesh-based Monte Carlo (MMC) in 2009 [56]. These simulators are two of the most advanced Monte Carlo programs available today, and researchers use them to simulate light propagation as photons across complex biological tissues [56,57]. Binary executable software was used to develop the first versions of MCX and MMC. Because of MATLAB's popularity among academic researchers, MEX variants such as MCXLAB, MMCLAB, and voxel-based MC (vMC) have been developed to make it more user-friendly for scientists. These open-source MC programs are essential resources for academics and students interested in modeling light interaction in tissue and comprehending fundamental theories [58,59]. Figure 6 depicts the basic steps of the MCX simulation process for the forward problem.

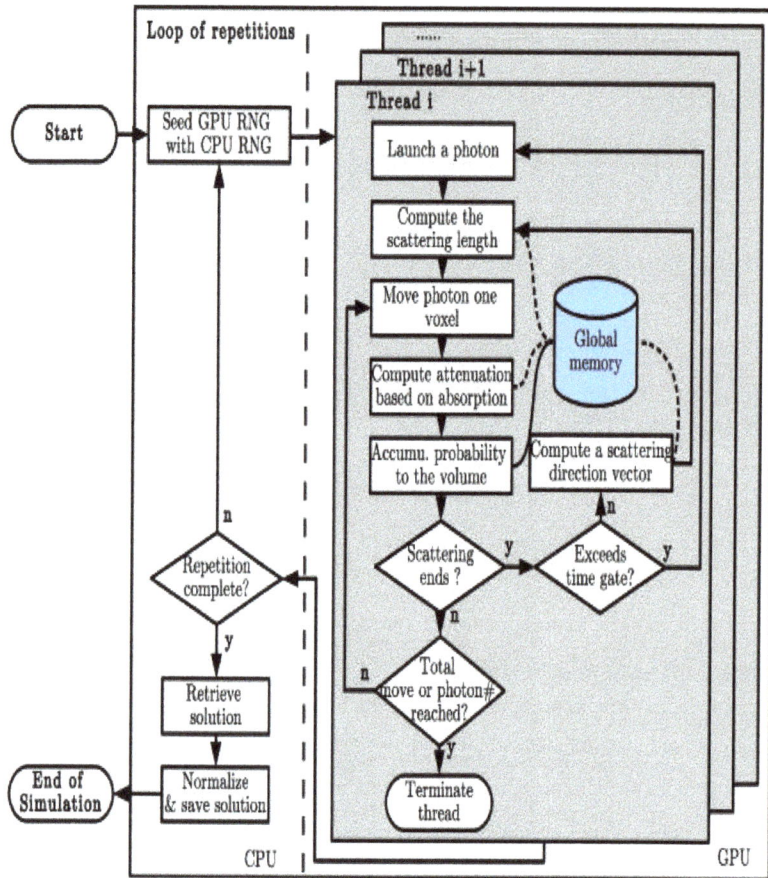

Figure 6. Basic steps of MCX technique (adapted from Ref. [56]).

4.5. ValoMC

Based on the MC method, Leino et al. [60] made ValoMC, an open-source program. With this software package, you can solve problems like the number of photons in the computing domain and their presence at the domain boundary. It is a useful tool for researchers because it can simulate complex measurement geometries with different light sources, intensity-modulated light, and optical parameter distributions that change in different places. Also, the interface for MATLAB (The Math Works Inc., Natick, MA) is made to be easy to use and to let users set up and solve problems quickly. The code for the software simulation is written in C++, and the Open MP parallelization library is used to make it work in multiple places at once. Visit the website at https://inverselight.github.io/ValoMC/ (accessed on 5 October 2022) and click on the "Download" button to get the software.

In the last few years, many ways to solve the forward problem have been written about. Table 1 provides an overview of these methods.

Table 1. Details about the various methods and types of toolboxes/software used for the simulation forward problem in fNIRs measurements.

References	Forward Simulation Method	Simulation Software/Toolbox	Data Type
B. W. Pogue et al., 1995 [61]	FDM	N/A	N/A
M. A. Ansari et al., 2014 [62]	BEM	N/A	N/A
Dehghani, Hamid, et al., 2009 [54]	FEM	NIRFAST	Breast model data
Yalavarthy, Phaneendra K. et al., 2007–2008 [7,63,64]	FEM	N/A	Phantom
Brigadoi, Sabrina, et al., [65]	FEM	Toast++	Real resting-state data
Chiarelli, Antonio M., et al., 2016 [66]	FEM	NIRFAST	Phantom
Lu, Wenqi, Daniel Lighter, and Iain B. Styles. 2018 [67]	FEM	NIRFAST	Realistic simulation data
Machado, A., et al., 2018 [68]	MC	MCX	Realistic simulation data
Yu, Leiming, et al., 2018 [58]	MC	MCX	Phantom
Jiang, Jingjing, et al., 2020 [69]	MC and FEM	MCX and Toast++	Silicon phantom experiment
Fu, Xiaoxue, and John E. Richards. 2021 [70]	MC	MCX	Realistic simulation data
Cai, Zhengchen, et al., 2021 [71]	MC	MCX	Realistic
Mazumder, Dibbyan, et al., 2021 [72]	MC	MCX	Realistic simulation data

5. Inverse Problem

In image reconstruction, the inverse problem is figuring out where the changes in absorption along the path of the diffuse light are. This can be done by using the relationship between the scalp and the law of propagation. In order to solve the image reconstruction problem, the forward model must be turned around, which can be written as the linear underdetermined inverse problem when there is noise.

$$y = Ax + \gamma \tag{8}$$

γ is the noise present in the data and A is the Jacobian/sensitivity matrix.

The Jacobian matrix shows the relationship between how sensitively light intensity is measured on the surface of the head and the optical properties of the head itself. The image reconstruction problem requires the direct inversion of the Jacobian/sensitivity matrix, which makes it a highly underdetermined and poorly posed problem. Because of the ill-conditioning of the system, regularization techniques must be employed to obtain a reliable solution. In the literature, several image reconstruction methods for the solution of inverse problems have been developed. Regularization-based methods and Bayesian estimating methods, which are two fundamental methodologies, have dominated the literature for a very long time.

6. Methods for Inverse Problem Solution

The various methods employed to solve the inverse problem (Equation (2)) will be explained in further detail in this section. Among these methods are back projection, singular value decomposition (SVD), truncated singular value decomposition (tSVD), lease square QR decomposition (LSQR), regularized lease square QR decomposition (rLSQR), minimum norm estimate (MNE), weighted minimum norm estimate (WMNE), low-resolution electromagnetic tomography (LORETA), L1-norm, hierarchical Bayesian (HB) as MAP estimate, expectation-maximization (EM), maximum entropy on the mean (MEM), and Bayesian model averaging (BMA).

The basic formulation of the inverse methods for the solution of fNIRs is given in the section. These methods are also described in terms of their mathematical form. According to the previously published literature, the performance of the inverse methods is thoroughly explained. The comparison is being made using a variety of parameters, including sparsity, spatial resolution, localization error, image quality, root mean square error, and quantitative and qualitative reconstructions, among other things.

6.1. Back Projection

Back projection is the inverse technique of projection. While projection aims to extract data from an image, back projection seeks to extract the image from the data calculated during the projection process. As a result, the back-projection process accepts as input the results matrix returned by the projection process, as well as all data related to the projection process that may be beneficial in completing the process. The BP method in image reconstruction is more straightforward and consists of back projecting the boundary measurements in the sensitivity matrix in the following manner [61,62]

$$x_{BP} = A^T y \qquad (9)$$

This method assumes that the sensitivity matrix is orthogonal in a broad sense (for example, that it is an estimate of its pseudo-inverse), which is not always the case. Nevertheless, this method has been employed in the literature [62–64] even though it typically overestimates the amplitude when multiple measurements are taken simultaneously.

Back projection is better than other iterative methods because it makes images faster with less processing power. But it can be hard to know how much oxygen is in the blood or to use breast mammography as a screening tool when there isn't enough quantitative information. Also, most diagnostic imaging techniques used today, like MRI and CT scans, use only qualitative information to make important diagnoses, like finding tumors and where they are. Back propagation is also efficient in terms of computing, but it has a low spatial resolution, which makes it hard to tell apart multiple objects that absorb light.

6.2. Singular Value Decomposition (SVD) and Truncated Singular Value Decomposition (tSVD)

The SVD and its hybrid version, the tSVD, try to find the pseudo-inverse of the sensitivity matrix while ignoring the smallest singular values that cause numerical instability (this solution will show the main contribution of the sensitivity matrix) [65].

Consider U^i and V^i to be the i-th column vectors of U and V correspondingly, the SVD decomposition as a decomposition of A into rank one matrices as

$$A = \sum_{i=1}^{n} \sigma_i U^i V^{iT}$$

U and V are orthonormal column vectors correspondingly, while σ_i are the nonnegative singular values (in descending order); If the inverted form of the solution is multiplied by the boundary measurements, the solution is found as follows:

$$x_{SVD/tSVD} = \sum_{i=1}^{n} \frac{U^{iT} y}{\sigma_i} V \qquad (10)$$

As the literature shows, Gupta, Saurabh, et al. [66] compare the SVD method to the Levenberg–Marquard method. SVD is computationally efficient and is applied to experimental data. Furthermore, prior information is used in conjunction with SVD by Zhan, Yuxuan, et al. [67] to significantly improve the crosswalk between the retrieved parameter. On the other hand, the tSVD solution is known for reconstructed images that are blurry [65].

6.3. Least Square by QR Decomposition (LSQR) and Regularized LSQR (rLSQR)

The LSQR method by Paige and Saunders [68] and its hybrid version, the rLSQR method, are both based on Tikhonov regularization, but they also add a term that makes the method more regular. The mathematical formulation for LSQR and rLSQR is given under [69]:

$$x_{LSQR/rLSQR} = argmin\left\{\|y - Ax\|^2 + \alpha\|x - x_{initial}\|^2\right\} \quad (11)$$

As opposed to the previous technique, this one does not require that the matrix A be saved; rather, it requires that one matrix-vector product with A and one matrix-vector product with A^T be assessed for each iteration.

The LSQR was presented by Prakash, Jaya, and Phaneendra K. Yalavarthy [70] in comparison to the regularized minimum residual approach (MRM). Compared to the MRM method, the LSQR method outperforms it in terms of computational time, the number of iterations, and image quality. It is applied to experimental data obtained from gelatine phantoms. Furthermore, C. B. Shaw et al. [71] demonstrate the computational efficiency and effectiveness of the LSQR using a simulated blood—vascular phantom experiment. Both quantitative and qualitative reconstructions benefit from the LSQR technique. However, hybrid algorithms, which incorporate the variation and modification of least square image reconstruction algorithms, have been developed and used in the literature [72–74].

6.4. Minimum Norm Estimate (MNE) and Weighted Minimum Norm Estimate (WMNE)

MNE is the most common inverse method. It was created to solve the inverse problem of MEG, and the norm solution is used to find the location of the EEG source. The mathematical formulation for MNE is given as under:

$$x_{MNE} = argmin\left\{\|y - Ax\|^2 + \alpha\|x\|^2\right\} \quad (12)$$

Similarly, the WMNE can be written as follow:

$$x_{WMNE} = argmin\left\{\|y - Ax\|^2 + \alpha\|Wx\|^2\right\} \quad (13)$$

The MNE solution, like tSVD, is known for producing scattered and blurry reconstruction images [75].

6.5. Low-Resolution Electromagnetic Tomographt (LORETA)

LORETA was initially created and used to locate EEG sources by Pascual-Marqui et al. [76]. LORETA has been used as a regularization method for fNIRs, which also considers L2-norm formulation as described for the MNE method by incorporating the Laplacian operator [11]. The mathematical formula for LORETA is given as follows:

$$x_{LORETA} = argmin\left\{\|y - Ax\|^2 + \alpha\|Lx\|^2\right\} \quad (14)$$

It is possible to interpret it as a weighted form of the MNE solution that aims to achieve maximum smoothness across space. Despite this, it continues to generate results with a vast spatial extent.

6.6. L1-Norm

L1-norm method has been developed and applied for EEG/MEG localization problem. The mathematical formulation for the L1-norm is given as under:

$$x_{L1-norm} = argmin\left\{\|y - Ax\|^2 + \alpha\|x\|^1\right\} \quad (15)$$

The L1-norm method has been demonstrated to have improved noise tolerance qualities and enhanced convergence features. It has also been shown to make solutions to other linear estimating problems more L1-norm sparse.

According to Habermehl, Christina, et al. [65], the L1-norm delivers the best results on experimental data (Gelatine cylindrical phantom that simulates breast tissues) compared to L0, L2, tSVD, and wMNE. Additionally, it demonstrates that the incorporation of the sparse algorithm into the procedure has the potential to improve accuracy. Meanwhile, the inclusion of sparsity in the lp norm minimization ($0 < p < 1$) as presented by Prakash, Jaya, et al. holds promise in improving the image quality compared to the L0-norm method [77,78]. The results of a numerical experiment conducted by S. Okawa et al. [79] demonstrate that lp sparsity regularisation improves spatial resolution. In addition, it describes how the reconstructed region is affected by the value of p. A lower p-value suggests that the target is highly localized.

Another image reconstruction approach is Bayesian estimation, which relies on a probabilistic model of observations and constraints called the likelihood function and prior distribution.

6.7. Hierarchical Bayesian as MAP Estimate

HB approach was initially developed and applied for the MEG localization problem [80]. In this method, observation and regularization are described as hierarchical probabilistic models. The HB estimation method uses an ARD prior to introduce the regularization parameter at each voxel position, which controls the degree of penalty. The basic formulation of the HB method for fNIRs is presented here (see [81] for detailed information).

i. Considering the measurement noise γ as a Gaussian distribution $N(0, \nu)$ and the forward problem as a probabilistic model as

$$P(y/x) \sim N(Ax, \nu) \quad (16)$$

where ν is the covariance matrix.

ii. Assuming the data prior distribution and likelihood function as $logP(x/y)$ and $logP(x/C)$ respectively.

iii. Computation of the posterior distribution of the unknown as

$$x_{MAP} = argmax\{logP(x/y) + logP(x/C)\} \quad (17)$$

where C anatomical prior image.

$$P(x, y, \theta, \vartheta) = P(y/x)P(x/\theta, \vartheta)P(\theta)P(\vartheta) \quad (18)$$

iv. By applying the variational Bayesian (VB) method, the posterior could be written as variational free energy

$$F(Q(x, \theta, \vartheta)) = \int Q(x, \theta, \vartheta) log\left(\frac{P(x, y, \theta, \vartheta)}{Q(x, \theta, \vartheta)}\right) d\beta d\alpha dx \quad (19)$$

with

$$Q(x, \theta, \vartheta) = Q(x)Q(\theta)Q(\vartheta)$$

image by maximizing the free energy, providing the reconstruction, and applying the Bayes rule to the posterior distribution.

In contrast to more traditional ways of regularizing, the idea of using Bayesian regularization to solve fNIRs has only been around for a short time. In a Bayesian paradigm, where all unknowns are thought of as random variables, the prior density is what is thought about the solution before the facts are considered. As a result, in conventional regularization, the prior functions similarly to the penalty term. The traditional Tikhonov regularized solution and the Bayesian maximum a posteriori (MAP) estimate have a well-established relationship, with classes of penalty functions and priors favoring similar types of solutions [82].

The HB algorithm for fNIRs has been proposed and used to make the changes in blood flow in the cortex and scalp less random and smoother. Using phantoms to test the performance and improve the accuracy of depth and spatial resolution [83]. Recent research by Shimokawa, Takeaki, et al. [83] provides the HB method with an ARD prior for fNIRs, as well as the inclusion of the two-step method. The sensitivity-normalized Tikhonov regularisation is utilised in the initial step of the process to locate a preliminary. In the second step, the result is refined through applying the hierarchical Bayesian estimate method. Furthermore, in another study, T. Shimokawa et al. [84] provide the HB method with Laplacian smooth prior to spatially variant Tikhonov regularization. This study include Two-layer phantom experiments, as well as the inclusion of MRI-based head-model simulations, are carried outBased on the results of that experiment, the proposed algorithm estimates the smooth, superficial activity in the scalp while also assessing the deep, localized activity in the cortical region. T. Aihara et al. also used the HB method to estimate spontaneous changes in cortical hemodynamic [85], in contrast to the task-related changes discussed in [86] for fMRI data. P. Hiltunen et al. [87] used the Bayesian and EM methods, as well as Tikhonov regularisation, in another study. Estimates of both the spatial organisation and the physical parameters can be obtained concurrently by using a Bayesian technique with a Gaussian prior. The reconstructed images' contrast is improved by the algorithm that was proposed, which has a high degree of spatial precision.

6.8. Expectation-Maximization (EM)

The Expectation-Minimization (EM) method for fNIRs sense was developed and employed by Cao et al. [88], and the mathematical description of the EM method can be described as follows:

By incorporating misplaced data and maximising the comprehensive penalised log-likelihood estimator, the maximum penalised log-likelihood estimator (MPLE) can be obtained.

$$x_{EM} = argmax\left\{-\frac{\|y - Ax\|^2}{2\delta^2} - \alpha\|x\|^1\right\} \quad (20)$$

The EM procedure generates a sequence of approximations x^k by alternating two phases (as shown below) until some stopping requirement is fulfilled.

➢ E-step given the observed data y and the current estimate μ^k, the conditional anticipation of the whole log-likelihood could be computed as

$$x^k = \mu^k + \frac{\beta^2}{\delta^2}A^T\left(y - A\mu^k\right) \quad (21)$$

➢ M-step: Update the estimated value of x^k

$$x^{k+1} = argmax\left\{-\|\mu - x^k\|^2 - 2\delta^2\alpha\|x\|^1\right\} \quad (22)$$

Equation can be explained separately for each element x_l^{k+1} as

$$x_l^{k+1} = argmax\left\{-\mu_l^2 + 2\mu_l x_l - 2\delta^2\alpha\|x\|^1\right\} \quad (23)$$

x_l is the element. It can be resolved using the soft threshold technique.

6.9. Maximum Entropy on the Mean (MEM)

The MEM method was first introduced by [89], and it has since been utilised and rigorously analysed in the context of EEG/MEG source imaging research [90,91]. MEM is not a new statistical method in the traditional sense, but rather a novel stochastic approach that leads to deterministic methods when some discretization step trends toward zero. Cai et al. [92] recently employed and evaluated the MEM approach to solving the inverse problem of fNIRs reconstruction.

Consider the variable x as an arbitrary variable with the probability distribution $dP(x) = P(x)dx$ then the unique solution $dP(x)$ could be attained as

$$dP^*(x) = argmax_{dP(x) \in C_m}(S_v(dP(x))) \qquad (24)$$

where $S_v(dP(x))$ is the Kullback-Leiber divergence or v-entropy of $dP(x)$ and define it as

$$S_v(dP(x)) = -\int_x \log\left(\frac{dP(x)}{dv(x)}\right)dP(x) = -\int_x f(x)\log(f(x))dv(x) \qquad (25)$$

$dv(x)$ is the prior distribution, the MEM solution from the gradient of free energy F_v is obtained as follows?

$$x_{MEM} = \nabla_\xi F_v(\xi) = A^T \lambda^* \qquad (26)$$

where $\lambda^* = argmax_\lambda D(\lambda)$, with the cost function $D(\lambda) = \lambda^T y - F_v(A^T \lambda) - \frac{1}{2}\lambda^T v(v)^T \lambda$.

6.10. Bayesian Model Averaging

The fundamental concept of BMA theory, which was initially developed and applied to MEG/EEG, is a mixture of Bayesian hierarchical models that can be used to estimate highly parameterized models [93]. Using Bayesian inference (BI) assumptions based on the given model or data (prior probability distribution), BMA may be used to construct the posterior distribution for quantities of interest [94]. The following is the basic mathematical description of BMA for fNIRs image-based model reconstruction (see [11] for additional information) and is given in more detail below:

i. Consider the basic assumption of the Bayesian formulization of the given problem as a normal probability density function as

$$p(y/x, \varphi) = N(Ax, \varphi)$$

where φ represents as hyperparameters which is unknown [11].

ii. The estimation of the parameter as the first level of inference using the Bayes theorem is described as the posterior probability density function a

$$(x/y, \varphi, H_k) = \frac{p(y/x, \varphi, H_k)p(x/\varphi, H_k)}{\int p(y/x, \varphi, H_k)p(x/\varphi, H_k)d\varphi}$$

where H_k represents as k-th model which is to be considered for the given problem.

iii. The estimation of the hyperparameters as 2nd level of inference is describing as the posterior probability density function as

$$p(\varphi/y, H_k) = \frac{p(y/\varphi, H_k)p(\varphi/H_k)}{\int p(y/\varphi, H_k)p(\varphi/H_k)d\varphi}$$

iv. The estimation of the model as the third level of inference as the posterior probability density function

$$p(H_k/y) = \frac{p(y/H_k)p(H_k)}{\int p(y/H_k)p(H_k)d\varphi}$$

v. Lastly, marginalizing the first, second, and third level of inference as posterior *pdf* as

$$p(x/y) = \int_{forall H_k} p(x/y, H_k)p(H_k) = \sum_k p(x/y, H_k)p(H_k) \qquad (27)$$

This procedure considers all possible solutions for every model (using 1st and 2nd level of inference) and averages weighted by each model's posterior model probability (PMP).

Furthermore, J. Tremblay et al. [11] applied the BMA for fNIRs and their results show that in terms of localization error, ROI, and RMSE, the BMA produces better results.

7. Conclusions

fNIRs is a practical approach due to their portability, little interference in magnetic and electrical fields, hyper-scanning, ease of use for neonates, and the fact that they require no ongoing maintenance. As a result of the rapid development of fNIRS devices and analytic toolboxes and its findings' reliability in various fields, the fNIRs approach can be considered a versatile and promising instrument. In fNIRs, the image reconstruction problem is divided into two parts: the model used to predict light distribution in tissue (the forward problem) and the method used to estimate the optical properties of the domain in tissue (the inverse problem). In order to achieve correct image reconstruction, it is essential to do accurate forward model simulation and develop methods to address inverse problems.

Concerning how to solve the problem, many researchers have used and presented a wide range of methods, such as toolboxes. FEM and MC are the two most advanced forward model simulation technologies today. Various toolboxes are being built and put into operation to improve the accuracy and efficiency of the forward model simulations. Regarding forward models, NIRFAST for FEM and MCX for the MC method are the most often used and developed software packages up to this moment.

When it comes to the solution of the inverse problem, the inverse methods such as back projection, SVD, tSVD, LSQR, rLSQR, MNE, WMNE, LORETA, $l1$-norm, HB as a MAP estimate, EM, MEM, and BMA, have been employed thusly. According to the research, while considering inverse methods, it is vital to consider factors such as computational time, localization ability, localization error, energy error, system complexity, improved resolution, and improved image quality, among others. According to the research reviewed above, when numerous measurements are collected at the same time, the back-projection method gives an overestimation of the amplitude. The SVD, tSVD, LSQR, and rLSQR methods are all efficient in terms of computational resources. On the other hand, the L1-norm and lp regularisation approaches have been found to be sparser than the other inverse methods, which is a positive development.

Incorporating priors into the inverse approach improves image quality and spatial accuracy. For this reason, the HB method has been employed in the literature and has produced satisfactory outcomes. Based on the prior information, the EM method for fNIRs has been used to increase the image quality and resolution by incorporating sparsity regularisation into the image. Furthermore, in terms of localization error, ROI, and RMSE, the BMA produces better results. Recently the MEM method has been used for fNIRs, and it has been proven to be more accurate and robust than both MNE and wMNE.

Considering the preceding, it is evident and apparent that, while the methods employed thus far have produced satisfactory results, continuous improvement in inverse problem solutions is ongoing. As a result, it may be possible to utilize the inverse method, which incorporates the sparse algorithm and prior information, to improve image quality and reduce localization error.

Author Contributions: Conceptualization, A.H. and I.F.; methodology, A.H.; software, M.Z.; validation, M.S.M., I.F. and T.B.T.; formal analysis, T.B.T.; investigation, I.F.; resources, I.F.; writing—original draft preparation, A.H.; writing—review and editing, A.H.; visualization, M.Z.; supervision, I.F.; funding acquisition, I.F. All authors have read and agreed to the published version of the manuscript.

Funding: This research received no external funding.

Data Availability Statement: Not applicable.

Acknowledgments: This research was funded by PETRONAS through YUTP grant (015LC0-372).

Conflicts of Interest: The authors declare no conflict of interest.

References

1. Ferrari, M.; Mottola, L.; Quaresima, V. Principles, techniques, and limitations of near infrared spectroscopy. *Can. J. Appl. Physiol.* **2004**, *29*, 463–487. [CrossRef] [PubMed]
2. Wolf, M.; Ferrari, M.; Quaresima, V. Progress of near-infrared spectroscopy and topography for brain and muscle clinical applications. *J. Biomed. Opt.* **2007**, *12*, 062104. [PubMed]
3. Bérubé-Lauzière, Y.; Crotti, M.; Boucher, S.; Ettehadi, S.; Pichette, J.; Rech, I. Prospects on time-domain diffuse optical tomography based on time-correlated single photon counting for small animal imaging. *J. Spectrosc.* **2016**, *2016*, 1947613. [CrossRef]
4. Lo, P.A.; Chiang, H.K. Three-dimensional fluorescence diffuse optical tomography using the adaptive spatial prior approach. *J. Med. Biol. Eng.* **2019**, *39*, 827–834. [CrossRef]
5. Applegate, M.; Istfan, R.; Spink, S.; Tank, A.; Roblyer, D. Recent advances in high speed diffuse optical imaging in biomedicine. *APL Photonics* **2020**, *5*, 040802. [CrossRef]
6. Pellicer, A.; del Carmen Bravo, M. Near-infrared spectroscopy: A methodology-focused review. In *Seminars in Fetal and Neonatal Medicine*; Elsevier: Amsterdam, The Netherlands, 2011; Volume 16, pp. 42–49.
7. Rahim, R.A.; Chen, L.L.; San, C.K.; Rahiman, M.H.F.; Fea, P.J. Multiple fan-beam optical tomography: Modelling techniques. *Sensors* **2009**, *9*, 8562–8578. [CrossRef]
8. Klose, A.D.; Netz, U.; Beuthan, J.; Hielscher, A.H. Optical tomography using the time-independent equation of radiative transfer—Part 1: Forward model. *J. Quant. Spectrosc. Radiat. Transf.* **2002**, *72*, 691–713. [CrossRef]
9. Hoshi, Y.; Yamada, Y. Overview of diffuse optical tomography and its clinical applications. *J. Biomed. Opt.* **2016**, *21*, 091312. [CrossRef]
10. Arridge, S.R. Optical tomography in medical imaging. *Inverse Probl.* **1999**, *15*, R41. [CrossRef]
11. Tremblay, J.; Martínez-Montes, E.; Vannasing, P.; Nguyen, D.K.; Sawan, M.; Lepore, F.; Gallagher, A. Comparison of source localization techniques in diffuse optical tomography for fNIRS application using a realistic head model. *Biomed. Opt. Express* **2018**, *9*, 2994–3016. [CrossRef]
12. Madsen, S.J. *Optical Methods and Instrumentation in Brain Imaging and Therapy*; Springer Science & Business Media: Berlin/Heidelberg, Germany, 2012.
13. Kavuri, V.C.; Lin, Z.-J.; Tian, F.; Liu, H. Sparsity enhanced spatial resolution and depth localization in diffuse optical tomography. *Biomed. Opt. Express* **2012**, *3*, 943–957. [CrossRef]
14. Yamada, Y.; Suzuki, H.; Yamashita, Y. Time-domain near-infrared spectroscopy and imaging: A review. *Appl. Sci.* **2019**, *9*, 1127. [CrossRef]
15. Patterson, M.S.; Chance, B.; Wilson, B.C. Time resolved reflectance and transmittance for the noninvasive measurement of tissue optical properties. *Appl. Opt.* **1989**, *28*, 2331–2336. [CrossRef] [PubMed]
16. Arridge, S.R.; Hebden, J.C. Optical imaging in medicine: II. Modelling and reconstruction. *Phys. Med. Biol.* **1997**, *42*, 841. [CrossRef] [PubMed]
17. Arridge, S.R.; Cope, M.; Delpy, D. The theoretical basis for the determination of optical pathlengths in tissue: Temporal and frequency analysis. *Phys. Med. Biol.* **1992**, *37*, 1531. [CrossRef] [PubMed]
18. Sikora, J.; Zacharopoulos, A.; Douiri, A.; Schweiger, M.; Horesh, L.; Arridge, S.R.; Ripoll, J. Diffuse photon propagation in multilayered geometries. *Phys. Med. Biol.* **2006**, *51*, 497. [CrossRef]
19. Liemert, A.; Kienle, A. Light diffusion in N-layered turbid media: Frequency and time domains. *J. Biomed. Opt.* **2010**, *15*, 025002. [CrossRef]
20. Zhang, A.; Piao, D.; Bunting, C.F.; Pogue, B.W. Photon diffusion in a homogeneous medium bounded externally or internally by an infinitely long circular cylindrical applicator. I. Steady-state theory. *JOSA A* **2010**, *27*, 648–662. [CrossRef]
21. Liemert, A.; Kienle, A. Light diffusion in a turbid cylinder. I. Homogeneous case. *Opt. Express* **2010**, *18*, 9456–9473. [CrossRef]
22. Erkol, H.; Nouizi, F.; Unlu, M.; Gulsen, G. An extended analytical approach for diffuse optical imaging. *Phys. Med. Biol.* **2015**, *60*, 5103. [CrossRef]
23. Arridge, S.R. Methods in diffuse optical imaging. *Philos. Trans. R. Soc. A Math. Phys. Eng. Sci.* **2011**, *369*, 4558–4576. [CrossRef] [PubMed]
24. Martelli, F.; Sassaroli, A.; Yamada, Y.; Zaccanti, G. Analytical approximate solutions of the time-domain diffusion equation in layered slabs. *JOSA A* **2002**, *19*, 71–80. [CrossRef] [PubMed]
25. Pogue, B.; Patterson, M.; Jiang, H.; Paulsen, K. Initial assessment of a simple system for frequency domain diffuse optical tomography. *Phys. Med. Biol.* **1995**, *40*, 1709. [CrossRef]
26. Hielscher, A.H.; Alcouffe, R.E.; Barbour, R.L. Comparison of finite-difference transport and diffusion calculations for photon migration in homogeneous and heterogeneous tissues. *Phys. Med. Biol.* **1998**, *43*, 1285. [CrossRef] [PubMed]
27. Hielscher, A.H.; Klose, A.D.; Hanson, K.M. Gradient-based iterative image reconstruction scheme for time-resolved optical tomography. *IEEE Trans. Med. Imaging* **1999**, *18*, 262–271. [CrossRef]

28. Tanifuji, T.; Chiba, N.; Hijikata, M. FDTD (finite difference time domain) analysis of optical pulse responses in biological tissues for spectroscopic diffused optical tomography. In Proceedings of the Technical Digest. CLEO/Pacific Rim 2001. 4th Pacific Rim Conference on Lasers and Electro-Optics (Cat. No. 01TH8557), Chiba, Japan, 15–19 July 2001; p. TuD3_5.
29. Tanifuji, T.; Hijikata, M. Finite difference time domain (FDTD) analysis of optical pulse responses in biological tissues for spectroscopic diffused optical tomography. *IEEE Trans. Med. Imaging* **2002**, *21*, 181–184. [CrossRef]
30. Ichitsubo, K.; Tanifuji, T. Time-resolved noninvasive optical parameters determination in three-dimensional biological tissue using finite difference time domain analysis with nonuniform grids for diffusion equations. In Proceedings of the 2005 IEEE Engineering in Medicine and Biology 27th Annual Conference, Shanghai, China, 17–18 January 2006; pp. 3133–3136.
31. Ren, K.; Abdoulaev, G.S.; Bal, G.; Hielscher, A.H. Algorithm for solving the equation of radiative transfer in the frequency domain. *Opt. Lett.* **2004**, *29*, 578–580. [CrossRef]
32. Montejo, L.D.; Kim, H.-K.K.; Hielscher, A.H. A finite-volume algorithm for modeling light transport with the time-independent simplified spherical harmonics approximation to the equation of radiative transfer. In Proceedings of the Optical Tomography and Spectroscopy of Tissue IX, San Francisco, CA, USA, 22–27 January 2011; p. 78960J.
33. Soloviev, V.Y.; D'Andrea, C.; Mohan, P.S.; Valentini, G.; Cubeddu, R.; Arridge, S.R. Fluorescence lifetime optical tomography with discontinuous Galerkin discretisation scheme. *Biomed. Opt. Express* **2010**, *1*, 998–1013. [CrossRef]
34. Zacharopoulos, A.D.; Arridge, S.R.; Dorn, O.; Kolehmainen, V.; Sikora, J. Three-dimensional reconstruction of shape and piecewise constant region values for optical tomography using spherical harmonic parametrization and a boundary element method. *Inverse Probl.* **2006**, *22*, 1509. [CrossRef]
35. Grzywacz, T.; Sikora, J.; Wojtowicz, S. Substructuring methods for 3-D BEM multilayered model for diffuse optical tomography problems. *IEEE Trans. Magn.* **2008**, *44*, 1374–1377. [CrossRef]
36. Srinivasan, S.; Ghadyani, H.R.; Pogue, B.W.; Paulsen, K.D. A coupled finite element-boundary element method for modeling Diffusion equation in 3D multi-modality optical imaging. *Biomed. Opt. Express* **2010**, *1*, 398–413. [CrossRef]
37. Srinivasan, S.; Carpenter, C.M.; Ghadyani, H.R.; Taka, S.J.; Kaufman, P.A.; Wells, W.A.; Pogue, B.W.; Paulsen, K.D. Image guided near-infrared spectroscopy of breast tissue in vivo using boundary element method. *J. Biomed. Opt.* **2010**, *15*, 061703. [CrossRef] [PubMed]
38. Elisee, J.P.; Gibson, A.; Arridge, S. Combination of boundary element method and finite element method in diffuse optical tomography. *IEEE Trans. Biomed. Eng.* **2010**, *57*, 2737–2745. [CrossRef]
39. Xie, W.; Deng, Y.; Lian, L.; Wang, K.; Luo, Z.; Gong, H. Boundary element method for diffuse optical tomography. In Proceedings of the 2013 Seventh International Conference on Image and Graphics, Qingdao, China, 26–28 July 2013; pp. 5–8.
40. Arridge, S.; Schweiger, M.; Hiraoka, M.; Delpy, D. A finite element approach for modelig photon transport in tissue. *Med. Phys.* **1993**, *20*, 299–309. [CrossRef] [PubMed]
41. Schweiger, M.; Arridge, S.R.; Delpy, D.T. Application of the finite-element method for the forward and inverse models in optical tomography. *J. Math. Imaging Vis.* **1993**, *3*, 263–283. [CrossRef]
42. Jiang, H.; Paulsen, K.D. Finite-element-based higher order diffusion approximation of light propagation in tissues. In Proceedings of the Optical Tomography, Photon Migration, and Spectroscopy of Tissue and Model Media: Theory, Human Studies, and Instrumentation, San Jose, CA, USA, 1–28 February 1995; pp. 608–614.
43. Schweiger, M.; Arridge, S.; Hiraoka, M.; Delpy, D. The finite element method for the propagation of light in scattering media: Boundary and source conditions. *Med. Phys.* **1995**, *22*, 1779–1792. [CrossRef] [PubMed]
44. Gao, F.; Niu, H.; Zhao, H.; Zhang, H. The forward and inverse models in time-resolved optical tomography imaging and their finite-element method solutions. *Image Vis. Comput.* **1998**, *16*, 703–712. [CrossRef]
45. Jiang, H. Frequency-domain fluorescent diffusion tomography: A finite-element-based algorithm and simulations. *Appl. Opt.* **1998**, *37*, 5337–5343. [CrossRef]
46. Klose, A.D.; Hielscher, A.H. Iterative reconstruction scheme for optical tomography based on the equation of radiative transfer. *Med. Phys.* **1999**, *26*, 1698–1707. [CrossRef]
47. Dehghani, H.; Srinivasan, S.; Pogue, B.W.; Gibson, A. Numerical modelling and image reconstruction in diffuse optical tomography. *Philos. Trans. R. Soc. A Math. Phys. Eng. Sci.* **2009**, *367*, 3073–3093. [CrossRef]
48. Paulsen, K.D.; Jiang, H. Spatially varying optical property reconstruction using a finite element diffusion equation approximation. *Med. Phys.* **1995**, *22*, 691–701. [CrossRef]
49. Gao, H.; Zhao, H. A fast-forward solver of radiative transfer equation. *Transp. Theory Stat. Phys.* **2009**, *38*, 149–192. [CrossRef]
50. Wang, L.; Jacques, S.L.; Zheng, L. MCML—Monte Carlo modeling of light transport in multi-layered tissues. *Comput. Methods Programs Biomed.* **1995**, *47*, 131–146. [CrossRef] [PubMed]
51. Chen, J.; Intes, X. Comparison of Monte Carlo methods for fluorescence molecular tomography—Computational efficiency. *Med. Phys.* **2011**, *38*, 5788–5798. [CrossRef]
52. Chen, J.; Intes, X. Time-gated perturbation Monte Carlo for whole body functional imaging in small animals. *Opt. Express* **2009**, *17*, 19566–19579. [CrossRef]
53. Periyasamy, V.; Pramanik, M. Advances in Monte Carlo simulation for light propagation in tissue. *IEEE Rev. Biomed. Eng.* **2017**, *10*, 122–135. [CrossRef]

54. Dehghani, H.; Eames, M.E.; Yalavarthy, P.K.; Davis, S.C.; Srinivasan, S.; Carpenter, C.M.; Pogue, B.W.; Paulsen, K.D. Near infrared optical tomography using NIRFAST: Algorithm for numerical model and image reconstruction. *Commun. Numer. Methods Eng.* **2009**, *25*, 711–732. [CrossRef]
55. Schweiger, M.; Arridge, S.R. The Toast++ software suite for forward and inverse modeling in optical tomography. *J. Biomed. Opt.* **2014**, *19*, 040801. [CrossRef]
56. Fang, Q.; Boas, D.A. Monte Carlo simulation of photon migration in 3D turbid media accelerated by graphics processing units. *Opt. Express* **2009**, *17*, 20178–20190. [CrossRef] [PubMed]
57. Fang, Q. Mesh-based Monte Carlo method using fast ray-tracing in Plücker coordinates. *Biomed. Opt. Express* **2010**, *1*, 165–175. [CrossRef] [PubMed]
58. Yu, L.; Nina-Paravecino, F.; Kaeli, D.R.; Fang, Q. Scalable and massively parallel Monte Carlo photon transport simulations for heterogeneous computing platforms. *J. Biomed. Opt.* **2018**, *23*, 010504. [CrossRef] [PubMed]
59. Yan, S.; Fang, Q. Hybrid mesh and voxel based Monte Carlo algorithm for accurate and efficient photon transport modeling in complex bio-tissues. *Biomed. Opt. Express* **2020**, *11*, 6262–6270. [CrossRef] [PubMed]
60. Leino, A.A.; Pulkkinen, A.; Tarvainen, T. ValoMC: A Monte Carlo software and MATLAB toolbox for simulating light transport in biological tissue. *OSA Contin.* **2019**, *2*, 957–972. [CrossRef]
61. Walker, S.A.; Fantini, S.; Gratton, E. Image reconstruction by backprojection from frequency-domain optical measurements in highly scattering media. *Appl. Opt.* **1997**, *36*, 170–179. [CrossRef] [PubMed]
62. Boas, D.; Chen, K.; Grebert, D.; Franceschini, M. Improving the diffuse optical imaging spatial resolution of the cerebral hemodynamic response to brain activation in humans. *Opt. Lett.* **2004**, *29*, 1506–1508. [CrossRef] [PubMed]
63. Zhai, Y.; Cummer, S.A. Fast tomographic reconstruction strategy for diffuse optical tomography. *Opt. Express* **2009**, *17*, 5285–5297. [CrossRef] [PubMed]
64. Das, T.; Dileep, B.; Dutta, P.K. Generalized curved beam back-projection method for near-infrared imaging using banana function. *Appl. Opt.* **2018**, *57*, 1838–1848. [CrossRef]
65. Habermehl, C.; Steinbrink, J.M.; Müller, K.-R.; Haufe, S. Optimizing the regularization for image reconstruction of cerebral diffuse optical tomography. *J. Biomed. Opt.* **2014**, *19*, 096006. [CrossRef]
66. Gupta, S.; Yalavarthy, P.K.; Roy, D.; Piao, D.; Vasu, R.M. Singular value decomposition based computationally efficient algorithm for rapid dynamic near-infrared diffuse optical tomography. *Med. Phys.* **2009**, *36*, 5559–5567. [CrossRef]
67. Zhan, Y.; Eggebrecht, A.T.; Culver, J.P.; Dehghani, H. Singular value decomposition based regularization prior to spectral mixing improves crosstalk in dynamic imaging using spectral diffuse optical tomography. *Biomed. Opt. Express* **2012**, *3*, 2036–2049. [CrossRef]
68. Paige, C.C.; Saunders, M.A. LSQR: An algorithm for sparse linear equations and sparse least squares. *ACM Trans. Math. Softw. TOMS* **1982**, *8*, 43–71. [CrossRef]
69. Hussain, A.; Faye, I.; Muthuvalu, M.S.; Boon, T.T. Least Square QR Decomposition Method for Solving the Inverse Problem in Functional Near Infra-Red Spectroscopy. In Proceedings of the 2021 IEEE 19th Student Conference on Research and Development (SCOReD), Kota Kinabalu, Malaysia, 23–25 November 2021; pp. 362–366.
70. Prakash, J.; Yalavarthy, P.K. A LSQR-type method provides a computationally efficient automated optimal choice of regularization parameter in diffuse optical tomography. *Med. Phys.* **2013**, *40*, 033101. [CrossRef] [PubMed]
71. Shaw, C.B.; Prakash, J.; Pramanik, M.; Yalavarthy, P.K. Least squares QR-based decomposition provides an efficient way of computing optimal regularization parameter in photoacoustic tomography. *J. Biomed. Opt.* **2013**, *18*, 080501. [CrossRef] [PubMed]
72. Yalavarthy, P.K.; Pogue, B.W.; Dehghani, H.; Paulsen, K.D. Weight-matrix structured regularization provides optimal generalized least-squares estimate in diffuse optical tomography. *Med. Phys.* **2007**, *34*, 2085–2098. [CrossRef] [PubMed]
73. Yalavarthy, P.K.; Pogue, B.W.; Dehghani, H.; Carpenter, C.M.; Jiang, S.; Paulsen, K.D. Structural information within regularization matrices improves near infrared diffuse optical tomography. *Opt. Express* **2007**, *15*, 8043–8058. [CrossRef] [PubMed]
74. Yalavarthy, P.K.; Lynch, D.R.; Pogue, B.W.; Dehghani, H.; Paulsen, K.D. Implementation of a computationally efficient least-squares algorithm for highly under-determined three-dimensional diffuse optical tomography problems. *Med. Phys.* **2008**, *35*, 1682–1697. [CrossRef]
75. Haufe, S.; Nikulin, V.V.; Ziehe, A.; Müller, K.-R.; Nolte, G. Combining sparsity and rotational invariance in EEG/MEG source reconstruction. *NeuroImage* **2008**, *42*, 726–738. [CrossRef]
76. Pascual-Marqui, R.D.; Michel, C.M.; Lehmann, D. Low resolution electromagnetic tomography: A new method for localizing electrical activity in the brain. *Int. J. Psychophysiol.* **1994**, *18*, 49–65. [CrossRef]
77. Prakash, J.; Shaw, C.B.; Manjappa, R.; Kanhirodan, R.; Yalavarthy, P.K. Sparse recovery methods hold promise for diffuse optical tomographic image reconstruction. *IEEE J. Sel. Top. Quantum Electron.* **2013**, *20*, 74–82. [CrossRef]
78. Shaw, C.B.; Yalavarthy, P.K. Performance evaluation of typical approximation algorithms for nonconvex ℓ p-minimization in diffuse optical tomography. *JOSA A* **2014**, *31*, 852–862. [CrossRef]
79. Okawa, S.; Hoshi, Y.; Yamada, Y. Improvement of image quality of time-domain diffuse optical tomography with lp sparsity regularization. *Biomed. Opt. Express* **2011**, *2*, 3334–3348. [CrossRef] [PubMed]
80. Sato, M.-A.; Yoshioka, T.; Kajihara, S.; Toyama, K.; Goda, N.; Doya, K.; Kawato, M. Hierarchical Bayesian estimation for MEG inverse problem. *NeuroImage* **2004**, *23*, 806–826. [CrossRef]

81. Guven, M.; Yazici, B.; Intes, X.; Chance, B. Hierarchical bayesian algorithm for diffuse optical tomography. In Proceedings of the 34th Applied Imagery and Pattern Recognition Workshop (AIPR'05), Washington, DC, USA, 19 October–21 December 2005; pp. 6–145.
82. Calvetti, D.; Pragliola, M.; Somersalo, E.; Strang, A. Sparse reconstructions from few noisy data: Analysis of hierarchical Bayesian models with generalized gamma hyperpriors. *Inverse Probl.* **2020**, *36*, 025010. [CrossRef]
83. Shimokawa, T.; Kosaka, T.; Yamashita, O.; Hiroe, N.; Amita, T.; Inoue, Y.; Sato, M.A. Hierarchical Bayesian estimation improves depth accuracy and spatial resolution of diffuse optical tomography. *Opt. Express* **2012**, *20*, 20427–20446. [CrossRef] [PubMed]
84. Shimokawa, T.; Kosaka, T.; Yamashita, O.; Hiroe, N.; Amita, T.; Inoue, Y.; Sato, M.A. Extended hierarchical Bayesian diffuse optical tomography for removing scalp artifact. *Biomed. Opt. Express* **2013**, *4*, 2411–2432. [CrossRef] [PubMed]
85. Aihara, T.; Shimokawa, T.; Ogawa, T.; Okada, Y.; Ishikawa, A.; Inoue, Y.; Yamashita, O. Resting-state functional connectivity estimated with hierarchical bayesian diffuse optical tomography. *Front. Neurosci.* **2020**, *14*, 32. [CrossRef]
86. Yamashita, O.; Shimokawa, T.; Aisu, R.; Amita, T.; Inoue, Y.; Sato, M.-A. Multi-subject and multi-task experimental validation of the hierarchical Bayesian diffuse optical tomography algorithm. *Neuroimage* **2016**, *135*, 287–299. [CrossRef]
87. Hiltunen, P.; Prince, S.; Arridge, S. A combined reconstruction–classification method for diffuse optical tomography. *Phys. Med. Biol.* **2009**, *54*, 6457. [CrossRef]
88. Cao, N.; Nehorai, A.; Jacob, M. Image reconstruction for diffuse optical tomography using sparsity regularization and expectation-maximization algorithm. *Opt. Express* **2007**, *15*, 13695–13708. [CrossRef]
89. Amblard, C.; Lapalme, E.; Lina, J.-M. Biomagnetic source detection by maximum entropy and graphical models. *IEEE Trans. Biomed. Eng.* **2004**, *51*, 427–442. [CrossRef]
90. Grova, C.; Daunizeau, J.; Lina, J.-M.; Bénar, C.G.; Benali, H.; Gotman, J. Evaluation of EEG localization methods using realistic simulations of interictal spikes. *Neuroimage* **2006**, *29*, 734–753. [CrossRef] [PubMed]
91. Chowdhury, R.A.; Lina, J.M.; Kobayashi, E.; Grova, C. MEG source localization of spatially extended generators of epileptic activity: Comparing entropic and hierarchical bayesian approaches. *PLoS ONE* **2013**, *8*, e55969. [CrossRef] [PubMed]
92. Cai, Z.; Machado, A.; Chowdhury, R.A.; Spilkin, A.; Vincent, T.; Aydin, Ü.; Pellegrino, G.; Lina, J.-M.; Grova, C. Diffuse optical reconstructions of fNIRS data using Maximum Entropy on the Mean. *bioRxiv* **2021**, *23*, 2021-02. [CrossRef]
93. Trujillo-Barreto, N.J.; Aubert-Vázquez, E.; Valdés-Sosa, P.A. Bayesian model averaging in EEG/MEG imaging. *NeuroImage* **2004**, *21*, 1300–1319. [CrossRef] [PubMed]
94. Fragoso, T.M.; Bertoli, W.; Louzada, F. Bayesian model averaging: A systematic review and conceptual classification. *Int. Stat. Rev.* **2018**, *86*, 1–28. [CrossRef]

Disclaimer/Publisher's Note: The statements, opinions and data contained in all publications are solely those of the individual author(s) and contributor(s) and not of MDPI and/or the editor(s). MDPI and/or the editor(s) disclaim responsibility for any injury to people or property resulting from any ideas, methods, instructions or products referred to in the content.

Article

Extending Normality: A Case of Unit Distribution Generated from the Moments of the Standard Normal Distribution

Miguel S. Concha-Aracena [1], Leonardo Barrios-Blanco [1], David Elal-Olivero [1], Paulo Henrique Ferreira da Silva [2,3] and Diego Carvalho do Nascimento [1,*]

1 Departamento de Matemática, Facultad de Ingeniería, Universidad de Atacama, Copiapó 1530000, Chile
2 Department of Statistics, Federal University of Bahia, Salvador 40170110, Brazil
3 Centro de Pesquisa em Matemática Aplicada à Indústria (CeMEAI), University of São Paulo, São Carlos 13566590, Brazil
* Correspondence: diego.nascimento@uda.cl

Abstract: This paper presents an important theorem, which shows that, heading from the moments of the standard normal distribution, one can generate density functions originating a family of models. Additionally, we discussed that different random variable domains are achieved with transformations. For instance, we adopted the moment of order two, from the proposed theorem, and transformed it, which enabled us to exemplify this class as a unit distribution. We named it as Alpha-Unit (AU) distribution, which contains a single positive parameter α (AU(α) $\in [0,1]$). We presented its properties and demonstrated two estimation methods for the α parameter, the maximum likelihood estimator (MLE) and uniformly minimum-variance unbiased estimator (UMVUE) methods. In order to analyze the statistical consistency of the estimators, a Monte Carlo simulation study was carried out, in which the robustness was demonstrated. As a real-world application, we adopted two sets of unit data, the first regarding the dynamics of Chilean inflation in the post-military period, and the other one regarding the daily maximum relative humidity of the air in the Atacama Desert. In both cases presented, the AU model is competitive, whenever the data present a range greater than 0.4 and extremely heavy asymmetric tail. We compared our model with other commonly used unit models, such as the beta, Kumaraswamy, logit-normal, simplex, unit-half-normal, and unit-Lindley distributions.

Keywords: asymmetry accommodation; rates and proportions; single-parameter distribution; unit distribution; water monitoring

1. Introduction

Statistical methodology plays an important role in quantitative methods, given the hypothesis testing and inferential procedures. Nonetheless, the comparison across features is given based on a generated function estimated from the data information. Most often, mild suppositions are assumed, which compromises the generalization of the results.

Under the perspective of statistical generalization (inferential method), some challenges are found for bounded distribution estimation. For instance, the confidence interval, which is often adopted from the maximum likelihood estimation approach and asymptotic supposition, is also assumed. Specially, interval estimation can be seen as the parameter space domain.

One exemplification is the case in which bounded information data are observed and, nonetheless, normality is commonly assumed to be true. This is the case of proportion/rate data, which are double bounded in the lower limit equal to zero and upper limit equal to one. Relative humidity is an example of this scenario in which every decision-making should be $\in [0,1]$ [1,2], or rates commonly used in the fields of finance, economics and demography, to number a few.

In the case of rates and proportions processes, as well as other processes whose variables of interest assume values in the range $(0,1)$, there is a well-represented class of models, the unit distributions family, which deals with this type of double-bounded data. Among the many existing unit distributions, it is noteworthy mentioning the power distribution, beta distribution [3], Kumaraswamy distribution [4], unit-logistic distribution [5], simplex distribution [6], unit-Weibull distribution [7,8], unit-Lindley distribution [9], unit-half-normal distribution [10], unit log-log distribution [11], modified Kumaraswamy and reflected modified Kumaraswamy distributions [12], unit-Teissier distribution [13], unit extended Weibull families of distributions [14], lognormal distribution [15], unit folded normal distribution [16], Marshall-Olkin reduced Kies distribution [17], and unit-Chen distribution [18].

Despite the applicability of the unit distributions in double-bounded variables, another important fact is that the interval estimation for the parameter may also be limited in a domain (like positive real number). In the face of it, we also presented an inferential alternative through the delta method.

This study starts with a presentation of an important theorem that changes from a modification of the standard normal distribution into a class of density functions that can be seen as a unit. Then, as an exemplification, a second moment case was chosen to illustrate the usefulness of this class of probabilistic models. This class of distributions shows to be competitive for high-frequency data with range greater than 0.4, important to real-world applications, whereas a classical unit distribution fails [19]. Additionally, two different data sets were selected to illustrate the adjustment of the proposed model. The first one is related to the Chilean inflation (ultimate post-military era), and the second one comes from the driest area of the planet (excluding the north and south poles).

This paper is structured in four parts. Section 2 presents the proposed one-parameter unit distribution. In Section 3, the inferences for the distribution parameter adopting the uniformly minimum-variance unbiased estimator (UMVUE) and maximum likelihood estimator (MLE) as point estimators, as well as interval estimations, are discussed. A simulation study is also presented in this section. In Section 4, two real data sets are used to illustrate the proposed methodology, one from the Chilean inflation in the post-military period, and other one from the relative humidity water monitoring in the Atacama Desert. Finally, Section 5 lists the conclusions of this study. Nevertheless, before moving on into the described structure, a wide class of models that can be generated in many different random variable supports is presented. Therefore, a theorem is elicited and, as a special case, the whole paper will consider an order two for exemplification of this powerful class of distributions.

Motivation

The normal (or Gaussian) distribution is very important to the history of statistics, and numerous modifications to this distribution have been proposed in the literature [20,21]. An interesting fact related to the normal distribution is that its even moments can be used to generate new distributions, which is the case presented below, through a definition and a result embodied in a theorem that accounts for the characterization of these new distributions.

Definition 1. *A random variable B is said to be distributed according to a Bimodal Normal (BN) distribution of order k, that is, $B \sim BN(k)$ (discussed in [22]), if its probability density function (PDF) is given by*

$$f(b \mid k) = \frac{1}{c} b^{2k} \phi(b), \qquad b \in \mathbb{R},$$

in which $\phi(\cdot)$ is the PDF of the standard normal distribution, $c = \prod_{j=1}^{k}(2j-1)$ and $k = \{1, 2, 3, \ldots\}$.

This class of distributions is always bimodal, which means that the observed modes move away from each other when the order k increases (as depicted by Figure 1).

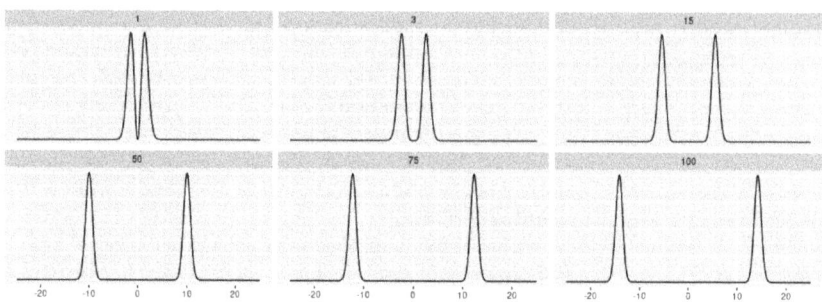

Figure 1. Density function of the BN distribution by varying the parameter k (displayed at the top of each chart).

It is noteworthy mentioning that transformations derived from the BN(k) distribution may lead to other domains of interest, e.g., the unit domain. For example, let $B \sim$ BN(k), then a scale parameter α, the transformation $\alpha|B| \in \mathbb{R}^+$, and then the transformation $e^{-\alpha|B|} \in [0,1]$. Thus, the stochastic characterization of a BN(k) distribution can be obtained according to the following theorem.

Theorem 1. *Let W_1 and W_2 be independent random variables, in which W_1 is such that $\mathbb{P}(W_1 = 1) = \mathbb{P}(W_1 = -1) = 1/2$ and $W_2 \sim \chi^2_{2k+1}$. Then,*

$$W_1\sqrt{W_2} \sim \mathrm{BN}(k). \tag{1}$$

So, this theorem is mainly motivated by the result that shows that if $X \sim$ BN(k), then $X^2 \sim \chi^2_{2k+1}$. The entire demonstration is presented in Appendix A.

2. The Model

In this section, a new unit distribution, named Alpha-Unit, which presents a single parameter, α, is discussed. Its stochastic representations (probability density and cumulative distribution functions), moments (including mean and variance), moment-generating function, and how to generate pseudo-random numbers from it will be presented. Moreover, a proposal of statistical control chart for unit data based on the Alpha-Unit distribution will also be shown.

The Alpha-Unit density is originated from the general theorem (Theorem 1), by considering $k = 1$. Moreover, it represents the second moment of the standard normal distribution and, later, transformed its domain. However, as k increases, the concentration of the distribution intensifies and other densities could be obtained.

Properties and Characterization

Definition 2. *(Alpha-Unit distribution). A random variable X follows an Alpha-Unit (AU) distribution with parameter $\alpha > 0$, that is, $X \sim AU(\alpha)$, if its PDF is given by*

$$f_X(x \mid \alpha) = \frac{2}{x\alpha}\left(\frac{\ln(x)}{\alpha}\right)^2 \phi\left(\frac{\ln(x)}{\alpha}\right), \quad 0 < x \leq 1. \tag{2}$$

Remark 1. *If $X \sim AU(\alpha)$, then its PDF is unimodal.*

Proof. The maxima of the AU distribution are studied, to which the criterion of the first derivative is first considered:

$$\frac{df_X(x \mid \alpha)}{dx} = \frac{2}{x\alpha^2} \frac{\ln(x)}{\alpha} \phi\left(\frac{\ln(x)}{\alpha}\right) \left[\frac{2}{x} - \frac{\ln(x)}{x} - \frac{[\ln(x)]^2}{\alpha} \frac{1}{x\alpha}\right] = 0.$$

By solving algebraically for x, we obtain:

$$x = \begin{cases} e^{\left(\frac{\alpha^2 + \sqrt{\alpha^4 + 8\alpha^2}}{2}\right)} & \text{(i)} \\ e^{\left(\frac{\alpha^2 - \sqrt{\alpha^4 + 8\alpha^2}}{2}\right)} & \text{(ii)} \end{cases}.$$

By working algebraically, it can be seen that this is only true for (ii), and is a global maximum, given that the solution is in between 0 and 1. Therefore, the AU distribution is unimodal. □

Proposition 1. *If $X \sim AU(\alpha)$, then its r-th order moment is given by*

$$\mathbb{E}[X^r] = 2e^{\left(\frac{r^2\alpha^2}{2}\right)} \left[\left(1 + r^2\alpha^2\right)(1 - \Phi(r\alpha)) - r\alpha\phi(r\alpha)\right],$$

in which $\Phi(\cdot)$ is the cumulative distribution function (CDF) of the standard normal distribution.

Proof. From the definition of the r-th order moment, we have:

$$\mathbb{E}[X^r] = \int_0^1 x^r f_X(x \mid \alpha) dx = \int_0^1 x^r \frac{2}{x\alpha} \left(\frac{\ln(x)}{\alpha}\right)^2 \phi\left(\frac{\ln(x)}{\alpha}\right) dx. \quad (3)$$

By changing the variables:

$$\begin{cases} u = \frac{1}{\alpha} \ln(x) & \Rightarrow \quad e^{u\alpha} = x \\ du = \frac{1}{\alpha x} dx & \Rightarrow \quad \alpha e^{u\alpha} du = dx \end{cases},$$

then substituting into Equation (3) and developing algebraically, we obtain:

$$\mathbb{E}[X^r] = 2e^{\frac{\alpha^2 r^2}{2}} \int_{-\infty}^0 u^2 \frac{1}{\sqrt{2\pi}} e^{-\frac{(u-\alpha r)^2}{2}} du.$$

Then, by making another change of variables: $h = u - \alpha r$, $dh = du$; and replacing these expressions in the previous equation, we have:

$$\mathbb{E}[X^r] = 2e^{\frac{\alpha^2 r^2}{2}} \int_{-\infty}^{-\alpha r} (h + \alpha r)^2 \frac{1}{\sqrt{2\pi}} e^{-\frac{h^2}{2}} dh$$

$$= 2e^{\frac{\alpha^2 r^2}{2}} \int_{-\infty}^{-\alpha r} \left(h^2 + 2h\alpha r + \alpha^2 r^2\right) \phi(h) dh$$

$$= 2e^{\frac{\alpha^2 r^2}{2}} \left(\int_{-\infty}^{-\alpha r} h^2 \phi(h) dh + 2\alpha r \int_{-\infty}^{-\alpha r} h\phi(h) dh + \alpha^2 r^2 \int_{-\infty}^{-\alpha r} \phi(h) dh\right).$$

By solving the integrals, we get to:

$$\mathbb{E}[X^r] = 2e^{\frac{\alpha^2 r^2}{2}} \left[\alpha r \phi(\alpha r) + (1 - \Phi(\alpha r)) - 2\alpha r \phi(\alpha r) + \alpha^2 r^2 (1 - \Phi(\alpha r))\right].$$

Then, by solving algebraically, we go down to the expression of Proposition 1. □

Out of Proposition 1, we obtain the mean and variance of the $AU(\alpha)$ model as it follows:

$$\mathbb{E}[X] = 2e^{\frac{\alpha^2}{2}}\left[(1+\alpha^2)(1-\Phi(\alpha))-\alpha\phi(\alpha)\right],$$

$$\mathrm{Var}[X] = \mathbb{E}[X^2] - (\mathbb{E}[X])^2$$
$$= 2e^{2\alpha^2}\left[(1+4\alpha^2)(1-\Phi(2\alpha))-2\alpha\phi(2\alpha)\right] - 4e^{\alpha^2}\left[(1+\alpha^2)(1-\Phi(\alpha))-\alpha\phi(\alpha)\right]^2.$$

Remark 2. *As an illustration, Figure 2 displays the generated asymmetry and kurtosis based on the chosen α parameter of the AU distribution.*

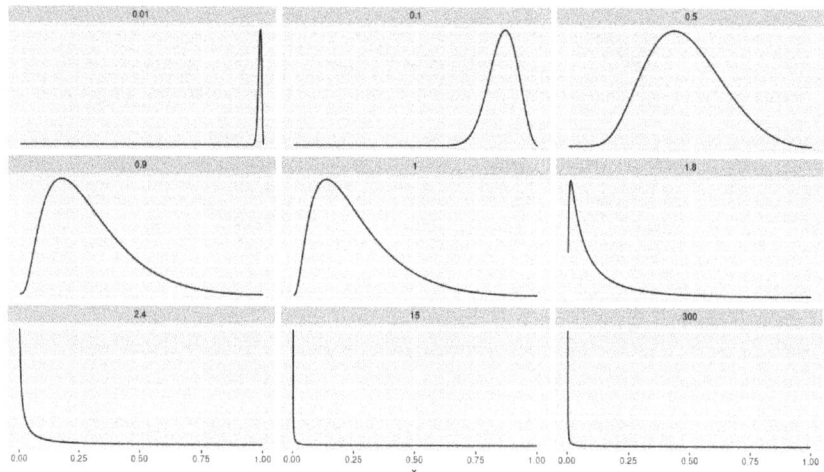

Figure 2. Density function of the AU distribution by varying the parameter α (displayed at the top of each chart). Whereas $B \sim BN(1) \to B^2 \sim \chi_3^2$, then the AU model was generated from $X = e^{-\alpha|B|}$.

Proposition 2. *If $X \sim AU(\alpha)$, then its CDF is given by*

$$F_X(x \mid \alpha) = 2\Phi\left(\frac{\ln(x)}{\alpha}\right) - 2\left(\frac{\ln(x)}{\alpha}\right)\phi\left(\frac{\ln(x)}{\alpha}\right).$$

Proof. By definition, the CDF is:

$$F_X(x \mid \alpha) = \int_0^x \frac{2}{t\alpha}\left(\frac{\ln(t)}{\alpha}\right)^2 \phi\left(\frac{\ln(t)}{\alpha}\right) dt. \qquad (4)$$

By making the change of variables:

$$\begin{cases} u = \frac{\ln(t)}{\alpha} & \Rightarrow \quad e^{u\alpha} = t \\ du = \frac{1}{\alpha t}dt & \Rightarrow \quad \alpha e^{u\alpha} du = dt \end{cases},$$

then substituting into Equation (4) and reducing expressions algebraically, we get to:

$$F_X(x \mid \alpha) = 2\int_{-\infty}^{\frac{\ln(x)}{\alpha}} u^2 \phi(u) du.$$

By calculating the integral, we find:

$$F_X(x \mid \alpha) = 2\left[-u\phi(u)\Big|_{-\infty}^{\ln(x)/\alpha} + \int_{-\infty}^{\ln(x)/\alpha} \phi(u)du\right]$$

$$= 2\left[-\left(\frac{\ln(x)}{\alpha}\right)\phi\left(\frac{\ln(x)}{\alpha}\right) + \Phi\left(\frac{\ln(x)}{\alpha}\right)\right].$$

Then, by multiplying and commuting, we get to the expression of Proposition 2. □

Additionally, if X denotes the monitored variable, then the PDF of X is given by (2). Also, consider that the probability of false alarm (known as type I error) is π. Thus, we get to:

$$\mathbb{P}(X < \text{LCL} \mid \alpha) = \mathbb{P}(X > \text{UCL} \mid \alpha) = \pi/2,$$

in which α is the in-control process parameter (that is, the parameter that controls the quality characteristic based on the in-control state), and LCL and UCL are the lower and upper control chart limits, respectively. Given the CDF $F_X(x \mid \alpha)$, then the quantile function of X is defined by $Q(p \mid \alpha) = F_X^{-1}(p \mid \alpha)$, $0 < p < 1$, which can be obtained by setting to zero and solving (numerically) for x the following equation:

$$\Phi\left(\frac{\ln(x)}{\alpha}\right) - \left(\frac{\ln(x)}{\alpha}\right)\phi\left(\frac{\ln(x)}{\alpha}\right) - \frac{p}{2}, \quad \text{for } 0 < p < 1.$$

Following [23], the control limits and centerline (CL) of the proposed control chart for unit data based on the AU distribution or, simply, AU control chart, are given by

$$\text{LCL} = Q(\pi/2 \mid \alpha), \quad \text{CL} = \mathbb{E}[X \mid \alpha], \quad \text{UCL} = Q(1 - \pi/2 \mid \alpha),$$

in which $Q(.)$ is the quantile function of the $AU(\alpha)$ distribution.

Proposition 3. *If $X \sim AU(\alpha)$, then its moment-generating function (MGF) is given by*

$$\psi_X(t \mid \alpha) = 2\sum_{k=0}^{\infty} \frac{t^k}{k!} e^{\left(\frac{k^2\alpha^2}{2}\right)} \left[\left(1 + k^2\alpha^2\right)(1 - \Phi(k\alpha)) - k\alpha\phi(k\alpha)\right].$$

Proof. By definition, the MGF is:

$$\psi_X(t \mid \alpha) = \mathbb{E}\left[e^{tx}\right] = \int_0^1 e^{tx} \frac{2}{x\alpha}\left(\frac{\ln(x)}{\alpha}\right)^2 \phi\left(\frac{\ln(x)}{\alpha}\right) dx. \tag{5}$$

By making the following change of variables:

$$\begin{cases} u = \frac{\ln(x)}{\alpha} & \Rightarrow \quad e^{u\alpha} = x \\ du = \frac{1}{\alpha x}dx & \Rightarrow \quad \alpha e^{u\alpha}du = dx \end{cases},$$

then substituting and simplifying into Equation (5), we get to:

$$\psi_X(t \mid \alpha) = 2\int_{-\infty}^{0} e^{(te^{u\alpha})} u^2 \phi(u) du$$

$$= 2\int_{-\infty}^{0} \sum_{k=0}^{\infty} \frac{t^k e^{u\alpha k}}{k!} u^2 \phi(u) du.$$

Working algebraically, we obtain:

$$\psi_X(t\mid\alpha) = 2\sum_{k=0}^{\infty}\frac{t^k}{k!}e^{\left(\frac{\alpha^2 k^2}{2}\right)}\int_{-\infty}^{0}u^2\frac{1}{\sqrt{2\pi}}e^{\left(\frac{-(u-\alpha k)^2}{2}\right)}du.$$

By making the following change of variables: $h = u - \alpha k$, $dh = du$; then substituting it into the previous equation, we get to:

$$\psi_X(t\mid\alpha) = 2\sum_{k=0}^{\infty}\frac{t^k}{k!}e^{\left(\frac{\alpha^2 k^2}{2}\right)}\int_{-\infty}^{-\alpha k}(h+\alpha k)^2\phi(h)dh.$$

Then, by solving the integral and adjusting algebraically, we get to the expression of Proposition 3. □

The pseudo-code presented in Algorithm 1 describes the important steps for the generation of random (in fact, pseudo-random) numbers from the AU(α) distribution. Further proofs are attached under Appendix B.

Algorithm 1 Random number generation from the AU(α) model.

Step 1. Generate a random number $x_1 \sim \chi_3^2$.

Step 2. Generate a random number $u \sim$ Uniform$(0,1)$. If $u \leq 1/2$, set $v = \sqrt{X_1}$; otherwise, $v = -\sqrt{X_1}$.

Step 3. Based on the numbers obtained, generate $y = \alpha|v|$, in which α is a (positive) scale parameter and $|v|$ follows a Bimodal Half-Normal (BHN) distribution.

Step 4. Conclude with the number generated by Step 3 as a negative power of base e, that is, $x = e^{-y} = e^{-\alpha|v|} \in [0,1]$.

Step 5. Repeat Steps 1–4 n times to obtain a random sample of size n from the AU(α) model.

---

3. Inference

In this section, the parameter estimation adopting the UMVUE and MLE approaches are discussed. At first, it will be demonstrated that the UMVUE can be obtained straightforwardly, since the proposed AU distribution is part of the exponential family. Later, the MLE will also be discussed, which will help to estimate not only the point estimation of the α parameter, but also the interval estimation. We enrolled the reasoning considering the asymptotic convergence in distribution of the parameter estimator, as well as adapted a transformation that ensures that the interval of the parameter will always be on its domain (the delta method). The delta transformation procedure will enable the correct inferences and the standard error calculation associated with the parameter estimate. Later on, a simulation study to illustrate these theoretical results is presented.

3.1. UMVUE through the Exponential Family

Many of the distributions used in statistics belong to the exponential family, thereby implying in a considerable advantage over other models that do not belong to this family. Such an advantage is significantly declared when it comes to calculating the statistic $T(\mathbf{X})$ of a random sample $\mathbf{X} = (X_1, X_2, \ldots, X_n)$. Next, it is shown that the proposed AU(α) distribution belongs to this family.

A random variable X is said to belong to the *one-parameter exponential family* if its associated PDF $f(\cdot \mid \theta)$ can be written in the form of:

$$f(x\mid\theta) = \exp\{c(\theta)T(x) + d(\theta) + S(x)\}.$$

Let $X \sim AU(\alpha)$, then the PDF of X can be written in exponential form as it follows:

$$f(x \mid \alpha) = \exp\left\{-\frac{1}{2\alpha^2}[\ln(x)]^2 - 3\ln(\alpha) + \ln\left(\frac{[\ln(x)]^2}{x\sqrt{2\pi}}\right)\right\}.$$

Then, X belongs to the one-parameter exponential family if we define:

$$c(\alpha) = -\frac{1}{2\alpha^2}, \quad T(x) = [\ln(x)]^2, \quad d(\alpha) = -3\ln(\alpha), \quad S(x) = \ln\left(\frac{[\ln(x)]^2}{x\sqrt{2\pi}}\right).$$

Let $x = (x_1, x_2, \ldots, x_n)$ be an observation (or realization) of the random sample $X = (X_1, X_2, \ldots, X_n)$, with $X_i \sim AU(\alpha)$, for $i = 1, 2, \ldots, n$. Then, the joint PDF presented in exponential form is

$$f(x \mid \alpha) = \exp\left\{-\frac{1}{2\alpha^2}\sum_{i=1}^{n}[\ln(x_i)]^2 - 3n\ln(\alpha) + \sum_{i=1}^{n}\ln\left(\frac{[\ln(x_i)]^2}{x_i\sqrt{2\pi}}\right)\right\},$$

from which it can be concluded that the statistic $T(X) = \sum_{i=1}^{n}[\ln(X_i)]^2$ is sufficient and complete, once the AU distribution is part of the exponential family.

Proposition 4. *Let $X = (X_1, X_2, \ldots, X_n)$ be a random sample, with $X_i \sim AU(\alpha)$, for $i = 1, 2, \ldots, n$, and $T(X) = \sum_{i=1}^{n}[\ln(X_i)]^2$. Then,*

$$W_n = \frac{1}{\alpha^2}T(X) \sim \chi^2_{3n}.$$

Proof. If $G = \left[\frac{\ln(X)}{\alpha}\right]^2$, then $G \sim \chi^2_3$. Thus, n independent and identically distributed samples of G will have the sum of n χ^2_3, which will result in a chi-squared distribution with degrees of freedom equal to $3n$, that is, χ^2_{3n}, since

$$F_G(g) = \mathbb{P}(G \leq g) = \mathbb{P}\left(\left[\frac{\ln(X)}{\alpha}\right]^2 \leq g\right) = \mathbb{P}\left(-\sqrt{g} \leq \frac{\ln(X)}{\alpha} \leq \sqrt{g}\right)$$

$$= \mathbb{P}(-\alpha\sqrt{g} \leq \ln(X) \leq \alpha\sqrt{g}) = \mathbb{P}(\ln(X) \leq \alpha\sqrt{g}) - \mathbb{P}(\ln(X) \leq -\alpha\sqrt{g})$$

$$= 1 - \mathbb{P}(\ln(X) \leq -\alpha\sqrt{g}) = 1 - \mathbb{P}\left(X \leq e^{-\alpha\sqrt{g}}\right) = 1 - F_X\left(e^{-\alpha\sqrt{g}}\right),$$

so,

$$f_G(g) = \frac{dF_G(g)}{dg} = f_X\left(e^{-\alpha\sqrt{g}}\right)\left(e^{-\alpha\sqrt{g}}\right)\left(\frac{\alpha}{2\sqrt{g}}\right)$$

$$= \frac{2}{\alpha e^{-\alpha\sqrt{g}}}\left(\frac{-\alpha\sqrt{g}}{\alpha}\right)^2 \phi\left(\frac{-\alpha\sqrt{g}}{\alpha}\right)e^{-\alpha\sqrt{g}}\frac{\alpha}{2\sqrt{g}}$$

$$= \frac{1}{\sqrt{g}}(\sqrt{g})^2\frac{1}{\sqrt{2\pi}}e^{-\frac{(\sqrt{g})^2}{2}} = \frac{1}{\sqrt{2\pi}}g^{1/2}\exp(-g/2) \equiv \chi^2_3.$$

□

Proposition 5. *Let $X = (X_1, X_2, \ldots, X_n)$ be a random sample, with $X_i \sim AU(\alpha)$, for $i = 1, 2, \ldots, n$, and $T(X) = \sum_{i=1}^{n}[\ln(X_i)]^2$. Then,*

$$S(X) = \frac{\Gamma\left(\frac{3n}{2}\right)\sqrt{2}}{\Gamma\left(\frac{3n+1}{2}\right)}\sqrt{T(X)}$$

is an unbiased estimator of α.

Proof. First, remember that if $X \sim \text{Gamma}(a,b)$ distribution, then $\mathbb{E}[X^k] = \frac{\Gamma(a+b)}{b^k \Gamma(a)}$. Since the α parameter is observed to be squared, it will be necessary to apply it to find an unbiased estimator. So, considering the random variable $W_n^{1/2}$ (with W_n as defined in Proposition 4), it follows that:

$$\mathbb{E}\left[(W_n)^{1/2}\right] = \frac{\Gamma\left(\frac{3n}{2} + \frac{1}{2}\right)}{2^{1/2}\Gamma\left(\frac{3n}{2}\right)},$$

so,

$$\mathbb{E}\left[\left(\frac{1}{\alpha^2}T(X)\right)^{1/2}\right] = \frac{\Gamma\left(\frac{3n}{2} + \frac{1}{2}\right)}{2^{1/2}\Gamma\left(\frac{3n}{2}\right)}$$

$$\mathbb{E}\underbrace{\left[\sqrt{T(X)}\frac{\Gamma\left(\frac{3n}{2}\right)\sqrt{2}}{\Gamma\left(\frac{3n}{2} + \frac{1}{2}\right)}\right]}_{S(X)} = \alpha.$$

□

Remark 3. *Considering the two previous propositions and resorting to the Lehmann-Scheffé theorem, one can conclude that $S(X)$ is UMVUE for α.*

3.2. Estimation using the Maximum Likelihood Method

Let $x = (x_1, x_2, \ldots, x_n)$ be a realization of the random sample $X = (X_1, X_2, \ldots, X_n)$ taken from the AU(α) distribution. Then, the log-likelihood function is given by

$$\ell(\alpha) = \text{constant} - 3n\ln(\alpha) - \Sigma_{i=1}^n \ln(x_i) + 2\Sigma_{i=1}^n \ln(\ln(x_i)) - \frac{1}{2\alpha^2}\Sigma_{i=1}^n [\ln(x_i)]^2.$$

The MLE of α, i.e., $\widehat{\alpha}$, is found by solving the following equation:

$$\frac{d\ell(\alpha)}{d\alpha} = -\frac{3n}{\alpha} + \frac{1}{\alpha^3}\Sigma_{i=1}^n [\ln(x_i)]^2 = 0,$$

resulting

$$\widehat{\alpha} = \left\{\frac{1}{3n}\sum_{i=1}^n [\ln(x_i)]^2\right\}^{1/2}.$$

On the other hand, the second derivative of $\ell(\alpha)$ evaluated at $\alpha = \widehat{\alpha}$ is negative, therefore concluding that $\widehat{\alpha}$ is MLE for α.

It is known that, under certain regularity conditions,

$$\sqrt{n}(\widehat{\alpha} - \alpha) \xrightarrow{D} N\left(0, I^{-1}(\alpha)\right),$$

in which $I(\alpha) = -\mathbb{E}\left[\frac{d^2 \ell(\alpha)}{d\alpha^2}\right] = \frac{6n}{\alpha^2}$.

A two-sided $100(1 - \pi)\%$ confidence interval for α can be calculated by

$$\left[\widehat{\alpha} - z_{1-\pi/2}\sqrt{\text{Var}[\widehat{\alpha}]}, \ \widehat{\alpha} + z_{1-\pi/2}\sqrt{\text{Var}[\widehat{\alpha}]}\right], \quad (6)$$

in which z_q is the q-th percentile of the standard normal distribution. The variance of $\widehat{\alpha}$ can be approximated by the inverse of the observed Fisher information, as

$$\text{Var}[\widehat{\alpha}] = I^{-1}(\widehat{\alpha}) = \frac{\widehat{\alpha}^2}{6n}.$$

Since α is a positive value and we cannot guarantee that the lower limit of the interval (6) is positive, we resort to the delta method to remedy such situation. For this, we define the function $g : [0, \infty) \to \mathbb{R}$ as $g(\alpha) = \ln(\alpha)$, and knowing that

$$\sqrt{n}(g(\widehat{\alpha}) - g(\alpha)) \xrightarrow{D} N\left(0, I^{-1}(\alpha)\left[\frac{dg(\alpha)}{d\alpha}\right]^2\right),$$

we can, then, obtain an approximate two-sided $100(1 - \pi)\%$ confidence interval for α through

$$\left[\widehat{\alpha} \exp\left(-\frac{z_{1-\pi/2}}{\sqrt{6n}}\right), \frac{\widehat{\alpha}}{\exp\left(-\frac{z_{1-\pi/2}}{\sqrt{6n}}\right)}\right]. \tag{7}$$

3.3. Simulation Study

In order to illustrate the presented inferences for the estimation of the AU distribution, the MLE versus the UMVUE are compared (via simulation study) in this subsection. Moreover, we considered the scenarios in which the parameter $\alpha = \{0.1, 0.3, 0.5, 0.7, 1.1, 1.5\}$, considering sample sizes $n = \{100, 200, 500\}$, through the Monte Carlo method with $N = 1000$ repetitions. This entire procedure took into account the random number generator for the $AU(\alpha)$ distribution shown in Algorithm 1. All analyses carried out in this study adopted the open-source R software [24].

For the performance comparison of the proposed estimators (MLE and UMVUE), since the true parameter value is known, the bias and mean squared error (MSE) metrics were adopted, and they are defined, respectively, as it follows:

$$\text{Bias}(\alpha) = \frac{1}{N}\sum_{i=1}^{N}(\widehat{\alpha}_i - \alpha) \quad \text{and} \quad \text{MSE}(\alpha) = \frac{1}{N}\sum_{i=1}^{N}(\widehat{\alpha}_i - \alpha)^2,$$

in which $\widehat{\alpha}_i$ is the estimate for α in the i-th iteration (point estimation). Additionally, based on the asymptotic results presented in this study, we also calculated the 95% confidence interval (CI) length by adopting the delta method from Equation (7) (interval estimation). That is, it analyzed the average of all the upper limits of the 95% confidence interval, as well as the average of all the lower limits, and then calculated their difference.

Table 1 presents the obtained average estimates (AvE) of the α parameter, for each sample size n, as well as the corresponding bias, MSE and 95% CI length (this last one only for MLE) results.

The asymptotic convergence of the MLE towards the robustness is noticed as the sample size increases. In addition, both MLE and UMVUE's bias and MSE are small and tend to decrease as n gets larger. On the other hand, the CI length also decreases as the sample size increases.

Finally, regarding the robustness of the estimators, the difference between the MLE and UMVUE estimates was taken, considering each different sample size n. Then, the interquartile range (IQR) was calculated per sample size group. That is, $\text{IQR}^{(ni)}\left(\widehat{\alpha}_{1\text{MLE}}^{(ni)} - \widehat{\alpha}_{1\text{UMVUE}}^{(ni)}, \ldots, \widehat{\alpha}_{j\text{MLE}}^{(ni)} - \widehat{\alpha}_{j\text{UMVUE}}^{(ni)}, \ldots, \widehat{\alpha}_{6\text{MLE}}^{(ni)} - \widehat{\alpha}_{6\text{UMVUE}}^{(ni)}\right)$, in which $ni = \{100, 200, 500\}$ and $\alpha_j = \{\alpha_1 = 0.1, \alpha_2 = 0.3, \ldots, \alpha_6 = 1.5\}$. For instance, the IQR for $n = 100$ was 0.00053, whereas for $n = 200$ and $n = 500$, it went down to 0.00025 and 0.00012, respectively. This points out, in short, that as the sample size gets larger, the error range gets smaller, regardless of the value of the α parameter.

Table 1. AvE, bias, MSE and 95% CI length (only for MLE) for the proposed estimators (MLE and UMVUE) of the single parameter (α) of the AU distribution, considering different sample sizes (n).

n	α	MLE				UMVUE		
		AvE	Bias	MSE	CI Length	AvE	Bias	MSE
100	0.1	0.0998	−0.0002	1.6930×10^{-5}	0.0160	0.0999	-8.2264×10^{-5}	1.6165×10^{-5}
200		0.0999	-9.8758×10^{-5}	8.7306×10^{-6}	0.0113	0.0999	-5.7124×10^{-5}	8.7314×10^{-6}
500		0.0999	-3.3400×10^{-6}	3.5542×10^{-6}	0.0071	0.1000	1.3327×10^{-5}	3.5555×10^{-6}
100	0.3	0.2996	−0.0004	0.0002	0.0480	0.2999	-8.0656×10^{-5}	0.0002
200		0.2997	−0.0003	7.8575×10^{-5}	0.0339	0.2998	−0.0002	7.8582×10^{-5}
500		0.2999	-1.0020×10^{-5}	3.1987×10^{-5}	0.0214	0.3002	0.0002	3.0979×10^{-5}
100	0.5	0.4994	−0.0006	0.0004	0.0800	0.4999	−0.0001	0.0004
200		0.4997	−0.0003	0.0002	0.0565	0.4997	−0.0003	0.0002
500		0.4999	-1.6700×10^{-5}	8.8855×10^{-5}	0.0357	0.5000	6.6637×10^{-5}	8.8888×10^{-5}
100	0.7	0.6992	−0.0008	0.0008	0.1120	0.6998	−0.0002	0.0008
200		0.6993	−0.0007	0.0004	0.0791	0.6996	−0.0004	0.0004
500		0.6999	-2.3380×10^{-5}	0.0001	0.0501	0.7000	9.3291×10^{-5}	0.0001
100	1.1	1.0987	−0.0013	0.0020	0.1760	1.0997	−0.0003	0.0020
200		1.0989	−0.0011	0.0010	0.1244	1.0994	−0.0006	0.0010
500		1.0999	-3.6741×10^{-5}	0.0004	0.0787	1.1001	0.0001	0.0004
100	1.5	1.4983	−0.0017	0.0038	0.2400	1.4996	−0.0004	0.0038
200		1.4985	−0.0015	0.0019	0.1696	1.4991	−0.0009	0.0019
500		1.4999	-5.0101×10^{-5}	0.0008	0.1073	1.5002	0.0002	0.0007

4. Real-World Exemplifications

In this section, two applications adopting the AU distribution with real-world issues are exemplified. The first case is related to the dynamics of the Chilean inflation in the post-military dictatorship period. The second case pertains to the relative humidity of the air in the northern Chilean city of Copiapó (Atacama region).

The Chilean inflation data are recorded annually, whose values considered the range from 1992 to 2021. These are based on the period after the military dictatorship of 1973–1990. It was analyzed the dynamics of the inflation data (in %), which were standardized by min-max transformation, resulting in a unit response variable (value between zero and one). The years 1990 and 1991 were excluded, since they are considered to be a period of transition. Then, the total amount of observations was of 30 years (from 1992 to 2021).

On the other hand, the relative air humidity data cover the period from February 2015 to October 2022, with a one-hour recording format (104,415 observations). Then, this data set was transformed into daily maximum observation (6226 observations).

4.1. Chilean Inflation (Post-Military Era)

Figure 3 presents the dynamics of the Chilean inflation in the post-military dictatorship period, demonstrating stability between the years of 1999 and 2008. The right panel displays the time series of inflation, in which time is measured in years, from year 1 (1992) to year 30 (2021). The left panel depicts the accumulation of the values throughout the time series, in which a predominant trend is shown around 0.1 of the inflation rate.

Once the empirical dynamics of these data was analyzed, the most common unit distributions, presented in the statistical literature, were fitted. The upper panel of Figure 4 illustrates the histogram for the inflation data, in which it is compared with different fitted densities based on the MLE: AU, beta (BE), Kumaraswamy (KUM), logit-normal (LOGITNO), simplex (SIMPLEX), unit-half-normal (UHN), and unit-Lindley (ULINDLEY). The lower panel of the same figure presents the fitted CDFs superimposed to the empirical CDF (ECDF).

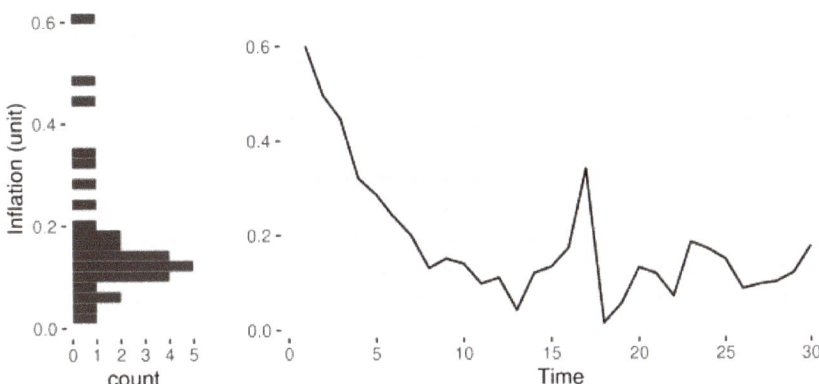

Figure 3. Chilean inflation in the period 1992–2021 (post-military era). The histogram on the left presents a skewness of the data. The dynamics is represented in the right panel, in which a disturbance (outlier) is observed in the year 2008 (observation #17).

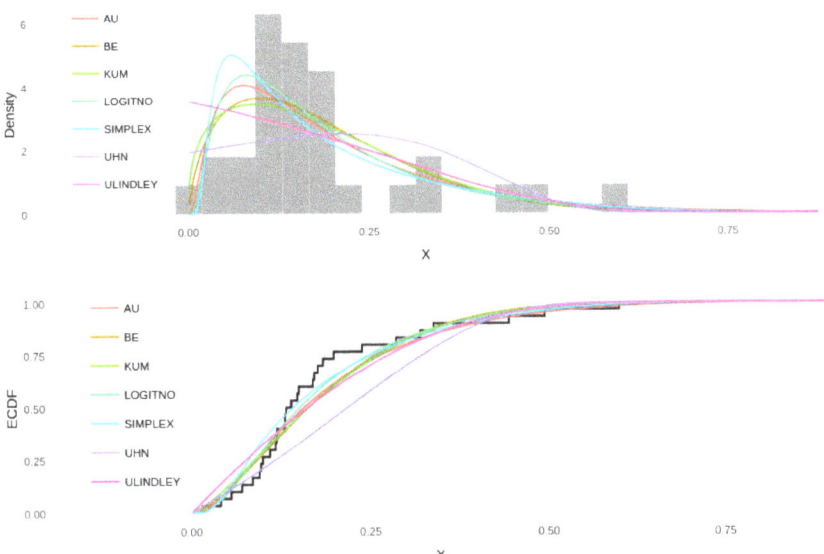

Figure 4. Estimated densities superimposed to the histogram (**top-chart**), and estimated CDFs superimposed to the ECDF (**bottom-chart**) (Chilean inflation data).

In order to quantify the performance of the fitted models, the Akaike Information Criterion (AIC) [25] and the Bayesian (or Schwarz) Information Criterion (BIC) [26] were analyzed. The obtained results (see Table 2) indicated the AU model as the best-fitted model to this data set. In addition, it is possible to make an inference about the average of the phenomenon, that is, the expectation of the AU($\hat{\alpha} = 1.2059$) model, resulting in $\mathbb{E}[X_{\text{Inflation}}] = 0.1948$. In other words, the average Chilean inflation, in post-military era, is of 19.49%.

In the following subsection, it is illustrated the performance of the AU model when adopting a high-frequency data set originated from the relative humidity from a city located in the Atacama Desert.

Table 2. Parameter estimates, AIC and BIC values (Chilean inflation data). S.E. = standard error.

Model	Parameter Estimate (S.E.)	AIC	BIC
AU(α)	$\hat{\alpha} = 1.205943\ (0.008079)$	-47.89	-46.49
BE(μ, σ)	$\hat{\mu} = 0.185857\ (0.000496)$ $\hat{\sigma} = 0.314688\ (0.001304)$	-44.58	-41.78
KUM(μ, σ)	$\hat{\mu} = 1.370127\ (0.045522)$ $\hat{\sigma} = 7.968427\ (7.750459)$	-43.63	-40.83
LOGITNO(μ, σ)	$\hat{\mu} = 0.150323\ (0.000457)$ $\hat{\sigma} = 0.916938\ (0.014013)$	-46.23	-43.43
SIMPLEX(μ, σ)	$\hat{\mu} = 0.182462\ (0.000584)$ $\hat{\sigma} = 2.854833\ (0.135834)$	-43.17	-40.37
UHN(σ)	$\hat{\sigma} = 0.413894\ (0.002855)$	-33.62	-32.22
ULINDLEY(μ)	$\hat{\mu} = 0.186834\ (0.000575)$	-41.99	-40.58

4.2. Water Monitoring in Air Humidity

The hydrological regime of the main rivers of Atacama is characterized by ice sources: water flows from the peaks following the melting of snowfall, glaciers, and permafrost located in the upper parts of the Andes range. In the context of climate change, it is, therefore, essential to understand the hydrological cycle of these regions, in order to set up a sustainable management policy to them. Understanding the hydrological cycle requires the implementation of tools for forecasting river flows, relative humidity, groundwater reservoirs, or any other water-related quantity monitoring, which inevitably demands an in-depth knowledge with respect to the physical phenomena that rule the entire hydrological cycle and, more precisely, the complex interaction between atmosphere, climate, landforms, ice, snow and river flows.

Additionally, a unique phenomenon called *Camanchaca* happens, which consists in a fog passing by the Copiapó city, recurrent only between midnight to around 10 a.m. Here, we demonstrate the variation of the relative humidity of Copiapó city, proposing a methodology that can be efficient, adjustable to these data. Using the daily maximum relative humidity, six different unit distributions were compared: AU, BE, KUM, LOGITNO, SIMPLEX, and UHN, as shown in Figure 5.

After comparing the commonly used unit models, we demonstrate the advantage of fitting the AU model over others (visually). Table 3 confirms the best fit of the AU model, based on information criteria (AIC and BIC), as well as depicts the estimation of the parameter(s) of each model.

Table 3. Parameter estimates, AIC and BIC values (relative air humidity data).

Model	Parameter Estimate (S.E.)	AIC	BIC
AU(α)	$\hat{\alpha} = 0.1092\ (3.1902 \times 10^{-7})$	$-14{,}023.49$	$-14{,}016.76$
BE(μ, σ)	$\hat{\mu} = 0.8476\ (1.2027 \times 10^{-6})$ $\hat{\sigma} = 0.2410\ (4.1119 \times 10^{-6})$	$-13{,}927.89$	$-13{,}914.41$
KUM(μ, σ)	$\hat{\mu} = 9.4004\ (0.0141)$ $\hat{\sigma} = 2.3882\ (0.0019)$	$-13{,}605.90$	$-13{,}592.43$
LOGITNO(μ, σ)	$\hat{\mu} = 0.8693\ (3.1376 \times 10^{-6})$ $\hat{\sigma} = 1.2299\ (1.2148 \times 10^{-4})$	-7600.43	-7586.95
SIMPLEX(μ, σ)	$\hat{\mu} = 0.9735\ (1.2959 \times 10^{-6})$ $\hat{\sigma} = 94.0480\ (0.7103)$	$32{,}477.13$	$32{,}490.61$
UHN(σ)	$\hat{\sigma} = 99.9900\ (6.5334 \times 10^{-7})$	$5{,}101{,}018{,}733.13$	$5{,}101{,}018{,}739.86$

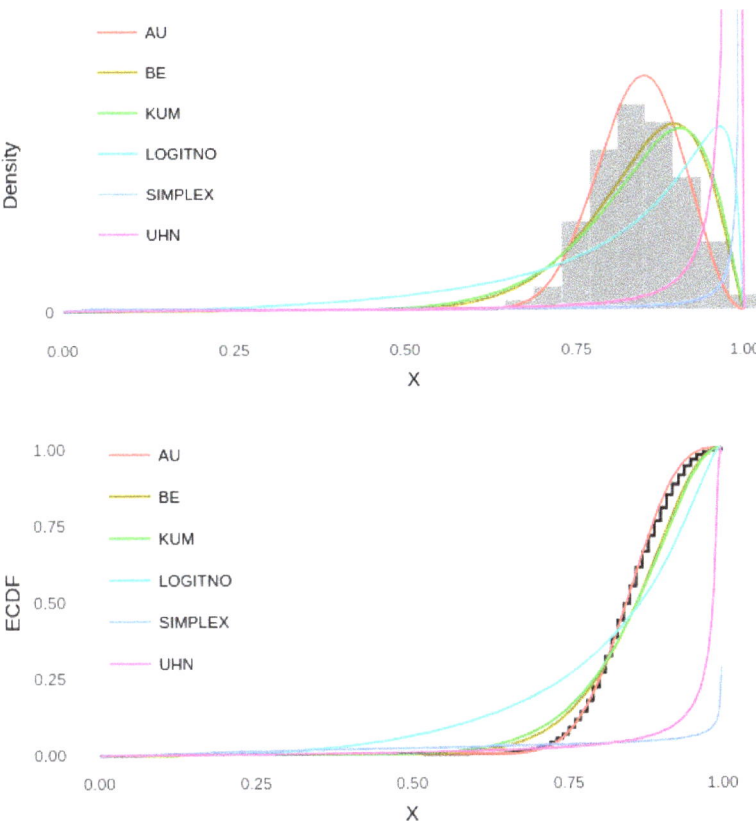

Figure 5. Estimated densities superimposed to the histogram (**top-chart**), and estimated CDFs superimposed to the ECDF (**bottom-chart**) (relative air humidity data).

After obtaining the parameter estimate for α, the AU model (best-fitted model) was used to construct a Statistical Process Control (SPC) chart [27], by calculating a tolerance upper-lower bound. Moreover, the Highest Density Interval (HDI) was adopted, considering a confidence degree of 99%, to monitor the daily maximum relative humidity records (as displayed by Figure 6).

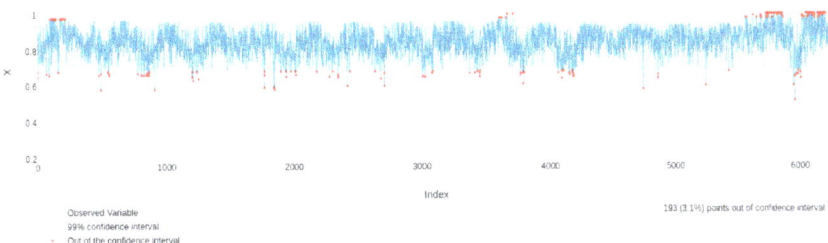

Figure 6. SPC control chart, considering a 99% of tolerance based on the AU model fitted to the daily maximum relative humidity of Copiapó city, Chile, from 1 February 2015 to 4 October 2022. It is observed that 193 days (3.1%) presented anomaly values (out-of-control signals). The obtained control limits were: LCL = 68.56% and UCL = 97.73%.

The expected daily maximum water relative humidity is of 84.23% (based on the fitted AU model). The obtained control limits, considering a confidence (or tolerance) level of 99%, were: LCL = 68.56% and UCL = 97.73%. Thus, the control chart based on the AU model (AU control chart) is another exciting and valuable alternative to some well-known SPC tools, which enlightens the forecasting and opens new doors to discuss extreme events in the Atacama water particles monitored by probabilistic reasoning.

5. Conclusions

This study showed the competitiveness of the developed Theorem 1 (Equation (1)), which enables for a great class of distributions that belong all to the exponential family. As an exemplification, we adopted the special case for $k = 1$, which is equivalent to the moment of order two of the standard normal distribution, and after some transformations, we developed the Alpha-Unit (AU) distribution. Also, we dedicated to the unit range, given the importance of this stochasticity representation.

Unit distributions are useful for values that oscillate between zero and one, such as fractions, proportions and rates, among others, or for a set of values in which there is a minimum or maximum limitation, resorting to standardization through the min-max transformation. Most distributions of this type come from transforming a random variable with certain distribution so that it takes values between zero and one, as in the case of unit-Lindley distribution [9], which comes from the Lindley distribution [28,29].

There are numerous studies based on (e.g., unit) distributions, by extending a model and applying it to several areas [11,14,16]. In this study, we introduced and showed the competitiveness of the AU distribution, especially for data with a range greater than 0.4, or which present high asymmetry and low decay. Further studies shall investigate this hypothesis in a wider amount of data sets (through different sorts of wide data range). Additionally, an implementation of this model adopting hierarchical estimation and spatio-temporal dependence would be useful for forecast/predictable problems.

Author Contributions: Conceptualization and methodology, D.E.-O. and D.C.d.N.; software, M.S.C.-A. and L.B.-B.; validation, formal analysis, investigation, resources, data curation, M.S.C.-A. and D.C.d.N.; writing—original draft preparation, D.E.-O., D.C.d.N., M.S.C.-A. and L.B.-B.; writing—review and editing, P.H.F.d.S.; visualization, D.C.d.N.; supervision, project administration, funding acquisition, D.E.-O. All authors have read and agreed to the published version of the manuscript.

Funding: This research was funded by Universidad de Atacama grant number ATA1956–CC88433.

Institutional Review Board Statement: Not applicable.

Informed Consent Statement: Not applicable.

Data Availability Statement: All adopted data and R script developed in this study are available at https://github.com/ProfNascimento/AlphaUnit (accessed on 12 November 2022).

Acknowledgments: This study was partially supported by the Vicerrectoría de Investigación y Postgrado (VRIP) and Dirección de Postgrado of the Universidad de Atacama (UDA). The author David Elal-Olivero was supported by the DIUDA REGULAR project No. 22409 from the Universidad de Atacama, Chile.

Conflicts of Interest: The authors declare no conflict of interest.

Appendix A

This appendix shows the proof that for a random variable

$$X \sim \mathrm{BN}(k) \quad \rightarrow \quad X^2 \sim \chi^2_{2k+1}.$$

Then,

$$F_{X^2}(x) = \mathbb{P}\left(X^2 \leq x\right) = \mathbb{P}(-\sqrt{x} \leq X \leq \sqrt{x}) = 2\mathbb{P}(X \leq \sqrt{x}) - 1 = 2F_X(\sqrt{x}) - 1.$$

It follows that

$$f_{X^2}(x) = 2f_X(\sqrt{x})\frac{1}{2\sqrt{x}} = \frac{1}{c}(\sqrt{x})^{2k}\phi(\sqrt{x})\frac{1}{\sqrt{x}} = \frac{1}{\prod_{j=1}^{k}(2j-1)}(\sqrt{x})^{2k-1}\frac{1}{\sqrt{2\pi}}e^{-\frac{x}{2}}.$$

Knowing that $\Gamma\left(\frac{2k+1}{2}\right) = \prod_{j=1}^{k}(2j-1)\frac{\sqrt{\pi}}{2^k}$, then

$$f_{X^2}(x) = \frac{1}{\prod_{j=1}^{k}(2j-1)}x^{\frac{2k-1}{2}}\frac{1}{\sqrt{2\pi}}e^{-\frac{x}{2}} = \frac{\sqrt{\pi}}{2^k\Gamma\left(\frac{2k+1}{2}\right)}\frac{x^{\frac{2k-1}{2}}}{2^{1/2}\sqrt{\pi}}e^{-\frac{x}{2}}$$

$$= \frac{1}{\Gamma\left(\frac{2k+1}{2}\right)2^{\frac{2k+1}{2}}}x^{\frac{2k-1}{2}}e^{-\frac{x}{2}}.$$

Therefore, $X^2 \sim \chi^2_{2k+1}$.

Besides that, complementation can be taken into account by saying that, considering $W_2 \sim \chi^2_{2k+1}$ and $\mathbb{P}(W_1 = \pm 1) = 1/2$, then $B = W_1\sqrt{W_2} \sim \text{BN}(k)$.

Let $b \geq 0$, then

$$F_B(b) = \mathbb{P}(B \leq b) = \mathbb{P}\left(W_1\sqrt{W_2} \leq b\right)$$

$$= \mathbb{P}\left(W_1\sqrt{W_2} \leq b \mid W_1 = 1\right)\mathbb{P}(W_1 = 1) + \mathbb{P}\left(W_1\sqrt{W_2} \leq b \mid W_1 = -1\right)\mathbb{P}(W_1 = -1)$$

$$\stackrel{\text{ind.}}{=} \mathbb{P}\left((1)\sqrt{W_2} \leq b\right)\frac{1}{2} + \mathbb{P}\left((-1)\sqrt{W_2} \leq b\right)\frac{1}{2}.$$

Since $b \geq 0$, then $\mathbb{P}\left((-1)\sqrt{W_2} \leq b\right) = 1$:

$$= \mathbb{P}\left(\sqrt{W_2} \leq b\right)\frac{1}{2} + \frac{1}{2} = \mathbb{P}\left(|W_2| \leq b^2\right)\frac{1}{2} + \frac{1}{2} = \mathbb{P}\left(-b^2 \leq W_2 \leq b^2\right)\frac{1}{2} + \frac{1}{2}$$

$$= \frac{1}{2}\left[\mathbb{P}\left(X \leq b^2\right) - \underbrace{\mathbb{P}\left(X \leq -b^2\right)}_{0}\right] + \frac{1}{2} = \frac{1}{2}\mathbb{P}\left(X \leq b^2\right) + \frac{1}{2} = \frac{1}{2}F_X\left(b^2\right) + \frac{1}{2}$$

Therefore,

$$f_B(b) = \frac{dF_B(b)}{db} = \frac{1}{2}f_X\left(b^2\right)2b = bf_X\left(b^2\right) = b\frac{1}{\Gamma\left(\frac{2k+1}{2}\right)2^{\frac{2k+1}{2}}}\left(b^2\right)^{\frac{2k+1}{2}-1}e^{-\frac{b^2}{2}}$$

$$= b\frac{1}{\Gamma\left(\frac{2k+1}{2}\right)2^{\frac{2k+1}{2}}}b^{2k-1}e^{-\frac{b^2}{2}} = \frac{1}{\frac{\sqrt{\pi}\prod_{j=1}^{k}(2j-1)}{2^k}2^{\frac{2k+1}{2}}}b^{2k}e^{-\frac{b^2}{2}}$$

$$= \frac{1}{\prod_{j=1}^{k}(2j-1)}\frac{b^{2k}}{\sqrt{2\pi}}e^{-\frac{b^2}{2}} = \frac{1}{\underbrace{\prod_{j=1}^{k}(2j-1)}_{c}}b^{2k}\phi(b).$$

Analogously, it is proved for $b < 0$.

Appendix B

The proposed theorem (Theorem 1) will be illustrated considering $k = 1$, to show the origin of the random numbers that generate the AU distribution.

Proposition A1. *If $X \sim \text{BN}(1)$, then $f_X(x) = x^2\phi(x)$ is a bimodal density function.*

Proof. If $f_X(x)$ is bimodal, it would have two maxima, to which the first and second derivative criteria would be applied:

$$\frac{df_X(x)}{dx} = 0 \Rightarrow$$

$$\frac{d(x^2\phi(x))}{dx} = 2x\phi(x) + x^2[-x\phi(x)] = 2x\phi(x) - x^3\phi(x) = x\phi(x)\left(2 - x^2\right) = 0.$$

Then, it can be seen that the solutions for the previous equation would be: $x_1 = 0$, $x_2 = \sqrt{2}$, $x_3 = -\sqrt{2}$. Hence, by applying the second derivative criterion:

$$\frac{d^2 f_X(x)}{dx^2} < 0 \Rightarrow$$

$$\frac{d(x\phi(x)(2-x^2))}{dx} = \phi(x)\left(2 - x^2\right) + x[-x\phi(x)]\left(2 - x^2\right) + x\phi(x)(-2x).$$

Reducing algebraically, we get to:

$$\frac{d^2 f_X(x)}{dx^2} = \phi(x)\left(2 - 5x^2 + x^4\right) < 0.$$

The only solutions that satisfy the previous inequality are: $x_2 = \sqrt{2}$, $x_3 = -\sqrt{2}$. Therefore, there are two maxima and the BN distribution is bimodal. □

Definition A1 (Bimodal Half-Normal distribution). *Let $Y \sim BN(1)$. If $Q = \alpha|Y|$, with $\alpha > 0$, then we say that Q is distributed according to a Bimodal Half-Normal (BHN) distribution with parameter α, and we denote it by $Q \sim BHN(\alpha)$.*

Proposition A2. *If $Q \sim BHN(\alpha)$, then the PDF of Q is given by*

$$f_Q(q \mid \alpha) = \frac{2}{\alpha}\left(\frac{q}{\alpha}\right)^2 \phi\left(\frac{q}{\alpha}\right), \quad q > 0.$$

Proof. Since $Q = \alpha|Y|$, with $Y \sim BN(1)$, then

$$F_Q(q) = \mathbb{P}(Q \leq q) = \mathbb{P}(\alpha|Y| \leq q) = \mathbb{P}\left(-\frac{q}{\alpha} \leq Y \leq \frac{q}{\alpha}\right) = 2\mathbb{P}\left(Y \leq \frac{q}{\alpha}\right) - 1 = 2F_Y\left(\frac{q}{\alpha}\right) - 1.$$

Hence, by deriving the previous expression, one has that

$$f_Q(q) = 2f_Y\left(\frac{q}{\alpha}\right)\frac{1}{\alpha} = \frac{2}{\alpha}\left(\frac{q}{\alpha}\right)^2 \phi\left(\frac{q}{\alpha}\right).$$

□

Proposition A3. *If $Q \sim BHN(\alpha)$, then*

$$X = e^{-Q} \sim AU(\alpha).$$

Proof. Let $X = e^{-Q}, 0 < x \leq 1$, then

$$F_X(x) = \mathbb{P}(X \leq x) = \mathbb{P}\left(e^{-Q} \leq x\right) = \mathbb{P}(-Q \leq \ln(x)) = \mathbb{P}(Q \geq -\ln(x))$$
$$= 1 - \mathbb{P}(Q \leq -\ln(x)) = 1 - F_Q(-\ln(x)).$$

By deriving the previous expression, we have:

$$f_X(x) = f_Q(-\ln(x))\frac{1}{x} = \frac{2}{\alpha}\left(\frac{-\ln(x)}{\alpha}\right)^2 \phi\left(\frac{-\ln(x)}{\alpha}\right)\frac{1}{x} = \frac{2}{\alpha x}\left(\frac{\ln(x)}{\alpha}\right)^2 \phi\left(\frac{\ln(x)}{\alpha}\right).$$

□

References

1. Fonseca, A.; Ferreira, P.H.; Nascimento, D.C.d.; Fiaccone, R.; Ulloa-Correa, C.; García-Piña, A.; Louzada, F. Water particles monitoring in the atacama desert: SPC approach based on proportional data. *Axioms* **2021**, *10*, 154. [CrossRef]
2. Bayer, F.M.; Cintra, R.J.; Cribari-Neto, F. Beta seasonal autoregressive moving average models. *J. Stat. Comput. Simul.* **2018**, *88*, 2961–2981. [CrossRef]
3. Ferrari, S.; Cribari-Neto, F. Beta regression for modelling rates and proportions. *J. Appl. Stat.* **2004**, *31*, 799–815. [CrossRef]
4. Kumaraswamy, P. A generalized probability density function for double-bounded random processes. *J. Hydrol.* **1980**, *46*, 79–88. [CrossRef]
5. Tadikamalla, P.R.; Johnson, N.L. Systems of frequency curves generated by transformations of logistic variables. *Biometrika* **1982**, *69*, 461–465. [CrossRef]
6. Barndorff-Nielsen, O.E.; Jørgensen, B. Some parametric models on the simplex. *J. Multivar. Anal.* **1991**, *39*, 106–116. [CrossRef]
7. Mazucheli, J.; Menezes, A.F.B.; Ghitany, M.E. The unit-Weibull distribution and associated inference. *J. Appl. Probab. Stat.* **2018**, *13*, 1–22.
8. Mazucheli, J.; Menezes, A.; Fernandes, L.; De Oliveira, R.; Ghitany, M. The unit-Weibull distribution as an alternative to the Kumaraswamy distribution for the modeling of quantiles conditional on covariates. *J. Appl. Stat.* **2020**, *47*, 954–974. [CrossRef]
9. Mazucheli, J.; Menezes, A.F.B.; Chakraborty, S. On the one parameter unit-Lindley distribution and its associated regression model for proportion data. *J. Appl. Stat.* **2019**, *46*, 700–714. [CrossRef]
10. Bakouch, H.S.; Nik, A.S.; Asgharzadeh, A.; Salinas, H.S. A flexible probability model for proportion data: Unit-half-normal distribution. *Commun. Stat.-Case Stud. Data Anal. Appl.* **2021**, *7*, 271–288. [CrossRef]
11. Korkmaz, M.Ç.; Korkmaz, Z.S. The unit log–log distribution: A new unit distribution with alternative quantile regression modeling and educational measurements applications. *J. Appl. Stat.* **2021**, *1*, 1–20. [CrossRef]
12. Sagrillo, M.; Guerra, R.R.; Bayer, F.M. Modified Kumaraswamy distributions for double bounded hydro-environmental data. *J. Hydrol.* **2021**, *603*, 127021. [CrossRef]
13. Krishna, A.; Maya, R.; Chesneau, C.; Irshad, M.R. The Unit Teissier Distribution and Its Applications. *Math. Comput. Appl.* **2022**, *27*, 12. [CrossRef]
14. Guerra, R.R.; Peña-Ramírez, F.A.; Bourguignon, M. The unit extended Weibull families of distributions and its applications. *J. Appl. Stat.* **2021**, *48*, 3174–3192. [CrossRef]
15. Aitchison, J.; Brown, J.A.C. *The Lognormal Distribution with Special Reference to Its Uses in Economics*; Cambridge University Press: Cambridge, UK, 1957.
16. Korkmaz, M.Ç.; Chesneau, C.; Korkmaz, Z.S. The Unit Folded Normal Distribution: A New Unit Probability Distribution with the Estimation Procedures, Quantile Regression Modeling and Educational Attainment Applications. *J. Reliab. Stat. Stud.* **2022**, *15*, 261–298. [CrossRef]
17. Afify, A.Z.; Nassar, M.; Kumar, D.; Cordeiro, G.M. A new unit distribution: properties, inference, and applications. *Electron. J. Appl. Stat. Anal.* **2022**, *15*, 460–484.
18. Korkmaz, M.Ç.; Altun, E.; Chesneau, C.; Yousof, H.M. On the unit-Chen distribution with associated quantile regression and applications. *Math. Slovaca* **2022**, *72*, 765–786. [CrossRef]
19. Santana-e Silva, J.J.; Cribari-Neto, F.; Vasconcellos, K.L. Beta distribution misspecification tests with application to Covid-19 mortality rates in the United States. *PLoS ONE* **2022**, *17*, e0274781. [CrossRef]
20. Stahl, S. The evolution of the normal distribution. *Math. Mag.* **2006**, *79*, 96–113. [CrossRef]
21. Limpert, E.; Stahel, W.A. Problems with using the normal distribution–and ways to improve quality and efficiency of data analysis. *PLoS ONE* **2011**, *6*, e21403. [CrossRef]
22. Elal-Olivero, D. Alpha-skew-normal distribution. *Proyecciones (Antofagasta)* **2010**, *29*, 224–240. [CrossRef]
23. Bayer, F.M.; Tondolo, C.M.; Müller, F.M. Beta regression control chart for monitoring fractions and proportions. *Comput. Ind. Eng.* **2018**, *119*, 416–426. [CrossRef]
24. R Core Team. *R: A Language and Environment for Statistical Computing*; R Foundation for Statistical Computing: Vienna, Austria, 2022.
25. Akaike, H. On entropy maximization principle. *Appl. Stat.* **1977**, *1*, 27–41.
26. Schwarz, G. Estimating the dimension of a model. *Ann. Stat.* **1978**, *6*, 461–464. [CrossRef]
27. Montgomery, D.C. *Introduction to Statistical Quality Control*, 6th ed.; John Wiley & Sons: Hoboken, NJ, USA, 2009.
28. Lindley, D.V. Fiducial distributions and Bayes' theorem. *J. R. Stat. Soc. Ser. B (Methodol.)* **1958**, *20*, 102–107. [CrossRef]
29. Lindley, D.V. *Introduction to Probability and Statistics from a Bayesian Viewpoint, Part II: Inference*; Cambridge University Press: Cambridge, UK, 1965.

Article

A Study on the Beech Wood Machining Parameters Optimization Using Response Surface Methodology

Sajjad Pakzad [1,*], Siamak Pedrammehr [1] and Mahsa Hejazian [2]

[1] Faculty of Design, Tabriz Islamic Art University, Tabriz 5164736931, Iran
[2] Faculty of Mechanical Engineering, University of Tabriz, Tabriz 5166616471, Iran
* Correspondence: s.pakzad@tabriziau.ac.ir

Abstract: The surface quality of wooden products is of great importance to production industries. The best surface quality requires a thorough understanding of the cutting parameters' effects on the wooden material. In this paper, response surface methodology, which is one of the conventional statistical methods in experiment design, has been used to design experiments and investigate the effect of different machining parameters as feed rate, spindle speed, step over, and depth of cut on surface quality of the beech wood. The mathematical model of the examined parameters and the surface roughness have also been obtained by the method. Finally, the optimal machining parameters have been obtained to achieve the best quality of the machined surface, which reduced the surface roughness up to 4.2 (µm). Each of the machining parameters has a considerable effect on surface quality, although it is noted that the feed rate has the greatest effect.

Keywords: optimization; response surface method; surface roughness; machining parameters

1. Introduction

In recent years, the wood industry has gained significant attention for its applications in various industries and because the wood and its products are very important in industrial production. The surface roughness, as the main parameter of surface quality, is among the requirements for quality production. The examination of the methods conducive to achieve the optimal cutting parameters for the minimum surface roughness of wooden products is one of the vital research issues that fill the gap existing in the literature in this respect.

Fujiwara et al. [1] have investigated the surface roughness of Japanese oak and beech that were polished with different sandpapers, and after paying attention to the distribution of the respective area the peaks of the roughness profile were checked. Usta et al. [2] have studied the effect of the number of grater knife blades, feed speed and depth of cut on the surface roughness of Acacia locust and European oak in the planning process. The samples have been tested with two and four blades, feeding speed of 5 and 9 (m/min) and cutting depth of 1, 2 and 4 (mm), respectively. It should be noted that under the same conditions, Acacia Locust has a smoother surface than European oak. They found that the surface roughness decreases by reducing the feed speed and depth of cut and increasing the number of grater blades. The lowest surface roughness in the experiment with the highest number of grater blades (4 blades), feed rate of 5 m per minute and cutting depth of 1 (mm) is achieved. Hernández et al. [3] have investigated the effect of cutting width and height on the surface quality of black spruce timber in the process of turning the trunk into lumber. So that the spindle speed and feed rate are kept constant, surface roughness tests have been performed in two conditions of summer and winter temperature and different cutting width and height. Finally, they obtained the suitable surface quality in summer temperature where the width and height of cut of the black spruce was less. Kilic et al. [4] have evaluated the effect of different machining techniques on the surface roughness of beech and spruce wood. They designed a test to consider the characteristics of sawn and

sanded surfaces with 60 and 80 sandpapers. Pinkowski et al. [5] have studied the effect of cutting angle and feed rate on the surface roughness of different woods in the planning process. They performed experiments with four different cutting angles of the blade, four different feed rates, and constant rotational speed. They found that surface roughness decreases with decreasing cutting angle and surface roughness increases with increasing feed rate. The optimal cutting angle is 40 degrees. Moreover, the surface area decreases with increasing wood density. Extensive research [6–10] has been conducted to investigate cutting parameters on different woods in the planning process. Koch et al. [11] have studied the effects of feed rate and spindle rotational speed on two types of wood and MDF in the CNC milling process. They used the factorial method in the design of the experiment and found that a smoother surface was obtained by increasing the rotational speed of the spindle and decreasing the feed rate. Bal and AKÇAKAYA [12] have studied the effect of step over, feed rate, and cutting depth on fiber surface roughness in the CNC machining process. They performed experiments on two cutting depths of 2 and 6 (mm), step over of 40, 60, and 80% of the tool diameter, feed rate of 3, 5, 7 (m/min) and a constant spindle speed of the spindle. They found that the feed rate and surface roughness increase with increasing the depth of cut. In the design of traditional experimental methods, only one factor was considered as a variable and other factors were constant. In this method, due to the existence of one variable, the effects between the variables are not studied and the full effect of the variables on the response is not displayed. In addition, to do the project in the mentioned method, many tests are needed, which leads to an increase in time and cost as well as an increase in the consumption of materials. To overcome this problem, the response surface methodology (RSM) was proposed by Box and Wilson for optimization studies [13]. RSM is a mathematical tool that determines the relationship between a set of responses and independent variables. An important aspect of RSM is design of experiments, commonly known as DOE. This strategy was originally developed to fit experimental models but can also be used for numerical experiments. DOE's goal is to select the points where the response should be evaluated. The test design can have a great impact on the accuracy of the estimation and the cost of constructing the response surface model. Rao and Murthy [14] have studied the effect of cutting parameters on the surface roughness and workpiece vibrations using experimental design methods including the RSM in the drilling process. Moreover, Hazir and Koc [15] have investigated the optimization of cutting parameters in the CNC process of Lebanese Cedar and European black pine with the aim of minimum surface roughness using RSM. Extensive research [16–19] has been done on modeling and optimization of cutting parameters to achieve the desired surface roughness by using the RSM method.

This research has been conducted to determine the effective parameters in machining of beech wood to achieve the best surface quality. Afterwards, the effect of machining parameters such as feed rate, spindle speed, cutting depth, and step over on beech wood surface roughness have been studied. Finally, Optimization modeling has been performed under RSM, and the mentioned parameters have been optimized to achieve the minimum surface roughness of the workpiece.

2. Materials and Methods

Woodworking with CNC technologies is an integral part of the woodworking industry, and there are various methods to achieve the desired smooth surface that is important in high-performance machining and high-quality production. In this section, the workpiece material and the utilized CNC machine and tool are introduced. The conditions and methods of testing and machining and the optimization method are also explained.

2.1. Test Materials and Conditions

The wood used in this research is beech wood, which is widely used for wooden products due to its stable internal structure, high density and good compressive strength performance. The physical and mechanical properties of beech wood have been studied in recently published literature [20–22]. Here, the details for the under-study wood mechanical properties are listed in Table 1. Pieces of this wood with dimensions of 10*30 (cm) and a thickness of 15 (mm) in the radial direction have been prepared for testing. The machine used for milling is a three-axis cartesian CNC with a Mach3 control system. The zigzag strategy has been used for the end milling of the desired surface in ArtCAM software. Here, the end mill series used are ARDEN 214, which are ideal for high volume end mills with medium feed rates due to their hard materials and diamond crystal structure. The end mill tool code 214,214 has a working height of 12 (mm) and a diameter of 20 (mm) with two tungsten carbide teeth.

Table 1. Mechanical properties of under study beech wood [21].

Bending Strength	Elasticity Modulus	Grain Parallel Compression	Grain Parallel Shear Strength	Grain Parallel Tensile Strength	Grain Normal Tensile Strength	Impact Bending
99.01 (MPa)	11,224 (MPa)	57.05 (MPa)	10.47 (MPa)	131.15 (MPa)	3.71 (MPa)	11.081 (KJ/m^2)

2.2. Experimentation

As the response surface method is one of the common statistical methods in the design of experiments, in the present study Design-Expert software and the response surface method have been used to design the experiments and analyze the results. In this method, the variables affecting the response and the minimum and maximum limits are determined, and based on these limits and the model the test matrix is designed. One of the main advantages of this method over the full factorial method is the reduction in the number of experiments while the number of variables is high, which reduces the costs and time of the research. The three main types of response surface methods are the central composite, Box Benken, and Dehlert models, in which the central composite model used in this paper is more valid than the others [23]. Work piece material, machine tool type, and geometric factors may be varied during machining [24]. Required surface quality can be attained by proper machining parameters selection. Here, in a milling condition with the given factors for the machine tool and work piece material, surface quality can be determined and improved depending on the geometric factors' selection which includes feed rate, cutting speed, step over, and depth of cut [25–27]. The effective variables considered on the surface roughness method and their minimum and maximum values are presented in Table 2.

Table 2. Minimum and maximum input data.

Parameter	Maximum	Minimum
Depth of cut (mm)	10	4
Feed rate (mm/s)	55	30
Spindle speed (rpm)	15,000	9000
Step over (mm)	7.75	5.25

By importing the data listed in Table 1 into the Design-Expert environment and using the central composite model for the response surface method, the test conditions have been designed according to the Table 3. The total number of experiments can also be obtained by the following equation:

$$N = 2^k + 2k \tag{1}$$

where N is the total number of experiments and k is the number of independent variables.

Table 3. Experimental test conditions.

No.	Step Over (mm)	Spindle Speed (rpm)	Feed Rate (mm/s)	Depth of Cut (mm)
1	7.75	9000	30	10
2	7.75	12,000	40	10
3	7.75	15,000	50	10
4	7.75	9000	35	8
5	7.75	12,000	45	8
6	5.25	12,000	55	8
7	5.25	15,000	55	8
8	7.75	15,000	45	8
9	6.5	15,000	45	8
10	5.25	9000	50	6
11	6.5	12,000	55	6
12	7.75	15,000	55	6
13	7.75	12,000	30	6
14	5.25	12,000	40	6
15	6.5	15,000	50	6
16	7.75	9000	40	6
17	7.75	9000	30	6
18	7.75	15,000	40	6
19	7.75	15,000	55	4
20	6.5	12,000	45	8
21	7.75	15,000	55	4
22	6.5	15,000	30	6
23	5.25	12,000	50	6
24	7.75	12,000	45	6

Surface roughness can be measured by tracing the probe across the workpiece surface. The arithmetical mean of the absolute values of the profile deviations, Ra, is a vertical parameter that shows the average roughness of a surface. After performing 24 designed tests the average roughness parameter (Ra) has been measured using a TIME 3202 digital roughness meter according to ISO 4287 standard [28], which uses five sampling lengths for Ra measurement. Figure 1 shows the machining process and average surface roughness measurement.

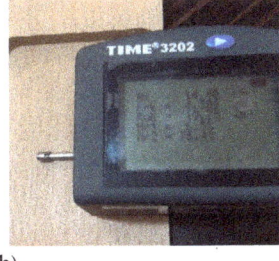

(a) (b)

Figure 1. (a) CNC machining of beech wood; (b) surface roughness measurement.

2.3. Response Surface Analysis

Response surface analysis is known as a time and cost economic method that makes it easy to identify the outlier data. This method has been adopted in various fields of study, and particularly in manufacturing research works [29–38]. Since the adjusted coefficient of determination R^2 represents the accuracy of the estimation concerning the roughness regression, it should be more than 90% to achieve the appropriate relation. Table 4 shows R^2 coefficient values for different equations. The value of this coefficient in the cubic equation is 100%, and it indicates the high accuracy of the estimated equation which has been utilized in this study.

Table 4. Regression models validation.

Regression Model	$Adj-R^2$	Valid
Linear $R_a(\mu m) = a_0 + a_1 f + a_2 n + a_3 a + a_4 s$	0.4480	
Linear + 2 factor interaction $R_a(\mu m) = a_0 + a_1 f + a_2 n + a_3 a + a_4 s + a_5 fn + a_6 na + a_7 as + a_8 sf$ $+ a_9 fa + a_{10} ns$	0.5732	
Quadratic $R_a(\mu m) = a_0 + a_1 f + a_2 n + a_3 a + a_4 s + a_5 f^2 + a_6 n^2 + a_7 a^2 + a_8 s^2$ $+ a_9 fn + a_{10} na + a_{11} as + a_{12} sf + a_{13} fa + a_{14} ns$	0.4278	
Cubic $R_a(\mu m) = a_0 + a_1 f + a_2 n + a_3 a + a_4 s + a_5 f^2 + a_6 n^2 + a_7 a^2 + a_8 s^2$ $+ a_9 fn + a_{10} na + a_{11} as + a_{12} sf + a_{13} fa + a_{14} ns$ $+ a_{15} f^3 + a_{16} n^3 + a_{17} a^3 + a_{18} s^3 + a_{19} afn + a_{20} afs$ $+ a_{21} ans + a_{22} fns + a_{23} a^2 f + a_{24} a^2 n + a_{25} a^2 s$ $+ a_{26} af^2 + a_{27} an^2 + a_{28} as^2 + a_{29} f^2 n + a_{30} f^2 s$ $+ a_{31} fn^2 + a_{32} fs^2 + a_{33} ns^2 + a_{34} n^2 s$	1	×

2.4. Variance Analysis

ANOVA (analysis of variance) is a statistical analysis used to determine the model's suitability. Table 5 shows the results of ANOVA for the third-order equation of Ra, where the p-value shows the significance of each coefficient. If the p-value becomes less than 0.05 it indicates the coefficient's significance and importance. Considering Table 5, all parameters of a third-order equation, including the third power of the parameters, are presented in the estimated equation. The total p-value of the equation is 0.0014, and therefore the estimated model is valid. The estimated coefficient of each parameter is also shown on the general model, which has the greatest effect on the feed rate that is equal to 31.47.

Table 5. Analysis of variance results.

Parameter	p-Value	Predicted Coefficient
Constant		22.26
Linear		
a	0.0031	10.75
f	0.0016	31.47
n	0.0013	−11.24
s	0.0012	9.88
Quadratic		
a^2	0.0072	2.80
f^2	0.0015	15.89
n^2	0.0012	1.93
s^2	0.0016	2.04
2 Factor interaction		
af	0.0026	19.51
an	0.0012	−11.87
as	0.0015	7.04
fn	0.0017	−9.14
fs	0.0012	10.44
ns	0.0015	−5.62
afn	0.0015	−8.44
afs	0.0014	7.62
ans	0.0022	1.58
fns	0.0014	−5.08
$a^2 f$	0.0061	2.31

Table 5. Cont.

Parameter	p-Value	Predicted Coefficient
2 Factor interaction		
$a^2 n$	0.0075	−1.41
$a f^2$	0.0021	10.83
$f^2 n$	0.0048	−1.10
Total	0.0014 (Significant)	

3. Results and Discussions

3.1. The Effect of Different Machining Parameters on Surface Roughness of Beech Wood

The effect of different machining parameters on surface roughness of other workpiece materials has been studied in several research works. In the literature [39–41] it was reported that the control parameters having the most effect on surface quality are the spindle speed, feed rate and depth of cut rate, and that better surface quality was obtained at higher spindle speeds, lower feed rates and depth of cut. In this study similar results have been obtained for the effect of spindle speed, feed rate, and depth of cut on surface quality of the beech wood. Particularly, the step-over effect on the surface roughness has been investigated in this study.

Figure 2 shows the effect of machining parameters on surface roughness. According to Figure 2a, which presents the effect of spindle speed on surface roughness, when the spindle speed increases the surface roughness increases as well. Moreover, this figure shows that the surface roughness increases with the increase in cutting depth. Figure 2b shows the effects of feed rate and surface roughness on cutting depth, where it is seen that if the feed rate increases the surface roughness increases, and with the increase in the cutting depth the surface roughness also increases. Figure 2c also shows the effects of cutting depth and surface roughness on step over. It can also be obtained from this figure that increasing the depth of cut leads to an increase in surface roughness. Significantly, with the increase in the step over, the surface roughness continues to increase.

Figure 2d illustrates the effects of spindle speed and surface roughness on the step over. As the spindle speed increases the surface roughness increases. With an increase in step over the surface roughness increases as well. Figure 2e shows the effects of step over and surface roughness on to the feed rate, and it is apparent that the step-over increase leads to the surface roughness increase. Per Figure 2f that presents the effects of spindle speed and surface roughness on feed rate, one can understand that the higher spindle speed or feed rate results in the higher surface roughness increases.

3.2. Parameter Optimization

The focus of the present work is to reduce the surface roughness of the workpiece to achieve the desired surface quality. Optimal machining parameters can be used to minimize the desired workpiece surface roughness. Table 6 shows the optimal machining parameters that are obtained here using the response surface method.

Table 6. Goal and optimized value of parameters.

Parameter	Goal	Description	Optimized Value
Depth of cut	Maximum	Increase in production rate	10
Feed rate	Maximum	Increase in production rate	66.262
Spindle speed	In range		15,000
Step over	In range		5.25
Surface roughness	Minimum	Increase in product quality	4.2
		Desirability	0.812

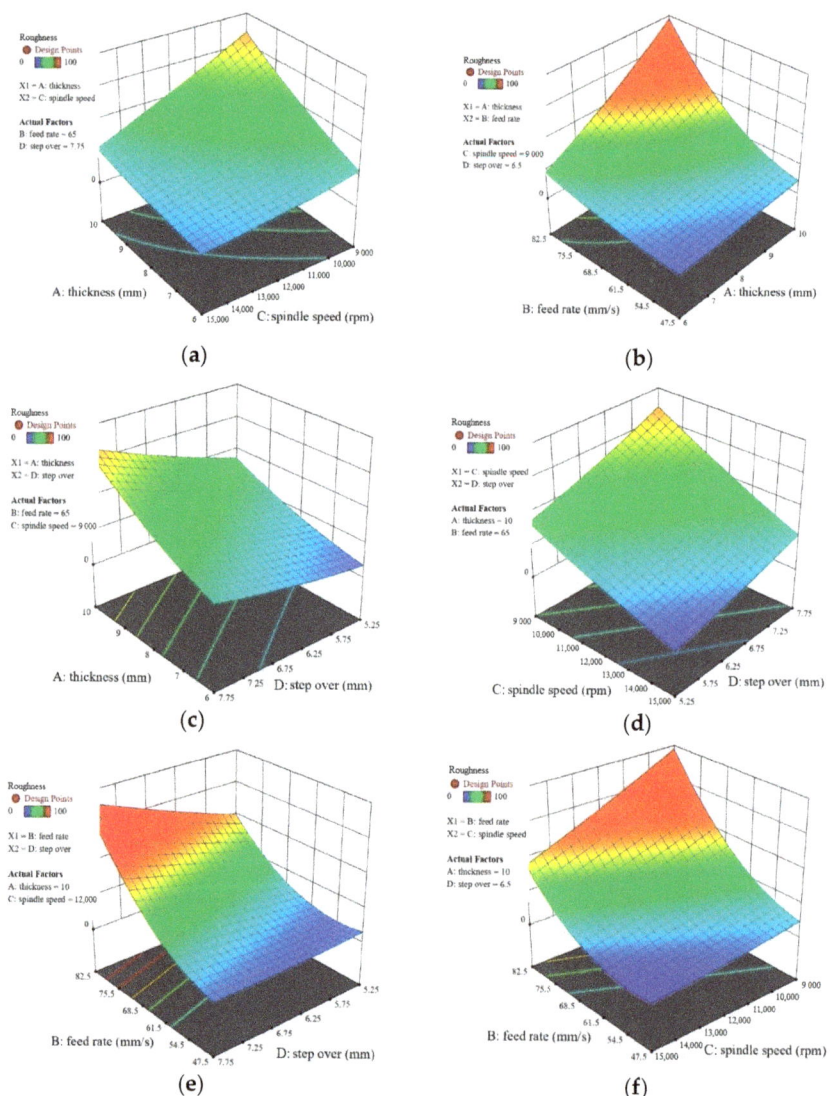

Figure 2. Effect of machining parameters on surface roughness: (**a**) effects of spindle speed and depth of cut on surface roughness; (**b**) effects of feed rate and depth of cut on surface roughness; (**c**) effects of depth of cut and step over on surface roughness; (**d**) effects of spindle speed and step over on surface roughness; (**e**) effects of step over and feed rate on surface roughness; (**f**) effects of spindle speed and feed rate on surface roughness.

By analyzing the results obtained from the optimization, the optimal value of *Ra* can be obtained based on the estimated model. This value is equal to 4.2 (µm) (Figure 3). As the desirability value approaches 1, a better optimization result will be obtained.

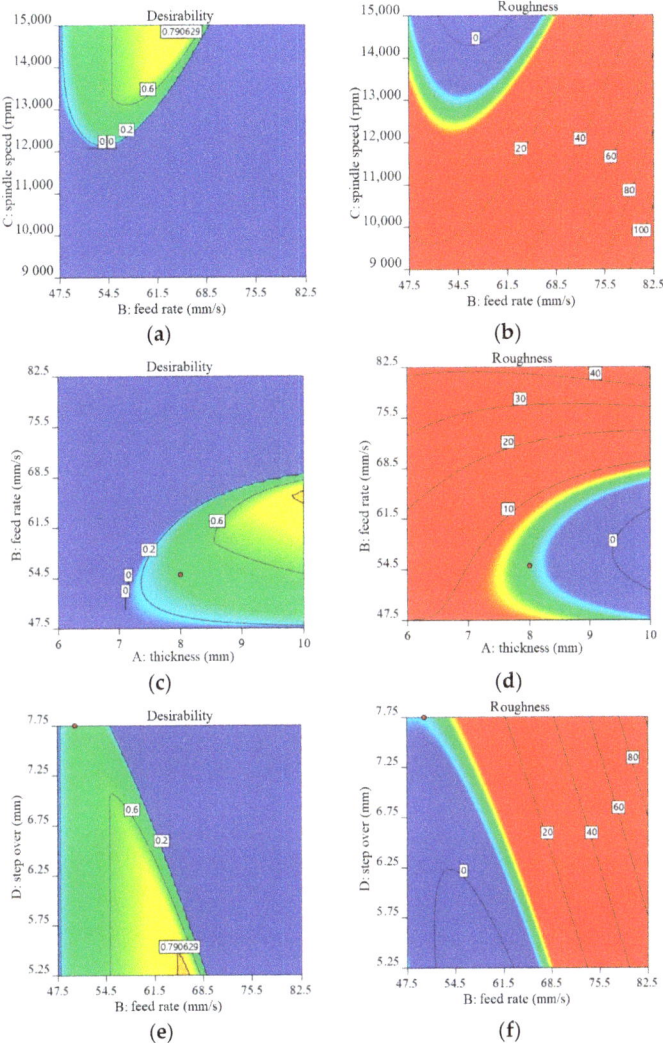

Figure 3. Effect of machining parameters and graphical analysis for surface roughness and desirability: (**a**) spindle speed and feed rate on desirability; (**b**) spindle speed and feed rate on roughness; (**c**) feed rate and thickness on desirability; (**d**) feed rate and thickness on roughness; (**e**) feed rate and step over on desirability; (**f**) feed rate and step over on roughness.

The optimized results' ramps are illustrated in Figure 4. The red bullets represent the optimized values and the blue bullet represents how well the surface quality increased. The relevant bar graph of desirability for the machining condition, replies, and the combined desirability of 0.812 is presented in Figure 5 that shows the overall desirability of all the parameters and the response.

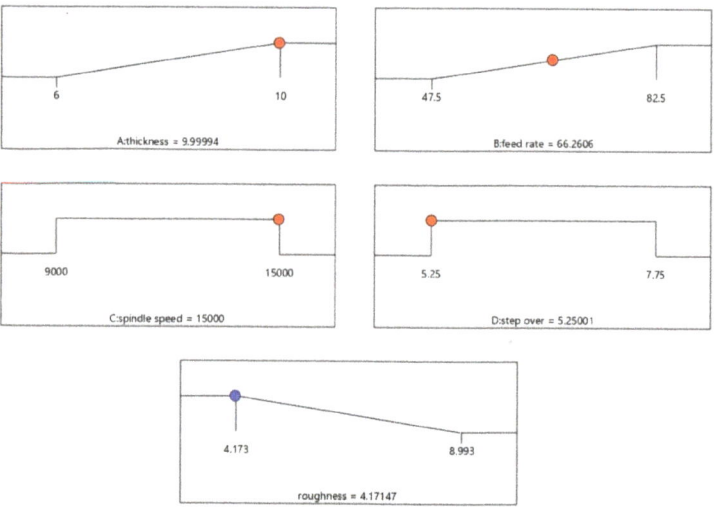

Figure 4. The graphs for optimal parameter ramp's function and combined optimization.

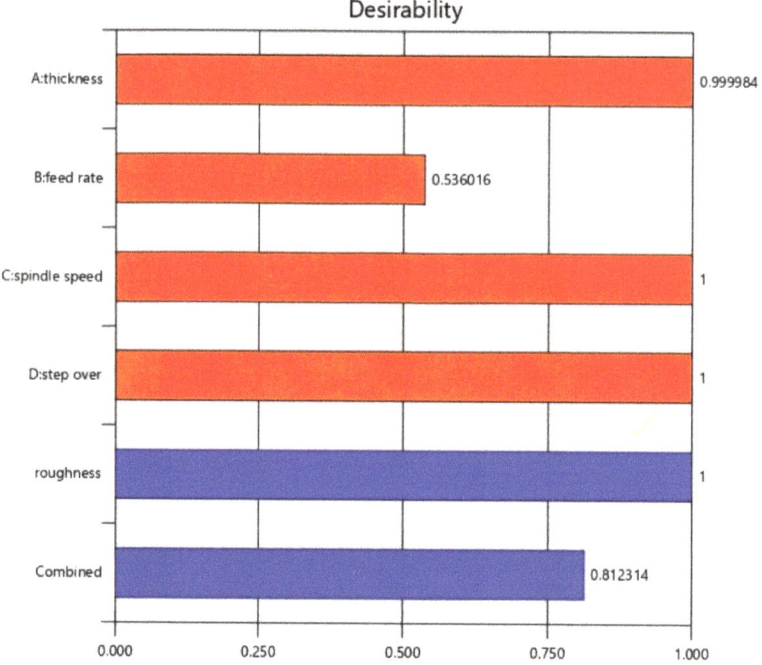

Figure 5. Desirability bar graph for combined optimization.

3.3. Model Validation

To validate the proposed model, the estimated surface roughness value and the value obtained from the model measurement have been compared here. Table 7 shows the estimated and measured values in different model conditions. According to this table the measured and estimated values are equal or have a slight difference with each other. Therefore, the estimated model has enough accuracy to calculate surface roughness based on different machining parameters (feed rate, spindle speed, depth of cut, step over).

Table 7. Comparison of surface roughness values measured and predicted by the model.

Condition	95 % PI High	95 % PI Low	Std Dev	Roughness Measured Value	Roughness Predicted Value by Model
1	8.52612	8.44988	0.003	8.488	8.488
2	7.38712	7.31088	0.003	7.349	7.349
3	5.25612	5.17988	0.003	5.218	5.218
4	6.70112	6.62488	0.003	6.663	6.663
5	7.06512	6.98888	0.003	7.027	7.027
6	7.63512	7.55888	0.003	7.597	7.597
7	5.92112	5.84488	0.003	5.883	5.883
8	6.95712	6.88088	0.003	6.919	6.919
9	6.79412	6.71788	0.003	6.756	6.756
10	7.53112	7.45488	0.003	7.493	7.493
11	7.84812	7.77188	0.003	7.81	7.81
12	8.01412	7.93788	0.003	7.976	7.976
13	5.27812	5.20188	0.003	5.24	5.24
14	7.52612	7.44988	0.003	7.488	7.488
15	6.78812	6.71188	0.003	6.75	6.75
16	9.03112	8.95488	0.003	8.993	8.993
17	8.02412	7.94788	0.003	7.986	7.986
18	5.10712	5.03088	0.003	5.069	5.069
19	7.87251	7.80649	0.002598	7.838	7.8395
20	7.08212	7.00588	0.003	7.044	7.044
21	7.87251	7.80649	0.002598	7.841	7.8395
22	4.21112	4.13488	0.003	4.173	4.173
23	7.46212	7.38588	0.003	7.424	7.424
24	6.30112	6.22488	0.003	6.263	6.263

4. Conclusions

This research mainly focuses on parameters investigation and optimization to achieve the best surface quality for the machined beech wood. The effect of machining parameters on the surface roughness of a piece of beech wood was investigated. RSM method is used to design experiments and the results are analyzed using Design-Expert. The studied parameters were optimized to achieve the minimum surface roughness. The summary of the obtained results is as follows:

- The roughness of surface decreased with decreasing feed rate. Changes in surface roughness due to the feed rate changes at high load depth, low spindle speed, and high step were very significant. Moreover, the surface roughness increased with an increasing pitch;
- The surface roughness increased with increasing the depth of cut. At this step, changes in surface roughness were very noticeable due to the changes in cutting depth, low spindle speed and high feed rate. In addition, as the spindle speed decreased, the surface roughness increased accordingly. Changes in surface roughness due to changes in spindle speed at high depth of cut, step over, and feed rate were very noticeable;
- The third-order mathematical model was modeled by the response surface method to estimate surface roughness based on machining parameters (feed rate, spindle speed, depth of cut and step by step). ANOVA showed that the greatest effect on surface roughness was related to the feed rate.

Finally, the optimal parameters for minimizing the surface roughness were obtained by the response surface method. Feed rate 66.262 (mm/s), spindle speed 15000 (rpm), cutting depth 10 (mm) and pitch 5.25 (mm). Moreover, the best surface roughness was obtained 4.2 (μm).

The results of the proposed model for the estimated surface roughness value were evaluated by the value obtained from the model measurement. The measured and estimated values are equal or have a slight difference. Finally, it can be concluded that the model has a good accuracy to predict surface roughness based on different machining parameters. As RSM allows investigating the influences of multiple factors and their interactions on one or more response variables, for future works this method can be applied to other factors influential on surface quality, and can even be employed to investigate the effects of the mentioned parameters on other response variables such as tool wear. This produces high-precision machining and high-quality wooden products. The study can also be continued on other wood types to study the product cost and quality. This, moreover, clearly shows the applicability and significance of the method in other studies in terms of economical cost, time, and any other limitations.

Author Contributions: Conceptualization, S.P. (Ssjjad Pakzad); methodology, S.P. (Ssjjad Pakzad) and S.P. (Siamak Pedrammehr); software, S.P. (Ssjjad Pakzad) and M.H.; validation, S.P. (Ssjjad Pakzad) and S.P. (Siamak Pedrammehr); formal analysis, S.P. (Ssjjad Pakzad), and M.H.; investigation, S.P. (Ssjjad Pakzad); resources S.P. (Ssjjad Pakzad) and M.H.; writing—original draft preparation, S.P. (Ssjjad Pakzad); writing—review and editing, S.P. (Siamak Pedrammehr) and M.H.; visualization, S.P. (Ssjjad Pakzad) and M.H.; supervision, S.P. (Siamak Pedrammehr); project administration, S.P. (Ssjjad Pakzad). All authors have read and agreed to the published version of the manuscript.

Funding: This research received no external funding.

Institutional Review Board Statement: Not applicable.

Informed Consent Statement: Not applicable.

Data Availability Statement: Not Applicable.

Conflicts of Interest: The authors declare no conflict of interest.

References

1. Fujiwara, Y.; Fujii, Y.; Sawada, Y.; Okumura, S. Assessment of wood surface roughness: Comparison of tactile roughness and three-dimensional parameters derived using a robust Gaussian regression filter. *J. Wood Sci.* **2004**, *50*, 35–40. [CrossRef]
2. Usta, I.; Demirci, S.; Kiliç, Y. Comparison of surface roughness of Locust acacia (*Robinia pseudoacacia* L.) and European oak (*Quercus petraea* (Mattu.) Lieble.) in terms of the preparative process by planing. *Build. Environ.* **2007**, *42*, 2988–2992. [CrossRef]
3. Hernández, R.E.; Kuljich, S.; Koubaa, A. Effect of cutting width and cutting height on the surface quality of black spruce cants produced by a chipper-canter. *Wood Fiber Sci.* **2010**, *42*, 273–284.
4. Kılıç, M.; Hiziroglu, S.; Burdurlu, E. Effect of machining on surface roughness of wood. *Build. Environ.* **2006**, *41*, 1074–1078. [CrossRef]
5. Pinkowski, G.; Szymański, W.; Krauss, A.; Stefanowski, S. Effect of sharpness angle and feeding speed on the surface roughness during milling of various wood species. *BioResources* **2018**, *13*, 6952–6962. [CrossRef]
6. Hiziroglu, S.; Kosonkorn, P. Evaluation of surface roughness of Thai medium density fiberboard (MDF). *Build. Environ.* **2006**, *41*, 527–533. [CrossRef]
7. Keturakis, G.; Juodeikiene, I. Investigation of milled wood surface roughness. *Mater. Sci.* **2007**, *13*, 47–51.
8. Malkoçoğlu, A. Machining properties and surface roughness of various wood species planed in different conditions. *Build. Environ.* **2007**, *42*, 2562–2567. [CrossRef]
9. Davim, J.P.; Clemente, V.C.; Silva, S. Surface roughness aspects in milling MDF (medium density fibreboard). *Int. J. Adv. Manuf. Technol.* **2008**, *40*, 49–55. [CrossRef]
10. Barcík, Š.; Pivolusková, E.; Kminiak, R.; Wieloch, G. The influence of cutting speed and feed speed on surface quality at plane milling of poplar wood. *Wood Res.* **2009**, *54*, 109–116.
11. Koc, K.H.; Erdinler, E.S.; Hazir, E.; Öztürk, E. Effect of CNC application parameters on wooden surface quality. *Measurement* **2017**, *107*, 12–18. [CrossRef]
12. Bal, B.C.; Akçakaya, E. The effects of step over, feed rate and finish depth on the surface roughness of fiberboard processed with CNC machine. *Furnit. Wooden Mater. Res. J.* **2018**, *1*, 86–93. [CrossRef]
13. Box, G.E.P.; Wilson, K.B. On the Experimental Attainment of Optimum Conditions. *J. R. Stat. Soc. Ser. B* **1951**, *13*, 1–38. [CrossRef]
14. Venkata Rao, K.; Murthy, P.B.G.S.N. Modeling and optimization of tool vibration and surface roughness in boring of steel using RSM, ANN and SVM. *J. Intell. Manuf.* **2018**, *29*, 1533–1543. [CrossRef]
15. Hazir, E.; Koc, K.H. Optimization of wood machining parameters in CNC routers: Taguchi orthogonal array based simulated angling algorithm. *Maderas Cienc. Tecnol.* **2019**, *21*, 493–510. [CrossRef]
16. Selaimia, A.-A.; Yallese, M.A.; Bensouilah, H.; Meddour, I.; Khattabi, R.; Mabrouki, T. Modeling and optimization in dry face milling of X2CrNi18-9 austenitic stainless steel using RMS and desirability approach. *Measurement* **2017**, *107*, 53–67. [CrossRef]

17. Asiltürk, I.; Neşeli, S.; Ince, M.A. Optimisation of parameters affecting surface roughness of Co28Cr6Mo medical material during CNC lathe machining by using the Taguchi and RSM methods. *Measurement* **2016**, *78*, 120–128. [CrossRef]
18. Sarıkaya, M.; Güllü, A. Taguchi design and response surface methodology based analysis of machining parameters in CNC turning under MQL. *J. Clean. Prod.* **2014**, *65*, 604–616. [CrossRef]
19. Prakash, S.; Palanikumar, K. Modeling for prediction of surface roughness in drilling MDF panels using response surface methodology. *J. Compos. Mater.* **2010**, *45*, 1639–1646. [CrossRef]
20. Skarvelis, M.; Mantanis, G.I. Physical and mechanical properties of beech wood harvested in the Greek public forests. *Wood Res.* **2013**, *58*, 123–130.
21. Najafian Ashrafi, M.; Shaabani Asrami, H.; Vosoughi Rudgar, Z.; Ghorbanian Far, M.; Heidari, A.; Rastbod, E.; Jafarzadeh, H.; Salehi, M.; Bari, E.; Ribera, J. Comparison of Physical and Mechanical Properties of Beech and Walnut Wood from Iran and Georgian Beech. *Forests* **2021**, *12*, 801. [CrossRef]
22. Purba, C.Y.C.; Dlouha, J.; Ruelle, J.; Fournier, M. Mechanical properties of secondary quality beech (*Fagus sylvatica* L.) and oak (*Quercus petraea* (Matt.) Liebl.) obtained from thinning, and their relationship to structural parameters. *Ann. For. Sci.* **2021**, *78*, 81. [CrossRef]
23. Montgomery, D.C. *Design and Analysis of Experiments*, 7th ed.; John and Wiley and Sons: Hoboken, NJ, USA, 2009.
24. Groover, M.P. *Fundamentals of Modern Manufacturing: Materials, Processes, and Systems*, 4th ed.; John and Wiley and Sons: Hoboken, NJ, USA, 2010.
25. Sharma, A.; Dwivedi, V.K. Effect of milling parameters on surface roughness: An experimental investigation. *Mater. Today Proc.* **2019**, *25*, 868–871. [CrossRef]
26. Arun Premnath, A.; Alwarsamy, T.; Abhinav, T.; Krishnakant, C.A. Surface roughness prediction by response surface methodology in milling of hybrid aluminium composites. *Procedia Eng.* **2012**, *38*, 745–752. [CrossRef]
27. Sanjeevi, R.; Nagaraja, R.; Radha Krishnan, B. Vision-based surface roughness accuracy prediction in the CNC milling process (Al6061) using ANN. *Mater. Today Proc.* **2021**, *37*, 245–247. [CrossRef]
28. *ISO 4287:1997*; Geometrical Product Specifications (GPS)—Surface Texture: Profile Method—Terms, Definitions and Surface Texture Parameters. International Organization for Standardization: Geneva, Switzerland, 1997.
29. Bakhaidar, R.B.; Naveen, N.R.; Basim, P.; Murshid, S.S.; Kurakula, M.; Alamoudi, A.J.; Bukhary, D.M.; Jali, A.M.; Majrashi, M.A.; Alshehri, S.; et al. Response Surface Methodology (RSM) Powered Formulation Development, Optimization and Evaluation of Thiolated Based Mucoadhesive Nanocrystals for Local Delivery of Simvastatin. *Polymers* **2022**, *14*, 5184. [CrossRef]
30. Gutema, E.M.; Gopal, M.; Lemu, H.G. Minimization of Surface Roughness and Temperature during Turning of Aluminum 6061 Using Response Surface Methodology and Desirability Function Analysis. *Materials* **2022**, *15*, 7638. [CrossRef]
31. Chen, C.-P.; Su, H.-Z.; Shih, J.-K.; Huang, C.-F.; Ku, H.-Y.; Chan, C.-W.; Li, T.-T.; Fuh, Y.-K. A Comparison and Analysis of Three Methods of Aluminum Crown Forgings in Processing Optimization. *Materials* **2022**, *15*, 8400. [CrossRef]
32. Oniszczuk-Świercz, D.; Świercz, R.; Michna, Š. Evaluation of Prediction Models of the Microwire EDM Process of Inconel 718 Using ANN and RSM Methods. *Materials* **2022**, *15*, 8317. [CrossRef]
33. Kang, H.; Liu, Y.; Li, D.; Xu, L. Study on the Removal of Iron and Manganese from Groundwater Using Modified Manganese Sand Based on Response Surface Methodology. *Appl. Sci.* **2022**, *12*, 11798. [CrossRef]
34. Khashi'Ie, N.S.; Waini, I.; Mukhtar, M.F.; Zainal, N.A.; Bin Hamzah, K.; Arifin, N.M.; Pop, I. Response Surface Methodology (RSM) on the Hybrid Nanofluid Flow Subject to a Vertical and Permeable Wedge. *Nanomaterials* **2022**, *12*, 4016. [CrossRef] [PubMed]
35. Equbal, A.; Equbal, M.A.; Equbal, M.I.; Ravindrannair, P.; Khan, Z.A.; Badruddin, I.A.; Kamangar, S.; Tirth, V.; Javed, S.; Kittur, M.I. Evaluating CNC Milling Performance for Machining AISI 316 Stainless Steel with Carbide Cutting Tool Insert. *Materials* **2022**, *15*, 8051. [CrossRef] [PubMed]
36. Alawad, M.O.; Alateyah, A.I.; El-Garaihy, W.H.; BaQais, A.; Elkatatny, S.; Kouta, H.; Kamel, M.; El-Sanabary, S. Optimizing the ECAP Parameters of Biodegradable Mg-Zn-Zr Alloy Based on Experimental, Mathematical Empirical, and Response Surface Methodology. *Materials* **2022**, *15*, 7719. [CrossRef] [PubMed]
37. Yanis, M.; Mohruni, A.S.; Sharif, S.; Yani, I.; Arifin, A.; Khona'Ah, B. Application of RSM and ANN in Predicting Surface Roughness for Side Milling Process under Environmentally Friendly Cutting Fluid. *J. Phys. Conf. Ser.* **2019**, *1198*, 042016. [CrossRef]
38. Zerti, A.; Yallese, M.A.; Zerti, O.; Nouioua, M.; Khettabi, R. Prediction of machining performance using RSM and ANN models in hard turning of martensitic stainless steel AISI 420. *Proc. Inst. Mech. Eng. Part C J. Mech. Eng. Sci.* **2019**, *233*, 4439–4462. [CrossRef]
39. Ghazali, M.H.M.; Mazlan, A.Z.A.; Wei, L.M.; Tying, C.T.; Sze, T.S.; Jamil, N.I.M. Effect of Machining Parameters on the Surface Roughness for Different Type of Materials. *IOP Conf. Ser. Mater. Sci. Eng.* **2019**, *530*, 012008. [CrossRef]
40. Zaidi, S.R.; Khan, M.; Jaffery, S.H.I.; Warsi, S. Effect of Machining Parameters on Surface Roughness During Milling Operation. *Adv. Manuf. Technol.* **2021**, *15*, 175–180. [CrossRef]
41. Zhenchao, Y.; Yang, X.; Yan, L.; Jin, X.; Quandai, W. The effect of milling parameters on surface integrity in high-speed milling of ultrahigh strength steel. *Procedia CIRP* **2018**, *71*, 83–88. [CrossRef]

Disclaimer/Publisher's Note: The statements, opinions and data contained in all publications are solely those of the individual author(s) and contributor(s) and not of MDPI and/or the editor(s). MDPI and/or the editor(s) disclaim responsibility for any injury to people or property resulting from any ideas, methods, instructions or products referred to in the content.

Article
On Λ-Fractional Derivative and Human Neural Network

D. Karaoulanis [1], A. K. Lazopoulos [2,*], N. Lazopoulou [3] and K. Lazopoulos [3]

[1] School of Electrical and Computer Engineering, National Technical University of Athens, 15780 Athen, Greece
[2] Mathematical Sciences Department, Hellenic Army Academy, 16673 Vari, Greece
[3] Independent Researcher, 19009 Rafina, Greece
* Correspondence: orfeakos74@gmail.com

Abstract: Fractional derivatives can express anomalous diffusion in brain tissue. Various brain diseases such as Alzheimer's disease, multiple sclerosis, and Parkinson's disease are attributed to the accumulation of proteins in axons. Discrete swellings along the axons cause other neuro diseases. To model the propagation of voltage in axons with all those causes, a fractional cable geometry has been adopted. Although a fractional cable model has already been presented, the non-existence of fractional differential geometry based on the well-known fractional derivatives raises questions. These minute parts of the human neural system are modeled as cables that function with a non-uniform cross-section in the fractional realm based upon the Λ-fractional derivative (Λ-FD). That derivative is considered the unique fractional derivative generating differential geometry. Examples are presented so that fruitful conclusions can be made. The present work is going to help medical and bioengineering scientists in controlling various brain diseases.

Keywords: human neural network; axons; dendrites; Λ-fractional derivative

MSC: 92B20; 53Z16; 26A33

1. Introduction

Fractional calculus (FC) is a mathematical procedure with global characteristics demanded by many scientific fields, from mechanics (Drapaca et al. [1], Di Paola et al. [2], Carpinteri et al. [3]) to economics, and from medicine and biology (Magin [4]) to physics (Hilfer [5], West et al. [6]), so that mathematical procedure expresses non-locality, generating in addition non-uniform geometry. Eringen [7] has already presented non-local theories in physics and mechanics applied to micro and nanoparticles and mechanics. He states that problems in micro or nano fields should be considered in the context of non-local theories. To be more precise, fractional calculus is based on fractional derivatives (FD), mainly Riemann-Liouville, Grunwald-Letnikov, and Caputo (Kilbas et al. [8], Podlubny [9]). Of course, many other fractional derivatives are applied in the scientific field, such as Riesz, Miller–Ross, Hadamard, Caputo Fabrizio, and Atangana-Baleanu fractional derivatives, to name a few. The main advantage of all these derivatives is their non-local behavior in space as well as in time. That means fractional calculus appeals to global phenomena and not local ones (Podlubny [9]). However, these derivatives are not derivatives in the mathematical sense. Indeed, they do not satisfy the fundamental perquisites of differential topology to correspond to differentials generating geometry (Chillingworth [10]). Therefore, their use, although very fruitful in results, is questionable. Replacing derivatives in differential equations with relative fractional derivatives is unjustifiable from the perspective of mathematical accuracy; therefore, one cannot develop a sound theory or model based on those derivatives.

On the other hand, the Λ-fractional derivative tackles that problem best. That derivative, introduced in 2018 (Lazopoulos [11]), aspires to provide a way out of the dead end that fractional derivatives face. Along with the Λ-transform (Λ-T) and Λ-space (Λ-S), that derivative transforms the initial fractional differential equation (FDE) into an ordinary equation in Λ-space and then transfers the results of Λ-space to the initial space, using a special transform formula. Therefore, the solution of the ordinary transformed equation is developed in Λ-space, where all topological perquisites are satisfied and then transferred back to the initial space.

Dendrites and axons are the building blocks of the human neural system. They carry electric signals to each other, thus allowing the neural system to work harmoniously. Their behavior is not local but mainly global, making them truly appealing to fractional calculus. Hence, the model of the electric potential is discussed in the present article concerning the dendrites and axons of the human neural network, where it is supposed that the behavior of the system has non-local dependence due to the microphysics of the electric neural network. To accomplish that, we model dendrites and axons as cables. Therefore, we focus on the solution for the coaxial cylindrical cable problem (the radius of the cable R = R_0 is constant), where the fractional derivatives in the corresponding differential equation are thought to be the ones defined by K. Lazopoulos et al. [11]. According to Λ-fractional analysis, we make the necessary transformation of the equation to Λ-space with the normal derivatives, resulting in a solution for the voltage in Λ-space, thus solving the problem.

This article is structured thus: In Section 2, a brief description of the behavior of Λ-fractional derivative, Λ-space, and Λ-transformation is given. In Section 3, the role of fractional calculus in the study of dendrites and axons as cables is described. Finally, a discussion is made in Section 4, and conclusions are drawn.

2. Foundations of Λ-Fractional Derivative, Λ-Transform, and Dual Λ-Space

To study fractional calculus, there are many thought-provoking books that the interested reader can refer to; Kilbas et al. [8], Podlubny [9], Samko et al. [12], Oldham [13], and Mainardi [14] are some very intriguing propositions. Nevertheless, we will summarize some essential points of FC to present them to the reader briefly.

Let us assume $\Omega = [\alpha, b]$ ($-\infty < \alpha < b < \infty$) to be a finite interval on the real axis. The left and right Riemann-Liouville fractional integrals are then defined by (Kilbas [8]):

$$^{RL}_{a}I^{\gamma}_{x}f(x) = \frac{1}{\Gamma(\gamma)} \int_{a}^{x} \frac{f(s)}{(x-s)^{1-\gamma}} ds \tag{1}$$

$$^{RL}_{x}I^{\gamma}_{b}f(x) = \frac{1}{\Gamma(\gamma)} \int_{x}^{b} \frac{f(s)}{(s-x)^{1-\gamma}} ds \tag{2}$$

with γ ($0 < \gamma \leq 1$) being the order of fractional integrals and $\Gamma(x) = (x-1)!$ ($\Gamma(\gamma)$ is called Euler's Gamma function). Furthermore, since $0 < \gamma \leq 1$ applies, the Riemann-Liouville (RL) Fractional Derivatives are defined by (Kilbas [8]):

$$^{RL}_{a}D^{\gamma}_{x}f(x) = \frac{d}{dx}\left(^{RL}_{a}I^{1-\gamma}_{x} f(x)\right) \tag{3}$$

and

$$^{RL}_{x}D^{\gamma}_{b}f(x) = -\frac{d}{dx}\left(^{RL}_{x}I^{1-\gamma}_{b} f(x)\right) \tag{4}$$

where Equation (3) defines the left and Equation (4) the right Fractional Derivatives. Moreover, the fractional integrals with the corresponding Riemann-Liouville FDs are related by the equation:

$$^{RL}_{a}D^{\gamma}_{x}\left(^{RL}_{a}I^{\gamma}_{x}f(x)\right) = f(x) \tag{5}$$

The Riemann-Liouville Fractional Derivative is also essential to our methodology since Λ-Derivative is defined as the fraction of two such derivatives (see Lazopoulos [10]):

$$^\Lambda_a D^\gamma_x f(x) = \frac{^{RL}_a D^\gamma_x f(x)}{^{RL}_a D^\gamma_x x} = \frac{\frac{d\, ^{RL}_a I^{1-\gamma}_x f(x)}{dx}}{\frac{d\, ^{RL}_a I^{1-\gamma}_x x}{dx}} = \frac{d\, ^{RL}_a I^{1-\gamma}_x f(x)}{d\, ^{RL}_a I^{1-\gamma}_x x} \qquad (6)$$

It is clear that $^{RL}_a D^\gamma_x f(x)$ is the Riemann-Liouville Derivative of F(X), as described in FC (Equations (4) and (5)), and $^{RL}_a I^{1-\gamma}_x f(x)$ is the Riemann-Liouville fractional integral of the real fractional dimension. In this article, $0 < \gamma \leq 1$ is considered (see Samko et al. [12], Podlubny [9]).

Λ-transform consists of defining new variables and functions in Λ-space using the transformation

$$F(X) = {}_aI^{1-\gamma}_x f(x(X)) \qquad (7)$$

for functions F(X) and

$$X = {}_aI^{1-\gamma}_x x \qquad (8)$$

for variables x.

F(X) and X then belong to Λ-space, and from there, they can form Λ-derivative (Equation (6)) and Λ-fractional differential equations (Λ-FDE). These equations in Λ-space have ordinary form; therefore, they can be treated conventionally, satisfying all perquisites of differential topology and allowing a proper geometry to be formed. The solution H(X) of the Λ-FDE is then transferred to the initial space using the formula

$$h(x) = {}^{RL}_a D^{1-\gamma}_x H(X(x)) \qquad (9)$$

(where h(x) is the solution in the initial space).

3. Λ-Fractional Calculus Studying Dendrites and Axons

Dendrites and axons transfer potential electric signals of potential V. We model these minute parts of the neural system using fractional calculus and assume that these are cables of constant radius R_0. Since the phenomenon is non-local, fractional derivatives are most suitable to describe this phenomenon. Λ-fractional derivative (introduced by K.A. Lazopoulos in 2018 (Lazopoulos [11])) is used to model the electric current passing through these building blocks of the neural system while Λ-transform and Λ-space are also participating. The equation that governs the voltage of the electric current inside the cable is (Lopez et al. [15])

$$C_M \frac{\partial V(x,t)}{\partial t} = \frac{d_0}{4r_L} \frac{\partial^2 V(x,t)}{\partial x^2} - i_{ion} \qquad (10)$$

where d_0 is the constant diameter of the cable, V(x,t) is the voltage of the current passing through the cable, where C_M denotes the specific membrane capacitance, r_L denotes the longitudinal resistance and i_{ion} is the ionic current per unit area into and out of the cable. In the passive cable case, namely when $i_{ion} = V/r_M$, with r_M the specific membrane resistance, we have this equation processed geometrically in Lopez et al. [15], so the final cable equation can be extracted:

$$\frac{\partial V(s,t)}{\partial t} = \frac{1}{r_L C_M \int_0^{2\pi} d\theta \sqrt{det g(\theta,s)}} \frac{\partial}{\partial s}\left(a(s)\frac{\partial V(s,t)}{\partial s}\right) - \frac{V(s,t)}{r_M C_M} \qquad (11)$$

where s is the length of the cable, θ is the angle in the cross-section of the cable, a(s) is the cross-sectional area of the cable, and g(θ,s) is the metric of the cable. It is important to stress that this equation was solved using the Caputo derivative in Lopez et al. [15].

According to the Lazopoulos approach, we make the necessary transformation of the equation to Λ-space with the ordinary derivatives, resulting in the following solution for the voltage in Λ-space (Lopez et al. [15]):

$$V^{\Lambda}(T,S) = V_0 l_0 \sqrt{\frac{r_L \cdot c_M}{2 \cdot \pi \cdot R_0 \cdot T}} \cdot e^{-\frac{r_L \cdot c_M \cdot S^2}{2 R_0 \cdot T}} \cdot e^{-\frac{T}{r_L \cdot c_M}} \tag{12}$$

where T, S is the time and arc length of the cable in Λ-space. They are connected with the ones in real space with the relations for fractional order γ:

$$t = [\Gamma(3-\gamma) \cdot T]^{\frac{1}{2-\gamma}}, s = [\Gamma(3-\gamma) \cdot S]^{\frac{1}{2-\gamma}} \tag{13}$$

Following [15], the other parameters in Equation (12) are constants and take the values

$$c_M = 0.001 F/cm^2, r_M = 3000 \cdot \Omega \cdot cm^2, r_L = 100 \cdot \Omega \cdot cm \ R_0 = 10^{-4} \text{ cm}, V_0 = 1.3 \times 10^{-6} V, l_0 = 0.13 \text{ cm}$$

Firstly, we will examine the case where the values of arc lengths S in Λ-space are constants. In order to find the values of the voltage V(t,s) in the initial space, we impose the following inverse transformation:

$$V(t,s) = {}_0^{RL}D_t^{1-\gamma}\left(V^{\Lambda}(t,s)\right) = \frac{1}{\Gamma(\gamma)} \cdot \frac{d}{dt}\int_0^t \frac{V^{\Lambda}(\tau,s)}{(t-\tau)^{1-\gamma}} d\tau \tag{14}$$

The results for voltage V(t, s) for various values of s and fractional order γ in real space are shown in Figures 1–4. In these figures, we can see that as the value of arc length s increases, we shift the voltage's maximum to higher time values. We believe this delay in maximum response is expected due to increased cable length. Also, for the same reason, we have a decrease in the maximum value of voltage and broadness of the voltage curve as the arc length s increases, denoting an inertial behavior across the cable.

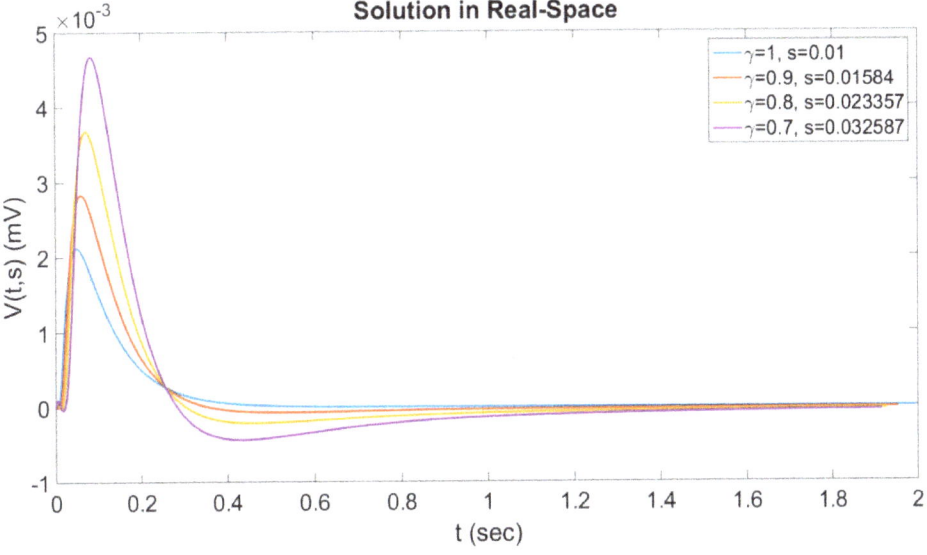

Figure 1. The voltage V(t,s) for various values of fractional order γ and corresponding values of s in real space (S = 0.01).

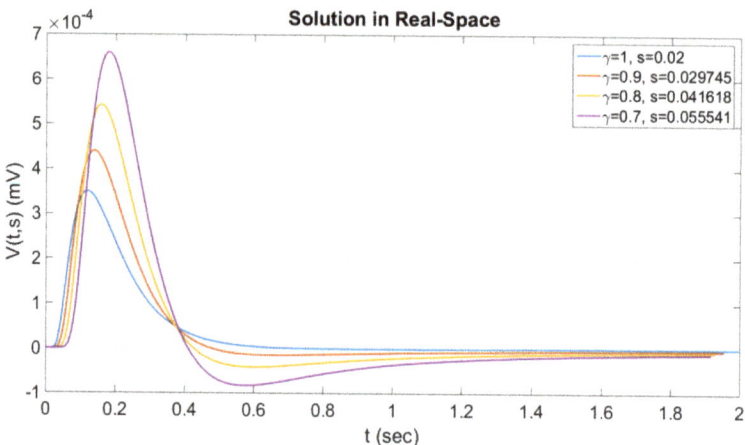

Figure 2. The voltage V(t,s) for various values of fractional order γ and corresponding values of s in real space (S = 0.02).

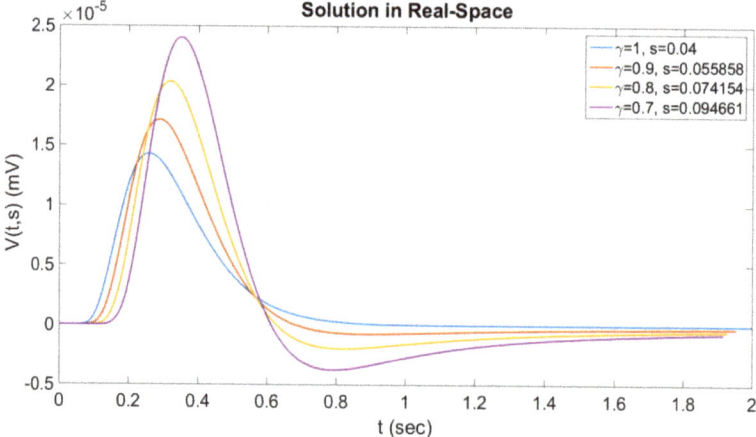

Figure 3. The voltage V(t,s) for various values of fractional order γ and corresponding values of s in real space (S = 0.04).

Finally, we must mention that in all cases of arc length values, the decrease of fractional order γ gives greater maximum values in voltage and reverses the polarity of the resulting voltage (from positive values to negative ones) as time passes.

Now, we will examine the voltage $V^\Lambda(T,S)$ (Equation (12)) as a two-variable function in Λ-space. In order to transform it to the initial space, we will use the following formula of inverse transformation for both t and s, according to K. Lazopoulos' [11] fractional approach:

$$V(t,s) = {}_0^{RL}D_t^{1-\gamma_2}({}_0^{RL}D_s^{1-\gamma_1}(V^\Lambda(\tau,q))) = \frac{1}{\Gamma(\gamma_2)\cdot\Gamma(\gamma_1)} \cdot \frac{d}{dt}\int_0^t \frac{1}{(t-\tau)^{1-\gamma_2}}(\frac{d}{ds}\int_0^s \frac{V^\Lambda(\tau,q)}{(s-q)^{1-\gamma_1}}dq)d\tau \quad (15)$$

where the relation gives $V^\Lambda(\tau,q)$:

$$V^\Lambda(\tau,q) = V_0 l_0 \sqrt{\frac{r_L \cdot c_M \cdot \Gamma(3-\gamma_2)}{2\cdot\pi\cdot R_0 \cdot \tau^{2-\gamma_2}}} \cdot e^{-\frac{r_L \cdot c_M \cdot \Gamma(3-\gamma_2)\cdot q^{4-2\gamma_1}}{2R_0\cdot(\Gamma(3-\gamma_1))^2 \cdot \tau^{2-\gamma_2}}} \cdot e^{-\frac{\tau^{2-\gamma_2}}{r_L \cdot c_M \cdot \Gamma(3-\gamma_2)}} \quad (16)$$

Here, the fractional orders (γ_2, γ_1) for the inverse transformation are different for time t and arc length s. Figures 5–11 present the voltage V(t,s) in real space for various values of fractional orders. The constants in Equation (16) take the same values as in Equation (12).

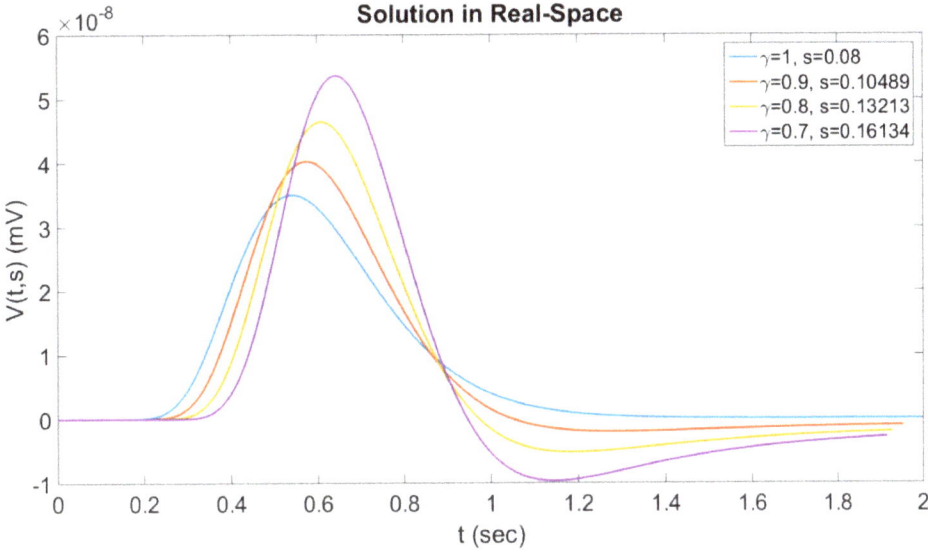

Figure 4. The voltage V(t,s) for various values of fractional order γ and corresponding values of s in real space (S = 0.08).

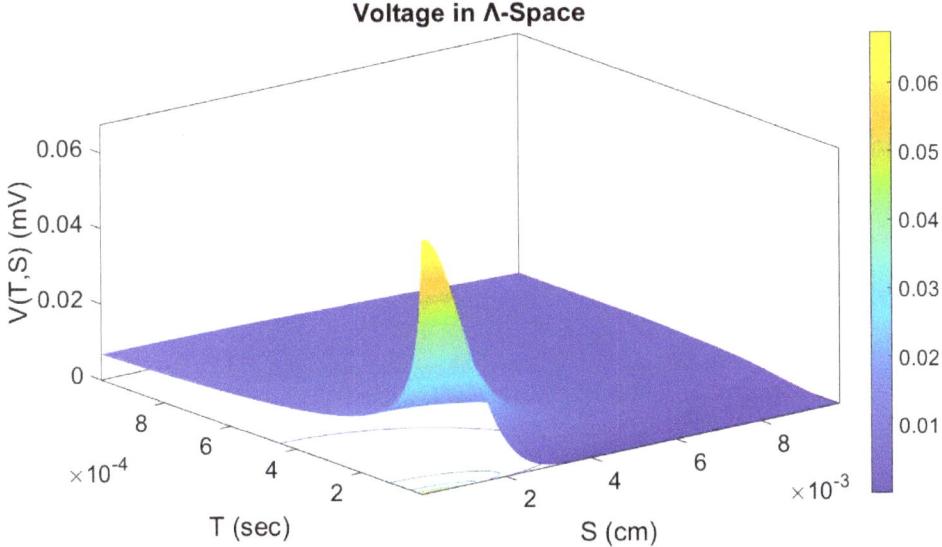

Figure 5. The voltage $V^\Lambda(T,S)$ in Λ-space as a function of time T and arc length S.

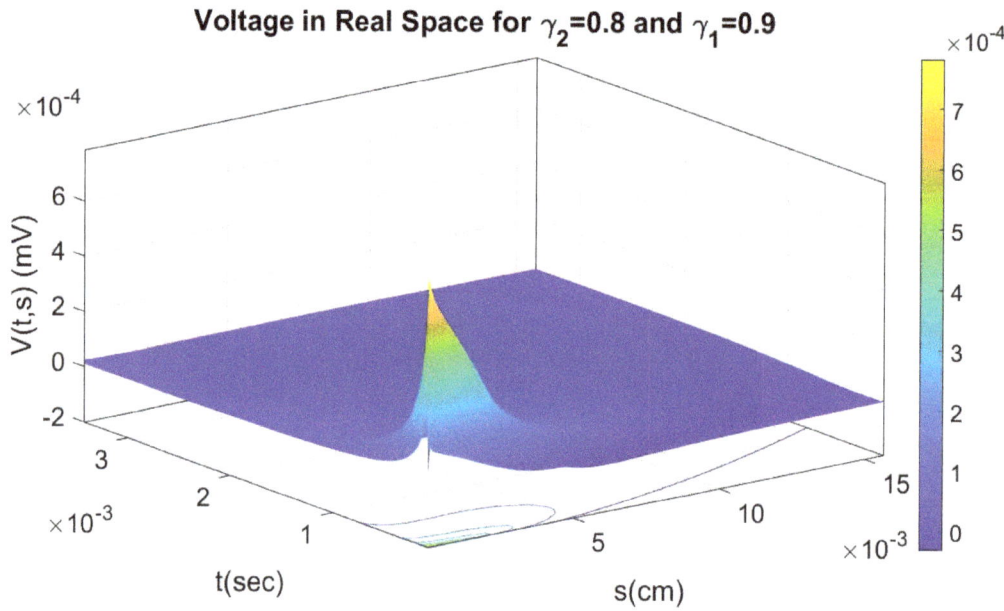

Figure 6. The voltage V(t,s) in real space as a function of time and arc length s, for fractional orders $\gamma_2 = 0.8$ and $\gamma_1 = 0.9$.

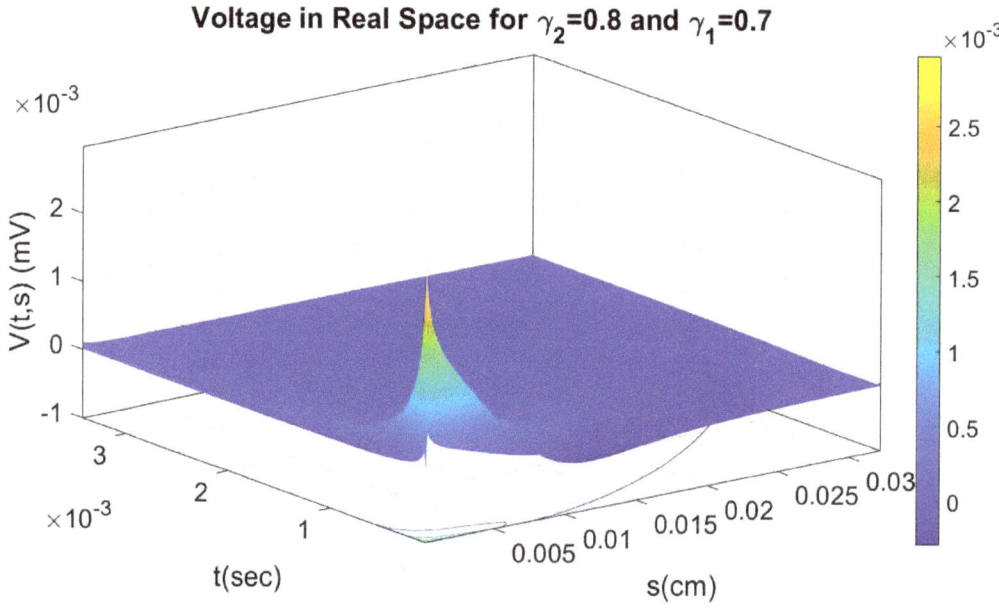

Figure 7. The voltage V(t,s) in real space as a function of time and arc length s, for fractional orders $\gamma_2 = 0.8$ and $\gamma_1 = 0.7$.

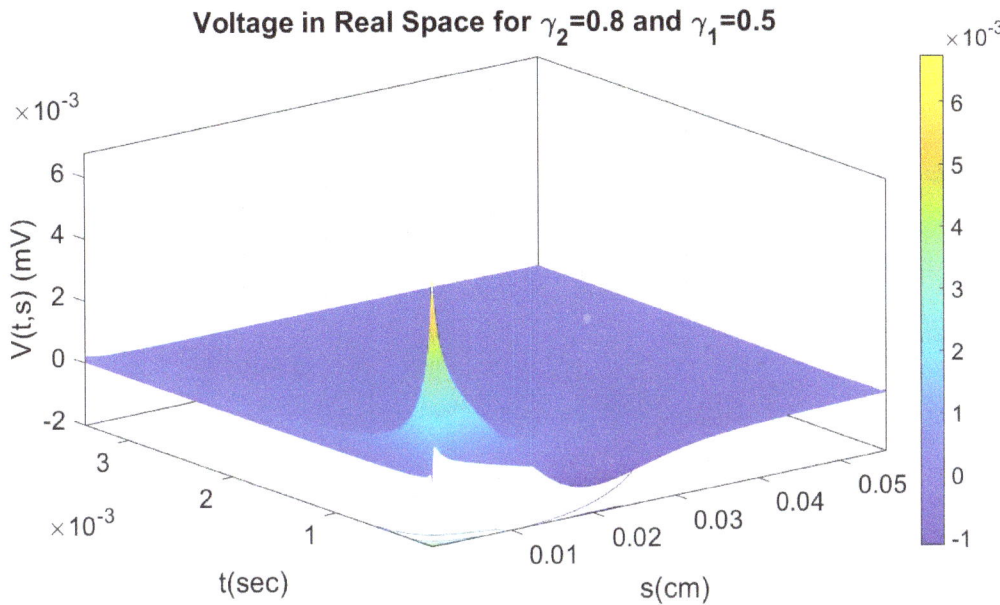

Figure 8. The voltage V(t,s) in real space as a function of time and arc length s, for fractional orders $\gamma_2 = 0.8$ and $\gamma_1 = 0.5$.

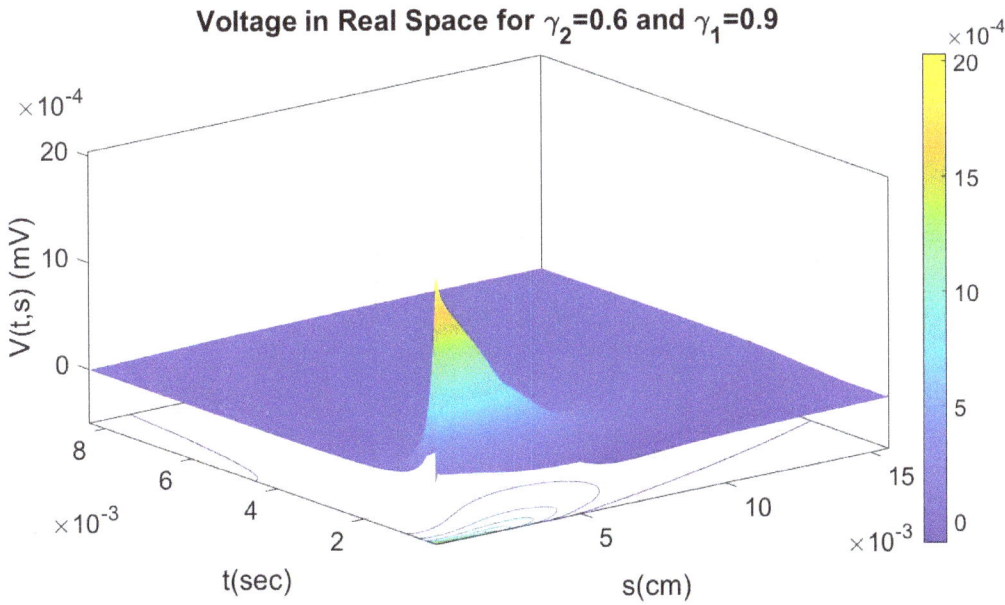

Figure 9. The voltage V(t,s) in real space as a function of time and arc length s, for fractional orders $\gamma_2 = 0.6$ and $\gamma_1 = 0.9$.

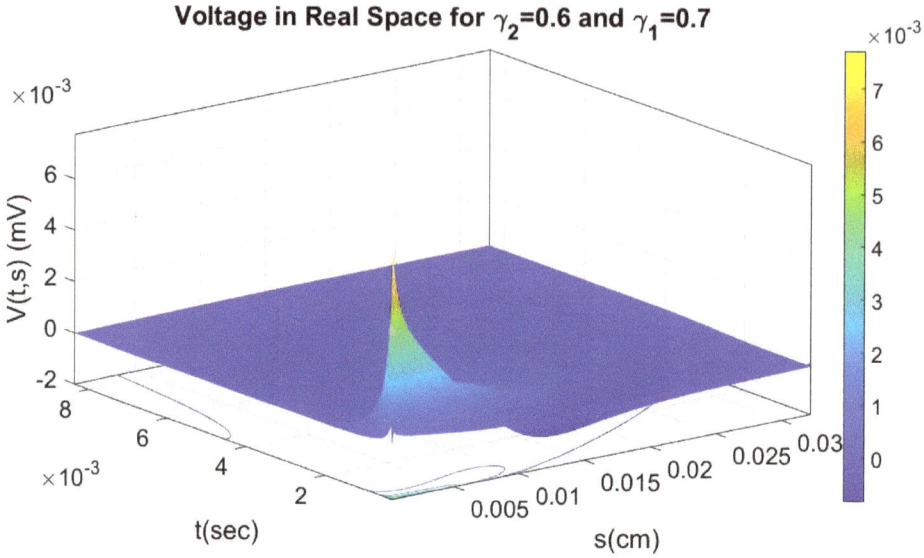

Figure 10. The voltage V(t,s) in real space as a function of time and arc length s, for fractional orders $\gamma_2 = 0.6$ and $\gamma_1 = 0.7$.

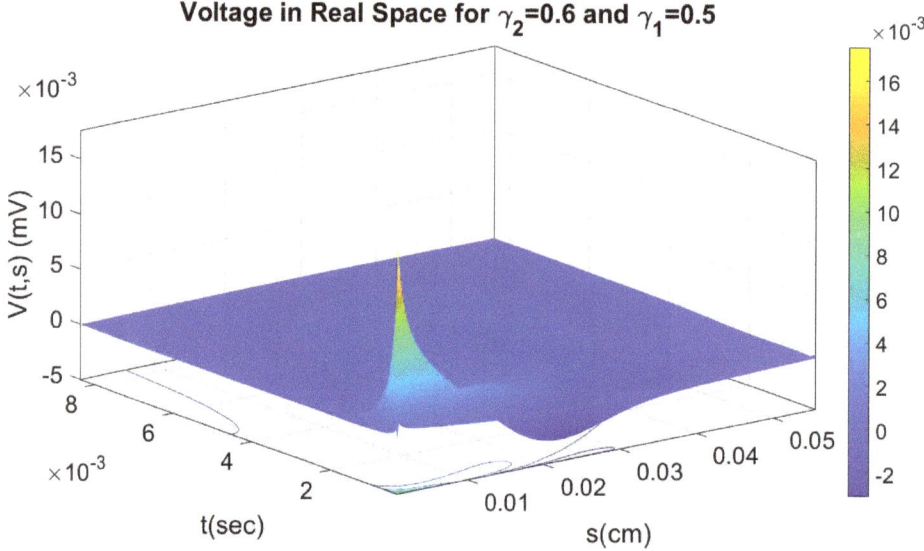

Figure 11. The voltage V(t,s) in real space as a function of time and arc length s, for fractional orders $\gamma_2 = 0.6$ and $\gamma_1 = 0.5$.

Based on Figures 5–11, we can indeed conclude that as the fractional order for time t (γ_2) or arc length s (γ_1) decreases, the maximum value reached by the voltage V(t,s) increases. Also, in all cases, we have a change in the polarity of the voltage (positive to negative) along the cable. Finally, we can observe that as fractional order for time t (γ_2) or arc length s (γ_1) decreases, we have non-zero voltage values for higher values of arc length s (longer cable).

4. Conclusions

Dendrites and axons are modeled as cables using fractional calculus. The voltage potential is transferred from Λ-space to the initial space. During this procedure, many interesting conclusions can be addressed, such as the high influence of the length of the cable s and the critical impact of the fractional order. More precisely, an increasing s results in the increase of voltage, while the decrease in fractional order also increases the voltage. The present work is addressed to medical and bioengineering researchers for controlling the evolution of various brain diseases, refs. [16–19].

Author Contributions: Conceptualization, K.L.; Data curation, D.K.; Investigation, D.K. and K.L.; Methodology, D.K., K.L. and A.K.L.; Writing—original draft, K.L.; Writing—review & editing, A.K.L.; Validation, N.L. All authors have read and agreed to the published version of the manuscript.

Funding: This research received no external funding.

Data Availability Statement: Data is unavailable.

Conflicts of Interest: The authors declare no conflict of interest.

References

1. Drapaca, C.S.; Sivaloganathan, S.A. Fractional model of continuum mechanics. *J. Elast.* **2012**, *107*, 107–123. [CrossRef]
2. Di Paola, M.; Failla, G.; Zingales, M. Physically-based approach to the mechanics of strong non-local linear elasticity theory. *J. Elast.* **2009**, *97*, 103–130. [CrossRef]
3. Carpinteri, A.; Cornetti, P.; Sapora, A. A Fractional calculus approach to non-local elasticity. *Eur. Phys. J. Spec. Top.* **2011**, *193*, 193–204. [CrossRef]
4. Magin, R.L. Fractional calculus in bioengineering, Parts 1–3. *Crit. Rev. Biomed. Eng.* **2004**, *32*, 1–377. [CrossRef] [PubMed]
5. Hilfer, R. *Applications of Fractional Calculus in Physics*; World Scientific: River Edge, NJ, USA, 2000.
6. West, B.J.; Bologna, M.; Grigolini, P. *Physics of Fractal Operators*; Springer: New York, NY, USA, 2003.
7. Eringen, A.C. *Nonlocal Continuum Field Theories*; Springer: New York, NY, USA, 2002.
8. Kilbas, A.A.; Srivastava, H.M.; Trujillo, J.J. *Theory and Applications of Fractional Differential Equations*; Elsevier: Amsterdam, The Netherlands, 2006.
9. Podlubny, I. *Fractional Differential Equations (An Introduction to Fractional Derivatives, Fractional Differential Equations, Some Methods of Their Solution and Some of Their Applications)*; Academic Press: San Diego, CA, USA; Boston, MA, USA; New York, NY, USA; London, UK; Tokyo, Japan; Toronto, ON, Canada, 1999.
10. Chillingworth, D. *Differential Topology with a View to Applications*; Pitman: London, UK; San Francisco, CA, USA, 1976.
11. Lazopoulos, K.A.; Lazopoulos, A.K. On the Mathematical Formulation of Fractional Derivatives. *Prog. Fract. Differ. Appl.* **2019**, *5*, 261–267.
12. Samko, S.G.; Kilbas, A.A.; Marichev, O.I. *Fractional Integrals and Derivatives: Theory and Applications*; Gordon and Breach: Amsterdam, The Netherlands, 1993.
13. Oldham, K.B.; Spanier, J. *The Fractional Calculus*; Academic Press: New York, NY, USA; London, UK, 1974.
14. Mainardi, F. *Fractional Calculus and Waves in Linear Viscoelasticity*; Imperial College Press: London, UK, 2010.
15. Lopez-Sanchez, E.J.; Romero, J.M. Cable equation for general geometry. *Phys. Rev. E* **2017**, *95*, 022403. [CrossRef] [PubMed]
16. Haugh, J.M. Analysis of reaction-diffusion systems with anomalous subdiffusion. *Biophys. J.* **2009**, *97*, 435–442. [CrossRef] [PubMed]
17. Saxon, M.J. A biological interpretation of transient anomalous subdiffusion. I, Qualitative model. *Biophys. J.* **2007**, *92*, 1178–1191. [CrossRef] [PubMed]
18. Weiss, M.; Elsner, M.; Kartberg, F.; Nilsson, T. Anomalous subdiffusion is a measure for cytoplasmic crowding in living cells. *Biophys. J.* **2004**, *87*, 3518–3524. [CrossRef] [PubMed]
19. Saxon, M.J. Anomalous subdiffusion in fluorescence photobleaching recovery: A Monte Carlo study. *Biophys. J.* **2001**, *81*, 2226–2240. [CrossRef] [PubMed]

Disclaimer/Publisher's Note: The statements, opinions and data contained in all publications are solely those of the individual author(s) and contributor(s) and not of MDPI and/or the editor(s). MDPI and/or the editor(s) disclaim responsibility for any injury to people or property resulting from any ideas, methods, instructions or products referred to in the content.

Article

Multiplicative Mixed-Effects Modelling of Dengue Incidence: An Analysis of the 2019 Outbreak in the Dominican Republic

Adelaide Freitas [1,2,†], Helena Sofia Rodrigues [2,3,*,†], Natália Martins [1,2,*,†], Adela Iutis [1], Michael A. Robert [4,5,†], Demian Herrera [6] and Manuel Colomé-Hidalgo [7]

1. Department of Mathematics, University of Aveiro, 3810-193 Aveiro, Portugal
2. Center for Research and Development in Mathematics and Applications (CIDMA), University of Aveiro, 3810-193 Aveiro, Portugal
3. Business School, Instituto Politécnico de Viana do Castelo, 4930-600 Valença, Portugal
4. Department of Mathematics, Virginia Tech, Blacksburg, VA 24061, USA
5. Center for Emerging, Zoonotic, and Arthropod-Borne Pathogens, Virginia Tech, Blacksburg, VA 24060, USA
6. Centro de Investigación en Salud Dr. Hugo Mendoza, Hospital Pediátrico Dr. Hugo Mendoza, Santo Domingo 10117, Dominican Republic
7. Instituto Tecnológico de Santo Domingo (INTEC), Santo Domingo 10602, Dominican Republic
* Correspondence: sofiarodrigues@esce.ipvc.pt (H.S.R.); natalia@ua.pt (N.M.)
† These authors contributed equally to this work.

Abstract: Dengue is a vector-borne disease that is endemic to several countries, including the Dominican Republic, which has experienced dengue outbreaks for over four decades. With outbreaks growing in incidence in recent years, it is becoming increasingly important to develop better tools to understand drivers of dengue transmission. Such tools are critical for providing timely information to assist healthcare authorities in preparing human, material, and medical resources for outbreaks. Here, we investigate associations between meteorological variables and dengue transmission in the Dominican Republic in 2019, the year in which the country's largest outbreak to date occurred. We apply generalized linear mixed modelling with gamma family and log link to model the weekly dengue incidence rate. Because correlations in lags between climate variables and dengue cases exhibited different behaviour among provinces, a backward-type selection method was executed to find a final model with lags in the explanatory variables. We find that in the best models, meteorological conditions such as temperature and rainfall have an impact with a delay of 2–5 weeks in the development of an outbreak, ensuring breeding conditions for mosquitoes.

Keywords: dengue; Dominican Republic; climate variables; lags; generalized linear mixed models

MSC: 92B15; 62P10; 62J12

1. Introduction

Dengue is one of the most significant mosquito-borne diseases to threaten human populations, particularly in tropical and subtropical regions. The number of dengue cases reported to the World Health Organization (WHO) has increased sharply from less than 0.5 million in 2000 to 5.2 million in 2019, and the number of dengue-induced deaths increased from 960 in 2000 to 4032 in 2015 [1], leading WHO to name dengue as one of the ten biggest threats to global health in 2019 [2]. Given the global increases in dengue in recent years, it is increasingly important to develop tools to better understand drivers of dengue transmission and to predict future outbreaks.

One country where dengue has long been endemic is the Dominican Republic. In the past decade, however, dengue outbreaks have grown in incidence, with the 2019 outbreak being the largest outbreak in the country to date [3,4]. In fact, 2019 was the year in which the WHO recorded the highest number of global dengue cases ever to occur within a year [1], suggesting that dengue in the Dominican Republic is mirroring global trends.

In an exploratory analysis of dengue in the Dominican Republic, Iutis et al. [3] showed there is no single meteorological, demographic or geographic factor that affects the incidence rate of dengue. They instead suggest that a combination of different factors could be responsible for increases in dengue cases. Among these factors is climate, which plays a very important role in dengue transmission and in the life cycle of the mosquitos that transmit dengue virus. For example, it is well known that the mosquito must have certain meteorological conditions to survive and reproduce [5,6]. Herein, we aim to characterize relationships between dengue cases and meteorological variables such as temperature, humidity, and precipitation by considering the 2019 outbreak of dengue in multiple provinces of the Dominican Republic. It is important to study not only the impact of climate variables on dengue transmission, but also lags between dengue cases and these variables because there are inherent lags in the dengue transmission process that arise from the mosquito life cycle. To that end, we also explore the relevance of time between meteorological conditions and reported dengue incidence by studying lags between climate and dengue variables.

By using 2019 dengue case data collected by hospitals in geographically distinct areas of the Dominican Republic, we implement gamma generalized linear mixed models (gamma-GLMM) to model relationships between dengue incidence rate and climatic variables, such as temperature, humidity, and precipitation. We emphasize here that 2019 is an important year in the evolution of dengue in the Dominican Republic and globally because the highest number of dengue cases ever reported both in the country and globally was in 2019 [1], and an investigation such as the present one will contribute to a better understanding of the drivers of this large outbreak.

This paper is organized as follows. First, we review literature of recent research on dengue. In Section 3, we introduce the response variable and discuss possible explanatory variables. We analyze the effect of lags between variables by studying correlations between the response variable and the meteorological variables with delays. Section 4 describes the gamma-GLMM method implemented for this study. In Section 5, we present two regression models and their results and discuss implications for modelling the weekly dengue incidence rate. Finally, in Section 6, we present some conclusions and directions for future work.

2. Literature Overview

2.1. Disease Transmission

Dengue virus is transmitted to humans by female mosquitoes, mainly of the species *Aedes aegypti* and *Aedes albopictus*. There are four strains of the dengue virus, and people can be infected with the virus more than once [7]. Infection in humans begins when an infectious female mosquito bites a human and injects dengue virus from one strain into the blood of the human host. Then the dengue virus develops and causes symptomatic or asymptomatic infection in humans. Symptoms of the disease can range from mild forms such as sudden fever, severe headache, nausea, vomiting, myalgia, and skin erythema, to more severe forms including dengue hemorrhagic fever and dengue shock syndrome. Severe dengue can cause death due to plasma leakage, fluid accumulation, severe bleeding, and respiratory failure [1].

On average, dengue infection persists for approximately 2 weeks [8]. The infected person has permanent immunity to the strain of dengue virus that caused the illness and temporary immunity to the other three strains. It should be noted that, in many cases, a second infection with a different strain of dengue virus can lead to a more virulent form of the disease [9]. Dengue virus transmission depends on four factors: the presence of the virus, the human host, the mosquito vector, and the suitability of environmental conditions [10]. With regard to environmental conditions, the transmission of the dengue virus is influenced by several factors, such as temperature, precipitation, relative humidity, and rapid urbanization [1].

2.2. Disease Control

To date, there are no effective antiviral therapies and the only treatment is to control the symptoms with medication. Vaccination is a measure of reduced effectiveness because currently there is only one licensed dengue vaccine which has several limitations. In particular, it can only be administered to people between 9 and 45 years old who have already been infected with one of the dengue viruses [1,11]. Vector control is the only available strategy against dengue.To this end, it is possible to implement measures including the use of insecticides and educational campaigns. Although insecticides have been effective in controlling dengue, increasing trends in mosquito-borne diseases may indicate an increase in insecticide resistance or ineffectiveness in controlling dengue transmission. Therefore, it is of great importance to understand mechanisms of resistance and the susceptibility of the mosquitoes to insecticides in order to develop more effective *Aedes* mosquito-control methods [12]. Educational campaigns are of great importance in preventing and controlling the spread of dengue. It is very important that the population recognize the symptoms of dengue, to be aware of the importance of having medical treatment in case of severe dengue, and to know how to control populations of the *Aedes* mosquito. In [13] the authors concluded that the population of Sri Lanka in 2019 has better awareness of dengue prevention compared to awareness of dengue mortality and dengue management. This study on knowledge, attitudes, and practices regarding dengue fever identified as a weak point the patient awareness of the patient's role in the management of dengue and identification of warning signs that precede hospitalization. If dengue hemorrhagic fever is detected early, the mortality is 2–5% but is can increase to 20% if there is no immediate treatment.

2.3. Dengue Modelling

Simulation models are useful for understanding the drivers and spread of dengue and for helping to understand the efficacy of potential control methods. Many simulation model studies use dynamical models based on ordinary differential equations [14–16]. However, in general, these models do not describe the effects that arise from delays between drivers and reported cases. There are inherent delays in the dengue transmission cycle that arise from the mosquito life cycle, the incubation period of the pathogen in the mosquito, and the incubation period of the pathogen in humans. Delay differential equations can model delayed effects because these models take into account not only the present time but also the past. For instance, in [10], the authors developed a model involving delayed (deterministic) differential equations that predicts locations of mosquito occurrence with a high accuracy, and the model realistically replicates mosquito population dynamics. The model depends on environmental drivers (temperature, precipitation, photoperiod, latitude, day of year) and human population density, and was tested with data from the *Aedes albopictus* mosquito, the most common dengue vector in Asia. By using this model, the authors analyzed the risk of dengue transmission in mainland China and concluded that temperature plays a key role in dengue outbreaks. Based on a dengue virus transmission model with maturation delay for mosquito production and seasonality, in [17] it is also found that the temperature change causes periodic oscillations of dengue fever cases.

Other usual approaches in the literature to investigate relationships between climatic factors and dengue incidence are based on regression models where overdispersion, which is often observed in dengue datasets, is taken into consideration. For instance, applying negative binomial regression models with climatic, spatial, cyclical and seasonal features as explanatory variables, ref. [18] found that precipitation, air pressure and climatic season significantly affected dengue transmission in Sri Lanka during the study period (2017–2019). In [18], all the variables were calculated with zero lags. In [19] a generalized additive model also considering a negative binomial distribution for the dengue cases (but adjusted for seasonality) was built by using climatic features with lags of 0–10 weeks and correlations were determined via Spearman's coefficient test. The model revealed that the relative humidity (with a lag of 1 week), minimum temperature (with a lag of 10 weeks) and wind (with a lag of 4 weeks) are associated with dengue cases in Asunción, Paraguay. These authors, however, did not evaluate the fitting of the proposed model to their data. In [20], generalized linear mixed models are fitted to the number of dengue cases and allow for specific effects for different data groupings. Concretely, negative binomial regression models, with random effects related to the localization (city), the time period (year), and their interaction (city:year) are constructed to describe the associations between the dengue cases reported in 20 cities in the Brazilian state of Goiás. Spearman's correlation test is also used to identify which lags in climate factors are more correlated with cases. The authors conclude that weekly precipitation, minimum temperature, maximum temperature, and relative humidity are positively associated with dengue cases, with lags of 10,10,10, and 6 weeks, respectively.

Another way to analyse dengue data is based on stochastic models. For instance, in [21], discrete time–space stochastic SIR-SI models (susceptible-infective-recovered for human populations; susceptible-infective for vector populations) were adapted from their deterministic analogs in order to estimate the relative risk for dengue disease mapping in Malaysian states during the years 2008–2009. The authors concluded that all the states have similar patterns of expected relative risk for all epidemiological weeks.

Concerning the modelling of dengue datasets from the Dominican Republic, we highlight [22] where a generalized linear model was fitted to the cumulative reported cases for each outbreak between 2012 and 2018. In that work, the authors concluded that emerging dengue outbreaks were robust to climatological and spatiotemporal conditions, indicating that constant surveillance is necessary to prevent future outbreaks. In addition, they showed that reported dengue cases occurred mainly in the 0–15 year age group, indicating that the older age groups had higher levels of immunity. However, the effect of a time delay is not considered in this study.

In this work, we study the dependence of the dengue incidence rate in the Dominican Republic in 2019 on delayed meteorological characteristics (temperature, rainfall, and humidity) by using gamma regression models with a normal random effects structure. The random effect is determined by geographical area (namely, the provinces) which means, in a broader sense, the modelling is conditioned to the geographical conditions of each considered area. To account for delays in transmission of dengue that arise from timing the mosquito life cycle that may be climate-dependent, we analyze relationships between dengue case data and independent meteorological variables at different times (considering lag time). For the selection of the lags, cross-correlation analysis (conditional to each province) and simple gamma regressions (one for each meteorological variable and lag) will be discussed and used to identify significant lag periods which will then be included in the final multiple regression model.

3. Material
3.1. Geographical Area and Period of Time

This study focuses on dengue cases reported in 2019 in the Dominican Republic when a total of 20,230 dengue cases were reported corresponding to 195.3 cases per 100,000 inhabitants. The Dominican Republic is a Caribbean country on the eastern two-thirds of the Island of Hispaniola. Divided into 31 provinces plus one autonomous district (Distrito Nacional, to which we refer hereafter as one of the provinces for simplicity), the country's estimated population in 2019 was over 10.3 million people, with the metropolitan area of Santo Domingo comprising 32% of the total population [23]. The country largely experiences a tropical climate for most of the regions.

Epidemiological surveillance data for dengue and weather records were reported during 2019 for each of the 32 provinces; however, due to the lack of completeness of the data available to us, this study focuses only on eight provinces for which the total percentage of missing values was very low: Barahona, Distrito Nacional, La Romana, Monte Cristi, Puerto Plata, Samaná, Santiago, and Santo Domingo (see provinces labeled in Figure 1).

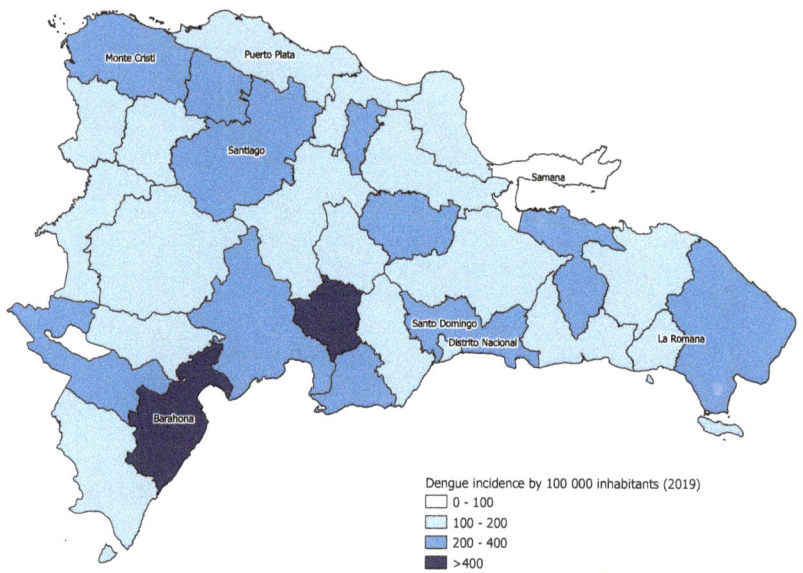

Figure 1. Dengue incidence per 100,000 inhabitants, in Dominican Republic in 2019. We include labels for the eight provinces included in this study.

3.2. Dependent Variable

The observed number of dengue cases officially diagnosed in hospitals of the Dominican Republic during 2019, is the dependent variable used for modelling the weekly dengue incidence rate. The data were recorded weekly and were aggregated by province. We let y_{ij} be the number of cases in province i ($i = 1, \ldots, 8$) reported in epidemiological week j ($j = 1, \cdots, 52$).

We compute five descriptive summary statistics: minimum (Min), maximum (Max), mean, standard deviation (Std.Dev), and coefficient of variation (in percentage, C.Var(%)) for the eight provinces in the study (Table 1). Throughout 2019, dengue incidence per week was, on average, highest in Santo Domingo and lowest in Samaná. Barahona had the least variability in relation to its mean comparatively among the eight provinces. For three of eight provinces, namely Barahona, Distrito Nacional, and Santo Domingo, there were dengue cases reported every week of the year.

Table 1. Summary statistics for dengue cases by province and by week in 2019 along with calculations of the annual dengue incidence rate ($aDIR$) and estimates of population size (Population).

	Barahona	Distrito Nacional	La Romana	Monte Cristi	Puerto Plata	Samana	Santiago	Santo Domingo
Min	4	5	0	0	0	0	0	17
Max	46	89	42	15	21	7	132	287
Mean	16.6	32.9	8.0	5.7	6.7	1.6	43.4	117.7
Std.Dev	10.9	23.7	9.9	4.9	6.4	1.7	40.3	90.2
C.Var(%)	65.9	72.0	123.5	86.4	94.6	106.7	92.89	76.6
aDIR	456.2	163.9	153.0	250.8	104.7	72.2	216.1	210.7
Population	189,149	1,036,494	270,166	116,605	332,386	111,217	1,038,044	2,855,892

Std.Dev, standard deviation; C.Var(%), standard deviation/mean × 100% (coefficient of variation); Population, total number of inhabitants.

Because the eight provinces vary greatly in population size, the total number of diagnosed dengue cases y_{ij} does not always give enough information about the severity of transmission, so we calculate the total weekly incidence per 100,000 people. We calculate the incidence rate in week j in province i as

$$y_{ij}/n_i \times 100{,}000, \tag{1}$$

where n_i denotes the total number of inhabitants in province i. This variable will be used in our analyses in Section 4. Additionally, we analyse the annual dengue incidence rate per 100,000 inhabitants, $aDIR_i$, for each province i:

$$aDIR_i = \sum_j y_{ij}/n_i \times 100{,}000. \tag{2}$$

We include the annual dengue incidence rate per 100,000 inhabitants in Table 1 for each province studied. Additionally, Figure 1 shows the annual dengue incidence rate per 100,000 inhabitants for all 32 provinces of the Dominican Republic. Although we only have reliable meteorological data from eight provinces, it can be seen in Figure 1 that these provinces are representative of all geographic regions of the country (in the figure, provinces with name labels in the figure are those included in this study). Spatially, it is possible to observe that the disease was spread across the country. Barahona exhibited the highest value of $aDIR$ ($\approx$456 cases per 100,000 inhabitants) followed by Monte Cristi ($\approx$251 cases per 100,000 inhabitants), which is the second-largest province by population among the eight provinces. Two provinces in the north and north east, Samaná and Puerto Plata exhibited the lowest values of $aDIR$, with Samaná having the lowest $aDIR$ of fewer than 73 cases per 100,000 inhabitants.

3.3. Independent Variables

In this study, meteorological conditions such as temperature, rainfall, and humidity are the factors considered to influence dengue incidence. Environmental data were obtained from the Oficina Nacional de Meteorologia (ONAMET), Dominican Republic, and supplemented with data from the National Aeronautics and Space Administration (NASA), of the United States of America, when some data were missing. The data include daily information on temperature (Temp; minimum, average, and maximum), precipitation (Precip; cumulative and average), relative humidity (RH; average) and daily temperature range (DTR; minimum, average, and maximum), in a total of nine variables.

3.3.1. Preliminary Analysis

For each province and meteorological variable, daily data were aggregated into the 52 epidemiological weeks of 2019, giving the corresponding statistical measure per week. For instance, Temp.min is the weekly minimum of daily minimum temperatures and Temp.avg is the average temperature of the week calculated from the mean of the daily average temperatures.

For the 24 provinces not included in this study, there were missing values for many weeks (14 or more) for some independent variables. For the eight remaining provinces and the nine meteorological independent variables over the 70 weeks (=the last 18 weeks of 2018 + the 52 weeks of 2019) considered in a preliminary analysis, only about 0.7% of values were missing. Interpolations of those values were then executed by using the average of the values observed in the week before and after the occurrence of each missing value. Then, statistical measures for all the nine independent variables with respect to 2019 were calculated by province and are displayed in Table 2.

As shown in Table 2, average, maximum, and minimum temperature measurements across provinces were mostly similar. The exceptions are Monte Cristi and La Romana which both presented very low minimum values for the weekly minimum temperatures (Temp.min). For Monte Cristi, we also observed the largest coefficients of variation for both weekly minimum temperatures and maximum temperatures with C.Var(%) values of 20% and 12%, respectively. For DTR, Monte Cristi was the province whose measurements deviated the most from the others, with low average, maximum, and minimum DTR values and higher C.Var(%) values.

Table 2. Summary statistics for weekly meteorological variables across the eight provinces in 2019.

Variables	Statistics	Barahona	Distrito Nacional	La Romana	Monte Cristi	Puerto Plata	Samaná	Santiago	Santo Domingo
Temp.avg	Min	24.94	26.06	22.90	20.34	24.21	24.69	23.40	26.06
	Max	29.88	30.42	28.54	26.87	29.85	29.84	29.25	30.42
	Mean	27.44	28.30	26.26	24.51	27.25	27.61	26.69	28.30
	Std.Dev	1.34	1.33	1.48	1.48	1.76	1.36	1.69	1.33
	C.Var(%)	4.87	4.70	5.65	6.05	6.47	4.93	6.33	4.70
Temp.max	Min	30.60	31.00	30.50	23.00	30.20	29.50	30.20	31.00
	Max	35.80	37.00	35.80	35.90	37.70	35.00	37.40	37.00
	Mean	32.83	33.82	32.97	27.34	33.83	32.80	33.80	33.82
	Std.Dev	1.29	1.66	1.39	3.30	2.18	1.53	1.71	1.66
	C.Var(%)	3.92	4.91	4.20	12.06	6.43	4.67	5.07	4.91
Temp.min	Min	18.00	20.10	0.00	2.20	15.60	14.00	15.00	20.10
	Max	25.00	26.00	23.20	25.00	23.60	25.00	22.00	26.00
	Mean	21.68	22.90	19.08	21.40	20.86	22.11	19.17	22.90
	Std.Dev	1.71	1.49	3.50	4.18	1.94	2.16	2.08	1.49
	C.Var(%)	7.88	6.53	18.35	19.55	9.31	9.77	10.87	6.53
DTR.avg	Min	5.99	6.94	8.99	0.00	8.54	5.26	8.76	6.94
	Max	11.30	10.50	14.10	10.20	12.57	10.39	15.47	10.50
	Mean	8.72	8.47	11.09	2.29	10.31	8.18	11.98	8.47
	Std.Dev	1.15	0.88	1.15	3.99	0.85	1.07	1.18	0.88
	C.Var(%)	13.20	10.43	10.33	174.08	8.21	13.13	9.81	10.43
DTR.max	Min	7.10	7.50	10.20	0.00	10.10	6.50	10.80	7.50
	Max	12.70	12.60	32.20	13.30	18.10	18.00	18.60	12.60
	Mean	10.44	9.96	13.18	2.97	12.25	9.90	13.91	9.96
	Std.Dev	1.29	1.04	3.00	4.98	1.40	1.84	1.58	1.04
	C.Var(%)	12.39	10.45	22.78	167.78	11.41	18.61	11.34	10.45
DTR.min	Min	3.50	3.60	4.10	0.00	5.00	-4.00	5.40	3.60
	Max	9.60	9.70	12.20	9.50	11.20	8.80	13.80	9.70
	Mean	6.82	6.97	8.99	1.55	8.50	6.67	9.77	6.97
	Std.Dev	1.41	1.03	1.53	3.04	1.20	1.85	1.82	1.03
	C.Var(%)	20.69	14.80	16.98	196.30	14.07	27.77	18.62	14.80
Precip.avg	Min	0.00	0.00	0.00	0.00	0.00	0.00	0.00	0.00
	Max	14.23	11.97	21.44	15.36	21.29	21.14	20.03	11.97
	Mean	2.19	2.23	3.10	1.09	2.56	4.42	2.48	2.23
	Std.Dev	3.27	2.81	.57	2.39	3.98	4.29	3.95	2.81
	C.Var(%)	149.05	125.98	147.80	219.66	155.78	97.06	159.05	125.98
Precip.total	Min	0.00	0.00	0.00	0.00	0.00	0.00	0.00	0.00
	Max	99.60	83.80	150.10	107.50	149.00	148.00	140.20	83.80
	Mean	15.00	13.73	20.98	7.63	17.63	30.69	16.94	13.73
	Std.Dev	22.65	18.23	31.32	16.86	27.76	29.84	27.48	18.23
	C.Var(%)	151.07	132.75	149.30	221.04	157.39	97.25	162.22	132.75
RH.avg	Min	64.23	72.56	76.29	60.66	75.44	77.03	69.66	72.56
	Max	83.10	84.06	90.20	77.56	90.46	89.43	88.83	84.06
	Mean	72.51	78.57	82.59	69.34	81.76	83.20	79.84	78.57
	Std.Dev	4.12	2.56	3.32	3.69	3.91	2.67	4.06	2.56
	C.Var(%)	5.69	3.26	4.02	5.33	4.78	3.21	5.08	3.26

Temp. avg., average of daily temperature observed during a week. Similar extension for the other variables: Precip., precipitation; RH, relative humidity; DTR, daily temperature range. C. Var(%), standard deviation/mean × 100% (coefficient of variation).

Although all eight provinces experienced weeks without rain in 2019, the maximum and average values of precipitation in 2019 tend to vary greatly among provinces. Precipitation is perhaps the factor that differs most among provinces of all the meteorological variables, with very high C.Var(%) values for both average and total weekly precipitation.

Most of the provinces present a coefficient of variation higher than 100% for both measurements with the only exception being Samaná province. Concerning the relative humidity, the weekly averages and variability therein were similar across all provinces.

3.3.2. Spearman's Rank Correlation in Lags

Because dengue infection relies on transmission by a mosquito vector, which in turn, along with the virus, experiences a life cycle regulated by meteorological conditions, it is important to study the time between meteorological conditions and reported cases. We consider here lags between environmental data and dengue cases. In this analysis, we include meteorological data from September 2018–December 2019 in order to consider potential impacts of weather conditions in late 2018 on transmission in early 2019.

We calculate Spearman's rank correlation coefficients between each one of the nine meteorological variables indicated in Table 2 and the weekly dengue incidence rate with time lags of 0–18 weeks, globally (by aggregating the eight provinces: $\sum_i y_{ij}/n_i \times 100{,}000$) and locally (by province, given by (Equation (1))). For the local analyses, because there are eight simultaneous null hypotheses for each pair lag-variable in test, the Holm procedure for multiple testing correction was applied to control the family-wise error rate at level 0.05. We show correlation coefficients for each lag for each province in Figures 2–4. In these figures, solid dots and plus points correspond to statistically significant correlations with adjusted p-values < 0.05 and p-values < 0.05, respectively, with nongray colour corresponding to each of the provinces, and gray colour corresponding to the global observations.

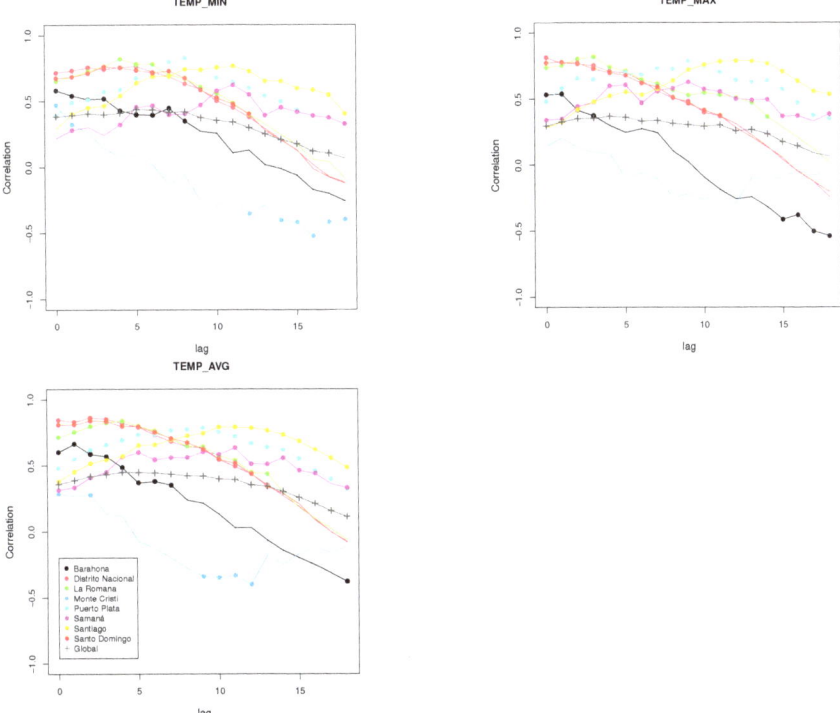

Figure 2. Spearman's rank correlation coefficient between the dengue incidence rate (1) and the minimum temperature (**top left**), the maximum temperature (**top right**) and the average temperature (**bottom center**) by week at lag 0–18 weeks.

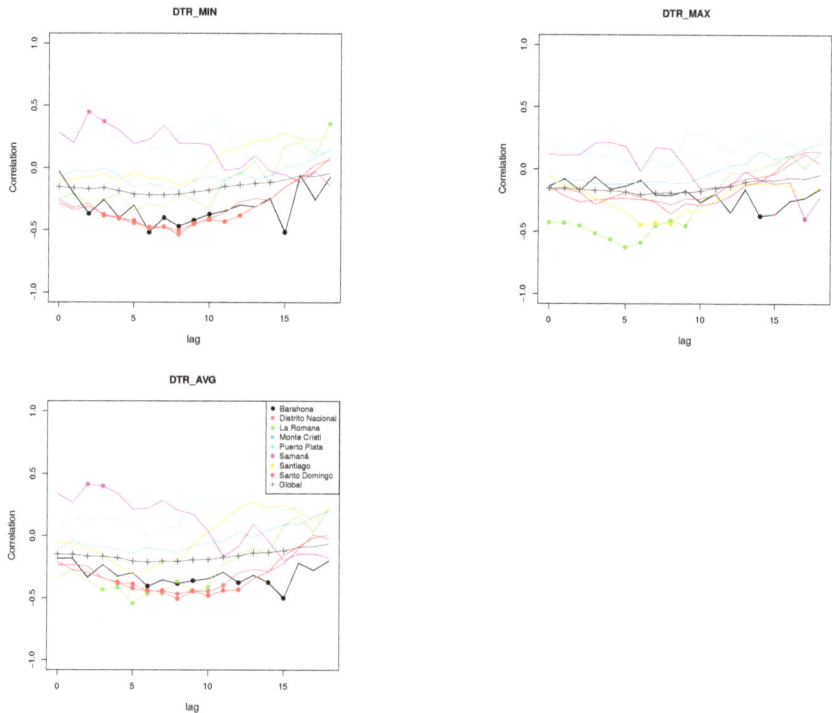

Figure 3. Spearman's rank correlation coefficient between the dengue incidence rate (1) and the minimum DTR (**top left**), the maximum DTR (**top right**) and the average DTR (**bottom center**) by week at lag 0–18 weeks.

These graphs show that the effect of time lag of meteorological variables on dengue incidence rate is varied among the eight provinces. For temperature variables, almost all provinces had significant positively correlated lags between dengue incidence rate and minimum, maximum, and average temperatures for many of the 19 time points we considered. Notably, Monte Cristi and Barahona were the only two provinces in which temperature variables were significantly negatively correlated with temperature. Correlation of lags with daily temperature range were much more mixed, with some provinces having negative correlations with lags in the same week that others had positive correlations in lags. However, in general, correlations in lags between dengue incidence rate and DTR were negative for most weeks studied. Regarding precipitation, very few lags were significantly correlated with dengue incidence. In fact, there are only two provinces where precipitation with lags less than 18 weeks was positively correlated with dengue cases: Samaná taking lag = 2 and Santiago taking lag = 8. Correlations in lags between dengue incidence rate and relative humidity exhibited a downward trend as the length of the lag increased: in general, correlations in smaller lags with average relative humidity were positive while correlations in larger lags were negative and often significantly so. This could be indicative of seasonal fluctuations in relative humidity.

Moreover, when we compared lags at the global level with those of provinces, we saw that correlations between climate variables, particularly temperature and DTR measurements, and dengue incidence rate in some provinces differed from the global correlations in direction and trends with increasing lag time. This potential province-specific lag effect introduces more complexity in the modelling of dengue incidence because global trends in meteorological variables may not be useful for predicting dengue at a local level, suggesting that the inclusion of lags in variables for each province may be necessary to understand and predict dengue transmission at the province level.

To avoid increasing complexity, a singular lag per independent variable was outlined for the present work. Hence, a lag selection criterion was first established based on a positive lower lag for which there are significant associations between the independent variable, and each dependent variable for the largest number of provinces and, at the same time, preferably, for the global level. Inspecting again Figures 2–4, some lag values might visually be suggested for each climatic variable. Concretely, in Figure 2, it is observed that statistically significant associations of dengue incidence with (weekly) minimum and average temperature are only found simultaneously for all the eight provinces and globally when lag is equal to 1 and 2 weeks, respectively. However, for the remaining climatic variables, the selection of a lag value following that criterion for the eight provinces and at the global level simultaneously is more difficult. In this sense, to avoid subjectivity, further on, in Section 4, a more objective lag-selection criterion will be established.

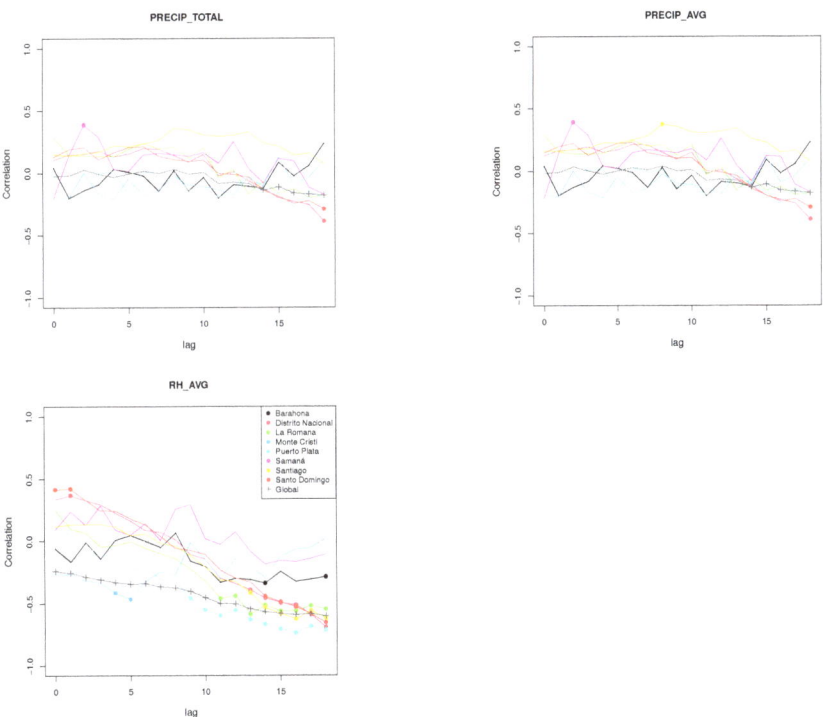

Figure 4. Spearman's rank correlation coefficient between the dengue incidence rate (1) and the cumulative precipitation (**top left**), the average precipitation (**top right**) and the average relative humidity (**bottom center**) by week at lag 0–18 weeks.

4. Method

For analyzing the effect of the meteorological variables on dengue incidence rate that follows a gamma distribution, gamma regressions defined by generalized linear models with fixed effects (gamma-GLM) or mixed effects (gamma-GLMM) can be adequate. Although both types of models have been applied in many studies, the latter has the advantage of being able to model clustered data structures and then incorporate within-group variability.

4.1. Gamma Distribution

The gamma distribution is a probability distribution for a positive continuous random variable Y with density function given by

$$f(y; k, \theta) = \frac{1}{\Gamma(k)\theta^k} y^{k-1} \exp(-y/\theta), \quad y > 0,$$

where k and θ are the shape parameter and the scale parameter of the distribution of Y, respectively, and $\Gamma(k)$ is the gamma function evaluated at k. For lower values of k, the density function is right-skewed.

The expected value μ and the variance value σ^2 of Y are related to the shape and scale parameters in the following way:

$$\mu = k\theta \quad \text{and} \quad \sigma^2 = \mu\theta.$$

4.2. Gamma Regression

Let $\{(x_{j1}, \cdots, x_{jp}, Y_j), j = 1, 2, \cdots, n\}$ be a random sample defined by n independent random variables $Y_j, j = 1, 2, \cdots, n$, such that $Y_j | (x_{j1}, \cdots, x_{jp})$ follows a gamma distribution, and consequently, its mean depends on p explanatory variables $(x_{j1}, \cdots, x_{jp})$, i.e.,

$$\mu_j = E(Y_j | x_{j1}, \cdots, x_{jp}), \quad j = 1, \cdots, n.$$

In a generalized linear model with gamma responses (gamma-GLM), each mean μ_j is described as a function of the p covariates using the link log on a linear predictor in the following form,

$$\log(\mu_j) = \beta_0 + \beta_1 x_{j1} + \cdots + \beta_p x_{jp}, \quad j = 1, \cdots, n, \qquad (3)$$

where $[\beta_0 \cdots \beta_p]$ is a vector of $p+1$ unknown parameters. Because the log function is invertible, then the Gamma-GLM provides a multiplicative model to the arithmetic mean:

$$\mu_j = \exp(\beta_0 + \beta_1 x_{j1} + \cdots + \beta_p x_{jp}).$$

The generalized linear mixed model with gamma responses (gamma-GLMM) is an extension of the gamma-GLM in which random effects are added to the fixed-effect parameters $\beta_0, \beta_1, \cdots, \beta_p$ in the linear predictor (3). This class of regression models is useful when there is a grouping structure of k object clusters in the set of the n data points. In such conditions, the response variable $Y_j^{(i)}$ corresponds to the jth observation into the ith group with values of the independent variables $x_{j1}^{(i)}, \cdots, x_{jp}^{(i)}$. Denoting $\mathbf{b}^{(i)} = [b_1^{(i)} \cdots b_q^{(i)}]$ a vector of q random effects, which are specific to the group i, the conditional response $Y_j^{(i)} | (x_{j1}, \cdots, x_{jp}, \mathbf{b}^{(i)})$ follows a gamma distribution with expected value μ_{ij} satisfying:

$$\log(\mu_{ij}) = \beta_0^{(i)} + \beta_1^{(i)} x_{j1}^{(i)} + \cdots + \beta_p^{(i)} x_{jp}^{(i)} + b_1^{(i)} z_1^{(i)} + \cdots + b_q^{(i)} z_q^{(i)} \qquad (4)$$

for $j = 1, \cdots, n_i$, $i = 1, \cdots, k$, where $\sum_i n_i = n$, the variables $z_1^{(i)}, z_2^{(i)}, \cdots, z_q^{(i)}$ depend on the independent variables and define the specific random effect for the ith predefined object cluster, and the vector of random effects $\mathbf{b}^{(i)}$ is assumed to follow a q-multivariate normal distribution $N(0, \Sigma_b)$, where Σ_b is a positive definite covariance matrix independent of the cluster i.

In this work, the modelling of the dengue incidence rate in terms of the environmental variables is analyzed assuming the eight provinces as $k = 8$ clusters in the dataset and random effect models with $q = 1$ and $z_1^{(i)} = 1$ in (4), and, consequently, $\Sigma_b = \sigma^2 > 0$.

Therefore, generalized regression models with gamma responses and a specific Y-intercept for each level of the random effects were fitted to the following models:

$$\log(\mu_{ij}) = \beta_0^{(i)} + \beta_1^{(i)} x_{j1}^{(i)} + \cdots + \beta_p^{(i)} x_{jp}^{(i)} + b^{(i)}, \quad j = 1, \cdots, 52, \, i = 1, \cdots, 8. \quad (5)$$

The beta parameter $\beta_k^{(i)}$, for $k = 1, \cdots, p$, can be interpreted by comparing the expected value of incidence rate μ_{ij} at week j in the province i with that obtained when the independent x_k increases a unit and the remaining ones are not changed. In fact, from (Equation (5)) we have

$$\frac{\mu_{ij} \text{ when } x_{jk}^{(i)} + 1}{\mu_{ij} \text{ when } x_{jk}^{(i)}} = \exp(\beta_k^{(i)}), \quad j = 1, \cdots, 52, \, i = 1, \cdots, 8. \quad (6)$$

Hence, these beta parameters correspond to the logarithm of the rate ratio. Therefore, if $\exp(\beta_k^{(i)}) > 1$, it is expected that the dengue incidence rate, at kth epidemiological week in the province i, increases $(\exp(\beta_1^{(i)}) - 1) \times 100\%$ for each one-unit increase in the independent variable $x_{jk}^{(i)}$. Otherwise, if $\exp(\beta_1^{(i)}) < 1$, it is expected that the dengue incidence rate, at kth epidemiological week in the province i, decreases $(1 - \exp(\beta_k^{(i)})) \times 100\%$ for each one-unit increase in the independent variable $x_{jk}^{(i)}$.

4.3. Gamma Fitting for the Dependent Variable

The dengue incidence rate (Equation (1)) is a continuous variable limited to the interval $[0, +\infty)$. It is asymmetrically distributed due to the greater presence of lower values. Given the presence of zero, the rate (Equation (1)) was (artificially) rescaled to guarantee strict positive outcomes and, consequently, a more suitable fitting of a gamma distribution. Then, an auxiliary constant equal to 0.5 was added to the numerator of (1) resulting in the adjusted rate

$$y_{ij}^* = \frac{y_{ij} + 0.5}{n_i} \times 100{,}000 \quad (7)$$

for the jth week and province i.

This strategy of adding an amount of 0.5 becomes relevant whenever there are no weekly records of dengue (a similar approach was also reported in other nonnormal regression models (e.g., [24]). We note that we considered alternative constants (such as 0.0001, 0.1, and 1), but numerical experiments showed that 0.5 provides good results in terms of convergence in the estimation process of the gamma-GLMM regression.

4.4. Lag Selection of the Independent Variables

Because certain climatic conditions can favor the development of the mosquito and virus, and consequently, dengue transmission at a later time, effects of meteorological conditions on dengue infections were analyzed with lags. From the cross-correlation analysis of lags of 0–18 weeks performed in Section 3.3.2, it was observed that there was no clear identification of which delay week for each meteorological variable is the most important to dengue incidence rate. Thus, a more objective lag selection procedure was then established.

Concretely, the effect of each independent meteorological variable, with lags from 0 up to 5 weeks, on the adjusted incidence rate (Equation (7)) were then separately examined by using (simple) gamma-GLMM models with a single independent variable (i.e., model (5) with $p = 1$). The period until 5 weeks in lags is justified, as it is a biologically plausible period of time that includes the combined time for *Ae. aegypti* egg hatching and larval development to adult mosquitoes. So, an exhaustive study with lags until 5 weeks seems to provide an adequate choice from a practical point of view.

Thus, for each meteorological variable, six simple models (simple in that there is only one independent variable and the random intercept) were considered: one for each lag-week. The lag-weeks that led to significant association (p-value < 0.05) to the adjusted incidence rate (Equation (7)) were identified so they could be present in the final multiple model. To determine the best lag-week of each meteorological variable, four different selection criteria were then established as follows. Three criteria are based on the Akaike Information Criterion (AIC). Because all the models have the same number of parameters, comparing AIC is equivalent to comparing deviance (i.e., -2 log (likelihood function)). For each meteorological variable, the best lag-week was defined among the simple models with significant independent variables as

- Criterion I: the first week ($0 \leq$ weeks ≤ 5) where a local minimum value of AIC occurred;
- Criterion II: the shortest delay ($1 \leq$ weeks ≤ 5) where a local minimum value of AIC occurred;
- Criterion III: the delay ($1 \leq$ weeks ≤ 5) where the global minimum value of AIC occurred;
- Criterion IV: the shortest delay ($1 \leq$ weeks ≤ 5) where a significant association was first achieved.

In Table 3, the best lag is identified for each independent variable, in accordance with each Criterion I-IV. For RH avg., there is no significant association with the adjusted incidence rate (7), with the lowest p-value of 0.1891 calculated for a lag of 5 weeks (data not shown). For the variable DTR.min and for both rainfall variables, Precip.total and Precip.avg, the same lag was identified by all criteria: five and two delayed weeks, respectively. For the other five meteorological variables, the four criteria are not consensual about the lag set selection for the independent variables.

Table 3. Selection of the best lag-week based on the criteria I-IV for each independent variable.

	Criterion I		Criterion II		Criterion III		Criterion IV	
	Best Lag	AIC	Best Lag	AIC	Best Lag	AIC	Best Lag	p-Value
Temp.avg	2	1767.1 **	2	1767.1 **	5	1750.2 **	0	0.0000
Temp.max	2	1847.6 **	2	1847.6 **	4	1846.7 **	0	0.0000
Temp.min	0	1876.1 **	2	1869.6 **	5	1869.3 **	0	0.0000
DTR.avg	5	1921.5 **	5	1921.5 **	5	1921.5 **	2	0.0420
DTR.max	3	1923.6 **	3	1923.6 **	5	1922.1 **	2	0.0192
DTR.min	5	1925.4 *	5	1925.4 *	5	1925.4 *	5	0.0119
Precip.avg	2	1925.1 *	2	1925.1 *	2	1925.1 *	2	0.0137
Precip.total	2	1925.6 *	2	1925.6 *	2	1925.6 *	2	0.0178
RH.avg	—		—		—		—	

*: $0.01 \leq p$-value < 0.05; **: p-value < 0.01.

4.5. Selection of the Final Gamma-GLMMs

Given that the four criteria I-IV suggest that the lags 0, 2, 4, and 5 could be assigned to the different temperature variables and the lags 2, 3, and 5 could be assigned to the variables DTR.avg and DTR.max, multiple regression models combining these lags for the (meteorological) independent variables were constructed. One of the two precipitation variable, either Precip.average or Precip.total, was also included in the constructed models. Both precipitation variables are not simultaneously considered in the same model. For both, lag = 2 was selected in accordance with the four criteria (Table 3). The remaining variables, DTR.min and RH.avg, were also included in the models and with lag equal to 5 and 2, respectively, in accordance with the four criteria. An exhaustive comparative analysis of the constructed multiple regression models was performed to find the best multiple gamma-GLMM (Equation (5)) for estimating the adjusted incidence rate (Equation (7)). Normal and independent random intercepts $b^{(i)}$, $i = 1, \cdots, 8$ (defined by the eight provinces) were assumed for all the constructed models. The best-fitting final model was identified by the lowest AIC. At the end, two multiple gamma-GLMMs, both incorporating only intercept random effects determined by provinces, were established.

4.6. Validation of the Gamma-GLMMs

For checking the fitting of the gamma distribution to the observed values of the adjusted rates (7), a QQ-plot and the test based on the ratio V of two variance estimators proposed in [25] were used. For analyzing the fitting of the two final gamma GLMMs to the data, the behavior of the deviance residuals of the fitted models was examined: (i) the existence of residual patterns, globally and by province, was visually evaluated using adequate residual plots; and (ii) the normality of the deviance residuals was assessed by using QQ-plot and the Shapiro–Wilks test. To assess how well the two final gamma GLMMs performs on each province, a 95% confidence interval of the weekly average of the adjusted dengue incidence rate estimated from these two developed final models was constructed by province and verified whether the provinces contain the correspondent weekly average observed from the data.

4.7. Software

All the statistical analyses were performed in the R statistical environment (R Core Team, 2020) by using the package `EnvStats` [26] for construction of gamma QQ-plot, the package `goft` [27] for goodness-of-fit test of the gamma distribution with unknown shape and scale parameters [25], and the package `lme4` [28] for modelling of the data by gamma-GLMMs with normal random intercept. The maps of the Dominican Republic was constructed by using QGIS software.

5. Results

5.1. Selected Models

Based on the lags suggested by Criterion I-IV (Section 4.5), twelve multiple gamma-GLMMs for estimating the adjusted incidence rate (Equation (7)) in terms of meteorological regressors were constructed: models M01-M12 with lags of meteorological variables as indicated in Table 4. For the construction of these models, we considered the variable Precip.avg as the precipitation regressor. For six of these models, the process of estimating the parameters was not convergent (i.e., the iteration process in the optimizer via the R-function `glmer` was stopped without an optimum value for the objective function) as noted in the last column in Table 4. Among the remaining six models, the lowest AIC was achieved by the model M12, which employs as explanatory variables the weekly average and minimum temperatures and average DTR with a lag of 5 weeks, the weekly maximum temperature with a lag of 4 weeks, and the average weekly precipitation with a lag of 2 weeks. M12 also included the maximum and minimum DTR with a lag of 5 weeks, but these variables were not significant to predictions.

In fact, the variable DTR.max was not a significant predictor in any of the previous models, so it was removed, and we replicated the procedure as before. With DTR.max removed, a total of eight models were developed, M13-M20 as indicated in Table 4. Among the convergent models, the lowest AIC was achieved to the model M20, which included all of the same predictors as M12 excepting DTR.max.

For both models, M12 and M20, the same set of independent variables was obtained as statistically significant: Temp.avg, Temp.max, Temp.min, DTR.avg, DTR.min and Precip.avg with lag equals to 5, 4, 5, 5, 5, and 2 weeks, respectively. Finally, because the variable DTR.min (with lag = 5 weeks) is not statistically significantly in the model, it was removed at this stage to obtain the final model (M21 in Table 4) which reached a slightly lower AIC value than the previous ones.

In this final model, temperature and DTR variables have larger lags. Therefore, this model could represent a long-term alarm based on both temperature and DTR conditions. Therefore, it will be called a longer-term model. Given this result, we aimed to next answer the question: could these same variables predict adjusted dengue incidence rate in a shorter time? Consequently, an extra model (M22 in Table 4), called a shorter-term model, with all these variables with a delay of 2 weeks was analyzed. All variables with a delay of 2 weeks were significant predictors; however, the AIC for M22 was not lower than that of M21, indicating that it is not a better model overall.

Table 4. Lag for the meteorological regressors in 22 multiple gamma-GLMMs constructed for fitting the dengue incidence rate. Statistical significance of the regressors are identified.

Model	Temperature avg.	Temperature max.	Temperature min.	DTR avg.	DTR max.	DTR min.	Precipitation avg.	AIC
M01	0	0	0	2	2	5	2	nc
M02	0	0	0	5	3	5	2	1806.5
	(0.0003)			(0.0659)				
M03	0	0	0	5	5	5	2	nc
M04	2	2	0	2	2	5	2	1738.9
	(<0.0001)	(0.0905)		(0.0174)		(0.0744)	(<0.0001)	
M05	2	2	0	5	3	5	2	1729.5
	(<0.0001)	(0.0309)		(0.0021)			(<0.0001)	
M06	2	2	0	5	5	5	2	nc
M07	2	2	2	2	2	5	2	nc
M08	2	2	2	5	3	5	2	1728.1
				(0.0026)			(<0.0001)	
M09	2	2	2	5	5	5	2	1728.6
	(<0.0001)			(0.0038)		(0.0950)	(<0.0001)	
M10	5	4	5	2	2	5	2	nc
M11	5	4	5	5	3	5	2	nc
M12	5	4	5	5	5	5	2	1699.3
	(<0.0001)	(0.0006)	(0.0153)	(0.0076)			(0.0296)	
M13	0	0	0	2	–	5	2	1804.8
	(0.0002)			(0.0086)			(0.0001)	
M14	0	0	0	5	–	5	2	1804.8
	(0.0002)			(0.0086)			(0.0001)	
M15	2	2	0	2	–	5	2	nc
M16	2	2	0	5	–	5	2	1728.6
	(<0.0001)	(0.0523)		(<0.0001)			(<0.0001)	
M17	2	2	2	2	–	5	2	nc
M18	2	2	2	5	–	5	2	1727.2
	(<0.0001)			(<0.0001)			(<0.0001)	
M19	5	4	5	2	–	5	2	nc
M20	5	4	5	5	–	5	2	1697.3
	(<0.0001)	(0.0006)	(0.0120)	(<0.0001)			(0.0250)	
M21	5	4	5	5	–	–	2	1695.5
	(<0.0001)	(0.0004)	(0.0120)	(<0.0001)			(0.0258)	
M22	2	2	2	2	–	–	2	1736.8
	(<0.0001)	(0.1260)	(<0.0001)	(<0.00005)			(0.0258)	

The p-value is indicated in parentheses; nc means the optimization routine was non-convergent.

We note that the procedure described above was replicated substituting the variable Precip.avg by Precip.total as a precipitation regressor. Under this condition, more nonconvergent models emerged, and slightly higher values of AIC were in general produced for the convergent homologous models (data not shown). We also note that when the random intercepts $b^{(i)}$ are not included in the multiple model (5) (i.e., where the approach GLM is used for modelling of the adjusted dengue incidence rate (Equation (7))), substantially higher values of AIC would be obtained for the correspondent GLMs, namely AIC = 1923.7 and AIC = 1936.8) for the fitted longer-term model and shorter-term model, respectively, justifying the modelling of the dengue data set by GLMM than by GLM.

As indicated in Table 4, in the longer-term model (M21), the weekly dengue incidence rate is described in of terms the average and the minimum values of the temperature both delayed by 5 weeks (Temp.avg5 and Temp.min5), the maximum value of the temperature delayed by 4 weeks (Temp.max4), and the average value of precipitation delayed by 2 weeks (Precip.avg2). In the *shorter-term* model (M22), the weekly dengue incidence rate is described by effects of those five meteorological features all with a delay of 2 weeks (Temp.avg2, Temp.max2, Temp.min2, DTR.avg2, and Precip.avg2).

Formally, these two models are defined as follows,

$$\log(\mu_{ij}) = \beta_0 + \beta_1 \text{Temp.avg5}_j + \beta_2 \text{Temp.max4}_j + \beta_3 \text{Temp.min5}_j + \beta_4 \text{DTR.avg5}_j + \beta_5 \text{Precip.avg2}_j + \text{Province}^{(i)}$$

and

$$\log(\mu_{ij}) = \beta_0 + \beta_1 \text{Temp.avg2}_j + \beta_2 \text{Temp.max2}_j + \beta_3 \text{Temp.min2}_j + \beta_4 \text{DTR.avg2}_j + \beta_5 \text{Precip.avg2}_j + \text{Province}^{(i)}$$

respectively, for each province $i = 1, \cdots, 8$, and meteorological conditions summarized in epidemiological week $j = 1, \cdots, 52$ of 2019. The variable Province$^{(i)}$ is assumed to be normally distributed with zero mean and constant variance σ_i^2 in the estimation process of the regressor coefficients in each model and represents the random effect specific (Y-intercept) to the ith province.

5.2. Validation

The histogram and the QQ-plot presented in Figure 5 suggest that the empirical right-skewed distribution of the adjusted rates (Equation (7)) for the set of the eight provinces is close to a gamma distribution (with $\mu \approx 4.29$ and $\sigma \approx 4.09$). There was no significant evidence that a gamma distribution did not provide an adequate fit ($V = 0.51294$, p-value = 0.7168).

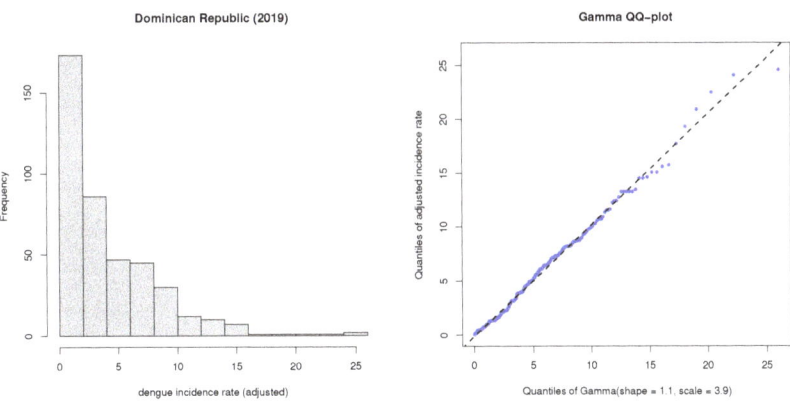

Figure 5. Histogram and gamma QQ-plot for the adjusted dengue incidence rate.

In Figure 6, for both models, it is observed that almost all of the deviance residuals vary between -2 and 2 and there is a higher spread of points for higher observed values of the incidence rate (7). When the observed incidence rate is close to zero, there are many negative residuals suggesting that both models tend to predict higher incidence rates than the observed rates. For higher observed values (e.g., for weekly incidence rate between approximately 6 and 15 per 100,000 inhabitants), both the smoothed average curves (red lines in the graphs) tend to increase, indicating that the values predicted by both models will be lower than the observed. Nevertheless, for situations with the highest incidence rates, the fitted curve is closer to zero in the shorter-term model. This suggests that meteorological conditions of temperature, DTR and precipitation of 2 weeks earlier tend to provide better predictions for dengue incidence when outbreaks are larger than than those predictions using longer delays.

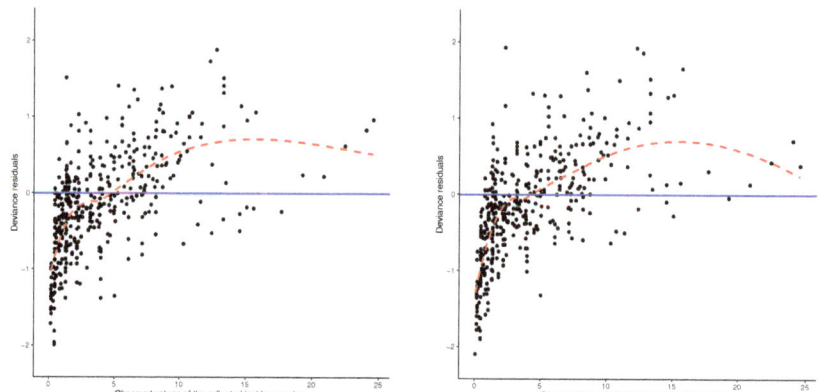

Figure 6. Deviance residuals versus observed values of the longer-term model (on the **left**) and the shorter-term model (on the **right**) with smooth loess curve (in red).

In Figure 7, the comparative boxplots of the deviance residuals for the eight provinces show that (i) the deviance residuals only exceeds the interval $[-2, 2]$ in Santiago, and only slightly; (ii) there are outliers, suggesting that there are a few weeks when the model estimates of the incidence rates could be atypical (in Distrito Nacional, Puerta Plata and Santiago); and (iii) the variability in two provinces, Santo Domingo and Distrito Nacional, seems to be lower than in other provinces. Although these results indicate the models do not always predict the true incidence rates in some weeks and some provinces, both the models fit relatively well to the data.

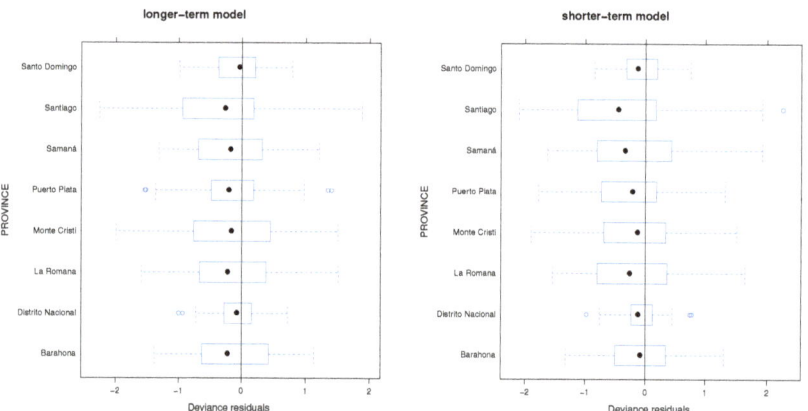

Figure 7. Comparative boxplots for deviance residuals across the eight provinces.

In Figure 8, the good alignment of the points with the diagonal line in both the QQ-plots suggests a normal distribution to the deviance residuals for both models. From the Shapiro–Wilks test, there was no significant evidence that the distributions of deviance residuals of both models were nonnormal (p-value = 0.818 for longer-term model and p-value = 0.136 for the shorter-term model).

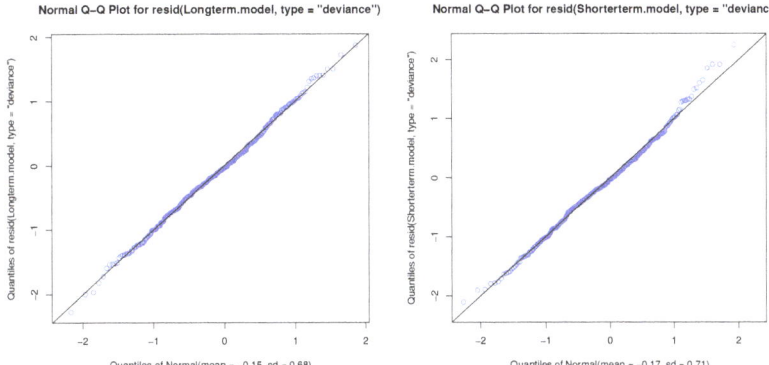

Figure 8. QQ-plots for the deviance residual related to the longer-term model (on the **left**) and the shorter-term model (on the **right**).

5.3. Interpretation

The estimates of the fixed effects and the effect variance of the two fitted models are displayed in Table 5. Only a single covariate coefficient (Temp.max2 for the *shorter-term* model) was not statistically significantly different from zero at a 5% significance level. Therefore, associations between each significant meteorological variable and the dengue incidence rate for the eight provinces of Dominican Republic can be then described assuming that the remaining variables are fixed. Variations in the daily average temperature (Temp.avg) have the greatest effect on the dependent variable (dengue incidence rate) with an increase of 1 °C leading to an increase in the dengue incidence rate by 52.4% ($\exp(0.4212) = 1.5238$) 2 weeks later and 44.4% ($\exp(0.3674) = 1.4440$) 5 weeks later. Although the same increase of the maximum temperature (Temp.max) increases the dengue incidence rate by 3.5% ($\exp(0.0341) = 1.0347$) 2 weeks later and 13% ($\exp(0.1218) = 1.1295$) 4 weeks later, the minimum temperature (Temp.min) reduces the rate of reported cases by 5.0% ($\exp(-0.0510) = 0.9503$) 2 weeks later and 6.0% ($\exp(-0.0618) = 0.9401$) 5 weeks later. If the average daily temperature range (DTR.avg) is 1 °C higher, then a decrease of 18.3% ($\exp(-0.2025) = 0.8167$) and 11.5% ($\exp(-0.1224) = 0.8848$) in dengue incidence rate is observed 5 and 2 weeks later, respectively. A 1-mm increase in the weekly average precipitation (Precip.avg) triggers an increase in the dengue incidence rate of 2.0% ($\exp(0.0210) = 1.0212$) and 4.5% ($\exp(0.0436) = 1.0446$) 2 weeks later for the longer-term and shorter-term models, respectively.

Table 5. Parameter estimates of two fitted gamma-GLMMs for modelling the adjusted incidence dengue rate.

| Parameter | Lag | Longer-Term Model | | | Lag | Shorter-Term Model | | |
		Beta	Std. Error	*p*-Value		Beta	Std. Error	*p*-Value
(Intercept)		−9.7579	0.7087	0.0000		−9.3166	0.7250	0.0000
Temp.avg	5	0.3674	0.0526	0.0000	2	0.4212	0.0676	0.0000
Temp.max	4	0.1218	0.0343	0.0004	2	0.0341	0.0476	0.4743
Temp.min	5	−0.0618	0.0247	0.0122	2	−0.0510	0.0247	0.0388
DTR.avg	5	−0.2025	0.0249	0.0000	2	−0.1224	0.0296	0.0000
Precip.avg	2	0.0210	0.0094	0.0258	2	0.0436	0.0101	0.0000

The variances of the random effects, $\sigma^2_{province}$, were estimated to be equal to 0.2363 and 0.2764 for the longer-term and shorter-term models, respectively. This result indicates slightly lower variability among the eight provinces for the Y-intercept of the fitted model when the meteorological variables are considered with more delays.

In Table 6, we show the observed adjusted dengue incidence rate along with 95% confidence intervals in the weekly average adjusted dengue incidence rate estimated by using both longer-term and shorter-term models across the eight provinces under study. The observed values fall within the estimated 95% confidence interval in all cases except for in Barahona for the longer-term model. Consequently, the longer-term model overestimates the dengue incidence rate in Barahona.

Table 6. Weekly average of the observed value and 95% confidence intervals (CI) for the weekly average of the estimated value from the two fitted gamma-GLMMs across the 52 weeks of 2019 for the adjusted dengue incidence rate for each province.

Provinces	Longer-Term Model			Shorter-Term Model		
	Lower CI	Upper CI	Observed	Lower CI	Upper CI	Observed
Barahona	9.377	13.160	9.038	8.549	11.732	9.038
Distrito Nacional	2.767	3.826	3.221	2.685	3.597	3.221
La Romana	2.257	3.193	3.153	2.289	3.177	3.153
Monte Cristi	4.788	6.356	5.278	4.473	5.869	5.278
Puerto Plata	1.726	2.472	2.117	1.788	2.518	2.170
Samaná	1.709	2.333	1.850	1.837	2.459	1.850
Santiago	3.160	4.504	4.233	3.764	5.406	4.233
Santo Domingo	3.357	4.642	4.140	3.274	4.386	4.140

In Table 7, estimates of the random effects are presented. Comparing longer-term and shorter-term models, we observe very similar negative estimates of random intercepts between models among four provinces: Santo Domingos, Puerto Plata, Distrito Nacional and Samaná. This indicates that, based on meteorological variables with shorter and longer delays, with lags as described in Table 5 for both models, lower expected values for the adjusted dengue incidence rate are predicted for these four provinces, with Samaná presenting the lowest one. Among the other four provinces, which have positive estimates, similar values between the two models are only observed for Santiago's province. The highest estimate of the random intercept of the longer-term model occurs for the province of Barahona and for the shorter-term model the highest estimate occurs for Monte Cristi. Therefore, although the adjusted dengue incidence rate based on 2 week-lag meteorological variables is expected to be higher in Monte Cristi, meteorological variables with a longer delay, with lags as indicated in the longer-term model will lead to a higher estimated rate in Barahona.

Table 7. Estimated intercept random effects for each of the eight provinces for the two fitted gamma-GLMMs.

Provinces	Random Effects	
	Longer-Term Model	Shorter-Term Model
Barahona	0.977	0.873
Distrito Nacional	−0.648	−0.646
La Romana	0.240	0.136
Monte Cristi	0.747	0.908
Puerto Plata	−0.550	−0.535
Samaná	−0.841	−0.851
Santiago	0.536	0.567
Santo Domingo	−0.454	−0.448

6. Conclusions

Dengue outbreaks are a consequence of complex interactions among multiple factors. In particular, dengue disease depends on the development of mosquitoes through a four-stage life cycle that is heavily influenced by environmental conditions [29]. This implies that the current number of cases can be influenced by past conditions that impact the mosquito life cycle. By using consistent methods for fitting gamma-GLMM models, we have analysed the effect of meteorological conditions with lags on the incidence of dengue conditioned to the human population density of eight provinces of the Dominican Republic. We defined two relationships in terms of province-specific effects and different statistics for meteorological variables related to temperature (average, maximum, minimum), daily temperature range (average), and precipitation (average) to explain the dengue incidence rate. Although one model provides estimates of dengue incidence by using meteorological variables in the short term (2 weeks), the other describes dengue incidence in terms of meteorological conditions reported after passage of more time. Our results showed a significant effect from temperatures with delay of 2, 4, and 5 weeks, from daily temperature range with delay of 2 and 5 weeks and from precipitation with delay of 2 weeks. Additionally, variations in average temperature (Temp.avg) have the greatest effect on dengue cases. These results are in agreement with similar studies that found significant risk of dengue when considering lags in climate variables of 2–5 weeks [3,4]. Our findings provide a better understanding of the relationships between meteorological conditions and weekly trends in dengue cases during the outbreak that occurred in the Dominican Republic in 2019.

Different geographical and spatial locations may have local effects that lead to different dengue models. We note that the focus of this work is on the effects of meteorological variables and the modelling of the dengue cases is conditioned to the population size of each province. But other influencers of dengue transmission are likely. We included province-specific random effects to account for some of the variability that could be produced by these influencers. In particular, geographical and sociopolitical features of each province could play a role in dengue transmission; however, these features are not considered as independent variables in this study. Analysing the variances of random effects, it is possible to conclude that among the eight provinces studied there is lower variability. But the distribution of values for random effects (Table 7) suggest that it is important to question whether other factors could be considered to improve model predictions. Our results highlight that dengue prediction models developed at local scales are important to understanding the risk of dengue because conditions at a higher level (such as at the national level), may not be useful for predicting dengue cases that have high heterogeneity driven by different geographic, climatic, sociodemographic, or other factors.

The analysis of the deviance residuals shows that, overall, both the models fit relatively well to the data. A normal distribution is fitted to the deviance residuals; however, there is a variability of the incidence rate within the provinces which suggest that both models might be improved by the addition of more random effects. The diagnostic model showed that there is variability in the incidence rate between provinces. Using the same lag for all provinces could not be the best choice; instead, it is important to investigate whether the selected lags in the meteorological variables are province-specific. For this reason, further studies are needed to develop a better understanding of variability in dengue incidence rates.

The lack of reliable data for a long period of time was a limitation of this work. There is a lack of long-term spatiotemporal and climate data for dengue incidence in the Dominican Republic. In spite of having data for 32 provinces, we only had reliable data for eight of them. Even considering eight provinces, it was necessary to supplement climate data collected in the Dominican Republic with data collected from other sources (NASA) to reduce missing values in the database. For future works, complete climate data from other provinces in the Dominican Republic is necessary. Having data from more provinces would allow us to assess how well the two final models perform in other provinces. Moreover, having data from more provinces and years could allow us to establish a better final model by using another strategies like cross-validation by splitting the data into two sets: a training data set for model-selection and a testing data set for inference. In order to develop better models aimed at understanding the intensification of dengue transmission in the Dominican Republic and to develop reliable warning systems for predicting future dengue incidence, it is important to gather more long-term data and to build robust systems for continuous collection of this data.

This research contributes to developing a better understanding of the dynamics of dengue and their relationship with climatological variables in the Dominican Republic, a tropical country where, despite minor differences in climate across the country, dengue incidence can vary greatly. This paper has practical implications for preparing vector control and public health departments by providing potential warning indicators for dengue outbreaks, which will in turn contribute to the development of comprehensive dengue management programs.

Author Contributions: Conceptualization, A.F., H.S.R. and N.M.; methodology, A.F., H.S.R. and N.M.; software, A.F., H.S.R. and A.I.; formal analysis, A.F., H.S.R. and N.M. and M.A.R.; validation, M.A.R., D.H. and M.C.-H.; data curation, A.I., M.A.R., D.H. and M.C.-H.; writing—original draft preparation, A.F., H.S.R., N.M. and M.A.R.; writing—review and editing, A.F., H.S.R., N.M., A.I., M.A.R., D.H. and M.C.-H.; supervision, A.F. and H.S.R.; project administration, A.F. and H.S.R. All authors have read and agreed to the published version of the manuscript.

Funding: Fund for Innovation and Scientific and Technological Development—Ministry of Higher Education, Science and Technology of the Dominican Republic. Work supported by Portuguese funds through the CIDMA—Center for Research and Development in Mathematics and Applications, and the Portuguese Foundation for Science and Technology (FCT-Fundação para a Ciência e a Tecnologia), within project UIDB/04106/2020.

Data Availability Statement: Not applicable.

Conflicts of Interest: The authors declare no conflict of interest.

References

1. Dengue and Severe Dengue, World Health Organization. 2021. Available online: https://www.who.int/news-room/fact-sheets/detail/dengue-and-severe-dengue (accessed on 22 March 2022).
2. Ten Threats to Global Health in 2019, World Health Organization. Available online: https://www.who.int/news-room/spotlight/ten-threats-to-global-health-in-2019 (accessed on 9 April 2022).
3. Iutis, A.; Rodrigues, H.S.; Freitas, A.; Martins, N. A preliminary analysis of weekly dengue incidence rate in the Dominican Republic during 2019. *J. Stat. Health Decis.* **2021**, *3*, 6–9.
4. Robert, M.A.; Rodrigues, H.; Sofia, H.D.; Donado Campos, J.M.; Morilla, F.; Aguila Mejia, J.; Guardado, M.E.; Skews, R.; Colome-Hidalgo, M. Spatiotemporal and Meteorological Trends in Dengue Transmission in the Dominican Republic, 2015–2019. Available online: https://medrxiv.org/cgi/content/short/2023.01.05.23284205v1 (accessed on 10 January 2023).
5. Brady, O.J.; A Johansson, M.; A Guerra, C.; Bhatt, S.; Golding, N.; Pigott, D.M.; Delatte, H.; Grech, M.G.; Leisnham, P.T.; Maciel-De-Freitas, R.; et al. Modelling adult Aedes aegypti and Aedes albopictus survival at different temperatures in laboratory and field settings. *Parasites Vectors* **2013**, *6*, 351. [CrossRef] [PubMed]
6. Reinhold, J.M.; Lazzari, C.R.; Lahondère, C. Effects of the Environmental Temperature on Aedes aegypti and Aedes albopictus Mosquitoes: A Review. *Insects* **2018**, *9*, 158. [CrossRef] [PubMed]
7. Halstead, S.B. Dengue. *Lancet* **2007**, *70*, 1644–1652. [CrossRef]
8. Srisuphanunt, M.; Puttaruk, P.; Kooltheat, N.; Katzenmeier, G.; Wilairatana, P. Prognostic Indicators for the Early Prediction of Severe Dengue Infection: A Retrospective Study in a University Hospital in Thailand. *Trop. Med. Infect. Dis.* **2022**, *31*, 162. [CrossRef]
9. Patanarapelert, K.; Tang, I.M. *Effect of Time Delay on the Transmission of Dengue Fever*; World Academy of Science, Engineering and Technology: Chicago, IL, USA, 2007.
10. Metelmann, S.; Liu, X.; Lu, L.; Caminade, C.; Liu, K.; Cao, L.; Medlock, J.M.; Baylis, M.; Morse, A.P.; Liu, Q. Assessing the suitability for Aedes albopictus and dengue transmission risk in China with a delay differential equation model. *PLoS Neglected Trop. Dis.* **2021**. [CrossRef]
11. Rodrigues, H.S.; Monteiro, M.T.T.; Torres, D.F.M. Vaccination Models and Optimal Control Strategies to Dengue. *Math. Biosci.* **2014**, *247*, 1–12. [CrossRef]
12. Gan, S.J.; Leong, Y.Q.; Bin Barhanuddin, M.F.H.; Wong, S.T.; Wong, S.F.; Mak, J.W.; Ahmad, R.B. Dengue fever and insecticide resistance in Aedes mosquitoes in Southeast Asia: A review. *Parasites Vectors* **2021**, *14*, 315. [CrossRef]
13. Jayawickreme, K.P.; Jayaweera, D.K.; Weerasinghe, S.; Warapitiya, D.; Subasinghe, S. A study on knowledge, attitudes and practices regarding dengue fever, its prevention and management among dengue patients presenting to a tertiary care hospital in Sri Lanka. *BMC Infect. Dis.* **2021**, *21*, 981. [CrossRef]

14. Brito da Cruz, A.M.C.; Rodrigues, H.S. Economic Burden of Personal Protective Strategies for Dengue Disease: An Optimal Control Approach. In *Optimization, Learning Algorithms and Applications*; OL2A 2021; Communications in Computer and Information Science; Springer: Cham, Switzerland, 2021; Volume 1488.
15. Brito da Cruz, A.M.C.; Rodrigues, H.S. Personal protective strategies for dengue disease: Simulations in two coexisting virus serotypes scenarios. *Math. Comput. Simul.* **2021**, *188*, 254–267. [CrossRef]
16. Sebastião, C.S.; Neto, Z.; Jandondo, D.; Mirandela, M.; Morais, J.; Brito, M. Dengue virus among HIV-infected pregnant women attending antenatal care in Luanda, Angola: An emerging public health concern. *Sci. Afr.* **2022**, *17*, e01356. [CrossRef]
17. Song, H.; Tian, D.; Shan, C. Modeling the effect of temperature on dengue virus transmission with periodic delay differential equations. *Math. Biosci. Eng.* **2020**, *17*, 4147–4164. [CrossRef] [PubMed]
18. Faruk, M.O.; Jannat, S.N.; Rahman, M.S. Impact of environmental factors on the spread of dengue fever in Sri Lanka. *Int. J. Environ. Sci. Technol.* **2022**, *19*, 10637–10648. [CrossRef]
19. Gómez-Gómez, R.E.; Kim, J.; Hong, K.; Jang, J.Y.L.; Kisiju, T.L.; Kim, S.; Chun, B.C. Association between Climate Factor and Dengue Fever in Asuncion, Paraguay: A Generalized Additive Model. *Int. J. Environ. Res. Public Health* **2022**, *19*, 12192. [CrossRef] [PubMed]
20. Oliveira, A.N.; Menezes, R.; Faria, S.; Afonso, P. Mixed-effects modelling for crossed and nested data: An analysis of dengue fever in the state of Goiás, Brazil. *J. Appl. Stat.* **2020**, *47*, 2912–2926. [CrossRef]
21. Samat, N.A.; Percy, D.F. Vector-borne infectious disease mapping with stochastic difference equations: An analysis of dengue disease in Malaysia. *J. Appl. Stat.* **2012**, *39*, 2029–2046. [CrossRef]
22. Petrone, M.E.; Earnest, R.; Lourenço, J.; Kraemer, M.U.; Paulino-Ramirez, R.; Grubaugh, N.D.; Tapia, L. Asynchronicity of endemic and emerging mosquito-borne disease outbreaks in the Dominican Republic. *Nat. Commun.* **2021**, *12*, 151. [CrossRef]
23. Oficinal Nacional de Estadística. Available online: https://www.one.gob.do/datos-y-estadisticas/temas/estadisticas-demograficas/estimaciones-y-proyecciones-demograficas/ (accessed on 15 February 2022).
24. Sciandra, M.; Spera, I. A model-based approach to Spotify data analysis: A Beta GLMM. *J. Appl. Stat.* **2022**, *49*, 214–229. [CrossRef]
25. Villasenor, J.A.; Gonzalez-Estrada, E. A variance ratio test of fit for Gamma distributions. *Stat. Probab. Lett.* **2015**, *96*, 281–286. [CrossRef]
26. Millard, S.P. *EnvStats: An R Package for Environmental Statistics*; Springer: New York, NY, USA, 2013.
27. Gonzalez-Estrada, E.; Villasenor-Alva, J.A. Goft: Tests of Fit for Some Probability Distributions. R Package Version 1.3.6. 2020. Available online: https://CRAN.R-project.org/package=goft (accessed on 5 December 2022)
28. Bates, D.; Maechler, M.; Bolker, B.; Walker, S. Linear mixed-effects models using lme4. *J. Stat. Softw.* **2015**, *67*, 1–48. [CrossRef]
29. Navarro Valencia, V.; Díaz, Y.; Pascale, J.M.; Boni, M.F.; Sanchez-Galan, J.E. Assessing the Effect of Climate Variables on the Incidence of Dengue Cases in the Metropolitan Region of Panama City. *Int. J. Environ. Res. Public Health* **2021**, *18*, 12108. [CrossRef] [PubMed]

Disclaimer/Publisher's Note: The statements, opinions and data contained in all publications are solely those of the individual author(s) and contributor(s) and not of MDPI and/or the editor(s). MDPI and/or the editor(s) disclaim responsibility for any injury to people or property resulting from any ideas, methods, instructions or products referred to in the content.

Article

An Accelerated Double-Integral ZNN with Resisting Linear Noise for Dynamic Sylvester Equation Solving and Its Application to the Control of the SFM Chaotic System

Luyang Han [1], Yongjun He [2], Bolin Liao [1,*] and Cheng Hua [1]

[1] College of Computer Science and Engineering, Jishou University, Jishou 416000, China
[2] School of Mathematics and Statistics, Hunan Normal University, Changsha 410081, China
* Correspondence: bolinliao@jsu.edu.cn; Tel.: +86-137-8791-8516

Abstract: The dynamic Sylvester equation (DSE) is frequently encountered in engineering and mathematics fields. The original zeroing neural network (OZNN) can work well to handle DSE under a noise-free environment, but may not work in noise. Though an integral-enhanced zeroing neural network (IEZNN) can be employed to solve the DSE under multiple-noise, it may fall flat under linear noise, and its convergence speed is unsatisfactory. Therefore, an accelerated double-integral zeroing neural network (ADIZNN) is proposed based on an innovative design formula to resist linear noise and accelerate convergence. Besides, theoretical proofs verify the convergence and robustness of the ADIZNN model. Moreover, simulation experiments indicate that the convergence rate and anti-noise ability of the ADIZNN are far superior to the OZNN and IEZNN under linear noise. Finally, chaos control of the sine function memristor (SFM) chaotic system is provided to suggest that the controller based on the ADIZNN has a smaller amount of error and higher accuracy than other ZNNs.

Keywords: dynamic Sylvester equation; linear noise; accelerated double integral ZNN; chaos control

MSC: 15A24; 34A34; 34H10; 93D20

Citation: Han, L.; He, Y.; Liao, B.; Hua, C. An Accelerated Double-Integral ZNN with Resisting Linear Noise for Dynamic Sylvester Equation Solving and Its Application to the Control of the SFM Chaotic System. *Axioms* **2023**, *12*, 287. https://doi.org/10.3390/axioms12030287

Academic Editors: Nuno Bastos, Touria Karite and Amir Khan

Received: 3 February 2023
Revised: 23 February 2023
Accepted: 3 March 2023
Published: 9 March 2023

Copyright: © 2023 by the authors. Licensee MDPI, Basel, Switzerland. This article is an open access article distributed under the terms and conditions of the Creative Commons Attribution (CC BY) license (https://creativecommons.org/licenses/by/4.0/).

1. Introduction

The Sylvester equation is a crucial matrix equation. It has a crucial position in many fields, such as image fusion [1], object detection [2], control configuration selection [3], fast tensor product solution [4], robotics [5–8], permanent magnet synchronous motors [9] and mobile manipulators [10]. Therefore, finding a quick solution to handle the dynamic Sylvester equation (DSE) is exceptionally crucial. Many scholars previously utilized numerical methods to solve the Sylvester equation, such as the Hessenberg–Schur iteration method [11] and Krylov subspace methods [12]. Nevertheless, numerical methods are only suitable for small-scale matrix issues and cannot solve DSE well. In recent years, the advantages of feedforward neural networks and recurrent neural networks (RNNs) with the parallel process and easy implementation in hardware have been gradually excavated [13–16]. The gradient neural network (GNN), an important type of RNN, has become increasingly popular in high-dimensional Sylvester equation solving [17,18]. Nevertheless, when the GNN approach was extended to dynamic domains, researchers discovered the two defects of GNN: first, the GNN method cannot make the residual value reach zero; second, its convergence rate is deficient.

After that, the original zeroing neural network (OZNN) was reported, aiming at the shortcomings of the GNN [19]. With the development of the zeroing neural network (ZNN) model, many scholars have focused on ZNN because it can deal with many dynamic mathematical problems [20–22]. Simultaneously, scholars constantly improved and innovated on the basis of the ZNN and they obtained many derived ZNN models for specific problems [7,9,23–25]. For instance, He et al. presented a double-accelerated ZNN for handling dynamic matrix inversion [23]. Xiao et al. proposed two nonlinear ZNN models and applied them to the 3D moving target location [24]. A noise-suppression variable parameter ZNN was proposed to handle the DSE [26]. In addition, there is much related work on the universal DSE [27,28].

It is worth noting that noise cannot be ignored, and it will affect the stability of the system [29–31]. Therefore, we should consider both convergence and robustness when designing ZNN models [32–34]. In order to better suppress noise, the PID control method is usually used by the public [35]. The control principle also mentions that the integral term can eliminate noise so that the error in the system is continuously reduced. Thus, the integral-enhanced ZNN model (IEZNN) was designed [32], and the integral term made up for the defect that the original ZNN could not suppress noise. Besides, many anti-noise ZNNs were researched and applied [36–38].

Nevertheless, the IEZNN model cannot suppress linear noise well. Many researchers point out that the activation functions can accelerate convergence and suppress noise [39–41]. Utilizing double integration and the fixed-time activation function (FTAF), we propose an accelerated double integral ZNN (ADIZNN) model with anti-linear noise interference to settle the DSE under linear noise. In brief, the ADIZNN has the characteristic of accelerated convergence and enhanced robustness due to the introduction of the FTAF and the double integral term. In addition, the theoretical proofs and simulation experiments under the linear noise environments are given. At last, the design ideas of ZNNs are extended to chaos control of the SFM chaotic system to show that the controller based on the ADIZNN has significant advantages compared with other controllers.

The remaining part of this paper is divided into five sections. Section 2 introduces the OZNN, IEZNN and ADIZNN models. Theoretical analyses of the ADIZNN are provided in Section 3. Section 4 offers two specific examples under linear noise. Besides, the chaos control experiment of the SFM chaotic system is provided in Section 5. Section 6 is the summary part of paper. These are the significant contributions of this research.

- Based on the novel ZNN design formula, an innovative ADIZNN is constructed for settling the dynamic Sylvester equation under the linear noise.
- The ADIZNN model has a novel double integral structure and activation function, which guarantees accelerated convergence and enhanced anti-noise capacity.
- Theoretical analyses and simulation results are provided to ensure that the ADIZNN model can handle the DSE with excellent convergence and robustness.
- Chaos control schemes of the TFM chaotic system are established to display that the controller based on the ADIZNN has superior performance than that based on the OZNN and IEZNN.

2. DSE Description and Models Design

Firstly, the general dynamic Sylvester equation (DSE), OZNN and IEZNN are offered. Posteriorly, the novel ADIZNN model proposed is particularly elaborated.

2.1. Description of DSE

The definition of the DSE is described in detail as follows:

$$U(t)P(t) - P(t)V(t) + G(t) = 0, \qquad (1)$$

in which $U(t), V(t), G(t) \in \mathbb{R}^{n \times n}$ are time-varying matrices, and $P(t) \in \mathbb{R}^{n \times n}$ is an unknown matrix.

The purpose of the ZNN model is to solve the unknown $P(t)$ in Equation (1) under noise, and the theoretical solution is denoted by $P^*(t)$. Moving matrix $G(t)$ of (1), we have

$$U(t)P(t) - P(t)V(t) = -G(t). \qquad (2)$$

For further derivation, we need to vectorize Equation (2) and obtain

$$\left(I_n \otimes U(t) - V^T(t) \otimes I_n\right)\text{vec}(P(t)) = -\text{vec}(G(t)), \tag{3}$$

in which $I_n \in \mathbb{R}^{n \times n}$ is an identity matrix, and $\text{vec}(\cdot)$ and the symbol $\otimes$ signify the vectorization and Kronecker product operation. Setting $Q(t) = I_n \otimes U(t) - V^T(t) \otimes I_n \in \mathbb{R}^{nn \times nn}$, $p(t) = \text{vec}(P(t)) \in \mathbb{R}^{nn \times 1}$, $g(t) = \text{vec}(G(t)) \in \mathbb{R}^{nn \times 1}$ of (3), the DSE is transformed into a linear equation:

$$Q(t)p(t) = -g(t).$$

For monitoring the solution process, we define

$$W(t) = Q(t)p(t) + g(t) \tag{4}$$

as an error function. The derivative of (4) with respect to time can be written as

$$\dot{W}(t) = \dot{Q}(t)p(t) + Q(t)\dot{p}(t) + \dot{g}(t). \tag{5}$$

2.2. Relevant Models Design

A detailed description of the relevant models are introduced in this subsection. The design formula of error in the ZNN model is defined as

$$\dot{W}(t) = -\xi \Phi(W(t)), \tag{6}$$

in which $\xi \in \mathbb{R}^+$ and $\Phi(\cdot)$ is a mapping array composed by the activation function. The elemental form of (6) is as follows

$$\dot{w}_i(t) = -\xi \phi(w_i(t)),$$

where $\phi(\cdot)$ denotes the nonlinear monotone non-decreasing odd activation function, and $w_i(\cdot)$ and $\phi(\cdot)$ are element forms of the $W(\cdot)$ and $\Phi(\cdot)$, where $i = 1, 2, \ldots, n^2$. When $\phi(\cdot)$ is the linear activation function (i.e., $\phi(\imath) = \imath$), we get the design formula of the OZNN model:

$$\dot{W}(t) = -\xi W(t). \tag{7}$$

Considering the case of linear noise, the design formula of the OZNN is

$$\dot{W}(t) = -\xi W(t) + Z(t), \tag{8}$$

where $Z(t) \in \mathbb{R}^{nn \times 1}$ refers to linear noise. Linear noise is a significant kind of noise, and it is generally shaped like $Z(t) = At + B$, where $A, B \in \mathbb{R}^{nn \times 1}$. Let $z_i(t)$, a_i and b_i stand for the ith elements of $Z(t)$, A and B. Then, the element form of $Z(t)$ is rewritten as $z_i(t) = a_i t + b_i$. Substituting Equations (4) and (5) into (8), the OZNN model to solve the DSE is obtained

$$Q(t)\dot{p}(t) = -\dot{Q}(t)p(t) - \dot{g}(t) - \xi(Q(t)p(t) + g(t)) + Z(t). \tag{9}$$

On this basis, Jin et al. added an integral term to suppress the noise and proposed an integral-enhanced ZNN (IEZNN) [32], and its design formula is

$$\dot{W}(t) = -\xi W(t) - \lambda \int_0^t W(\tau) \mathrm{d}\tau, \tag{10}$$

with ξ and $\lambda \in \mathbb{R} > 0$. Then, we obtain the case of (10) under noise:

$$\dot{W}(t) = -\xi W(t) - \lambda \int_0^t W(\tau) \mathrm{d}\tau + Z(t). \tag{11}$$

Substituting (4) and (5) into (11), the model of the IEZNN can be rewritten as

$$Q(t)\dot{p}(t) = -\dot{Q}(t)p(t) - \dot{g}(t) - \xi(Q(t)p(t) + g(t)) \\ - \lambda \int_0^t (Q(\tau)p(\tau) + g(\tau))d\tau + Z(t). \quad (12)$$

Now that all the relevant models descriptions are complete, the accelerated double integral ZNN will be introduced.

2.3. ADIZNN Model Design

In this subsection, an accelerated double integral ZNN (ADIZNN) model is proposed, which can resist the linear noise effectively. We know that $\dot{W}(t) = -\xi\Phi(W(t))$ from Section 2.2, to describe the evolution of the model more intuitively, set

$$\Theta(t) = \dot{W}(t) + \xi\Phi(W(t)), \quad (13)$$

where $\Phi(\cdot)$ denotes the fixed-time activation function (FTAF) here, and its element form is

$$\phi(\iota) = (\varepsilon_1|\iota|^\mu + \varepsilon_2|\iota|^\sigma)\text{sign}(\iota) + \varepsilon_3\iota + \varepsilon_4\text{sign}(\iota), \quad (14)$$

in which ε_1 and $\varepsilon_2 > 0$, ε_3 and $\varepsilon_4 \geq 0$, $0 < \mu < 1$, $\sigma > 1$.

Remark 1. *We make some detailed remarks about FTAF (14).*

- *The $\varepsilon_1|\iota|^\mu \text{sign}(\iota)$ and $\varepsilon_2|\iota|^\sigma \text{sign}(\iota)$ of FTAF (14) are to accelerate convergence.*
- *The $\varepsilon_3\iota$ and $\varepsilon_4\text{sign}(\iota)$ of FTAF (14) are to suppress noise;*

In addition, let

$$\Theta(t) = -\lambda \int_0^t \Theta(\tau)d\tau,$$

with $\lambda \in \mathbb{R}^+$. We define

$$Y(t) = \Theta(t) + \lambda \int_0^t \Theta(\tau)d\tau. \quad (15)$$

Substituting (13) into (15), one can get

$$Y(t) = \dot{W}(t) + \xi\Phi(W(t)) + \lambda \int_0^t (\dot{W}(\tau) + \xi\Phi(W(\tau)))d\tau. \quad (16)$$

Similarly, set

$$Y(t) = -\lambda \int_0^t Y(\tau)d\tau. \quad (17)$$

Substituting (16) into (17), we obtain

$$\dot{W}(t) + \xi\Phi(W(t)) + \lambda W(t) + \lambda\xi \int_0^t \Phi(W(\tau))d\tau \\ = -\lambda \int_0^t \left(\dot{W}(\tau) + \xi\Phi(W(\tau)) + \lambda W(\tau) + \lambda\xi \int_0^\tau \Phi(W(\sigma))d\sigma\right)d\tau \\ = -\lambda W(t) - \lambda\xi \int_0^t \Phi(W(\tau))d\tau - \lambda^2 \int_0^t W(\tau)d\tau - \lambda^2\xi \int_0^t \int_0^\tau \Phi(W(\sigma))d\sigma d\tau.$$

Thus, the design formula of the ADIZNN for DSE is obtained:

$$\dot{W}(t) = -2\lambda W(t) - \xi\Phi(W(t)) - \lambda^2 \int_0^t W(\tau)d\tau \\ - 2\lambda\xi \int_0^t \Phi(W(\tau))d\tau - \lambda^2\xi \int_0^t \int_0^\tau \Phi(W(\sigma))d\sigma d\tau. \quad (18)$$

Furthermore, the design formula of the ADIZNN with noise can be written as

$$\dot{W}(t) = -2\lambda W(t) - \xi\Phi(W(t)) - \lambda^2 \int_0^t W(\tau)d\tau$$
$$- 2\lambda\xi \int_0^t \Phi(W(\tau))d\tau - \lambda^2\xi \int_0^t \int_0^\tau \Phi(W(\sigma))d\sigma d\tau + Z(t).$$

Furthermore, $W(t) = Q(t)p(t) + g(t)$ and $\dot{W}(t) = \dot{Q}(t)p(t) + Q(t)\dot{p}(t) + \dot{g}(t)$ are already known. Hence, the ADIZNN model that included noise can be further obtained:

$$\begin{aligned} Q(t)\dot{p}(t) = & -\dot{Q}(t)p(t) - \dot{g}(t) - 2\lambda(Q(t)p(t) + g(t)) - \xi\Phi(Q(t)p(t) + g(t)) \\ & - 2\lambda\xi \int_0^t \Phi(Q(\tau)p(\tau) + g(\tau))d\tau - \lambda^2 \int_0^t (Q(\tau)p(\tau) + g(\tau))d\tau \\ & - \lambda^2\xi \int_0^t \int_0^\tau \Phi(\dot{Q}(\sigma)p(\sigma) + Q(\sigma)\dot{p}(\sigma) + \dot{g}(\sigma))d\sigma d\tau + Z(t). \end{aligned} \quad (19)$$

Remark 2. *We make some detailed remarks about ADIZNN (19).*

- Based on the novel ZNN design formula, an innovative ADIZNN is constructed for settling the DSE under the linear noise.
- The novel double integral structure and activation function, which guarantees accelerated convergence and enhanced anti-noise capacity.

3. Theoretical Analyses

We mainly discuss and prove properties of the ADIZNN in this section. In order to better express the Frobenius norm of $W(t)$, we introduce the error norm $\|W(t)\|_F = \|Q(t)p(t) + g(t)\|_F$.

3.1. Convergence

The convergence performance of ADIZNN (19) is investigated and studied under the ideal noise-free condition in this subsection.

Theorem 1. *Given matrices $U(t) \in \mathbb{R}^{n \times n}$, $V(t) \in \mathbb{R}^{n \times n}$ and $G(t) \in \mathbb{R}^{n \times n}$. From any initial value $P(0)$, the error norm $\|W(t)\|_F$ of ADIZNN (19) can reach zero under the ideal noise-free condition, that is,*

$$\lim_{t \to \infty} \|W(t)\|_F = 0.$$

Proof of Theorem 1. In order to give a clearer proof process, let $w_i(t)$, $\theta_i(t)$, $\gamma_i(t)$ and $\phi(\cdot)$ represent the elements form of $W(t)$, $\Theta(t)$, $Y(t)$ and $\Phi(\cdot)$. First, considering

$$Y(t) = \dot{W}(t) + \xi\Phi(W(t)) + \lambda \int_0^t (\dot{W}(\tau) + \xi\Phi(W(\tau)))d\tau, \quad (20)$$

ADIZNN model (19) under the noiseless environment can be transformed into

$$Y(t) = -\lambda \int_0^t Y(\tau)d\tau. \quad (21)$$

The element form of (21) is

$$\gamma_i(t) = -\lambda \int_0^t \gamma_i(\tau)d\tau. \quad (22)$$

Then, the derivative of (22) is

$$\dot{\gamma}_i(t) = -\lambda \gamma_i(t). \quad (23)$$

Setting a Lyapunov equation

$$\ell(t) = \gamma_i^2(t),$$

its derivative is
$$\dot{\ell}(t) = 2\dot{\gamma}_i(t)\gamma_i(t). \tag{24}$$

Substituting (23) into (24), we have
$$\dot{\ell}(t) = -2\lambda\gamma_i(t)\gamma_i(t) = -2\lambda\gamma_i^2(t).$$

Because $\ell(t)$ is positive definite and $\dot{\ell}(t)$ is negative definite, $\ell(t)$ is globally asymptotically stable, and we have
$$\lim_{t\to\infty}|\ell(t)| = \lim_{t\to\infty}\left|\gamma_i^2(t)\right| = \lim_{t\to\infty}|\gamma_i(t)| = 0. \tag{25}$$

Thus, $\gamma_i = \dot{w}_i(t) + \xi\phi(w_i(t)) + \lambda\int_0^t(\dot{w}_i(\tau) + \xi\phi(w_i(\tau)))d\tau = 0$ as $t \to \infty$ based on (20) and (25). Considering $\theta_i(t) = \dot{w}_i(t) + \xi\phi(w_i(t))$, then we have
$$\theta_i(t) = -\lambda\int_0^t \theta_i(\tau)d\tau, t \to \infty. \tag{26}$$

Therefore,
$$\lim_{t\to\infty}\left|\theta_i(t) + \lambda\int_0^t \theta_i(\tau)d\tau\right| = 0.$$

It is not difficult to know
$$\lim_{t\to\infty}|\theta_i(t)| = \lim_{t\to\infty}\left|-\lambda\int_0^t \theta_i(\tau)d\tau\right|.$$

The derivative of the above equation is
$$\lim_{t\to\infty}|\dot{\theta}_i(t)| = \lim_{t\to\infty}|-\lambda\theta_i(t)| + \Delta, \Delta \to 0,$$

where Δ is a small error in the derivative of $\theta_i(t)$. Setting another Lyapunov equation
$$\hbar(t) = \theta_i^2(t). \tag{27}$$

The derivative of (27) is
$$\dot{\hbar}(t) = 2\dot{\theta}_i(t)\theta_i(t) = -2\lambda\theta_i^2(t).$$

According to the Lyapunov theorem, we get
$$\lim_{t\to\infty}|\theta_i(t)| = 0.$$

Because $\theta_i(t) = \dot{w}_i(t) + \xi\phi(w_i(t))$, thus,
$$\lim_{t\to\infty}|\theta_i(t)| = \lim_{t\to\infty}|\dot{w}_i(t) + \xi\phi(w_i(t))| = 0. \tag{28}$$

Thus,
$$\dot{w}_i(t) = -\xi\phi(w_i(t)).$$

Clearly, we get
$$\lim_{t\to\infty}|w_i(t)| = 0.$$

Thus, writing it in matrix form gives the following
$$\lim_{t\to\infty}\|W(t)\|_F = 0.$$

The proof is completed now. □

3.2. Robustness

Furthermore, the ADIZNN model can still approximate the theoretical solution infinitely when solving the DSE in a noisy environment. In other words, the ADIZNN model has strong robustness. Its robustness proof process is presented below.

Theorem 2. *Given matrices $U(t) \in \mathbb{R}^{n \times n}$, $V(t) \in \mathbb{R}^{n \times n}$ and $G(t) \in \mathbb{R}^{n \times n}$, the identity matrix $I_n \in \mathbb{R}^{n \times n}$. From any initial value $P(0)$, $P(t)$ of the proposed ADIZNN can reach $P^*(t)$ in solving the DSE under the linear noise condition, that is,*

$$\lim_{t \to \infty} \|W(t)\|_F = 0.$$

Proof of Theorem 2. Linear noise can be written as

$$Z(t) = At + B, \tag{29}$$

where $A \in \mathbb{R}^{nn \times 1}$ and $B \in \mathbb{R}^{nn \times 1}$ are constant matrices. Its element form can be written as

$$z_i(t) = a_i t + b_i.$$

According to (20) and (21) of Theorem 1, the ADIZNN model (19) can be converted to

$$Y(t) = -\lambda \int_0^t Y(\tau) d\tau + Z(t). \tag{30}$$

Its element is

$$\gamma_i(t) = -\lambda \int_0^t \gamma_i(\kappa) d\kappa + z_i(t). \tag{31}$$

Taking the derivative of γ_i twice, we get

$$\ddot{\gamma}_i(t) = -\lambda \dot{\gamma}_i(t) + \ddot{z}_i(t). \tag{32}$$

Differentiating the linear noise once and twice yield $\dot{z}_i(t) = a$ and $\ddot{z}_i(t) = 0$. Then,

$$\ddot{\gamma}_i(t) = -\lambda \dot{\gamma}_i(t).$$

We set up a Lyapunov function $\Im(t) = \dot{\gamma}_i^2(t)$, so

$$\dot{\Im}(t) = 2\ddot{\gamma}_i(t)\dot{\gamma}_i(t) = -\lambda \dot{\gamma}_i^2(t).$$

Due to the $\Im(t)$ being positive definite and $\dot{\Im}(t)$ being negative definite, $\Im(t)$ is globally asymptotically stable, and we have

$$\lim_{t \to \infty} |\Im(t)| = \lim_{t \to \infty} |\dot{\gamma}_i^2(t)| = \lim_{t \to \infty} |\dot{\gamma}_i(t)| = 0. \tag{33}$$

According to (31) and (33), we obtain

$$\lim_{t \to \infty} |\dot{\gamma}_i(t)| = \lim_{t \to \infty} |-\lambda \gamma_i(t) + \dot{z}_i(t)| = 0.$$

We know that $\dot{z}_i(t) = a$, so it is not hard to figure out

$$\lim_{t \to \infty} |-\lambda \gamma_i(t) + a| = 0.$$

Then it is concluded that

$$\lim_{t \to \infty} |\lambda \gamma_i(t)| = |a|.$$

Thus we get
$$\lim_{t\to\infty} |\gamma_i(t)| = \left|\frac{a}{\lambda}\right|.$$

Thus $|\gamma_i(t)| = \left|\dot{w}_i(t) + \xi\phi(w_i(t)) + \lambda\int_0^t (\dot{w}_i(\tau) + \xi\phi(w_i(\tau)))\mathrm{d}\tau\right| = |a/\lambda|$ as $t \to \infty$. Let
$$\theta_i(t) = \dot{w}_i(t) + \xi\phi(w_i(t)), \tag{34}$$

then we have $|\gamma_i(t)| = \left|\theta_i(t) + \lambda\int_0^t \theta_i(\tau)\mathrm{d}\tau\right| = |a/\lambda|$ as $t \to \infty$. Thus we can infer that
$$\lim_{t\to\infty} \left(\dot{\theta}_i(t) + \lambda\theta_i(t)\right) = 0.$$

Then, we can draw
$$\lim_{t\to\infty} \dot{\theta}_i(t) = \lim_{t\to\infty} -\lambda\theta_i(t).$$

Obviously, due to $\lambda > 0$, $\dot{\theta}_i(t)$ and $\theta_i(t)$ having different signs, thus we get
$$\lim_{t\to\infty} |\theta_i(t)| = 0.$$

In addition, $\theta_i(t) = \dot{w}_i(t) + \xi\phi(w_i(t))$ is known from (34), that means
$$\lim_{t\to\infty} |\theta_i(t)| = \lim_{t\to\infty} |\dot{w}_i(t) + \xi\phi(w_i(t))| = 0.$$

The above equation and (28) are the same, we can say
$$\lim_{t\to\infty} |w_i(t)| = 0.$$

The corresponding matrix form is
$$\lim_{t\to\infty} \|W(t)\|_F = 0.$$

Thus, the proof is accomplished now. □

4. Examples Verification

In Section 3, the properties of the ADIZNN are proved. In this section, comparative experiments are adopted to highlight the outstanding performance of ADIZNN (19). The OZNN (9), IEZNN (12) and ADIZNN (19) models are applied in solving the dynamic Sylvester equation problem. Besides, $P^*(t)$ refers to the theoretical value of $P(t)$ in the experiment 1 and experiment 2.

Remark 3. *Sylvester matrix equations play an important role in the field of control [3,42,43], and they are widely used in the fields of manipulators [10], signal processing [1,44] and statistics [45]. For example, the redundant decomposition of manipulator in the Ref. [10] can first be represented by the quadratic programming problem with equality constraints, then this problem can be further converted into a dynamic linear equation (i.e., a special case of the DSE when $V(t) = 0$) by the Lagrange multiplier method. Therefore, this paper only verifies the effect of the proposed model to solve the DSE, which can be extended to related fields.*

4.1. Experiment 1

The dynamic matrices $U(t)$, $V(t)$ and $G(t)$ are provided

$$U(t) = \begin{bmatrix} s(-2t) & -c(-2t) \\ c(-2t) & s(-2t) \end{bmatrix}, V(t) = \begin{bmatrix} t & 0 \\ 0 & 2 \end{bmatrix}, G(t) = \begin{bmatrix} s(3t) & c(3t) \\ 2s(3t) & -2c(3t) \end{bmatrix}, \tag{35}$$

where $s(\cdot)$ and $c(\cdot)$ represent the sine function and cosine function. The default model parameters are: $\xi = 2, \lambda = 1, \varepsilon_1 = \varepsilon_2 = \varepsilon_3 = \varepsilon_4 = 0.5$ and $\mu = 0.5, \sigma = 2$.

Figure 1 presents state trajectories synthesized by the OZNN model (9), IEZNN model (12) and ADIZNN model (19) using FTAF (14) for the DSE with (35) in the noiseless environment. It is obvious that the OZNN model (9), IEZNN model (12) and ADIZNN model (19) can fit the theoretical solutions in a noiseless environment. Even without linear noise, ADIZNN (19) has the fastest convergence speed, which means that its convergence performance is better than the other two models.

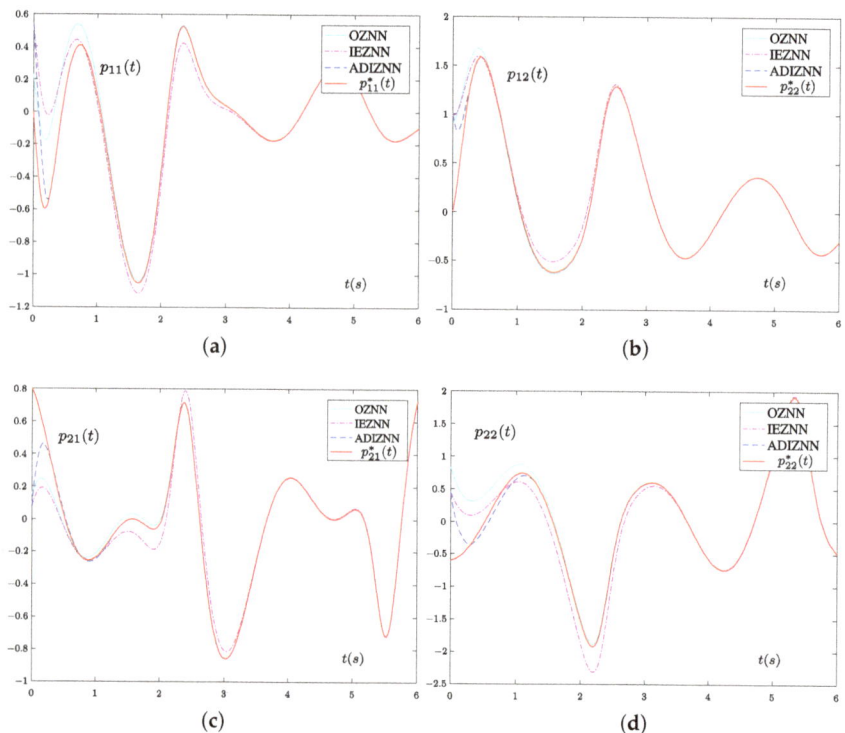

Figure 1. State trajectories of OZNN (9), IEZNN (12) and ADIZNN (19) for the DSE with (35) in the absence of the noise. (**a**) State trajectory of $p_{11}(t)$. (**b**) State trajectory of $p_{12}(t)$. (**c**) State trajectory of $p_{21}(t)$. (**d**) State trajectory of $p_{22}(t)$.

Although in the noiseless environment, all three models can fit the theoretical value, model testing in noisy environment is more important. In Figure 2, we explore the state trajectories of these three models under linear noise $z_i(t) = t/4 + 4$ for the DSE with (35). Obviously, the OZNN's state trajectory completely deviates from the theoretical results, that is to say, OZNN (9) cannot calculate the theoretical result of DSE under $z_i(t) = t/4 + 4$. In Figure 2, the fitting trend of IEZNN (12) is closer and closer to $P^*(t)$ with the increase of t, $p_{11}(t)$, $p_{12}(t)$, $p_{21}(t)$ and $p_{22}(t)$ of IEZNN (12) still cannot converge to $p_{11}^*(t)$, $p_{12}^*(t)$, $p_{21}^*(t)$ and $p_{22}^*(t)$. However, the $p_{11}(t)$, $p_{12}(t)$, $p_{21}(t)$ and $p_{22}(t)$ of ADIZNN (19) converge to theoretical values within 1.3 s. The above results are sufficient to illustrate that ADIZNN (19) can suppress $z_i(t) = t/4 + 4$ when solving the DSE problem.

Remark 4. *Here, we have a discussion of the results of the comparison about Figures 1 and 2. Since the OZNN model (9) does not contain an integral term, it has no ability to suppress linear noise. The IEZNN model (12) contains an integral term, which can resist linear noise to a certain extent, and the error results obtained by solving the DSE with the IEZNN model (12) are not satisfactory.*

However, the ADIZNN model (19) contains the double integral term and FTAF (14), which can effectively suppress linear noise, and its convergence time is much faster than IEZNN.

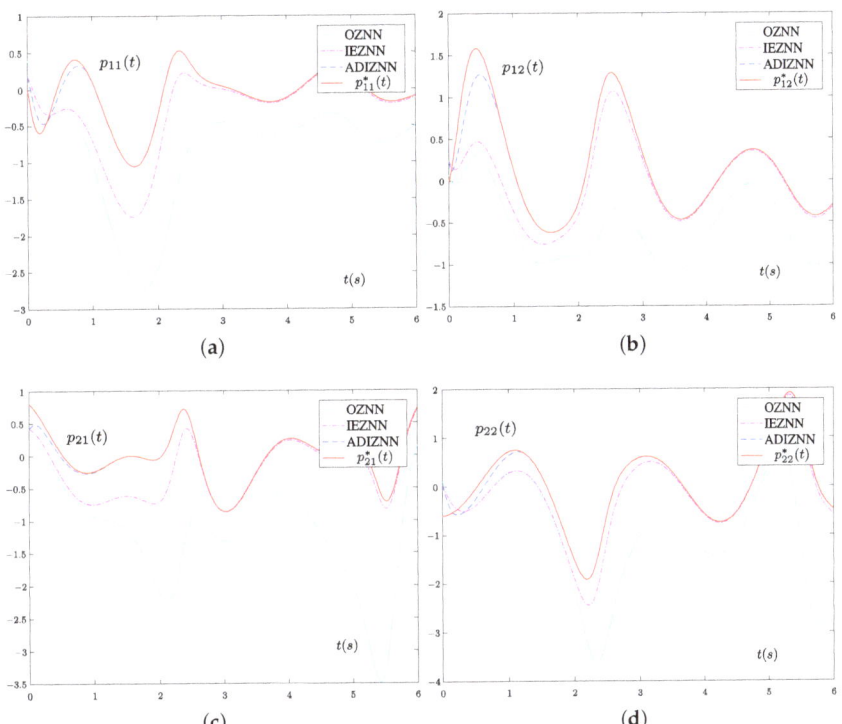

Figure 2. State trajectories of OZNN (9), IEZNN (12) and ADIZNN (19) for the DSE with (35) under the linear noise $z_i(t) = t/4 + 4$. (**a**) State trajectory of $p_{11}(t)$. (**b**) State trajectory of $p_{12}(t)$. (**c**) State trajectory of $p_{21}(t)$. (**d**) State trajectory of $p_{22}(t)$.

In Figure 3, we study the error norms $\|W(t)\|_F$ of OZNN model (9), IEZNN model (12) and ADIZNN model (19) with $\xi = 2$ and $\lambda = 1$ under the different noise environments for the two-dimensional matrices (35). Figure 3a–d correspond to $z_i(t) = 0$, $z_i(t) = t/4 + 4$, $z_i(t) = 4t + 4$ and $z_i(t) = 16t + 4$, respectively. From Figure 3a, $\|W(t)\|_F$ of the OZNN model (9), IEZNN model (12) and ADIZNN model (19) can achieve convergence to zero. However, in the comparison of convergence time, the OZNN model (9) is the slowest, and the IEZNN (12) and ADIZNN model (19) can converge within 1.3 and 4.7 s, respectively. Under linear noise, the information suggested by the Figure 3b–d is that the error norms $\|W(t)\|_F$ of the OZNN model (9) and IEZNN model (12) present a divergence trend. However, $\|W(t)\|_F$ of the ADIZNN model (19) can converge under the linear noise, and the convergence accuracy can reach 1×10^{-3}. It can be seen that the convergence accuracy of the ADIZNN model (19) does not decrease with the increase of linear noise $z_i(t)$. Besides, the detailed comparison of the three models under the four different noises is given in Table 1.

Furthermore, the different parameters of ADIZNN (19) are reported for the DSE with (35) under the noise $z_i(t) = 16t + 4$ in Figure 4. The parameter $\lambda = 1$ of the ADIZNN is fixed, and $\xi = 1.2$, $\xi = 2.4$, $\xi = 3.6$ are selected respectively in Figure 4a. Then, the parameter $\xi = 1$ of the ADIZNN is fixed, and $\lambda = 0.8$, $\lambda = 1.6$, $\lambda = 2.4$ are investigated respectively in Figure 4b. From Figure 4a,b, as ξ and λ increase, the convergence speed of ADIZNN (19) becomes faster. By contrast, the gain of parameter λ on the convergence rate of the model is greater than that of parameter ξ.

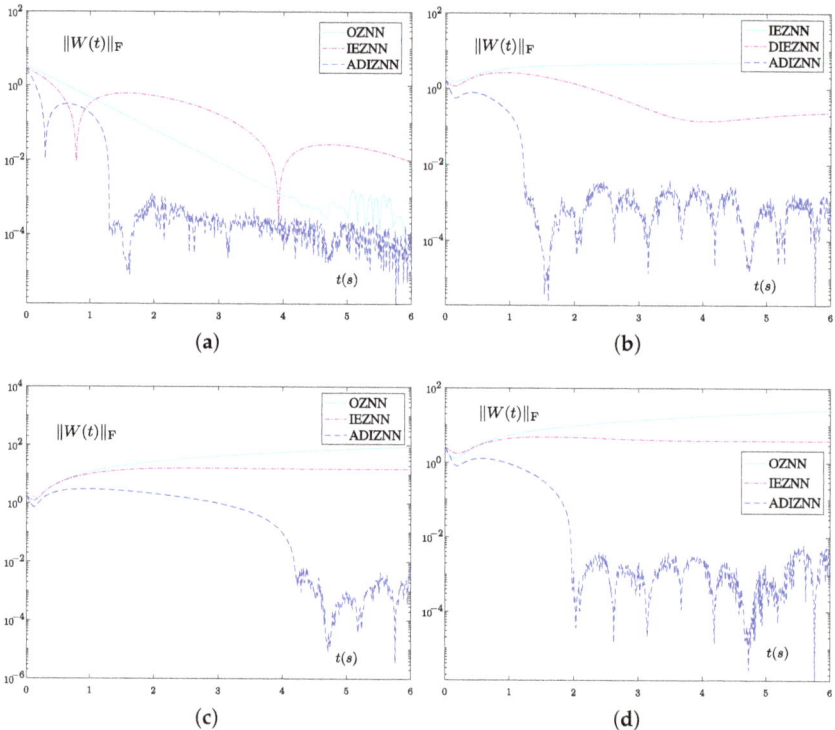

Figure 3. Error norms $\|W(t)\|_F$ of OZNN (9), IEZNN (12) and ADIZNN (19) for the DSE with (35) in different noise environments. (**a**) No noise $z_i(t) = 0$. (**b**) Linear noise $z_i(t) = t/4 + 4$. (**c**) Linear noise $z_i(t) = 4t + 4$. (**d**) Linear noise $z_i(t) = 16t + 4$.

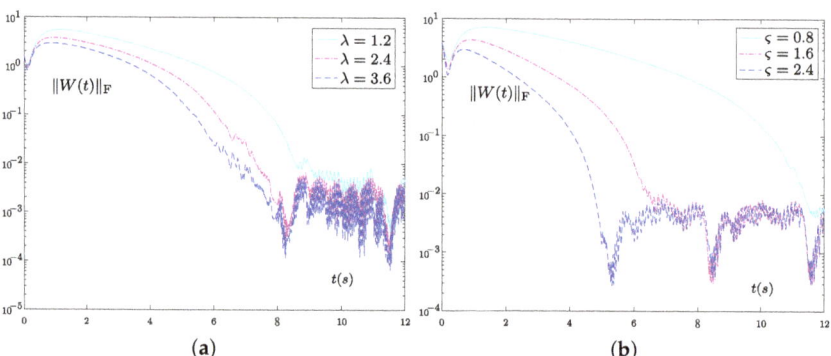

Figure 4. Error norms $\|W(t)\|_F$ of ADIZNN (19) with different parameters for the DSE with (35) in linear noise $z_i(t) = 16t + 4$. (**a**) Fixed $\lambda = 1$, different ς. (**b**) Fixed $\varsigma = 1$, different λ.

Table 1. The detailed comparison of OZNN (9), IEZNN (12) and ADIZNN (19) with $\xi = 2$ and $\lambda = 1$ for the DSE with (35) under the different noise environments.

Noise	OZNN Model (9)	IEZNN Model (12)	ADIZNN Model (19)
$z_i(t) = 0$	convergent	convergent	convergent
$z_i(t) = t/4 + 4$	diverging	diverging	convergent
$z_i(t) = 4t + 4$	diverging	diverging	convergent
$z_i(t) = 16t + 4$	diverging	diverging	convergent

4.2. Experiment 2

Furthermore, the two-dimensional matrices are extended to the four-dimensional matrices are considered:

$$U(t) = \begin{bmatrix} s(t) & -s(t) & -s(t) & c(t) \\ s(t) & c(t) & c(t) & s(t) \\ s(t) & -c(t) & c(t) & -s(t) \\ -c(t) & -s(t) & s(t) & c(t) \end{bmatrix},$$

$$V(t) = \begin{bmatrix} t & 0 & 0 & 0 \\ 0 & \frac{1}{t+1} & 0 & 0 \\ 0 & 0 & t+2 & 0 \\ 0 & 0 & 0 & 1 \end{bmatrix}, G(t) = \begin{bmatrix} s(3t) & s(3t) & s(3t) & c(3t) \\ 0 & s(3t) & c(3t) & c(3t) \\ 0 & 0 & c(3t) & c(3t) \\ 0 & 0 & 0 & c(3t) \end{bmatrix}. \qquad (36)$$

The parameters of FTAF (14) are $\varepsilon_1 = \varepsilon_2 = \varepsilon_3 = \varepsilon_4 = 0.5$ and $\mu = 0.5, \sigma = 2$.

Figure 5 presents the error norms $\|W(t)\|_F$ of OZNN (9), IEZNN (12) and ADIZNN (19) with $\xi = 2$ and $\lambda = 1$ under the different noise environments for the four-dimensional matrices (36). In Figure 5a, all three models can achieve convergence in a noiseless environment, but the convergence rate of ADIZNN (19) is much faster than OZNN (9) and IEZNN (12). However, the convergence time of these three models is very different. ADIZNN (19) can achieve convergence within 1.1 s, OZNN (9) can achieve convergence within 5.2 s, and IEZNN (12) takes a longer time to achieve convergence. Figure 5b–d presents the error norms $\|W(t)\|_F$ of ADIZNN (19) can achieve convergence, while the error norms of the other two models are diverging. It can be seen that when the noise are $z_i(t) = t/4 + 4$, $z_i(t) = 4t + 4$ and $z_i(t) = 16t + 4$, the convergence time of ADIZNN (19) are 1.1 s, 2.1 s and 4.3 s, respectively. It shows that only ADIZNN (19) can still solve the DSE problem under linear noise well for the high-dimensional matrices.

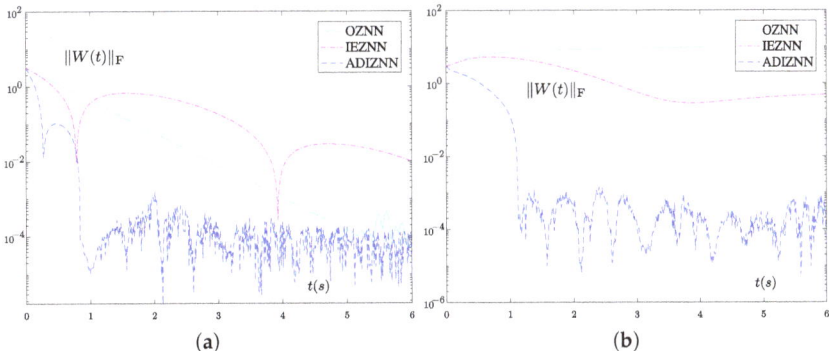

Figure 5. *Cont.*

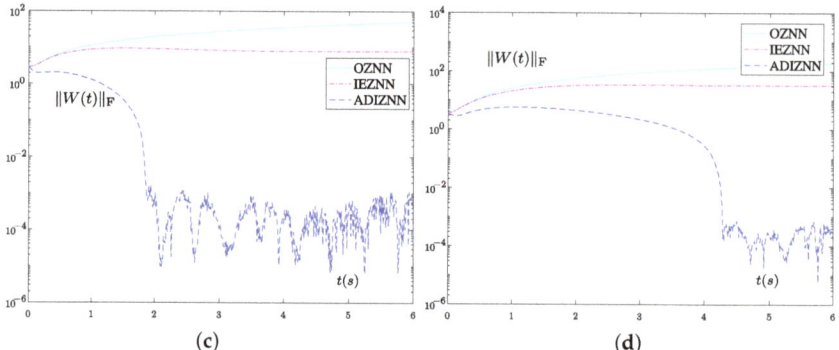

Figure 5. Error norms $\|W(t)\|_F$ of OZNN (9), IEZNN (12) and ADIZNN (19) for the DSE with (36) in different noise environments. (**a**) $z_i(t) = 0$. (**b**) $z_i(t) = t/4 + 4$. (**c**) $z_i(t) = 4t + 4$. (**d**) $z_i(t) = 16t + 4$.

5. Application to the Control of the Sine Function Memristor Chaotic System

The design method of ZNN can not only be effectively used to solve the DSE, but also can be utilized for the control of the chaotic system. Chaotic system [46] is a kind of common nonlinear systems, which is widely used in secure communication [47,48], power systems and network systems [49–51]. Hence, the SFM chaotic control system [52] and three controllers based on ZNNs are presented in this section.

The SFM [52] is introduced in detail as follows:

$$\begin{cases} \dot{x}_1(t) = s(x_2(t)), \\ \dot{x}_2(t) = -\frac{1}{3}s(x_1(t)) + \frac{1}{2}s(x_2(t)) - \frac{1}{2}\eta^2 s(x_2(t))s^2(x_3(t)), \\ \dot{x}_3(t) = -s(x_2(t)) - 0.6s(x_3(t)) + \eta s(x_2(t))s(x_3(t)), \end{cases} \quad (37)$$

where $X(t) = [x_1(t), x_2(t), x_3(t)]^T$ are state variables.

When considering uncertainties, noise and the controller, (37) is rewritten as

$$\begin{cases} \dot{x}_1(t) = s(x_2(t)) + \Delta f_1(x) + \hbar_1(t) + u_1(t), \\ \dot{x}_2(t) = -\frac{1}{3}s(x_1(t)) + \frac{1}{2}s(x_2(t)) - \frac{1}{2}\eta^2 s(x_2(t))s^2(x_3(t)) + \Delta f_2(x) + \hbar_2(t) + u_2(t), \\ \dot{x}_3(t) = -s(x_2(t)) - 0.6s(x_3(t)) + \eta s(x_2(t))s(x_3(t)) + \Delta f_3(x) + \hbar_3(t) + u_3(t), \end{cases} \quad (38)$$

where $\Delta f_1(x)$, $\Delta f_2(x)$ and $\Delta f_3(x)$ are uncertainties of the system, $\hbar_1(t)$, $\hbar_2(t)$ and $\hbar_3(t)$ refer to external disturbances, $u_1(t)$, $u_2(t)$ and $u_3(t)$ represent the controllers.

Define error $\mathcal{E}(t) = X(t) - 0$, where $\mathcal{E}(t) = [e_1(t), e_2(t), e_3(t)]^T$.

According to design Formula (7), we have

$$\dot{\mathcal{E}}(t) = -\xi \mathcal{E}(t). \quad (39)$$

Thus, combining (38) and (39), the controller based on OZNN (39) is

$$\begin{cases} u_1(t) = -\xi x_1(t) - s(x_2(t)), \\ u_2(t) = -\xi x_2(t) + \frac{1}{3}s(x_1(t)) - \frac{1}{2}s(x_2(t)) + \frac{1}{2}\eta^2 s(x_2(t))s^2(x_3(t)), \\ u_3(t) = -\xi x_3(t) + s(x_2(t)) + 0.6s(x_3(t)) - \eta s(x_2(t))s(x_3(t)). \end{cases} \quad (40)$$

Based on the (10), we get

$$\dot{\mathcal{E}}(t) = -\xi \mathcal{E}(t) - \lambda \int_0^t \mathcal{E}(\tau) d\tau. \quad (41)$$

Similarly, combining (38) and (41), we have the controller based on IEZNN (41) as follows:

$$\begin{cases} u_1(t) = -\xi x_1(t) - \lambda \int_0^t x_1(\tau)d\tau - s(x_2(t)), \\ u_2(t) = -\xi x_2(t) - \lambda \int_0^t x_2(\tau)d\tau + \frac{1}{3}s(x_1(t)) - \frac{1}{2}s(x_2(t)) + \frac{1}{2}\eta^2 s(x_2(t))s^2(x_3(t)), \\ u_3(t) = -\xi x_3(t) - \lambda \int_0^t x_3(\tau)d\tau + s(x_2(t)) + 0.6s(x_3(t)) - \eta s(x_2(t))s(x_3(t)). \end{cases} \quad (42)$$

Analogously, the design formula of the ADIZNN is

$$\begin{aligned} \dot{\mathcal{E}}(t) = &-2\lambda \mathcal{E}(t) - \xi\Phi(\mathcal{E}(t)) - \lambda^2 \int_0^t \mathcal{E}(\tau)d\tau - 2\lambda\xi \int_0^t \Phi(\mathcal{E}(\tau))d\tau \\ &- \lambda^2 \xi \int_0^t \int_0^\tau \Phi(\mathcal{E}(\sigma))d\sigma d\tau. \end{aligned} \quad (43)$$

Thus, combining (38) and (43), the controller based on ADIZNN (43) is

$$\begin{cases} u_1(t) = -2\lambda x_1(t) - \xi\phi(x_1(t)) - \lambda^2 \int_0^t x_1(\tau)d\tau - 2\lambda\xi \int_0^t \phi(x_1(\tau))d\tau \\ \qquad - \lambda^2 \xi \int_0^t \int_0^\tau \phi(x_1(\sigma))d\sigma d\tau - s(x_2(t)), \\ u_2(t) = -2\lambda x_2(t) - \xi\phi(x_2(t)) - \lambda^2 \int_0^t x_2(\tau)d\tau - 2\lambda\xi \int_0^t \phi(x_2(\tau))d\tau \\ \qquad - \lambda^2 \xi \int_0^t \int_0^\tau \phi(x_2(\sigma))d\sigma d\tau + \frac{1}{3}s(x_1(t)) - \frac{1}{2}s(x_2(t)) + \frac{1}{2}\eta^2 s(x_2(t))s^2(x_3(t)), \\ u_3(t) = -2\lambda x_3(t) - \xi\phi(x_3(t)) - \lambda^2 \int_0^t x_3(\tau)d\tau - 2\lambda\xi \int_0^t \phi(x_3(\tau))d\tau \\ \qquad - \lambda^2 \xi \int_0^t \int_0^\tau \phi(x_3(\sigma))d\sigma d\tau + \frac{1}{3}s(x_1(t)) + \frac{1}{2}s(x_2(t)) - \frac{1}{2}\eta^2 s(x_2(t))s^2(x_3(t)). \end{cases} \quad (44)$$

Let $\Delta f(x) = [s(x_2(t)), 2c(x_1(t)), 3s(x_1(t))c(x_3(t))]^T$, $\hbar(t) = [t/4 + 4] \in \mathbb{R}^{3 \times 1}$ and set the $\eta = 3$, $\xi = 2$ and $\lambda = 1$, the ADIZNN model using the FTAF with $\varepsilon_1 = \varepsilon_2 = \varepsilon_3 = \varepsilon_4 = 0.5$ and $\mu = 0.5$, $\sigma = 2$. Figure 6a presents space tracks of the original system (37) under no controller. Figure 6b–d indicate space tracks of system (38) under controller (40), controller (42) and controller (44) from initial values $X(0) = [0.1, 0.1, 0.1]^T$. The end points of system (38) under controller (40), controller (42) and controller (44) are respectively $[1266, 1266, 1266]^T$, $[0.9748, 0.9918, -0.0518]^T$ and $[-0.0033, 0.0047, 9.952 \times 10^{-7}]^T$. Figure 7a presents states of original system (37). It is obvious from the Figure 7b–d that the state (i.e., errors) of system (38) under controller (40) and controller (42) cannot reach zero in a three-dimensional space. At the same time, the state of and controller (44) can stable to zero. From the above data, it can be seen that the phase of the SFM system under controller (44) is fairly close to zero with a tiny error, and we hope that the end point of the phase of controller is the closest to zero, so as to achieve the smallest error as possible. The experimental results substantiate the effectiveness and feasibility of the controller (44). In other words, a double integral design scheme can also effectively suppress the existing linear noise and other additional interference items in the application of sine function memristor chaotic system control.

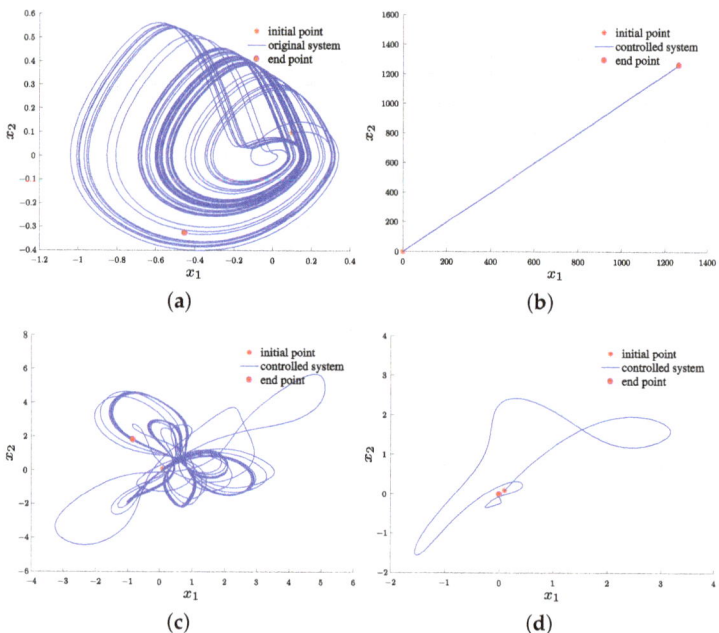

Figure 6. Phases of the original SFM system and the SFM under controller (40), controller (42) and controller (44) from $X(0) = [0.1, 0.1, 0.1]^T$. (**a**) Original SFM system; (**b**) By controller (40); (**c**) By controller (42); (**d**) By controller (44).

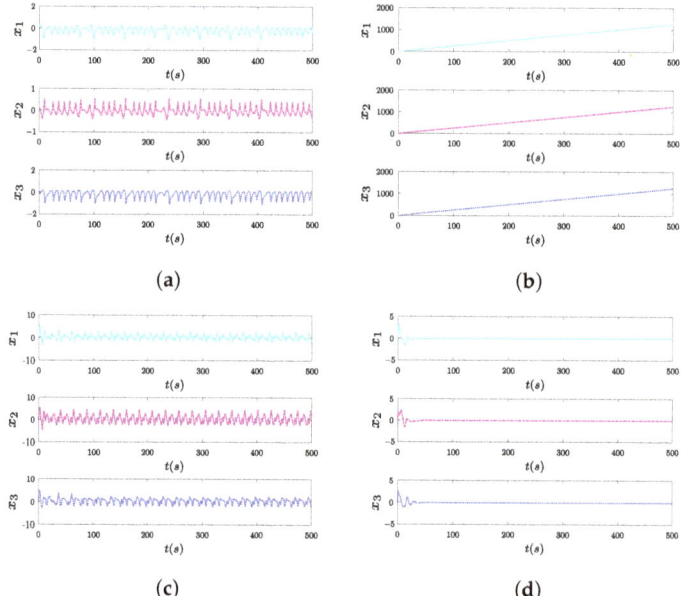

Figure 7. State trajectories of the original SFM system and the SFM under controller (40), controller (42) and controller (44) from $X(0) = [0.1, 0.1, 0.1]^T$. (**a**) Original SFM system; (**b**) By controller (40); (**c**) By controller (42); (**d**) By controller (44).

6. Conclusions

An innovative ZNN with a double integral was proposed, which can settle the DSE under linear noise. It is worth mentioning that the ADIZNN model has excellent convergence and robustness, which has been verified by theory. Additionally, two different dimensional experiments have revealed that the ADIZNN has more remarkable convergence and antinoise ability than the OZNN and IEZNN under various linear noises. Finally, phases and states trajectories of the SFM chaotic system synthesized by several controllers have been given to indicate that the controller based on ADIZNN has the highest convergence rate in three-dimensional space.

Author Contributions: Conceptualization, L.H. and Y.H.; methodology, C.H. and B.L.; software, Y.H.; validation, L.H. and B.L.; formal analysis, C.H.; investigation, Y.H.; data curation, Y.H. and C.H.; writing—original draft preparation, L.H.; writing—review and editing, B.L. and L.H.; visualization, Y.H.; supervision, B.L. and Y.H.; project administration, B.L.; funding acquisition, B.L. and L.H. All authors have read and agreed to the published version of the manuscript.

Funding: This work was funded by the National Natural Science Foundation of China under Grants 62066015 and 61962023; the Natural Science Foundation of Hunan Province of China under grant 2020JJ4511; and the Research Foundation of Education Bureau of Hunan Province of China under Grant 20A396; and the Hunan Provincial Innovation Foundation For Postgraduate under grant CX20221105.

Institutional Review Board Statement: Not applicable.

Informed Consent Statement: Not applicable.

Data Availability Statement: Not applicable.

Conflicts of Interest: The authors declare no conflict of interest.

Abbreviations

The following abbreviations are used in this manuscript:

DSE	Dynamic Sylvester equation
ZNN	Zeroing neural network
OZNN	Original zeroing neural network
ADIZNN	Accelerated double integral ZNN
SFM	Sine function memristor
RNNs	recurrent neural networks
GNN	Gradient neural network
IEZNN	integral enhanced ZNN model
FTAF	fixed-time activation function

References

1. Wei, Q.; Dobigeon, N.; Tourneret, J.Y.; Bioucas-Dias, J.; Godsill, S. R-FUSE: Robust fast fusion of multiband images based on solving a Sylvester equation. *IEEE Signal Process. Lett.* **2016**, *23*, 1632–1636. [CrossRef]
2. Huo, L.; Yang, S.; Jiao, L.; Wang, S.; Shi, J. Local graph regularized coding for salient object detection. *Infrared Phys. Technol.* **2016**, *77*, 124–131. [CrossRef]
3. Shaker, H.R.; Tahavori, M. Control configuration selection for bilinear systems via generalised Hankel interaction index array. *Int. J. Control* **2015**, *88*, 30–37. [CrossRef]
4. Dolgov, S.; Pearson, J.W.; Savostyanov, D.V.; Stoll, M. Fast tensor product solvers for optimization problems with fractional differential equations as constraints. *Appl. Math. Comput.* **2016**, *273*, 604–623. [CrossRef]
5. Jin, L.; Yan, J.; Du, X.; Xiao, X.; Fu, D. RNN for solving time-variant generalized Sylvester equation with applications to robots and acoustic source localization. *IEEE Trans. Ind. Inform.* **2020**, *16*, 6359–6369. [CrossRef]
6. Katsikis, V.N.; Mourtas, S.D.; Stanimirović, P.S.; Zhang, Y. Solving complex-valued time-varying linear matrix equations via QR decomposition with applications to robotic motion tracking and on angle-of-arrival localization. *IEEE Trans. Neural Netw. Learn. Syst.* **2021**, *33*, 3415–3424. [CrossRef] [PubMed]
7. Li, W.; Han, L.; Xiao, X.; Liao, B.; Peng, C. A gradient-based neural network accelerated for vision-based control of an RCM-constrained surgical endoscope robot. *Neural Comput. Appl.* **2022**, *34*, 1329–1343. [CrossRef]

8. Li, Z.; Liao, B.; Xu, F.; Guo, D. A new repetitive motion planning scheme with noise suppression capability for redundant robot manipulators. *IEEE Trans. Syst. Man Cybern. Syst.* **2018**, *50*, 5244–5254. [CrossRef]
9. Liao, B.; Han, L.; Cao, X.; Li, S.; Li, J. Double integral-enhanced Zeroing neural network with linear noise rejection for time-varying matrix inverse. *CAAI Trans. Intell. Technol.* **2023**, 1–14. [CrossRef]
10. Yan, X.; Liu, M.; Jin, L.; Li, S.; Hu, B.; Zhang, X.; Huang, Z. New zeroing neural network models for solving nonstationary Sylvester equation with verifications on mobile manipulators. *IEEE Trans. Ind. Inform.* **2019**, *15*, 5011–5022. [CrossRef]
11. Song, C.; Feng, J.; Wang, X.; Zhao, J. Finite iterative method for solving coupled Sylvester-transpose matrix equations. *J. Appl. Math. Comput.* **2014**, *46*, 351–372. [CrossRef]
12. Ali Beik, F.P.; Movahed, F.S.; Ahmadi-Asl, S. On the Krylov subspace methods based on tensor format for positive definite Sylvester tensor equations. *Numer. Linear Algebra Appl.* **2016**, *23*, 444–466. [CrossRef]
13. Wu, H.C.; Chen, T.C.T.; Chiu, M.C. Constructing a precise fuzzy feedforward neural network using an independent fuzzification approach. *Axioms* **2021**, *10*, 282. [CrossRef]
14. Tuyen, D.N.; Tuan, T.M.; Le, X.H.; Tung, N.T.; Chau, T.K.; Van Hai, P.; Gerogiannis, V.C.; Son, L.H. RainPredRNN: A new approach for precipitation nowcasting with weather radar echo images based on deep learning. *Axioms* **2022**, *11*, 107. [CrossRef]
15. Su, L.; Zhou, L. Exponential synchronization of memristor-based recurrent neural networks with multi-proportional delays. *Neural Comput. Appl.* **2019**, *31*, 7907–7920. [CrossRef]
16. Khan, A.H.; Li, S.; Luo, X. Obstacle avoidance and tracking control of redundant robotic manipulator: An RNN-based metaheuristic approach. *IEEE Trans. Ind. Inform.* **2019**, *16*, 4670–4680. [CrossRef]
17. Jin, L.; Li, S.; Hu, B. RNN models for dynamic matrix inversion: A control-theoretical perspective. *IEEE Trans. Ind. Inform.* **2017**, *14*, 189–199. [CrossRef]
18. He, X.; Liu, Q.; Yang, Y. MV-GNN: Multi-view graph neural network for compression artifacts reduction. *IEEE Trans. Image Process.* **2020**, *29*, 6829–6840. [CrossRef]
19. Zhang, Y.; Jiang, D.; Wang, J. A recurrent neural network for solving Sylvester equation with time-varying coefficients. *IEEE Trans. Neural Netw.* **2002**, *13*, 1053–1063. [CrossRef]
20. Zhang, Z.; Zheng, L.; Weng, J.; Mao, Y.; Lu, W.; Xiao, L. A new varying-parameter recurrent neural-network for online solution of time-varying Sylvester equation. *IEEE Trans. Cybern.* **2018**, *48*, 3135–3148. [CrossRef] [PubMed]
21. Xiao, L.; Zhang, Z.; Zhang, Z.; Li, W.; Li, S. Design, verification and robotic application of a novel recurrent neural network for computing dynamic Sylvester equation. *Neural Netw.* **2018**, *105*, 185–196. [CrossRef]
22. Qiu, B.; Zhang, Y.; Yang, Z. New discrete-time ZNN models for least-squares solution of dynamic linear equation system with time-varying rank-deficient coefficient. *IEEE Trans. Neural Netw. Learn. Syst.* **2018**, *29*, 5767–5776. [CrossRef] [PubMed]
23. He, Y.; Liao, B.; Xiao, L.; Han, L.; Xiao, X. Double accelerated convergence ZNN with noise-suppression for handling dynamic matrix inversion. *Mathematics* **2021**, *10*, 50. [CrossRef]
24. Xiao, L.; He, Y.; Li, Y.; Dai, J. Design and analysis of two nonlinear ZNN models for matrix LR and QR factorization with application to 3D moving target location. *IEEE Trans. Ind. Inform.* **2022**, 1–11. [CrossRef]
25. Katsikis, V.N.; Mourtas, S.D.; Stanimirović, P.S.; Zhang, Y. Continuous-time varying complex QR decomposition via zeroing neural dynamics. *Neural Process Lett.* **2021**, *53*, 3573–3590. [CrossRef]
26. Xiao, L.; He, Y. A noise-suppression ZNN model with new variable parameter for dynamic Sylvester equation. *IEEE Trans. Ind. Inform.* **2021**, *17*, 7513–7522. [CrossRef]
27. Tang, G.; Li, X.; Xu, Z.; Li, S.; Zhou, X. An integration-enhanced noise-resistant RNN model with superior performance illustrated via time-varying sylvester equation solving. In Proceedings of the IEEE 2020 Chinese Control And Decision Conference (CCDC), Hefei, China, 22–24 August 2020; pp. 1906–1911.
28. Gong, J.; Jin, J. A faster and better robustness zeroing neural network for solving dynamic Sylvester equation. *Neural Process Lett.* **2021**, *53*, 3591–3606. [CrossRef]
29. Han, L.; Liao, B.; He, Y.; Xiao, X. Dual noise-suppressed ZNN with predefined-time convergence and its application in matrix inversion. In Proceedings of the IEEE 2021 11th International Conference on Intelligent Control and Information Processing (ICICIP), Denver, CO, USA, 28–30 September 2021; pp. 410–415.
30. Xiao, L.; He, Y.; Dai, J.; Liu, X.; Liao, B.; Tan, H. A variable-parameter noise-tolerant zeroing neural network for time-variant matrix inversion with guaranteed robustness. *IEEE Trans. Neural Netw. Learn. Syst.* **2020**, *33*, 1535–1545. [CrossRef]
31. Guo, D.; Li, S.; Stanimirović, P.S. Analysis and application of modified ZNN design with robustness against harmonic noise. *IEEE Trans. Ind. Inform.* **2019**, *16*, 4627–4638. [CrossRef]
32. Jin, L.; Zhang, Y.; Li, S. Integration-enhanced Zhang neural network for real-time-varying matrix inversion in the presence of various kinds of noises. *IEEE Trans. Neural Netw. Learn. Syst.* **2015**, *27*, 2615–2627. [CrossRef]
33. Dzieciol, H.; Sillekens, E.; Lavery, D. Extending phase noise tolerance in UDWDM access networks. In Proceedings of the 2020 IEEE Photonics Society Summer Topicals Meeting Series (SUM), Virtual, 13–15 July 2020; pp. 1–2.
34. Xiang, Q.; Liao, B.; Xiao, L.; Jin, L. A noise-tolerant Z-type neural network for time-dependent pseudoinverse matrices. *Optik* **2018**, *165*, 16–28. [CrossRef]
35. Johnson, M.A.; Moradi, M.H. *PID Control*; Springer: Berlin/Heidelberg, Germany, 2005.
36. Liao, B.; Han, L.; He, Y.; Cao, X.; Li, J. Prescribed-time convergent adaptive ZNN for time-varying matrix inversion under harmonic noise. *Electronics* **2022**, *11*, 1636. [CrossRef]

37. Jin, J.; Qiu, L. A robust fast convergence zeroing neural network and its applications to dynamic Sylvester equation solving and robot trajectory tracking. *J. Frankl. Inst.* **2022**, *359*, 3183–3209. [CrossRef]
38. Zhang, Y.; Yi, C.; Guo, D.; Zheng, J. Comparison on Zhang neural dynamics and gradient-based neural dynamics for online solution of nonlinear time-varying equation. *Neural Comput. Appl.* **2011**, *20*, 1–7. [CrossRef]
39. Zhang, Y.; Jin, L.; Ke, Z. Superior performance of using hyperbolic sine activation functions in ZNN illustrated via time-varying matrix square roots finding. *Comput. Sci. Inf. Syst.* **2012**, *9*, 1603–1625. [CrossRef]
40. Yang, Y.; Zhang, Y. Superior robustness of power-sum activation functions in Zhang neural networks for time-varying quadratic programs perturbed with large implementation errors. *Neural Comput. Appl.* **2013**, *22*, 175–185. [CrossRef]
41. Zhang, Y.; Ding, Y.; Qiu, B.; Zhang, Y.; Li, X. Signum-function array activated ZNN with easier circuit implementation and finite-time convergence for linear systems solving. *Inf. Process. Lett.* **2017**, *124*, 30–34. [CrossRef]
42. Benner, P. Factorized solution of Sylvester equations with applications in control. *Sign (H)* **2004**, *1*, 2.
43. Castelan, E.B.; da Silva, V.G. On the solution of a Sylvester equation appearing in descriptor systems control theory. *Syst. Control Lett.* **2005**, *54*, 109–117. [CrossRef]
44. Wei, Q.; Dobigeon, N.; Tourneret, J.Y. Fast fusion of multi-band images based on solving a Sylvester equation. *IEEE Trans. Image Process.* **2015**, *24*, 4109–4121. [CrossRef]
45. Diao, H.; Shi, X.; Wei, Y. Effective condition numbers and small sample statistical condition estimation for the generalized Sylvester equation. *Sci. China Math.* **2013**, *56*, 967–982. [CrossRef]
46. Zhang, R.; Xi, X.; Tian, H.; Wang, Z. Dynamical analysis and finite-time synchronization for a chaotic system with hidden attractor and surface equilibrium. *Axioms* **2022**, *11*, 579. [CrossRef]
47. Rasouli, M.; Zare, A.; Hallaji, M.; Alizadehsani, R. The synchronization of a class of time-delayed chaotic systems using sliding mode control based on a fractional-order nonlinear PID sliding surface and its application in secure communication. *Axioms* **2022**, *11*, 738. [CrossRef]
48. He, W.; Luo, T.; Tang, Y.; Du, W.; Tian, Y.C.; Qian, F. Secure communication based on quantized synchronization of chaotic neural networks under an event-triggered strategy. *IEEE Trans. Neural Netw. Learn. Syst.* **2019**, *31*, 3334–3345. [CrossRef] [PubMed]
49. Xiao, L.; He, Y.; Liao, B. A parameter-changing zeroing neural network for solving linear equations with superior fixed-time convergence. *Expert Syst. Appl.* **2022**, *208*, 118086. [CrossRef]
50. Su, H.; Luo, R.; Huang, M.; Fu, J. Robust fixed time control of a class of chaotic systems with bounded uncertainties and disturbances. *Int. J. Control Autom. Syst.* **2022**, *20*, 813–822. [CrossRef]
51. Singer, J.; Wang, Y.; Bau, H.H. Controlling a chaotic system. *Phys. Rev. Lett.* **1991**, *66*, 1123. [CrossRef]
52. Sun, J.; Zhao, X.; Fang, J.; Wang, Y. Autonomous memristor chaotic systems of infinite chaotic attractors and circuitry realization. *Nonlinear Dyn.* **2018**, *94*, 2879–2887. [CrossRef]

Disclaimer/Publisher's Note: The statements, opinions and data contained in all publications are solely those of the individual author(s) and contributor(s) and not of MDPI and/or the editor(s). MDPI and/or the editor(s) disclaim responsibility for any injury to people or property resulting from any ideas, methods, instructions or products referred to in the content.

Article

Tolerance Limits and Sample-Size Determination Using Weibull Trimmed Data

Arturo J. Fernández

Departamento de Matemáticas, Estadística e Investigación Operativa and Instituto de Matemáticas y Aplicaciones (IMAULL), Universidad de La Laguna (ULL), 38071 Santa Cruz de Tenerife, Spain; ajfernan@ull.es

Abstract: Guaranteed-coverage and expected-coverage tolerance limits for Weibull models are derived when, owing to restrictions on data collection, experimental difficulties, the presence of outliers, or some other extraordinary reasons, certain proportions of the extreme sample values have been censored or disregarded. Unconditional and conditional tolerance bounds are presented and compared when some of the smallest observations have been discarded. In addition, the related problem of determining minimum sample sizes for setting Weibull tolerance limits from trimmed data is discussed when the numbers or proportions of the left and right trimmed observations are fixed. Step-by-step procedures for determining optimal sampling plans are also presented. Several numerical examples are included for illustrative purposes.

Keywords: missing or discarded data; guaranteed-coverage and expected-coverage tolerance limits; optimal sampling plans; unconditional and conditional tolerance limits

MSC: 62F25; 62N05; 62N01; 62G30

Citation: Fernández, A.J. Tolerance Limits and Sample-Size Determination Using Weibull Trimmed Data. *Axioms* **2023**, *12*, 351. https://doi.org/10.3390/axioms12040351

Academic Editors: Nuno Bastos, Touria Karite and Amir Khan

Received: 10 February 2023
Revised: 20 March 2023
Accepted: 29 March 2023
Published: 2 April 2023

Copyright: © 2023 by the author. Licensee MDPI, Basel, Switzerland. This article is an open access article distributed under the terms and conditions of the Creative Commons Attribution (CC BY) license (https://creativecommons.org/licenses/by/4.0/).

1. Introduction

Tolerance limits are extensively employed in some statistical fields, including statistical quality control, economics, medical and pharmaceutical statistics, environmental monitoring, and reliability analysis. In essence, a tolerance interval describes the behavior of a fraction of individuals. Roughly speaking, the tolerance limits are bounds within which one expects a stated proportion of the population to lie. Two basic types of such limits have received considerable attention, β-content and β-expectation tolerance limits; see Wilks [1], Guttman [2] and Fernández [3] and references therein. Succinctly, a β-content tolerance interval contains at least $100\beta\%$ of the population with certain confidence, whereas a β-expectation tolerance interval covers, on the average, a fraction β of the population.

In life-testing and reliability analysis, the tolerance limits are frequently computed from a complete or right-censored sample. In this paper, the available empirical information is provided by a trimmed sample, i.e., it is assumed that determined proportions q_1 and q_2 of the smallest and largest observations have been eliminated or censored. These kinds of data are frequently used in several areas of statistical practice for deriving robust inferential procedures and detecting influential observations, e.g., Prescott [4], Huber [5], Healy [6], Welsh [7], Wilcox [8], and Fernández [9,10]. In various situations, some extreme sample values may not be recorded due to restrictions on data collection (generally for reasons of economy of money, time, and effort), experimental difficulties or some other extraordinary reasons, or be discarded (especially when some observations are poorly known or the presence of outliers is suspected). In particular, a known number of observations in an ordered sample might be missing at either end (single censoring) or at both ends (double censoring) in failure censored experiments. Specifically, double censoring has been treated by many authors in the statistical literature (among others, Healy [11], Prescott [12], Schneider [13], Bhattacharyya [14], LaRiccia [15], Schneider and Weissfeld [16], Fernández [17,18], Escobar and Meeker [19], Upadhyay and Shastri [20], and Ali Mousa [21]).

The Weibull distribution provides a versatile statistical model for analyzing time-to-event data, which is useful in many fields, including biometry, economics, engineering, management, and the environmental, actuarial, and social sciences. In survival and reliability analysis, this distribution plays a prominent role and has successfully been used to describe animal and human disease mortality, as well as the reliability of both components and equipments in industrial applications. This probability model has many practical applications; e.g., Chen et al. [22], Tsai et al. [23], Aslam et al. [24], Fernández [25], Roy [26], Almongy et al. [27], and Algarni [28]. If the Weibull shape parameter $\alpha = 1$, the distribution is exponential, which plays an notable role in engineering; see Fernández et al. [29], Lee et al. [30], Chen and Yang [31], and Yousef et al. [32]. The random variable is Rayleigh distributed when $\alpha = 2$. This case is also important in various areas; see Aminzadeh [33,34], Raqab and Madi [35], Fernández [36], and Lee et al. [37].

This paper is devoted to deriving tolerance limits using a trimmed sample drawn from a Weibull $W(\theta, \alpha)$ population. It is assumed that α is appropriately chosen while the Weibull scale parameter, θ, is unknown. The conditionality principle, proposed primarily by Fisher, is adopted when some of the smallest observations have been disregarded. The related problem of determining minimum sample sizes is also tackled. In the exponential case, Fernández [38,39] presented optimal two-sided tolerance intervals and tolerance limits for k-out-of-n systems, respectively. On the basis of a complete Rayleigh sample (i.e., $\alpha = 2$), Aminzadeh [33] found β-expectation tolerance limits and discussed the determination of sample size to control stability of coverage, whereas Aminzadeh [34] derived approximate tolerance limits when θ depends on a set of explanatory variables. Weibull tolerance limits based on complete samples were obtained in Thoman et al. [40].

The structure of the remainder of this work is as follows. The sampling distribution of a Weibull trimmed sample is provided in the next section. Section 3 presents β-content tolerance limits based on $W(\theta, \alpha)$ trimmed data. In addition, the problem of determining optimal sample sizes is discussed. Mean-coverage tolerance limits are derived in Section 4. Optimal sampling plans for setting β-expectation tolerance limits are also deduced. The corresponding unconditional and conditional bounds are compared in Sections 3 and 4 when the lower trimming proportion, q_1, is positive, whereas Section 5 includes several numerical examples, reported by Sarhan and Greenberg [41], Meeker and Escobar [42], and Lee and Wang [43], for illustrative purposes. Finally, Section 6 offers some concluding remarks.

2. Weibull Trimmed Samples

The probability density function (pdf) of a random variable X which has a Weibull distribution with positive parameters θ and α, i.e., $X \sim W(\theta, \alpha)$, is defined by

$$f_X(x \mid \theta, \alpha) = \frac{\alpha x^{\alpha-1}/\theta^\alpha}{\exp\{(x/\theta)^\alpha\}}, \quad x > 0. \tag{1}$$

Its k-th moment is obtained to be $E[X^k \mid \theta, \alpha] = \theta^k \Gamma(1 + k/\alpha)$, $k = 1, 2, ...$, where $\Gamma(\cdot)$ is the well-known gamma function. The parameter α controls the shape of the density whereas θ determines its scaling. Since the hazard rate is $h(x \mid \theta, \alpha) = (\alpha/\theta^\alpha)x^{\alpha-1}$ for $x > 0$, the Weibull law may be used to model the survival distribution of a population with increasing ($\alpha > 1$), decreasing ($\alpha < 1$), or constant ($\alpha = 1$) risk. Examples of increasing and decreasing hazard rates are, respectively, patients with lung cancer and patients who undergo successful major surgery. Davis [44] reports several cases in which a constant risk is reasonable, including payroll check errors and radar set component failures.

In many practical applications, Weibull distributions with α in the range 1 to 3 seem appropriate. If $3 \leq \alpha \leq 4$, the $W(\theta, \alpha)$ pdf has a near normal shape; for large α (e.g., $\alpha \geq 10$), the shape of the density is close to that of the (smallest) extreme value density. The Weibull density becomes more symmetric as α grows. In Weibull data analysis it is quite habitual to assume that the shape parameter, α, is a known constant. Among other authors, Soland [45], Tsokos and Rao [46], Lawless [47], and Nordman and Meeker [48] provide justifications. The α value may come from previous or related data or may be a widely accepted value for the problem, or even an expert guess. In reliability analysis, α is often tied to the failure mechanism of the product and so engineers might have some knowledge of it. Klinger et al. [49] provide tables of Weibull parameters for various devices. Abernethy [50] supplies useful information about past experiments with Weibull data. Several situations in which it is appropriate to consider that α is constant are described in Nordman and Meeker [48]. Among many others, Danziger [51], Tsokos and Canavos [52], Moore and Bilikam [53], Kwon [54], and Zhang and Meeker [55] also utilize a given Weibull shape parameter.

Consider a random sample of size n from a Weibull distribution (1) with unknown scale parameter $\theta \in \Theta = (0, \infty)$, and let $X_{r:n}, ..., X_{s:n}$ be the ordered observations remaining when the $(r-1)$ smallest observations and the $(n-s)$ largest observations have been discarded or censored, where $1 \le r \le s \le n$. The trimming proportions $q_1 = (r-1)/n$ and $q_2 = 1 - s/n$, as well as the shape parameter α, are assumed to be predetermined constants.

The pdf of the (q_1, q_2)-trimmed sample $\mathbf{X} = (X_{r:n}, ..., X_{s:n})$ at $\mathbf{x} = (x_{r:n}, ..., x_{s:n})$ is then defined by

$$f_\mathbf{X}(\mathbf{x} \mid \theta, \alpha) = \frac{n! \alpha^{s-r+1}\{1 - \exp(-x_{r:n}^\alpha/\theta^\alpha)\}^{r-1} \prod_{i=r}^{s} x_{i:n}^{\alpha-1}}{(r-1)!(n-s)! \theta^{(s-r+1)\alpha} \exp\{T(\mathbf{x})/\theta^\alpha\}}, \quad (2)$$

for $0 < x_{r:n} < \cdots < x_{s:n}$, where $T(\mathbf{x})$ is the observed value of

$$T \equiv T(\mathbf{X}) = \sum_{i=r}^{s} X_{i:n}^\alpha + (n-s) X_{s:n}^\alpha.$$

Clearly, T is sufficient when $r = 1$, whereas the sample evidence is contained in the sufficient statistic $(X_{r:n}, T)$ if $r > 1$.

The maximum likelihood estimator (MLE) of θ, denoted by $\widehat{\theta} \equiv \widehat{\theta}(\mathbf{X})$, can be derived from the equation $\partial \ln f_\mathbf{X}(\mathbf{X} \mid \theta, \alpha) / \partial \theta = 0$. It is well-known that $\widehat{\theta}$ is the unique solution to the equation

$$(\widehat{\theta})^\alpha = \frac{X_{r:n}^\alpha (r-1)/(s-r+1)}{1 - \exp([X_{r:n}^\alpha/(\widehat{\theta})^\alpha])} + \frac{T}{s-r+1}. \quad (3)$$

See, e.g., Theorem 1 in Fernández et al. [29]. Therefore, the MLE of θ is given explicitly by $\widehat{\theta} = (T/s)^{1/\alpha}$ when $r = 1$. Otherwise, $\widehat{\theta}$ must be found upon using an iterative procedure.

3. Guaranteed-Coverage Tolerance Limits

Given the Weibull (q_1, q_2)-trimmed sample $\mathbf{X} = (X_{r:n}, ..., X_{s:n})$ and $\beta, \gamma \in (0,1)$, a statistic $L_{\beta,\gamma} \equiv L_{\beta,\gamma}(\mathbf{X})$ is called a lower β-content tolerance limit at level of confidence γ (or simply a lower (β, γ)-TL for short) of the $W(\theta, \alpha)$ distribution if

$$\Pr{}^{\mathbf{X}|\theta,\alpha}\left\{\Pr{}^{X|\theta,\alpha}(X > L_{\beta,\gamma}) \ge \beta\right\} = \gamma \quad (4)$$

for all $\theta > 0$, where $\Pr^{\mathbf{X}|\theta,\alpha}\{\cdot\}$ and $\Pr^{X|\theta,\alpha}(\cdot)$ refer to the respective sampling distribution of $\mathbf{X}$ and X under the nominal values of θ and α, which are defined in (1) and (2), respectively.

According to (4), one may guarantee with confidence γ that at least $100\beta\%$ of population measurements will exceed $L_{\beta,\gamma}$. In other words, with confidence γ, the probability that a future observation of $X \sim W(\theta, \alpha)$ will surpass $L_{\beta,\gamma}$ is at least β. Clearly, an upper (β, γ)-TL, $U_{\beta,\gamma} \equiv U_{\beta,\gamma}(\mathbf{X})$, is provided by $L_{1-\beta,1-\gamma}$. In this manner, one can be $100\gamma\%$ confident that at least $100\beta\%$ of Weibull $W(\theta, \alpha)$ observations will be less than $U_{\beta,\gamma}$.

Assuming that $1 < r = s$, as $X_{r:n}$ is minimal sufficient for θ, it is logical to consider a lower (β, γ)-TL for the form $L_{\beta,\gamma} = C_{\beta,\gamma} X_{r:n}$, where, from (4), $C_{\beta,\gamma}$ must satisfy

$$\Pr\left(\exp\left\{-(C_{\beta,\gamma} X_{r:n}/\theta)^\alpha\right\} \ge \beta\right) = \gamma.$$

Since $\exp(-X_{r:n}^\alpha/\theta^\alpha) \sim Beta(n-r+1,r)$, it follows that $\beta^{1/(C_{\beta,\gamma})^\alpha}$ is merely the $(1-\gamma)$-quantile of the $Beta(n-r+1,r)$ distribution. Thus, $C_{\beta,\gamma}$ satisfies the equation

$$\sum_{k=0}^{r-1} \frac{\binom{n}{k}\{1-\beta^{1/(C_{\beta,\gamma})^\alpha}\}^k}{\beta^{(k-n)/(C_{\beta,\gamma})^\alpha}} = 1-\gamma.$$

Alternatively, $C_{\beta,\gamma}$ may be expressed explicitly as

$$C_{\beta,\gamma} = \left(\frac{-\ln\beta}{\ln\{1+rF_{2r,2(n-r+1);\gamma}/(n-r+1)\}} \right)^{1/\alpha}, \tag{5}$$

where $F_{2r,2(n-r+1);\gamma}$ denotes the γ-quantile of the F-distribution with $2r$ and $2(n-r+1)$ degrees of freedom (df). In particular, $C_{\beta,\gamma} = \{n \ln\beta/\ln(1-\gamma)\}^{1/\alpha}$ when $r=s=1$, whereas $C_{\beta,\gamma} = \{\ln\beta/\ln(1-\gamma^{1/n})\}^{1/\alpha}$ if $r=s=n$.

If $1=r \leq s$, it is clear that T is minimal sufficient for θ, which implies that it is sensible to assume that $L_{\beta,\gamma}$ is proportional to $T^{1/\alpha}$, i.e., $L_{\beta,\gamma} = C_{\beta,\gamma} T^{1/\alpha}$. In this situation, it can be shown that $2T/\theta^\alpha \sim \chi^2_{2s}$, where χ^2_{2s} represents the chi-square distribution with $2s$ df. Observe that, letting $X_{0:n} \equiv 0$, the pivotal $2T/\theta^\alpha$ coincides with $\sum_{i=1}^s Z_i$, where $Z_i = 2(n-i+1)(X_{i:n}^\alpha - X_{i-1:n}^\alpha)/\theta^\alpha$, $i=1,..,s$, are mutually independent χ^2_2 variables. Since, in view of (4),

$$\Pr(\exp\{-(C_{\beta,\gamma})^\alpha T/\theta^\alpha\} \geq \beta) = \Pr(2T/\theta^\alpha \leq -2\ln\beta/(C_{\beta,\gamma})^\alpha) = \gamma,$$

it turns out that $C_{\beta,\gamma} = (-2\ln\beta/\chi^2_{2s;\gamma})^{1/\alpha}$. Consequently, $L_{\beta,\gamma} = (-2T\ln\beta/\chi^2_{2s;\gamma})^{1/\alpha}$.

3.1. Unconditional and Conditional Tolerance Limits

When focusing on the more general case, in which $1 < r < s$, obviously $(X_{r:n}, T)$ is a sufficient statistic for θ. Moreover, if $R = T - (n-r+1)X_{r:n}^\alpha$, then $2R/\theta^\alpha \sim \chi^2_{2(s-r)}$ since this pivotal quantity can be expressed as the sum of the $(s-r)$ independent χ^2_2 variables $Z_{r+1}, Z_{r+2}, ..., Z_s$. Therefore, it can be shown that

$$L_{\beta,\gamma} = C_{\beta,\gamma} R^{1/\alpha} = (-2R\ln\beta/\chi^2_{2(s-r);\gamma})^{1/\alpha}$$

constitutes a (unconditional) lower (β,γ)-TL. Notice, however, that this limit is based on an insufficient statistic R.

An alternative and more appropriate TL can be constructed assuming that $A = X_{r:n}^\alpha/R$ is an ancillary statistic. Note that, by itself, A does not contain any information about θ, and that the statistic (R, A) is minimal sufficient for θ. Therefore, given A, the statistic R is conditionally sufficient. In accordance with the conditional principle suggested by Fisher, a tolerance limit should be based on the distribution of R given the observed value of the ancillary statistic A. Then, adopting the above principle and assuming that $A = a$, it is sensible to look for a conditional lower (β,γ)-TL of the form $L_{\beta,\gamma}^a = C_{\beta,\gamma}^a R^{1/\alpha}$, where

$$\Pr{}^{X|\theta,\alpha}\left\{ \Pr{}^{X|\theta,\alpha}\left(X > L_{\beta,\gamma}^a \right) \geq \beta \mid A = a \right\} = \gamma. \tag{6}$$

Thus, as $\Pr(R/\theta^\alpha \leq -\ln\beta/(C_{\beta,\gamma}^a)^\alpha \mid A=a) = \gamma$, it follows that $-\ln\beta/(C_{\beta,\gamma}^a)^\alpha$ is precisely the γ-quantile of the distribution of R/θ^α conditional to $A=a$.

The pdf of $Y = R/\theta^\alpha$ given $A = a$ is derived to be

$$f_Y(y \mid a) = \frac{y^{s-r}\exp[-\{1+(n+1-r)a\}y]}{(s-r)!G[a]\{1-\exp(-ay)\}^{1-r}}, \quad y > 0,$$

where

$$G[a] = \sum_{k=0}^{r-1} \frac{(-1)^i \binom{r-1}{k}}{\{(k+n+1-r)a+1\}^{s-r+1}},$$

whereas the cumulative distribution function of Y conditional to $A = a$ is defined by

$$\Pr(Y \leq y \mid a) = 1 - G^*[y;a]/G[a], \quad y > 0,$$

where

$$G^*[y;a] = \sum_{i=0}^{r-1}\sum_{j=0}^{s-r} \frac{(-1)^i \binom{r-1}{i} y^j \{1+(n-r+1+i)a\}^{j-s+r-1}}{j! \exp[\{1+(n-r+1+i)a\}y]}.$$

Consequently, if y_γ^a denotes the γ-quantile of the distribution of Y given $A = a$, i.e., y_γ^a satisfies the equation $G^*[y_\gamma^a;a] = (1-\gamma)G[a]$, it is obvious that $C_{\beta,\gamma}^a = (-\ln \beta/y_\gamma^a)^{1/\alpha}$. In this way, it follows that $L_{\beta,\gamma}^a = (-R\ln \beta/y_\gamma^a)^{1/\alpha}$.

Of course, $L_{\beta,\gamma}^A \equiv L_{\beta,\gamma}^A(\mathbf{X})$ is also a lower (β,γ)-TL in the ordinary unconditional sense because

$$\Pr{}^{\mathbf{X}|\theta,\alpha}\left\{\Pr{}^{X|\theta,\alpha}\left(X > L_{\beta,\gamma}^A\right) \geq \beta\right\}$$

coincides with

$$E\left[\Pr{}^{\mathbf{X}|\theta,\alpha}\left\{\Pr{}^{X|\theta,\alpha}\left(X > L_{\beta,\gamma}^A\right) \geq \beta \mid A\right\}\right] = E[\gamma] = \gamma.$$

Table 1 compares, for selected values of r, s, and n, the unconditional and conditional lower (β,γ) tolerance factors, $C_{\beta,\gamma}$ and $C_{\beta,\gamma}^{a_\varepsilon}$, corresponding to the $W(\theta,\alpha)$ distribution when $\alpha = 1$, $(\beta,\gamma) = (0.90, 0.95)$ and $A = a_\varepsilon$, $\varepsilon = 0.01, 0.25, 0.75, 0.99$, where a_ε denotes the ε-quantile of the distribution of A. It can be proven that a_ε is the unique positive solution in a to the following equation

$$\sum_{i=0}^{r-1} \frac{(-1)^i r\binom{r-1}{i}\binom{n}{r}/(n-r+1+i)}{\{1+(n-r+1+i)a\}^{s-r}} = 1 - \varepsilon.$$

Table 1. Unconditional and conditional lower (β,γ) tolerance factors, $C_{\beta,\gamma}$ and $C_{\beta,\gamma}^{a_\varepsilon}$, for the $W(\alpha,\theta)$ model based on $\mathbf{X} = (X_{r:n}, \ldots, X_{s:n})$ when $\alpha = 1$, $\beta = 0.90$, and $\gamma = 0.95$.

r	s	n	$C_{\beta,\gamma}$	$C_{\beta,\gamma}^{a_{0.01}}$	$C_{\beta,\gamma}^{a_{0.25}}$	$C_{\beta,\gamma}^{a_{0.75}}$	$C_{\beta,\gamma}^{a_{0.99}}$
2	6	10	0.0135885	0.0103609	0.0124313	0.0183526	0.0450331
	10	20	0.00801336	0.00682716	0.00751394	0.00921814	0.0147077
4	8	30	0.0135885	0.00934313	0.0129005	0.0211442	0.0562717
	20	40	0.00456163	0.00396171	0.00437034	0.00506643	0.00673139
6	10	50	0.0135885	0.00894574	0.0133632	0.0230475	0.0636906
	30	60	0.00323337	0.00285084	0.00312617	0.00353006	0.00438183

It is worthwhile to mention that the difference between $C_{\beta,\gamma}$ and $C_{\beta,\gamma}^{a_\varepsilon}$ might be large when A takes extreme percentiles (i.e., when ε is near to 0 or 1). For instance, if $(r,s,n) = (4,8,30)$, the unconditional factor is $C_{\beta,\gamma} = 0.01359$, whereas the respective conditional factors $C_{\beta,\gamma}^{a_{0.01}}$ and $C_{\beta,\gamma}^{a_{0.99}}$ are given by 0.009343 and 0.05627. The difference between $C_{\beta,\gamma}$ and $C_{\beta,\gamma}^{a_\varepsilon}$ becomes smaller when n grows to infinity and the trimming proportions, q_1 and q_2, are fixed. Indeed, provided that $s - r$ is large, $C_{\beta,\gamma}$ and $C_{\beta,\gamma}^a$ are quite similar. In addition, it turns out that

$$C_{\beta,\gamma} \simeq C_{\beta,\gamma}^* = \left(\frac{-\ln \beta}{s-r+z_\gamma\sqrt{s-r}}\right)^{1/\alpha}$$

from the Wilson–Hilferty transformation (see, e.g., Lawless [47], p. 158), where z_γ is the γ-quantile of the standard normal distribution. For instance, $C_{\beta,\gamma} = 0.001862$ and

$C^*_{\beta,\gamma} = 0.001880$ when $(r,s,n) = (5,50,55)$, $\alpha = 1$ and $(\beta,\gamma) = (0.90, 0.95)$. In this case, $(C^{a_{0.01}}_{\beta,\gamma}, C^{a_{0.99}}_{\beta,\gamma})$ is $(0.001741, 0.002170)$. If one assumes now that $(r,s,n) = (5,90,95)$, then $C_{\beta,\gamma} = 0.001046$ and $C^*_{\beta,\gamma} = 0.001051$, whereas $(C^{a_{0.01}}_{\beta,\gamma}, C^{a_{0.99}}_{\beta,\gamma}) = (0.001007, 0.001134)$.

3.2. Sample-Size Determination

The choice of sample size plays a primordial role in the design of most statistical studies. A traditional approach is to assume that it is desired to find the smallest value of n (and the corresponding values of r and s), such that the lower (β,γ)-TL based of a (q_1, q_2)-trimmed sample $\mathbf{X} = (X_{r:n}, ..., X_{s:n})$ drawn from $X \sim W(\alpha, \theta)$, $L_{\beta,\gamma} \equiv L_{\beta,\gamma}(\mathbf{X})$, satisfies

$$\Pr{}^{X|\theta,\alpha}\left\{\Pr{}^{X|\theta,\alpha}(X > L_{\beta,\gamma}) \geq \beta'\right\} \leq \gamma' \tag{7}$$

for all $\theta > 0$, and certain $\beta' > \beta$ and γ'. In this way, one could affirm that at least $100\beta\%$ of population measurements will exceed $L_{\beta,\gamma}$ with confidence γ, and that at least $100\beta'\%$ of population measurements will surpass $L_{\beta,\gamma}$ with confidence at most γ'. That is to say, the random coverage of $(L_{\beta,\gamma}(\mathbf{X}), +\infty)$ is at least β with probability γ and it is at least $\beta' > \beta$ with a probability not exceeding γ'.

In this subsection, a sampling plan (r,s,n) satisfying condition (7) will be named feasible. Our target is obtaining the optimal (minimum sample size) feasible plan (r,s,n) for setting the lower (β,γ)-TL. For later use, $\lceil x \rceil$ and $\lfloor x \rfloor$ will represent the rounded-up and -down values of x to integer numbers.

Supposing that $1 < r = s \leq n$, it is clear that $L_{\beta,\gamma} = C_{\beta,\gamma} X_{r:n}$ and $L_{\beta',\gamma'} = C_{\beta',\gamma'} X_{r:n}$, where $C_{\beta,\gamma}$ and $C_{\beta',\gamma'}$ are defined in accordance with (5). Thus, condition (7) will hold if and only if $C_{\beta,\gamma} \geq C_{\beta',\gamma'}$. Therefore, (r,r,n) is a feasible sampling plan if and only if $g_1(r,n) \geq 0$, where

$$g_1(r,n) = \frac{\ln\{1 + rF_{2r,2(n-r+1);\gamma'}/(n-r+1)\}}{\ln\{1 + rF_{2r,2(n-r+1);\gamma}/(n-r+1)\}} - \frac{\ln \beta'}{\ln \beta}.$$

Since $F_{2r,2(n-r+1);\gamma} \longrightarrow \chi^2_{2r;\gamma}/(2r)$ when $n \to \infty$ and $\ln(1+t)/t \longrightarrow 1$ as $t \to 0$, there exists a value of n, such that (r,r,n) is feasible if $h_1(r) > 0$, where

$$h_1(r) = \chi^2_{2r;\gamma'}/\chi^2_{2r;\gamma} - \ln \beta' / \ln \beta.$$

Otherwise, the inequation $g_1(r,n) \geq 0$ has no solution in n. On the other hand, provided that $1 = r \leq s \leq n$, as $L_{\beta,\gamma} = (-2T \ln \beta / \chi^2_{2s;\gamma})^{1/\alpha}$ is the lower (β,γ)-TL, the sampling plan $(1,s,n)$ will be feasible if and only if $h_1(s) \geq 0$. Similarly, if $1 < r < s \leq n$, the plan (r,s,n) would be feasible if and only if $h_1(s-r) \geq 0$ because $L_{\beta,\gamma} = (2R \ln \beta / \chi^2_{2(s-r);\gamma})^{1/\alpha}$.

The determination of the optimal feasible sampling plan for setting the lower (β,γ)-TL assuming fixed numbers of trimmed observations (Case I) or fixed trimming proportions (Case II) will be discussed in the remainder of this subsection.

Case I: *Fixed numbers of left and right trimmed observations*

Suppose that the researcher wishes to find the optimal feasible plan (r,s,n), such that $(r-1) = \delta_1$ and $(n-s) = \delta_2$, where δ_1 and δ_2 are prespecified non-negative integers. Then, if $g_1(r,n) \geq 0$ with $r = \delta_1 + 1$ and $n = \delta_1 + \delta_2 + 1$, it follows that $(\delta_1 + 1, \delta_1 + 1, \delta_1 + \delta_2 + 1)$ would be the optimal plan. Otherwise, if m denotes the smallest integer value, such that $h_1(m) \geq 0$, it turns out that

$$(r,s,n) = (\delta_1 + 1, \delta_1 + m + \mathrm{I}(\delta_1 > 0), \delta_1 + \delta_2 + m + \mathrm{I}(\delta_1 > 0))$$

would be the optimal plan, where $\mathrm{I}(\cdot)$ is the indicator function. Observe that m will always exist because $\chi^2_{2k;\gamma'}/\chi^2_{2k;\gamma} \longrightarrow 1$ as $k \to \infty$ and $\ln \beta' / \ln \beta < 1$. It is worthwhile to point out that $m = 1$ if and only if $\gamma' \geq 1 - (1-\gamma)^{\ln \beta'/\ln \beta}$ since $\chi^2_{2;\varepsilon} = -2\ln(1-\varepsilon)$ for $\varepsilon \in (0,1)$. In particular, m is always 1 when $\gamma' \geq \gamma$. Note also that $(\delta_1+1, \delta_1+1, \delta_1+\delta_2+1)$ is not feasible when $m > \delta_1 + 1$.

Due to the fact that $\chi^2_{2k;\varepsilon} \simeq 2k\{1 - 1/(9k) + z_\varepsilon/(9k)^{1/2}\}^3$ when $k \geq 5$ and $\varepsilon \in (0,1)$ from Wilson–Hilferty transformation, it can be proven that m is approximately equal to the smallest integer greater than or equal to ρ, i.e., $m \simeq \lceil \rho \rceil$, where

$$\rho = \{\omega + (\omega^2 + 1/9)^{1/2}\}^2 \quad \text{and} \quad \omega = \frac{z_{\gamma'} - z_\gamma (\ln \beta'/\ln \beta)^{1/3}}{6\{(\ln \beta'/\ln \beta)^{1/3} - 1\}}. \tag{8}$$

It can be proven that the approximation $m \simeq \lceil \rho \rceil$ is exact in practically all cases. Nonetheless, a method for determining the proper value of m would be immediate: using $m_0 = \lceil \rho \rceil$ as initial the guess of m, calculate $h_1(m_0)$ and $h_1(m_0 - 1)$. If $h_1(m_0) \geq 0$ and $h_1(m_0 - 1) < 0$, then $m = m_0$; otherwise, set $m_0 = m_0 - 1$ if $h_1(m_0) < 0$ or set $m_0 = m_0 + 1$ if $h_1(m_0) \geq 0$, and repeat again this process.

Case II: *Fixed left and right trimming proportions*

Assuming that $\pi_i \geq 0$, $i = 1,2$, and $\pi_1 + \pi_2 < 1$, consider now that the researcher desires to obtain the minimum sample size feasible plan (r_n, s_n, n) with $r_n = \lfloor n\pi_1 + 1 \rfloor$ and $s_n = \lceil n(1-\pi_2) \rceil$. In such a case, the left and right trimming proportions, q_1 and q_2, are approximately π_1 and π_2, respectively. Furthermore, $r_n \leq s_n$ and the available observations would be at least $\lceil n(1 - \pi_1 - \pi_2) \rceil$.

Our aim is to determine the smallest integer n, such that $g_1(r_n, n) \geq 0$ if $1 < r_n = s_n$ or such that $h_1(s_n - r_n + I(r_n = 1)) \geq 0$ otherwise. As before, m will represent the smallest integer satisfying $h_1(m) \geq 0$. It is important to take into account that if (r_n, s_n, n) is a feasible plan, then r_n must be greater than or equal to m when $r_n = s_n$. Otherwise, as

$$s_n - r_n + I(r_n = 1) = m, \quad s_n \geq m + 1 - I(r_n = 1) \quad \text{and} \quad n \geq s_n,$$

it follows that $n \geq n_0$, where

$$n_0 = \max\left\{\left\lceil \frac{m - 1 - I(r_n = 1)}{1 - \pi_1 - \pi_2}\right\rceil, \left\lceil \frac{m - I(r_n = 1)}{1 - \pi_2}\right\rceil, m + 1 - I(r_n = 1)\right\}. \tag{9}$$

In addition, since $n(1 - \pi_2) - (n\pi_1 + 1) \leq m - I(r_n = 1)$, it turns out that

$$n \leq \lfloor \{m + 1 - I(r_n = 1)\}/(1 - \pi_1 - \pi_2) \rfloor. \tag{10}$$

On the other side, if $r_n = s_n = k > 1$, it is clear that $k \leq n\pi_1 + 1$ and $n(1 - \pi_2) \leq k$. As a consequence,

$$\lceil (k-1)/\pi_1 \rceil \leq n \leq \lfloor k/(1 - \pi_2) \rfloor.$$

The above results may be helpful for finding the optimal sampling plan. Once the researcher chooses the desired values of $\beta, \gamma, \beta', \gamma', \pi_1, \pi_2 \in (0,1)$, with $\beta < \beta'$ and $\pi_1 + \pi_2 < 1$, a step-by-step procedure for determining the smallest sample size plan (r_n, s_n, n) satisfying (7), where $r_n = \lfloor n\pi_1 + 1 \rfloor$ and $s_n = \lceil n(1-\pi_2) \rceil$, may be described as follows:

- Step 1: If $\gamma' \geq 1 - (1-\gamma)^{\ln \beta'/\ln \beta}$, then set $(r_n, s_n, n) = (1,1,1)$ and go to step 10. Otherwise, find the smallest integer m, such that $h_1(m) \geq 0$ using $m_0 = \lceil \rho \rceil$ as initial guess (see Case I), where ρ is given in (8).
- Step 2: Define $n = n_0$ assuming that $r_n = 1$, where n_0 is provided in (9), and compute r_n and s_n. If $r_n > 1$, redefine $n = n_0$ and recalculate r_n and s_n.
- Step 3: While $(s_n - r_n + I(r_n = 1)) < m$ set $n = n + 1$ and recompute r_n and s_n.
- Step 4: If $r_n < m$, then go to step 10. Otherwise, take $k = m$.
- Step 5: If $k > \lfloor 1/\{1 - \pi_1/(1-\pi_2)\} \rfloor$, go to step 10.

- *Step 6:* Take $n_1 = \lceil (k-1)/\pi_1 \rceil$.
- *Step 7:* If $n_1 > n$, go to step 10.
- *Step 8:* If $n_1 > \lfloor k/(1-\pi_2) \rfloor$, set $k = k+1$ and go to step 7.
- *Step 9:* If $g_1(r_{n_1}, n_1) \geq 0$, then set $(r_n, s_n, n) = (k, k, n_1)$ and $k = k+1$, and go to step 6. Otherwise, let $n_1 = n_1 + 1$ and go to step 7.
- *Step 10:* The optimal sampling plan is given by (r_n, s_n, n).

Table 2 reports the optimal sampling plans (r, s, n) for setting lower (β, γ)-TLs based on the Weibull $W(\theta, \alpha)$ trimmed sample $\mathbf{X} = (X_{r:n}, \ldots, X_{s:n})$ when (i) $q_1 \simeq 0.2$ and $q_2 \simeq 0.3$ and (ii) $r - 1 = 2$ and $n - s = 3$.

Table 2. Optimal sampling plans (r, s, n) for setting lower (β, γ)-TLs for the $W(\alpha, \theta)$ model based on $\mathbf{X} = (X_{r:n}, \ldots, X_{s:n})$ when (i) $q_1 \simeq 0.2$ and $q_2 \simeq 0.3$ and (ii) $r - 1 = 2$ and $n - s = 3$.

				$q_1 \simeq 0.2, q_2 \simeq 0.3$			$r = 3, n - s = 3$		
β	β'	γ	γ'	r	s	n	r	s	n
0.80	0.85	0.90	0.25	16	54	76	3	41	44
			0.50	6	21	29	3	18	21
		0.95	0.25	21	73	103	3	55	58
			0.50	10	35	49	3	28	31
0.90	0.95	0.90	0.25	4	12	16	3	11	14
			0.50	1	3	3	3	3	6
		0.95	0.25	4	14	19	3	13	16
			0.50	2	7	9	3	8	11

For instance, consider that $(\beta, \gamma) = (0.8, 0.9)$ and $(\beta', \gamma') = (0.85, 0.25)$. Assuming that the researcher desires around, 20% and 30% of the smallest and the largest observations be trimmed, respectively, (i.e., $q_1 \simeq \pi_1 = 0.2$ and $q_2 \simeq \pi_2 = 0.3$), as $m = \lceil \rho \rceil = 38$, it follows from (9) and (10) that $72 \leq n \leq 78$. The optimal sampling plan would be precisely $(16, 54, 76)$, i.e., one needs a sample of size $n = 76$, but the smallest 16 and the largest 24 observations are disregarded or censored. The left and right trimming proportions are exactly $q_1 = 0.1974$ and $q_2 = 0.2895$. If it was required that the first two and last three data are discarded or censored (i.e., $r - 1 = 2$ and $n - s = 3$), the optimal sampling would be $(3, 41, 44)$. On the other hand, suppose that $(\beta, \gamma) = (0.9, 0.9)$ and $(\beta', \gamma') = (0.95, 0.50)$. In that case, m also coincides with $\lceil \rho \rceil = 3$. If the researcher assumes that $\pi_1 = 0.2$ and $\pi_2 = 0.3$, then $n_0 = 3$ from (9), whereas $(r_n, s_n, n) = (1, 3, 3)$ is the optimal plan since $s_n - r_n + \mathrm{I}(r_n = 1) \geq m$. The minimum sample size plan would be $(3, 3, 6)$ provided that $r - 1 = 2$ and $n - s = 3$.

4. Expected-Coverage Tolerance Limits

Given the Weibull (q_1, q_2)-trimmed sample $\mathbf{X} = (X_{r:n}, \ldots, X_{s:n})$ and $\beta \in (0, 1)$, a statistic $\mathcal{L}_\beta \equiv \mathcal{L}_\beta(\mathbf{X})$ is called a lower β-expectation tolerance limit (or lower β-ETL for simplicity) of the $W(\theta, \alpha)$ distribution if it satisfies

$$E^{\mathbf{X}|\theta,\alpha}\left[\Pr{}^{X|\theta,\alpha}(X > \mathcal{L}_\beta)\right] = \beta \tag{11}$$

for all $\theta > 0$. In this way, the probability that a future observation of X will surpass $\mathcal{L}_\beta$ is expected to be β. Obviously, an upper β-ETL, $\mathcal{U}_\beta \equiv \mathcal{U}_\beta(\mathbf{X})$, is given by $\mathcal{L}_{1-\beta}$.

Provided that $\beta \in (0, 1)$, our purpose is determining β-ETLs based on the trimmed sample $\mathbf{X} = (X_{r:n}, \ldots, X_{s:n})$ drawn from $X \sim W(\theta, \alpha)$.

Suppose that $1 < r = s$, in which case $X_{r:n}$ is minimal sufficient for θ. It is therefore rational to consider a lower β-ETL of the form $\mathcal{L}_\beta = D_\beta X_{r:n}$, where, from (11), the constant D_β must satisfy

$$E^{\mathbf{X}|\theta,\alpha}\left[\exp\left\{-(D_\beta X_{r:n}/\theta)^\alpha\right\}\right] = \beta.$$

Since $\exp(-X_{r:n}^\alpha/\theta^\alpha) \sim Beta(n-r+1,r)$, D_β is the unique positive solution to the following equation in D

$$\zeta(D) = B(n-r+1+D^\alpha, r)/B(n-r+1, r) = \beta,$$

where $B(\cdot, \cdot)$ is the beta function, i.e., $D_\beta = \zeta^{-1}(\beta)$. Note that $\zeta(\cdot)$ is continuous and decreasing with $\zeta(0) = 1$ and $\zeta(+\infty) = 0$. Therefore, D_β is the positive constant which satisfies the equation

$$\sum_{i=0}^{r-1} \frac{(-1)^i \binom{r-1}{i} r \binom{n}{r}}{n-r+1+i+(D_\beta)^\alpha} = \beta.$$

Observe that $D_\beta = \{n(1-\beta)/\beta\}^{1/\alpha}$ when $r = s = 1$. In general, as

$$\prod_{i=0}^{r-1} \{1 + (D_\beta)^\alpha/(n-i)\} = 1/\beta,$$

it is clear that

$$(n-r+1)^{1/\alpha}(\beta^{-1/r}-1)^{1/\alpha} \leq D_\beta \leq n^{1/\alpha}(\beta^{-1/r}-1)^{1/\alpha}.$$

The above lower and upper bounds on D_β might serve as a starting point for iterative interpolation methods, such as regula falsi. In addition,

$$D_\beta \simeq (n-r/2+1/2)^{1/\alpha}(\beta^{-1/r}-1)^{1/\alpha}$$

when r/n is small.

If $1 = r \leq s$, as T is minimal sufficient for θ, it is evident that $\mathcal{L}_\beta = D_\beta T^{1/\alpha}$ is an appropriate lower β-ETL. Since $2T/\theta^\alpha \sim \chi_{2s}^2$, the tolerance factor is given by $D_\beta = (\beta^{-1/s}-1)^{1/\alpha}$.

4.1. Unconditional and Conditional Tolerance Limits

In the more general case in which $1 < r < s$, the statistic $(X_{r:n}, T)$ is minimal sufficient. Since $2R/\theta^\alpha \sim \chi_{2(s-r)}^2$, where $R = T - (n-r+1)X_{r:n}^\alpha$, it is obvious that $\mathcal{L}_\beta = D_\beta R^{1/\alpha}$ is a (unconditional) lower β-ETL when $D_\beta = \{\beta^{1/(r-s)} - 1\}^{1/\alpha}$. The lower and upper β-ETLs are then given by

$$\mathcal{L}_\beta = \left[\{\beta^{1/(r-s)} - 1\}R\right]^{1/\alpha} \quad \text{and} \quad \mathcal{U}_\beta = \left[\{(1-\beta)^{1/(r-s)} - 1\}R\right]^{1/\alpha}.$$

Nonetheless, as in Section 3, these limits are based on an insufficient statistic R. As mentioned previously, (R, A) is minimal sufficient for θ and $A = X_{r:n}^\alpha/R$ is pivotal for θ. Thus, if ones adopts the conditionality principle and assumes that $A = a$, it is then natural to seek a conditional lower β-ETL of the form $\mathcal{L}_\beta^a = D_\beta^a R^{1/\alpha}$, where

$$E^{\mathbf{X}|\theta,\alpha}\left[\Pr^{X|\theta,\alpha}\left(X > \mathcal{L}_\beta^a\right) \mid A = a\right] = \beta. \tag{12}$$

After some calculations, it follows from (12) that

$$E\left[\exp\{-(D_\beta^a)^\alpha R/\theta^\alpha\} \mid A = a\right] = \frac{G[a/\{1+(D_\beta^a)^\alpha\}]}{G[a]\{1+(D_\beta^a)^\alpha\}^{s-r+1}} = \beta.$$

Manifestly, the conditional lower β-ETL given A, $\mathcal{L}_\beta^A$, is also an unconditional lower β-ETL because

$$E^{\mathbf{X}|\theta,\alpha}\left[\Pr^{X|\theta,\alpha}\left(X > \mathcal{L}_\beta^A\right)\right] = E\left[E\left[\Pr^{X|\theta,\alpha}\left(X > \mathcal{L}_\beta^A\right) \mid A\right]\right] = E[\beta] = \beta$$

Table 3 compares unconditional and conditional lower β-expectation $W(\alpha, \theta)$ tolerance factors, D_β and $D_\beta^{a_\varepsilon}$, for selected values of r, s, and n when $\alpha = 1$, $\beta = 0.90$ and $A = a_\varepsilon$, $\varepsilon = 0.01, 0.25, 0.75, 0.99$.

Table 3. Unconditional and conditional lower β-expectation tolerance factors, D_β and $D_\beta^{a_\varepsilon}$, for the $W(\alpha, \theta)$ model based on $\mathbf{X} = (X_{r:n}, \ldots, X_{s:n})$ when $\alpha = 1$ and $\beta = 0.90$.

r	s	n	D_β	$D_\beta^{a_{0.01}}$	$D_\beta^{a_{0.25}}$	$D_\beta^{a_{0.75}}$	$D_\beta^{a_{0.99}}$
2	6	10	0.0266901	0.0183145	0.0219756	0.0324522	0.0796828
	10	20	0.0132572	0.0107789	0.0118633	0.0145544	0.0232244
4	8	30	0.0266901	0.0154573	0.0213445	0.0349895	0.0931401
	20	40	0.00660676	0.00553705	0.00610823	0.00708131	0.00940913
6	10	50	0.0266901	0.0141242	0.0211005	0.0363961	0.100592
	30	60	0.00439967	0.00376406	0.00412769	0.00466106	0.00578604

As before, the difference between D_β and $D_\beta^{a_\varepsilon}$ might be considerable when ε is near to 0 or 1. Nevertheless, D_β and $D_\beta^{a_\varepsilon}$ are quite similar when $s - r$ is large. For instance, $D_\beta = 0.001240$, $D_\beta^{a_{0.01}} = 0.001189$, and $D_\beta^{a_{0.99}} = 0.001339$ when $(r, s, n) = (5, 90, 95)$, $\alpha = 1$, and $\beta = 0.90$.

4.2. Sample-Size Determination

Frequently, the researcher wishes to choose the minimum sample size to achieve a specified criterion for β-ETLs. In our circumstances, a classical criterion is to require the maximum variation of the content of the β-expectation tolerance interval $(\mathcal{L}_\beta, +\infty)$ around its mean value, β, to be sufficiently small (say, less than $\varepsilon \in (0, \min\{\beta, 1-\beta\})$) with a determined minimum stability (say $\lambda \in (0, 1)$). In other words, the coverage of the random interval $(\mathcal{L}_\beta(\mathbf{X}), +\infty)$ must be contained in $(\beta - \varepsilon, \beta + \varepsilon)$ with a probability of at least λ, i.e.,

$$\Pr{}^{\mathbf{X}|\theta,\alpha} \left(\left| \Pr{}^{X|\theta,\alpha}(X > \mathcal{L}_\beta) - \beta \right| < \varepsilon \right) \geq \lambda \tag{13}$$

or, equivalently, $\Pr^{\mathbf{X}|\theta,\alpha} \{ \ln(\beta - \varepsilon) < -(\mathcal{L}_\beta/\theta)^\alpha < \ln(\beta + \varepsilon) \} \geq \lambda$ for all $\theta > 0$. In this subsection, if condition (13) is satisfied, the corresponding sampling plan (r, s, n) will be called feasible.

Assuming that $1 < r = s \leq n$, as $\exp(-X_{r:n}^\alpha/\theta^\alpha) \sim \text{Beta}(n - r + 1, r)$ and $\mathcal{L}_\beta = D_\beta X_{r:n}$, where $D_\beta = \zeta^{-1}(\beta)$, it is deduced that the sampling plan (r, r, n) is feasible if and only if $g_2(r, n) \geq 0$, in which

$$g_2(r, n) = \sum_{k=0}^{r-1} \binom{n}{k} \left[\frac{\{1 - (\beta + \varepsilon)^{1/(D_\beta)^\alpha}\}^k}{(\beta + \varepsilon)^{(k-n)/(D_\beta)^\alpha}} - \frac{\{1 - (\beta - \varepsilon)^{1/(D_\beta)^\alpha}\}^k}{(\beta - \varepsilon)^{(k-n)/(D_\beta)^\alpha}} \right] - \lambda.$$

Provided that $1 = r \leq s \leq n$, the sampling plan $(1, s, n)$ will be feasible if and only if $h_2(s) \geq 0$, where

$$h_2(s) = \sum_{i=0}^{s-1} \frac{(\beta^{i/s}/i!)}{(1 - \beta^{1/s})^i} \left[\frac{\{-\ln(\beta + \varepsilon)\}^i}{(\beta + \varepsilon)^{1/(1 - \beta^{-1/s})}} - \frac{\{-\ln(\beta - \varepsilon)\}^i}{(\beta - \varepsilon)^{1/(1 - \beta^{-1/s})}} \right] - \lambda,$$

in view of that $\mathcal{L}_\beta = D_\beta T^{1/\alpha}$ with $D_\beta = (\beta^{-1/s} - 1)^{1/\alpha}$ and $2T/\theta^\alpha \sim \chi_{2s}^2$. In particular, the plan $(1, 1, n)$ would be feasible if and only if $(\beta + \varepsilon)^{\beta/(1-\beta)} - (\beta - \varepsilon)^{\beta/(1-\beta)} \geq \lambda$. Finally, if $1 < r < s \leq n$, it can be shown that (r, s, n) is feasible if and only if $h_2(s - r) \geq 0$.

The determination of the optimal feasible sampling plan for setting the lower β-ETL assuming fixed numbers of trimmed observations (Case I) or fixed trimming proportions (Case II) will be tackled in the remainder of this subsection.

Case I: *Fixed numbers of left and right trimmed observations*

In this situation, the researcher desires to find the optimal feasible plan (r, s, n), such that $(r-1) = \delta_1$ and $(n-s) = \delta_2$, where δ_1 and δ_2 are prespecified non-negative integers. Then, $(\delta_1 + 1, \delta_1 + 1, \delta_1 + \delta_2 + 1)$ would be the optimal plan if $g_2(r, n) \geq 0$ with $r = \delta_1 + 1$ and $n = \delta_1 + \delta_2 + 1$. Otherwise, if m is now the smallest integer value, such that $h_2(m) \geq 0$, it turns out that the optimal plan would be

$$(r, s, n) = (\delta_1 + 1, \delta_1 + m + I(\delta_1 > 0), \delta_1 + \delta_2 + m + I(\delta_1 > 0))$$

Note that m will always exist because $h_2(k) > 0$ when k is sufficiently large. It is important to mention that $m = 1$ if and only if

$$h_2(1) = (\beta + \varepsilon)^{\beta/(1-\beta)} - (\beta - \varepsilon)^{\beta/(1-\beta)} - \lambda \geq 0.$$

Moreover, if $r = s$ and $n \to \infty$, as $2nX_{r:n}^\alpha/\theta^\alpha$ converges in law to a χ_{2r}^2 distribution and $D_\beta / n^{1/\alpha} \longrightarrow (\beta^{-1/r} - 1)^{1/\alpha}$, it follows that $g_2(r, n) \longrightarrow h_2(r)$. Consequently, if (r, r, n) is a feasible plan, it is indispensable that $r \geq m$. Hence, $(\delta_1 + 1, \delta_1 + 1, \delta_1 + \delta_2 + 1)$ is not feasible when $m > \delta_1 + 1$.

Case II: *Fixed left and right trimming proportions*

Consider that it is now needed to obtain the minimum sample size feasible plan (r_n, s_n, n) with $r_n = \lfloor n\pi_1 + 1 \rfloor$ and $s_n = \lceil n(1 - \pi_2) \rceil$, where $\pi_i \geq 0, i = 1, 2$, and $\pi_1 + \pi_2 < 1$. Our goal in this case is to determine the smallest integer n such that $g_2(r_n, n) \geq 0$ if $1 < r_n = s_n$ or such that $h_2(s_n - r_n + I(r_n = 1)) \geq 0$ otherwise.

Assume that (r_n, s_n, n) is a feasible plan and also that m is the smallest integer satisfying $h_2(m) \geq 0$. Then, it turns out that $r_n \geq m$ when $r_n = s_n$, whereas $n \geq n_0$ if $r_n < s_n$, where n_0 is given in (9).

Given $\beta, \varepsilon, \lambda, \pi_1, \pi_2 \in (0, 1)$, with $\varepsilon < \min\{\beta, 1 - \beta\}$, and $\pi_1 + \pi_2 < 1$, a step-by-step procedure for determining the minimum sample size plan (r_n, s_n, n) satisfying (13), where $r_n = \lfloor n\pi_1 + 1 \rfloor$ and $s_n = \lceil n(1 - \pi_2) \rceil$, would be similar to that presented in Section 3.2, except that $g_1(r_{n_1}, n_1)$ is replaced by $g_2(r_{n_1}, n_1)$ in step 9, and step 1 is now as follows:

- *Step 1:* If $(\beta + \varepsilon)^{\beta/(1-\beta)} - (\beta - \varepsilon)^{\beta/(1-\beta)} \geq \lambda$, then set $(r_n, s_n, n) = (1, 1, 1)$ and go to step 10. Otherwise, find the smallest integer m, such that $h_2(m) \geq 0$.

Table 4 shows the optimal sampling plans (r, s, n) for setting lower β-ETLs based on the Weibull $W(\theta, \alpha)$ trimmed sample $\mathbf{X} = (X_{r:n}, ..., X_{s:n})$ for selected values of β, ε and δ when (i) $q_1 \simeq 0.2$ and $q_2 \simeq 0.3$ and (ii) $r - 1 = 2$ and $n - s = 3$.

In particular, if $\beta = 0.9$, $\varepsilon = 0.03$, $\delta = 0.9$ and the experimenter desires that at least 20% of the smallest and 30% of the largest observations were trimmed, the minimum sample size for setting the lower β-ETL would be $n = 53$, whereas the smallest 10 and the largest 15 data would be disregarded or censored (i.e., $r = 11$ and $s = 38$). On the other hand, if the experimenter wishes to discard the first two and last three data, the required sample size is $n = 33$; obviously, the optimal sampling plan would be $(3, 30, 33)$.

Table 4. Optimal sampling plans (r, s, n) for setting lower β-ETLs for the $W(\alpha, \theta)$ model based on $\mathbf{X} = (X_{r:n}, ..., X_{s:n})$ when (i) $q_1 \simeq 0.2$ and $q_2 \simeq 0.3$ and (ii) $r - 1 = 2$ and $n - s = 3$.

β	ε	δ	$q_1 \simeq 0.2, q_2 \simeq 0.3$			$r = 3, n - s = 3$		
			r	s	n	r	s	n
0.80	0.03	0.70	16	54	76	3	41	44
		0.90	39	135	192	3	99	102
	0.06	0.70	4	14	19	3	13	16
		0.90	10	34	48	3	27	30
0.90	0.03	0.70	5	16	22	3	14	17
		0.90	11	38	53	3	30	33
	0.06	0.70	1	3	3	3	3	6
		0.90	3	10	13	3	10	13

5. Illustrative Examples

Three numerical examples are considered in this section to illustrate the results developed above.

5.1. Example 1

An experiment in which students were learning to measure strontium-90 concentrations in samples of milk was considered by Sarhan and Greenberg [41]. The test substance was supposed to contain 9.22 microcuries per liter. Ten measurements, each involving readings and calculations, were made. However, since the measurement error was known to be relatively larger at the extremes, especially the upper one, a decision was made to censor the two smallest and the three largest observations, leaving the following trimmed sample: $\mathbf{x} = (8.2, 8.4, 9.1, 9.8, 9.9)$. Thus, $n = 10$, $r = 3$, and $s = 7$, which imply that $q_1 = 0.2$ and $q_2 = 0.3$.

Fernández [10] assumed that the above data arisen from a Weibull model (1) with $\alpha = 3$, which has a near normal shape. In such a case, $T = 6720.03$, $R = 2309.09$ and $A = a = 0.238782$. Furthermore, in view of (3), the MLEs of θ and the mean concentration, $\mu = E[X \mid \theta, \alpha]$, are given by $\hat{\theta} = 10.1049$ and $\hat{\mu} = 9.02343$.

Table 5 contains the unconditional and conditional lower and upper (β, γ)-TLs and β-ETLs for selected values of β and γ when $\alpha = 3$. For instance, if $\beta = \gamma = 0.9$, $L_{\beta,\gamma} = 3.315$ and $L^a_{\beta,\gamma} = 4.162$, whereas $\mathcal{L}_\beta = 3.950$ and $\mathcal{L}^a_\beta = 4.783$. In particular, the experimenter might assert with confidence $\gamma = 0.9$ that at least 90% of strontium-90 concentrations will exceed 3.315 (4.162) if the unconditional (conditional) approach is adopted. Moreover, under the unconditional (conditional) perspective, one can be 90% confident that a future strontium-90 concentration will surpass 3.950 (4.783). The corresponding unconditional and conditional upper (β, γ)-TLs and β-ETLs are derived to be $U_{\beta,\gamma} = 14.50$, $U^a_{\beta,\gamma} = 16.23$, $\mathcal{U}_\beta = 12.16$ and $\mathcal{U}^a_\beta = 14.12$.

Table 5. Unconditional and conditional lower and upper (β, γ)-TLs and β-ETLs in Example 1.

β	γ	$L_{\beta,\gamma}$	$L^a_{\beta,\gamma}$	$\mathcal{L}_\beta$	$\mathcal{L}^a_\beta$	$U_{\beta,\gamma}$	$U^a_{\beta,\gamma}$	$\mathcal{U}_\beta$	$\mathcal{U}^a_\beta$
0.80	0.90	4.257	5.345	5.098	6.160	12.87	14.40	10.46	12.31
	0.95	4.050	5.139			13.96	15.24		
0.90	0.90	3.315	4.162	3.950	4.783	14.50	16.23	12.16	14.12
	0.95	3.154	4.002			15.73	17.18		

Suppose the experimenter wish to determine the optimal sampling plan (r, s, n) for setting the lower $(0.9, 0.9)$-TL based on a Weibull trimmed sample under the premise that the left and right trimming proportions are nearly 0.2 and 0.3, respectively. According to Table 2, if (β', γ') is $(0.95, 0.25)$, the needed sample size would be $n = 16$, whereas $r = 4$ and $s = 12$. On the other side, if the experimenter wants to ignore the smallest two and the largest three observations, the optimal sampling plan would be $(3, 11, 14)$.

In addition, consider now the experimenter desires to find the optimal sampling plan (r, s, n) for setting a lower 0.9-ETL, $\mathcal{L}_{0.9}(\mathbf{X})$, such that the coverage of $(\mathcal{L}_{0.9}(\mathbf{X}), +\infty)$ is contained in $(0.87, 0.93)$ with a probability of at least 0.7. If it is also required that about 20% and 30% of the smallest and largest observations were trimmed, respectively, the optimal sampling plan is given by $(5, 16, 22)$ based on Table 4 with $\beta = 0.9$, $\varepsilon = 0.3$ and $\delta = 0.7$. Likewise, in the case of it was demanded that $r = 3$ and $n - s = 3$, the smallest sample size would be $n = 17$.

In order to explore the effect of α on the tolerance limits, the unconditional and conditional lower and upper (β, γ)-TLs and β-ETLs for selected values of α around 3 are displayed in Table 6. In general, as expected, the influence of α is quite appreciable, especially in the unconditional case.

Table 6. Unconditional and conditional lower and upper (β, γ)-TLs and β-ETLs for selected values of α around 3 in Example 1.

α	$\beta = 0.80, \gamma = 0.90$				$\beta = 0.90, \gamma = 0.95$			
	$L_{\beta,\gamma}$	$L_{\beta,\gamma}^a$	$\mathcal{L}_\beta$	$\mathcal{L}_\beta^a$	$U_{\beta,\gamma}$	$U_{\beta,\gamma}^a$	$\mathcal{U}_\beta$	$\mathcal{U}_\beta^a$
2.8	3.936	5.133	4.775	5.976	2.855	3.764	3.633	4.557
2.9	4.100	5.241	4.940	6.071	3.006	3.885	3.794	4.673
3.0	4.257	5.345	5.098	6.160	3.154	4.002	3.950	4.783
3.1	4.408	5.444	5.248	6.245	3.298	4.114	4.100	4.889
3.2	4.552	5.538	5.391	6.326	3.437	4.222	4.244	4.990

5.2. Example 2

Meeker and Escobar [42] (pp. 151, 198) present the results of a failure-censored fatigue crack-initiation experiment in which 100 specimens of a type of titanium alloy were put on test. Only the nine smallest times to crack-initiation were recorded. In this way, $n = 100$, $r = 1$ and $s = 9$. The observed times in units of 1000 cycles were 18, 32, 39, 53, 59, 68, 77, 78, and 93. Based on experience with fatigue tests on similar alloys, it was assumed the adequacy of the Weibull model (1) with $\alpha = 2$ to describe the above data. Hence, $T = 821504$ and $R = 789104$, whereas $\hat{\theta} = 302.123$ and $\hat{\mu} = 267.749$ are the MLEs of θ and the expected failure-time μ.

Table 7 shows the unconditional and conditional lower and upper (β, γ)-TLs and β-ETLs when $r = 1, 2, ..., 9$ for selected values of β and γ. For example, if the engineer wants to discard the smallest two data (i.e., $r = 3$) and $(\beta, \gamma) = (0.8, 0.9)$, it turns out that $T = 820156$, $R = 671098$, $\hat{\theta} = 302.154$ and $\hat{\mu} = 267.777$, whereas $A = \chi^2_{3;100}/R$ takes the value $a = 0.00226644$. In such a case, it follows that $L_{\beta,\gamma} = 127.1$, $L_{\beta,\gamma}^a = 118.8$, $\mathcal{L}_\beta = 159.5$, and $\mathcal{L}_\beta^a = 143.6$. Hence, the reliability engineer could affirm with confidence $\gamma = 0.9$ that at least 80% of the times to crack-initiation (in units of 1000 cycles) of specimens of that type of titanium alloy will be greater than 127.1 (118.8) when the unconditional (conditional) viewpoint is considered. Likewise, adopting the unconditional (conditional) perspective, the engineer may be 80% sure that a future time to crack-initiation will surpass 159,500 (143,600) cycles.

It is interesting to point out that the variability of $L_{\beta,\gamma}^a$ when $r = 2, ..., 8$ is very small. In addition, observe that $L_{\beta,\gamma}^a$, $r = 2, ..., 8$, is quite similar to the unconditional lower (β, γ)-TL, $L_{\beta,\gamma}$, for $r = 1$. Analogous results are obtained for the β-ETLs when $r = 2, ..., 5$.

Table 7. Unconditional and conditional lower and upper (β,γ)-TLs and β-ETLs when $r = 1, \ldots, 9$ in Example 2.

	$\beta = 0.80, \gamma = 0.90$				$\beta = 0.90, \gamma = 0.95$			
r	$L_{\beta,\gamma}$	$L^a_{\beta,\gamma}$	$\mathcal{L}_\beta$	$\mathcal{L}^a_\beta$	$U_{\beta,\gamma}$	$U^a_{\beta,\gamma}$	$\mathcal{U}_\beta$	$\mathcal{U}^a_\beta$
1	118.8		143.6		77.44		98.35	
2	123.5	118.8	152.7	143.6	80.03	77.44	104.5	98.37
3	127.1	118.8	159.5	143.6	82.01	77.44	109.0	98.36
4	123.5	118.9	157.9	143.7	79.29	77.50	107.8	98.43
5	126.8	118.9	166.2	143.7	80.90	77.49	113.4	98.43
6	125.1	118.9	169.7	145.3	79.01	77.54	115.5	108.5
7	119.9	119.0	171.9	152.0	74.57	77.61	116.4	105.8
8	151.2	118.9	242.9	150.9	91.10	77.50	161.9	105.2
9	119.4		144.3		77.81		98.84	

5.3. Example 3

Lee and Wang [43] (p. 205) consider that 21 patients with acute leukemia have the following remission times in months: 1, 1, 2, 2, 3, 4, 4, 5, 5, 6, 8, 8, 9, 10, 10, 12, 14, 16, 20, 24, and 34. The available sample is now complete, since $r = 1$ and $s = n = 21$.

In accordance with previous tests, the researcher assumes that the remission time follows the exponential distribution. A probability plot also indicates that the Weibull model (1) with $\alpha = 1$ fits the above data very well. In this situation, $T = \sum_{i=1}^n x_i = 198$ and $\widehat{\theta} = T/n = 9.42857$. Supposing that $(\beta, \gamma) = (0.8, 0.9)$, it follows that $L_{\beta,\gamma} = 1.634$ and $\mathcal{L}_\beta = 2.115$.

Table 8 provides the unconditional and conditional lower and upper (β, γ)-TLs and β-ETLs when $r = 1, 3, 5, 7, 9, 11$, and $n - s = r - 1$ (i.e., $q_1 = q_2$). For instance, if the two smallest and largest observations are missing, and the unconditional (conditional) perspective is adopted, the researcher might state with confidence $\gamma = 0.9$ that at least 80% of patients with acute leukemia will have remission times greater than $L_{\beta,\gamma} = 1.467$ ($L^a_{\beta,\gamma} = 1.622$) months. In the same manner, one might be 80% confident that a future remission time will exceed $\mathcal{L}_\beta = 1.966$ ($\mathcal{L}^a_\beta = 2.126$) months.

Table 8. Unconditional and conditional lower and upper (β,γ)-TLs and β-ETLs for $r = 1, 3, 5, 7, 9, 11$ and $s = n + 1 - r$ in Example 3.

		$\beta = 0.80, \gamma = 0.90$				$\beta = 0.90, \gamma = 0.95$			
r	s	$L_{\beta,\gamma}$	$L^a_{\beta,\gamma}$	$\mathcal{L}_\beta$	$\mathcal{L}^a_\beta$	$U_{\beta,\gamma}$	$U^a_{\beta,\gamma}$	$\mathcal{U}_\beta$	$\mathcal{U}^a_\beta$
1	21	1.634		2.115		0.7178		0.9959	
3	19	1.467	1.622	1.966	2.126	0.6386	0.7102	0.9249	1.001
5	17	1.385	1.586	1.933	2.110	0.5960	0.6920	0.9083	0.9926
7	15	1.232	1.507	1.839	2.039	0.5209	0.6542	0.8617	0.9591
9	13	1.436	1.580	2.467	2.184	0.5843	0.6817	1.148	1.027
11	11	1.768		2.518		0.7563		1.182	

6. Concluding Remarks

Weibull tolerance limits with certain guaranteed or expected coverages are obtained in this paper when the available empirical information is provided by a trimmed sample. These bounds are valid, even when some of the smallest and largest observations have been disregarded or censored. Single (right or left) and double failure-censoring are allowed. Unconditional and conditional tolerance bounds have been obtained and compared when $s > r > 1$. The difference between these limits might be large when the auxiliary statistic A takes extreme percentiles. In our case, it is preferable to use the suggested conditional tolerance limits. Optimal sampling plans for setting β-content and β-expectation tolerance limits have also been determined. Efficient step-by-step procedures for computing the corresponding test plans with smallest sample sizes have been proposed. These methods can be easily applied and require little computational effort. Several numerical examples have been studied for illustrative and comparative purposes. An extension of the frequency-based perspective presented in this work the Bayesian approach is currently under investigation.

Funding: This research was partially supported by MCIN/AEI/10.13039/501100011033 under grant PID2019-110442GB-I00.

Data Availability Statement: Data are contained within the article.

Acknowledgments: The author thanks the Editor and Reviewers for providing valuable comments and suggestions.

Conflicts of Interest: The author declares no conflict of interest.

References

1. Wilks, S.S. Determination of sample sizes for setting tolerance limits. *Ann. Math. Stat.* **1941**, *12*, 91–96. [CrossRef]
2. Guttman, I. *Statistical Tolerance Regions: Classical and Bayesian*; Charles W. Griffin and Co.: London, UK, 1970.
3. Fernández, A.J. Computing tolerance limits for the lifetime of a k-out-of-n:F system based on prior information and censored data. *Appl. Math. Model.* **2014**, *38*, 548–561. [CrossRef]
4. Prescott, P. Selection of trimming proportions for robust adaptive trimmed means. *J. Amer. Statist. Assoc.* **1978**, *73*, 133–140. Erratum in *J. Amer. Statist. Assoc.* **1978**, *73*, 691. [CrossRef]
5. Huber, P.J. *Robust Statistics*; Wiley: New York, NY, USA, 1981.
6. Healy, M.J.R. Algorithm AS 180: A linear estimator of standard deviation in symmetrically trimmed normal samples. *Appl. Stat.* **1982**, *31*, 174–175. [CrossRef]
7. Welsh, A.H. The trimmed mean in the linear model (with discussion). *Ann. Stat.* **1987**, *15*, 20–45.
8. Wilcox, R.R. Simulation results on solutions to the multivariate Behrens-Fisher problem via trimmed means. *Statistician* **1995**, *44*, 213–225. [CrossRef]
9. Fernández, A.J. Bayesian estimation based on trimmed samples from Pareto populations. *Comput. Stat. Data Anal.* **2006**, *51*, 1119–1130. [CrossRef]
10. Fernández, A.J. Weibull inference using trimmed samples and prior information. *Stat. Pap.* **2009**, *50*, 119–136. [CrossRef]
11. Healy, M.J.R. A mean difference estimator of standard deviation in symmetrically censored samples. *Biometrika* **1978**, *65*, 643–646. [CrossRef]
12. Prescott, P. A mean difference estimator of standard deviation in asymmetrically censored normal samples. *Biometrika* **1979**, *66*, 684–686. [CrossRef]
13. Schneider, H. Simple and highly efficient estimators for censored normal samples. *Biometrika* **1984**, *71*, 412–414. [CrossRef]
14. Bhattacharyya, G.K. On asymptotics of maximum likelihood and related estimators based on Type II censored data. *J. Am. Stat. Assoc.* **1985**, *80*, 398–404. [CrossRef]
15. LaRiccia, V.N. Asymptotically chi-squared distributed tests of normality for Type II censored samples. *J. Am. Stat. Assoc.* **1986**, *81*, 1026–1031. [CrossRef]
16. Schneider, H.; Weissfeld, L. Inference based on Type II censored samples. *Biometrics* **1986**, *42*, 531–536. [CrossRef] [PubMed]
17. Fernández, A.J. Highest posterior density estimation from multiply censored Pareto data. *Stat. Pap.* **2008**, *49*, 333–341. [CrossRef]
18. Fernández, A.J. Smallest Pareto confidence regions and applications. *Comput. Stat. Data Anal.* **2013**, *62*, 11–25. [CrossRef]
19. Escobar, L.A.; Meeker, W.Q. Algorithm AS 292: Fisher information matrix for the extreme value, normal and logistic distributions and censored data. *Appl. Stat.* **1994**, *43*, 533–554. [CrossRef]
20. Upadhyay, S.K.; Shastri, V. Bayesian results for classical Pareto distribution via Gibbs sampler, with doubly-censored observations. *IEEE Trans. Reliab.* **1997**, *46*, 56–59. [CrossRef]
21. Ali Mousa, M.A.M. Bayesian prediction based on Pareto doubly censored data. *Statistics* **2003**, *37*, 65–72. [CrossRef]
22. Chen, J.W.; Li, K.H.; Lam, Y. Bayesian single and double variable sampling plans for the Weibull distribution with censoring. *Eur. J. Oper. Res.* **2007**, *177*, 1062–1073. [CrossRef]
23. Tsai, T.-R.; Lu, Y.-T.; Wu, S.-J. Reliability sampling plans for Weibull distribution with limited capacity of test facility. *Comput. Ind. Eng.* **2008**, *55*, 721–728. [CrossRef]
24. Aslam, M.; Jun, C.-H.; Fernández, A.J.; Ahmad, M.; Rasool, M. Repetitive group sampling plan based on truncated tests for Weibull models. *Res. J. Appl. Sci. Eng. Technol.* **2014**, *7*, 1917–1924. [CrossRef]
25. Fernández, A.J. Optimum attributes component test plans for k-out-of-n:F Weibull systems using prior information. *Eur. J. Oper. Res.* **2015**, *240*, 688–696. [CrossRef]
26. Roy, S. Bayesian accelerated life test plans for series systems with Weibull component lifetimes. *Appl. Math. Model.* **2018**, *62*, 383–403. [CrossRef]

27. Almongy, H.M.; Alshenawy, F.Y.; Almetwally, E.M.; Abdo, D.A. Applying Transformer Insulation Using Weibull Extended Distribution Based on Progressive Censoring Scheme. *Axioms* **2021**, *10*, 100. [CrossRef]
28. Algarni, A. Group Acceptance Sampling Plan Based on New Compounded Three-Parameter Weibull Model. *Axioms* **2022**, *11*, 438. [CrossRef]
29. Fernández, A.J.; Bravo, J.I.; De Fuentes, Í. Computing maximum likelihood estimates from Type II doubly censored exponential data. *Stat. Methods Appl.* **2002**, *11*, 187–200. [CrossRef]
30. Lee, W.-C.; Wu, J.-W.; Hong, C.-W. Assessing the lifetime performance index of products with the exponential distribution under progressively type II right censored samples. *J. Comput. Appl. Math.* **2009**, *231*, 648–656. [CrossRef]
31. Chen, K.-S.; Yang, C.-M. Developing a performance index with a Poisson process and an exponential distribution for operations management and continuous improvement. *J. Comput. Appl. Math.* **2018**, *343*, 737–747. [CrossRef]
32. Yousef, M.M.; Hassan, A.S.; Alshanbari, H.M.; El-Bagoury, A.-A.H.; Almetwally, E.M. Bayesian and Non-Bayesian Analysis of Exponentiated Exponential Stress–Strength Model Based on Generalized Progressive Hybrid Censoring Process. *Axioms* **2022**, *11*, 455. [CrossRef]
33. Aminzadeh, M.S. β-expectation tolerance intervals and sample-size determination for the Rayleigh distribution. *IEEE Trans. Reliab.* **1991**, *40*, 287–289. [CrossRef]
34. Aminzadeh, M.S. Approximate 1-sided tolerance limits for future observations for the Rayleigh distribution, using regression. *IEEE Trans. Reliab.* **1993**, *42*, 625–630. [CrossRef]
35. Raqab, M.Z.; Madi, M.T. Bayesian prediction of the total time on test using doubly censored Rayleigh data. *J. Stat. Comput. Simul.* **2002**, *72*, 781–789. [CrossRef]
36. Fernández, A.J. Bayesian estimation and prediction based on Rayleigh sample quantiles. *Qual. Quant.* **2010**, *44*, 1239–1248. [CrossRef]
37. Lee, W.-C.; Wu, J.-W.; Hong, M.-L.; Lin, L.-S.; Chan, R.-L. Assessing the lifetime performance index of Rayleigh products based on the Bayesian estimation under progressive type II right censored samples. *J. Comput. Appl. Math.* **2011**, *235*, 1676–1688. [CrossRef]
38. Fernández, A.J. Two-sided tolerance intervals in the exponential case: Corrigenda and generalizations. *Comput. Stat. Data Anal.* **2010**, *54*, 151–162. [CrossRef]
39. Fernández, A.J. Tolerance Limits for k-out-of-n Systems With Exponentially Distributed Component Lifetimes. *IEEE Trans. Reliab.* **2010**, *59*, 331–337. [CrossRef]
40. Thoman, D.R.; Bain, L.J.; Antle, C.E. Maximum likelihood estimation, exact confidence intervals for reliability and tolerance limits in the Weibull distribution. *Technometrics* **1970**, *12*, 363–373. [CrossRef]
41. Sarhan, A.E.; Greenberg, B.G. *Contributions to Order Statistics*; Wiley: New York, NY, USA, 1962.
42. Meeker, W.Q.; Escobar, L.A. *Statistical Methods for Reliability Data*; Wiley: New York, NY, USA, 1998.
43. Lee, E.T.; Wang, J.W. *Statistical Methods for Survival Data Analysis*, 3rd ed.; Wiley: Hoboken, NJ, USA, 2003.
44. Davis, D.J. An analysis of some failure data. *J. Am. Stat. Assoc.* **1952**, *47*, 113–150. [CrossRef]
45. Soland, R.M. Bayesian analysis of the Weibull process with unknown scale parameter and its application to acceptance sampling. *IEEE Trans. Reliab.* **1968**, *17*, 84–90. [CrossRef]
46. Tsokos, C.P.; Rao, A.N.V. Bayesian analysis of the Weibull failure model under stochastic variation of the shape and scale parameters. *Metron* **1976**, *34*, 201–217.
47. Lawless, J.F. *Statistical Models and Methods for Lifetime Data*; Wiley: New York, NY, USA, 1982.
48. Nordman, D.J.; Meeker, W.Q. Weibull prediction intervals for a future number of failures. *Technometrics* **2002**, *44*, 15–23. [CrossRef]
49. Klinger, D.J.; Nakada, Y.; Menéndez, M.A. *AT&T Reliability Manual*; Van Nostrand Reinhold: New York, NY, USA, 1990.
50. Abernethy, R.B. *The New Weibull Handbook*; Robert B. Abernethy: North Palm Beach, FL, USA, 1998.
51. Danziger, L. Planning censored life tests for estimation of the hazard rate of a Weibull distribution with prescribed precision. *Technometrics* **1970**, *12*, 408–412. [CrossRef]
52. Tsokos, C.P.; Canavos, G.C. Bayesian concepts for the estimation of reliability in the Weibull life testing model. *Int. Stat. Rev.* **1972**, *40*, 153–160. [CrossRef]
53. Moore, A.H.; Bilikam, J.E. Bayesian estimation of parameters of life distributions and reliability from type II censored samples. *IEEE Trans. Reliab.* **1978**, *27*, 64–67. [CrossRef]
54. Kwon, Y.I. A Bayesian life test sampling plan for products with Weibull lifetime distribution sold under warranty. *Reliab. Eng. Syst. Saf.* **1996**, *53*, 61–66. [CrossRef]
55. Zhang, Y.; Meeker, W.Q. Bayesian life test planning for the Weibull distribution with given shape parameter. *Metrika* **2005**, *61*, 237–249. [CrossRef]

Disclaimer/Publisher's Note: The statements, opinions and data contained in all publications are solely those of the individual author(s) and contributor(s) and not of MDPI and/or the editor(s). MDPI and/or the editor(s) disclaim responsibility for any injury to people or property resulting from any ideas, methods, instructions or products referred to in the content.

Article

Reliability Estimation under Normal Operating Conditions for Progressively Type-II XLindley Censored Data

Refah Alotaibi [1], Mazen Nassar [2,3] and Ahmed Elshahhat [4,*]

1. Department of Mathematical Sciences, College of Science, Princess Nourah bint Abdulrahman University, P.O. Box 84428, Riyadh 11671, Saudi Arabia
2. Department of Statistics, Faculty of Science, King Abdulaziz University, Jeddah 21589, Saudi Arabia
3. Department of Statistics, Faculty of Commerce, Zagazig University, Zagazig 44519, Egypt
4. Faculty of Technology and Development, Zagazig University, Zagazig 44519, Egypt
* Correspondence: aelshahhat@ftd.zu.edu.eg

Abstract: This paper assumes constant-stress accelerated life tests when the lifespan of the test units follows the XLindley distribution. In addition to the maximum likelihood estimation, the Bayesian estimation of the model parameters is acquired based on progressively Type-II censored samples. The point and interval estimations of the model parameters and some reliability indices under normal operating conditions at mission time are derived using both estimation methods. Using the Markov chain Monte Carlo algorithm, the Bayes estimates are calculated using the squared error loss function. Simulating the performances of the different estimation methods is performed to illustrate the proposed methodology. As an example of how the proposed methods can be applied, we look at two real-life accelerated life test cases. According to the numerical outcomes and based on some criteria, including the root of the mean square error and interval length, we can conclude that the Bayesian estimation method based on the Markov chain Monte Carlo procedure performs better than the classical methods in evaluating the XLindley parameters and some of its reliability measures when a constant-stress accelerated life test is applied with progressively Type-II censoring.

Keywords: XLindley distribution; accelerated life tests; reliability analysis; Bayes inference; progressive Type-II censoring

1. Introduction

Under normal operating conditions, the life test for high-reliability products is frequently time-consuming and expensive because it would take a considerable amount of time before acquiring a sufficient number of failures for the necessary analysis. To rapidly and cheaply gather data regarding such products under experimental time constraints, accelerated life tests (ALTs) are typically conducted. As part of the ALTs, stress variables are typically set, including the temperature, humidity, voltage, pressure, etc. To determine the life characteristics of the products, the data gathered throughout the accelerated testing can be analyzed and extrapolated to the normal operating conditions. Nelson [1], Meeker and Escobar [2], Tang [3] and Balakrishnan [4] have all offered substantial reviews on past findings on the topic of ALTs. One of the most often utilized tests in reliability engineering is the constant-stress ALT (CSALT). As a result of the CSALT, the researchers can divide the products into several groups and test each group at a specific level of stress. A constant level of stress is applied during the entire test duration, for example, to semiconductors and microelectronics, see Luo et al. [5]. There are usually two or more levels at which products are tested separately. For time saving, tests are even run simultaneously when possible. Numerous studies have been conducted on the statistical inferences for the CSALT under various lifetime distributions using both classical and Bayesian approaches. For instance, when the product lifetime follows the Weibull distribution, Wang [6] discussed the inference of the CSALT. Lin et al. [7] investigated the inferences of the CSALT for log-location-scale lifetime distributions. Sief et al. [8] studied the inference of the CSALT from the generalized half-normal distribution. Nassar et al. [9] investigated the estimation issues of the Lindley distribution with the CSALT. See also Hakamipour [10], Kumar et al. [11] and Wu et al. [12] for more detail.

Although the main objective of the ALTs is to shorten the period of the experiment, the researchers spend a lot of time waiting for all test units to fail. In such situations, it is crucial to deal with censored data. In general, censoring means that actual failure times are known for just a part of the units under investigation. The Type-I, Type-II, and progressive Type-II censoring (PT-IIC) schemes are the most frequently utilized censoring schemes in ALTs. The PT-IIC is more powerful than traditional Type-I and Type-I censoring which enables researchers to withdraw live units at various testing stages. Consider an experiment in which n identical units are put on a life test with a predetermined censoring plan $(R_1, R_2, \ldots, R_m)$, where m is the desired number of observed failures. For $i = 1, \ldots, m-1$, at the time of the ith failure, R_i units from the remaining units are picked at random and removed from the test. Immediately, upon the occurrence of the last failure, all the remaining units R_m are removed and the test is ended, i.e., $R_m = n - m - \sum_{i=1}^{m-1} R_i$. In engineering experiments, some items must be removed for a more in-depth inspection or saved for use as test samples in future investigations. In this case, the PT-IIC plan naturally arises from such experiments. The test procedure of the CSALT in the presence of PT-IIC data will be discussed in detail in the next section. The PT-IIC scheme has received a lot of attention in the literature, for example, see Balakrishnan et al. [13], Balakrishnan and Lin [14], Chen and Gui [15], Wu and Gui [16], Dey et al. [17] and Alotaibi et al. [18]. A good introduction to the idea of progressive censoring as well as a leading review article is provided by Balakrishnan [19].

In view of the importance of the CSALT in rapidly ending the life test and the flexibility of the PT-IIC scheme over the conventional censoring schemes, our main aim in this paper is to investigate the estimation issues of the XLindley (XL) distribution when the data are gathered based on the PT-IIC plan with the CSALT. As far as we are aware, no work has yet addressed the CSALT model when PT-IIC data from the XL distribution are utilized. Although numerous studies investigated the estimation problems in the presence of CSALTs, few works studied the estimations of the reliability function (RF) and hazard rate function (HRF) under normal use conditions. In other words, the majority of the available studies considered only the estimation problems of the unknown parameters and say nothing regarding the estimation of the reliability indices under operating settings. Therefore, we think it is of interest to reliability engineers and other practitioners to identify the reliability measures under normal operating conditions in the case of the XL distribution. For more detail about the reliability estimation, see Wang et al. [20], Wang et al. [21] and Zhuang et al. [22]. In this study, the model parameters are estimated using both classical and Bayesian approaches and then after some reliability measures are evaluated under normal use conditions. Using the maximum likelihood method, as a classical approach, the maximum likelihood estimates (MLEs) of the different quantities are acquired and the associated approximate confidence intervals (ACIs) are also obtained. On the other hand, the Bayes estimates are investigated based on the squared error (SE) loss function. Due to the complex form of the joint posterior distribution, the Markov chain Monte Carlo (MCMC) procedure is implemented to obtain the required Bayes estimates as well as the Bayes credible intervals (BCIs). It is important to mention here that the derived estimators from the two estimation procedures cannot be theoretically compared because of their complicated structures. To get over this problem, we consider carrying out simulation research to compare the effectiveness of different estimators (point or interval) based on some statistical standards. Additionally, two examples are provided to illustrate how different approaches can be used. The simulation findings show that the MCMC procedure provides more accurate estimates of the model parameters as well as the RF and HRF under normal operating settings than those acquired based on the classical maximum likelihood method. Moreover, the real data analysis demonstrates that the XL distribution can be considered as a suitable model to fit constant-stress accelerated data sets, namely the oil of insulating fluid and transformer life-testing (TLT) data.

The article's structure is as follows: A description of the model, the test method, and the assumptions are given in Section 2. The MLEs as well as the ACIs confidence intervals are covered in Section 3. The Bayes estimation and BCIs of the unknown parameters are provided in Section 4. Section 5 presents the findings of the simulation research that was carried out to assess the effectiveness of the various estimators. Finally, two data sets are examined in Section 6, and some concluding remarks are offered in Section 7.

2. Model Description, Test Procedure, and Assumptions

A special combination of the exponential and Lindley distributions, known as the XL distribution, was introduced by Chouia and Zeghdoudi [23] as a new variant of the Lindley distribution. They demonstrated that compared to other one-parameter models like the Xgamma, exponential, and Lindley distributions, the XL has greater flexibility. They demonstrated the flexibility and suitability of the XL distribution as a model for representing time-to-event data in the real world. In addition to having an increasing hazard function, which is typical in many fields, it also has a single parameter which considerably reduces the mathematical challenges in reliability estimation. Using an adaptive Type-II progressive hybrid censoring plan, Alotaibi et al. [24] addressed the estimation problems, including both classical and Bayesian methods, of the XL distribution. They also demonstrated that data sets from chemical engineering may be modeled using the XL distribution rather than some other classical distributions, including gamma and Weibull distributions. Assume that Y is an experimental unit's lifetime random variable that follows the XL distribution with scale parameter α. As a result, the probability density function (PDF), distribution function (DF), RF and HRF corresponding to Y are expressed, respectively, by

$$g(y;\alpha) = \frac{\alpha^2 e^{-\alpha y}(1 + \bar{\alpha} + y)}{\bar{\alpha}^2}, \quad y > 0, \ \alpha > 0, \tag{1}$$

$$G(y;\alpha) = 1 - e^{-\alpha y}\left(1 + \frac{\alpha y}{\bar{\alpha}^2}\right), \tag{2}$$

$$\bar{G}(y;\alpha) = e^{-\alpha y}\left(1 + \frac{\alpha y}{\bar{\alpha}^2}\right), \tag{3}$$

and

$$H(y;\alpha) = \frac{\alpha^2(1 + \bar{\alpha} + y)}{\bar{\alpha}^2 + \alpha y}, \tag{4}$$

where $\bar{\alpha} = 1 + \alpha$.

2.1. Test Procedure

Under CSALT, assume that we have r accelerated stress levels $x_1 < x_2 < \cdots < x_r$, where the stress level under usual conditions is x_u. Let $n_j, j = 1, \ldots, r$ be r subgroups created from a total of N identical test items, where $n_1 + \cdots + n_r = N$. Assume that x_j is the level of stress applied to the n_j test units. The number of observed failure m_j is fixed before starting the experiment with a prefixed progressive censoring plan $(R_{j1}, R_{j2}, \ldots, R_{jm_j})$, with the awareness that $n_j = m_j + \sum_{i=1}^{m_j} R_{ji}$. At stress level x_j, when the first failure, say Y_{j1}, occurred, from the remaining surviving items, R_{j1} items are randomly removed. Similarly, at Y_{j2}, R_{j1} items are randomly removed from the remaining items, and so on. At the time of the m_j^{th} failure, say Y_{jm_j}, all the remaining items are withdrawn. The PT-IIC data that were observed under the stress level x_i were collected in this manner

$$y_{j1} < y_{j2} < \cdots < y_{jm_j}, \ j = 1, \ldots, r.$$

2.2. Basic Assumptions

In the context of CSALT, the following assumptions are applied across the whole paper:

1. Under the designed stress x_u and the accelerated stress levels x_j, the lifetime of test items follows the XL distribution with DF given by

$$G_j(y;\alpha_j) = 1 - e^{-\alpha_j y}\left(1 + \frac{\alpha_j y}{\alpha_j^2}\right), y > 0, j = 1,\ldots,r.$$

2. It is assumed that the life-stress model for the scale parameter $\alpha_j, j = 1,\ldots,r$ of the XL distribution is log-linear, i.e.,

$$\log(\alpha_j) = \lambda + \beta x_j, j = 1,\ldots,r,$$

where λ and β are unknown parameters depending on the product's characteristics and need to be estimated.

Based on the above assumptions, without the normalized constant, we can write the joint likelihood function of the unknown parameters λ and β, given the observed data, as follows

$$L(\lambda,\beta|y) = \prod_{j=1}^{r}\prod_{i=1}^{m_j} g_j(y_{ji};\lambda,\beta)[1 - G_j(y_{ji};\lambda,\beta)]^{R_{ji}}, \tag{5}$$

where $y = (y_{j1},\ldots,y_{jm_j})$.

3. Maximum Likelihood Estimation

In this section, the MLEs of the unknown parameters λ and β as well as the RF under designed stress are investigated. Moreover, the ACIs of these different parameters are discussed, employing the asymptotic properties of the MLEs. Using the aforementioned assumptions and by substituting the PDF and DF in the joint likelihood function presented in (5) by the PDF and DF of the XL distribution given by (1) and (2), respectively, we obtain

$$L(\lambda,\beta|y) = \frac{e^{2m\lambda + \beta \sum_{j=1}^{r} m_j x_j}}{e^{2\sum_{j=1}^{r} m_j \log(1+e^{\lambda+\beta x_j})}} \exp\left[-\sum_{(j,i)}(1+R_{ji})y_{ji}e^{\lambda+\beta x_j} + \sum_{(j,i)}\log\left(2 + e^{\lambda+\beta x_j} + y_{ji}\right)\right]$$

$$\times \prod_{j=1}^{r}\prod_{i=1}^{m_j}\left[1 + \frac{y_{ji}e^{\lambda+\beta x_j}}{(1+e^{\lambda+\beta x_j})^2}\right]^{R_{ji}}, \tag{6}$$

where $m = \sum_{j=1}^{r} m_j$ and $\sum_{(j,i)} = \sum_{j=1}^{r}\sum_{i=1}^{m_j}$. The log-likelihood function of (6) is obtained as follows:

$$l(\lambda,\beta|y) = 2m\lambda + \beta\sum_{j=1}^{r} m_j x_j - 2\sum_{j=1}^{r} m_j \log\left(1 + e^{\lambda+\beta x_j}\right) - \sum_{(j,i)}(1+R_{ji})y_{ji}e^{\lambda+\beta x_j}$$

$$+ \sum_{(j,i)}\log\left(2 + e^{\lambda+\beta x_j} + y_{ji}\right) + \sum_{(j,i)} R_{ji}\log\left[1 + \frac{y_{ji}e^{\lambda+\beta x_j}}{(1+e^{\lambda+\beta x_j})^2}\right]. \tag{7}$$

The MLEs of the model parameters, indicated by $\hat{\lambda}$ and $\hat{\beta}$, can be determined by solving the following non-linear likelihood equations which are obtained by setting the derivatives of the log-likelihood function in (7) with respect to λ and β to zero

$$\frac{\partial l(\lambda,\beta|y)}{\partial \lambda} = 2m - 2\sum_{j=1}^{r}\frac{m_j e^{\lambda+\beta x_j}}{1 + e^{\lambda+\beta x_j}} - \sum_{(j,i)}(1+R_{ji})y_{ji}e^{\lambda+\beta x_j} + \sum_{(j,i)}\frac{e^{\lambda+\beta x_j}}{2 + e^{\lambda+\beta x_j} + y_{ji}}$$

$$+ \sum_{(j,i)}\frac{R_{ji}y_{ji}e^{\lambda+\beta x_j}(1 - e^{\lambda+\beta x_j})}{(1+e^{\lambda+\beta x_j})\left[1 + e^{\lambda+\beta x_j}\left(2 + y_{ji} + e^{\lambda+\beta x_j}\right)\right]} = 0 \tag{8}$$

and

$$\frac{\partial l(\lambda,\beta|\mathbf{y})}{\partial \beta} = \sum_{j=1}^{r} m_j x_j - 2\sum_{j=1}^{r} \frac{m_j x_j e^{\lambda+\beta x_j}}{1+e^{\lambda+\beta x_j}} - \sum_{(j,i)}(1+R_{ji})y_{ji}x_j e^{\lambda+\beta x_j} + \sum_{(j,i)} \frac{x_j e^{\lambda+\beta x_j}}{2+e^{\lambda+\beta x_j}+y_{ji}}$$
$$+ \sum_{(j,i)} \frac{R_{ji}y_{ji}x_j e^{\lambda+\beta x_j}(1-e^{\lambda+\beta x_j})}{(1+e^{\lambda+\beta x_j})\left[1+e^{\lambda+\beta x_j}\left(2+y_{ji}+e^{\lambda+\beta x_j}\right)\right]} = 0 \qquad (9)$$

Because the solutions to the previous equations cannot be found in a closed form, the Newton–Raphson method is frequently employed in these circumstances to produce the appropriate MLEs $\hat{\lambda}$ and $\hat{\beta}$. Based on the estimated values $\hat{\lambda}$ and $\hat{\beta}$, we can obtain the MLEs of RF and HRF under normal operating conditions x_u at mission time t, respectively, using the invariance property of the MLEs, as demonstrated below:

$$\hat{\overline{G}}_u(t) = e^{-\hat{\alpha}_u t}\left(1+\frac{\hat{\alpha}_u t}{\hat{\alpha}_u^2}\right)$$

and

$$\hat{H}_u(t) = \frac{\hat{\alpha}_u^2(1+\hat{\alpha}_u+t)}{\hat{\alpha}_u^2+\hat{\alpha}_u t},$$

where $\hat{\alpha}_u = e^{\hat{\lambda}+\hat{\beta}x_u}$.

After having the point estimates for the various parameters, it is now interesting to construct the confidence intervals for the unknown parameters λ and β, or any function of them, such as the RF and HRF. Here, we utilize the asymptotic normality of the MLEs to obtain the ACIs of the different parameters. According to Miller [25], the asymptotic distribution of the MLEs can be expressed as $(\hat{\lambda},\hat{\beta}) \sim N[(\lambda,\beta), \mathbf{I}^{-1}(\hat{\lambda},\hat{\beta})]$, where $\mathbf{I}^{-1}(\hat{\lambda},\hat{\beta})$ is the approximated variance–covariance matrix as presented below:

$$\mathbf{I}^{-1}(\hat{\lambda},\hat{\beta}) = \begin{pmatrix} -\frac{\partial^2 l(\lambda,\beta|\mathbf{y})}{\partial \lambda^2} & -\frac{\partial^2 l(\lambda,\beta|\mathbf{y})}{\partial \lambda \partial \beta} \\ -\frac{\partial^2 l(\lambda,\beta|\mathbf{y})}{\partial \beta \partial \lambda} & -\frac{\partial^2 l(\lambda,\beta|\mathbf{y})}{\partial \beta^2} \end{pmatrix}^{-1}_{(\lambda,\beta)=(\hat{\lambda},\hat{\beta})} = \begin{pmatrix} \hat{\sigma}_{11} & \hat{\sigma}_{12} \\ \hat{\sigma}_{21} & \hat{\sigma}_{22} \end{pmatrix}, \qquad (10)$$

where

$$\frac{\partial^2 l(\lambda,\beta|\mathbf{y})}{\partial \lambda^2} = -2\sum_{j=1}^{r} \frac{m_j e^{\lambda+\beta x_j}}{(1+e^{\lambda+\beta x_j})^2} - \sum_{(j,i)}(1+R_{ji})y_{ji}e^{\lambda+\beta x_j} + \sum_{(j,i)}\frac{(2+y_{ji})e^{\lambda+\beta x_j}}{(2+e^{\lambda+\beta x_j}+y_{ji})^2}$$
$$- \sum_{(j,i)} \frac{R_{ji}y_{ji}e^{\lambda+\beta x_j}\left\{2e^{\lambda+\beta x_j}+e^{2(\lambda+\beta x_j)}\left[6+2e^{\lambda+\beta x_j}-e^{2(\lambda+\beta x_j)}+2y_{ji}\right]-1\right\}}{(1+e^{\lambda+\beta x_j})^2\left[1+e^{\lambda+\beta x_j}\left(2+y_{ji}+e^{\lambda+\beta x_j}\right)\right]^2},$$

$$\frac{\partial^2 l(\lambda,\beta|\mathbf{y})}{\partial \beta^2} = -2\sum_{j=1}^{r} \frac{m_j x_j^2 e^{\lambda+\beta x_j}}{(1+e^{\lambda+\beta x_j})^2} - \sum_{(j,i)}(1+R_{ji})y_{ji}x_j^2 e^{\lambda+\beta x_j} + \sum_{(j,i)}\frac{x_j^2(2+y_{ji})e^{\lambda+\beta x_j}}{(2+e^{\lambda+\beta x_j}+y_{ji})^2}$$
$$- \sum_{(j,i)} \frac{R_{ji}y_{ji}x_j^2 e^{\lambda+\beta x_j}\left\{2e^{\lambda+\beta x_j}+e^{2(\lambda+\beta x_j)}\left[6+2e^{\lambda+\beta x_j}-e^{2(\lambda+\beta x_j)}+2y_{ji}\right]-1\right\}}{(1+e^{\lambda+\beta x_j})^2\left[1+e^{\lambda+\beta x_j}\left(2+y_{ji}+e^{\lambda+\beta x_j}\right)\right]^2},$$

and

$$\frac{\partial^2 l(\lambda,\beta|\mathbf{y})}{\partial\lambda\partial\beta} = -2\sum_{j=1}^{r}\frac{m_j x_j e^{\lambda+\beta x_j}}{(1+e^{\lambda+\beta x_j})^2} - \sum_{(j,i)}(1+R_{ji})y_{ji}x_j e^{\lambda+\beta x_j} + \sum_{(j,i)}\frac{x_j(2+y_{ji})e^{\lambda+\beta x_j}}{(2+e^{\lambda+\beta x_j}+y_{ji})^2}$$
$$- \sum_{(j,i)}\frac{R_{ji}y_{ji}x_j e^{\lambda+\beta x_j}\left\{2e^{\lambda+\beta x_j} + e^{2(\lambda+\beta x_j)}\left[6 + 2e^{\lambda+\beta x_j} - e^{2(\lambda+\beta x_j)} + 2y_{ji}\right] - 1\right\}}{(1+e^{\lambda+\beta x_j})^2\left[1+e^{\lambda+\beta x_j}\left(2+y_{ji}+e^{\lambda+\beta x_j}\right)\right]^2}.$$

Therefore, for $0 < \tau < 1$, the $100(1-\tau)\%$ ACIs for λ and β are provided by

$$\hat{\lambda} \pm z_{\tau/2}\sqrt{\hat{\sigma}_{11}} \text{ and } \hat{\beta} \pm z_{\tau/2}\sqrt{\hat{\sigma}_{22}},$$

where $\hat{\sigma}_{11}$ and $\hat{\sigma}_{22}$ are the main diagonal elements of (10) and $z_{\tau/2}$ is the upper $(\tau/2)^{th}$ percentile point of the standard normal distribution.

As a matter of fact, in order to establish the confidence bounds of the RF and HRF under normal operating conditions, we should first determine the variances of their estimators. Here, we approximate the necessary estimated variances of $\hat{\overline{G}}_u(t)$ and $\hat{H}_u(t)$ using the delta method. To apply this approach, we need the first derivatives of RF and HRF with respect to the parameters λ and β as follows:

$$\frac{\partial \overline{G}_u(t)}{\partial \lambda} = -\frac{te^{-te^{\lambda+\beta x_u}+2(\lambda+\beta x_u)}\left[4+t+e^{\lambda+\beta x_u}(3+t+e^{\lambda+\beta x_u})\right]}{(1+e^{\lambda+\beta x_u})^2}, \quad \frac{\partial \overline{G}_u(t)}{\partial \beta} = x_u\frac{\partial \overline{G}_u(t)}{\partial \lambda}$$

$$\frac{\partial H_u(t)}{\partial \lambda} = \frac{e^{2(\lambda+\beta x_u)}\left\{2t+e^{\lambda+\beta x_u}\left[7+4e^{\lambda+\beta x_u}+e^{2(\lambda+\beta x_u)}+t(4+t^2+2e^{\lambda+\beta x_u})\right]\right\}}{[(1+e^{\lambda+\beta x_u})^2 + te^{\lambda+\beta x_u}]^2},$$

and

$$\frac{\partial H_u(t)}{\partial \beta} = x_u\frac{\partial H_u(t)}{\partial \lambda}.$$

Let $\Lambda_1 = (\frac{\partial \overline{G}_u(t)}{\partial \lambda}, \frac{\partial \overline{G}_u(t)}{\partial \beta})$ and $\Lambda_2 = (\frac{\partial H_u(t)}{\partial \lambda}, \frac{\partial H_u(t)}{\partial \beta})$, evaluated at the MLEs of λ and β. Then, the approximate estimated variances of $\hat{\overline{G}}_u(t)$ and $\hat{H}_u(t)$ are obtained as follows:

$$\hat{\sigma}_{\overline{G}} \approx [\Lambda_1 I^{-1}(\hat{\lambda},\hat{\beta})\Lambda_1^\top] \text{ and } \hat{\sigma}_H \approx [\Lambda_2 I^{-1}(\hat{\lambda},\hat{\beta})\Lambda_2^\top].$$

Consequently, the ACIs of $\overline{G}_u(t)$ and $H_u(t)$ can be constructed, respectively, as

$$\hat{\overline{G}}_u(t) \pm z_{\tau/2}\sqrt{\hat{\sigma}_{\overline{G}}}, \text{ and } \hat{H}_u(t) \pm z_{\tau/2}\sqrt{\hat{\sigma}_H}.$$

4. Bayesian Estimation

When the sample size is large or the data are well collected, MLEs usually produce results that are reasonably accurate. However, when there is a lot of information missing from the data or the sample size is limited, the Bayesian paradigm produces a more precise inference. We discuss the Bayesian inference for the model parameters as well as the RF and HRF in this section. As we are aware, in a Bayesian investigation, the model parameters are generally treated as random variables that follow a set of predetermined prior distributions. On the basis of the prior knowledge and the observed data, it is then possible to acquire the posterior distributions of the model parameters and obtain the Bayes estimators as well. Keep in mind that the mean time to failure of the testing units is often lower in ALTs because of the stress conditions. In our case and for the XL distribution, one can see from Chouia and Zeghdoudi [23] that the mean is a decreasing function of the parameter α. Under the log-linear model, this can be achieved for positive β with any value for the parameter λ. This idea can be incorporated into the priors. We assume that the parameters are independent, where the parameter λ follows the normal distribution, which allows the parameter λ to be negative or positive. On the other hand, the parameter β is assumed to follow the gamma distribution which is more flexible than other prior distributions and adapts the support of the parameter β, i.e., $\lambda \sim N(a,b)$ and $\beta \sim Gamma(c,d)$. Then, the joint prior distribution can be expressed as

$$p(\lambda, \beta) \propto \beta^{c-1} e^{-0.5(\lambda-a)^2/b^2 - d\beta}, \quad -\infty < \lambda < \infty, \beta > 0, \qquad (11)$$

where $b, c, d > 0$ and $-\infty < a < \infty$ are the hyperparameters. Equations (6) and (11), when combined, can provide the following as the joint posterior density function of λ and β:

$$q(\lambda, \beta|\mathbf{y}) = \frac{\beta^{c-1} e^{2m\lambda + \beta \sum_{j=1}^{r} m_j x_j - 0.5(\lambda-a)^2/b^2 - d\beta}}{A \, e^{2\sum_{j=1}^{r} m_j \log\left(1 + e^{\lambda + \beta x_j}\right)}} \prod_{j=1}^{r} \prod_{i=1}^{m_j} \left[1 + \frac{y_{ji} e^{\lambda + \beta x_j}}{\left(1 + e^{\lambda + \beta x_j}\right)^2}\right]^{R_{ji}}$$

$$\times \exp\left[-\sum_{(j,i)} (1 + R_{ji}) y_{ji} e^{\lambda + \beta x_j} + \sum_{(j,i)} \log\left(2 + e^{\lambda + \beta x_j} + y_{ji}\right)\right], \qquad (12)$$

where A is the normalized constant given by

$$A = \int_0^\infty \int_{-\infty}^\infty p(\lambda, \beta) \, L(\lambda, \beta|\mathbf{y}) \, d\lambda \, d\beta.$$

We can draw Bayes estimators with respect to parameters of interest and/or functions of parameters, say $\psi(\lambda, \beta)$, using the SE loss function as follows:

$$\tilde{\psi}(\lambda, \beta) = \frac{\int_0^\infty \int_{-\infty}^\infty \psi(\lambda, \beta) p(\lambda, \beta) \, L(\lambda, \beta|\mathbf{y}) \, d\lambda \, d\beta}{\int_0^\infty \int_{-\infty}^\infty p(\lambda, \beta) \, L(\lambda, \beta|\mathbf{y}) \, d\lambda \, d\beta}. \qquad (13)$$

Due to the ratio of two intractable integrals in (13), it appears that the Bayes estimator cannot be derived analytically. Due to this difficulty, the MCMC method is used, which does not require the computation of a normalizing constant. First, we must derive the conditional distributions of the parameters λ and β to apply the MCMC technique. In light of (12), the following are the conditional posterior distributions of λ and β, respectively,

$$q(\lambda|\beta, \mathbf{y}) \propto \frac{e^{2m\lambda - 0.5(\lambda-a)^2/b^2}}{e^{2\sum_{j=1}^{r} m_j \log\left(1 + e^{\lambda + \beta x_j}\right)}} \prod_{j=1}^{r} \prod_{i=1}^{m_j} \left[1 + \frac{y_{ji} e^{\lambda + \beta x_j}}{\left(1 + e^{\lambda + \beta x_j}\right)^2}\right]^{R_{ji}}$$

$$\times \exp\left[-\sum_{(j,i)} (1 + R_{ji}) y_{ji} e^{\lambda + \beta x_j} + \sum_{(j,i)} \log\left(2 + e^{\lambda + \beta x_j} + y_{ji}\right)\right] \qquad (14)$$

and

$$q(\beta|\lambda, \mathbf{y}) = \frac{\beta^{c-1} e^{\beta \sum_{j=1}^{r} m_j x_j - d\beta}}{e^{2\sum_{j=1}^{r} m_j \log\left(1 + e^{\lambda + \beta x_j}\right)}} \prod_{j=1}^{r} \prod_{i=1}^{m_j} \left[1 + \frac{y_{ji} e^{\lambda + \beta x_j}}{\left(1 + e^{\lambda + \beta x_j}\right)^2}\right]^{R_{ji}}$$

$$\times \exp\left[-\sum_{(j,i)} (1 + R_{ji}) y_{ji} e^{\lambda + \beta x_j} + \sum_{(j,i)} \log\left(2 + e^{\lambda + \beta x_j} + y_{ji}\right)\right]. \qquad (15)$$

It is noted that no analytical reduction to any well-known distributions can be achieved for the conditional distributions of λ and β provided by (14) and (15), respectively. The main goal of MCMC algorithms is to generate samples from a given probability distribution. The "Monte Carlo" part of the method's name is due to the sampling purpose, whereas the "Markov Chain" part comes from the kind of Markov chains. As a result, the Metropolis–Hastings (M-H) procedure is used to generate samples from these distributions in order to obtain the Bayes estimates and the BCIs. To implement the M-H procedure, we consider the normal distribution as the proposal distribution for both parameters. Thus, follow the steps listed below for the sample generation process:

Step 1. Put $l = 1$.

Step 2. Start with the primary guesses $(\lambda^{(0)}, \beta^{(0)}) = (\hat{\lambda}, \hat{\beta})$.

Step 3. Obtain $\lambda^{(l)}$ from (14) using the M-H algorithm.

Step 4. Acquire $\beta^{(l)}$ using (15) via the M-H algorithm.

Step 5. Use $\lambda^{(l)}$ and $\beta^{(l)}$ to obtain $\alpha_u^{(l)}$, and then compute

$$\overline{G}_u^{(l)}(t) = e^{-\hat{\alpha}_u^{(l)} t}\left(1 + \frac{\hat{\alpha}_u^{(l)} t}{[\hat{\alpha}_u^{(l)}]^2}\right)$$

and

$$H_u^{(l)}(t) = \frac{[\hat{\alpha}_u^{(l)}]^2(1 + \hat{\alpha}_u^{(l)} + t)}{[\hat{\alpha}_u^{(l)}]^2 + \hat{\alpha}_u^{(l)} t}$$

Step 6. Set $l = l + 1$.

Step 7. Perform Steps 3–6 M times to acquire

$$\left[\lambda^{(l)}, \beta^{(l)}, \overline{G}_u^{(l)}(t), H_u^{(l)}(t)\right], l = 1, 2, \ldots, M.$$

To guarantee convergence and avoid the appeal of starting values, the first D generated samples are eliminated. In this case, we have $\phi^{(l)}$, where $l = D+1, \ldots, M$, where $\phi = \lambda, \beta, \overline{G}_u(t), H_u(t)$. Based on large M, one can compute the Bayes estimates of ϕ based on the SE loss function as

$$\tilde{\phi} = \frac{1}{M^\circ}\sum_{l=D^\circ}^{M} \phi^{(l)},$$

where $M^\circ = M - D$ and $D^\circ = D + 1$. To obtain the BCI of ϕ, sort $\phi^{(l)}$ as $\phi^{[l]}, l = D^\circ, \ldots, M$. Then, the $100(1 - \tau)\%$ BCI of the ϕ takes the form

$$\left\{\phi^{[0.5\tau M^\circ]}, \phi^{[M^\circ(1 - 0.5\tau)]}\right\}.$$

5. Monte Carlo Simulations

To compare the behavior of the proposed point and interval estimators of the XL model parameter α and its reliability characteristics RF $\overline{G}_u(t)$ and HRF $H_u(t)$, extensive simulation studies are conducted based on several combinations of x_j, $j = 1, 2, \ldots, r$ (stress levels), n_j (group size), m_j (effective sample size) and R_{ji}, $j = 1, 2, \ldots, r$ $i = 1, 2, \ldots, m_j$ (censoring pattern). We replicated the PT-IIC mechanism 1000 times when the true value of (λ, β) is taken as $(0.2, 0.5)$. At the same time, for the usual condition $x_u = 0.1$, the acquired estimates of $\overline{G}_u(t)$ and $H_u(t)$ at time $t = 0.1$ are evaluated when their actual values are taken as 0.9011 and 1.0438, respectively. Take 2 choices of stress levels (x_1, x_2), namely $(1, 2)$ and $(3, 5)$, $n_1 = n_2 = n(= 30, 80)$, without loss of generality, and the failure percentages (FPs) are taken as $\frac{m}{n} \times 100\% = (40, 80)\%$ to a specific amount m of each n. Moreover, for each setting, different progressive censoring mechanisms are considered as follows:

$$\text{Scheme-1}: R_1 = n - m, \quad R_i = 0 \quad \text{for} \quad i \neq 1;$$
$$\text{Scheme-2}: R_{\frac{m}{2}} = n - m, \quad R_i = 0 \quad \text{for} \quad i \neq \frac{m}{2};$$
$$\text{Scheme-3}: R_m = n - m, \quad R_i = 0 \quad \text{for} \quad i \neq m.$$

Once 1000 constant stress PT-IIC samples are collected, the maximum likelihood and Bayes estimates of λ, β, α (based on normal condition $x_u = 0.1$), $\overline{G}_u(t)$ and $H_u(t)$ along with their asymptotic and credible interval estimates are calculated. To perform the desired numerical evaluations, using R 4.2.2 software, we suggest to install both the 'maxLik' (proposed by Henningsen and Toomet [26]) and 'coda' (proposed by Plummer et al. [27]) packages in order to carry out the maximum likelihood and Bayesian analysis.

Following the mean and variance criteria of the proposed density priors, we have chosen different sets of the prior parameters (a, b, c, d) of λ and β, called Prior[1]:(0.2, 5, 0.5, 1) and Prior[2]:(0.2, 1, 2.5, 5). These values are determined in such a way that the expected prior refers to the sample mean for the coefficient of interest. Alternatively, the hyperparameter values can also easily be specified using the past-sample technique. Following the M-H sampler described in Section 4, to obtain the Bayes point (or credible) estimates of λ, β, α_u, $\overline{G}_u(t)$ or $H_u(t)$, we simulated $D = 2000$ and $M° = 10,000$ samples.

To evaluate the convergence of the simulated MCMC draws of λ, β, α_u, $\overline{G}_u(t)$ or $H_u(t)$, when $(x_1, x_2) = (1, 2)$, $n[\text{FP}] = 30[40\%]$ and Scheme-1 (as an example), both the autocorrelation and trace convergence diagnostic plots are shown in Figure 1. It shows that the samples drawn from the Markov chain of all the unknown parameters are mixed adequately, and thus the calculated estimates are satisfactory.

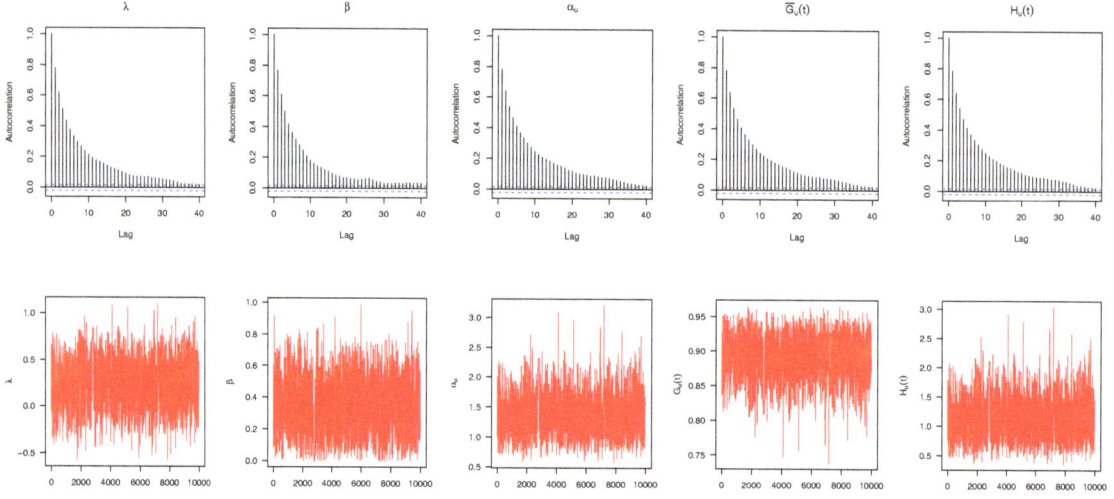

Figure 1. Autocorrelation (**top**) and trace (**bottom**) plots for MCMC draws in Monte Carlo simulation.

Now, the comparison between the acquired point estimates of λ is made based on their root mean squared errors (RMSEs) and mean absolute biases (RABs), respectively, as

$$\text{RMSE} = \sqrt{\frac{1}{1000} \sum_{i=1}^{1000} \left(\breve{\lambda}^{(i)} - \lambda\right)^2}$$

and

$$\text{MAB} = \frac{1}{1000} \sum_{i=1}^{1000} \left|\breve{\lambda}^{(i)} - \lambda\right|,$$

respectively, where $\breve{\lambda}^{(i)}$ is the calculated estimate at ith sample of λ.

Additionally, taking $\tau = 5\%$, the comparison between the acquired interval estimates of λ is made based on their average confidence lengths (ACLs) and coverage percentages (CPs) as

$$\text{ACL}_{95\%}(\lambda) = \frac{1}{1000} \sum_{i=1}^{1000} \left(\mathcal{U}_{\breve{\lambda}^{(i)}} - \mathcal{L}_{\breve{\lambda}^{(i)}}\right),$$

and

$$\text{CP}_{95\%}(\lambda) = \frac{1}{1000} \sum_{i=1}^{1000} \mathbf{1}_{\left(\mathcal{L}_{\breve{\lambda}^{(i)}}, \mathcal{U}_{\breve{\lambda}^{(i)}}\right)}(\lambda),$$

respectively, where $\mathbf{1}(\cdot)$ is the indicator function, $(\mathcal{L}(\cdot), \mathcal{U}(\cdot))$ is the two-sided interval estimate. In a similar fashion, both point and interval estimates of β, α_u, $\overline{G}_u(t)$ and $H_u(t)$ can easily be developed.

Nowadays, heat-map data visualization has become a popular tool for digital data representation as the value of each data point is indicated using specific colors. Therefore, all the simulated results (including the RMSE, MAB, ACL and CP) of λ, β, α_u, $\overline{G}_u(t)$ and $H_u(t)$ are displayed by a heat-map tool in Figures 2–6, respectively. Specifically, for Prior-1 (say P1) as an example, the Bayes estimates are mentioned as "BE-P1", whereas the BCI estimates are mentioned as "BCI-P1". All the numerical tables are also available as Supplementary Materials.

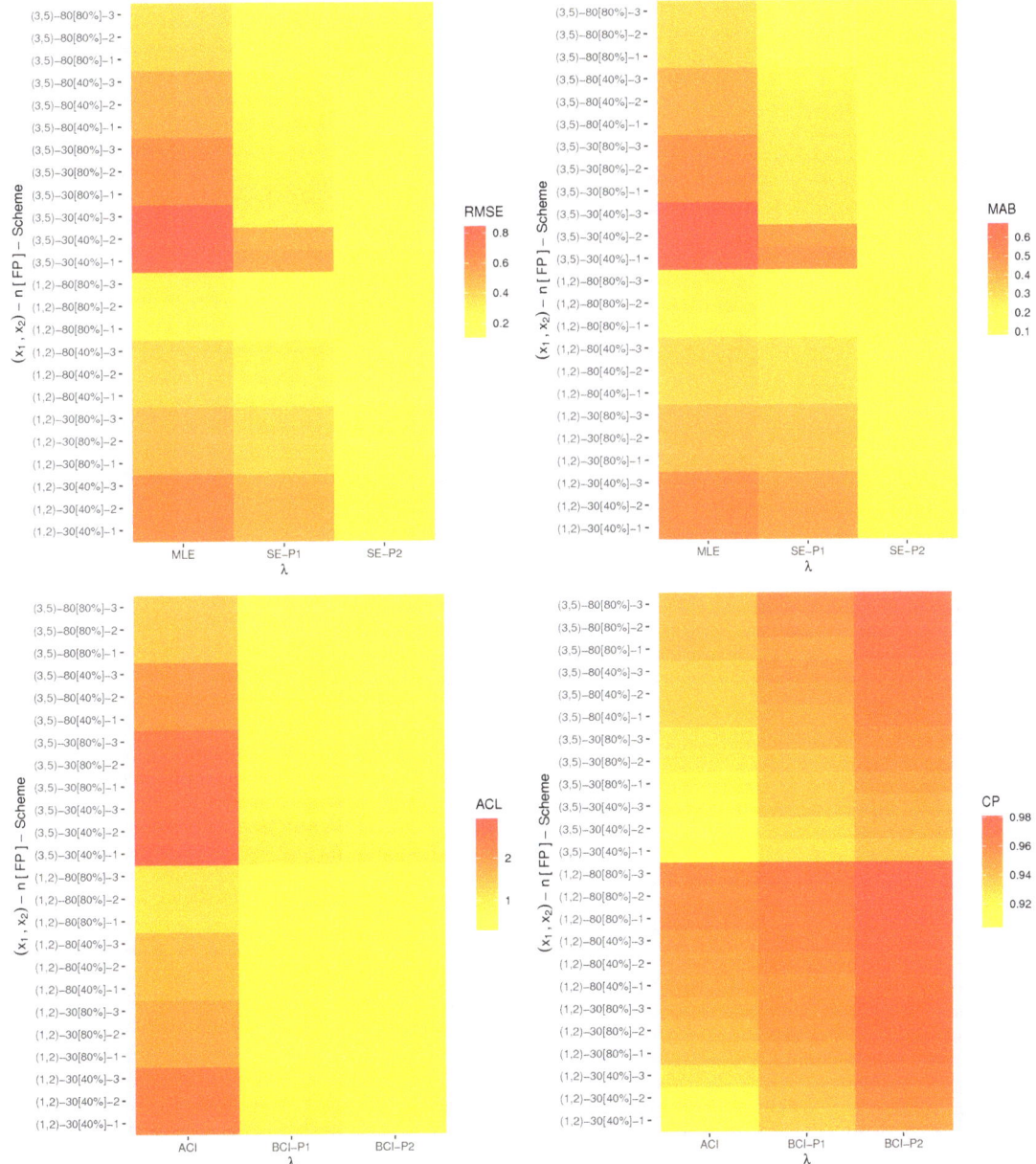

Figure 2. Heat map for the simulation results of λ.

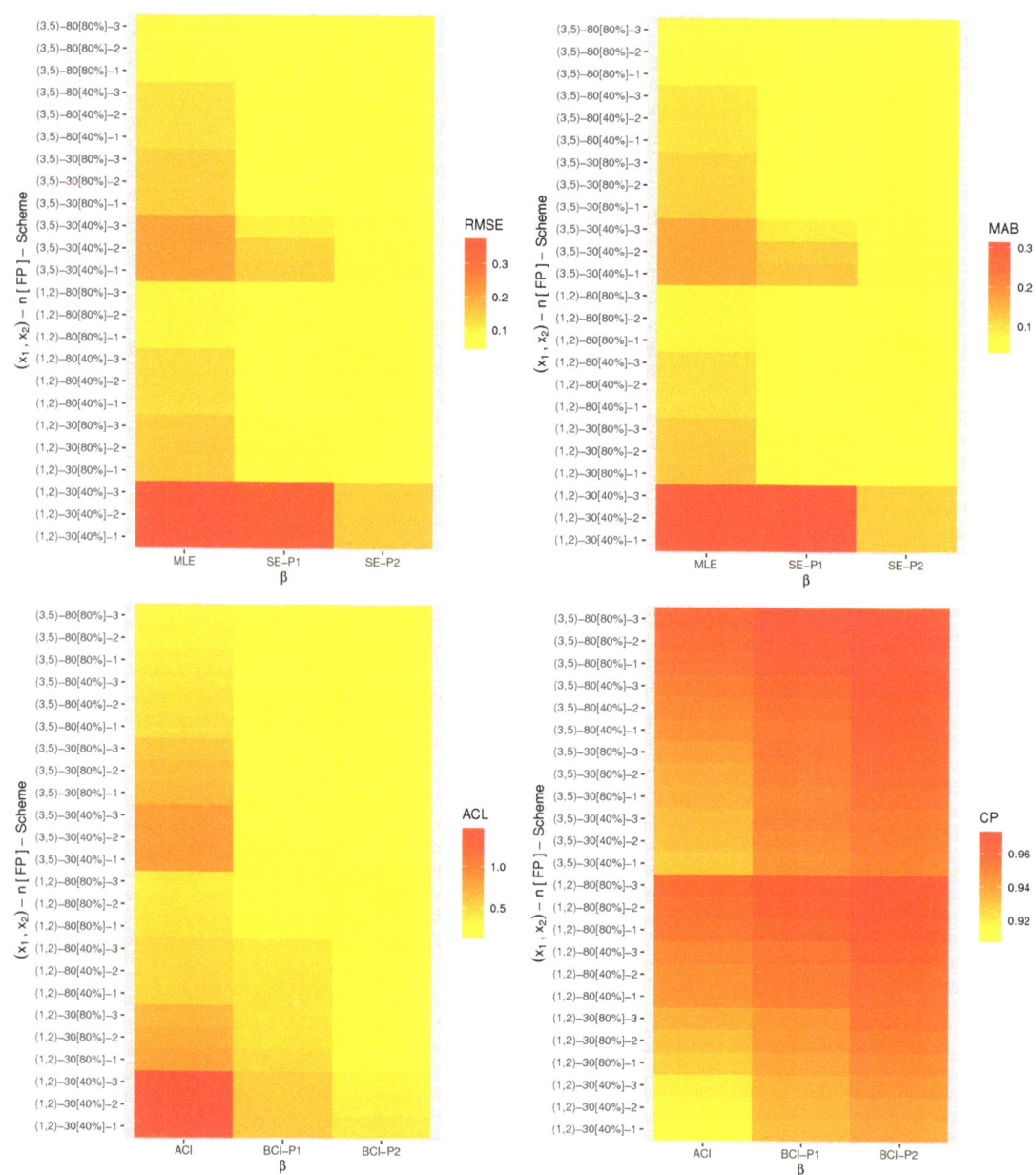

Figure 3. Heat map for the simulation results of β.

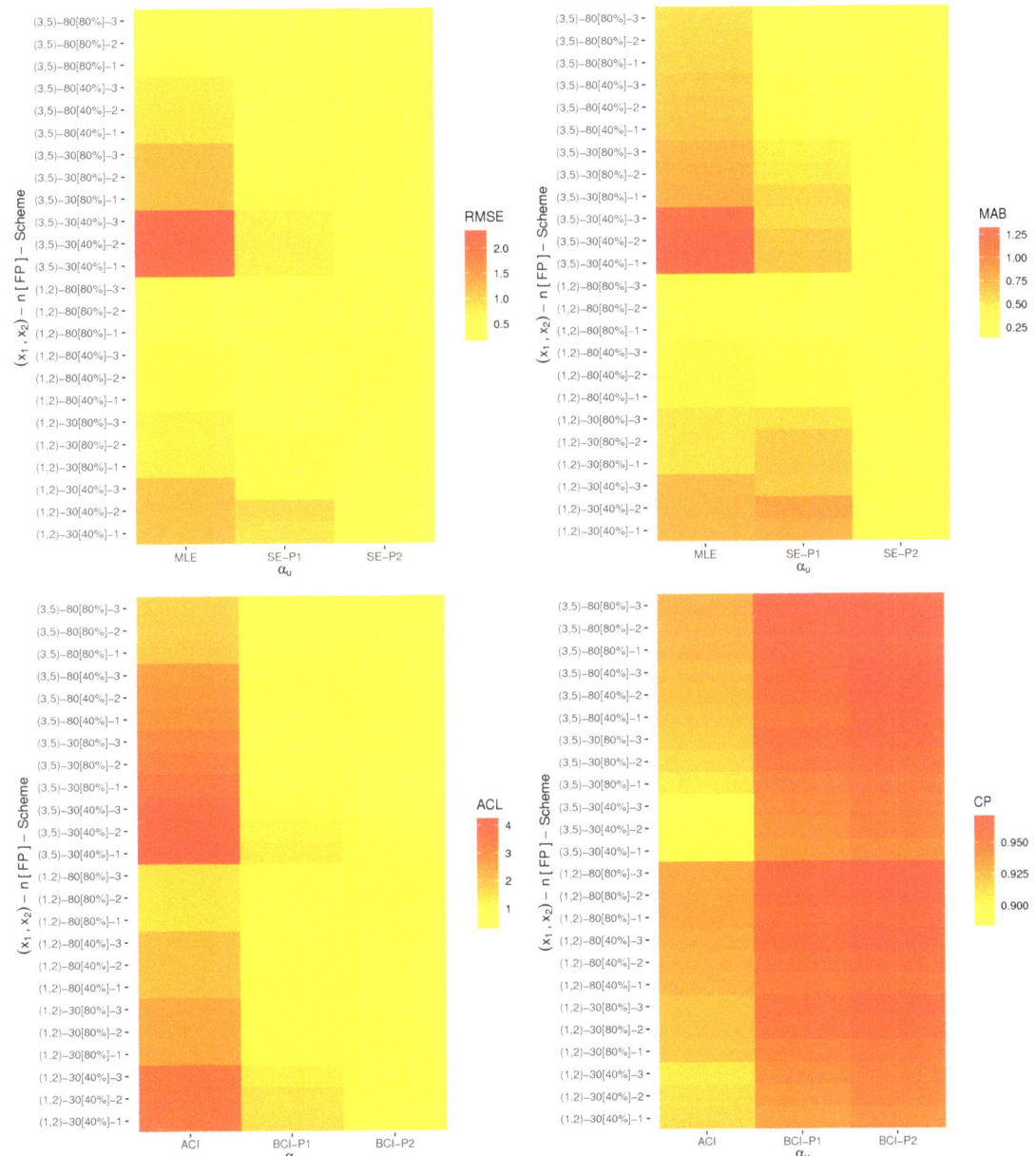

Figure 4. Heat map for the simulation results of α_u.

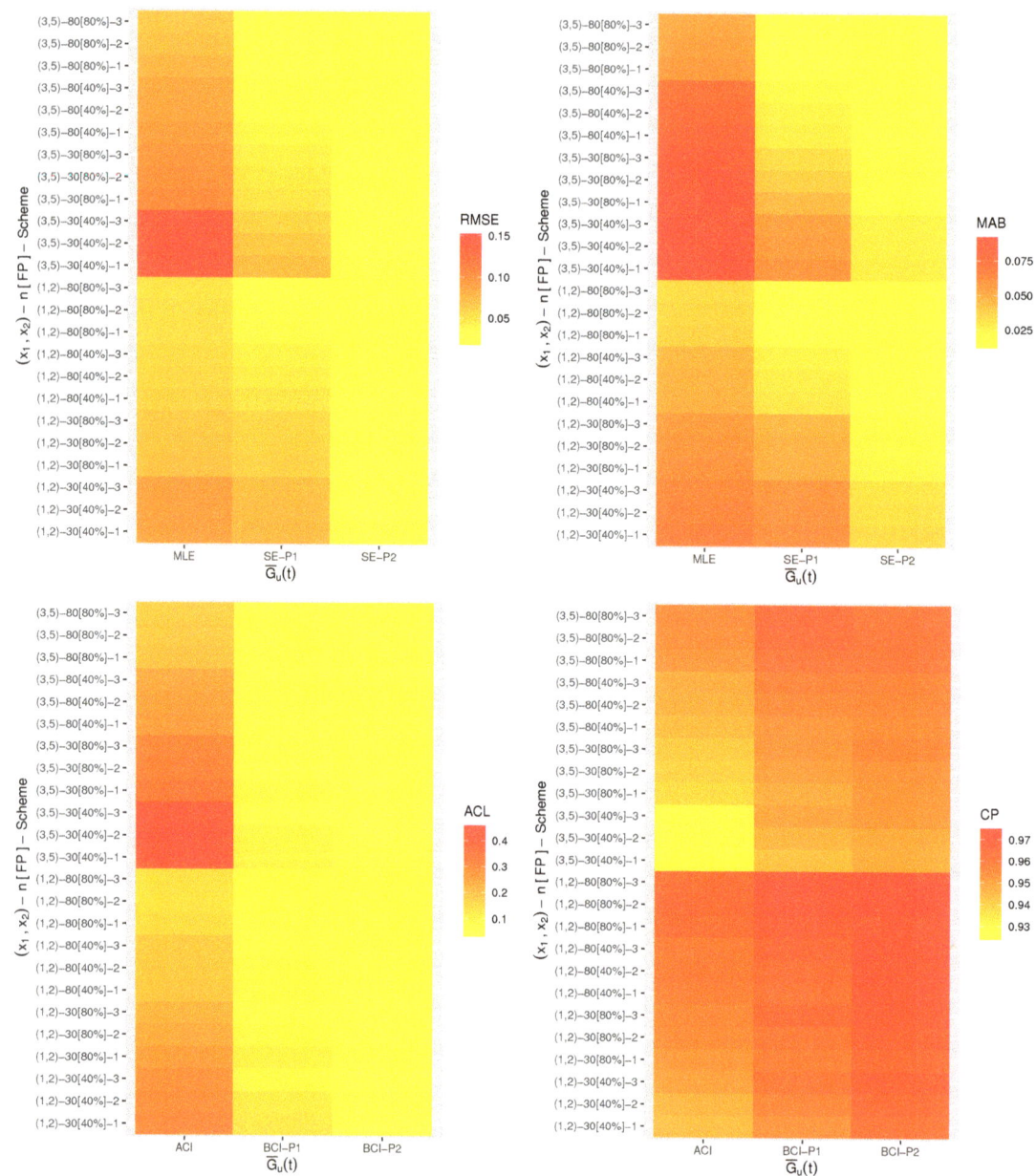

Figure 5. Heat map for the simulation results of $\overline{G}_u(t)$.

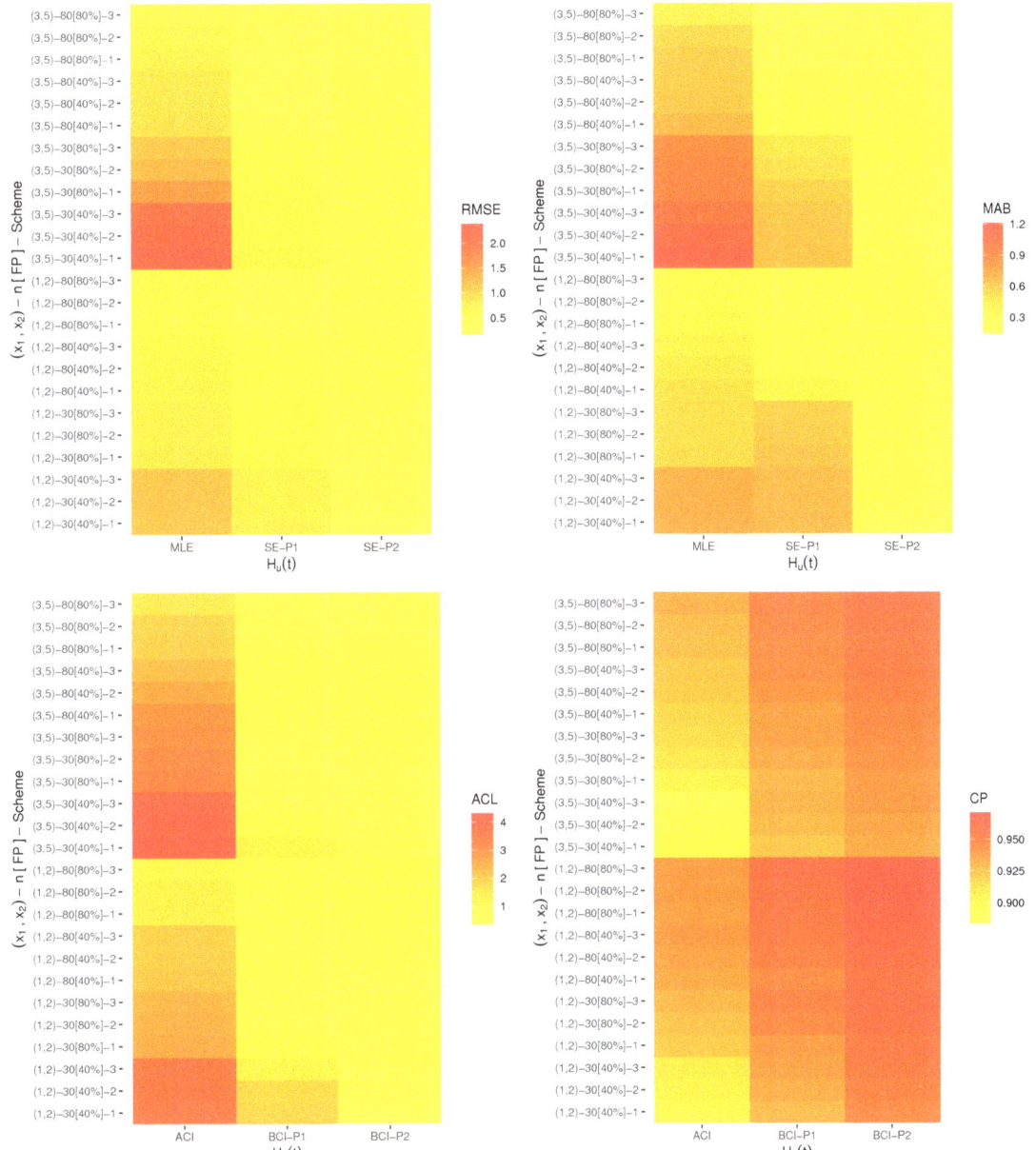

Figure 6. Heat map for the simulation results of $H_u(t)$.

From Figures 2–6, in terms of the lowest level of the RMSE, MAB and ACL values as well as the highest level of the CP values, we list the following conclusions:

1. As a general comment, it is clear that the derived point (or interval) estimates of λ, β, α_u, $\overline{G}_u(t)$ or $H_u(t)$ have a good performance.
2. As n (or m or both) increases, all the calculated estimates provide better results and hold the consistency property. An equivalent observation is also reached when $\sum_{i=1}^{m_j} R_{ji}$ decreases.

3. As x_j, $j = 1, 2$ increase, the following can be seen:
   - The RMSEs and MRABs of all the estimates of λ increase while of β they decrease.
   - The RMSEs and MRABs of α_u, $\overline{G}_u(t)$ and $H_u(t)$ derived from the likelihood method increase while those derived from the Bayes method decrease.
   - The ACLs of λ increase while of β they decrease. The CPs of λ decrease while of β they increase.
   - The ACLs of α_u, $\overline{G}_u(t)$ and $H_u(t)$ obtained from the ACI method increase while those obtained from the BCI decrease. Regarding their CPs, the opposite result is noted.
4. It is known that more accurate estimates will be obtained when the priors are used more accurately. Thus, for all settings, the MCMC estimates of λ, β, α_u, $\overline{G}_u(t)$ and $H_u(t)$ provide more accurate results compared to those obtained from the likelihood method.
5. Because the calculated variance of Prior[1] is higher than that associated with Prior[2], as anticipated, all the MCMC (or BCI) estimates using Prior[2] have more accurate results than the others, and both are better than those obtained from the MLE (or ACI) estimates.
6. Comparing the proposed censoring schemes 1, 2 and 3, for both the point and interval estimates, it is observed that the proposed estimation procedures of λ, β, α_u, $\overline{G}_u(t)$ or $H_u(t)$ perform better based on Scheme-3 (right censoring) than the others.
7. To sum up, the simulation facts showed that the Bayes estimation method according to the M-H sampler for evaluating the XL parameters of life has a good performance and is recommended across different scenarios.

6. Real-Life Applications

To highlight the adaptability of acquired estimators to real-life situations, this section demonstrates two applications from the engineering field using two real data sets. These applications showed that the proposed estimation approaches work satisfactorily in practice.

6.1. Oil of Insulating Fluid

This application provides an analysis of the oil breakdown times (OBTs) of an insulating fluid subjected to various high test voltages. From Nelson [28], two data sets (in seconds) under different stress levels (kilovolor or kV) are considered; one is taken from 30 kV (normal use condition) and the other is taken from 32 kV (stress use condition). For computational convenience, each breakdown time point is divided by one hundred. So, the new transformed OBT data are presented in Table 1. Before addressing our inference, to check whether the XL model provides a significant fit to the OBT data or not, the Kolmogorov–Smirnov (KS) statistics along its p-value at a 5% significance level are considered. First, from Table 1, the MLE (standard error (SE)) of α based on the normal and stress use OBT data sets is 1.5101(0.3835) and 2.6212(0.6097), respectively. Correspondingly, the KS (p-value) of the normal and stress use data sets is 0.203(0.682) and 0.309(0.089), respectively. It indicates, for both given stress levels, that the XL model fits the OBT data appropriately. Graphically, from Table 1, the fitted/empirical RFs as well as the probability–probability (PP) plots are plotted and shown in Figure 7. As we anticipated, Figure 7 shows that the proposed XL model provides a suitable fit to the OBT data sets.

Table 1. Oil breakdown times of insulating fluid.

Normal Use										
0.1705	0.1774	0.2046	0.2102	0.2266	0.4340	0.4730	1.3907	1.4412	1.7588	1.9490
Stress Use										
0.0027	0.0040	0.0069	0.0079	0.0275	0.0391	0.0988	0.1395	0.1593	0.2780	0.5324
0.8285	0.8929	1.0058	2.1510							

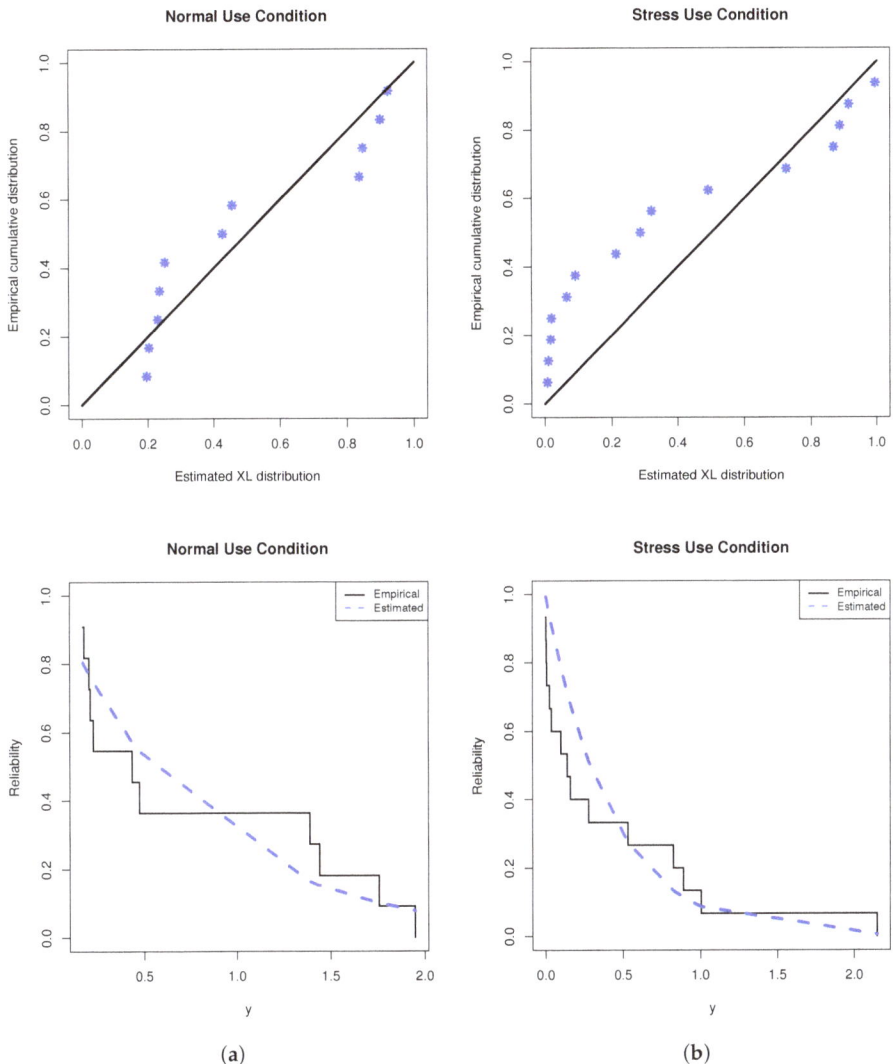

Figure 7. Fitted RF (**right**) and PP (**left**) plots from OBT data. (**a**) Normal condition; (**b**) stress condition.

In this part, to see the usefulness of the derived point/interval estimators, several PT-IIC samples from the OBT data sets are obtained. From Table 1, taking different options of the effective samples m_j, $i = 1, 2$ and censoring plans $(R_{j1}, R_{j2}, \ldots, R_{jm_j})$, 3 artificial samples are created and listed in Table 2. Here, for brevity, the scheme $(1, 1, 1, 1, 1)$ is considered as (1^5). So, for each generated sample, the point estimates (including the maximum likelihood and Bayes estimates) and the interval estimates (including the asymptotic and credible interval estimates) of λ, β, α_u, $\overline{G}_u(t)$ and $H_u(t)$ (for distinct time $t = 1$ and the normal operating level $x_u = 25$) are calculated. Obviously, we do not have any prior information about λ and β; thus, we set $a = b = c = d = 0.001$ which means that the posterior density becomes quite close to the likelihood function. We also run the proposed MCMC procedure with a burn-in of 10,000 followed by 40,000 iterations. Thus, the Bayes point (or credible interval) estimates are evaluated. The initial values of β and δ for beginning our iterations are taken as $\hat{\lambda}$ and $\hat{\beta}$, respectively. However, in Table 3, the point estimates (with their

SEs) and the interval estimates (with their lengths) are presented. It shows that both the frequentist and Bayesian estimates are very close to each other while the latter performed better than the former with respect to the minimum standard errors and interval lengths. A similar behavior is also noted in the case of the interval estimates.

Moreover, to display the convergence of the generated Markovian chains, the histograms plot with the Gaussian kernel as well as the trace plot based on 40,000 MCMC variates are shown in Figure 8. Specifically, in Figure 8, the Bayes estimate of λ, β, α_u, $\overline{G}_u(t)$ and $H_u(t)$ is highlighted by a solid line while their BCI bounds are highlighted by dashed lines. As a result, from Figure 8, it is observed that (i) the proposed estimates developed by the MCMC algorithm have sufficient convergence, (ii) the burn-in sample has enough size to eliminate the effect of the starting points and (iii) the density distribution of λ or δ is almost fairly symmetrical, of α_u or $H_u(t)$ it is positively skewed and of $\overline{G}_u(t)$ it is negatively skewed.

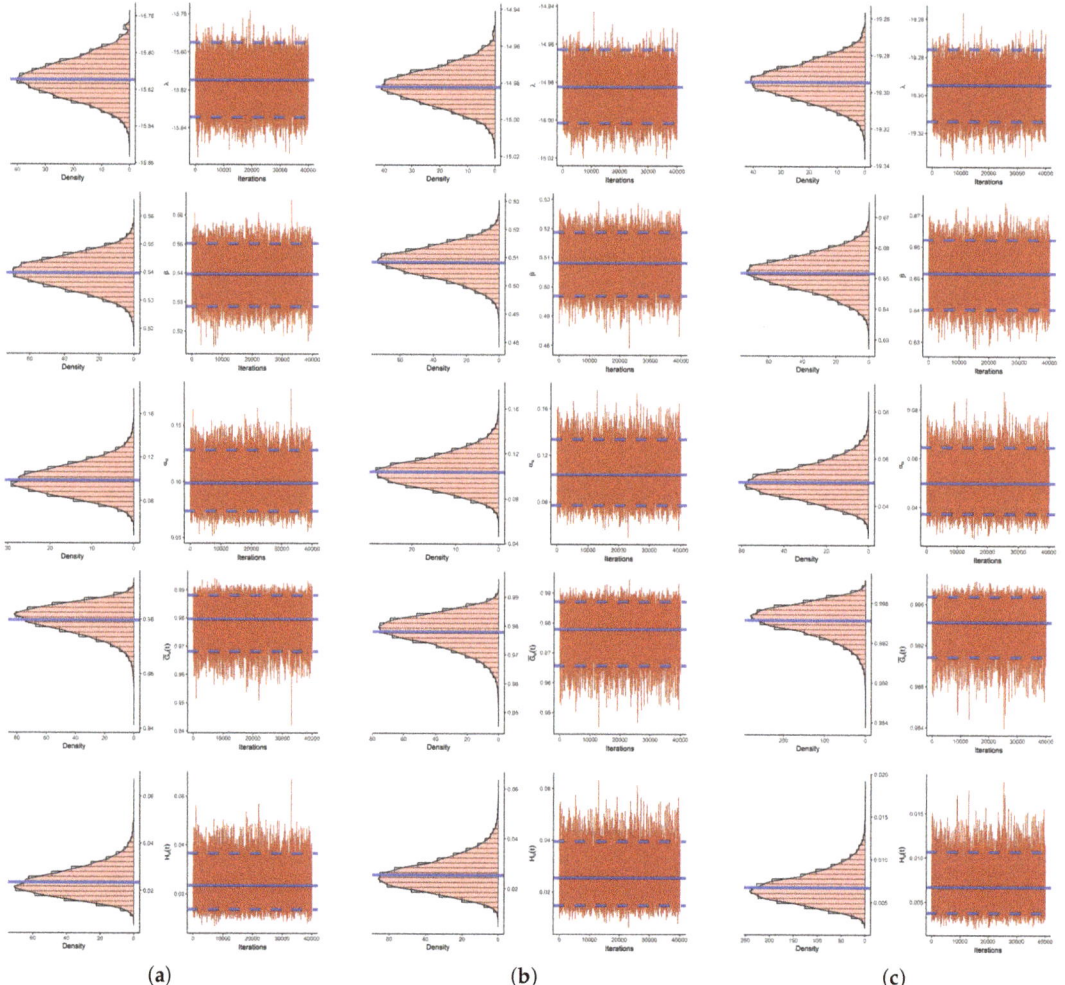

Figure 8. Density (**left**) and trace (**right**) plot of λ, β, α_u, $\overline{G}_u(t)$ and $H_u(t)$ from OBT data. (**a**) Sample 1; (**b**) Sample 2; (**c**) Sample 3.

Table 2. Various constant stress PC-T-II samples from OBT data.

Sample	Scheme	Normal Use Censored Data from $(n_1, m_1) = (11, 8)$
1	$(3, 0^7)$	0.1705, 0.2046, 0.2102, 0.2266, 0.4340, 1.3907, 1.4412, 1.7588
2	$(0^3, 3, 0^4)$	0.1705, 0.1774, 0.2046, 0.2102, 0.4730, 1.3907, 1.4412, 1.7588
3	$(0^7, 3)$	0.1705, 0.1774, 0.2046, 0.2102, 0.2266, 0.4340, 0.4730, 1.3907
Sample	Scheme	Stress Use Censored Data from $(n_2, m_2) = (15, 10)$
1	$(5, 0^9)$	0.0027, 0.0069, 0.0079, 0.0275, 0.0391, 0.1395, 0.1593, 0.2780, 0.8285, 0.8929
2	$(0^4, 5, 0^5)$	0.0027, 0.0040, 0.0069, 0.0079, 0.0275, 0.1593, 0.2780, 0.5324, 0.8285, 0.8929
3	$(0^9, 5)$	0.0027, 0.0040, 0.0069, 0.0079, 0.0275, 0.0391, 0.0988, 0.1395, 0.1593, 0.2780

Table 3. Point and interval estimates from OBT data.

Sample	Par.	MLE Est.	MLE SE	MCMC Est.	MCMC SE	95% ACI Lower	95% ACI Upper	95% ACI Length	95% BCI Lower	95% BCI Upper	95% BCI Length
1	λ	−15.821	5.0750	−15.815	0.0122	−25.768	−5.874	19.894	−15.834	−15.795	0.0394
	β	0.5402	0.1637	0.5397	0.0056	0.2192	0.8611	0.6418	0.5286	0.5504	0.0218
	α_u	0.0986	0.0985	0.0990	0.0139	−0.0946	0.2917	0.3863	0.0742	0.1282	0.0540
	$\bar{G}_u(t)$	0.9801	0.0359	0.9797	0.0052	0.9098	0.9995	0.0897	0.9683	0.9882	0.0199
	$H_u(t)$	0.0231	0.0413	0.0235	0.0059	−0.0578	0.1040	0.1618	0.0138	0.0367	0.0229
2	λ	−14.988	5.5623	−14.982	0.0116	−25.890	−4.0865	21.804	−15.001	−14.963	0.0388
	β	0.5088	0.1795	0.5083	0.0056	0.1570	0.8605	0.7034	0.4970	0.5189	0.0219
	α_u	0.1034	0.1129	0.1037	0.0144	−0.1178	0.3246	0.4424	0.0775	0.1339	0.0564
	$\bar{G}_u(t)$	0.9784	0.0425	0.9780	0.0055	0.8951	0.9942	0.0991	0.9657	0.9872	0.0215
	$H_u(t)$	0.0251	0.0489	0.0256	0.0063	−0.0706	0.1208	0.1915	0.0149	0.0396	0.0247
3	λ	−19.302	7.2219	−19.295	0.0125	−33.457	−5.1476	28.309	−19.314	−19.276	0.0381
	β	0.6521	0.2332	0.6516	0.0056	0.1951	1.1092	0.9141	0.6403	0.6623	0.0220
	α_u	0.0498	0.0700	0.0500	0.0070	−0.0874	0.1870	0.2744	0.0374	0.0647	0.0273
	$\bar{G}_u(t)$	0.9944	0.0149	0.9943	0.0015	0.9652	0.9996	0.0344	0.9908	0.9968	0.0059
	$H_u(t)$	0.0066	0.0174	0.0067	0.0018	−0.0275	0.0406	0.0681	0.0038	0.0107	0.0069

6.2. Transformer Life-Testing

In this application, to show the usefulness of the proposed estimation approaches and to verify how our estimates work in practice, the failure times (in hours) of the TLT at high voltage are analyzed. These data were first given by Nelson [28] and later re-analyzed by Nassar et al. [9]. Under three accelerating stresses, 35.4, 42.2 and 46.7 kV, the TLT data sets were generated. In Table 4, each failure time in 35.4 kV (as normal use data) and 42.2 kV (as stress use data) is divided by 1000 for computational purposes, and the new transformed TLT data are presented. From Table 4, the MLE (SE) of α based on the normal and stress use TLT data sets is 5.0778(1.7186) and 37.968(12.640), respectively. Next, the KS distance and its (p-value) from the normal and stress use TLT data sets is 0.185(0.901) and 0.287(0.374), respectively. This result is evidence that the XL model fits the TLT data sets well. On the other hand, in Figure 9, two plots, namely the fitted/empirical RFs and PP of the XL model, are displayed. It supports the same goodness-of-fit findings.

Table 4. Failure times of transformer life-testing.

Normal Use								
0.0401	0.0594	0.0712	0.1665	0.2047	0.2297	0.3083	0.5379	
Stress Use								
0.0006	0.0134	0.0152	0.0199	0.0250	0.0302	0.0328	0.0444	0.0562

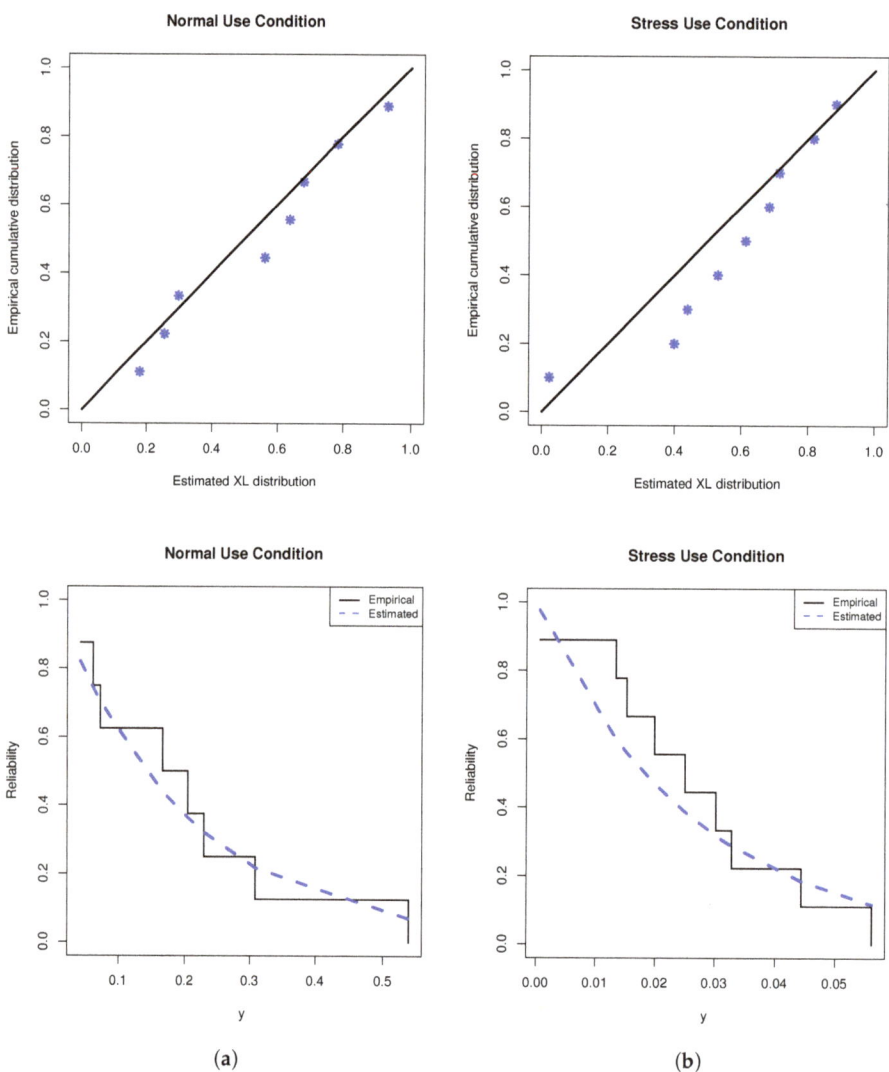

Figure 9. Fitted RF (**right**) and PP (**left**) plots from TLT data. (**a**) Normal condition; (**b**) stress condition.

From Table 4, based on several choices of $m_j = 5$, $i = 1, 2$ and $(R_{j1}, R_{j2}, \ldots, R_{jm_j})$, some artificial constant stress PT-IIC samples are generated and provided in Table 5. For each sample, in Table 6, the Bayes and maximum likelihood estimates along with their SEs as well as the 95% ACI/BCI estimates along with their lengths of λ, β, α_u, $\overline{G}_u(t)$ and $H_u(t)$ (at $t = 1$ and $x_u = 20$) are calculated and provided. Just like our assumption about the prior parameters in Section 6.1, the acquired Bayes point/interval analyses are made. It is seen that the calculated point and interval estimates of λ, β, α_u, $\overline{G}_u(t)$ and $H_u(t)$, derived from the Bayes MCMC and likelihood estimation methods, are quite similar to each other. It also supports the same findings established in Table 3. To evaluate the behavior of 40,000 simulated Markovian chains of λ, β, α_u, $\overline{G}_u(t)$ or $H_u(t)$, for each generated sample in Table 4, the density and trace plots are shown in Figure 10. It indicates that the MCMC estimates converged adequately. It also depicts that the simulated posteriors of λ are distributed as fairly symmetric while of (β or $\overline{G}_u(t)$) and (α_u or $H_u(t)$) they are distributed as negatively and positively skewed, respectively.

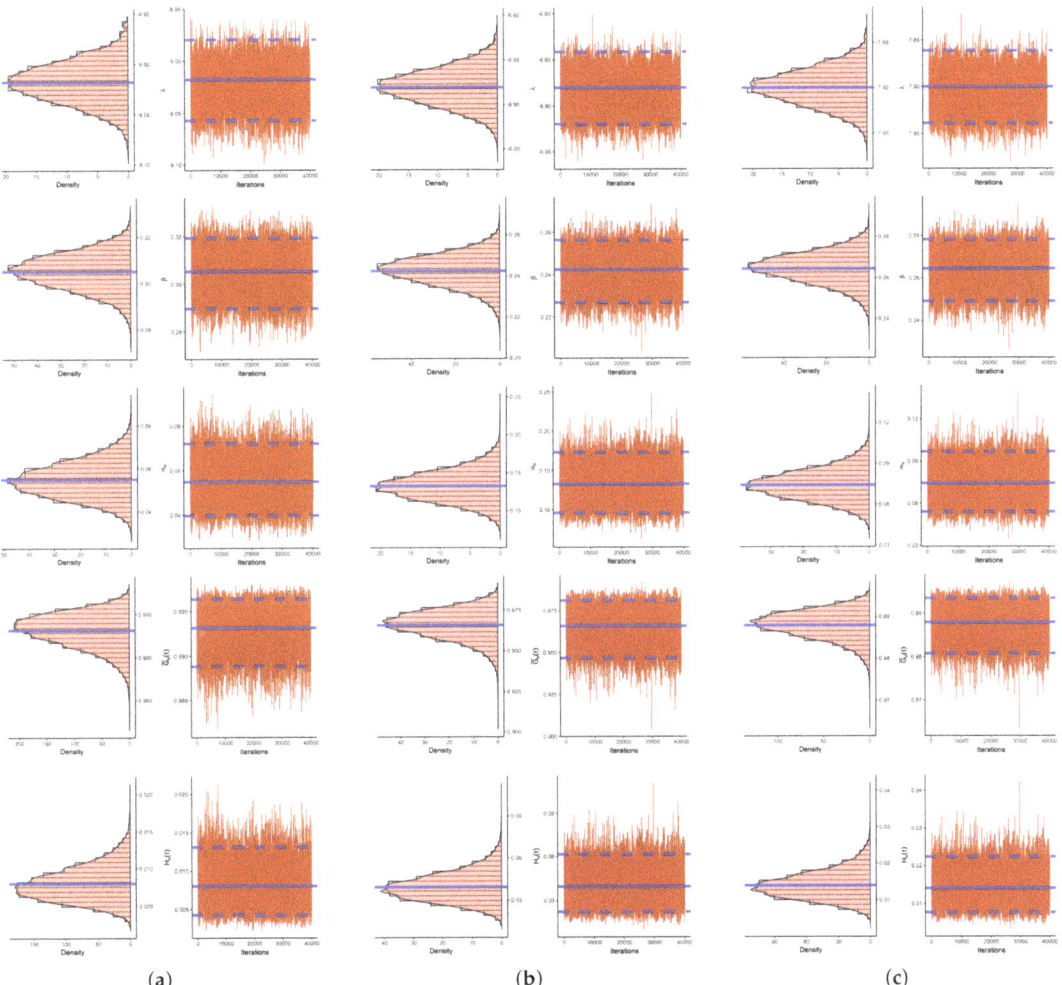

(a)   (b)   (c)

Figure 10. Density (**left**) and trace (**right**) plot of λ, β, α_u, $\overline{G}_u(t)$ and $H_u(t)$ from TLT data. (**a**) Sample 1; (**b**) Sample 2; (**c**) Sample 3.

Table 5. Various constant stress PC-T-II samples from TLT data.

Sample	Scheme	Normal Use Censored Data from $(n_1, m_1) = (8, 5)$
1	$(3, 0^4)$	0.0401, 0.0594, 0.1665, 0.2047, 0.2297
2	$(0^2, 3, 0^2)$	0.0401, 0.0594, 0.0712, 0.2047, 0.3083
3	$(0^4, 3)$	0.0401, 0.0594, 0.0712, 0.1665, 0.2047
Sample	Scheme	Stress Use Censored Data from $(n_2, m_2) = (9, 5)$
1	$(4, 0^4)$	0.0006, 0.0134, 0.0199, 0.0250, 0.0328
2	$(0^2, 4, 0^2)$	0.0006, 0.0134, 0.0152, 0.0250, 0.0444
3	$(0^4, 4)$	0.0006, 0.0134, 0.0152, 0.0199, 0.0250

As a summary, the numerical results developed from the OBT or TLT data revealed that the proposed XL model is useful for addressing the proposed inferential issues and is also beneficial for addressing the engineering problems.

Table 6. Point and interval estimates from TLT data.

Sample	Par.	MLE		MCMC		95% ACI			95% BCI		
		Est.	SE	Est.	SE	Lower	Upper	Length	Lower	Upper	Length
1	λ	−9.0329	3.4227	−9.0180	0.0249	−15.741	−2.3244	13.417	−9.0572	−8.9797	0.0775
	β	0.3067	0.0879	0.3052	0.0078	0.1345	0.4790	0.3445	0.2896	0.3193	0.0297
	α_u	0.0551	0.0926	0.0549	0.0083	−0.1264	0.2367	0.3631	0.0397	0.0720	0.0323
	$\bar{G}_u(t)$	0.9932	0.0215	0.9932	0.0020	0.9511	0.9993	0.0482	0.9888	0.9964	0.0075
	$H_u(t)$	0.0079	0.0250	0.0080	0.0023	−0.0410	0.0569	0.0979	0.0043	0.0131	0.0088
2	λ	−6.8924	3.2927	−6.8806	0.0231	−13.346	−0.4388	12.907	−6.9197	−6.8415	0.0782
	β	0.2438	0.0846	0.2425	0.0076	0.0780	0.4097	0.3316	0.2269	0.2563	0.0295
	α_u	0.1333	0.2154	0.1327	0.0196	−0.2888	0.5553	0.8442	0.0961	0.1731	0.0770
	$\bar{G}_u(t)$	0.9661	0.0958	0.9659	0.0087	0.7783	0.9985	0.2202	0.9468	0.9810	0.0342
	$H_u(t)$	0.0393	0.1101	0.0394	0.0100	−0.1765	0.2550	0.4315	0.0221	0.0614	0.0393
3	λ	−7.9132	3.3983	−7.8999	0.0238	−14.574	−1.2526	13.321	−7.9386	−7.8612	0.0775
	β	0.2658	0.0874	0.2645	0.0075	0.0945	0.4372	0.3426	0.2491	0.2783	0.0292
	α_u	0.0746	0.1241	0.0744	0.0109	−0.1687	0.3178	0.4865	0.0540	0.0968	0.0428
	$\bar{G}_u(t)$	0.9881	0.0367	0.9880	0.0032	0.9161	0.9968	0.0807	0.9808	0.9935	0.0127
	$H_u(t)$	0.0139	0.0424	0.0141	0.0037	−0.0693	0.0971	0.1663	0.0076	0.0223	0.0147

7. Conclusions and Future Work

A statistical analysis of constant-stress accelerated life tests for the XLIndley distribution based on progressive Type-II censoring is investigated in this article. Even though there have been many studies looking into estimating problems when constant-stress accelerated life tests are present, there have been relatively few studies looking into the estimation of reliability and hazard rate functions in the context of normal use conditions. To fill this gap, we utilized classical and Bayesian inferential approaches to estimate the unknown parameters and reliability measures under normal use situations. Based on the maximum likelihood approach, the point estimates and the approximate confidence intervals based on the asymptotic normality of the maximum likelihood estimators are obtained. The squared error loss function is used in the Bayesian technique to derive the Bayes estimates. The Markov chain Monte Carlo approach is employed to obtain the Bayes estimates and the Bayes credible intervals of the unknown parameters due to the joint posterior distribution's complex expression. The effectiveness of the various estimation techniques is demonstrated through a simulation study, and the applicability of the different estimators is verified through the analysis of two data sets from accelerated life tests. Based on the root mean square error, absolute bias and interval length of the estimates, the numerical results show that the Bayes estimates, whether point or interval, perform quite well. It is observed that the various estimates based on the right censoring scheme perform better than other censoring schemes. Moreover, the accuracy of the Bayes estimates increases as the prior distribution's variance decreases. In general, when prior knowledge about the unknown parameters is available, the Bayes estimates outperform the maximum likelihood method. It is preferable to utilize the classical method when there is no information about the unknown parameters because the Bayesian method requires more calculation time. On future work, one can perform the same estimation procedures for the XLindley distribution described in the current study based on adaptive progressively censored samples. Referring to Opheim and Roy [29] and Avdović and Jevremović [30], the concepts of these two papers can be extended to test the XLindley distribution empirically by providing cut-off values for the required number of samples to attain predetermined nominal significance levels.

Supplementary Materials: The following supporting information can be downloaded at: https://www.mdpi.com/article/10.3390/axioms12040352/s1, Table S1: Average estimates (1st column), RMSEs (2nd column) and MABs (3rd column) of λ; Table S2: Average estimates (1st column), RMSEs (2nd column) and MABs (3rd column) of β; Table S3: Average estimates (1st column), RMSEs (2nd column) and MABs (3rd column) of α_u; Table S4: Average estimates (1st column), RMSEs (2nd column) and MABs (3rd column) of $\bar{G}_u(t)$; Table S5: Average estimates (1st column), RMSEs (2nd column) and MABs (3rd column) of $H_u(t)$; Table S6: The ACLs (1st column) and CPs (2nd column) of 95% ACI/BCI of λ; Table S7: The ACLs (1st column) and CPs (2nd column) of 95% ACI/BCI of β; Table S8: The ACLs (1st column) and CPs (2nd column) of 95% ACI/BCI of α_u; Table S9: The ACLs (1st column) and CPs (2nd column) of 95% ACI/BCI of $\bar{G}_u(t)$; Table S10: The ACLs (1st column) and CPs (2nd column) of 95% ACI/BCI of $H_u(t)$.

Author Contributions: Methodology, M.N. and R.A.; funding acquisition, R.A.; software, A.E.; supervision, A.E.; writing—original draft, R.A. and M.N.; writing—review and editing, M.N. and A.E. All authors have read and agreed to the published version of the manuscript.

Funding: This research was funded by the Princess Nourah bint Abdulrahman University Researchers Supporting Project number (PNURSP2023R50), Princess Nourah bint Abdulrahman University, Riyadh, Saudi Arabia.

Data Availability Statement: The authors confirm that the data supporting the findings of this study are available within the article.

Acknowledgments: Princess Nourah bint Abdulrahman University Researchers Supporting Project number (PNURSP2023R50), Princess Nourah bint Abdulrahman University, Riyadh, Saudi Arabia. The authors would also like to express their thanks to the editor and the anonymous referees for valuable comments and helpful observations.

Conflicts of Interest: The authors declare no conflict of interest.

References

1. Nelson, W.B. *Accelerated Testing: Statistical Models, Test Plans, and Data Analysis*; John Wiley and Sons: New York, NY, USA, 1990.
2. Meeker, W.Q.; Escobar, L.A. *Statistical Methods for Reliability Data*; John Wiley and Sons: New York, NY, USA, 1998.
3. Tang, L.C. Multiple-steps step-stress accelerated life test. In *Handbook of Reliability Engineering*; Pham, H., Ed.; Springer: New York, NY, USA, 2003; pp. 441–455.
4. Balakrishnan, N. A synthesis of exact inferential results for exponential step-stress models and associated optimal accelerated life-tests. *Metrika* **2009**, *69*, 351–396. [CrossRef]
5. Luo, C.; Shen, L.; Xu, A. Modelling and estimation of system reliability under dynamic operating environments and lifetime ordering constraints. *Reliab. Eng. Syst. Saf.* **2022**, *218*, 108136. [CrossRef]
6. Wang, L. Estimation of constant-stress accelerated life test for Weibull distribution with nonconstant shape parameter. *J. Comput. Appl. Math.* **2018**, *343*, 539–555. [CrossRef]
7. Lin, C.T.; Hsu, Y.Y.; Lee, S.Y.; Balakrishnan, N. Inference on constant stress accelerated life tests for log-location-scale lifetime distributions with type-I hybrid censoring. *J. Stat. Comput. Simul.* **2019**, *89*, 720–749. [CrossRef]
8. Sief, M.; Liu, X.; Abd El-Raheem, A.E.R.M. Inference for a constant-stress model under progressive type-I interval censored data from the generalized half-normal distribution. *J. Stat. Comput. Simul.* **2021**, *91*, 3228–3253. [CrossRef]
9. Nassar, M.; Dey, S.; Wang, L.; Elshahhat, A. Estimation of Lindley constant-stress model via product of spacing with Type-II censored accelerated life data. *Commun.-Stat.-Simul. Comput.* **2021**. [CrossRef]
10. Hakamipour, N. Comparison between constant-stress and step-stress accelerated life tests under a cost constraint for progressive type I censoring. *Seq. Anal.* **2021**, *40*, 17–31 [CrossRef]
11. Kumar, D.; Nassar, M.; Dey, S.; Alam, F.M.A. On estimation procedures of constant stress accelerated life test for generalized inverse Lindley distribution. *Qual. Reliab. Eng. Int.* **2022**, *38*, 211–228. [CrossRef]
12. Wu, W.; Wang, B.X.; Chen, J.; Miao, J.; Guan, Q. Interval estimation of the two-parameter exponential constant stress accelerated life test model under Type-II censoring. *Qual. Technol. Quant. Manag.* **2022**. [CrossRef]
13. Balakrishnan, N.; Cramer, E.; Kamps, U.; Schenk, N. Progressive type II censored order statistics from exponential distributions. *Stat. J. Theor. Appl. Stat.* **2001**, *35*, 537–556. [CrossRef]
14. Balakrishnan, N.; Lin, C.T. On the distribution of a test for exponentiality based on progressively type-II right censored spacings. *J. Stat. Comput. Simul.* **2003**, *73*, 277–283. [CrossRef]
15. Chen, S.; Gui, W. Statistical analysis of a lifetime distribution with a bathtub-shaped failure rate function under adaptive progressive type-II censoring. *Mathematics* **2020**, *8*, 670. [CrossRef]
16. Wu, M.; Gui, W. Estimation and prediction for Nadarajah-Haghighi distribution under progressive type-II censoring. *Symmetry* **2021**, *13*, 999. [CrossRef]

17. Dey, S.; Elshahhat, A.; Nassar, M. Analysis of progressive type-II censored gamma distribution. *Comput. Stat.* **2022**, *38*, 481–508. [CrossRef]
18. Alotaibi, R.; Nassar, M.; Rezk, H.; Elshahhat, A. Inferences and engineering applications of alpha power Weibull distribution using progressive type-II censoring. *Mathematics* **2022**, *10*, 2901. [CrossRef]
19. Balakrishnan, N. Progressive censoring methodology: An appraisal. *Test* **2007**, *16*, 211–259. [CrossRef]
20. Wang, B.X.; Yu, K.; Jones, M.C. Inference under progressively type II right-censored sampling for certain lifetime distributions. *Technometrics* **2010**, *52*, 453–460. [CrossRef]
21. Wang, P.; Tang, Y.; Bae, S.J.; He, Y. Bayesian analysis of two-phase degradation data based on change-point Wiener process. *Reliab. Eng. Syst. Saf.* **2018**, *170*, 244–256. [CrossRef]
22. Zhuang, L.; Xu, A.; Wang, X.L. A prognostic driven predictive maintenance framework based on Bayesian deep learning. *Reliab. Eng. Syst. Saf.* **2023**, *234*, 109181. [CrossRef]
23. Chouia, S.; Zeghdoudi, H. The XLindley Distribution: Properties and Application. *J. Stat. Theory Appl.* **2021**, *20*, 318–327. [CrossRef]
24. Alotaibi, R.; Nassar, M.; Elshahhat, A. Computational Analysis of XLindley Parameters Using Adaptive Type-II Progressive Hybrid Censoring with Applications in Chemical Engineering. *Mathematics* **2022**, *10*, 3355. [CrossRef]
25. Miller, R. *Survival Analysis*; Wiley: New York, NY, USA, 1981.
26. Henningsen, A.; Toomet, O. maxLik: A package for maximum likelihood estimation in R. *Comput. Stat.* **2011**, *26*, 443–458. [CrossRef]
27. Plummer, M.; Best, N.; Cowles, K.; Vines, K. CODA: Convergence diagnosis and output analysis for MCMC. *R News* **2006**, *6*, 7–11.
28. Nelson, W.B. *Accelerated Testing: Statistical Model, Test Plan and Data Analysis*; Wiley: New York, NY, USA, 2004.
29. Opheim, T.; Roy, A. More on the supremum statistic to test multivariate skew-normality. *Computation* **2021**, *9*, 126. [CrossRef]
30. Avdović, A.; Jevremović, V. Quantile-zone based approach to normality testing. *Mathematics* **2022**, *10*, 1828. [CrossRef]

Disclaimer/Publisher's Note: The statements, opinions and data contained in all publications are solely those of the individual author(s) and contributor(s) and not of MDPI and/or the editor(s). MDPI and/or the editor(s) disclaim responsibility for any injury to people or property resulting from any ideas, methods, instructions or products referred to in the content.

Article

Application of the Optimal Homotopy Asymptotic Approach for Solving Two-Point Fuzzy Ordinary Differential Equations of Fractional Order Arising in Physics

Ali Fareed Jameel [1,2], Dulfikar Jawad Hashim [3], Nidal Anakira [4,*], Osama Ababneh [5], Ahmad Qazza [5], Abedel-Karrem Alomari [6] and Khamis S. Al Kalbani [1]

[1] Faculty of Education and Arts, Sohar University, Sohar 3111, Oman
[2] Institute of Strategic Industrial Decision Modelling (ISIDM), School of Quantitative Sciences (SQS), Universiti Utara Malaysia (UUM), Sintok 06010, Malaysia
[3] Computer Engineering Technique, Mazaya University College, Nasiriyah 64001, Thi-Qar, Iraq
[4] Department of Mathematics, Faculty of Science and Technology, Irbid National University, Irbid P.O. Box 2600, Jordan
[5] Department of Mathematics, Faculty of Science, Zarqa University, Zarqa 13110, Jordan
[6] Department of Mathematics, Faculty of Science, Yarmouk University, Irbid 21163, Jordan
* Correspondence: dr.nidal@inu.edu.jo

Abstract: This work focuses on solving and analyzing two-point fuzzy boundary value problems in the form of fractional ordinary differential equations (FFOBVPs) using a new version of the approximation analytical approach. FFOBVPs are useful in describing complex scientific phenomena that include heritable characteristics and uncertainty, and obtaining exact or close analytical solutions for these equations can be challenging, especially in the case of nonlinear problems. To address these difficulties, the optimal homotopy asymptotic method (OHAM) was studied and extended in a new form to solve FFOBVPs. The OHAM is known for its ability to solve both linear and nonlinear fractional models and provides a straightforward methodology that uses multiple convergence control parameters to optimally manage the convergence of approximate series solutions. The new form of the OHAM presented in this work incorporates the concepts of fuzzy sets theory and some fractional calculus principles to include fuzzy analysis in the method. The steps of fuzzification and defuzzification are used to transform the fuzzy problem into a crisp problem that can be solved using the OHAM. The method is demonstrated by solving and analyzing linear and nonlinear FFOBVPs at different values of fractional derivatives. The results obtained using the new form of the fuzzy OHAM are analyzed and compared to those found in the literature to demonstrate the method's efficiency and high accuracy in the fuzzy domain. Overall, this work presents a feasible and efficient approach for solving FFOBVPs using a new form of the OHAM with fuzzy analysis.

Keywords: fuzzy sets theory; fuzzy fractional derivative; caputo derivative; fuzzy boundary value problems; fuzzy fractional differential equations; optimal homotopy asymptotic method

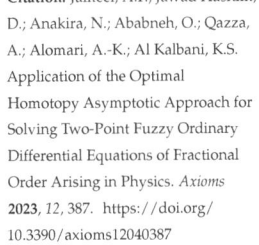

Citation: Jameel, A.F.; Jawad Hashim, D.; Anakira, N.; Ababneh, O.; Qazza, A.; Alomari, A.-K.; Al Kalbani, K.S. Application of the Optimal Homotopy Asymptotic Approach for Solving Two-Point Fuzzy Ordinary Differential Equations of Fractional Order Arising in Physics. *Axioms* **2023**, *12*, 387. https://doi.org/10.3390/axioms12040387

Academic Editors: Nuno Bastos, Touria Karite and Amir Khan

Received: 27 January 2023
Revised: 26 March 2023
Accepted: 3 April 2023
Published: 17 April 2023

Copyright: © 2023 by the authors. Licensee MDPI, Basel, Switzerland. This article is an open access article distributed under the terms and conditions of the Creative Commons Attribution (CC BY) license (https:// creativecommons.org/licenses/by/ 4.0/).

1. Introduction

Fractional-order models are more accurate than integer-order models since there are more degrees of freedom in the fractional-order models. Fractional calculus apparently captures some of the hereditary properties of the system [1]. Fractional calculus is not modern; it is a generalization of traditional calculus theory, which deals with the integer order [2]. In fractional calculus, the derivative and integral found in classical calculus are generalized to the arbitrary real or complex order, that is, to non-integer order [3]. Fractional calculus is seen as an essential tool for managing such complicated problems that are reliant on long-term memory terms, even though classical calculus is a great tool for modeling many complex real-world phenomena [4]. Memory is the term used to describe the output or results that depend on the history of the variables from a previous period. Classical calculus cannot solve issues that depend on the memory of the variables [5].

During the past decade, fractional differential equations under the effect of uncertainty (FFDEs) have appeared more and more practically in different research areas, such as physics and engineering [6,7], in addition to many other fields [8]. FFDEs are characterized by a nonlocal derivative operator. This, in turn, contributes to modeling the complicated real-world problems that are based on the long memory term. Unfortunately, the stemming uncertainty caused by a lack of data or the difficulty of exactly determining the supplementary conditions will lead to errors in measurement, so using the nonlocal fractional derivative operators in the fuzzy environment will ensure a more accurate mathematical model that simulates human thinking.

Accurate modeling of complex real-world problems helps us provide a clear and explicit concept of complex dynamics by employing the definitions and theories of the fractional calculus theory and the fuzzy calculus theory. However, these models remain impractical until they are solved because the solutions provide a comprehensive view, in addition to the fact that the solutions aid in studying and understanding the physical and engineering properties of real-world problems [8]

In solving some of the FFODEs, the analytical approach aims to present a closed-form solution [9,10]. A closed-form solution is considered the exact solution to the problem [11]. The solution may be expressed as the sum of a finite number of elementary functions, such as polynomial, exponential, trigonometric, and hyperbolic functions. The advantage of a closed-form solution is that it provides an overall view of the solution to the problem. Moreover, in the analysis of results, using closed-form solutions generally does not require a huge amount of computation [12]. In many instances, analytical solutions cannot be found [13–16]. Nevertheless, the solutions to such equations are always in demand due to practical interests. Therefore, to deal with such instances in a more realistic manner, FFODEs are commonly solved using the approximation approach, which includes the numerical and approximate analytical methods.

Numerous methods were proposed for solving FFOBVPs; for instance, we refer the reader to explore [16–19]. These numerical methods demonstrated their ability to solve only linear cases of FFODEs. In the numerical approach, the aim is to obtain an approximate solution, where an open-form solution is sought instead of a closed-form. However, the numerical class of methods directly solves FFODEs of high orders; instead, they require a transformation into a system of the first order. Further, most studies employ numerical methods for linear first-order problems [20,21]. Unfortunately, most of the complicated real-world problems were modeled using nonlinear differential equations, which makes these methods inappropriate to deal with them—especially the problems governed by strong nonlinearity.

In addition to the optimal homotopy asymptotic method (OHAM) presented in this work, several other approximate analytical methods have been used to solve different types of FFOBVPs. These include the variational iteration method (VIM) [22,23], the reproducing kernel Hilbert space method (RKHSM) [24], the spectral collocation method (SCM) [7], the Adomian decomposition method (ADM) [25], the differential transform method [26], the residual power series method (RPSM) [27], and the fractional residual power series method (FRPSM) [28].

Hashim et al. [29] solved fuzzy IVPs with fractional derivative orders between 0 and 1 using the optimal homotopy asymptotic method (OHAM), and the paper presented the defuzzification of fuzzy fractional IVPs. The authors then introduced a framework for solving the considered problem using the OHAM. Upper and lower solutions were investigated in terms of the accuracy and convergence of the method by finding optimal values of the convergent parameters using a few terms of the series solution with higher accuracy than the fractional residual power method. The paper did not discuss the fuzzification of the boundary value problem or its solution. As one more section of this work, we will investigate the fuzzy theory and the OHAM to solve the fuzzy boundary value problem with a fractional derivative order between 1 and 2.

While these methods have shown promise in solving FFOBVPs, they often fail to provide a simple way to control and adjust the convergence area. This can be a significant obstacle in obtaining accurate solutions, especially for nonlinear problems. Therefore, the development of new approximate analytical methods is necessary to overcome these challenges and improve the accuracy of solutions.

The OHAM presented in this work addresses this issue by using multiple convergence control parameters to optimally manage the convergence of approximate series solutions. This allows for greater flexibility in controlling and adjusting the convergence area, resulting in more accurate solutions for FFOBVPs. This is due to the proposed methods' inability to control the convergence region. Nowadays, homotopy methods are the most promising approaches for solving nonlinear real-world problems [30] due to their ability to simplify complicated problems, provide the freedom to choose the auxiliary functions, and provide a simple way to control the convergence, which helps us optimize the convergence series solutions for the strong nonlinearity problems. The OHAM has been used to solve various types of differential equations, including classical differential equations [31], fuzzy differential equations [32], and fractional differential equations [33]. The method's effectiveness in controlling the convergence area has been demonstrated through numerical results for both linear and nonlinear problems. The OHAM provides multiple convergence control parameters that allow for greater flexibility in adjusting the convergence area and obtaining accurate solutions. This makes OHAM a promising method for solving complex differential equations encountered in science and engineering applications.

In order to solve FFOBVPs, this study intended to create novel approximative analytical techniques with convergence-control capabilities. The fundamental idea of the OHAM will be applied to the development of the new approach, which will be able to manage the significant challenge of managing the convergence of the approximative analytical solutions. This work also focuses on the development of the fuzzy OHAM's fractional form, represented by the abbreviation FF-OHAM, on two different types of application problems that fall under the Caputo definitions of differentiability and involve linear and nonlinear application problems. This starts with the introduction of the basic tools of fuzzy fractional calculus in the second section, followed by providing the defuzzification procedure for the FFOBVPs in Section 3. Section 4 provides the new version of the FF-OHAM for solving FFOBVPs; then, the numerical simulation of the physical applications of the FF-OHAM will be provided in Section 5. Then, we will end with the conclusions regarding the effectiveness of the proposed method and the gained results.

2. Mathematical Background

In this section, we will present the basic concepts and definitions linked with fractional calculus theory in the fuzzy domain, which will help us comprehend the work in the next sections, such as the fuzzy fractional integral [34], which is a generalization of the classical fractional integral concept to the fuzzy-valued functions. It is a fuzzy operator that takes a fuzzy-valued function [35] as an input and produces another fuzzy-valued function as an output. The fuzzy fractional integral can be interpreted as a generalization of the fuzzy integral and the classical Riemann–Liouville integral of fractional order [36]. The Caputo derivative of fractional order is used to define the fuzzy fractional integral in the sense of Caputo [37]. It is worth noting that the concept of α-cut is also used in the fuzzy fractional integral theory to define the α-cut of a fuzzy fractional integral. The α-cut of a fuzzy fractional integral is a fuzzy number that corresponds to the fuzzy α-cut [38]. The fuzzy-valued function is obtained by taking the fuzzy fractional integral and the Riemann–Liouville integral of fractional order [24]. On the other hand, the following fundamental definition of the fuzzy fractional integral needs to be recalled:

Definition 1 ([7]). *For any continuous fuzzy valued function, $\widetilde{g} \in C^{\mathcal{F}}[a,b] \cap L^{\mathcal{F}}[a,b]$, the fuzzy fractional Riemann–Liouville integration of $\widetilde{g}(x)$ will be defined by the following form:*

$$\widetilde{\mathcal{J}}^{\omega}\widetilde{g}(x) = \frac{1}{\Gamma(\omega)} \int_0^x \widetilde{g}(y)(x-y)^{\omega-1} dy, \text{ for } \omega, x \in \mathbb{R} \text{ and } \omega, x > 0 \quad (1)$$

$\forall \alpha \in [0,1]$, α-cuts for fuzzy-valued function, $\widetilde{g}$, can be represented by

$$\widetilde{g}(x;\alpha) = \left[\underline{g}(x;\alpha), \overline{g}(x;\alpha)\right] \quad (2)$$

where $\widetilde{\mathcal{J}}^{\omega}$ is the Riemann–Liouville integral operator of order ω; $\Gamma(\omega)$ is the famous Gamma function; $C^{\mathcal{F}}[a,b]$ is the set of all fuzzy-valued measurable functions, $\widetilde{g}$, on $[a,b]$; and $L^{\mathcal{F}}[a,b]$ is the space of fuzzy-valued functions, which are continuous on $[a,b]$.

Definition 2 ([24]). *Let $\omega \in (1,2]$, and $\widetilde{g} : [a,b] \to \widetilde{U}$, such that $\widetilde{g}$ and $\widetilde{g}' \in C^{\mathcal{F}}[0,b] \cap L^{\mathcal{F}}[0,b]$. Then, $\mathcal{F}$ can define the fuzzy fractional derivative in the sense of the Caputo of the fuzzy function $\widetilde{g}$ at $x \in (a,b)$, as follows:*

$$\left(\widetilde{D}^{\omega}\widetilde{g}\right)(x) = \frac{1}{\Gamma(2-\omega)} \int_0^x \frac{\widetilde{g}''(x)}{(y-x)^{\omega-1}} dx, x > 0 \quad (3)$$

where D is the Housdorff metric of the fuzzy set $\widetilde{U}$. Note that the fuzzy fractional Riemann–Liouville integration represents the left inverse operator of the fuzzy fractional Caputo derivative sense, such that $\forall \widetilde{g}(x) \in C^{\mathcal{F}}[a,b] \cap L^{\mathcal{F}}[a,b]$. We have

$$\widetilde{\mathcal{J}}^{\omega}\left(\widetilde{D}^{\omega}\widetilde{g}\right)(x) = \widetilde{g}(x) - x g'(0) - g(0), x \in \mathbb{R}, \text{ and } x > 0. \quad (4)$$

3. Fuzzification and Defuzzification of FFODEs

The first step of the development of the proposed FF-OHAM for solving second-order FFOBVPs is the defuzzification step. This is a general step that applies to the general form of second-order FFOBVPs, as shown below.

Consider the second-order FFOBVP as follows:

$$\begin{cases} \widetilde{y}^{(\omega)}(x) = \widetilde{g}\left(x, \widetilde{y}(x), \widetilde{y}^{(1)}(x)\right), x \in [x_0, X], \\ 1 < \omega \leq 2, \end{cases} \quad (5)$$

subject to the following boundary conditions:

$$\begin{cases} \widetilde{y}(x_0) = \widetilde{a}_0, \widetilde{y}^{(1)}(x_0) = \widetilde{a}_1, \\ \widetilde{y}(X) = \widetilde{b}_0, \widetilde{y}^{(1)}(X) = \widetilde{b}_1, \end{cases} \quad (6)$$

where $\widetilde{g}$ is the fuzzy function, while $\widetilde{y}^{(\omega)}(x)$ is the fractional Caputo derivative of the fuzzy function $\widetilde{y}(x)$; and the boundary conditions at the points x_0 and X are fuzzy numbers.

For $x \in [x_0, X]$ and $\forall \alpha \in [0,1]$, the fuzzy function will be defined by $\left[\widetilde{y}\right]_\alpha = \left[\underline{y}, \overline{y}\right]_\alpha$ $\forall x \in [x_0, X]$ as follows:

$$\begin{cases} \left[\widetilde{y}(x_0)\right]_\alpha = \left[\underline{y}(x_0;\alpha), \overline{y}(x_0;\alpha)\right], \\ \left[\widetilde{y}^{(1)}(x_0)\right]_\alpha = \left[\underline{y}^{(1)}(x_0;\alpha), \overline{y}^{(1)}(x_0;\alpha)\right], \\ \left[\widetilde{y}(X)\right]_\alpha = \left[\underline{y}(X;\alpha), \overline{y}(X;\alpha)\right], \\ \left[\widetilde{y}^{(1)}(X)\right]_\alpha = \left[\underline{y}^{(1)}(X;\alpha), \overline{y}^{(1)}(X;\alpha)\right]. \end{cases} \qquad (7)$$

Now, by assuming $\widetilde{\hat{Y}}(x) = \left\{\widetilde{y}(x), \widetilde{y}^{(1)}(x)\right\}$, for defuzzification we have:

$$\widetilde{\hat{Y}}(x,\alpha) = \left[\underline{\hat{Y}}(x,\alpha), \overline{\hat{Y}}(x,\alpha)\right] = \left[\underline{y}(x,\alpha), \underline{y}^{(1)}(x,\alpha), \overline{y}(x;\alpha), \overline{y}^{(1)}(x;\alpha)\right]. \qquad (8)$$

In addition, by utilizing the concepts of the extension principle theory, we can write the α-cut of the fuzzy function, as shown below:

$$\left[\widetilde{g}\left(x, \widetilde{\hat{Y}}\right)\right]_\alpha = \widetilde{g}\left(x, \widetilde{\hat{Y}}(x;\alpha)\right) = \left[\underline{g}\left(x, \widetilde{\hat{Y}};\alpha\right), \overline{g}\left(x, \widetilde{\hat{Y}};\alpha\right)\right], \qquad (9)$$

where

$$\begin{cases} \underline{g}\left(x, \widetilde{\hat{Y}}(x;\alpha)\right) = g_l\left(x, \underline{\hat{Y}}(t;\alpha), \overline{Y}(x;\alpha)\right) = g_l\left(x, \widetilde{\hat{Y}}(x;\alpha)\right), \\ \overline{g}\left(x, \widetilde{\hat{Y}}(x;\alpha)\right) = g_u\left(x, \underline{\hat{Y}}(x;\alpha), \overline{Y}(x;\alpha)\right) = g_u\left(x, \widetilde{\hat{Y}}(x;\alpha)\right). \end{cases} \qquad (10)$$

which means that $\forall \alpha \in [0,1]$. We have

$$\begin{cases} \underline{y}^{(\omega)}(x;\alpha) = g_l\left(x, \widetilde{\hat{Y}}(x;\alpha)\right), \\ \overline{y}^{(\omega)}(x;\alpha) = g_u\left(x, \widetilde{\hat{Y}}(x;\alpha)\right). \end{cases} \qquad (11)$$

where

$$\begin{cases} g_l\left(x, \widetilde{\hat{Y}}(x;\alpha)\right) = \min\left\{\widetilde{y}^{(\omega)}\left(x, \widetilde{\mu}(\alpha)\right)\Big|\widetilde{\mu}(\alpha) \in \left[\widetilde{\hat{Y}}(x;\alpha)\right]_\alpha\right\}, \\ g_u\left(x, \widetilde{\hat{Y}}(x;\alpha)\right) = \max\left\{\widetilde{y}^{(\omega)}\left(x, \widetilde{\mu}(\alpha)\right)\Big|\widetilde{\mu}(\alpha) \in \left[\widetilde{\hat{Y}}(x;\alpha)\right]_\alpha\right\}. \end{cases} \qquad (12)$$

4. FF-OHAM for FFTBVPs

In this section, the F-OHAM presented by [21] for solving the integer order of ODEs is fuzzified and then defuzzified using some concepts of the fuzzy set theory in Section 2 to create a new form of the method denoted by the FF-OHAM for solving linear and nonlinear second-order FFOBVPs approximately.

$$\begin{cases} \widetilde{y}^{(\omega)}(x) = \widetilde{g}\left(x, \widetilde{y}(x), \widetilde{y}^{(1)}(x)\right) + \widetilde{G}(x) \; x \in [x_0, X], \\ \widetilde{y}(x_0) = \widetilde{a}_0, \; \widetilde{y}'(x_0) = \widetilde{a}_1, \\ \widetilde{y}(X) = \widetilde{b}_0, \; \widetilde{y}'(X) = \widetilde{b}_1, \\ \omega \in (1, 2], \end{cases} \qquad (13)$$

Followed by the defuzzification of Equation (5), such that for all $\alpha \in [0,1]$, we have the following lower bound:

$$\begin{cases} \mathcal{L}_{\beta_1}\left(\underline{y}(x;\alpha)\right) - g_l\left(x, \widetilde{\hat{Y}}(x)\right) - \underline{G}(x) = 0, \ x \in [x_0, X], \\ \text{ß}\left(\underline{y}(x;\alpha), \dfrac{\partial [\underline{y}]_\alpha}{\partial x}\right) = 0. \end{cases} \quad (14)$$

and the following upper bound:

$$\begin{cases} \overline{\mathcal{L}}_{\beta_1}\left(\widetilde{y}(x;\alpha)\right) - g_u\left(x, \widetilde{\hat{Y}}(x)\right) - \overline{G}(x) = 0, \ x \in [x_0, X], \\ \text{ß}\left(\overline{y}(x;\alpha), \dfrac{\partial [\overline{y}]_\alpha}{\partial x}\right) = 0. \end{cases} \quad (15)$$

According to [3], Equations (14) and (15) can be written as the following lower and upper zeroth order deformation homotopy equation:

$$\begin{cases} (1-q)\left[\underline{\mathcal{L}}_\omega\left(\left[\underline{y}(x;q)\right]_\alpha\right) - \underline{G}(x;\alpha)\right] = \underline{\mathcal{H}}(q;\alpha)\left[\underline{\mathcal{L}}_\omega\left(\left[\underline{y}(x;q)\right]_\alpha\right)\right] \\ \quad - \underline{\mathcal{H}}(q;\alpha)[\underline{G}(x;\alpha)] - \underline{\mathcal{H}}(q;\alpha)\left[g_l\left(\left[\widetilde{y}(x;q)\right]_\alpha\right)\right], \\ (1-q)\left[\overline{\mathcal{L}}_\omega([\overline{y}(x;q)]_\alpha) - \overline{G}(x;\alpha)\right] = \overline{\mathcal{H}}(q;\alpha)\left[\overline{\mathcal{L}}_\omega([\overline{y}(x;q)]_\alpha)\right] \\ \quad - \overline{\mathcal{H}}(q;\alpha)[\overline{G}(x;\alpha)] - \overline{\mathcal{H}}(q;\alpha)\left[g_l\left(\left[\widetilde{y}(x;q)\right]_\alpha\right)\right], \end{cases} \quad (16)$$

subject to the following fuzzy boundary conditions

$$\text{ß}\left(\left[\widetilde{y}(x;q)\right]_\alpha, \dfrac{\partial\left[\widetilde{y}(x;q)\right]_\alpha}{\partial x}\right) = 0, \quad (17)$$

where $\widetilde{\mathcal{L}}_\omega = [\underline{\mathcal{L}}_\omega, \overline{\mathcal{L}}_\omega] = \left[\dfrac{\partial^{(\omega)}[\underline{y}(x;q)]_\alpha}{\partial x^{(\omega)}}, \dfrac{\partial^{(\omega)}[\overline{y}(x;q)]_\alpha}{\partial x^{(\omega)}}\right]$ are the linear operators and $q \in [0,1]$ is an embedding parameter. Here, $\widetilde{\mathcal{H}}(q;\alpha) = [\underline{\mathcal{H}}(q), \overline{\mathcal{H}}(q)]_\alpha$ is a nonzero auxiliary fuzzy function for $q \neq 0$, and $\left[\widetilde{y}(x;q)\right]_\alpha$ is an unknown fuzzy function.

Obviously, for $q = 0$ and $q = 1$, we obtain the initial approximation, and the exact solution, respectively, as follows:

$$\begin{cases} \left[\underline{y}(x;0)\right]_\alpha = \underline{y}_0(x;\alpha), \left[\underline{y}(x;1)\right]_\alpha = \underline{Y}(x;\alpha), \\ [\overline{y}(x;0)]_\alpha = \overline{y}_0(t;\alpha). [\overline{y}(x;1)]_\alpha = \overline{Y}(x;\alpha). \end{cases} \quad (18)$$

Thus, as q increases from 0 to 1, the series solution, $\left[\widetilde{y}(x;q)\right]_\alpha$, changes from $\widetilde{y}_0(x;\alpha)$ to the solution of Equations (14) and (15), $\widetilde{Y}(x;\alpha)$, where $\widetilde{y}_0(x;\alpha)$ is obtained from Equation (16) for $q = 0$ as follows:

$$\begin{cases} \underline{y}_0(x;\alpha) = \widetilde{\mathcal{J}}^{(\beta_1)} \underline{G}(x;\alpha), \\ \overline{y}_0(x;\alpha) = \widetilde{\mathcal{J}}^{(\beta_1)} \overline{G}(x;\alpha), \end{cases} \quad (19)$$

subject to the following fuzzy boundary condition

$$\text{ß}\left(\widetilde{y}_0(x;\alpha), \dfrac{\partial [\widetilde{y}_0]_\alpha}{\partial x}\right) = 0 \quad (20)$$

We choose the auxiliary function $\widetilde{\mathcal{H}}(q;\alpha)$ for Equation (16) in the following form:

$$\begin{cases} \underline{\mathcal{H}}(q;\alpha) = \underline{S}_1(\alpha)q + \underline{S}_2(\alpha)q^2 + \ldots = \sum_{j=1}^{k} \underline{S}_j(\alpha)q^j, \\ \overline{\mathcal{H}}(q;\alpha) = \overline{S}_1(\alpha)q + \overline{S}_2(\alpha)q^2 + \ldots = \sum_{j=1}^{k} \overline{S}_j(\alpha)q^j, \end{cases} \quad (21)$$

where $\widetilde{S}_1(\alpha) = [\underline{S}_1(\alpha), \overline{S}_1(\alpha)]$, $\widetilde{S}_2(\alpha) = [\underline{S}_2(\alpha), \overline{S}_2(\alpha)]$, ... are the constants to be found for all $\alpha \in [0,1]$. Now, by expanding $\left[\widetilde{y}(x;q,S_j(\alpha))\right]_\alpha$ into Taylor's series about q, we obtain the following approximate series solution:

$$\begin{cases} \left[\underline{y}(x;q,\underline{S}_j(\alpha))\right]_\alpha = \underline{y}_0(x;\alpha) + \sum_{j=1}^{k} \left[\underline{y}_j(x,\underline{S}_j(\alpha))\right]_\alpha q^j, \\ \left[\overline{y}(x;q,\overline{S}_j(\alpha))\right]_\alpha = \overline{y}_0(x;\alpha) + \sum_{j=1}^{k} \left[\overline{y}_j(x,\overline{S}_j(\alpha))\right]_\alpha q^j. \end{cases} \quad (22)$$

According to [3], by substituting Equation (22) into Equation (16) and then collecting the coefficient of like powers of q, we will obtain the following system of linear equations—where the zeroth-order problem is given by Equation (19), while the first to k^{th}-order problems are given as in the general k^{th}-order formula with respect to $\widetilde{y}_k(x;\alpha)$, for $k \geq 1$:

$$\begin{cases} \underline{y}_k(x;\alpha) = \underline{y}_{k-1}(x;\alpha) + \sum_{j=1}^{k-1} \underline{S}_j(\alpha)\left(\underline{y}_{k-j}(x;\alpha)\right) \\ \underline{\mathcal{J}}^{(\omega)}\left(\underline{S}_k(\alpha)g_{l0}\left(\widetilde{y}_0(x;\alpha)\right) + \sum_{j=1}^{k-1}\underline{S}_j(\alpha)g_{l\,k-j}\left(\sum_{i=0}^{k-1}\widetilde{y}_i(x;\alpha)\right)\right) \\ \overline{y}_k(x;\alpha) = \overline{y}_{k-1}(x;\alpha) + \sum_{j=1}^{k-1} \overline{S}_j(\alpha)\left(\overline{y}_{k-j}(x;\alpha)\right) \\ \overline{\mathcal{J}}^{(\omega)}\left(\overline{S}_k(\alpha)g_{l0}\left(\widetilde{y}_0(x;\alpha)\right) + \sum_{j=1}^{k-1}\overline{S}_j(\alpha)g_{u\,k-j}\left(\sum_{i=0}^{k-1}\widetilde{y}_i(x;\alpha)\right)\right) \end{cases} \quad (23)$$

$$\beta\left(\widetilde{y}_k(x;\alpha), \frac{\partial[\widetilde{y}_k]_\alpha}{\partial x}\right) = 0 \quad (24)$$

where $g_{l\,k-j}\left(\sum_{i=0}^{k-1}\widetilde{y}_i(x;\alpha)\right)$ and $g_{u\,k-j}\left(\sum_{i=0}^{k-1}\widetilde{y}_i(x;\alpha)\right)$ are the coefficients of q^j in the expansion of $g_l\left[\widetilde{y}(x;q)\right]_\alpha$ and $g_u\left[\widetilde{y}(x;q)\right]_\alpha$ about the embedding parameter q. We have the lower and upper bounds as follows:

$$\begin{cases} g_l\left(\left[\widetilde{y}\left(x;q,\sum_{j=1}^{k}\widetilde{S}_j(\alpha)\right)\right]_\alpha\right) = g_{l0}(\widetilde{y}_0(x;\alpha)) + \sum_{j=1}^{k} g_{lj}\left(\sum_{j=0}^{k}[\widetilde{y}_j]_\alpha\right)q^j, \\ g_u\left(\left[\widetilde{y}\left(x;q,\sum_{j=1}^{k}\widetilde{S}_j(\alpha)\right)\right]_\alpha\right) = g_{u0}(\widetilde{y}_0(x;\alpha)) + \sum_{j=1}^{k} g_{uj}\left(\sum_{j=0}^{k}[\widetilde{y}_j]_\alpha\right)q^j. \end{cases} \quad (25)$$

It has been observed that the convergence of the series in Equation (22) depends upon the auxiliary constants $\widetilde{S}_1(\alpha), \widetilde{S}_2(\alpha), \ldots \widetilde{S}_k(\alpha)$, then, at $q = 1$, we obtain the exact solution shown below:

$$\begin{cases} \left[\underline{Y}\left(x, \sum_{j=1}^{\infty} \underline{S}_j(\alpha)\right)\right]_\alpha = \underline{y}_0(x;\alpha) + \sum_{j=1}^{\infty} \left[\underline{y}_j\left(x; \sum_{j=1}^{\infty} \underline{S}_j(\alpha)\right)\right]_\alpha, \\ \left[\overline{Y}\left(x, \sum_{j=1}^{\infty} \overline{S}_j(\alpha)\right)\right]_\alpha = \overline{y}_0(x;\alpha) + \sum_{j=1}^{\infty} \left[\overline{y}_j\left(x; \sum_{j=1}^{\infty} \overline{S}_j(\alpha)\right)\right]_\alpha. \end{cases} \quad (26)$$

5. Convergence Dynamic of the FF-OHAM

Substituting Equation (22) into Equations (14) and (15) yields the following residual:

$$\begin{cases} \underline{RE}\left(x, \sum_{j=1}^{k} \underline{\tilde{S}}_j(\alpha); \alpha\right) = \underline{\mathcal{L}}_\omega\left(\underline{y}\left(x, \sum_{j=1}^{k} \underline{\tilde{S}}_j(\alpha); \alpha\right)\right) - \underline{G}(x; \alpha) \\ \qquad - g_l\left(\tilde{\tilde{y}}\left(x, \sum_{j=1}^{k} \tilde{S}_j(\alpha); \alpha\right)\right), \\ \overline{RE}\left(x, \sum_{j=1}^{k} \overline{\tilde{S}}_j(\alpha); \alpha\right) = \overline{\mathcal{L}}_\omega\left(\overline{y}\left(x, \sum_{j=1}^{k} \overline{\tilde{S}}_j(\alpha); \alpha\right)\right) - \overline{G}(x; \alpha) \\ \qquad - g_u\left(\tilde{\tilde{y}}\left(x, \sum_{j=1}^{k} \tilde{S}_j(\alpha); \alpha\right)\right). \end{cases} \quad (27)$$

As mentioned in [22], if $\widetilde{RE} = 0$, then $\tilde{y}$ yields the exact solution $\tilde{Y}$, although, generally, it does not happen, especially in nonlinear FFOBVPs. To identify the auxiliary constants of $\tilde{S}_j(\alpha), j = 1, 2, \ldots k$, we choose x_0 and X, such that the optimum values of $\tilde{S}_j(\alpha)$ for the convergent solution of the desired problem is obtained. To find the optimal values of $\tilde{S}_j(\alpha)$ here, we apply the method of least squares as follows:

$$S\widetilde{RE}\left(x, \sum_{j=1}^{k} \tilde{S}_j(\alpha); \alpha\right) = \int_{x_0}^{X} \widetilde{RE}^2\left(x, \sum_{j=1}^{k} \tilde{S}_j(\alpha); \alpha\right) dx, \quad (28)$$

where $\widetilde{RE}$ is the residual,

$$\begin{cases} [\underline{RE}]_\alpha = \underline{\mathcal{L}}_\omega\left([\underline{y}]_\alpha\right) - \underline{G}(x; \alpha) - g_l\left([\tilde{y}]_\alpha\right) \\ [\overline{RE}]_\alpha = \overline{\mathcal{L}}_\omega([\overline{y}]_\alpha) - \overline{G}(x; \alpha) - g_u\left([\tilde{y}]_\alpha\right) \end{cases} \quad (29)$$

and

$$\frac{\partial S\widetilde{RE}}{\partial \tilde{S}_1(\alpha)} = \frac{\partial S\widetilde{RE}}{\partial \tilde{S}_2(\alpha)} = \ldots \frac{\partial S\widetilde{RE}}{\partial \tilde{S}_k(\alpha)} = 0. \quad (30)$$

It should be noted that our process included the fuzzy level set α, so the best values of $\tilde{S}_k(\alpha)$ are determined from Equation (30) for each $\alpha \in [0, 1]$, which provides us with an easy way to set and optimally control the convergent area and the rate of the solution series.

6. Numerical Simulation of the Physical Applications via FF-OHAM

This section reflects the use of the FF-OHAM from Sections 3 and 4 for some fuzzy models in physics. The method's performance is tested in two linear and nonlinear FFOBVPs applications.

- Mechanical Application: Fuzzy Fractional Bagley–Torvik Equation

Consider the fuzzy fractional Bagley–Torvik equation [7]:

$$D^{(1.5)}\tilde{y}(x) + \tilde{y}(x) = \tilde{F}(x; \alpha), \ x \in [0, 1], \quad (31)$$

such that

$$\tilde{F}(x; \alpha) = \begin{cases} \underline{F}(x; \alpha) \\ \overline{F}(x; \alpha) \end{cases} = \begin{cases} \alpha(x^2 - x) + 4\alpha\frac{\sqrt{x}}{\sqrt{\pi}}, \\ (2 - \alpha)(x^2 - x) + 4(2 - \alpha)\frac{\sqrt{x}}{\sqrt{\pi}}. \end{cases} \quad (32)$$

subject to the following fuzzy boundary condition

$$\begin{cases} \underline{y}(0;\alpha) = \underline{y}(1;\alpha) = (\alpha - 1), \\ \overline{y}(0;\alpha) = \overline{y}(1;\alpha) = (1 - \alpha). \end{cases} \tag{33}$$

with the following fuzzy exact solution

$$\begin{cases} \underline{Y}(x;\alpha) = \alpha(x^2 - x), \\ \overline{Y}(x;\alpha) = (2 - \alpha)(x^2 - x). \end{cases} \tag{34}$$

we can contract the FF-OHAM series solution for all $\alpha \in [0,1]$ of Equation (31) as follows:

$$\begin{cases} (1-q)\left[\widetilde{D}^{(1.5)}\left(\widetilde{y}(x;\alpha)\right) - \widetilde{F}(x;\alpha)\right] = \sum_{j=1}^{5} \widetilde{S}_j(\alpha)q^j \\ \widetilde{S}_j(\alpha)q^j\left[\widetilde{D}^{(1.5)}\left(\widetilde{y}(x;\alpha)\right) + \widetilde{y}(x;\alpha) - \left(\widetilde{F}(x;\alpha)\right)\right] \end{cases} \tag{35}$$

such that

$$\widetilde{y}(x;\alpha) = \widetilde{y}_0(x;\alpha) + \sum_{j=1}^{k} \widetilde{y}_j(x, S_1, \ldots, S_j; \alpha)q^j \tag{36}$$

Zeroth-order problem:

$$\begin{cases} \widetilde{y}_0(x,\alpha) = \widetilde{\mathcal{J}}^{(1.5)}\left[\alpha\left((x^2 - x) + 4\frac{\sqrt{x}}{\sqrt{\pi}}\right), (2-\alpha)\left((x^2 - x) + 4\frac{\sqrt{x}}{\sqrt{\pi}}\right)\right] \\ \text{\ss}\left(\widetilde{y}_0(x;\alpha), \frac{\partial[\widetilde{y}_0]_\alpha}{\partial x}\right) = 0 \end{cases} \tag{37}$$

First-order problem:

$$\begin{cases} \widetilde{y}_1\left(x, \widetilde{S}_1(\alpha); \alpha\right) = \left(1 + \widetilde{S}_1(\alpha)\right)\widetilde{y}_0(x;\alpha) + \widetilde{S}_1(\alpha)\widetilde{\mathcal{J}}^{(1.5)}\widetilde{y}_0(x;\alpha) \\ \qquad - \left(1 + \widetilde{S}_1(\alpha)\right)\widetilde{\mathcal{J}}^{(1.5)}\left(\widetilde{F}(x;\alpha)\right), \\ \text{\ss}\left(\widetilde{y}_1(x;\alpha), \frac{\partial[\widetilde{y}_1]_\alpha}{\partial x}\right) = 0. \end{cases} \tag{38}$$

Second-order problem:

$$\begin{cases} \widetilde{y}_2\left(x, \widetilde{S}_1(\alpha), \widetilde{S}_2(\alpha); \alpha\right) = \left(1 + \widetilde{S}_1(\alpha)\right)\widetilde{y}_1\left(x, \widetilde{S}_1(\alpha); \alpha\right) + \widetilde{S}_2(\alpha)\widetilde{y}_0(x;\alpha) + \\ \widetilde{S}_1(\alpha)\widetilde{\mathcal{J}}^{(1.5)}\widetilde{y}_1\left(x, \widetilde{S}_1(\alpha); \alpha\right) + \widetilde{S}_2(\alpha)\widetilde{\mathcal{J}}^{(1.5)}\widetilde{y}_0(x;\alpha) - \widetilde{S}_2(\alpha)\widetilde{\mathcal{J}}^{(1.5)}\left(\widetilde{F}(x;\alpha)\right) \\ \text{\ss}\left(\widetilde{y}_2(x;\alpha), \frac{\partial[\widetilde{y}_2]_\alpha}{\partial x}\right) = 0. \end{cases} \tag{39}$$

Third-order problem:

$$\begin{cases} \tilde{y}_3\left(x, \tilde{S}_1(\alpha), \tilde{S}_2(\alpha), \tilde{S}_3(\alpha); \alpha\right) = \left(1 + \tilde{S}_1(\alpha)\right)\tilde{y}_2\left(x, \tilde{S}_1(\alpha), \tilde{S}_2(\alpha); \alpha\right) + \\ \tilde{S}_2(\alpha)\tilde{y}_1\left(x, \tilde{S}_1(\alpha); \alpha\right) + \tilde{\mathcal{J}}^{(1.5)} \sum_{j=1}^{3} \tilde{S}_j(\alpha)\tilde{y}_{3-j}\left(x, \tilde{S}_1(\alpha), \ldots, \tilde{S}_{3-j}(\alpha); \alpha\right) \\ -\tilde{S}_3(\alpha)\tilde{\mathcal{J}}^{(1.5)}\left(\tilde{F}(x; \alpha)\right) + \tilde{S}_3(\alpha)\tilde{y}_0(x; \alpha) \\ \beta\left(\tilde{y}_3(x; \alpha), \frac{\partial[\tilde{y}_3]_\alpha}{\partial x}\right) = 0. \end{cases} \quad (40)$$

Fourth-order problem:

$$\begin{cases} \tilde{y}_4\left(x, \tilde{S}_1(\alpha), \ldots, \tilde{S}_4(\alpha); \alpha\right) = \left(1 + \tilde{S}_1(\alpha)\right)\tilde{y}_3\left(x, \tilde{S}_1(\alpha), \tilde{S}_2(\alpha), \tilde{S}_3(\alpha); \alpha\right) + \\ \tilde{S}_2(\alpha)\tilde{y}_2\left(x, \tilde{S}_1(\alpha), \tilde{S}_2(\alpha); \alpha\right) + \tilde{S}_3(\alpha)\tilde{y}_1\left(x, \tilde{S}_1(\alpha); \alpha\right) + \tilde{S}_4(\alpha)\tilde{y}_0(x; \alpha) + \\ \tilde{\mathcal{J}}^{(1.5)} \sum_{j=1}^{4} \tilde{S}_j(\alpha)\tilde{y}_{4-j}\left(x, \tilde{S}_1(\alpha), \ldots, \tilde{S}_{4-i}(\alpha); \alpha\right) - \tilde{S}_4(\alpha)\tilde{\mathcal{J}}^{(1.5)}\left(\tilde{F}(x; \alpha)\right) \\ \beta\left(\tilde{y}_4(x; \alpha), \frac{\partial[\tilde{y}_4]_\alpha}{\partial x}\right) = 0 \end{cases} \quad (41)$$

Fifth-order problem:

$$\begin{cases} \tilde{y}_5\left(x, \tilde{S}_1(\alpha), \ldots, \tilde{S}_5(\alpha); \alpha\right) = \left(1 + \tilde{S}_1(\alpha)\right)\tilde{y}_4\left(x, \tilde{S}_1(\alpha), \ldots, \tilde{S}_4(\alpha); \alpha\right) + \\ \tilde{S}_2(\alpha)\tilde{y}_3\left(x, \tilde{S}_1(\alpha), \tilde{S}_2(\alpha), \tilde{S}_3(\alpha); \alpha\right) + \tilde{S}_3(\alpha)\tilde{y}_2\left(x, \tilde{S}_1(\alpha), \tilde{S}_2(\alpha); \alpha\right) + \\ \tilde{S}_4(\alpha)\tilde{y}_1\left(x, \tilde{S}_1(\alpha); \alpha\right) + \tilde{S}_5(\alpha)\tilde{y}_0(x; \alpha) - \tilde{S}_5(\alpha)\tilde{\mathcal{J}}^{(1.5)}\left(\tilde{F}(x; \alpha)\right) + \\ \tilde{\mathcal{J}}^{(1.5)} \sum_{j=1}^{5} \tilde{S}_j(\alpha)\tilde{y}_{5-j}\left(x, \tilde{S}_1(\alpha), \ldots, \tilde{S}_{5-i}(\alpha); \alpha\right) \\ \beta\left(\tilde{y}_5(x; \alpha), \frac{\partial[\tilde{y}_5]_\alpha}{\partial x}\right) = 0. \end{cases} \quad (42)$$

Next, we will solve Equation (31) with a third-order series FF-OHAM using the Mathematica 13 Dsolve package

$$\tilde{y}(x; \alpha) = \tilde{y}_0(x; \alpha) + \sum_{j=1}^{3} \tilde{y}_j\left(x, \tilde{S}_1(0.5), \ldots, \tilde{S}_j(0.5); 0.5\right) \quad (43)$$

For this linear application, we found that the fuzzy convergence parameters at $\alpha = 0.5$ provide an appropriate and accurate series solution at each $\alpha \in [0,1]$, such that $\tilde{S}_1(0.5) = -1.065291064957493$, $\tilde{S}_2(0.5) = -0.00004338985509905724$, and $\tilde{S}_3(0.5) = -0.0020739269082325523$.

Next, we will employ the fuzzy convergence parameters $\tilde{S}_1(0.5)$, $\tilde{S}_2(0.5)$, and $\tilde{S}_3(0.5)$ in Equation (43) to find the third-order FF-OHAM approximate series solution for Equation (31), as shown in Table 1, as follows.

Table 1. The approximate solutions and errors for Equation (31) using the third-order FF-OHAM at $x = 0.5$ for all $\alpha \in [0,1]$.

α	$\left[\underline{ER}\right]_\alpha, \tilde{S}_j$	$\left[\overline{ER}\right]_\alpha, \tilde{S}_j$	$\left[\underline{y}\right]_\alpha, \tilde{S}_j$	$\left[\overline{y}\right]_\alpha, \tilde{S}_j$
0	-1.36061×10^{-5}	0	-0.49998	0
0.2	-1.22455×10^{-5}	-1.36061×10^{-6}	-0.44998	-0.04999
0.4	-1.08849×10^{-5}	-2.72123×10^{-6}	-0.39999	-0.09999
0.6	-9.52429×10^{-6}	-4.08184×10^{-6}	-0.34999	-0.14999
0.8	-8.16368×10^{-6}	-5.44245×10^{-6}	-0.29999	-0.19999
1	-6.80306×10^{-6}	-6.80306×10^{-6}	-0.24999	-0.24999

Using a three-dimensional graph, we summarize the solutions using the third-order FF-OHAM over all $x \in [0, 0.5]$ and $\alpha \in [0, 1]$ corresponding with the best optimal convergence control values—$\tilde{S}_1(0.5)$, $\tilde{S}_2(0.5)$, and $\tilde{S}_3(0.5)$—of Equation (31) in Figure 1.

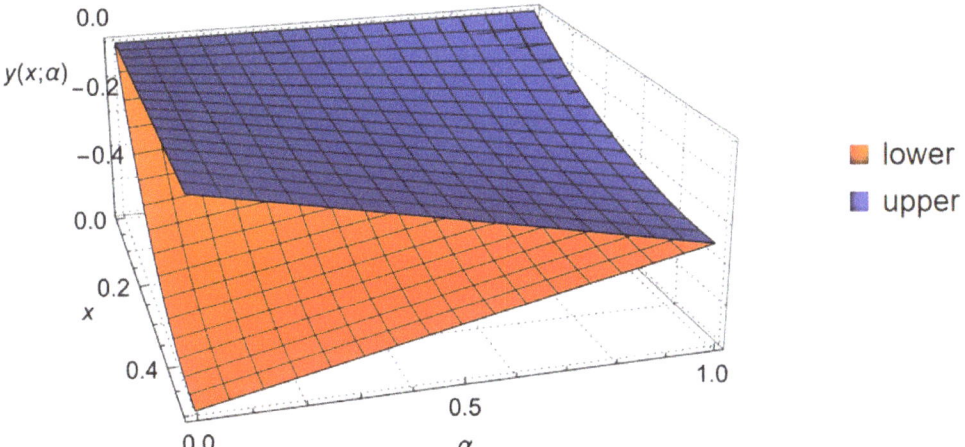

Figure 1. The three-dimensional approximate solution of Equation (31) given by the third-order FF-OHAM over all $x \in [0, 0.5]$, and for all $\alpha \in [0, 1]$.

To analyze the behavior of FF-OHAM for solving second-order FFOBVPs, we shall proceed to solve Equation (31) using the same data, $x \in [0, 0.5]$ and $\omega = 1.5$, and the fifth-order FF-OHAM instead of the third-order FF-OHAM to illustrate the convergence dynamic of FF-OHAM for different terms of the approximate series solution; therefore, the series solution will take the following form:

$$\tilde{y}(x;\alpha) = \tilde{y}_0(x;\alpha) + \sum_{j=1}^{5} \tilde{y}_j\left(x, \tilde{S}_1(0.5), \ldots, \tilde{S}_j(0.5); 0.5\right) \tag{44}$$

such that the optimal convergence control parameters calculated using the Mathematica 13 Dsolve package are

$\tilde{S}_1(0.5) = -1.0270653590282228$ $\tilde{S}_2(0.5) = 6.734609572815013 \times 10^{-7}$ $\tilde{S}_3(0.5) = -0.000025083072228706767$
$\tilde{S}_4(0.5) = 0.000131089732250741$ $\tilde{S}_5(0.5) = 0.0001858737255737089$

The above convergence parameters will be employed in Equation (44) to find the fifth-order FF-OHAM approximate series solution for Equation (31), as shown in Table 2, as follows.

Table 2. The approximate solutions and errors for Equation (31) using the fifth-order FF-OHAM at $x = 0.5$ for all $\alpha \in [0, 1]$.

α	$[\underline{ER}]_\alpha, \tilde{S}_j(0.5)$	$[\overline{ER}]_\alpha, \tilde{S}_j(0.5)$	$[\underline{y}]_\alpha, \tilde{S}_j(0.5)$	$[\overline{y}]_\alpha, \tilde{S}_j(0.5)$
0	-2.79607×10^{-8}	0	-0.50000	0
0.2	-2.51647×10^{-8}	-2.79607×10^{-9}	-0.45000	-0.05000
0.4	-2.23686×10^{-8}	-5.59214×10^{-9}	-0.40000	-0.10000
0.6	-1.95725×10^{-8}	-8.38822×10^{-9}	-0.35000	-0.15000
0.8	-1.67764×10^{-8}	-1.11843×10^{-8}	-0.30000	-0.20000
1	-1.39804×10^{-8}	-1.39804×10^{-8}	-0.25000	-0.25000

Figure 2 illustrates the summary of the solutions using the fifth-order FF-OHAM over all $x \in [0, 0.5]$ and $\alpha \in [0, 1]$ corresponding with the best optimal convergence control values—$\tilde{S}_1(0.5), \tilde{S}_2(0.5), \tilde{S}_3(0.5), \tilde{S}_4(0.5)$, and $\tilde{S}_5(0.5)$—of Equation (43) in a three-dimensional figure.

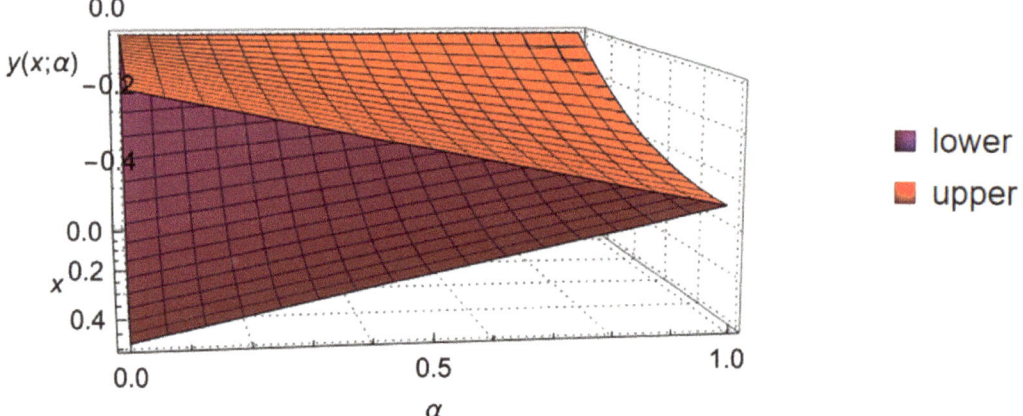

Figure 2. The three-dimensional approximate solution for Equation (31) given using the fifth-order FF-OHAM over all $x \in [0, 0.5]$, and for all $\alpha \in [0, 1]$.

Tables 1 and 2 and Figures 1 and 2 illustrate that the third- and fifth-order FF-OHAMs satisfy the triangular solution of the fuzzy differential equations for Equation (31) [2]. On the other hand, we can conclude that the series solution of the linear physical application involving FFOBVP using the FF-OHAM will approach the exact solutions whenever the order of the FF-OHAM increases. The developed FF-OHAM is compared with the spectral collection method (SCM) for solving the mechanical application described in Equation (31). Figures 3 and 4 illustrate the lower and upper accuracy of the fifth-order FF-OHAM in comparison to the fifth-order SCM for solving the mechanical pplication $\forall x \in [0, 1]$ at $\alpha = 0.5$ based on the absolute error defined below in Equation (45).

$$\begin{cases} \underline{ERR} = \left| \underline{Y}(x; \alpha) - \underline{y}(x; \alpha) \right| \\ \overline{ERR} = \left| \overline{Y}(x; \alpha) - \overline{y}(x; \alpha) \right| \end{cases}, \forall x \in [0, 1] \text{, and } \forall \alpha \in [0, 1] \qquad (45)$$

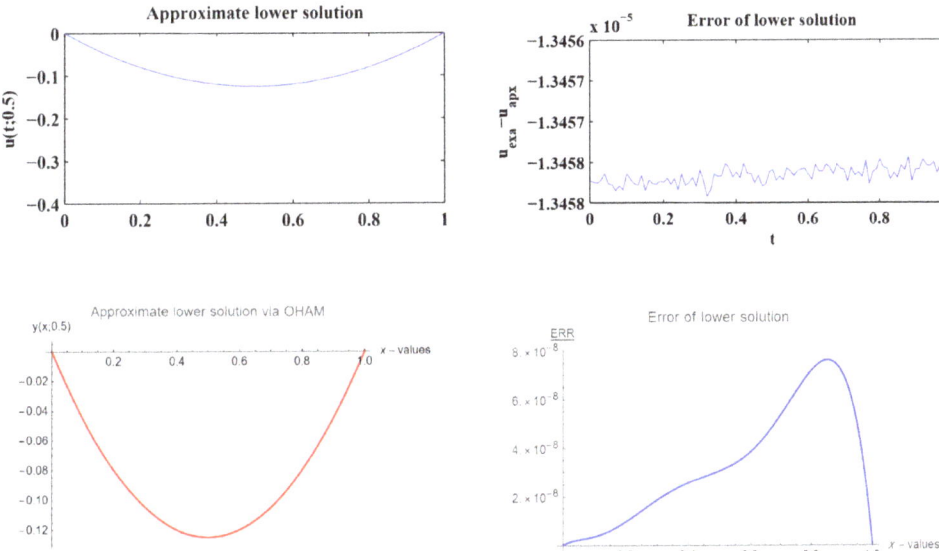

Figure 3. Comparison of the lower approximate solution for Equation (31) using the fifth-order FF-OHAM and the fifth-order SCM for $\alpha = 0.5$ and $\forall x \in [0,1]$.

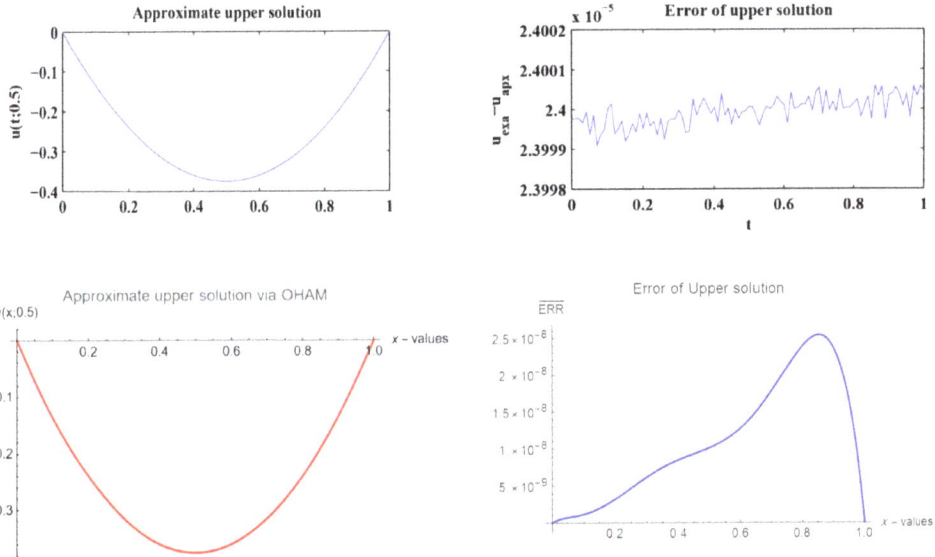

Figure 4. Comparison of the upper approximate solution for Equation (31) using the fifth-order FF-OHAM and the fifth-order SCM for $\alpha = 0.5$ and $\forall x \in [0,1]$.

We can conclude from Figures 3 and 4 that the accuracy of the approximate solution solved for using the fifth-order FF-OHAM series provides better accuracy compared to SCM for all $x \in [0,1]$.

- Thermal Conductivity of a Material: Nonlinear Fractional Temperature Distribution Equation

Consider the mathematical model, a nonlinear fractional temperature distribution equation of order $\omega \in (1,2]$, which explains the distribution of the temperature in the lumped convection system in a layer comprised of materials with varying thermal conductivity [39]:

$$\begin{cases} D^{(\omega)}y(x) - \eta(y(x))^4 = 0, \; x \in [0,1] \\ y'(0) = 0, \; y(1) = 1. \end{cases} \qquad (46)$$

where x is the time-independent variable, and $y(x)$ is the dimensionless temperature.

The following is the fuzzy version of Equation (46):

$$\begin{cases} \widetilde{D}^{(\omega)}\widetilde{y}(x;\alpha) - \eta(y(x;\alpha))^4 = 0, \; x \in [0,1] \\ \underline{y}'(0;\alpha) = (0.1\alpha - 0.1), \; \underline{y}(1;\alpha) = (0.1\alpha + 0.9), \\ \overline{y}'(0;\alpha) = (0.1 - 0.1\alpha), \; \overline{y}(1;\alpha) = (1.1 - 0.1\alpha). \end{cases} \qquad (47)$$

To solve the fuzzy fractional model of the thermal conductivity using the FF-OHAM, sccording to Section 3, we can build the approximate series solution for Equation (47) of order $\omega \in (1,2]$ for all $\alpha \in [0,1]$ as follows:

For $k \geq 0$, we can construct the following FF-OHAM form

$$(1-q)\left[\widetilde{D}^{(\omega)}\left(\widetilde{y}(x;\alpha)\right)\right] = \sum_{j=1}^{k} S_j(\alpha) q^j \left[\widetilde{D}^{(\omega)}\left(\widetilde{y}(x;\alpha)\right) - \eta\left(\widetilde{y}(x;\alpha)\right)^4\right], \qquad (48)$$

Then, the approximate series solution is introduced in Equation (49) below:

$$\widetilde{y}(x;\alpha) = \widetilde{y}_0(x;\alpha) + \sum_{j=1}^{k} \widetilde{y}_j(x, S_1, \ldots, S_j; \alpha) q^j \qquad (49)$$

For a zeroth-order problem:

$$\widetilde{y}_0(x;\alpha) = \left[\widetilde{0}\right]. \qquad (50)$$

For first- to tenth-order problems:

$$\begin{cases} (1-q)\left[\widetilde{D}^{(\omega)}\left(\widetilde{y}(x;\alpha)\right)\right] = \sum_{j=0}^{9} \widetilde{S}_j(\alpha) q^j \left[\widetilde{D}^{(\omega)}\left(\widetilde{y}(x;\alpha)\right) - \right. \\ \left. \eta\left(\sum_{i=0}^{9} \widetilde{y}_{9-i}(x;\alpha) \sum_{j=0}^{i} \widetilde{y}_{i-j}(x;\alpha) \sum_{s=0}^{j} \widetilde{y}_s(x;\alpha) \widetilde{y}_{j-s}(x;\alpha)\right)\right], \\ \widetilde{y}_k'(0;\alpha) = \widetilde{y}_k(1;\alpha) = \widetilde{0}. \end{cases} \qquad (51)$$

Next, using the Mathematica 13 Dsolve package to find the series solutions for the lower and the upper bounds of Equation (47), for $j = 1, 2, \ldots, 10$, we obtain

$$\widetilde{y}(x;\alpha) = \widetilde{y}_0(x;\alpha) + \sum_{j=1}^{10} \widetilde{y}_j(x, S_1, \ldots, S_j; \alpha) q^j \qquad (52)$$

such that the optimal lower and upper convergence control parameters calculated and coded using Mathematica 13 to find the most accurate solution for Equation (47) via the tenth-order FF-OHAM are listed in Tables 3 and 4 below.

Table 3. Lower auxiliary convergence parameters of the tenth-order FF-OHAM for solving Equation (47) at $\omega = 1.9$, $x = 0.1$, for all $\alpha \in [0,1]$.

α	$\underline{S}_j$		
0	$\underline{S}_1 = -0.427542431160988556$	$\underline{S}_2 = 0.10029988098228566$	$\underline{S}_3 = -0.13497958972180282$
	$\underline{S}_4 = 0.057027658640051423$	$\underline{S}_5 = -0.026736473824494192$	$\underline{S}_6 = -0.09334881995323582$
	$\underline{S}_7 = 0.14476539458261192$	$\underline{S}_8 = 2.6782513149178886$	$\underline{S}_9 = -3.1547021023298236$
		$\underline{S}_{10} = 0$	
0.5	$\underline{S}_1 = -0.4275424758687012$	$\underline{S}_2 = 0.10581949295995502$	$\underline{S}_3 = -0.1375566084081214$
	$\underline{S}_4 = 0.07545735284696302$	$\underline{S}_5 = -0.049825680470098175$	$\underline{S}_6 = -0.21083114235974942$
	$\underline{S}_7 = 0.33623100353843177$	$\underline{S}_8 = -1.780319356305217$	$\underline{S}_9 = 1.8279961729200187$
		$\underline{S}_{10} = 0$	
1	$\underline{S}_1 = -0.4275424759052609$	$\underline{S}_2 = 0.10838719398757574$	$\underline{S}_3 = -0.1393691078519383$
	$\underline{S}_4 = 0.0819534530845722$	$\underline{S}_5 = -0.05404354434171497<$	$\underline{S}_6 = -0.06431130239382181$
	$\underline{S}_7 = 0.12107016205095011$	$\underline{S}_8 = -0.9412597479377718$	$\underline{S}_9 = 1.0018880129871244$
		$\underline{S}_{10} = 0$	

Table 4. Upper auxiliary convergence parameters of the tenth-order FF-OHAM for solving Equation (47) at $\omega = 1.9$, $x = 0.1$, for all $\alpha \in [0,1]$.

α	$\overline{S}_j$		
0	$\overline{S}_1 = -0.4499999715464292$	$\overline{S}_2 = 0.07033774093204971$	$\overline{S}_3 = -0.08588077852784994$
	$\overline{S}_4 = 0.02200367504397761$	$\overline{S}_5 = -0.013738000249538687$	$\overline{S}_6 = -0.13177749373901043$
	$\overline{S}_7 = 0.20247748961630552$	$\overline{S}_8 = -1.167757698543094$	$\overline{S}_9 = 1.1715997608744646$
		$\overline{S}_{10} = 0$	
0.5	$\overline{S}_1 = -0.4500000000118868$	$\overline{S}_2 = 0.11085869384502318$	$\overline{S}_3 = -0.1322901831399701$
	$\overline{S}_4 = 0.053720614964490584$	$\overline{S}_5 = -0.019748829952898384$	$\overline{S}_6 = -0.12141795332965101$
	$\overline{S}_7 = 0.1700603758070842$	$\overline{S}_8 = -0.7863871032395353$	$\overline{S}_9 = 0.7686499426055967$
		$\overline{S}_{10} = 0$	
1	$\overline{S}_1 = -0.4499999999893346$	$\overline{S}_2 = 0.1095056263140715$	$\overline{S}_3 = -0.1302513333365527$
	$\overline{S}_4 = 0.0473415579627094$	$\overline{S}_5 = -0.0185338348210904$	$\overline{S}_6 = -0.14589007991813402$
	$\overline{S}_7 = 0.2076338115632854$	$\overline{S}_8 = -1.0720018208884141$	$\overline{S}_9 = 1.0605759385659808$
		$\overline{S}_{10} = 0$	

The above lower and upper convergence parameters in Tables 3 and 4 bare employed in Equation (52) to find the tenth-order FF-OHAM approximate series solution for Equation (47), as shown in Table 5 and summarized Figure 5 below.

Table 5. The approximate solutions and errors for Equation (47) using the tenth-order FF-OHAM when $\omega = 1.9$ at $x = 0.1$ for all $\alpha \in [0,1]$.

α	$\left[\underline{ER}\right]_\alpha, \underline{S}_j$	$\left[\overline{ER}\right]_\alpha, \overline{S}_j$	$\left[\underline{y}\right]_\alpha, \underline{S}_j$	$\left[\overline{y}\right]_\alpha, \overline{S}_j$
0	-7.73663×10^{-5}	-1.78658×10^{-5}	0.81730	0.83216
0.5	-6.65123×10^{-6}	1.68215×10^{-6}	0.82167	0.82909
1	6.42966×10^{-5}	-2.62733×10^{-5}	0.82560	0.82560

Figure 5 illustrates the summary of the solutions using the tenth-order FF-OHAM over all $x \in [0, 0.1]$ and $\alpha \in [0,1]$ corresponding with the best optimal convergence control values, $\tilde{S}_j$, of Equation (47) in the three-dimensional graph.

Morever, the fuzzy solutions, shown in Table 5 and Figure 5, clarify that the new construction of the FF-OHAM satisfies the fuzzy solution of the new fuzzy version of the distribution of the model of the temperature in the lumped convection system in a layer comprised of materials with varying thermal conductivity. Furthermore, the FF-OHAM provides an appropriate approximate series solution for the strong nonlinearity fractional differential equation with the presence of the uncertainty, which makes this approach applicable and suitable for solving the most complicated, nonlinear real-world problems.

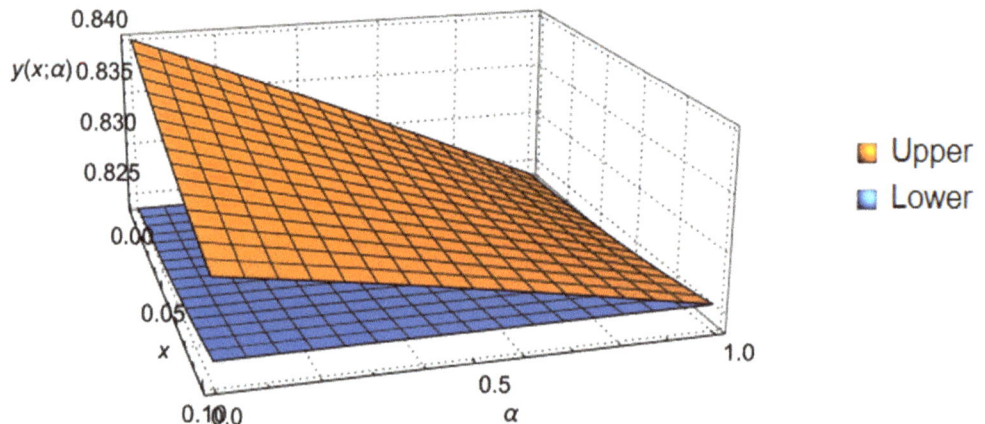

Figure 5. The three-dimensional approximate solution for Equation (47) given using the tenth-order FF-OHAM over all $x \in [0, 0.1]$ at $\omega = 1.9$ and for $\eta = 0.6$, and for all $\alpha \in [0, 1]$.

7. Conclusions

The present study focused on developing an approximate analytical method, called FF-OHAM, for solving linear and nonlinear fractional order boundary value problems (FFOBVPs). The FF-OHAM method has the ability to control the convergence of the series solution by selecting the optimal convergence parameter for each method. The Bagley–Torvik equation, which is an inhomogeneous linear FFOBVP, was used as a case study to demonstrate the accuracy of the FF-OHAM method in solving linear cases. The method was found to provide an accurate series solution as the series order increases and the obtained solution converges to the exact solution. The solutions obtained using the FF-OHAM were found to be more accurate than those obtained using the SCM. Furthermore, the study also introduced a new fuzzy version of the fractional temperature distribution equation and utilized the FF-OHAM to find the series solution for this nonlinear problem. The FF-OHAM method was found to provide an accurate series solution for solving nonlinear cases without needing an exact solution. The convergence dynamic of the FF-OHAM was also used to obtain optimal convergence parameters for this problem. Finally, it is noted that all the fuzzy fractional solutions obtained using the FF-HAM and the FF-OHAM satisfy the triangular fuzzy solution, which is a desirable property for fuzzy systems. It is a good idea to explore techniques to improve the computational efficiency of the developed FF-OHAM method, as this can lead to faster and more efficient solutions for FFOBVPs, such as parallelization. The FF-OHAM method can be parallelized to run on multiple processors or cores simultaneously. This can help to reduce the computational time required to obtain a solution, especially for large and complex problems.

Author Contributions: Conceptualization, A.F.J.; methodology, supervision, and editing, D.J.H.; writing—original draft preparation, N.A.; writing—review editing and funding, A.-K.A.; data curation and coding, A.-K.A.; review editing and funding, O.A.; review editing and funding, A.Q.; and paper review in terms of numerical results, K.S.A.K. All authors have read and agreed to the published version of the manuscript.

Funding: This research received no external funding.

Informed Consent Statement: Not applicable.

Data Availability Statement: Not applicable.

Conflicts of Interest: The authors declare no conflict of interest.

References

1. Machado, J.T.; Galhano, A.M.; Trujillo, J.J. On development of fractional calculus during the last fifty years. *Scientometrics* **2014**, *98*, 577–582. [CrossRef]
2. Failla, G.; Zingales, M. Advanced materials modelling via fractional calculus: Challenges and perspectives. *Philos. Trans. R. Soc. A Math. Phys. Eng. Sci.* **2020**, *378*, 20200050. [CrossRef] [PubMed]
3. Dalir, M.; Bashour, M. Applications of fractional calculus. *Appl. Math. Sci.* **2010**, *4*, 1021–1032.
4. Bonyah, E.; Atangana, A.; Chand, M. Analysis of 3D IS-LM macroeconomic system model within the scope of fractional calculus. *Chaos Solitons Fractals X* **2019**, *2*, 100007. [CrossRef]
5. Picozzi, S.; West, B.J. Fractional langevin model of memory in financial markets. *Phys. Rev. E* **2002**, *66*, 046118. [CrossRef]
6. You, X.; Li, S.; Kang, L.; Cheng, L. A Study of the Non-Linear Seepage Problem in Porous Media via the Homotopy Analysis Method. *Energies* **2023**, *16*, 2175. [CrossRef]
7. Esmaeilbeigi, M.; Paripour, M.; Garmanjani, G. Approximate solution of the fuzzy fractional Bagley-Torvik equation by the RBF collocation method. *Comput. Methods Differ. Equ.* **2018**, *6*, 186–214.
8. Chakraverty, S.; Tapaswini, S.; Behera, D. *Fuzzy Arbitrary Order System: Fuzzy Fractional Differential Equations and Applications*; John Wiley: Hoboken, NJ, USA, 2016.
9. Abdollahi, R.; Farshbaf Moghimi, M.B.; Khastan, A.; Hooshmandasl, M.R. Linear fractional fuzzy differential equations with Caputo derivative. *Comput. Methods Differ. Equ.* **2019**, *7*, 252–265.
10. Das, A.K.; Roy, T.K. Exact solution of some linear fuzzy fractional differential equation using Laplace transform method. *Glob. J. Pure Appl. Math.* **2017**, *13*, 5427–5435.
11. Kudryashov, N.A. Method for finding highly dispersive optical solitons of nonlinear differential equations. *Optik* **2020**, *206*, 163550. [CrossRef]
12. Bulut, H.; Baskonus, H.M.; Belgacem, F.B.M. The analytical solution of some fractional ordinary differential equations by the Sumudu transform method. *Abstr. Appl. Anal.* **2013**, *2013*, 203875. [CrossRef]
13. Ghanbari, B.; Akgul, A. Abundant new analytical and approximate solutions to the generalized schamel equation. *Phys. Scr.* **2020**, *95*, 075201. [CrossRef]
14. Verma, P.; Kumar, M. An analytical solution of linear/nonlinear fractional-order partial differential equations and with new existence and uniqueness conditions. *Proc. Natl. Acad. Sci. India Sect. A Phys. Sci.* **2022**, *92*, 47–55. [CrossRef]
15. Takači, D.; Takači, A.; Takači, A. On the operational solutions of fuzzy fractional differential equations. *Fract. Calc. Appl. Anal.* **2014**, *17*, 1100–1113. [CrossRef]
16. Ahmad, M.Z.; Hasan, M.K.; Abbasbandy, S. Solving fuzzy fractional differential equations using Zadeh's extension principle. *Sci. World J.* **2013**, *2013*, 454969. [CrossRef]
17. Ahmadian, A.; Senu, N.; Salahshour, S.; Suleiman, M. On a numerical solution for fuzzy fractional differential equation using an operational matrix method. In Proceedings of the 2015 International Symposium on Mathematical Sciences and Computing Research (iSMSC), Ipoh, Malaysia, 19–20 May 2015; pp. 432–437.
18. Ahmadian, A.; Suleiman, M.; Salahshour, S.; Baleanu, D. A Jacobi operational matrix for solving a fuzzy linear fractional differential equation. *Adv. Differ. Equ.* **2013**, *2013*, 104. [CrossRef]
19. Mazandarani, M.; Kamyad, A.V. Modified fractional Euler method for solving fuzzy fractional initial value problem. *Commun. Nonlinear Sci. Numer. Simul.* **2013**, *18*, 12–21. [CrossRef]
20. Ahmadian, A.; Ismail, F.; Salahshour, S.; Baleanu, D.; Ghaemi, F. Uncertain viscoelastic models with fractional order: A new spectral tau method to study the numerical simulations of the solution. *Commun. Nonlinear Sci. Numer. Simul.* **2017**, *53*, 44–64. [CrossRef]
21. Prakash, P.; Nieto, J.J.; Senthilvelavan, S.; Sudha Priya, G. Fuzzy fractional initial value problem. *J. Intell. Fuzzy Syst.* **2015**, *28*, 2691–2704. [CrossRef]
22. Khodadadi, E.; Çelik, E. The variational iteration method for fuzzy fractional differential equations with uncertainty. *Fixed Point Theory Appl.* **2013**, *2013*, 13. [CrossRef]
23. Panahi, A. Approximate solution of fuzzy fractional differential equations. *Int. J. Ind. Math.* **2017**, *9*, 111–118.
24. Hasan, S.; Alawneh, A.; Al-Momani, M.; Momani, S. Second order fuzzy fractional differential equations under Caputo's H-differentiability. *Appl. Math. Inf. Sci.* **2017**, *11*, 1597–1608. [CrossRef]
25. Ali, F.J.; Anakira, N.R.; Alomari, A.K.J.; Man, N.H. Solution and analysis of the fuzzy Volterra integral equations via homotopy analysis method. *Comput. Model. Eng. Sci.* **2021**, *127*, 875–899.
26. Rivaz, A.; Fard, O.S.; Bidgoli, T.A. Solving fuzzy fractional differential equations by a generalized differential transform method. *SeMA J.* **2016**, *73*, 149–170. [CrossRef]
27. Alshorman, M.A.; Zamri, N.; Ali, M.; Albzeirat, A.K. New implementation of residual power series for solving fuzzy fractional Riccati equation. *J. Model. Optim.* **2018**, *10*, 81–87. [CrossRef]

28. Alaroud, M.O.; Saadeh, R.A.; Al-smadi, M.O.; Ahmad, R.R.; Din, U.K.; Abu Arqub, O. Solving nonlinear fuzzy fractional IVPs using fractional residual power series algorithm. *IACM* **2019**, *2019*, 170–175.
29. Dulfikar, J.H.; Ali, F.J.; The, Y.Y.; Alomari, A.K.; Anakira, N.R. Optimal homotopy asymptotic method for solving several models of first order fuzzy fractional IVPs. *Alex. Eng. J.* **2022**, *61*, 4931–4943.
30. Mousa, M.M.; Alsharari, F. Convergence and error estimation of a new formulation of homotopy perturbation method for classes of nonlinear integral/integro-differential equations. *Mathematics* **2021**, *9*, 2244. [CrossRef]
31. Marinca, V.; Herişanu, N. Application of optimal homotopy asymptotic method for solving nonlinear equations arising in heat transfer. *Int. Commun. Heat Mass Transf.* **2008**, *35*, 710–715. [CrossRef]
32. Ali, F.J.; Akram, H.S.; Anakira, N.R.; Alomari, A.K.; Azizan, S. Comparison for the Approximate Solution of the Second-Order Fuzzy Nonlinear Differential Equation with Fuzzy Initial Conditions. *Math. Stat.* **2020**, *8*, 527–534.
33. Ali, F.J.; Anakira, N.R.; Alomari, A.K.; Hashim, I.; Shakhatreh, M. Numerical solution of n-th order fuzzy initial value problems by six stages Range Kutta method of order five. *Int. J. Electr. Comput. Eng.* **2019**, *9*, 6497–6506.
34. Yuldashev, T.K.; Karimov, E.T. Inverse problem for a mixed type integro-differential equation with fractional order Caputo operators and spectral parameters. *Axioms* **2020**, *9*, 121. [CrossRef]
35. Radi, D.; Sorini, L.; Stefanini, L. On the numerical solution of ordinary, interval and fuzzy differential equations by use of F-transform. *Axioms* **2020**, *9*, 15. [CrossRef]
36. Dulfikar, J.H.; Ali, F.J.; Teh, Y.Y. Approximate Solutions of Fuzzy Fractional Differential Equations via Homotopy Analysis Method. *Fract. Differ. Appl.* **2023**, *9*, 167–187.
37. Kaur, D.; Agarwal, P.; Rakshit, M.; Chand, M. Fractional calculus involving (p, q)-mathieu type series. *Appl. Math. Nonlinear Sci.* **2020**, *5*, 15–34. [CrossRef]
38. Bodjanova, S. Median alpha-levels of a fuzzy number. *Fuzzy Sets Syst.* **2002**, *157*, 879–891. [CrossRef]
39. Ismail, M.; Saeed, U.; Alzabut, J.; Rehman, M. Approximate solutions for fractional boundary value problems via green-CAS wavelet method. *Mathematics* **2019**, *7*, 1164. [CrossRef]

Disclaimer/Publisher's Note: The statements, opinions and data contained in all publications are solely those of the individual author(s) and contributor(s) and not of MDPI and/or the editor(s). MDPI and/or the editor(s) disclaim responsibility for any injury to people or property resulting from any ideas, methods, instructions or products referred to in the content.

Article

Dynamics of a Double-Impulsive Control Model of Integrated Pest Management Using Perturbation Methods and Floquet Theory

Fahad Al Basir [1], Jahangir Chowdhury [2] and Delfim F. M. Torres [3,*]

[1] Department of Mathematics, Asansol Girls' College, Asansol 713304, India
[2] Department of Applied Science, RCC Institute of Information Technology, Canal South Road, Kolkata 700015, India
[3] Center for Research and Development in Mathematics and Applications (CIDMA), Department of Mathematics, University of Aveiro, 3810-193 Aveiro, Portugal
* Correspondence: delfim@ua.pt; Tel.: +351-234-370-668

Abstract: We formulate an integrated pest management model to control natural pests of the crop through the periodic application of biopesticide and chemical pesticides. In a theoretical analysis of the system pest eradication, a periodic solution is found and established. All the system variables are proved to be bounded. Our main goal is then to ensure that pesticides are optimized, in terms of pesticide concentration and pesticide application frequency, and that the optimum combination of pesticides is found to provide the most benefit to the crop. By using Floquet theory and the small amplitude perturbation method, we prove that the pest eradication periodic solution is locally and globally stable. The acquired results establish a threshold time limit for the impulsive release of various controls as well as some valid theoretical conclusions for effective pest management. Furthermore, after a numerical comparison, we conclude that integrated pest management is more effective than single biological or chemical controls. Finally, we illustrate the analytical results through numerical simulations.

Keywords: integrated pest management (IPM); impulsive differential equations; stability; Floquet theory; perturbation method; numerical simulations

MSC: 92D45; 34D20

Citation: Al Basir, F.; Chowdhury, J.; Torres, D.F.M. Dynamics of a Double-Impulsive Control Model of Integrated Pest Management Using Perturbation Methods and Floquet Theory. *Axioms* **2023**, *12*, 391. https://doi.org/10.3390/axioms12040391

Academic Editors: Valery Y. Glizer and Feliz Manuel Minhós

Received: 20 January 2023
Revised: 31 March 2023
Accepted: 15 April 2023
Published: 18 April 2023

Copyright: © 2023 by the authors. Licensee MDPI, Basel, Switzerland. This article is an open access article distributed under the terms and conditions of the Creative Commons Attribution (CC BY) license (https:// creativecommons.org/licenses/by/ 4.0/).

1. Introduction

In today's farming systems, a variety of approaches are used for pest control. Maintaining high output while guaranteeing sustainability is crucial for the entire agriculture sector. Since the beginning of human civilization, insect and pest control has been one of the most significant difficulties in the agricultural sector [1,2]. Every day, people come up with fresh ideas for equipment and tactics to use in their fight against pests. As a result of human efforts to manage pests, our natural ecology and nature are on the verge of extinction [3].

Chemical controls are less expensive to implement, yet they result in significant environmental damage [4–6]. On the other hand, biological controls are more costly to implement but have less environmental impact [7]. However, frequently, the use of a single control method is not beneficial to control pest resistance and preserve environmental quality [8,9]. In order to reduce insect populations below economic levels, integrated pest management (IPM), a safer and more effective method, was developed. IPM is used for a variety of agronomic crops and is now widely used as an economical and environment-friendly pest control method in several nations [8–10]. When the ecological cost of management is added to the economic price of controls, a combination of chemical and biological controls yields a superior result when they are used with proper rate and with tolerable intervals. Modeling of this phenomenon leads naturally to the use of impulsive differential equations [11,12].

Many researchers have designed mathematical models for pest management through control strategies, some of which promote chemical agents [4,7], some advocate the use of biological agents to impose a total solution of pest and disease [1,2,10,13–15], and some researchers use both the chemical and biopesticides in their mathematical models [5,16–18]. Mathematical-model-based works using impulsive differential equations are also available in the literature, as already mentioned [19–26]. Recently, Li, Huang, and Liu proposed a pest management model to simulate the application of pesticides and build a pesticide function with residual and delayed effects of pesticides, proposing pest management with pollutant emission [27]. Liu et al. constructed a mathematical model for pest control in which susceptible and infected pests are separated from the pest population and only susceptible pests are harmful to crops [28]. They weighed the two approaches of spraying pesticides and releasing diseased pests and natural enemies to control vulnerable pests when completing their task. Alzabut established a mathematical model based on the sense of biological survey in the field of agriculture, and introduced various control methods to determine how to protect the crops from destructive pests [29]. In [24], an integrated pest management model using impulsive differential equations was proposed and analyzed for *Jatropha curcas* using the release of infective pests and spraying of chemical pesticides. The existence and stability of susceptible pest-eradication solutions were analyzed using Floquet theory and the small amplitude perturbation method. To the best of our knowledge, all available articles deal with single-impulse differential equation models where the stability analysis of the periodic pest extinction solution is obtained by the Floquet theory, the method of small amplitude perturbation, and the comparison theorem. However, none of the prior research available in the literature employs the concentration of chemical pesticides as a system variable as we do here. Moreover, in our study, we spray biological and chemical pesticides at two different time intervals, simultaneously varying the time period.

Pest control models using a single impulse are available (see, e.g., [30]), but using double-impulsive controls is rare [31,32]. The authors of [31] took a predator population along with biopesticides in an impulsive periodic way for the control of crop pests. The authors of [32] proposed a predator–prey model with disease in the prey and investigated it for the purpose of integrated pest management. The permanence of the system and global stability of the susceptible pest-eradication periodic solution were shown by means of the released amounts of infective prey and predator. In contrast, here, impulses on both chemical and biopesticides were assumed in the formulation of the mathematical model for crop pest management.

Our use of the concentration profile of the chemical pesticide as a model variable is a novel approach. We demonstrated the dynamics using both the chemical and biological pesticides in the system in an impulsive way, which is, to the best of our knowledge, a novel concept in crop pest control. The proposed double-impulsive system was analyzed with proper analytical methods, namely, using Floquet theory and the perturbation method.

Floquet theory is a powerful mathematical tool for analyzing periodic systems, and it can be extended to impulsive models with periodic impulses. In impulsive models, the system's behavior is characterized by a sequence of discrete impulses applied at regular intervals. These impulses may arise in many practical scenarios, including electrical circuits, control systems, and biological systems. Floquet theory provides a robust framework for analyzing and designing control strategies for impulsive models with periodic impulses. One can analyze the stability of the impulsive system by examining the eigenvalues of the Floquet matrix [33]. In our analysis, we utilize small amplitude perturbation techniques and Floquet theory and obtain some valid theoretical results for successful management of pests. Moreover, we also establish the threshold time limit for the impulsive release of control agents. Our approach for using the Floquet theory is novel. Additionally, we examined the dynamics of the system for biological and chemical pesticides used as a sole control measure.

The paper is organized as follows. In Section 2, we derive the model by using impulsive differential equations for capturing the IPM system dynamics, taking plant, pest, virus, and chemical pesticide as model variables. The mathematical analysis of the model is then discussed in Section 3, which contains three subsections. In Section 3.1, we determine susceptible pest-eradication periodic solutions and check the feasibility–boundedness of the system variables discussed in Section 3.2. The local and global stability conditions around the susceptible pest-eradication periodic solutions are explored in Section 3.3. In Section 4, we exhibit our mathematical results through numerical simulations. Finally, in Section 5, we provide a discussion on the three types of control strategies: spraying chemical pesticide only, impulsively incorporating of infected pest only, and integrated control with a fixed and a variable impulse period, to make the final conclusion.

2. Derivation of the Impulsive Control Model

The following assumptions are taken to formulate the desired model: the crop plant and susceptible pest populations are denoted by x and y, respectively, and we denote z as the infected pest population.

Due to the finite size of a crop field, which, however, may be large, we assume logistic growth for the biomass of the crop, with net growth rate r and carrying capacity k. Crops become affected by pests, thereby causing considerable crop reduction.

Let α be the contact rate between crop and susceptible pest; let $v(t)$ be the biopesticide (virus); and s be the concentration of chemical pesticide. A virus infects the susceptible pest at a rate, λ. The chemical pesticide kills the susceptible and infected pests at the rates m_1 and m_2, respectively. Parameters c_1 and c_2 are the conversion factors of susceptible and infected pests, respectively, due to consumption of crop; d and $d + \delta$ are the mortality rates of susceptible and infected pest, respectively; θ is the virus replication rate; and γ is the lysis rate of the virus. Finally, we introduce a periodic application of biopesticide and chemical pesticide with different time intervals.

Based on the above assumptions, the desired impulsive system for integrated pest management is given as

$$\begin{cases} \dfrac{dx}{dt} = rx\left(1 - \dfrac{x}{k}\right) - \alpha xy - \phi\alpha xz, & t \neq (n\tau_1, n\tau_2), \\ \dfrac{dy}{dt} = c_1\alpha xy - \lambda yv - dy - m_1 sy, & t \neq (n\tau_1, n\tau_2), \\ \dfrac{dz}{dt} = c_2\phi\alpha xz + \lambda yv - (d+\delta)z - m_2 sz, & t \neq (n\tau_1, n\tau_2), \\ \dfrac{dv}{dt} = \theta(d+\delta)z - \gamma v, & t \neq (n\tau_1, n\tau_2), \\ \dfrac{ds}{dt} = -\mu s, & t \neq (n\tau_1, n\tau_2), \\ v(t^+) = v(t^-) + v_i, & t = n\tau_1, \\ s(t^+) = s(t^-) + s_i, & t = n\tau_2, \end{cases} \quad (1)$$

where v_i and s_i are the strength of biopesticide and chemical pesticide application in the system at $t = n\tau_1$ and $t = n\tau_2$, respectively; $n = 0, 1, 2, 3, \ldots$, where τ_1 and τ_2 are the time periods. Here, $v(t^-)$ and $s(t^-)$ are the strength of biopesticide and chemical pesticide before the periodic input, and $v(t^+)$ and $s(t^+)$ are the strength of biopesticide and chemical pesticide after the periodic input.

In the impulsive model (1), we assumed the concentration of chemical pesticide as a model population, which is realistic and a novel idea. We use two different impulse intervals for two control agents (biopesticide and chemical pesticide) that will be analyzed both analytically and numerically. We proceed by analyzing the dynamics of model (1) by discussing the existence of equilibria with their stability.

3. Dynamics of the Impulsive Model

In this section, we analyze the boundedness of the solutions of system (1), we find out its pest-eradication steady state, and we analyze the local and global stability. Finally, we discuss the permanence of the impulsive system.

3.1. Boundedness of the Model Variables

Let $V(t) = x(t) + y(t) + z(t) + v(t) + s(t)$ and

$$\frac{dV}{dt} + mV \leq \left(rx + mx - \frac{rx^2}{k}\right) - (1-c_1)\alpha xy - (1-c_2)\phi\alpha xz - \{(d-m)\}y$$
$$-\{(1-\theta)(d+\delta) - m\}z - (\gamma - m)v - (\mu - m)s.$$

Now, let us define $m = \min\{d, \gamma, \mu, (d+\delta)(1-\theta)\}$. As $0 < c_1, c_2, \theta < 1$, then $1 - c_1 > 0, 1 - c_2 > 0$, and $1 - \theta > 0$, so we can write that

$$\frac{dV(t)}{dt} + mV(t) \leq M_0, \tag{2}$$

where $\frac{k(m+r)^2}{4r} = M_0$. At $t = n\tau_1$, we have

$$V(n\tau_1^+) \leq V(n\tau_1) + v_i. \tag{3}$$

By the comparison theorem, for $t \geq 0$ we have

$$V(t) \leq V(0)e^{-mt} + \frac{M_0(1-e^{-mt})}{m} + v_i \frac{e^{-m(t-\tau_1)}}{1-e^{m\tau_1}} + v_i \frac{e^{m\tau_1}}{e^{m\tau_1}-1}$$
$$\to \frac{M_0}{m} + v_i \frac{e^{m\tau_1}}{e^{m\tau_1}-1} \text{ as } t \to \infty. \tag{4}$$

When $t = n\tau_2$,

$$V(n\tau_2^+) \leq V(n\tau_2) + v_i \tag{5}$$

and from the comparison theorem it follows that

$$V(t) \leq V(0)e^{-mt} + \frac{M_0(1-e^{-mt})}{m} + v_i \frac{e^{-m(t-\tau_2)}}{1-e^{m\tau_2}} + v_i \frac{e^{m\tau_2}}{e^{m\tau_2}-1}$$
$$\to \frac{M_0}{m} + v_i \frac{e^{m\tau_2}}{e^{m\tau_2}-1} \text{ as } t \to \infty. \tag{6}$$

Thus, $V(t)$ is uniformly bounded and there exists a positive constant $M > 0$ such that $x(t) \leq M, y(t) \leq M, z(t) \leq M, v(t) \leq M$, and $s(t) \leq M$ for all t.

From the above discussion, we have the following theorem.

Theorem 1. *For the impulsive system (1), there exists a positive constant M such that $x(t) \leq M$, $y(t) \leq M, z(t) \leq M, v(t) \leq M$, and $s(t) \leq M$ for all t.*

For non-negative solutions, the following lemma follows from [13].

Lemma 1. *Let $X(t)$ be a solution of the impulsive system (1) with $X(0^+) \geq 0$. Then $X(t) \geq 0$ for all $t > 0$.*

3.2. Existence of the Pest-Free Periodic Orbit

Since both pests are assumed to be harmful for crops, we discuss stability at infected and susceptible pest-eradication solutions of the system when $y = 0$ and $z = 0$, $t \neq (n\tau_1, n\tau_2)$, and the linear forms of the fourth and fifth equation of (1) are

$$\frac{dv}{dt} = -\gamma v \quad \text{and} \quad \frac{ds}{dt} = -\mu s, \tag{7}$$

respectively. For an impulse control, we must have

$$\begin{aligned} v(t^+) &= v(t^-) + v_i, \quad \text{for } t = \tau_1, \\ s(t^+) &= s(t^-) + s_i, \quad \text{for } t = \tau_2. \end{aligned} \tag{8}$$

From (7) and (8) it is clear that v and s are independent of each other. Thus, the solution of Equation (7) can be given as follows:

$$\begin{aligned} v(t) &= \{v(0^+) - v^*(0^+)\}e^{-\gamma t} + v^*(t), \text{ for } t \in (\tau_1, (n+1)\tau_1], \\ s(t) &= \{s(0^+) - s^*(0^+)\}e^{-\mu t} + s^*(t), \text{ for } \in (\tau_2, (n+1)\tau_2], \end{aligned} \tag{9}$$

where $v^*(t)$ and $s^*(t)$, the positive periodic solution of (7), are given by

$$v^*(t) = \frac{v_i e^{-\gamma(t-n\tau_1)}}{1 - e^{-\gamma\tau_1}}, \quad s^*(t) = \frac{s_i e^{-\mu(t-n\tau_2)}}{1 - e^{-\mu\tau_2}}, \tag{10}$$

with initial values

$$v^*(0^+) = \frac{v_i}{1 - e^{-\gamma\tau_1}}, \quad s^*(0^+) = \frac{s_i}{1 - e^{-\mu\tau_2}}. \tag{11}$$

If $y(t) = 0$ and $z(t) = 0$, then the first equation of (1) is

$$\frac{dx}{dt} = rx\left(1 - \frac{x}{k}\right), \tag{12}$$

which is a logistic equation, and its solution is

$$x(t) = \frac{kx(0)}{x(0) + (k - x(0))e^{rt}} \quad \text{for } t \neq (n\tau_1, n\tau_2). \tag{13}$$

Clearly, (13) has two equilibria, such as $x = 0$ and $x = k$. Therefore, (1) has two pest-eradication solutions, $(0, 0, 0, v^*, s^*)$ and $(k, 0, 0, v^*, s^*)$. Obviously, at $x = 0$ the system (13) is impossible from the perspective of ecology. For this reason, in the following subsection we study the stability for the system (1) at $E = (k, 0, 0, v^*, s^*)$.

3.3. Stability of the Pest-Free Periodic Solution

We establish the following theorem for the stability of the pest-free periodic orbit.

Theorem 2. *System (1) is both locally and globally stable around the pest-free periodic solution $E = (k, 0, 0, v^*, s^*)$ for the following:*

(i) Application of biopesticide and chemical pesticide with same time interval $t = n\tau$, provided that

$$c_1\alpha - d - \frac{\lambda v_i e^{-\gamma(t-n\tau)}}{1 - e^{-\gamma\tau}} - \frac{m_1 s_i e^{-\mu(t-n\tau)}}{1 - e^{-\mu\tau}} < 0,$$

$$c_2\phi k\alpha - (d + \delta) - \frac{m_2 s_i e^{-\mu(t-n\tau)}}{1 - e^{-\mu\tau}} < 0; \tag{14}$$

(ii) Application of biopesticide with time interval $t = n\tau_1$ and chemical pesticide with time interval $t = n\tau_2$, i.e., for different time intervals, where $\tau_1 \neq \tau_2$, provided that

$$c_1\alpha - d - \frac{\lambda v_i e^{-\gamma(t-n\tau_1)}}{1 - e^{-\gamma\tau_1}} < 0,$$
$$c_2\phi k\alpha - (d + \delta) < 0, \qquad (15)$$
$$c_1\alpha - d - \frac{m_1 s_i e^{-\mu(t-n\tau_2)}}{1 - e^{-\mu\tau_2}} < 0.$$

Proof. We need to prove the stability of the system in two cases:
(i) Application of chemical pesticide and biopesticide with same time interval;
(ii) Application of biopesticide and chemical pesticide with different time intervals.
(i) In this case, let $t = nt_1 = nt_2 = n\tau$. We discuss the stability of the system through the small amplitude perturbation method at the periodic solution $(k, 0, 0, v^*, s^*)$. Let

$$x(t) = k + \epsilon_1(t), \quad y(t) = \epsilon_2(t), \quad z(t) = \epsilon_3(t),$$
$$v(t) = v^*(t) + \epsilon_4(t), \quad s(t) = s^*(t) + \epsilon_5(t). \qquad (16)$$

Here, $\epsilon_1, \epsilon_2, \epsilon_3, \epsilon_4$, and ϵ_5 denote small amplitude perturbations. Thus, the corresponding system of (1) at $(k, 0, 0, v^*, s^*)$ is given by

$$\begin{aligned}
\frac{d\epsilon_1}{dt} &= r\{k + \epsilon_1(t)\}\left(1 - \frac{k + \epsilon_1(t)}{k}\right) - \alpha\{k + \epsilon_1(t)\}\epsilon_2(t) \\
&\quad - \phi\alpha\{k + \epsilon_1(t)\}\epsilon_3(t), & t \neq n\tau, \\
\frac{d\epsilon_2}{dt} &= c_1\alpha\{k + \epsilon_1(t)\}\epsilon_2(t) - \lambda\epsilon_2(t)\{v^*(t) + \epsilon_4(t)\} \\
&\quad - d\epsilon_2(t) - m_1\{s^*(t) + \epsilon_5(t)\}\epsilon_2(t), & t \neq n\tau, \\
\frac{d\epsilon_3}{dt} &= c_2\phi\alpha\{k + \epsilon_1(t)\}\epsilon_3(t) + \lambda\epsilon_2(t)\{v^*(t) + \epsilon_4(t)\} - (d + \delta)\epsilon_3(t) \\
&\quad - m_2\{s^*(t) + \epsilon_5(t)\}\epsilon_3(t), & t \neq n\tau, \\
\frac{d\epsilon_4}{dt} &= \theta(d + \delta)\epsilon_3(t) - \gamma\{v^*(t) + \epsilon_4(t)\}, & t \neq n\tau, \\
\frac{d\epsilon_5}{dt} &= -\mu\{s^*(t) + \epsilon_5(t)\}, & t \neq n\tau, \\
\triangle\{v^*(t) + \epsilon_4(t)\} &= v_i, & t = n\tau, \\
\triangle\{s^*(t) + \epsilon_5(t)\} &= s_i, & t = n\tau.
\end{aligned} \qquad (17)$$

Now, the linear system corresponding to the system (17) is given as

$$\begin{aligned}
\frac{d\epsilon_1}{dt} &= -r\epsilon_1(t) - \alpha k\epsilon_2(t) - \phi\alpha k\epsilon_3(t), & t \neq n\tau, \\
\frac{d\epsilon_2}{dt} &= c_1\alpha k\epsilon_2(t) - \lambda\epsilon_2(t)v^*(t) - d\epsilon_2(t) - m_1 s^*(t)\epsilon_2(t), & t \neq n\tau, \\
\frac{d\epsilon_3}{dt} &= c_2\phi k\alpha\epsilon_3(t) + \lambda\epsilon_2(t)v^*(t) - (d + \delta)\epsilon_3(t) - m_2 s^*(t)\epsilon_3(t), & t \neq n\tau, \\
\frac{d\epsilon_4}{dt} &= \theta(d + \delta)\epsilon_3(t) - \gamma\epsilon_4(t), & t \neq n\tau, \\
\frac{d\epsilon_5}{dt} &= -\mu\epsilon_5(t), & t \neq n\tau, \\
\Delta\epsilon_4(t) &= v_i, \quad t = n\tau, \\
\Delta\epsilon_5(t) &= s_i, \quad t = n\tau.
\end{aligned} \qquad (18)$$

The fundamental matrix $M(t)$ of (18) is obtained as

$$\frac{dM(t)}{dt} = \frac{1}{m}\begin{bmatrix} -r & -\alpha k & -\phi\alpha k & 0 & 0 \\ 0 & c_1\alpha k - \lambda v^*(t) - d - m_1 s^*(t) & 0 & 0 & 0 \\ 0 & \lambda v^*(t) & m_{33} & 0 & 0 \\ 0 & 0 & \theta(d+\delta) & -\gamma & 0 \\ 0 & 0 & 0 & 0 & -\mu \end{bmatrix}$$

with initial condition $M(t) = I_5$ (the identity matrix) and $m_{33} = c_2\phi k\alpha - (d+\delta) - m_2 s^*(t)$.
Now, the fundamental solution matrix is given by

$$M(t) = \frac{1}{m}\begin{bmatrix} \exp(-rt) & M_1(t) & M_2(t) & 0 & 0 \\ 0 & M_3(t) & 0 & 0 & 0 \\ 0 & M_4(t) & M_5 & 0 & 0 \\ 0 & 0 & M_5(t) & \exp(-\gamma t) & 0 \\ 0 & 0 & 0 & 0 & \exp(-\mu t) \end{bmatrix}.$$

Here, $M_5 = \exp\int_0^t \{c_2\phi k\alpha - (d+\delta) - m_2 s^*(t)\}dt$,

$$M_3(t) = \exp\int_0^\tau \{c_1\alpha k - \lambda v^*(t) - d - m_1 s^*(t)\}dt,$$

where the other $M_i(t)$s are not required for our further analysis. According to Floquet theory [33], the periodic solution $E(k, 0, 0, v^*v, s^*)$ is asymptotically stable if the absolute values of the eigenvalues of $M(\tau)$ are less than one.

The eigenvalues of $M(t)$ are

$$\lambda_1 = \exp\{-r\tau\}, \lambda_2 = \exp\int_0^\tau \{c_1\alpha k - \lambda v^*(t) - d - m_1 s^*(t)\}dt,$$

$$\lambda_3 = \exp\int_0^\tau \{c_2\phi k\alpha - (d+\delta) - m_2 s^*(t)\}dt, \lambda_4 = \exp\{-\gamma\tau\},$$

$$\lambda_5 = \exp\{-\mu\tau\}.$$

Clearly, $0 < \lambda_1 < 1, 0 < \lambda_4 < 1$ and $0 < \lambda_5 < 1$. Thus, when both pesticides are applied with the same time interval, then the system is locally stable around the periodic solution $E = (k, 0, 0, v^*v, s^*)$ if $0 < \lambda_2 < 1$ and $0 < \lambda_3 < 1$. From this, we obtain

$$\exp\int_0^\tau \{c_1\alpha k - \lambda v^*(t) - d - m_1 s^*(t)\}dt < 1,$$

$$\exp\int_0^\tau \{c_2\phi k\alpha - (d+\delta) - m_2 s^*(t)\}dt < 1. \quad (19)$$

From Equation (19), we can choose $\delta_1 > 0$ such that

$$\eta_1 = \exp\int_{n\tau}^{(n+1)\tau} \{c_1\alpha - \lambda(v^*(t) - \delta_1) - d - m_1(s^*(t) - \delta_1)\}dt < 1,$$

$$\eta_2 = \exp\int_{n\tau}^{(n+1)\tau} \{c_2\phi k\alpha - (d+\delta) - m_2(s^*(t-\delta_1))\}dt < 1.$$

Since all state variables are positive,

$$\frac{dv}{dt} \geq -\gamma v; \quad \frac{ds}{dt} \geq -\mu s.$$

Thus, according to the comparison theorem and Equations (10) and (11), for $\delta_1 > 0$ there exists $t_0 > 0$ such that $v(t) \geq v^* - \delta_1, s(t) \geq s^* - \delta_1$ for all $t > t_0$.

From the second equation of system (1), it can be written that

$$\begin{aligned}\dot{y}(t) &\leq y(t)\{c_1\alpha - \lambda(v^*(t) - \delta_1) - d - m_1(s^*(t) - \delta_1)\}, \quad t \neq n\tau,\\ y(t^+) &= y(t), \quad t = n\tau.\end{aligned} \quad (20)$$

Integrating (20) into $[n\tau, (n+1)\tau]$, it can be shown that

$$\begin{aligned}y\{(n+1)\tau\} &\leq y(n\tau) \exp \int_{n\tau}^{(n+1)\tau} \{c_1\alpha - \lambda(v^*(t) - \delta_1) - d - m_1(s^*(t) - \delta_1)\} dt\\ &= y(n\tau)\eta_1.\end{aligned} \quad (21)$$

Similarly,

$$y\{n\tau\} \leq y\{(n-1)\tau\}\eta_1. \quad (22)$$

Hence, from (21) and (22),

$$y\{(n+1)\tau\} \leq y\{(n-1)\tau\}\eta_1^2.$$

Proceeding in this way, we obtain

$$y\{(n+1)\tau\} \leq y(\tau)\eta_1^n. \quad (23)$$

Since $\eta_1 < 1$, one has $\eta_1^n \to 0$ whenever $n \to \infty$. Hence, $y\{(n+1)\tau\} \to 0$ as $n \to \infty$. Now we take $n\tau < t \leq (n+1)\tau$. Then, clearly, $0 < y(t) \leq y(n\tau) \exp(n\tau)$. Thus, $y(t) \to 0$ as $t \to \infty$. For

$$\eta_2 = \exp \int_{n\tau}^{(n+1)\tau} \{c_2\phi k\alpha - (d+\delta) - m_2(s^*(t-\delta_1))\} dt < 1,$$

we can similarly prove that $z(t) \to 0$ as $t \to \infty$.

We now prove that $v(t) \to v^*(t)$ as $t \to \infty$. Since $z(t) \to 0$ as $t \to \infty$, then for some $0 < \delta_2 < \frac{\gamma}{\theta(d+\delta)}$ there exists $t_1 > 0$ such that $0 < z(t) < \delta_2$ for all $t > t_1$. Thus, for $t > t_1$ and from the fourth equation of system (1), we can write that

$$\theta(d+\delta)\delta_2 - \gamma v(t) \geq \dot{v}(t) \geq -\theta(d+\delta)\delta_2 - \gamma v(t). \quad (24)$$

Let $v_1(t)$ and $v_2(t)$ be the solutions of

$$\begin{aligned}\dot{v}_1(t) &= -\theta(d+\delta)\delta_2 - \gamma v_1(t), \quad t \neq n\tau,\\ v_1(t^+) &= v_1(t) + v_i, \quad t = n\tau,\end{aligned}$$

and

$$\begin{aligned}\dot{v}_2(t) &= \theta(d+\delta)\delta_2 - \gamma v_2(t), \quad t \neq n\tau,\\ v_2(t^+) &= v_2(t) + v_i, \quad t = n\tau,\end{aligned}$$

respectively. Then, the solution will be

$$\begin{aligned}v_1^*(t) &= \frac{v_i e^{-\gamma(t-n\tau)}}{1 - e^{-\gamma\tau}} + \theta(d+\delta)\delta_2,\\ v_2^*(t) &= \frac{v_i e^{-\gamma(t-n\tau)}}{1 - e^{-\gamma\tau}} - \theta(d+\delta)\delta_2.\end{aligned} \quad (25)$$

From (25), it is clear that when $\delta_2 \to 0$ we have $v_1^*(t) \to v^*(t)$ and $v_2^*(t) \to v^*(t)$. Hence, it follows from (24) that $v(t) \to v^*(t)$ as $t \to \infty$.

Similarly, we can choose $0 < \delta_3 < \mu$ and, in the same way, we can prove that $s(t) \to s^*(t)$ as $t \to \infty$.

Finally, we shall prove that $x(t) \to k$ as $t \to \infty$. We already proved that $y(t)$, $z(t) \to 0$ as $t \to \infty$. Thus, for $\delta_3 > 0$, there exists $t_3 > 0$ such that $y(t)$, $z(t) < \delta_3$ for all $t > t_3$. Hence, from the first equation of system (1), we can write that

$$rx(t) - \frac{rx^2(t)}{k} > \dot{x}(t) \geq \{r - \delta_3\alpha(1+\phi)\}x(t) - \frac{rx^2(t)}{k},$$

which implies that

$$\frac{kx_0}{x_0 + (k - x_0)e^{rt}} \geq x(t) \geq \frac{k\{r - \delta_3\alpha(1+\phi)\}x_0}{rx_0 + [k\{r - \delta_3\alpha(1+\phi)\} - rx_0]e^{-\{r-\delta_3\alpha(1+\phi)\}t}}. \quad (26)$$

Hence, for $\delta_3 \to 0$, $x(t) \to k$ as $t \to \infty$. Thus, for application of biopesticide and chemical pesticide together with the same time interval $t = n\tau$, we can say that system (1) is locally as well as globally stable if

$$c_1\alpha - d - \frac{\lambda v_i e^{-\gamma(t-n\tau)}}{1 - e^{-\gamma\tau}} - \frac{m_1 s_i e^{-\mu(t-n\tau)}}{1 - e^{-\mu\tau}} < 0,$$
$$c_2\phi k\alpha - (d+\delta) - \frac{m_2 s_i e^{-\mu(t-n\tau)}}{1 - e^{-\mu\tau}} < 0. \quad (27)$$

Two subcases arise here, namely,

Subcase I. Application of biopesticide with time interval $t = n\tau_1$.

In this case, $s_i = 0$. Hence, system (1) is locally as well as globally stable around the periodic solution if

$$c_1\alpha k - d - \frac{\lambda v_i e^{-\gamma(t-n\tau_1)}}{1 - e^{-\gamma\tau_1}} < 0,$$
$$c_2\phi k\alpha - (d+\delta) < 0. \quad (28)$$

Subcase II. Application of chemical pesticide with time interval $t = n\tau_2$.

In this case, $v_i = 0$, and hence system (1) is locally as well as globally stable around the periodic solution if

$$c_1\alpha k - d - \frac{m_1 s_i e^{-\mu(t-n\tau_2)}}{1 - e^{-\mu\tau_2}} < 0,$$
$$c_2\phi k\alpha - (d+\delta) - \frac{m_2 s_i e^{-\mu(t-n\tau_2)}}{1 - e^{-\mu\tau_2}} < 0. \quad (29)$$

The proof is complete. □

4. Numerical Simulations

Now we solve the impulsive system numerically and we graphically display the results found. We varied the crucial parameters within their feasible ranges to observe their impact on the impulsive model's solution trajectories and equilibria. Precisely, we solved the impulsive system and plotted the results in figures using the ode45 MATLAB solver.

In Figure 1, the impulsive time interval for microbial biological pesticide release is 5 days, and releasing of biopesticide was considered in different rates: $v_i = 0$ (i.e., without pesticides), $v_i = 6$, and $v_i = 12$. It is revealed that susceptible pest population decreases with an increase in the release rate of biopesticides.

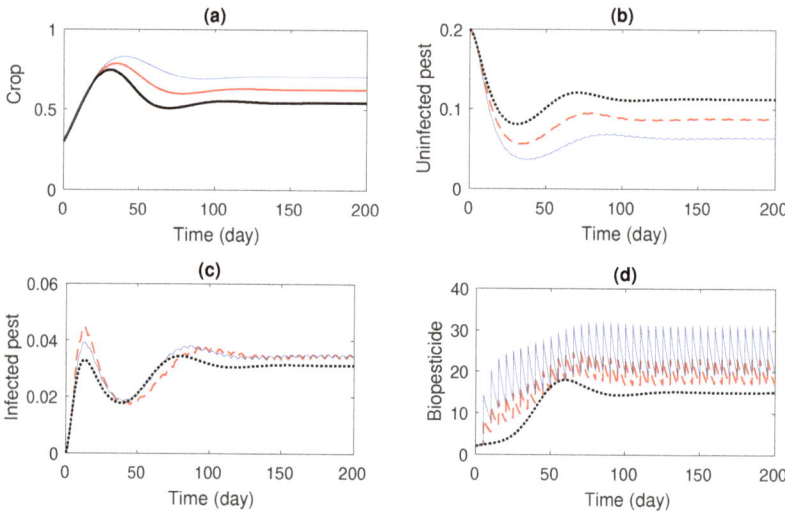

Figure 1. Impact of biopesticide application in impulsive mode on system (1). Evolution of (**a**) crop; (**b**) uninfected pest; (**c**) infected pest; (**d**) biopesticide. The set of parameters are $r = 0.1$, $k = 1$, $\alpha = 0.2$, $\beta = 0.003$, $m_1 = 0.8$, $m_2 = 0.6$, $c_1 = 0.5$, $c_2 = 0.8$, $\gamma = 0.15$, $\delta = 0.2$, $d = 0.05$, $\kappa = 100$, $s = 0.3$, and $\lambda = 0.35$. Here, the time interval is $\tau_1 = 5$ days and the rates of biopesticide release are $v_i = 0$ (black line), $v_i = 6$ (red line), and $v_i = 12$ (blue line).

In Figure 2, by taking different impulsive intervals, biopesticide is applied to the system. A better result is obtained for lower intervals (2 days) but, with a higher release of biopesticide, pests are present in the system. From Figures 1 and 2, we can conclude that pest control using only biopesticides is very costly and a time-consuming process.

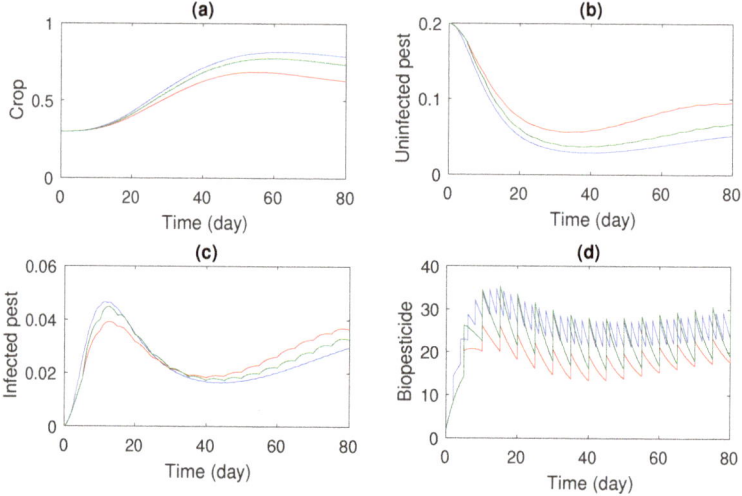

Figure 2. Impact of biopesticide on system (1) for different impulse intervals and rates. Evolution of (**a**) crop; (**b**) uninfected pest; (**c**) infected pest; (**d**) biopesticide. Red line indicates $v_i = 6$ and $\tau_1 = 5$, green line indicates $v_i = 12$ and $\tau_1 = 5$, and blue line indicates $v_i = 12$ and $\tau_1 = 2$.

Recall that in our model we take τ_1 as the time period for biopesticide spraying (generally a virus particle) and τ_2 as the time period for chemical pesticide sprays. In

Figure 3 we see the effect for the same time intervals, $\tau_1 = \tau_2 = 5$ days, whereas in Figure 4 we see the effect for different time intervals, $\tau_1 = 3$ days and $\tau_2 = 2$ days.

If both microbial biopesticides and chemical pesticides are released simultaneously, with an equal time interval of 5 days, then the extinction of both infected and susceptible pest populations is possible (see Figure 3).

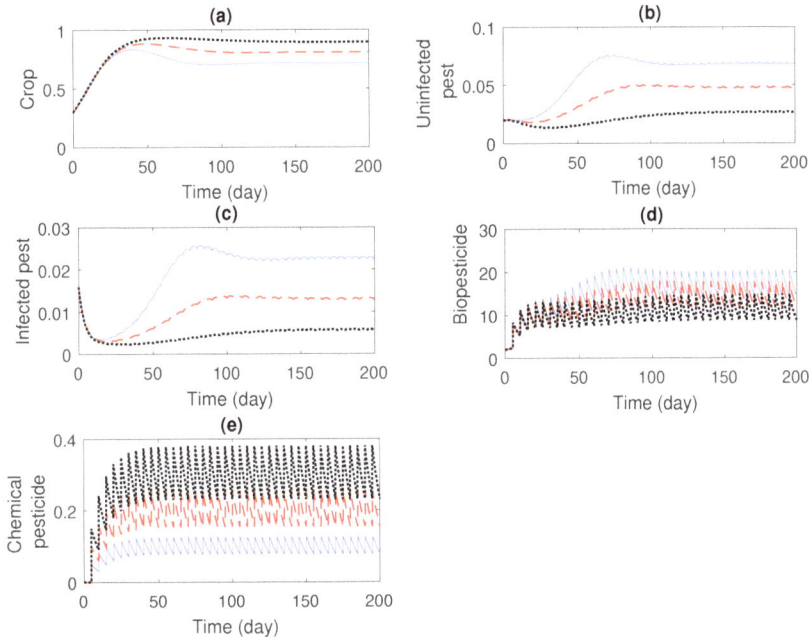

Figure 3. Impact of both biopesticide and chemical pesticide on system (1) with the same impulse interval, $\tau_1 = \tau_2 = 5$. Evolution of (**a**) crop; (**b**) uninfected pest; (**c**) infected pest; (**d**) biopesticide; (**e**) chemical pesticide. The rates of impulses are $s_i = 0.15$ and $v_i = 6$ for black dotted color; $s_i = 0.1$ and $v_i = 6$ for red dashed line; and $s_i = 0.05$ and $v_i = 6$ for blue solid line.

Figure 4 illustrates the dynamics of the double impulse with different impulse intervals. Double impulses occur at the time which is the common multiple of the two intervals. For example, if we take $\tau_1 = 2$ and $\tau_2 = 3$, then simultaneous impulses will occur at the times $t = 6$, $t = 12$, $t = 18$, and so on. Figure 4 is the most important figure characterizing the impact of two different but simultaneous impulses on the total pest population with different time intervals. It is observed that for $v_i = 12$, $s_i = 0.15$, $\tau_1 = 3$, and $\tau_2 = 2$, the total pest population becomes extinct. In Figure 4d, the impact of double impulses occurs at $t = 48$, $t = 54$, $t = 60$ days, etc., which are common multiples of the two intervals $\tau_1 = 2$ and $\tau_2 = 3$.

It is also numerically checked that when the rate of the impulse control is high, a comparatively lower interval can be taken for cost-effectiveness of the process.

Thus, the advantage of the impulsive control is that we can determine the proper rate and a suitable interval of giving controlling agents in the system.

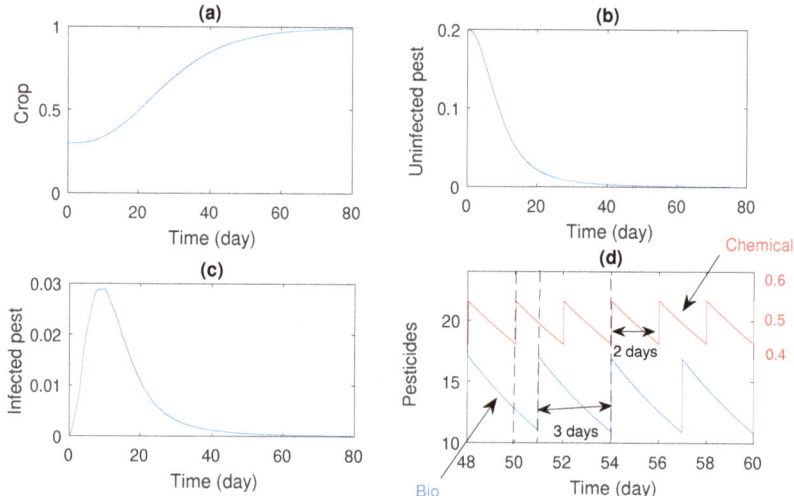

Figure 4. Impact of both biopesticide and chemical pesticide on system (1) with same impulse interval, $\tau_1 = 3$, $\tau_2 = 2$, and where the rates of impulses are $s_i = 0.15$ and $v_i = 6$. Evolution of (**a**) crop; (**b**) uninfected pest; (**c**) infected pest; (**d**) pesticides (biopesticide in blue, chemical pesticide in red).

5. Discussion and Conclusions

In the present research, we studied impulsive periodic applications of integrated pesticides, that is, simultaneous use of biopesticide and chemical pesticide in a pest management system. We proposed a two-impulse mathematical model using an impulsive differential equation to observe the impact of periodic application of the combined pesticides in impulsive modes.

In the previous models available in the literature, chemical and biological pesticides were used in the model in a continuous way. In contrast, here, we used them in an impulsive periodic way. Consequently, a two-impulse mathematical model was established. Moreover, in the proposed model, we took chemical pesticides concentration as the model population, which is a novel approach.

Stability theory (Floquet theory) and numerical calculations were used to examine the system dynamical behavior. We determined the conditions under which the impulsive system will be stable both locally and globally. For example, the local stability of a pest-free periodic orbit was established. The dynamics varied with the rate of both biopesticide recruitment and the chemical pesticide concentration.

Chemical pesticides minimize the oscillations in the system and make the system stable in a shorter time. Numerical and analytical analysis reveals that increasing frequency of pesticide application will require less administration of biopesticide and chemical pesticide, which is economically beneficial and environmentally safe.

Our research is directed to optimize and find the right combination of pesticides with maximum benefit to the crop plant. The numerical simulation also shows that control over the spraying of chemical pesticides is needed to control pests and minimize the cost of cultivation. On the other hand, chemical pesticides may have negative environmental implications due to their lingering effects; nonetheless, the best control approach provides the least amount of collateral damage to the environment.

In a nutshell, the promising feature of the system is the combined use of the pesticides in impulsive control methods that reduce the cost and negative effects on the environment. Using a combination of pesticides to deliver the pesticide can save the cost and reduce the side effects of chemical pesticides. Our obtained results will give a new perspective to farmers who implement this in a real-world setting.

In the future, one can extend this work to an optimal impulsive system for cost-effectiveness of the control process.

Author Contributions: Conceptualization, F.A.B. and J.C.; methodology, F.A.B., J.C. and D.F.M.T.; software, F.A.B. and J.C.; validation, F.A.B., J.C. and D.F.M.T.; formal analysis, F.A.B., J.C. and D.F.M.T.; investigation, F.A.B., J.C. and D.F.M.T.; writing—original draft preparation, F.A.B., J.C. and D.F.M.T.; writing—review and editing, F.A.B., J.C. and D.F.M.T.; visualization, F.A.B. and J.C. All authors have read and agreed to the published version of the manuscript.

Funding: Torres was funded by The Portuguese Foundation for Science and Technology (FCT) grant number UIDB/04106/2020.

Institutional Review Board Statement: Not applicable.

Informed Consent Statement: Not applicable.

Data Availability Statement: No new data were created or analyzed in this study. Data sharing is not applicable to this article.

Acknowledgments: The authors are very grateful to four anonymous reviewers for careful reading of the submitted manuscript and also for providing several important comments and suggestions.

Conflicts of Interest: The authors declare no conflicts of interest. The funders had no role in the design of the study; in the collection, analyses, or interpretation of data; in the writing of the manuscript; or in the decision to publish the results.

References

1. Al Basir, F.; Banerjee, A.; Ray, S. Role of farming awareness in crop pest management—A mathematical model. *J. Theor. Biol.* **2019**, *461*, 59–67. [CrossRef]
2. Ndolo, D.; Njuguna, E.; Adetunji, C.O.; Harbor, C.; Rowe, A.; Den Breeyen, A.; Sangeetha, J.; Singh, G.; Szewczyk, B.; Anjorin, T.S.; et al. Research and development of biopesticides: Challenges and prospects. *Outlooks Pest Manag.* **2019**, *6*, 267–276. [CrossRef]
3. Chattopadhyay, P.; Banerjee, G.; Mukherjee, S. Recent trends of modern bacterial insecticides for pest control practice in integrated crop management system. *3 Biotech* **2017**, *7*, 60. [CrossRef]
4. Perring, T.M.; Gruenhagen, N.M.; Farrar, C.A. Management of plant viral diseases through chemical control of insect vectors. *Annu. Rev. Entomol.* **1999**, *44*, 457–481. [CrossRef] [PubMed]
5. Ghosh, S.; Bhattacharya, D.K. Optimization in microbial pest control: An integrated approach. *Appl. Math. Model.* **2010**, *34*, 1382–1395. [CrossRef]
6. Bhattacharyya, S.; Bhattacharya, D.K. Pest control through viral disease: Mathematical modeling and analysis. *J. Theor. Biol.* **2006**, *238*, 177–197. [CrossRef] [PubMed]
7. Fest, C.; Schmidt, K. *The Chemistry of Organophosphorus Pesticides*; Springer: New York, NY, USA, 1973. [CrossRef]
8. Lenteren, J.C.V. Integrated pest management in protected crops. In *Integrated Pest Management*; Dent, D., Ed.; Chapman and Hall: London, UK, 1995; pp. 311–320. Available online: https://cir.nii.ac.jp/crid/1573950400276916864 (accessed on 20 January 2023).
9. Flint, M.L. *Integrated Pest Management for Walnuts*; University of California Statewide Integrated Pest Management Project; Division of Agriculture and Natural Resources, University of California: Davis, CA, USA, 1987; Volume 3270, p. 3641.
10. Stern, V.M. The bioeconomics of pest control. *Iowa State J. Res.* **1975**, *49*, 467–472. Available online: https://core.ac.uk/download/pdf/224978255.pdf (accessed on 20 January 2023).
11. Liu, B.; Teng, Z.; Chen, L. Analysis of a predator-prey model with Holling II functional response concerning impulsive control strategy. *J. Comput. Appl. Math.* **2006**, *193*, 347–362. [CrossRef]
12. Páez Chávez, J.; Jungmann, D.; Siegmund, S. Modeling and analysis of integrated pest control strategies via impulsive differential equations. *Int. J. Differ. Equ.* **2017**, *2017*, 1820607. [CrossRef]
13. Wang, L.; Chen, L.; Nieto, J.J. The dynamics of an epidemic model for pest control with impulsive effect. *Nonlinear Anal. Real World Appl.* **2010**, *11*, 1374–1386. [CrossRef]
14. Al Basir, F.; Noor, M.H. A Model for Pest Control using Integrated Approach: Impact of latent and gestation Delays. *Nonlinear Dyn.* **2022**, *108*, 1805–1820. [CrossRef]
15. Abraha, T.; Al Basir, F.; Obsu, L.L.; Torres, D.F.M. Pest control using farming awareness: Impact of time delays and optimal use of biopesticides. *Chaos Solitons Fractals* **2021**, *146*, 110869. [CrossRef]
16. Chowdhury, J.; Basir, F.A.; Takeuchi, Y.; Ghosh, M.; Roy, P.K. A mathematical model for pest management in Jatropha curcas with integrated pesticides—An optimal control approach. *Ecol. Complex.* **2019**, *37*, 24–31. [CrossRef]
17. Tang, S.; Chen, L. Modelling and analysis of integrated pest management strategy. *Discret. Contin. Dyn. Syst. Ser. B* **2004**, *4*, 759–768. [CrossRef]

18. Paez, Chavez, J.; Jungmann, D.; Siegmund, S. A comparative study of integrated pest management strategies based on impulsive control. *J. Biol. Dyn.* **2018**, *12*, 318–341. [CrossRef] [PubMed]
19. Kalra, P.; Kaur, M. Stability analysis of an eco-epidemiological SIN model with impulsive control strategy for integrated pest management considering stage-structure in predator. *Int. J. Math. Model. Numer. Optim.* **2022**, *12*, 43–68. [CrossRef]
20. Liu, J.; Hu, J.; Yuen, P. Extinction and permanence of the predator-prey system with general functional response and impulsive control. *Appl. Math. Model.* **2020**, *88*, 55–67. [CrossRef]
21. Tian, B.; Li, J.; Wu, X.; Zhang, Y. Dynamic behaviour of a predator-prey system with impulsive control strategy. *Int. J. Dyn. Syst. Differ. Equ.* **2022**, *12*, 493–509. [CrossRef]
22. Kumari, V.; Chauhan, S.; Dhar, J. Controlling pest by integrated pest management: A dynamical approach. *Int. J. Math. Eng. Manag. Sci.* **2020**, *5*, 769–786. [CrossRef]
23. Pang, Y.; Wang, S.; Liu, S. Dynamics analysis of stage-structured wild and sterile mosquito interaction impulsive model. *J. Biol. Dyn.* **2022**, *16*, 464–479. [CrossRef]
24. Chowdhury, J.; Al Basir, F.; Cao, X.; Roy, P.K. Integrated pest management for Jatropha Carcus plant: An impulsive control approach. *Math. Methods Appl. Sci.* **2021**, in press. [CrossRef]
25. Tian, Y.; Tang, S.; Cheke, R.A. Dynamic complexity of a predator-prey model for IPM with nonlinear impulsive control incorporating a regulatory factor for predator releases. *Math. Model. Anal.* **2019**, *24*, 134–154. [CrossRef]
26. Jose, S.A.; Ramachandran, R.; Cao, J.; Alzabut, J.; Niezabitowski, M.; Balas, V.E. Stability analysis and comparative study on different eco-epidemiological models: Stage structure for prey and predator concerning impulsive control. *Optim. Control. Appl. Methods* **2022**, *43*, 842–866. [CrossRef]
27. Li, J.; Huang, Q.D.; Liu, B. A pest control model with birth pulse and residual and delay effects of pesticides. *Adv. Differ. Equ.* **2019**, *2019*, 117. [CrossRef]
28. Liu, B.; Kang, B.-L.; Tao, F.-M.; Hu, G. Modelling the effects of pest control with development of pesticide resistance. *Acta Math. Appl. Sin. Engl. Ser.* **2021**, *37*, 109–125. [CrossRef]
29. Alzabut, J. An Integrated Eco-Epidemiological Plant Pest Natural Enemy Differential Equation Model with Various Impulsive Strategies. 2022. Available online: http://earsiv.ostimteknik.edu.tr:8081/xmlui/handle/123456789/207 (accessed on 20 January 2023).
30. Zhang, H.; Xu, W.; Chen, L. A impulsive infective transmission SI model for pest control. *Math. Methods Appl. Sci.* **2007**, *30*, 1169–1184. [CrossRef]
31. Al Basir, F.; Chowdhury, J.; Das, S.; Ray, S. Combined impact of predatory insects and bio-pesticide over pest population: Impulsive model-based study. *Energy Ecol. Environ.* **2022**, *7*, 173–185. [CrossRef]
32. Shi, R.; Jiang, X.; Chen, L. A predator-prey model with disease in the prey and two impulses for integrated pest management. *Appl. Math. Model.* **2009**, *33*, 2248–2256. [CrossRef]
33. Klausmeier, C.A. Floquet theory: A useful tool for understanding nonequilibrium dynamics. *Theor. Ecol.* **2008**, *1*, 153–161. [CrossRef]

Disclaimer/Publisher's Note: The statements, opinions and data contained in all publications are solely those of the individual author(s) and contributor(s) and not of MDPI and/or the editor(s). MDPI and/or the editor(s) disclaim responsibility for any injury to people or property resulting from any ideas, methods, instructions or products referred to in the content.

Article

Solutions of (2+1)-D & (3+1)-D Burgers Equations by New Laplace Variational Iteration Technique

Gurpreet Singh [1,2], Inderdeep Singh [2], Afrah M. AlDerea [3,*], Agaeb Mahal Alanzi [3] and Hamiden Abd El-Wahed Khalifa [3,4]

[1] Department of Applied Sciences, Chitkara University Institute of Engineering and Technology, Chitkara University, Rajpura 140401, India; gurpreet.2418@chitkara.edu.in
[2] Department of Physical Sciences, Sant Baba Bhag Singh University, Jalandhar 144030, India
[3] Department of Mathematics, College of Science and Arts, Qassim University, AL-Badaya 51951, Saudi Arabia
[4] Department of Operations and Management Research, Cairo University, Giza 12613, Egypt
* Correspondence: a.alderea@qu.edu.sa

Abstract: The new Laplace variational iterative method is used in this research for solving the (2+1)-D and (3+1)-D Burgers equations. This technique relies on the modified variational iteration method and the Laplace transform. To apply this approach, the differential problem is first transformed into an algebraic form using the Laplace transform, and then the algebraic equations are iteratively solved using the modified variational iterative approach. By utilizing this technique, the Burgers equations can be solved both numerically and analytically. The study demonstrates the effectiveness of the new Laplace variational iterative approach through three specific examples.

Keywords: partial differential equations; partial derivatives; (2+1)-D Burgers's equation; (3+1)-D Burgers's equation; system of two-dimensional Burgers's equation

MSC: 44A10; 35E15; 47J30

1. Introduction

The J.M. Burgers equation, also known as Burgers's equation, is a significant and commonly used non-linear PDE. It was first introduced by Bateman and later corrected by Burgers, and is sometimes referred to as the Bateman–Burgers equation. This equation is employed to simulate numerous physical phenomena, for example, acoustics, diffraction water waves, heat conduction, shock waves, and turbulence issues, among others.

This research focuses on the analytical solutions of the two-dimensional and three-dimensional Burgers equations. The new Laplace transform with the variational iteration method (LVIM) is utilized for solving these equations. Approximate results obtained using the LVIM approach are then compared with the analytical results of Burgers's equation, the numerical approximations of the Burgers equation obtained via the Laplace Homotopy Perturbation method (LHPM) [1], and the numerical results of the Burgers equation obtained via the EHPM [2]. To demonstrate the effectiveness of the proposed method, a comparison study is given in Section 3.

In addition, the suggested strategy's convergence is illustrated through graphs of both precise and approximate solutions. Various partial differential equations with linear and non-linear coefficients can be utilized to solve initial value and boundary value problems. To find approximate solutions to Burgers equations, several numerical schemes have been developed, including the spline FEM, ADM, Douglas FD scheme, exact explicit FDM, VIM, and others [3–10]. However, only a few analytical methods, such as the LHPM [11], Hopf–Cole Transformation [12], etc., have been developed to obtain the precise solution of certain PDEs. Laplace transform-based methods are extensively employed in mathematics to solve differential equations. Other techniques, such as the VIM and the HPM, can also

Citation: Singh, G.; Singh, I.; AlDerea, A.M.; Alanzi, A.M.; Khalifa, H.A.E.-W. Solutions of (2+1)-D & (3+1)-D Burgers Equations by New Laplace Variational Iteration Technique. *Axioms* **2023**, *12*, 647. https://doi.org/10.3390/axioms12070647

Academic Editors: Stefano De Marchi, Nuno Bastos, Touria Karite and Amir Khan

Received: 4 April 2023
Revised: 11 May 2023
Accepted: 8 June 2023
Published: 29 June 2023

Copyright: © 2023 by the authors. Licensee MDPI, Basel, Switzerland. This article is an open access article distributed under the terms and conditions of the Creative Commons Attribution (CC BY) license (https://creativecommons.org/licenses/by/4.0/).

be combined with it to make it hybrid. By combining these approaches with the Laplace Transform method, partial differential equations can be solved analytically. The VIM has been used to solve various differential equations [13]. It has been demonstrated that the VIM can also solve non-linear equations [14]. The Laplace Transformation and variational iteration approach have been used to solve Smoluchowski's coagulation equations [15]. A new modified variational iterative approach has been proposed for the solution of boundary value problems of higher order [16]. The variational iteration approach and Laplace transformation have been combined in [17]. In [18], certain issues with the variational iterative approach and how the Laplace transform method fixes them are detailed. Modified fractional derivatives have a Laplace variational approach built into them [19]. A new Laplace Transformation and variational iterative approach can solve non-linear PDEs [20]. The new Laplace and variational iterative approach has been used to solve numerous equations [21–24].

Consider, the (2+1)-D non-linear Burgers's equation can also be written as

$$\frac{\partial \varphi(\alpha,\beta,\tau)}{\partial \tau} + \rho\varphi(\alpha,\beta,\tau)\frac{\partial \varphi(\alpha,\beta,\tau)}{\partial \alpha} = \mu\left(\frac{\partial^2 \varphi(\alpha,\beta,\tau)}{\partial \alpha^2} + \frac{\partial^2 \varphi(\alpha,\beta,\tau)}{\partial \beta^2}\right) \quad (1)$$

with the initial conditions

$$\varphi(\alpha,\beta,0) = h(\alpha,\beta)$$

where u is the velocity component, μ is the kinematic viscosity, ρ is any constant, and t is the time.

Similarly, the (3+1)-D Non-linear Burgers equation is

$$\frac{\partial \varphi(\alpha,\beta,z,\tau)}{\partial \tau} + \rho\varphi(\alpha,\beta,z,\tau)\frac{\partial \varphi(\alpha,\beta,z,\tau)}{\partial \alpha} = \mu\left(\frac{\partial^2 \varphi(\alpha,\beta,z,\tau)}{\partial \alpha^2} + \frac{\partial^2 \varphi(\alpha,\beta,z,\tau)}{\partial \beta^2} + \frac{\partial^2 \varphi(\alpha,\beta,z,\tau)}{\partial z^2}\right)$$

with initial conditions

$$\varphi(\alpha,\beta,z,0) = j(\alpha,\beta,z)$$

where u is the velocity component, μ is the kinematic viscosity, ρ is any constant, and τ is the time.

Non-linear partial differential equations find wide application in the fields of engineering, physics, and applied mathematics. Various approaches have been suggested in the literature to solve the two-dimensional Burgers equations as well as the two-dimensional and three-dimensional Burgers equations. The importance of discovering exact solutions to PDEs for developing novel techniques to obtain precise or approximate solutions remains a topic of great interest in mathematics, engineering, and physics, as evidenced by recent publications [25–30].

2. Materials and Methods

2.1. New LVIM for Solving (2+1)-D Burgers's Equation

Consider the following (2+1)-D Burgers equation:

$$\frac{\partial \varphi(\alpha,\beta,\tau)}{\partial \tau} + \rho\varphi(\alpha,\beta,\tau)\frac{\partial \varphi(\alpha,\beta,\tau)}{\partial \alpha} = \mu\left(\frac{\partial^2 \varphi(\alpha,\beta,\tau)}{\partial \alpha^2} + \frac{\partial^2 \varphi(\alpha,\beta,\tau)}{\partial \beta^2}\right) \quad (2)$$

with given conditions as

$$\varphi(\alpha,\beta,0) = h(\alpha,\beta)$$

Rewriting Equation (2), we have

$$\frac{\partial \varphi(\alpha,\beta,\tau)}{\partial \tau} = \mu\left(\frac{\partial^2 \varphi(\alpha,\beta,\tau)}{\partial \alpha^2} + \frac{\partial^2 \varphi(\alpha,\beta,\tau)}{\partial \beta^2}\right) - \rho\varphi(\alpha,\beta,\tau)\frac{\partial \varphi(\alpha,\beta,\tau)}{\partial \alpha} \quad (3)$$

By applying Laplace transformation on (3), we have

$$L\left\{\frac{\partial \varphi(\alpha,\beta,\tau)}{\partial \tau}\right\} = L\left\{\mu\left(\frac{\partial^2\varphi(\alpha,\beta,\tau)}{\partial \alpha^2} + \frac{\partial^2\varphi(\alpha,\beta,\tau)}{\partial \beta^2}\right) - \rho\varphi(\alpha,\beta,\tau)\frac{\partial \varphi(\alpha,\beta,\tau)}{\partial \alpha}\right\} \quad (4)$$

$$sL\{\varphi(\alpha,\beta,\tau)\} - \varphi(\alpha,\beta,0) = L\left\{\mu\left(\frac{\partial^2\varphi}{\partial \alpha^2} + \frac{\partial^2\varphi}{\partial \beta^2}\right) - \rho\varphi\frac{\partial \varphi}{\partial \alpha}\right\} \quad (5)$$

$$sL\{\varphi(\alpha,\beta,\tau)\} - h(\alpha,\beta) = L\left\{\mu\left(\frac{\partial^2\varphi}{\partial \alpha^2} + \frac{\partial^2\varphi}{\partial \beta^2}\right) - \rho\varphi\frac{\partial \varphi}{\partial \alpha}\right\} \quad (6)$$

$$sL\{\varphi(\alpha,\beta,\tau)\} = h(\alpha,\beta) + L\left\{\mu\left(\frac{\partial^2\varphi}{\partial \alpha^2} + \frac{\partial^2\varphi}{\partial \beta^2}\right) - \rho\varphi\frac{\partial \varphi}{\partial \alpha}\right\} \quad (7)$$

$$L\{\varphi(\alpha,\beta,\tau)\} = \frac{h(\alpha,\beta)}{s} + \frac{1}{s}L\left\{\mu\left(\frac{\partial^2\varphi}{\partial \alpha^2} + \frac{\partial^2\varphi}{\partial \beta^2}\right) - \rho\varphi\frac{\partial \varphi}{\partial \alpha}\right\} \quad (8)$$

By using inverse Laplace transformation on (8), we obtain

$$\varphi(\alpha,\beta,\tau) = h(\alpha,\beta) + L^{-1}\left[\frac{1}{s}L\left\{\mu\left(\frac{\partial^2\varphi}{\partial \alpha^2} + \frac{\partial^2\varphi}{\partial \beta^2}\right) - \rho\varphi\frac{\partial \varphi}{\partial \alpha}\right\}\right] \quad (9)$$

Now, by modifying VIM from Equation (9), we obtain

$$\varphi_{n+1} = h(\alpha,\beta) + L^{-1}\left[\frac{1}{s}L\left\{\mu\left(\frac{\partial^2\varphi_n}{\partial \alpha^2} + \frac{\partial^2\varphi_n}{\partial \beta^2}\right) - \left(\rho\varphi_n\frac{\partial \varphi_n}{\partial \alpha}\right)\right\}\right] \quad (10)$$

Equation (10) represents the modified iteration formula of LVIM; the solution is given by

$$\varphi = \lim_{n\to\infty} \varphi_n$$

2.2. The Convergence of LVIM for (2+1)-D Partial Differential Equations

Consider the two-dimensional differential equation

$$l\varphi(\alpha,\beta,\tau) + n\varphi(\alpha,\beta,\tau) = g(\alpha,\beta,\tau) \quad (11)$$

with the initial conditions

$$\varphi(\alpha,\beta,0) = h(\alpha,\beta) \quad (12)$$

where l, n, and g are a linear operator of the first order, a non-linear operator, and a non-homogeneous term, respectively.

The iteration formula of the new LVIM is

$$\varphi_{m+1}(\alpha,\beta,\tau) = G(\alpha,\beta) + L^{-1}\left[\frac{1}{s}L\{n\varphi_m(\alpha,\beta,\tau)\}\right]$$

Now, define the operator $A[\varphi]$ as

$$A[\varphi] = L^{-1}\left[\frac{1}{s}L\{n\varphi_m(\alpha,\beta,\tau)\}\right] \quad (13)$$

define the components $v_m, m = 0, 1, 2, 3 \ldots$ as

$$\begin{cases} v_0 = u_0, \\ v_1 = A[v_0], \\ v_2 = A[v_1], \\ \quad \cdot \\ \quad \cdot \\ \quad \cdot \\ v_{m+1} = A[v_m] \end{cases} \tag{14}$$

Hence,

$$\varphi(\alpha, \beta, \tau) = \lim_{m \to \infty} \varphi_m(\alpha, \beta, \tau) \tag{15}$$

For the analysis of convergence of new LVIM, let us discuss the following theorem.

Theorem 1. *Let A, as defined in (14), be an operator from Hilbert space H to H; the solution, as defined in (16), converges if there exists $0 < \gamma < 1$ such that*

$$\|A[v_{m+1}]\| \leq \gamma \|A[v_m]\| \quad (i.e., \|v_{m+1}\| \leq \gamma \|v_m\|)$$

for all $m \in N \cup \{0\}$.

Proof. Define the sequence $\{S_n\}_{n=1}^{\infty}$ as

$$\begin{cases} S_1 = G(\alpha, \beta) + v_1, \\ S_2 = G(\alpha, \beta) + v_2, \\ S_3 = G(\alpha, \beta) + v_3, \\ \quad \cdot \\ \quad \cdot \\ \quad \cdot \\ S_m = G(\alpha, \beta) + v_m \end{cases} \tag{16}$$

Now, we will show that sequence $\{S_n\}_{n=1}^{\infty}$ is a Cauchy sequence in the Hilbert space H. Consider

$$\|S_{m+1} - S_m\| = \|v_{m+1} - v_m\| \leq \gamma \|v_m\| \leq \gamma^2 \|v_{m-1}\| \leq \ldots \leq \gamma^{m+1} \|v_0\|$$

For every $m, n \in N, m \geq n$, we have

$$\begin{aligned} \|S_m - S_n\| &= \|(S_m - S_{m-1}) + (S_{m-1} - S_{m-2}) + \ldots + (S_{n+1} - S_n)\| \\ &\leq \|(S_m - S_{m-1})\| + \|(S_{m-1} - S_{m-2})\| + \ldots + \|(S_{n+1} - S_n)\| \\ &\leq \gamma^m \|v_0\| + \gamma^{m-1} \|v_0\| + \ldots + \gamma^{n+1} \|v_0\| \\ &= \frac{1 - \gamma^{m-n}}{1 - \gamma} \gamma^{n+1} \|v_0\| \end{aligned}$$

Since $0 < \gamma < 1$, therefore,

$$\lim_{m,n \to \infty} \|S_m - S_n\| = 0 \tag{17}$$

Hence, $\{S_n\}_{n=1}^{\infty}$ is a Cauchy sequence in the Hilbert space H and it implies that the series solution (16) converges. □

2.3. New LVIM for Solving (3+1)-D Burgers's Equation

Consider the following (3+1)-D Burgers equation:

$$\frac{\partial \varphi(\alpha,\beta,\tau,z)}{\partial \tau} + \rho\varphi(\alpha,\beta,z,\tau)\frac{\partial \varphi(\alpha,\beta,z,\tau)}{\partial \alpha} = \mu\left(\frac{\partial^2 \varphi(\alpha,\beta,z,\tau)}{\partial \alpha^2} + \frac{\partial^2 \varphi(\alpha,\beta,z,\tau)}{\partial \beta^2} + \frac{\partial^2 \varphi(\alpha,\beta,z,\tau)}{\partial z^2}\right) \quad (18)$$

with given conditions as
$$\varphi(\alpha,\beta,z,0) = j(\alpha,\beta,z)$$

Rewriting Equation (18), we have

$$\frac{\partial \varphi(\alpha,\beta,z,\tau)}{\partial \tau} = \mu\left(\frac{\partial^2 \varphi(\alpha,\beta,z,\tau)}{\partial \alpha^2} + \frac{\partial^2 \varphi(\alpha,\beta,z,\tau)}{\partial \beta^2} + \frac{\partial^2 \varphi(\alpha,\beta,z,\tau)}{\partial z^2}\right) - \rho\varphi(\alpha,\beta,z,\tau)\frac{\partial \varphi(\alpha,\beta,z,\tau)}{\partial \alpha} \quad (19)$$

By applying Laplace transformation on (19), we have

$$L\left\{\frac{\partial \varphi(\alpha,\beta,z,\tau)}{\partial \tau}\right\} \\ = L\left\{\mu\left(\frac{\partial^2 \varphi(\alpha,\beta,z,\tau)}{\partial \alpha^2} + \frac{\partial^2 \varphi(\alpha,\beta,z,\tau)}{\partial \beta^2} + \frac{\partial^2 \varphi(\alpha,\beta,z,\tau)}{\partial z^2}\right) - \rho\varphi(\alpha,\beta,z,\tau)\frac{\partial \varphi(\alpha,\beta,z,\tau)}{\partial \alpha}\right\} \quad (20)$$

$$sL\{\varphi(\alpha,\beta,z,\tau)\} - \varphi(\alpha,\beta,z,0) = L\left\{\mu\left(\frac{\partial^2 \varphi}{\partial \alpha^2} + \frac{\partial^2 \varphi}{\partial \beta^2} + \frac{\partial^2 \varphi}{\partial z^2}\right) - \rho\varphi\frac{\partial \varphi}{\partial \alpha}\right\} \quad (21)$$

$$sL\{\varphi(\alpha,\beta,z,\tau)\} - j(\alpha,\beta,z) = L\left\{\mu\left(\frac{\partial^2 \varphi}{\partial \alpha^2} + \frac{\partial^2 \varphi}{\partial \beta^2} + \frac{\partial^2 \varphi}{\partial z^2}\right) - \rho\varphi\frac{\partial \varphi}{\partial \alpha}\right\} \quad (22)$$

$$sL\{\varphi(\alpha,\beta,z,\tau)\} = j(\alpha,\beta,z) + L\left\{\mu\left(\frac{\partial^2 \varphi}{\partial \alpha^2} + \frac{\partial^2 \varphi}{\partial \beta^2} + \frac{\partial^2 \varphi}{\partial z^2}\right) - \rho\varphi\frac{\partial \varphi}{\partial \alpha}\right\} \quad (23)$$

$$L\{\varphi(\alpha,\beta,z,\tau)\} = \frac{j(\alpha,\beta,z)}{s} + \frac{1}{s}L\left\{\mu\left(\frac{\partial^2 \varphi}{\partial \alpha^2} + \frac{\partial^2 \varphi}{\partial \beta^2} + \frac{\partial^2 \varphi}{\partial z^2}\right) - \rho\varphi\frac{\partial \varphi}{\partial \alpha}\right\} \quad (24)$$

By using inverse Laplace transformation on (24), we obtain

$$\varphi(\alpha,\beta,z,\tau) = j(\alpha,\beta,z) + L^{-1}\left[\frac{1}{s}L\left\{\mu\left(\frac{\partial^2 \varphi}{\partial \alpha^2} + \frac{\partial^2 \varphi}{\partial \beta^2} + \frac{\partial^2 \varphi}{\partial z^2}\right) - \rho\varphi\frac{\partial \varphi}{\partial \alpha}\right\}\right] \quad (25)$$

Now, by modifying VIM from Equation (25), we obtain

$$\varphi_{n+1} = j(\alpha,\beta,z) + L^{-1}\left[\frac{1}{s}L\left\{\mu\left(\frac{\partial^2 \varphi_n}{\partial \alpha^2} + \frac{\partial^2 \varphi_n}{\partial \beta^2} + \frac{\partial^2 \varphi_n}{\partial z^2}\right) - \left(\rho\varphi_n\frac{\partial \varphi_n}{\partial \alpha}\right)\right\}\right] \quad (26)$$

Equation (26) represents the modified iteration formula of LVIM; the solution is given by

$$\varphi = \lim_{n\to\infty} \varphi_n \quad (27)$$

2.4. The Convergence of LVIM for (3+1)-D Partial Differential Equations

Consider the three-dimensional differential equation

$$l\varphi(\alpha,\beta,z,\tau) + n\varphi(\alpha,\beta,\tau) = g(\alpha,\beta,\tau) \quad (28)$$

with the initial conditions
$$\varphi(\alpha,\beta,0) = h(\alpha,\beta) \quad (29)$$

where l, n, and g are a linear operator of the first order, a non-linear operator, and a non-homogeneous term, respectively.

The iteration formula of the new LVIM is

$$\varphi_{m+1}(\alpha,\beta,z,\tau) = G(\alpha,\beta) + L^{-1}\left[\frac{1}{s}L\{n\varphi_m(\alpha,\beta,z,\tau)\}\right]$$

Now, define the operator $A[\varphi]$ as

$$A[\varphi] = L^{-1}\left[\frac{1}{s}L\{n\varphi_m(\alpha,\beta,z,\tau)\}\right] \qquad (30)$$

define the components $v_m, m = 0, 1, 2, 3 \ldots$ as

$$\begin{cases} v_0 = u_0, \\ v_1 = A[v_0], \\ v_2 = A[v_1], \\ \quad \vdots \\ v_{m+1} = A[v_m] \end{cases} \qquad (31)$$

Hence,

$$\varphi(\alpha,\beta,z,\tau) = \lim_{m\to\infty}\varphi_m(\alpha,\beta,z,\tau) \qquad (32)$$

For the analysis of convergence of new LVIM, let us discuss the following theorem.

Theorem 2. *Let A, as defined in (30), be an operator from Hilbert space H to H; the solution, as defined in (32), converges if there exists $0 < \gamma < 1$ such that*

$$\|A[v_{m+1}]\| \leq \gamma \|A[v_m]\| \quad (i.e., \; \|v_{m+1}\| \leq \gamma\|v_m\|)$$

for all $m \in N \cup \{0\}$.

Proof. Define the sequence $\{S_n\}_{n=1}^{\infty}$ as

$$\begin{cases} S_1 = G(\alpha,\beta,z) + v_1, \\ S_2 = G(\alpha,\beta,z) + v_2, \\ S_3 = G(\alpha,\beta,z) + v_3, \\ \quad \vdots \\ S_m = G(\alpha,\beta,z) + v_m \end{cases} \qquad (33)$$

Now, we will show that sequence $\{S_n\}_{n=1}^{\infty}$ is a Cauchy sequence in the Hilbert space H. Consider

$$\|S_{m+1} - S_m\| = \|v_{m+1} - v_m\| \leq \gamma\|v_m\| \leq \gamma^2\|v_{m-1}\| \leq \ldots \leq \gamma^{m+1}\|v_0\|$$

For every $m, n \in N, m \geq n$, we have

$$\begin{aligned}
\|S_m - S_n\| &= \|(S_m - S_{m-1}) + (S_{m-1} - S_{m-2}) + \ldots + (S_{n+1} - S_n)\| \\
&\leq \|(S_m - S_{m-1})\| + \|(S_{m-1} - S_{m-2})\| + \ldots + \|(S_{n+1} - S_n)\| \\
&\leq \gamma^m\|v_0\| + \gamma^{m-1}\|v_0\| + \ldots + \gamma^{n+1}\|v_0\| \\
&= \frac{1 - \gamma^{m-n}}{1-\gamma}\gamma^{n+1}\|v_0\|
\end{aligned}$$

Since $0 < \gamma < 1$, therefore,

$$\lim_{m,n\to\infty}\|S_m - S_n\| = 0 \qquad (34)$$

Hence, $\{S_n\}_{n=1}^{\infty}$ is a Cauchy sequence in the Hilbert space H and it implies that the series solution (32) converges. □

3. Numerical Examples

Examples are provided in this part to illustrate the effectiveness and precision of the suggested Laplace variational iterative method.

Example 1. *Consider the following Two-Dimensional Burgers Equation*

$$\frac{\partial \varphi(\alpha,\beta,\tau)}{\partial \tau} = \frac{1}{A}\varphi(\alpha,\beta,\tau)\frac{\partial \varphi(\alpha,\beta,\tau)}{\partial \alpha} + \frac{\partial^2 \varphi(\alpha,\beta,\tau)}{\partial \alpha^2} + \frac{\partial^2 \varphi(\alpha,\beta,\tau)}{\partial \beta^2} \quad (35)$$

with conditions given as

$$\varphi(\alpha,\beta,0) = A(\alpha+\beta)$$

By applying the LT on (35), we have

$$L\left\{\frac{\partial \varphi(\alpha,\beta,\tau)}{\partial \tau}\right\} = L\left\{\frac{1}{A}\varphi(\alpha,\beta,\tau)\frac{\partial \varphi(\alpha,\beta,\tau)}{\partial \alpha} + \frac{\partial^2 \varphi(\alpha,\beta,\tau)}{\partial \alpha^2} + \frac{\partial^2 \varphi(\alpha,\beta,\tau)}{\partial \beta^2}\right\} \quad (36)$$

$$sL\{\varphi(\alpha,\beta,\tau)\} - \varphi(\alpha,\beta,0) = L\left\{\frac{1}{A}\varphi(\alpha,\beta,\tau)\frac{\partial \varphi(\alpha,\beta,\tau)}{\partial \alpha} + \frac{\partial^2 \varphi(\alpha,\beta,\tau)}{\partial \alpha^2} + \frac{\partial^2 \varphi(\alpha,\beta,\tau)}{\partial \beta^2}\right\}$$

$$sL\{\varphi(\alpha,\beta,\tau)\} - A(\alpha+\beta) = L\left\{\frac{1}{A}\varphi(\alpha,\beta,\tau)\frac{\partial \varphi(\alpha,\beta,\tau)}{\partial \alpha} + \frac{\partial^2 \varphi(\alpha,\beta,\tau)}{\partial \alpha^2} + \frac{\partial^2 \varphi(\alpha,\beta,\tau)}{\partial y^2}\right\}$$

$$L\{\varphi(\alpha,\beta,\tau)\} = \frac{A(\alpha+\beta)}{s} + \frac{1}{s}L\left\{\frac{1}{A}\varphi(\alpha,\beta,\tau)\frac{\partial \varphi(\alpha,\beta,\tau)}{\partial \alpha} + \frac{\partial^2 \varphi(\alpha,\beta,\tau)}{\partial \alpha^2} + \frac{\partial^2 \varphi(\alpha,\beta,\tau)}{\partial \beta^2}\right\} \quad (37)$$

By applying the inverse Laplace transformation on (37), we get

$$\varphi = A(\alpha+\beta) + L^{-1}\left[\frac{1}{s}L\left\{\frac{1}{A}\varphi(\alpha,\beta,t)\frac{\partial \varphi(\alpha,\beta,\tau)}{\partial \alpha} + \frac{\partial^2 \varphi(\alpha,\beta,\tau)}{\partial \alpha^2} + \frac{\partial^2 \varphi(\alpha,\beta,\tau)}{\partial \beta^2}\right\}\right] \quad (38)$$

Using the proposed variational method from (38), we obtain

$$\varphi_{m+1} = A(\alpha+\beta) + L^{-1}\left[\frac{1}{s}L\left\{\frac{1}{A}\varphi_m\frac{\partial \varphi_m}{\partial \alpha} + \frac{\partial^2 \varphi_m}{\partial \alpha^2} + \frac{\partial^2 \varphi_m}{\partial \beta^2}\right\}\right] \quad (39)$$

From (39), we obtain

$$\varphi_0 = A(\alpha+\beta),$$

$$\varphi_1 = A(\alpha+\beta)(1+\tau),$$

$$\varphi_2 = A(\alpha+\beta)\left(1+\tau+\tau^2+\frac{\tau^3}{3}\right),$$

$$\varphi_3 = A(\alpha+\beta)\left(1+\tau+\tau^2+\tau^3+\frac{2\tau^4}{3}+\frac{\tau^5}{3}+\frac{\tau^6}{9}+\frac{\tau^7}{63}\right)$$

Similarly, we can find the fourth, fifth, and other iterations. The solution can be found as

$$\varphi = \lim_{m\to\infty}\varphi_m$$

After simplification, we obtain

$$\varphi = A(\alpha+\beta)\left(1+\tau+\tau^2+\tau^3+\tau^4+\tau^5\ldots\right),$$

This implies

$$\varphi = A(\alpha + \beta)(1-\tau)^{-1}$$

or

$$\varphi = \frac{A(\alpha + \beta)}{(1-\tau)} \qquad (40)$$

This series solution is valid only if $|\tau| < 1$.

Table 1 shows the comparison study of solutions obtained by new Laplace variation iteration method (up to fourth term), variational homotopy perturbation method (up to fourth term (as discussed in [1])), and the exact solutions for $\alpha = 0.1$, $\beta = 0.1$ and A = 2 of Example 1. Table 2 shows the comparison of absolute errors obtained by new Laplace variation iteration method (up to fourth term) and variational homotopy perturbation method (up to fourth term (as discussed in [1])) for $\alpha = 0.1$, $\beta = 0.1$ and A = 2 of Example 1. Table 3 shows the comparison of absolute errors obtained by new Laplace variation iteration method (up to fourth term) for different value of τ. Figure 1 shows the physical behavior of solutions for $\tau = 0.2$ at different domain of α and β.

Table 1. The comparison study of new LVIM (up to fourth term), VHPM (up to fourth term (as mentioned in [1])), and the exact solution for $(\alpha, \beta) = (0.1, 0.1)$ and A = 2.

τ	Exact	LVIM	VHPM [1]
0.01	0.40404040	0.40404040	0.40404040
0.02	0.40816326	0.40816324	0.40816320
0.03	0.41237113	0.41237101	0.41237080
0.04	0.41666666	0.41666629	0.41666560
0.05	0.42105263	0.42105170	0.42105000
0.06	0.42553191	0.42552996	0.42552640
0.07	0.43010752	0.43010383	0.43009720
0.08	0.43478260	0.43477617	0.43476480
0.09	0.43956043	0.43954990	0.43953160
0.10	0.44444444	0.44442804	0.44440000

Table 2. The comparison of absolute errors obtained by new LVIM (up to fourth term) and VHPM (up to fourth term (as mentioned in [1])) for $(\alpha, \beta) = (0.1, 0.1)$ and A = 2.

τ	$|\varphi_{exact} - \varphi_{LVIM}|$	$|\varphi_{exact} - \varphi_{VHPM}|$ [1]
0.01	1.3604×10^{-9}	4.0404×10^{-9}
0.02	2.2210×10^{-8}	6.5306×10^{-8}
0.03	1.1475×10^{-7}	3.3402×10^{-7}
0.04	3.7016×10^{-7}	1.0667×10^{-6}
0.05	9.2255×10^{-7}	2.6316×10^{-6}
0.06	1.9531×10^{-6}	5.5149×10^{-6}
0.07	3.6948×10^{-6}	1.0327×10^{-5}
0.08	6.4373×10^{-6}	1.7809×10^{-5}
0.09	1.0532×10^{-5}	2.8840×10^{-5}
0.10	1.6399×10^{-5}	4.4444×10^{-5}

Table 3. The comparison of absolute errors obtained by new LVIM (up to fourth term) and VHPM (up to fourth term (as mentioned in [1])) for $(\alpha, \beta) = (0.1, 0.1)$ and A = 2 at different τ.

τ	Exact Solutions	$|\varphi_{exact} - \varphi_{LVIM}|$	$|\varphi_{exact} - \varphi_{VHPM}|$ [1]
0.2	0.50000000	3.2774×10^{-4}	8.0000×10^{-4}
0.3	0.57142857	2.1108×10^{-3}	4.6286×10^{-3}
0.4	0.66666666	8.6822×10^{-3}	1.7067×10^{-2}
0.5	0.80000000	2.8423×10^{-2}	5.0000×10^{-2}
0.6	1.00000000	8.2421×10^{-2}	1.2960×10^{-1}

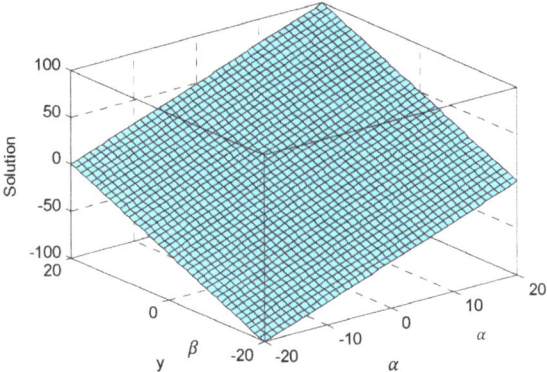

Figure 1. Description of solutions of Example 1 for $\tau = 0.2$.

Example 2. *Consider the following (3+1)-D Burgers equation*

$$\frac{\partial \varphi(\alpha,\beta,z,t)}{\partial \tau} = \frac{1}{B}\varphi(\alpha,\beta,z,\tau)\frac{\partial \varphi(\alpha,\beta,z,\tau)}{\partial \alpha} + \frac{\partial^2 \varphi(\alpha,\beta,z,\tau)}{\partial \alpha^2} + \frac{\partial^2 \varphi(\alpha,\beta,z,\tau)}{\partial \beta^2} + \frac{\partial^2 \varphi(\alpha,\beta,z,\tau)}{\partial z^2} \quad (41)$$

with the initial conditions

$$\varphi(\alpha,\beta,z,0) = B(\alpha + \beta + z)$$

By using the Laplace transformation on (41), we obtain

$$L\left\{\frac{\partial \varphi(\alpha,\beta,z,\tau)}{\partial \tau}\right\} = L\left\{\frac{1}{B}\varphi(\alpha,\beta,z,\tau)\frac{\partial \varphi(\alpha,v,z,\tau)}{\partial \alpha} + \frac{\partial^2 \varphi(\alpha,\beta,z,\tau)}{\partial \alpha^2} + \frac{\partial^2 \varphi(\alpha,\beta,z,\tau)}{\partial \beta^2} + \frac{\partial^2 \varphi(\alpha,\beta,z,\tau)}{\partial z^2}\right\}$$

$$sL\{\varphi(\alpha,\beta,z,\tau)\} - \varphi(\alpha,\beta,z,0)$$

$$= L\left\{\frac{1}{B}\varphi(\alpha,\beta,z,\tau)\frac{\partial \varphi(x,\beta,z,\tau)}{\partial \alpha} + \frac{\partial^2 \varphi(\alpha,\beta,z,\tau)}{\partial \alpha^2} + \frac{\partial^2 \varphi(\alpha,\beta,z,\tau)}{\partial \beta^2} + \frac{\partial^2 \varphi(\alpha,\beta,z,\tau)}{\partial z^2}\right\}$$

$$sL\{\varphi(\alpha,\beta,z,\tau)\} - (\alpha + \beta + z)\} \quad (42)$$

$$= L\left\{\frac{1}{B}\varphi(\alpha,\beta,z,\tau)\frac{\partial \varphi(\alpha,\beta,z,\tau)}{\partial \alpha} + \frac{\partial^2 \varphi(\alpha,\beta,z,\tau)}{\partial \alpha^2} + \frac{\partial^2 \varphi(\alpha,\beta,z,\tau)}{\partial \beta^2} + \frac{\partial^2 \varphi(\alpha,\beta,z,\tau)}{\partial z^2}\right\}$$

$$L\{\varphi(\alpha,\beta,z,\tau)\} = \frac{B(\alpha+\beta+z)}{s} +$$

$$\frac{1}{s}L\left\{\frac{1}{B}\varphi(\alpha,\beta,z,\tau)\frac{\partial \varphi(\alpha,\beta,z,t)}{\partial \alpha} + \frac{\partial^2 \varphi(\alpha,\beta,z,t)}{\partial \alpha^2} + \frac{\partial^2 \varphi(\alpha,\beta,z,t)}{\partial \beta^2} + \frac{\partial^2 u(\alpha,\beta,z,t)}{\partial z^2}\right\}$$

By the inverse Laplace transformation on (42), we obtain

$$\varphi = B(\alpha + \beta + z) +$$
$$L^{-1}\left[\frac{1}{s}L\left\{\frac{1}{B}\varphi(\alpha,\beta,z,\tau)\frac{\partial \varphi(\alpha,\beta,z,\tau)}{\partial \alpha} + \frac{\partial^2 \varphi(\alpha,\beta,z,\tau)}{\partial x^2} + \frac{\partial^2 \varphi(\alpha,\beta,z,\tau)}{\partial \beta^2} + \frac{\partial^2 \varphi(\alpha,\beta,z,t)}{\partial z^2}\right\}\right] \quad (43)$$

Using the modified variational iteration method from Equation (43), we obtain

$$\varphi_{m+1} = B(\alpha + \beta + z) + L^{-1}\left[\frac{1}{s}L\left\{\varphi_m\frac{\partial \varphi_m}{\partial x} + \frac{\partial^2 \varphi_m}{\partial x^2} + \frac{\partial^2 \varphi_m}{\partial \beta^2} + \frac{\partial^2 \varphi_m}{\partial z^2}\right\}\right] \quad (44)$$

From (44), we obtain

$$\varphi_0 = B(\alpha + \beta + z),$$

$$\varphi_1 = B(\alpha + \beta + z)(1 + \tau),$$

$$\varphi_2 = B(\alpha + \beta + z)\left(1 + \tau + \tau^2 + \frac{\tau^3}{3}\right),$$

$$\varphi_3 = B(\alpha + \beta + z)\left(1 + \tau + \tau^2 + \tau^3 + \frac{2\tau^4}{3} + \frac{\tau^5}{3} + \frac{\tau^6}{9} + \frac{\tau^7}{63}\right),$$

The solution can be obtained by

$$\varphi = \lim_{m\to\infty} \varphi_m$$

Now, after simplification, we obtain

$$\varphi = B(\alpha + \beta + z)\left(1 + \tau + \tau^2 + \tau^3 + \tau^4 + \tau^5 \ldots\right)$$

This implies

$$\varphi = B(\alpha + \beta + z)(1 - \tau)^{-1}$$

or

$$\varphi = \frac{B(\alpha + \beta + z)}{(1 - \tau)}$$

This series solution is valid only if $|\tau| < 1$.

Table 4 shows the comparison study of solutions obtained by new Laplace variation iteration method (up to fourth term), variational homotopy perturbation method (up to fourth term (as discussed in [1])), and the exact solutions for $\alpha = 0.1$, $\beta = 0.1$, $z = 0.1$ and B = 3 of Example 2. Table 5 shows the comparison of absolute errors obtained by new Laplace variation iteration method (up to fourth term) and variational homotopy perturbation method (up to fourth term (as discussed in [1])) for particular values of variables $\alpha = 0.1$, $\beta = 0.1$, $z = 0.1$ and B = 3 of Example 3. Table 6 shows the comparison of absolute errors obtained by new Laplace variation iteration method (up to fourth term) for different value of τ. Figure 2 shows the physical behavior of solutions for $\tau = 0.1$ at different domain of α, β and z.

Table 4. The comparison of new LVIM (up to fourth term), VHPM (up to fourth term (as mentioned in [1])), and exact solution for (α, β, z) = (0.1, 0.1, 0.1) and B = 3.

τ	Exact	NLVIM	VHPM [1]
0.01	0.90909090	0.90909090	0.90909090
0.02	0.91836734	0.91836729	0.91836720
0.03	0.92783505	0.92783479	0.92783430
0.04	0.93750000	0.93749916	0.93749760
0.05	0.94736842	0.94736634	0.94736250
0.06	0.95744680	0.95744241	0.95743440
0.07	0.96774193	0.96773362	0.96771870

Table 4. *Cont.*

τ	Exact	NLVIM	VHPM [1]
0.08	0.97826086	0.97824638	0.97822080
0.09	0.98901098	0.98898729	0.98894610
0.10	1.00000000	0.99996310	0.99990000

Table 5. The comparison of absolute errors obtained by new LVIM (up to fourth term) and VHPM (up to fourth term (as mentioned in [1])) for $(\alpha, \beta, z) = (0.1, 0.1, 0.1)$ and B = 3.

τ	$|\varphi_{exact} - \varphi_{LVIM}|$	$|\varphi_{exact} - \varphi_{VHPM}|$ [1]
0.01	3.0608×10^{-9}	9.0909×10^{-9}
0.02	4.9972×10^{-8}	1.4694×10^{-7}
0.03	2.5818×10^{-7}	7.5155×10^{-7}
0.04	8.3287×10^{-7}	2.4000×10^{-6}
0.05	2.0757×10^{-6}	5.9211×10^{-6}
0.06	4.3945×10^{-6}	1.2409×10^{-5}
0.07	8.3134×10^{-6}	2.3235×10^{-5}
0.08	1.4484×10^{-5}	4.0070×10^{-5}
0.09	2.3698×10^{-5}	6.4889×10^{-5}
0.10	3.6899×10^{-5}	1.0000×10^{-4}

Table 6. The comparison of absolute errors obtained by new LVIM (up to fourth term) and VHPM (up to fourth term (as mentioned in [1])) for $(\alpha, \beta, z) = (0.1, 0.1, 0.1)$ and B = 3 at different τ.

τ	Exact Solutions	$|\varphi_{exact} - \varphi_{LVIM}|$	$|\varphi_{exact} - \varphi_{VHPM}|$ [1]
0.2	1.12500000	7.3742×10^{-4}	1.8000×10^{-3}
0.3	1.28571428	4.7493×10^{-3}	1.0414×10^{-2}
0.4	1.50000000	1.9535×10^{-2}	3.8400×10^{-2}
0.5	1.80000000	6.3951×10^{-2}	1.1250×10^{-1}
0.6	2.25000000	1.8545×10^{-1}	2.9160×10^{-1}

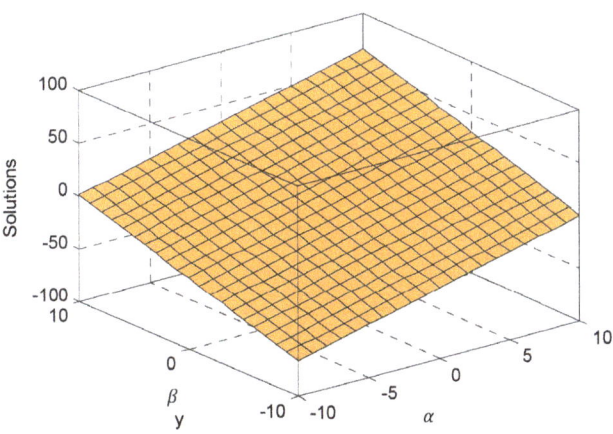

Figure 2. Description of solutions of Example 2 for $z = 0.2$ and $\tau = 0.1$.

4. Conclusions

Based on the preceding discussion and experiments, the combination of the Laplace transforms, and the variational iteration technique presents an effective approach to solve the (2+1)-D and (3+1)-D Burgers equations. Compared to the variational homotopy perturbation technique (VHPM), the new Laplace variational iteration method (LVIM) is more effective in obtaining an approximate solution that closely approximates the actual one. It is possible that this technique may be utilized in the future to solve the three-dimensional Burgers equation system.

Author Contributions: Conceptualization, G.S.; methodology, G.S.; software, G.S.; validation, I.S., A.M.A. (Afrah M. AlDerea) and A.M.A. (Agaeb Mahal Alanzi); formal analysis, G.S.; investigation, G.S.; resources, G.S.; data curation, G.S.; writing—original draft preparation, G.S.; writing—review and editing, G.S.; visualization, H.A.E.-W.K.; supervision, I.S.; This research work is related to the Ph.D research work of Gurpreet Singh (G.S.), no other person can use this research work for getting any degree from any institute/University. All authors have read and agreed to the published version of the manuscript.

Funding: The researchers would like to thank the Deanship of Scientific Research, Qassim University for funding the publication of this project.

Data Availability Statement: All data is available within the article.

Acknowledgments: The researchers would like to thank the Deanship of Scientific Research, Qassim University for funding the publication of this project.

Conflicts of Interest: The authors declare that they have no conflicts of interest.

References

1. Hendi, F.A.; Kashkari, B.S.; Alderremy, A.A. The variational Homotopy Perturbation method for solving ((n × n) + 1). Dimensional Burgers' equations. *J. Appl. Math.* **2016**, *2016*, 4146323. [CrossRef]
2. Suleman, M.; Wu, Q.; Abbas, G. Approximate analytic solution of (2 + 1) dimensional coupled differential Burger's equation using Elzaki Homotopy Perturbation Method. *Alex. Eng. J.* **2016**, *55*, 1817–1826. [CrossRef]
3. Kutluay, S.; Bahadir, A.; Özdeş, A. Numerical solution of one dimensional Burgers' equation by explicit and exact-explicit finite difference methods. *J. Comput. Appl. Math.* **1999**, *103*, 251–261. [CrossRef]
4. Kutluay, S.; Esen, A.; Dag, I. Numerical solutions of the Burgers' equations by the least squares quadratic B spline finite element method. *J. Comput. Appl. Math.* **2004**, *167*, 21–33. [CrossRef]
5. Pandey, K.; Verma, L.; Verma, A.K. On a finite difference scheme for Burgers' equations. *Appl. Math. Comput.* **2009**, *215*, 2206–2214. [CrossRef]
6. Aksan, E.N. A numerical solution of Burgers' equation by finite element method constructed on the method of discretization in time. *Appl. Math. Comput.* **2005**, *170*, 895–904. [CrossRef]
7. Abdou, M.A.; Soliman, A.A. Variational iteration method for solving Burgers' and coupled Burgers' equations. *J. Comput. Appl. Math.* **1996**, *181*, 245–251. [CrossRef]
8. Mittal, R.; Singhal, P. Numerical solution of Burgers' equation. *Commun. Num. Methods Eng.* **1993**, *9*, 397–406. [CrossRef]
9. Abbasbandy, S.; Darvishi, M.T. A numerical solution of Burgers' equation by modified Adomian Decomposition method. *Appl. Math. Comput.* **2005**, *163*, 1265–1272.
10. Öziş, T.; Aksan, E.N.; Özdeş, A. A finite element approach for solution of Burgers' equation. *Appl. Math. Comput.* **2003**, *139*, 417–428. [CrossRef]
11. Aminikhah, H. A new efficient method for solving two-dimensional Burgers' equation. *ISRN Comput. Math.* **2012**, *2012*, 603280. [CrossRef]
12. Hopf, E. The partial differential equation $u_t + uu_x = \mu u_{xx}$. *Commun. Pure Appl. Math.* **1950**, *3*, 201–230. [CrossRef]
13. He, J.H. Variational iteration method for delay differential equations. *Commun. Nonlinear Sci. Numer. Simul.* **1997**, *2*, 235–236. [CrossRef]
14. He, J.H. Variational iteration method-a kind of non-linear analytical technique: Some examples. *Int. J. Nonlinear Mech.* **1999**, *34*, 699–708. [CrossRef]
15. Hammouch, Z.; Mekkaoui, T. A Laplace-variational iteration method for solving the homogeneous Smoluchowski coagulation equation. *Appl. Math. Sci.* **2012**, *6*, 879–886.
16. Arife, A.S.; Yildirim, A. New modified variational iteration transform method (MVITM) for solving eighth-order boundary value problems in one step. *World Appl. Sci. J.* **2011**, *13*, 2186–2190.
17. Hesameddini, E.; Latifizadeh, H. Reconstruction of variational iteration algorithms using the Laplace transform. *Int. J. Nonlinear Sci. Numer. Simul.* **2009**, *10*, 1377–1382. [CrossRef]

18. Wu, G.C. Laplace transform overcoming principle drawbacks in application of the variational iteration method to fractional heat equations. *Therm. Sci.* **2012**, *16*, 1257–1261. [CrossRef]
19. Martinez, H.Y.; Gomez-Aguilar, J.F. Laplace variational iteration method for modified fractional derivatives with non-singular kernel. *J. Appl. Comput. Mech.* **2020**, *6*, 684–698.
20. Elzaki, T.M. Solution of Nonlinear Partial Differential Equations by New Laplace Variational Iteration Method. In *Differential Equations: Theory and Current Research*; IntechOpen: London, UK, 2018.
21. Singh, G.; Singh, I. Laplace variational iterative method for solving 3D Schrodinger equations. *J. Math. Comput. Sci.* **2020**, *10*, 2015–2024.
22. Singh, G.; Singh, I. Laplace variational iterative method for solving Two-dimensional Telegraph equations. *J. Math. Comput. Sci.* **2020**, *10*, 2943–2954.
23. Singh, G.; Singh, I. New Hybrid Technique for solving Three-dimensional Telegraph equations. *Adv. Differ. Equ. Control. Process.* **2021**, *24*, 153–165. [CrossRef]
24. Singh, G.; Singh, I. The exact solution of 3D Diffusion and wave equations using Laplace variational iterative method. *Int. J. Adv. Res. Eng. Technol.* **2020**, *11*, 36–43.
25. Aksan, E.N. Quadratic B-spline finite element method for numerical solution of the Burgers' equation. *Appl. Math. Comput.* **2006**, *174*, 884–896. [CrossRef]
26. Kutluay, S.; Esen, A. A lumped galerkin method for solving the burgers equation. *Int. J. Comput. Math.* **2004**, *81*, 1433–1444. [CrossRef]
27. Sirendaoreji. Exact solutions of the two-dimensional Burgers equation. *J. Phys. A* **1999**, *32*, 6897–6900. [CrossRef]
28. Sharma, K.D.; Kumar, R.; Kakkar, M.; Ghangas, S. Three dimensional waves propagation in thermos-viscoelastic medium with two temperature and void. *IOP Conf. Ser. Mater. Sci. Eng.* **2021**, *1033*, 012059. [CrossRef]
29. Singh, V.; Saluja, N.; Singh, C.; Malhotra, R. Computational and Experimental study of microwave processing of susceptor with multiple topologies of launcher waveguide. *AIP Conf. Proc.* **2022**, *2357*, 040019.
30. Khan, M. A novel solution technique for two-dimensional Burgers equation. *Alex. Eng. J.* **2014**, *53*, 485–490. [CrossRef]

Disclaimer/Publisher's Note: The statements, opinions and data contained in all publications are solely those of the individual author(s) and contributor(s) and not of MDPI and/or the editor(s). MDPI and/or the editor(s) disclaim responsibility for any injury to people or property resulting from any ideas, methods, instructions or products referred to in the content.

Article

An Extended AHP-Based Corpus Assessment Approach for Handling Keyword Ranking of NLP: An Example of COVID-19 Corpus Data

Liang-Ching Chen [1] and Kuei-Hu Chang [2,*]

[1] Department of Foreign Languages, R.O.C. Military Academy, Kaohsiung 830, Taiwan
[2] Department of Management Sciences, R.O.C. Military Academy, Kaohsiung 830, Taiwan
* Correspondence: evenken2002@yahoo.com.tw

Abstract: The use of corpus assessment approaches to determine and rank keywords for corpus data is critical due to the issues of information retrieval (IR) in Natural Language Processing (NLP), such as when encountering COVID-19, as it can determine whether people can rapidly obtain knowledge of the disease. The algorithms used for corpus assessment have to consider multiple parameters and integrate individuals' subjective evaluation information simultaneously to meet real-world needs. However, traditional keyword-list-generating approaches are based on only one parameter (i.e., the keyness value) to determine and rank keywords, which is insufficient. To improve the evaluation benefit of the traditional keyword-list-generating approach, this paper proposed an extended analytic hierarchy process (AHP)-based corpus assessment approach to, firstly, refine the corpus data and then use the AHP method to compute the relative weights of three parameters (keyness, frequency, and range). To verify the proposed approach, this paper adopted 53 COVID-19-related research environmental science research articles from the Web of Science (WOS) as an empirical example. After comparing with the traditional keyword-list-generating approach and the equal weights (EW) method, the significant contributions are: (1) using the machine-based technique to remove function and meaningless words for optimizing the corpus data; (2) being able to consider multiple parameters simultaneously; and (3) being able to integrate the experts' evaluation results to determine the relative weights of the parameters.

Keywords: corpus assessment approach; natural language processing (NLP); COVID-19; analytic hierarchy process (AHP); environmental science

Citation: Chen, L.-C.; Chang, K.-H. An Extended AHP-Based Corpus Assessment Approach for Handling Keyword Ranking of NLP: An Example of COVID-19 Corpus Data. *Axioms* **2023**, *12*, 740. https://doi.org/10.3390/axioms12080740

Academic Editors: Nuno Bastos, Touria Karite and Amir Khan

Received: 2 June 2023
Revised: 14 July 2023
Accepted: 17 July 2023
Published: 28 July 2023

Copyright: © 2023 by the authors. Licensee MDPI, Basel, Switzerland. This article is an open access article distributed under the terms and conditions of the Creative Commons Attribution (CC BY) license (https://creativecommons.org/licenses/by/4.0/).

1. Introduction

The corpus assessment approach has been applied in the Natural Language Processing (NLP) field for a long time, and it is seen as a critical technique for identifying linguistic patterns [1–3]. Since the end of 2019, the emergence of the novel coronavirus disease COVID-19 has caused serious impacts on global political and economic systems, and even endangered people's lives [4–6]. Diseases always do more harm than good to humans; nevertheless, during the pandemic, scientists discovered that a series of public health policies, such as city lockdowns, as well as decreasing unnecessary commercial activities and travel, can mitigate global environmental pollution issues that we have been helpless to address in the past, especially the air quality index (AQI), which has been shown to have significantly decreased in many modern cities [7–9]. COVID-19 does not seem to be completely eradicated so far; thus, to keep mining knowledge of the disease, it is critical to effectively integrate, process, and reproduce its corpus data.

Corpus assessment approaches have been utilized to process the corpus data of various domains to discover domain-oriented tokens and define linguistic patterns. For example, Poole [3] used the corpus-based approach to process the collected published judicial opinions from 12 geographic distribution areas of the U.S. Federal Court of Appeals (i.e., the target corpus), for analyzing stance adverbs in its target domain. The contributions of the research defined the linguistic patterns of legal writing styles and provided pedagogical suggestions for legal purposes in English. Otto [2] proposed a three-phase corpus-based data driven learning (DDL) approach to identify special-purpose tokens in the civil engineering domain. The results disclosed that the approach was able to unveil the tokens' functions and improve the efficiency of defining the linguistic patterns in the specialized context of civil engineering. However, when the traditional corpus assessment approach [10] encountered function words and meaningless letters in the keyword list, it could not automatically remove them to conduct corpus optimization, which decreased the efficiency of the corpus assessment. Moreover, the keyword list only adopted the likelihood ratio method [11] as an information retrieval (IR) mean to rank keywords. This caused inaccurate results, because other potential parameters such as frequency and range were not taken into consideration, which made the traditional approach unable to truly define the keywords' level of importance.

The equal weights (EW) method is a classic approach used to process multiple parameters simultaneously when the relative importance of the parameters is unknown. However, the EW method assumes that the relative weights of each parameter are equal, which ignores the relative importance between different parameters. Saaty [12] firstly proposed the analytic hierarchy process (AHP) method to handle the relative importance between different parameters in decision-making problems. The AHP method uses the pairwise comparison between different parameters to compute the eigenvector and eigenvalue and then obtains the relative weights of the parameters. Since then, the AHP method has been adopted in a wide range of applications. For example, Rezaei and Tahsili [13] adopted the AHP method to conduct urban and crisis management, for accessing the vulnerability and immunization parts to decrease the effects of earthquakes. In addition, Ristanovic et al. [14] demonstrated that the AHP method can obtain the best solutions in processing the operational risk management of banks. Prior studies have shown that the AHP method is usually applied in the fields of management and operational research (OR) [12–20]; nevertheless, properly modifying the AHP method can allow it to be used in NLP fields for the computer processing of natural languages, by considering the relative weights of multiple parameters simultaneously.

Corpus assessment approaches have been widely used as an NLP tool in the fields of social sciences and the sciences to explore the linguistic patterns of specific domains [1–3,10,21–23]. The traditional keyword-list-generating approach [10] is based on the likelihood ratio method, which is an IR approach utilized in many types of corpus software [1,23] to calculate a token's keyness value and rank tokens to form a keyword list. Many corpus-based approaches also adopt these types of corpus software to handle corpus analysis tasks [24,25]. However, for traditional keyword ranking, it is difficult to determine the actual importance of each keyword when the program only uses their keyness values for ranking. Namely, the traditional keyword-list-generating approach is only based on one parameter (i.e., the keyness values) to determine and rank keywords, which is insufficient. In the advanced information, communication, and technology (ICT) era, people have developed many algorithms for machine learning and optimizing prior algorithms or machines, with the expectation of machines being able to make more complete and accurate judgments and evaluation results. Thus, the corpus assessment approach should integrate with machine-based corpus optimization and consider multiple parameters (or vectors) simultaneously, to make the evaluation results more accurate. To optimize the deficiency of the traditional keyword-list-generating approach, this paper proposed an extended AHP-based corpus assessment approach to integrate the likelihood ratio method, the corpus optimization approach, and the AHP method, to improve the accuracy of keyword ranking in corpus assessments. The proposed approach firstly optimizes the likelihood ratio method results by removing function words and meaningless letters, and then simultaneously takes three parameters (i.e., the keyness, frequency, and range) into consideration to rank keywords while considering multiple parameters. More importantly, the relative importance of these parameters is evaluated and determined by experts. That is, the proposed approach not only conducts a complete assessment on the issue but also enables expert evaluation results to be integrated and transformed qualitatively and quantitatively, thereby further making the keyword ranking more complete, precise, and able to satisfy individuals' intentions. To verify the proposed extended AHP-based corpus assessment approach, this paper adopted 53 research articles from the Web of Science (WOS) as empirical examples of natural language data.

The remainder of this paper is organized as follows. Section 2 presents the background information of related methods and the COVID-19 impacts on environmental sciences. Section 3 describes each step of the proposed extended AHP-based corpus assessment approach. Section 4 uses COVID-19-related research articles as empirical examples to verify the proposed approach and compare it with the other two methods, and highlight the contributions. Section 5 is the concluding section.

2. Background

2.1. Likelihood Ratio Method

With the rise of ICT, people have started to rely on computers to process big natural language data. Dunning [11] first introduced the likelihood ratio method for computing the keyness values of tokens for keyword retrieval in corpus analysis tasks, and it is now considered a critical algorithm that is embedded in many types of corpus software. The logic behind the algorithm is that it compares a token's frequency values in two corpora (i.e., the target corpus and the benchmark corpus). When it finds a token with high frequency values in the target corpus and relatively low frequency values in the benchmark corpus, it will calculate the token's keyness values, after which the computation results of the tokens' keyness values will be ranked for generating a keyword list.

The definition of likelihood ratio method is described as follows:

Definition 1 ([11,21]). *Assume that two random variables, X_1 and X_2, follow the binomial distributions $B(N_1, p_1)$ and $B(N_2, p_2)$; p_1 and p_2 are a single trial's success probability, and n_1 and n_2 represent the number of successes that can occur anywhere among the N_1 and N_2 trials, respectively. The logarithm of the likelihood ratio (λ) can be defined as:*

$$-2\log\lambda = 2[\log L(p_1, n_1, N_1) + \log L(p_2, n_2, N_2) - \log L(p, n_1, N_1) - \log L(p, n_2, N_2)]$$

where

$$L(p, n, N) = p^n(1-p)^{N-n}$$
$$p_1 = \tfrac{n_1}{N_1}, p_2 = \tfrac{n_2}{N_2}, \text{ and } p = \tfrac{n_1+n_2}{N_1+N_2}$$

2.2. Environmental Science Perspective of COVID-19

The earth is the only planet that humans have detected so far in the vast universe to cultivate life [26]. Creatures on the earth depend on a pleasant environment to survive and grow from generation to generation. However, due to the rapid development of human civilization, people have caused serious damage to the earth's environmental and ecological systems. The emission of large amounts of carbon and toxic pollutants (e.g., PM2.5 and PM10 particulate matter, carbon monoxide (CO), ground-level ozone (O3), sulfur dioxide (SO2), and nitrogen dioxide (NO2)) has caused serious air pollution and global warming, leading to the emergence of extreme climates or weather events, and ultimately damaging the survival of organisms [26–29]. Many countries are continuously advocating pro-environmental behaviors to create sustainable development of the ecosystem and the environment. However, people may believe that environmental impacts are a future matter and that even vigorous efforts to promote environmental protection cannot achieve immediate mitigations [30].

Since 2019, the COVID-19 pandemic has impacted economic and political systems globally [31,32]. The COVID-19 virus has been classified as severe acute respiratory syndrome coronavirus 2 (SARS-CoV-2). It is related to SARS-CoV and Middle East Respiratory Syndrome (MERS-CoV), but it has a much higher infectious capability and a lower fatality rate than the former two coronavirus types [31,33–35]. In the middle of 2023, the WHO declared that there were over 765 million confirmed cases, with over 6 million deaths during the COVID-19 pandemic [36]. The genetic formation of the spike protein in SARS-CoV-2 has mutated and caused difficulties for the human immune system to resist the virus, hence causing the virus to have a have rapid infection rate [32,33,37]. Moreover, because of its low fatality rate, the virus can parasitize and remain in its hosts for an extended period, thus giving the virus opportunities to mutate and evolve [38]. Until now, many countries are still suffering from COVID-19 variants (such as the Alpha, Beta, Gamma, and Delta variants), which have caused this anti-virus battle to become endless [39]. Current measurements for fighting the COVID-19 pandemic rely on expanding viral detection, enhancing vaccination rates, and following public health policies [34,35]. In addition, the development and introduction of vaccines and specific medicines indicate that people are gradually gaining the dominant position in this anti-virus battle [40].

From the perspective of environmental science, the series of quarantine policies such as travel limitations, city lockdowns, prohibiting non-essential commercial activities, shutting down unnecessary industries, and banning large gatherings has unexpectedly and significantly mitigated pollution levels and the AQI [26,27,41–44]. Prior studies have taught an important lesson—do not think that the self-contribution of pro-environmental behaviors are insignificant—and the improved AQI has proved that restoration of the environment can be an immediate improvement as long as people are willing to strike a balance between economic development and the environment [27,42,43,45].

3. Methodology

Keyword ranking in the corpus assessment approach is an important technique for handling big natural language data and assisting humans in IR and language pattern recognition. For example, information about COVID-19 continuously spreads in our daily life. Although the vaccine has been invented and people are being vaccinated gradually, the SARS-CoV-2 variants keep mutating and causing the anti-virus war to become endless. To enhance our understanding and awareness of COVID-19, the algorithms used for NLP in corpus analysis must be optimized. Hence, this paper proposes an extended AHP-based corpus assessment approach to integrate the likelihood ratio method, the corpus optimization approach, and the AHP method to improve the accuracy of keyword ranking in corpus assessments. The proposed approach is mainly divided into 11 steps, and a detailed description is described as follows (see Figure 1):

Step 1. Create the target corpus.

Compile the natural language data as the target corpus, and convert the file format of the target corpus from the .docx or .pdf format into the .txt (UTF-8) format.

Step 2. Import the target corpus and the benchmark corpus to the program.

Input the compiled target corpus to AntConc 3.5.8 [1] (the corpus software adopted in this paper) to compute the frequency of each lexical unit's occurrence. In addition, before generating the keyword list, input the benchmark corpus data. English for general purposes (EGP) genres such as blogs, fictional works, magazines, and news of the Corpus of Contemporary American English (COCA) is adopted as the benchmark corpus.

Step 3. Optimize the target corpus.

Before initializing the likelihood ratio calculation, from a linguistic perspective, function words will decrease the accuracy of high frequency words and the keyword-generating process [21]. Therefore, to increase the accuracy and efficiency of soft computing in NLP tasks, this optimization process is inevitable. This step adopts the corpus optimization process of Chen et al. [21], which uses a machine-based processing approach to eliminate function words.

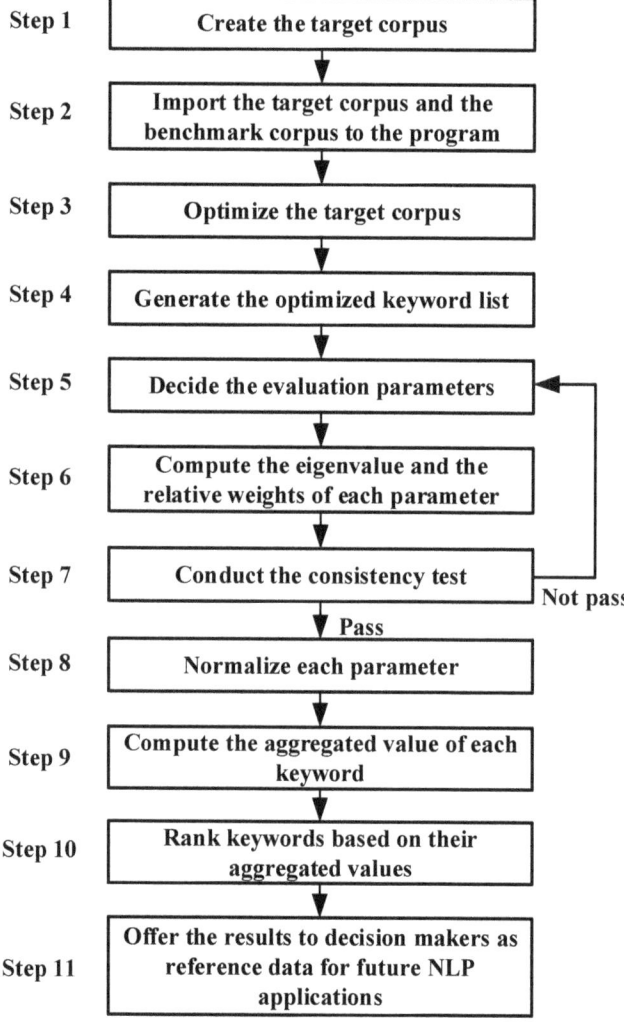

Figure 1. Flowchart of the proposed approach.

Step 4. Generate the optimized keyword list.

After all corpus data is inputted, Dunning's [11] likelihood ratio method will compute and extract words that appear highly frequently in the target corpus in comparison with the words in the benchmark corpus (i.e., computing words' keyness values and ranking them). These words can be considered to be characteristic of the target corpus. Namely, keywords of the target corpus will be retrieved and ranked on the keyword list.

Step 5. Decide the evaluation parameters.

Give experts questionnaires with a paired comparison based on Table 1 to conduct a pairwise comparison of each parameter, in order to, respectively, evaluate the two criteria's relative contribution or importance.

Table 1. Pairwise comparison scale [12].

Relative Importance Scale	Definition of Relatively Important Level	Explanation
1	Equal importance	Two indicators contribute equally to the objective
3	Moderate importance of one over another	From experience and judgment, a certain indicator is slightly important
5	Essential or strong importance	From experience and judgment, a certain indicator is quite important
7	Demonstrated or very strong importance	Practical aspects show that a certain indicator is extremely important
9	Absolute importance	The evidence indicates that a certain indicator is absolutely important
2, 4, 6, 8	The median value of adjacent measures	When a compromise is needed

Then, use Equation (1) to establish the pairwise comparison matrix and proceed with the computation process. If there are n influencing elements, an $\frac{n(n-1)}{2}$ pairwise comparisons must be conducted.

$$\begin{bmatrix} 1 & a_{12} & \cdots & a_{1n} \\ 1/a_{12} & 1 & \cdots & a_{2n} \\ \vdots & \vdots & \ddots & \vdots \\ 1/a_{1n} & 1/a_{2n} & \cdots & 1 \end{bmatrix} \quad (1)$$

Step 6. Compute the eigenvalue and the relative weights of each parameter.

The eigenvalues and eigenvectors are computed by Equation (2), in which A is the $n \times n$ pairwise comparison matrix, λ is the eigenvalue of matrix A, and X is the eigenvector of matrix A.

$$A \cdot X = \lambda \cdot X \quad (2)$$

After obtaining the maximal eigenvalue λ_{max}, use Equation (3) to calculate the relative weights, W, of each parameter.

$$A \cdot W = \lambda_{max} \cdot W \quad (3)$$

where $W = [w_1, w_2, \ldots, w_n]^T$, and $\sum_{i=1}^{n} w_i = 1$.

Step 7. Conduct the consistency test.

When conducting an expert questionnaire survey, relatively important level scores are usually given by the experts' subjective comments. In other words, the objective and ideal framework should satisfy the transitivity. To inspect whether the pairwise comparison matrix created by the experts' questionnaires is consistent, the consistency index (CI) must be computed by Equation (4) and the consistency ratio (CR) must be calculated by Equation (5) for verification. If the CR value is less than 0.1, the pairwise comparison matrix is consistent.

$$CI = \frac{\lambda_{max} - n}{n - 1} \quad (4)$$

$$CR = \frac{CI}{RI} \quad (5)$$

where n is the dimension of the pairwise comparison matrix, λ_{max} is the maximal eigenvalue of the matrix, and RI is the random index (see Table 2).

Table 2. Random index (RI) table [12].

n	1	2	3	4	5	6	7	8	9	10	11	12	13	14	15
RI	N/A	N/A	0.58	0.90	1.12	1.24	1.32	1.41	1.45	1.49	1.51	1.48	1.56	1.57	1.59

Step 8. Normalize each parameter.

This paper used three parameters, including the keyness, frequency, and range, to calculate the normalized value of each parameter.

Assume that the p_{ij} is the value of the ith item of keyword data and the jth parameter. The value of r_{ij} is the normalization of p_{ij}, defined as follows.

$$r_{ij} = \frac{p_{ij}}{p_j^{max}}, \ j = 1, 2, \ldots, 3 \tag{6}$$

Step 9. Compute the aggregated value of each keyword.

The aggregated value of each keyword is computed by the multiplication of the relative weights of the results for the three parameters from step 8 (shown as Equation (7)).

$$\text{aggregated value}_i = \sum_{j=1}^{3} w_j \times r_{ij} \tag{7}$$

Step 10. Rank keywords based on their aggregated values.

Re-rank the keywords based on their aggregated values from step 9, and generate the ultimate optimized keyword list.

Step 11. Offer the results to decision makers as reference data for future NLP applications.

The optimized keyword list can be provided as critical reference data for decision makers in future NLP applications, such as corpus analysis, keyword analysis, or key information extraction.

4. Empirical Analysis

4.1. Overviews of the Target Corpus

This paper adopted 53 research articles published in 2020–2021 from WOS, which is an internationally well-known academic database. These research articles were under the categorization of environmental science as defined by journal citation reports (JCR), and the topics were all centered on COVID-19. The selection of the research articles had to satisfy the following criteria: (1) the research article needed to correlate with COVID-19; (2) the research article needed to belong to the environmental science discipline; (3) the research article needed to be highly cited; and (4) the research article needed to have a science citation index (SCI) or a social science citation index (SSCI). The main reason to set these criteria was that there is bounteous fake news (information) about COVID-19. After the researchers used the above criteria to search for the relevant research articles from the WOS database, during that moment, there were 53 highly cited research articles showing in the search results. Thus, to verify and highlight the contributions of the proposed approach, the 53 research articles were selected as the target corpus for being the rigorous and non-controversial natural language data.

4.2. Traditional Keyword-List-Generating Approach for Ranking Keywords

The traditional keyword-list-generating approach [10] adopted by this study used Dunning's [11] likelihood ratio method as the main algorithm to determine the keywords of the target corpus. However, some deficiencies occurred in the traditional keyword-list-generating approach. First, without the corpus data optimization process, function words and meaningless letters would affect and reduce the tokens' keyness computation accuracy and cause the keyword list to contain unrelated or meaningless tokens; second, if the keyness value was the only parameter used to determine and rank keywords, it would be impossible to define which keyword was the most commonly used or the most widely dispersed. In other words, the tokens' keyness value needed to be computed with other parameters (e.g., frequency and range) to become a multiple-parameter calculation result that could be used to rank keywords.

4.3. The EW Method for Ranking Keywords

The EW method [46,47] assumes that each criterion has the same importance. If the problem to be solved contains n parameters, $P_1, P_2, \ldots, P_n$, the weight of the EW method is $\frac{1}{n}$. Let a_i be the assessment value of criterion P_i. The weights of the aggregated values for the EW method are shown in Equation (8).

$$\text{EW value} = \frac{1}{n}\sum_{i=1}^{n} a_i \qquad (8)$$

When the EW method was adopted for computing the parameters of this paper (i.e., the keyness, frequency, and range) for ranking keywords, several deficiencies emerged. First, from the linguistic perspective, under the circumstance that the target corpus was not optimized, the keyness calculation results would have interference from function words and meaningless letters, causing the keyness values to be biased at the beginning. Second, although the EW method can simultaneously consider all parameters, the relative importance level of each parameter should not be the same; hence, it was difficult to meet the experts' expectations.

4.4. The Proposed Extended AHP-Based Corpus Assessment Approach

To optimize and address the deficiencies of the two aforementioned methods, this paper adopted the target corpus as the empirical case, to demonstrate and verify the efficacy and practicality of the proposed approach. Detailed descriptions of each step were as follows.

Step 1. Create the target corpus.

The target corpus in this paper was based on 53 research articles with SCI from WOS. The lexical features included 10,595 word types, 189,680 tokens, and a type–token ratio (TTR) of 0.05586 (representing the lexical diversity).

Step 2. Import the target corpus and the benchmark corpus to the program.

To retrieve the keywords, the algorithm of the software will calculate a word's keyness value to determine whether it is the domain-oriented word, by finding the word that has high frequency in the target corpus but has low frequency in the benchmark corpus. From the perspective of linguistic analysis, when the target corpus is the textual data of professional fields, then the benchmark corpus should select more general-purpose-use data (i.e., EGP). In addition, COCA is considered as the biggest and genre-balanced EGP corpus data, and is widely adopted by many corpus-based researchers as the benchmark corpus [11,21], and so did this paper. After processing by the software, the lexical features of the benchmark corpus (i.e., COCA) included 109,306 word types, 8,266,198 tokens, and a TTR of 0.01322.

Step 3. Optimize the target corpus.

To increase the accuracy of keyword extraction, this step adopted the corpus-based machine optimization approach to eliminate function words and meaningless letters [21]. Table 3 shows the refined target corpus, which eliminated 217 word types and 81,097 tokens, and downsized the target corpus by 43%. Without the interference of function words and meaningless letters, the keyword generator could retrieve more domain-oriented or content words to form a more accurate keyword list.

Table 3. Data discrepancy between the original data and the refined data.

Lexical Feature	Original Data	Refined Data	Data Discrepancy
Word Types	10,595	10,378	−217 (decreasing 2%)
Tokens	189,680	108,583	−81,097 (decreasing 43%)
TTR	0.05586	0.09558	

Step 4. Generate the optimized keyword list.

Once the target corpus, the benchmark corpus, and the stop wordlist are input into AntConc 3.5.8 [1], the traditional keyword-list-generating approach is used to exclude function words and meaningless letters to calculate each token's keyness value and determine the keyword list (see Figure 2). However, during this step, the keyword list still remains at the single-parameter evaluation stage.

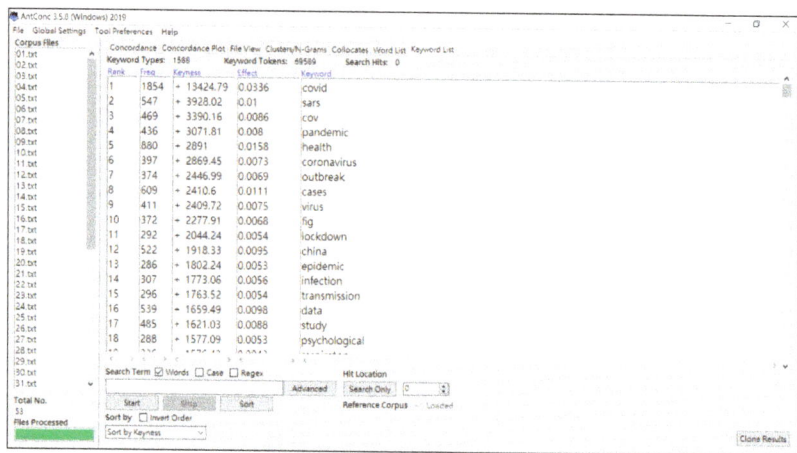

Figure 2. The optimized keyword list on AntConc 3.5.8 [1].

Step 5. Decide the evaluation parameters.

In this step, the evaluation parameters decided by experts are determined as the tokens' keyness, frequency, and range values for the following evaluation processes. The evaluation team in this study included three experts with academic specialties including NLP, corpus linguistics, teachers of English to speakers of other languages (TESOL), performance evaluation, and fuzzy logic. Based on Table 1, the three experts determined the pairwise comparison results of the evaluation parameters, respectively. The results are shown in Table 4.

Table 4. Pairwise comparison results of the parameters.

Criteria	Experts	Experts' Comments		
		Keyness	Frequency	Range
Keyness	Expert 1	1	1/2	1/3
	Expert 2	1	1	1/2
	Expert 3	1	1/2	1/3
Frequency	Expert 1	2	1	1/2
	Expert 2	1	1	1/2
	Expert 3	2	1	1/2
Range	Expert 1	3	2	1
	Expert 2	2	2	1
	Expert 3	3	2	1

Next, the researchers arithmetically averaged each element in the matrix given by the experts and summarized the results as shown in Table 5, and then used Equation (1) to create the matrix for computation in the following steps.

Table 5. The aggregated pairwise comparison matrix.

Criteria	Keyness	Frequency	Range
Keyness	1.000	0.667	0.389
Frequency	1.499	1.000	0.500
Range	2.571	2.000	1.000

Step 6. Compute the eigenvalue and the relative weights of each parameter.

After computing the aggregated pairwise comparison matrix (see Table 5) using Equations (2) and (3), the maximum of the eigenvalue, λ_{max} was 3.003, and the relative weights for the keyness, frequency, and range were 0.195, 0.278, and 0.527, respectively. The relative weights were given by the experts' evaluation and calculated through the AHP computing process, which indicated the relative importance between each vector. Based on the priority vector that range (0.527) > frequency (0.278) > keyness (0.195), we reasoned that the experts' overall assessments indicated that the so-called keywords should also occur widely and frequently in the corpus data.

Step 7. Conduct the consistency test.

To verify the reliability and validity of the relative weights, use Equations (4) and (5), and Table 2 to compute the CI and CR values. The CR value is 0.003, which is less than 0.1, which expressed that the results were acceptable.

Step 8. Normalize each parameter.

Use Equation (6) to normalize each parameter for further aggregated value computation.

Step 9. Compute the aggregated value of each keyword.

Once all parameters were nominalized, the researchers used Equation (7) to compute the aggregated value of the keywords. The partial results of the keywords' aggregated values are presented in Table 6.

Table 6. Keyword list results of the three compared approaches (partial data).

The Traditional Keyword List Generator [10]			The EW Method [47]			The Proposed Method		
Rank	Keyness Value	Token	Rank	EW Value	Token	Rank	AHP-Based Value	Token
1	14,098.08	COVID-19	1	0.717	COVID-19	1	1.000	COVID-19
2	6008.24	et	2	0.695	the	2	0.699	health
3	4803.88	al	3	0.592	of	3	0.608	coronavirus
4	4129.4	SARS	4	0.552	and	4	0.608	study
5	3562.98	CoV	5	0.488	in	5	0.598	cases
6	3232.45	pandemic	6	0.426	health	6	0.598	China
7	3195.11	health	7	0.406	et	7	0.591	disease
8	3015.85	coronavirus	8	0.403	coronavirus	8	0.587	data
9	2626.35	cases	9	0.377	pandemic	9	0.568	pandemic
10	2584.59	outbreak	10	0.377	al	10	0.557	SARS
11	2560.15	virus	11	0.377	SARS	11	0.555	public
12	2414.4	fig	12	0.376	study	12	0.548	reported
13	2358.18	of	13	0.374	cases	13	0.537	high
14	2151.97	lockdown	14	0.372	china	14	0.531	used
15	2101.9	china	15	0.372	disease	15	0.531	number
16	1907.4	epidemic	16	0.370	by	16	0.527	due
17	1885.46	infection	17	0.360	data	17	0.526	virus
18	1872.07	transmission	18	0.343	were	18	0.515	confirmed
19	1844.72	data	19	0.342	virus	19	0.513	countries
20	1789.67	study	20	0.342	reported	20	0.508	spread
21	1708.46	disease	21	0.336	during	21	0.503	analysis
22	1682.23	psychological	22	0.333	public	22	0.502	outbreak

Table 6. Cont.

The Traditional Keyword List Generator [10]			The EW Method [47]			The Proposed Method		
Rank	Keyness Value	Token	Rank	EW Value	Token	Rank	AHP-Based Value	Token
23	1663.43	respiratory	23	0.329	outbreak	23	0.500	level
24	1639.61	temperature	24	0.328	confirmed	24	0.497	table
25	1602.85	Wuhan	25	0.327	between	25	0.496	results
26	1580.8	confirmed	26	0.326	due	26	0.483	measures
27	1518.98	during	27	0.323	high	27	0.483	significant
28	1504.64	reported	28	0.320	number	28	0.483	period
29	1395.95	anxiety	29	0.319	used	29	0.476	respiratory
30	1307.22	emissions	30	0.318	spread	30	0.475	including
31	1292.84	concentrations	31	0.318	countries	31	0.471	impact
32	1206.96	measures	32	0.317	CoV	32	0.471	infection
33	1205.46	and	33	0.315	analysis	33	0.469	different
34	1182.21	the	34	0.310	respiratory	34	0.468	days
35	1164.24	spread	35	0.307	results	35	0.463	transmission
36	1143.28	march	36	0.307	level	36	0.463	CoV
37	1127.58	pollution	37	0.306	measures	37	0.463	Wuhan
38	1104.61	period	38	0.304	infection	38	0.462	increased
39	1095.2	countries	39	0.304	table	39	0.462	research
40	1079.93	infected	40	0.304	transmission	40	0.459	population
41	1073.05	analysis	41	0.302	Wuhan	41	0.454	March
42	1035.12	CI	42	0.301	significant	42	0.451	related
43	1029.14	emergency	43	0.299	period	43	0.449	studies
44	1022.27	RNA	44	0.296	impact	44	0.448	compared
45	1014.58	impact	45	0.292	e	45	0.448	epidemic
46	1008.79	in	46	0.292	epidemic	46	0.443	using
47	997.92	variables	47	0.289	increased	47	0.437	based
48	991.82	patients	48	0.287	population	48	0.437	associated
49	975.98	PM	49	0.287	march	49	0.434	total
50	958.18	results	50	0.285	related	50	0.433	case
51	942.67	infectious	51	0.283	research	51	0.431	increase
52	935.49	factors	52	0.283	studies	52	0.429	observed
53	933.81	air	53	0.281	compared	53	0.428	low
54	896.63	severe	54	0.278	associated	54	0.428	control
55	894.87	respondents	55	0.273	observed	55	0.426	severe
56	888.35	wastewater	56	0.273	using	56	0.422	February
57	869.62	concentration	57	0.272	based	57	0.421	affected
58	866.76	depression	58	0.271	severe	58	0.416	current
59	856.5	associated	59	0.270	total	59	0.416	patients
60	850.23	stress	60	0.270	affected	60	0.414	higher

* COVID-19: Corona Virus Disease 2019; CoV: Corona Virus; CI: Confinement Index; PM: Particulate Matter; RNA: Ribonucleic Acid; SARS: Severe Acute Respiratory Syndrome.

Step 10. Rank the keywords based on their aggregated values.

Based on each keyword's aggregated value, the researchers re-ranked the keyword list (see Table 6) to form the ultimate optimized keyword list.

Step 11. Offer the results to decision makers as reference data for future NLP applications.

The results of the ultimate optimized keyword list can be integrated with the complete evaluation results from the experts to provide a more complete benchmark for defining critical lexical units, thereby improving the efficiency and accuracy of NLP.

4.5. Comparison and Discussion

To enhance the accuracy of the corpus evaluation results, a corpus assessment approach must be able to compute multiple parameters at the same time and consider the relative importance between different parameters. However, the traditional keyword-list-generating approach [10] only uses the likelihood ratio method [11] to determine and rank keywords in the target corpus, which is a deficiency of corpus assessment [2,3,10,22]. Thus, to optimize the aforementioned issues, this paper proposed an extended AHP-based corpus assessment approach that integrated the likelihood ratio method, the corpus optimization approach, and the AHP method to refine corpus data, simultaneously handle multiple parameters, and consider the relative importance between different parameters for accurately evaluating keywords. COVID-19-related research articles (N = 53) from the environmental science discipline were adopted as the target corpus and used as an empirical example to verify the proposed approach.

This paper compared three approaches from three perspectives: (1) corpus optimization; (2) considering multiple parameters simultaneously; and (3) considering the relative importance between different parameters to highlight the contributions of the proposed approach (see Table 7).

Table 7. Comparison of the optimization features between three approaches.

Research Method	Optimization Feature		
	Corpus Optimization	Considering Multiple Parameters Simultaneously	Considering the Relative Importance between Different Parameters
The traditional keyword-list-generating approach [10]	No	No	No
The EW method [47]	No	Yes	No
The proposed extended AHP-based corpus assessment approach	Yes	Yes	Yes

Firstly, for corpus optimization, Table 6 indicates that function words, such as the, and, of, and in, appeared on the keyword lists generated by the traditional keyword-list-generating approach [10] and the EW method [47]. Due to function words being critical elements to form meaningful sentences, those tokens usually occupy over 40% of the corpus data. If the function words are not eliminated beforehand, the likelihood ratio method [11] will consider them as keywords because their extremely high frequency values will disguise the keyness computation results. Once the function words are included in the keyword list, content words that may be true keywords will be excluded; thus, causing bias in the computation results. Before entering the algorithm computation process, the proposed approach adopted the corpus optimization approach to eliminate function words and meaningless letters, to enhance the computation accuracy.

Secondly, when considering multiple parameters simultaneously, it is insufficient to use the traditional keyword-list-generating approach [10], as it is based on only one parameter (the keyness) to rank keywords. To make the evaluation results approach uncontroversial, the EW method [47] and the proposed approach were used to simultaneously take three parameters (i.e., the keyness, frequency, and range) into consideration, and each keyword's aggregated value was used to re-rank the keyword list.

Finally, in consideration of the relative importance of different parameters, the researchers soon discovered the major problem of the EW method [47]. Although the EW method could consider the three parameters at the same time, the importance between the three parameters would be considered as equal, and the relative importance between the parameters would not be confirmed. To compensate for this deficiency, the proposed approach integrated the AHP method [12] to calculate the relative weights of each parameter and identify the relative importance between parameters. After using the AHP method to calculate the experts' evaluation scores, the researchers discovered that the relative weights of the keyness, frequency, and range were 0.195, 0.278, and 0.528, respectively, which were not equal. The derived implications of the unequal relative weights indicated that, after generating the keyword list, the experts wanted to identify the most widely- and frequently-used keywords in the target corpus; hence, their assessment results determined the relative importance of the three parameters as range > frequency > keyness.

In summation, to handle the single-parameter evaluation deficiency of keyword ranking and optimize the traditional corpus-based assessment approach, the proposed extended AHP-based corpus assessment approach was able to exclude function words and meaningless letters, simultaneously compute multiple parameters, and consider the relative importance between different parameters.

5. Conclusions

The algorithms used for today's corpus analytical tasks are gradually being used for multiple-parameter and high-precision analysis. Keyword ranking is one of the critical techniques of corpus analysis to extract key information from the target corpus. COVID-19 is no longer limited to medical or public health issues, but also impacts other issues such as ecological systems, environmental science, and economics. High-precision COVID-19 corpus data analysis can enhance the efficiency of knowledge discovery for this novel disease. However, the traditional keyword-list-generating approach [10] is only based on the likelihood ratio method [11] to compute the tokens' keyness values, to determine and rank keywords. Thus, there is still room for optimization, as it does not automatically eliminate function words and meaningless letters or conduct multiple-parameter evaluations. Moreover, when the EW method [47] is adopted as the multiple-parameter evaluation approach to re-rank keywords, it cannot eliminate function words and meaningless letters or confirm the relative importance between each parameter to obtain more accurate results. Hence, this paper proposed an extended AHP-based corpus assessment approach to compensate the aforementioned problems, by optimizing the target corpus and conducting a multiple-parameter evaluation by using the relative weights of the parameters to determine the keywords' actual importance levels.

The proposed extended AHP-based corpus assessment approach has the following significant contributions. First, the proposed approach uses a machine-based approach to eliminate function words and meaningless letters for optimizing the target corpus, thereby further enhancing the accuracy of the followed algorithms' computations. Second, the proposed approach uses the AHP method to fully consider the relative weights of three parameters to provide calculation results with higher accuracy. Third, the proposed approach is a corpus-based assessment approach based on the perspectives of multiple parameters, which differs from traditional approaches that are based on the perspective of a single parameter. The optimized keyword list represents that each keyword has been fully considered as being truly important, which enhances the accuracy of keyword application. Fourth, the traditional corpus-based assessment approaches that were mentioned in this paper were just special cases of the proposed extended AHP-based corpus assessment approach. In addition to optimizing the traditional approaches, the proposed approach also makes itself more generally applicable. Once the keyword ranking results are optimized and improved by the proposed method, the important and domain-oriented words (i.e., keywords) will be ranked in the ahead ranks, which will improve users' IR efficiency through the corpus software. In other words, without the optimization, the ahead ranks will show the words of grammar, or those which are meaningless, unimportant, or even unrelated to the domain, which will rely on human's tasks to filter the unnecessary information. The target corpus (i.e., COVID-19 corpus data) used in this paper was only a specific case for verification and highlighted the advantages of the proposed approach; namely, any corpus data can be processed and optimized by the proposed approach.

This paper has some limitations for future researchers to overcome. With today's advanced information technology, future studies can be based on the proposed approach to develop other algorithms for optimizing corpus analytical tasks, such as the Term Frequency-Inverse Document Frequency (TF-IDF) method, high-precision NLP techniques e.g., [48,49], multiple-parameter evaluation models, and novel corpus programs.

Author Contributions: Conceptualization, L.-C.C. and K.-H.C.; methodology, L.-C.C.; software, L.-C.C.; validation, K.-H.C.; writing—original draft preparation, L.-C.C.; writing—review and editing, K.-H.C.; funding acquisition, K.-H.C. All authors have read and agreed to the published version of the manuscript.

Funding: The authors would like to thank the National Science and Technology Council, Taiwan, for financially supporting this research under Contract Nos. MOST 111-2221-E-145-003 and NSTC 111-2221-E-145-003.

Data Availability Statement: Data is unavailable due to privacy or ethical restrictions.

Conflicts of Interest: The authors declare no conflict of interest.

References

1. Anthony, L. AntConc (Version 3.5.8), Corpus Software. 2019. Available online: https://www.laurenceanthony.net/software/antconc/ (accessed on 1 January 2022).
2. Otto, P. Choosing specialized vocabulary to teach with data-driven learning: An example from civil engineering. *Engl. Specif. Purp.* **2021**, *61*, 32–46. [CrossRef]
3. Poole, R. A corpus-aided study of stance adverbs in judicial opinions and the implications for English for legal purposes instruction. *Engl. Specif. Purp.* **2021**, *62*, 117–127. [CrossRef]
4. Akhtaruzzaman, M.; Boubaker, S.; Sensoy, A. Financial contagion during COVID-19 crisis. *Financ. Res. Lett.* **2021**, *38*, 101604. [CrossRef]
5. Antonakis, J. Leadership to defeat COVID-19. *Group Process Intergroup Relat.* **2021**, *24*, 210–215. [CrossRef]
6. Chilamakuri, R.; Agarwal, S. COVID-19: Characteristics and therapeutics. *Cells* **2021**, *10*, 206. [CrossRef]
7. Aydin, S.; Nakiyingi, B.A.; Esmen, C.; Guneysu, S.; Ejjada, M. Environmental impact of coronavirus (COVID-19) from Turkish perceptive. *Environ. Dev. Sustain.* **2021**, *23*, 7573–7580. [CrossRef]
8. Sahraei, M.A.; Kuskapan, E.; Codur, M.Y. Public transit usage and air quality index during the COVID-19 lockdown. *J. Environ. Manag.* **2021**, *286*, 112166. [CrossRef]
9. SanJuan-Reyes, S.; Gomez-Olivan, L.M.; Islas-Flores, H. COVID-19 in the environment. *Chemosphere* **2021**, *263*, 127973. [CrossRef]
10. Ross, A.S.; Rivers, D.J. Discursive Deflection: Accusation of "fake news" and the spread of mis- and disinformation in the Tweets of president Trump. *Soc. Media Soc.* **2018**, *4*, 2056305118776010. [CrossRef]
11. Dunning, T. Accurate methods for the statistics of surprise and coincidence. *Comput. Linguist.* **1993**, *19*, 61–74.
12. Saaty, T.L. *The Analytic Hierarchy Process*; McGraw-Hill: New York, NY, USA, 1980.
13. Rezaei, A.; Tahsili, S. Urban vulnerability assessment using AHP. *Adv. Civ. Eng.* **2018**, *2018*, 2018601. [CrossRef]
14. Ristanovic, V.; Primorac, D.; Kozina, G. Operational risk management using multi-criteria assessment (AHP model). *Teh. Vjesn.* **2021**, *28*, 678–683.
15. Chang, K.H. Generalized multi-attribute failure mode analysis. *Neurocomputing* **2016**, *175*, 90–100. [CrossRef]
16. Chang, K.H.; Chang, Y.C.; Chain, K.; Chung, H.Y. Integrating soft set theory and fuzzy linguistic model to evaluate the performance of training simulation systems. *PLoS ONE* **2016**, *11*, e0162092. [CrossRef] [PubMed]
17. Durao, L.F.C.S.; Carvalho, M.M.; Takey, S.; Cauchick-Miguel, P.A.; Zancul, E. Internet of Things process selection: AHP selection method. *Int. J. Adv. Manuf. Technol.* **2018**, *99*, 2623–2634. [CrossRef]
18. Han, Y.; Wang, Z.H.; Lu, X.M.; Hu, B.W. Application of AHP to road selection. *ISPRS Int. J. Geo-Inf.* **2020**, *9*, 86. [CrossRef]
19. Saaty, T.L. Rank from comparisons and from ratings in the analytic hierarchy/network processes. *Eur. J. Oper. Res.* **2006**, *168*, 557–570. [CrossRef]
20. Chang, K.H.; Chain, K.; Wen, T.C.; Yang, G.K. A novel general approach for solving a supplier selection problem. *J. Test. Eval.* **2016**, *44*, 1911–1924. [CrossRef]
21. Chen, L.C.; Chang, K.H.; Chung, H.Y. A novel statistic-based corpus machine processing approach to refine a big textual data: An ESP case of COVID-19 news reports. *Appl. Sci.* **2020**, *10*, 5505. [CrossRef]
22. Chen, L.C.; Chang, K.H. A novel corpus-based computing method for handling critical word ranking issues: An example of COVID-19 research articles. *Int. J. Intell. Syst.* **2021**, *36*, 3190–3216. [CrossRef]
23. Scott, M. PC analysis of key words-and key key words. *System* **1997**, *25*, 233–245. [CrossRef]
24. Brookes, G. 'Lose weight, save the NHS': Discourses of obesity in press coverage of COVID-19. *Crit. Discourse Stud.* **2021**, *19*, 629–647. [CrossRef]
25. Ong, T.T.; McKenzie, R.M. The language of suffering: Media discourse and public attitudes towards the MH17 air tragedy in Malaysia and the UK. *Discourse Commun.* **2019**, *13*, 562–580. [CrossRef]
26. Gautam, S. The influence of COVID-19 on air quality in India: A boon or inutile. *B. Environ. Contam. Tox.* **2020**, *104*, 724–726. [CrossRef]
27. Gope, S.; Dawn, S.; Das, S.S. Effect of COVID-19 pandemic on air quality: A study based on Air Quality Index. *Environ. Sci. Pollut. R.* **2021**, *28*, 35564–35583. [CrossRef]

28. Liu, Q.; Harris, J.T.; Chiu, L.S.; Sun, D.L.; Houser, P.R.; Yu, M.Z.; Duffy, D.Q.; Little, M.M.; Yang, C.W. Spatiotemporal impacts of COVID-19 on air pollution in California, USA. *Sci. Total Environ.* **2021**, *750*, 141592. [CrossRef]
29. Yao, Y.; Pan, J.H.; Liu, Z.X.; Meng, X.; Wang, W.D.; Kan, H.D.; Wang, W.B. Ambient nitrogen dioxide pollution and spreadability of COVID-19 in Chinese cities. *Ecotox. Environ. Safe* **2021**, *208*, 111421. [CrossRef] [PubMed]
30. Lee, P.S.; Sung, Y.H.; Wu, C.C.; Ho, L.C.; Chiou, W.B. Using episodic future thinking to pre-experience climate change increases pro-environmental behavior. *Environ. Behav.* **2020**, *52*, 60–81. [CrossRef]
31. Baloch, S.; Baloch, M.A.; Zheng, T.L.; Pei, X.F. The coronavirus disease 2019 (COVID-19) pandemic. *Environ. Dev. Sustain.* **2020**, *250*, 271–278. [CrossRef] [PubMed]
32. Yi, H.S.; Ng, S.T.; Farwin, A.; Low, A.P.T.; Chang, C.M.; Lim, J. Health equity considerations in COVID-19: Geospatial network analysis of the COVID-19 outbreak in the migrant population in Singapore. *J. Travel. Med.* **2021**, *28*, taaa159. [CrossRef] [PubMed]
33. Huang, X.Y.; Wei, F.X.; Hu, L.; Wen, L.J.; Chen, K. Epidemiology and clinical characteristics of COVID-19. *Arch. Iran. Med.* **2020**, *23*, 268–271. [CrossRef] [PubMed]
34. Klopfenstein, T.; Kadiane-Oussou, N.J.; Toko, L.; Royer, P.Y.; Lepiller, Q.; Gendrin, V.; Zayet, S. Features of anosmia in COVID-19. *Med. Maladies Infect.* **2020**, *50*, 436–439. [CrossRef] [PubMed]
35. Pascarella, G.; Strumia, A.; Piliego, C.; Bruno, F.; Del Buono, R.; Costa, F.; Scarlata, S.; Agro, F.E. COVID-19 diagnosis and management: A comprehensive review. *J. Intern. Med.* **2020**, *288*, 192–206. [CrossRef] [PubMed]
36. World Health Organization (WHO). WHO Coronavirus (COVID-19) Dashboard. 2021. Available online: https://covid19.who.int/ (accessed on 1 May 2023).
37. Othman, H.; Bouslama, Z.; Brandenburg, J.T.; da Rocha, J.; Hamdi, Y.; Ghedira, K.; Srairi-Abid, N.; Hazelhurst, S. Interaction of the spike protein RBD from SARS-CoV-2 with ACE2: Similarity with SARS-CoV, hot-spot analysis and effect of the receptor polymorphism. *Biochem. Biophys. Res. Commun.* **2020**, *527*, 702–708. [CrossRef]
38. Wibmer, C.K.; Ayres, F.; Hermanus, T.; Madzivhandila, M.; Kgagudi, P.; Oosthuysen, B.; Lambson, B.E.; de Oliveira, T.; Vermeulen, M.; van der Berg, K.; et al. SARS-CoV-2 501Y.V2 escapes neutralization by South African COVID-19 donor plasma. *Nat. Med.* **2021**, *27*, 622–625. [CrossRef]
39. World Health Organization (WHO). SARS-CoV-2 Variants, Working Definitions and Actions Taken. 2021. Available online: https://www.who.int/en/activities/tracking-SARS-CoV-2-variants/ (accessed on 1 May 2023).
40. Forni, G.; Mantovani, A. COVID-19 vaccines: Where we stand and challenges ahead. *Cell Death Differ.* **2021**, *28*, 626–639. [CrossRef]
41. Berman, J.D.; Ebisu, K. Changes in US air pollution during the COVID-19 pandemic. *Sci. Total Environ.* **2020**, *739*, 139864. [CrossRef]
42. Bashir, M.F.; Ma, B.J.; Shahzad, L. A brief review of socio-economic and environmental impact of COVID-19. *Air Qual. Atmos. Health* **2020**, *13*, 1403–1409. [CrossRef]
43. Srivastava, A. COVID-19 and air pollution and meteorology-an intricate relationship: A review. *Chemosphere* **2021**, *263*, 128297. [CrossRef] [PubMed]
44. Travaglio, M.; Yu, Y.Z.; Popovic, R.; Selley, L.; Leal, N.S.; Martins, L.M. Links between air pollution and COVID-19 in England. *Environ. Pollut.* **2021**, *268*, 115859. [CrossRef] [PubMed]
45. Saadat, S.; Rawtani, D.; Hussain, C.M. Environmental perspective of COVID-19. *Sci. Total Environ.* **2020**, *728*, 138870. [CrossRef]
46. Cusmariu, A. A proof of the arithmetic mean geometric mean inequality. *Am. Math. Mon.* **1981**, *88*, 192–194. [CrossRef]
47. Chunaev, P. Interpolation by generalized exponential sums with equal weights. *J. Approx. Theory* **2020**, *254*, 105397. [CrossRef]
48. Stefano, M.; Siino, M.; Garbo, G. Improving Irony and Stereotype Spreaders Detection using Data Augmentation and Convolutional Neural Network. *CEUR Workshop Proc.* **2022**, *3180*, 2585–2593.
49. Siino, M.; Ilenia, T.; Marco, L.C. T100: A modern classic ensemble to profile irony and stereotype spreaders. *CEUR Workshop Proc.* **2022**, *3180*, 2666–2674.

Disclaimer/Publisher's Note: The statements, opinions and data contained in all publications are solely those of the individual author(s) and contributor(s) and not of MDPI and/or the editor(s). MDPI and/or the editor(s) disclaim responsibility for any injury to people or property resulting from any ideas, methods, instructions or products referred to in the content.

Article

A Flexible Dispersed Count Model Based on Bernoulli Poisson–Lindley Convolution and Its Regression Model

Hassan S. Bakouch [1,2], Christophe Chesneau [3], Radhakumari Maya [4], Muhammed Rasheed Irshad [5], Sreedeviamma Aswathy [5] and Najla Qarmalah [6,*]

1. Department of Mathematics, College of Science, Qassim University, Buraydah 51452, Saudi Arabia; h.bakouch@qu.edu.sa or hassan.bakouch@science.tanta.edu.eg
2. Department of Mathematics, Faculty of Science, Tanta University, Tanta 31111, Egypt
3. Department of Mathematics, University of Caen, 14032 Caen, France
4. Department of Statistics, University College, Thiruvananthapuram 695034, Kerala, India; publicationsofmaya@gmail.com
5. Department of Statistics, Cochin University of Science and Technology, Cochin 682022, Kerala, India; irshadmr@cusat.ac.in (M.R.I.)
6. Department of Mathematical Sciences, College of Science, Princess Nourah bint Abdulrahman University, Riyadh 11671, Saudi Arabia
* Correspondence: nmbinqurmalah@pnu.edu.sa

Abstract: Count data are encountered in real-life dealings. More understanding of such data and the extraction of important information about the data require some statistical analysis or modeling. One innovative technique to increase the modeling flexibility of well-known distributions is to use the convolution of random variables. This study examines the distribution that results from adding two independent random variables, one with the Bernoulli distribution and the other with the Poisson–Lindley distribution. The considered distribution is named as the two-parameter Bernoulli–Poisson–Lindley distribution. Many of its statistical properties are investigated, such as moments, survival and hazard rate functions, mode, dispersion behavior, mean deviation about the mean, and parameter inference based on the maximum likelihood method. To evaluate the effectiveness of the bias and mean square error of the produced estimates, a simulation exercise is carried out. Then, applications to two practical data sets are given. Finally, we construct a flexible count data regression model based on the proposed distribution with two practical examples.

Keywords: discrete statistical model; dispersion index; hazard rate function; parameter estimation; simulation; regression

MSC: 62E15

1. Introduction

In recent decades, count data analysis has drawn interest. There are many count data sets in practical as well as theoretical domains, including medicine, sports, engineering, finance, insurance, etc. (see [1]). However, we are unable to use methodologies or typical standard probability distributions to analyze them. Building adaptable models has attracted a lot of interest from statisticians and applied scientists in order to improve the modeling of count data. Therefore, it is critical to create models that are superior to standard distributions in order to successfully investigate real-world data and its attributes.

Recently, for the purpose of modeling count data, several models have evolved. The use of conventional discrete distributions as models for dependability, hazard rates, counts, etc., is limited. The widespread parametric models for analyzing such data are the Poisson, geometric, and negative binomial (NB) models (see [2]). The Poisson regression model is the most common model for modeling count data, but an obstacle arises: there is a fact that they may exhibit over- or under-dispersion, which is when a count's

conditional variance is greater or less than its conditional mean (see [3]). In these cases, the Poisson model's mean–variance relationship is a well-known drawback. This has led to the introduction of various Poisson distribution types (see [4,5]). A traditional way of overcoming over-dispersion is to allow the single parameter of the Poisson distribution to be a random variable following a given distribution. This is also known as the compounding method, and the idea was first proposed in [6]. The resultant compound distributions are also termed as mixture distributions. One such famous mixture distribution is the negative binomial distribution, obtained by mixing the Poisson distribution with a gamma distribution. In real-world count modeling applications, the negative binomial distribution with an additional dispersion parameter is widely accepted as a solution to the over-dispersion issue.

As a result, various discrete distributions based on widely used continuous distributions for reliability, hazard rates, etc., have been developed. The discrete Weibull distribution is the most well-liked of these. It was introduced in [7–9]. Since then, numerous applications have been made. There are many other recently constructed distributions with continuous analogues. The author in [10] introduced the discrete gamma distribution, which has received significant attention for applications in the areas of molecular biology and evolution. Discrete analogues of the continuous Burr and Pareto distributions were constructed in [11]. On the other hand, the authors in [12] introduced a discrete analogue of the continuous inverse Weibull distribution. The discrete Lindley distribution was proposed in [13].

There are so many models for studying over-dispersion, while only a few models are there to deal with under-dispersion, because over-dispersion exists more frequently (see [14]).

Various extensions and generalizations of the Poisson distributions were developed for both over-dispersed and under-dispersed count data in the literature over the last decade. The authors in [15] proposed the generalized Poisson (GP) regression model, whereas those of [16] introduced the Conway–Maxwell–Poisson (COM–Poisson) model. The COM–Poisson regression model was also created. The authors in [17] invented the Poisson–Tweedie regression model.

Each of the aforementioned models has some drawbacks. For instance, the GP model's range must be truncated in order to achieve under-dispersion, with the level of truncation depending on the actual model parameters. The issue is that because of the range's shortening, the probabilities no longer add up to 1. The convolutions (sum and difference) of two independent random variables are a clever way of broadening the modeling possibilities of well-known distributions.

The author in [18] proposed the discrete Poisson–Lindley distribution, a compound Poisson distribution obtained by compounding the Poisson distribution with the Lindley distribution. The authors in [19] introduced an efficient regression model for under-dispersed count data based on the Bernoulli–Poisson convolution (BerPoi) for under-dispersed count data. In it, the response variable is distributed according to the BerPoi distribution using a specific parameterization indexed by mean and dispersion parameters.

In this paper, we introduce a distribution generated from the sum of two independent random variables, one with the Bernoulli distribution and the other with the Poisson–Lindley distribution. The resulting distribution is known as the Bernoulli–Poisson–Lindley (BPL) distribution. One of its key advantages is that it is suitable for modeling both under-dispersed and over-dispersed count data, unlike the Poisson distribution. Furthermore, it has only two parameters, which reduces the complexity of the simulation study, unlike some Poisson generalizations with three parameters. Moreover, it has an increasing hazard rate, making it appropriate for modeling equipment wear and tear or ageing processes. The proposed model is appropriate for regression modeling since its moments may be retrieved in closed form.

The remaining sections of the paper are organized as follows: Section 2 presents the BPL distribution. Section 3 discusses the statistical properties of this distribution.

Section 4 introduces the parameter estimation using the maximum likelihood method, and its performance is assessed via a simulation study. The new model is shown to perform at least as well as other recently proposed two-parameter discrete models, and the conventional one-parameter discrete models using two real data sets are analyzed in Section 5. In Section 6, a regression model is developed. Finally, several key takeaways are outlined in Section 7.

2. Bernoulli-Poisson-Lindley Distribution

The BPL distribution is obtained by the distribution of the sum of two independent random variables, one with the Bernoulli distribution, and the other with the Poisson–Lindley distribution.

The result below presents a simple expression of the corresponding probability mass function (pmf).

Proposition 1. *The pmf of the BPL distribution with parameters α and θ can be expressed as*

$$p(x, \alpha, \theta) = \begin{cases} \dfrac{(1-\alpha)\theta^2(\theta+2)}{(\theta+1)^3} & if \ x = 0 \\[2mm] \dfrac{\theta^2\left[(1+\alpha\theta)(x+\theta+1) + (1-\alpha)\right]}{(\theta+1)^{x+3}} & if \ x = 1, 2, 3, \ldots \end{cases} \quad (1)$$

Proof. Let X_1 and X_2 be two independent random variables, with X_1 following the Bernoulli distribution with parameter $0 < \alpha < 1$, i.e., $P(X_1 = 0) = 1 - \alpha$ and $P(X_1 = 1) = \alpha$ and X_2 following the Poisson–Lindley distribution with parameter $\theta > 0$, i.e., $P(X_2 = x) = \dfrac{\theta^2(x+\theta+2)}{(\theta+1)^{x+3}}$ with $x = 0, 1, 2, 3, \ldots$ Then, by the definition, the BPL distribution is the distribution of $X = X_1 + X_2$. Let us now determine its pmf. For any $x = 0, 1, \ldots$, we have

$$p(x, \alpha, \theta) = P(X = x) = P(X_1 + X_2 = x)$$
$$= P(X_1 = 0)P(X_2 = x) + P(X_1 = 1)P(X_2 = x - 1).$$

In particular, for $x = 0$, we have

$$p(x, \alpha, \theta) = P(X_1 = 0)P(X_2 = 0) = \frac{(1-\alpha)\theta^2(\theta+2)}{(\theta+1)^3}.$$

For $x = 1, 2, \ldots$, we have

$$p(x, \alpha, \theta) = P(X = x)$$
$$= (1-\alpha)\frac{\theta^2(x+\theta+2)}{(\theta+1)^{x+3}} + \alpha\frac{\theta^2(x-1+\theta+2)}{(\theta+1)^{x-1+3}}$$
$$= \frac{\theta^2}{(\theta+1)^{x+3}}\left[\alpha(x+\theta+1)(\theta+1) + (1-\alpha)(x+2+\theta)\right]$$
$$= \frac{\theta^2}{(\theta+1)^{x+3}}\left[\alpha\theta(x+\theta+1) + \alpha(x+\theta+1) + (1-\alpha)(x+\theta+1+1)\right]$$
$$= \frac{\theta^2}{(\theta+1)^{x+3}}\left[\alpha\theta(x+\theta+1) + \alpha(x+\theta+1) + (1-\alpha)(x+\theta+1) + (1-\alpha)\right]$$
$$= \frac{\theta^2}{(\theta+1)^{x+3}}\left[(1+\alpha\theta)(x+\theta+1) + (1-\alpha)\right].$$

This ends the proof of Proposition 1. □

Remark 1. When $\alpha \to 0$, the Poisson–Lindley distribution is included in the BPL distribution as a special case.

Proposition 2. *The cumulative density function (cdf) of the BPL distribution can be expressed as, for any integer x,*

$$F(x, \alpha, \theta) = 1 + \frac{[-1 - \theta(3 + x + \theta + x\alpha\theta + \alpha\theta(2 + \theta))]}{(1 + \theta)^{x+3}}, \quad x = 0, 1, 2, \ldots \quad (2)$$

Proof. It follows from the geometric series expansions and some algebra, that

$$F(x, \alpha, \theta) = \sum_{k=0}^{x} p(k, \alpha, \theta)$$

$$= \frac{\theta^2(1 - \alpha)(\theta + 2)}{(\theta + 1)^3} + \sum_{k=1}^{x} \frac{\theta^2 \Big[[(1 + \alpha\theta)(k + \theta + 1)] + (1 - \alpha)\Big]}{(\theta + 1)^{k+3}}$$

$$= 1 + \frac{[-1 - \theta(3 + x + \theta + x\alpha\theta + \alpha\theta(2 + \theta))]}{(1 + \theta)^{x+3}}.$$

This ends the proof of Proposition 2. □

The corresponding survival function is given by

$$S(x, \alpha, \theta) = \frac{1 + \theta[3 + x + \theta + x\alpha\theta + \alpha\theta(2 + \theta)]}{(1 + \theta)^{x+3}}, \quad x = 0, 1, 2, \ldots \quad (3)$$

The hazard rate function (hrf) of the BPL distribution is obtained as

$$h(x, \alpha, \theta) = \begin{cases} \dfrac{(1 - \alpha)\theta^2(\theta + 2)}{1 + \theta[3 + \theta + \alpha\theta(2 + \theta)]} & \text{if } x = 0 \\ \dfrac{\theta^2[1 - \alpha + (1 + x + \theta)(1 + \alpha\theta)]}{1 + \theta[3 + x + \theta + x\alpha\theta + \alpha\theta(2 + \theta)]} & \text{if } x = 1, 2, 3, \ldots \end{cases} \quad (4)$$

Figure 1 shows the different shapes of the pmf. It clearly indicates that the BPL distribution is positively skewed, unimodal and as θ goes larger, the mass concentrates more on values closer to 0 than at higher values. Figure 2 also presents different shapes of the cdf.

Figure 3 presents different shapes of the hrf, indicating that the BPL distribution exhibits increasing hazard rates with respect to both α and θ.

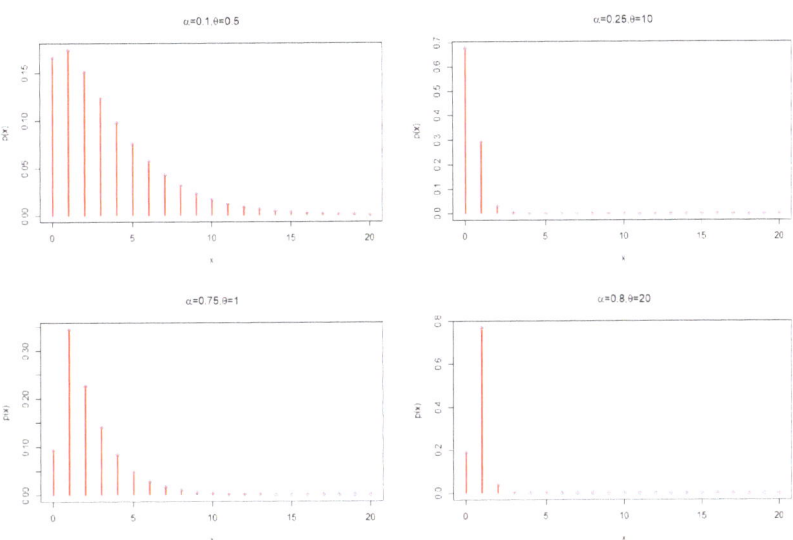

Figure 1. Pmfs of the BPL distribution for different values of the parameters.

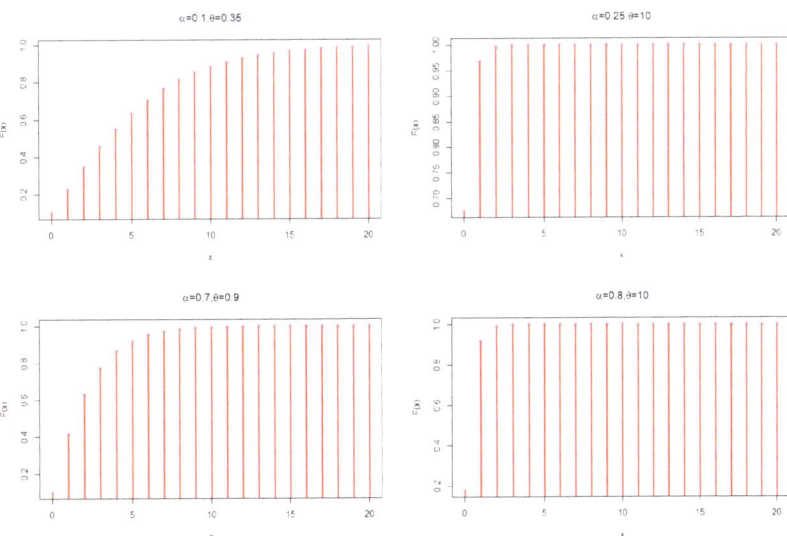

Figure 2. Cdfs of the BPL distribution for different values of the parameters.

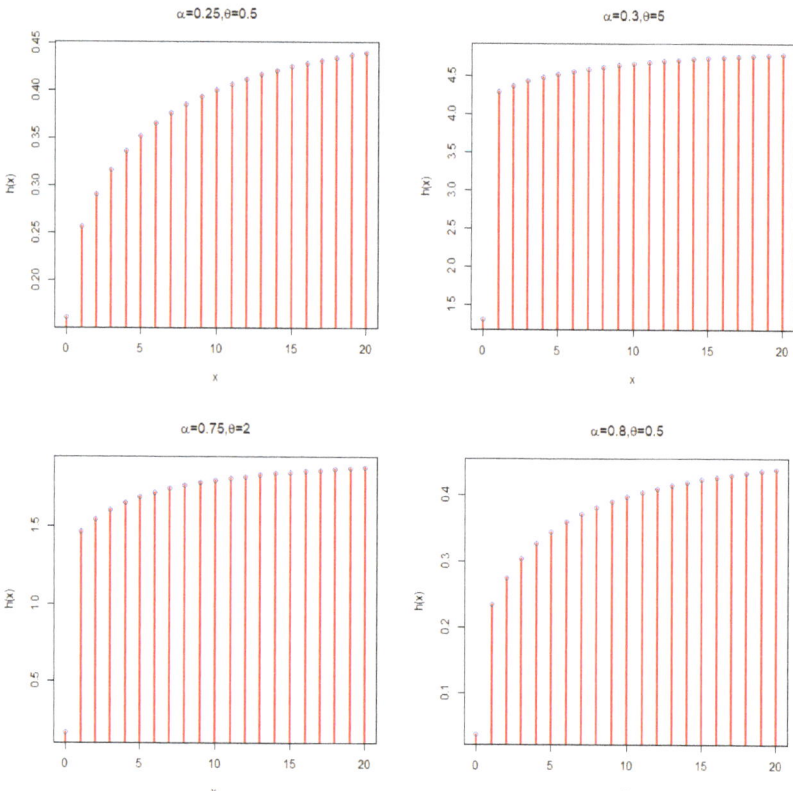

Figure 3. Hrfs of the BPL distribution for different values of the parameters.

3. Statistical Properties

3.1. Mode

We now provide some theory to the observation of the mode of the BPL distribution made in Figure 1.

Proposition 3. *Let X be a random variable following the BPL distribution. Then, the mode of X, denoted by x_m, exists in $\{0,1,2,\ldots\}$, and satisfies*

$$-1 + \frac{1}{\theta} - \theta + \frac{2+\alpha}{1+\alpha\theta} \leq x_m \leq \frac{1}{\theta} - \theta + \frac{\alpha-1}{1+\alpha\theta}, \tag{5}$$

with $x_m = 0$ if the upper bound is non-positive.

Proof. By the definition of the mode, it corresponds to the integer $x = x_m$ for which $p(x,\alpha,\theta)$ has the greatest value, where we recall that

$$p(x,\alpha,\theta) = \begin{cases} (1-\alpha)\theta^2 \dfrac{(\theta+2)}{(\theta+1)^3} & if \ x = 0 \\ \dfrac{\theta^2}{(\theta+1)^{x+3}}\left[(1+\alpha\theta)(x+\theta+1) + (1-\alpha)\right] & if \ x = 1,2,3,\ldots \end{cases} \tag{6}$$

To reach our aim, we need to solve $p(x_m, \alpha, \theta) \geq p(x_m - 1, \alpha, \theta)$ and $p(x_m, \alpha, \theta) \geq p(x_m + 1, \alpha, \theta)$. Obviously, $p(x_m, \alpha, \theta) \geq p(x_m - 1, \alpha, \theta)$ implies that

$$x_m \leq \frac{1}{\theta} - \theta + \frac{\alpha - 1}{1 + \alpha \theta}. \qquad (7)$$

Furthermore, $p(x_m, \alpha, \theta) \geq p(x_m + 1, \alpha, \theta)$ implies that

$$x_m \geq -1 + \frac{1}{\theta} - \theta + \frac{2 + \alpha}{1 + \alpha \theta}. \qquad (8)$$

By combining Equations (7) and (8), we obtain Equation (5), hence, the proof of Proposition 3. □

3.2. Moments, Skewness, and Kurtosis

Hereafter, let X be a random variable following the BPL distribution. Then, after some algebraic developments, the probability generating function of X is given by

$$P(s) = E(s^X) = \frac{[1 + (-1 + s)\alpha]\theta^2 (2 - s + \theta)}{(1 + \theta)(1 - s + \theta)^2},$$

for $s < \theta + 1$.

The moment-generating function of X can be obtained by replacing s by e^t, for $t < \log(\theta + 1)$, which gives

$$M(t) = E(e^{tX}) = \frac{[1 + (-1 + e^t)\alpha]\theta^2 (2 - e^t + \theta)}{(1 + \theta)(1 - e^t + \theta)^2}.$$

Basically, the r-th moment about the origin of X is derived as

$$E(X^r) = \sum_{x=0}^{\infty} x^r p(x, \alpha, \theta) = \sum_{x=1}^{\infty} x^r \frac{\theta^2}{(\theta + 1)^{x+3}} [(1 + \alpha\theta)(x + \theta + 1) + (1 - \alpha)].$$

Thus, after an intense use of the geometric series formulas (see Appendix A), the first four moments of X are

$$E(X) = \alpha + \frac{2 + \theta}{\theta(\theta + 1)},$$

$$E(X^2) = \frac{6 + \theta[4 + \theta + \alpha(4 + \theta(3 + \theta))]}{\theta^2(1 + \theta)},$$

$$E(X^3) = \frac{24 + \theta[24 + \theta(8 + \theta) + \alpha(3 + \theta)(6 + \theta(4 + \theta))]}{\theta^3(1 + \theta)},$$

and

$$E(X^4) = \frac{120 + \theta[168 + \theta[78 + \theta(16 + \theta)] + \alpha[96 + \theta(132 + \theta[64 + \theta(15 + \theta)])]]}{\theta^4(1 + \theta)}.$$

Now, the variance of X is calculated as

$$V(X) = E(X^2) - [E(X)]^2 = \frac{2 + \theta[6 + \theta(4 + \theta + (1 - \alpha)\alpha(1 + \theta)^2)]}{\theta^2(1 + \theta)^2}.$$

Figure 4 presents the plots of the variance of X for different values of the parameters α and θ. We see that the variance decreases when α is fixed and θ increases.

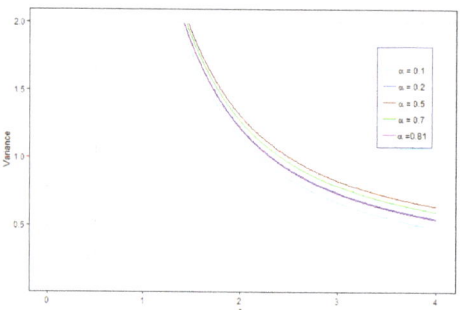

Figure 4. Variance of the BPL distribution for different values of the parameters.

On the other hand, based on the first four moments of X, the skewness of X is

$$Skewness(X) = \frac{[4 + \theta(18 + \theta[32 + \theta(22 + \alpha(1+\theta)^3 - 3\alpha^2(1+\theta)^3 + 2\alpha^3(1+\theta)^3 + \theta(7+\theta))])]^2}{[2 - \theta(6 - \theta[4 + \theta + (1-\alpha)\alpha(1+\theta^2)])]^3}.$$

Furthermore, the kurtosis of X is

$$Kurtosis(X) = \frac{1}{[-2 + \theta(-6 + \theta[-4 - \theta - (1-\alpha)\alpha(1+\theta)^2])]^2}\bigg[24 + \theta(144 + \theta[338 + 6\alpha^3\theta^2(1+\theta)^4 - 3\alpha^4\theta^2(1+\theta)^4 + \alpha(1+\theta)^2[12 + \theta(4+\theta)(9+\theta[4+\theta])] + \theta[406 + \theta(258 + \theta(87 + \theta[15+\theta]))] - 2\alpha^2(1+\theta)^2[6 + \theta(18 + \theta[14 + \theta(7+2\theta)])]])\bigg].$$

Figure 5 presents the plots of the skewness and kurtosis of X, respectively. From these plots, when the value of α is held constant, and θ increases, a significant effect on both the skewness and kurtosis is observed. Furthermore, when θ increases, the BPL distribution is rightly skewed and leptokurtic.

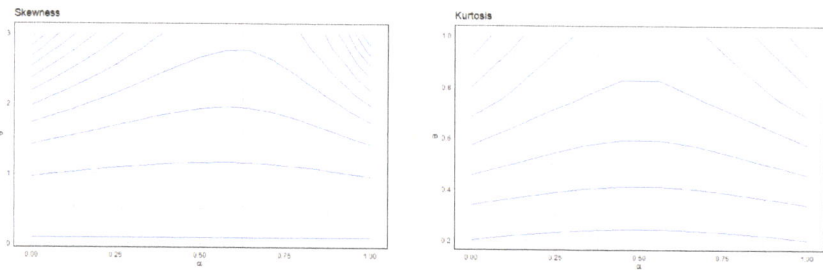

Figure 5. Skewness and kurtosis of the BPL distribution for different values of the parameters.

3.3. Dispersion Index and Coefficient of Variation

In this section, we discuss the dispersion index (DI) and coefficient of variation (CV) associated with the BPL distribution. The CV of X is obtained as

$$CV(X) = \frac{\sqrt{2 + \theta[6 + \theta(4 + \theta + (1-\alpha)\alpha(1+\theta)^2)]}}{2 + \theta + \alpha\theta(\theta+1)}.$$

The DI of X is given by

$$DI(X) = 1 + \frac{1}{\theta} + \frac{1}{1+\theta} - \left(\alpha + \frac{1-\alpha+\alpha\theta}{2+\theta(1+\alpha+\alpha\theta)}\right).$$

Clearly, $DI(X)$ is greater than 1 when θ tends to 0, and less than 1 when θ tends to ∞. Thus, the BPL distribution has under- or over-dispersed properties.

Numerical values for some moment measures, such as mean, variance, DI, skewness, and kurtosis for the BPL distribution for different sets of parameter values are given in Tables 1 and 2. It can be observed that the mean and variance decrease as θ tends to ∞ for fixed values of α.

Table 1. Numerical values for some moment measures associated with the BPL distribution for $\alpha = 0.1$ and different values of θ.

Measures	θ				
	0.1	10	50	99	999
Mean	19.1909	0.2091	0.1204	0.1102	0.1010
Variance	218.3545	0.2108	0.1108	0.1003	0.0910
DI	11.3780	1.0083	0.9204	0.9102	0.9010
Skewness	2.0459	5.1086	6.4470	6.7468	7.0719
Kurtosis	6.0496	8.5888	8.2779	8.2024	8.1209

Table 2. Numerical values for some moment measures associated with the BPL distribution for $\alpha = 0.3$ and different values of θ.

Measures	θ				
	0.1	10	50	99	999
Mean	19.3909	0.4091	0.3204	0.3102	0.3010
Variance	218.4745	0.3309	0.2308	0.2203	0.2110
DI	11.2669	0.8087	0.7204	0.7102	0.7010
Skewness	2.0426	1.4711	0.9079	0.8355	0.7692
Kurtosis	6.0462	4.3926	2.4144	2.1001	1.7964

3.4. Mean Deviation about the Mean

The mean deviation (MD) about the mean measures the amount of scatter in a population. Let μ be the mean of the BPL distribution, i.e., $\mu = E(X) = \alpha + \frac{2+\theta}{\theta(\theta+1)}$. Then the MD about the mean is defined as $MD(X) = E(|X - \mu|)$, and can be calculated as

$$MD(X) = \sum_{x=0}^{\infty} |x - \mu| p(x, \alpha, \theta)$$

$$= \mu p(0, \alpha, \theta) + \sum_{x=1}^{\lfloor\mu\rfloor} (\mu - x) p(x, \alpha, \theta) + \sum_{x=\lfloor\mu\rfloor+1}^{\infty} (x - \mu) p(x, \alpha, \theta)$$

$$= \frac{(1+\theta)^{-3-\lfloor\mu\rfloor}}{\theta} \Big[2(1+\theta)^2 [2 + \theta(1 + \alpha + \alpha\theta)] - 2\theta(1 + \theta[3 + \theta + \alpha\theta(2+\theta)])\mu$$

$$- (1+\theta)^{2+\lfloor\mu\rfloor} [2 + \theta(1 + \alpha + \alpha\theta - (1+\theta)\mu)]$$

$$+ 2\theta\lfloor\mu\rfloor(2 + \theta[4 + \alpha + \theta + \alpha\theta(3 + \theta - \mu) - \mu] + \theta(1+\alpha\theta)\lfloor\mu\rfloor)\Big],$$

where $\lfloor\mu\rfloor$ is the greatest integer less than or equal to μ.

Figure 6 shows the plot of the MD about the mean of X. From this plot, we observe that when θ increases, the values of the MD about the mean decrease.

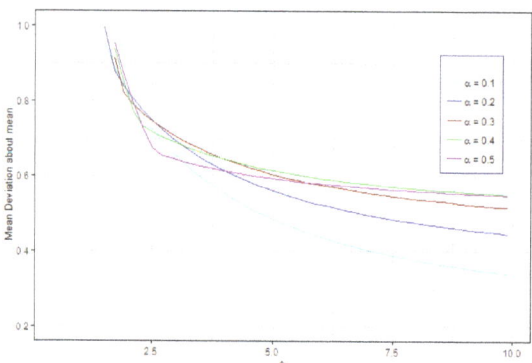

Figure 6. MD about the mean of the BPL distribution for different values of α and θ.

4. Parameter Estimation

Parameter estimation is an important step toward a deeper understanding of the process. The classical method of estimation, the maximum likelihood (ML) method, is used here to estimate the parameters. Let $X_1, X_2, \ldots, X_n$ be a random sample of size n from a BPL distribution with unknown parameters α and θ. Let $x_1, \ldots, x_n$ be the n observed values. Let y be the number of x_i taking the value 0 and $(n - y)$ of x_i's are taking the nonzero values. The log-likelihood function is given by

$$\log L(\alpha, \theta) = y \log(1 - \alpha) + 2y \log \theta + y \log(\theta + 2) - 3y \log(\theta + 1) + 2(n - y) \log \theta \\ - 3(n - y) \log(1 + \theta) \\ + \sum_{i=1, x_i \neq 0}^{n-y} \left\{ \log\left[(1 + \alpha\theta)(1 + \theta + x_i) + (1 - \alpha)\right] - x_i \log(\theta + 1) \right\}.$$

The maximum likelihood estimates (MLEs) of α and θ are the values that maximize $\log L(\alpha, \theta)$. They are denoted as $\hat{\alpha}$ and $\hat{\theta}$, respectively. The partial derivatives of $\log L(\alpha, \theta)$ with respect to each parameter are the following:

$$\frac{\partial}{\partial \alpha} \log L(\alpha, \theta) = \sum_{i=1}^{n-y} \left\{ \frac{\theta(1 + x_i + \theta) - 1}{(1 + \alpha\theta)(1 + x_i + \theta) + (1 - \alpha)} \right\} - \frac{y}{1 - \alpha},$$

$$\frac{\partial}{\partial \theta} \log L(\alpha, \theta) = \sum_{i=1}^{n-y} \left\{ \frac{(1 + \alpha\theta) + (1 + x_i + \theta)\alpha}{(1 + \alpha\theta)(1 + x_i + \theta) + (1 - \alpha)} \right\} - \frac{n(3 + \bar{x})}{\theta + 1} + \frac{y}{\theta + 2} + \frac{2n}{\theta}.$$

In order to obtain the MLEs, note that the above system of equations set to zero contains non-linear equations and does not have an explicit solution. Consequently, the system must be solved numerically, for example, using the statistical programming language **R** (see Appendix A).

Simulation Study

In this section, a brief simulation study is performed to evaluate the asymptotic behavior of the MLEs for different parametric combinations. Here the iteration is carried out for different sample sizes (50, 100, 200, 500, 1000) and $N = 1000$ replications are used for the same. The measures such as percentage relative bias (PRB) and mean square errors (MSEs) are calculated with the following formulas:

$$PRB = \frac{\sum_{i=1}^{N}(a - \hat{a}_i)}{\sum_{i=1}^{N} \hat{a}_i} \times 100,$$

where $a \in \{\alpha, \theta\}$, $\hat{a}_i$ is the MLE of a at the i-th replication, and

$$MSE = \frac{1}{N}\sum_{i=1}^{N}(a_i - \hat{a}_i)^2.$$

It is evident from Table 3 that all the estimates are asymptotically unbiased as n increases, i.e., with the PRBs approaching zero and the MSEs decreasing to zero.

Table 3. Simulation results.

	\multicolumn{6}{c}{$\alpha = 0.25, \theta = 0.6$}
n	MLE (α)	PRB (α)	MSE (α)	MLE (θ)	PRB (θ)	MSE (θ)
50	0.24715	1.15434	0.29785	0.61781	−2.88305	0.10035
100	0.24663	1.36523	0.19457	0.60301	−0.49874	0.06998
200	0.23642	3.74246	0.15031	0.60426	−0.70581	0.05007
500	0.24617	1.55751	0.08833	0.60124	−0.20587	0.03022
1000	0.25123	−0.88448	0.06078	0.60058	−0.09602	0.02079
	\multicolumn{6}{c}{$\alpha = 0.5, \theta = 1.2$}
n	MLE (α)	PRB (α)	MSE (α)	MLE (θ)	PRB (θ)	MSE (θ)
50	0.49695	0.61431	0.15829	1.24485	−3.60276	0.24016
100	0.50188	−0.37455	0.10670	1.22124	−1.73911	0.16789
200	0.49925	0.15014	0.07770	1.21047	−0.86520	0.11252
500	0.50077	−0.15318	0.04811	1.20429	−0.35658	0.06926
1000	0.50027	−0.05312	0.03408	1.20472	−0.39213	0.04991
	\multicolumn{6}{c}{$\alpha = 0.65, \theta = 3$}
n	MLE (α)	PRB (α)	MSE (α)	MLE (θ)	PRB (θ)	MSE (θ)
50	0.64882	0.18225	0.02067	3.26433	−8.09744	1.14048
100	0.65254	−0.38979	0.06712	3.10000	−3.22588	0.60840
200	0.64524	0.73814	0.04595	3.03897	−1.28222	0.41492
500	0.65194	−0.29778	0.09402	3.03066	−1.01156	0.26135
1000	0.65068	−0.10485	0.02939	3.00499	−0.16592	0.17036

5. Empirical Studies

This section describes a comparison of the BPL model with other competing models given in Table 4, to demonstrate the BPL model's practical effectiveness. Two practical data sets are considered. The comparison of the fitted models is based on conventional metrics: the Akaike information criterion (AIC), the Bayesian information criterion (BIC), the Kolmogorov–Smirnov test (KS) and the resulting p-value. In particular, the formulas for the AIC and BIC are

$$AIC = -2\log L + 2r$$

and

$$BIC = -2\log L + r\log n,$$

respectively, where $\log L$ is the estimation of the log-likelihood function and r is the number of parameters.

The pmfs of the competing models are given as follows:

- For the DG model:

$$p(x, \beta, \gamma) = e^{-\beta\gamma^{x+1}} - e^{-\beta\gamma^x}, \ x = 0, 1, 2, \ldots, \beta > 0, 0 < \gamma < 1.$$

- For the DIW model:

$$p(x, \beta, \gamma) = \begin{cases} \beta & if \ x = 1 \\ \beta^{x^{-\gamma}} - \beta^{(x-1)^{-\gamma}} & if \ x = 2, 3, 4, \ldots, 0 < \beta < 1, \gamma > 0. \end{cases}$$

- For the PQX model:

$$p(x, \beta, \gamma) = \frac{2\beta\gamma(\gamma+1)^2 + \gamma^3(x+1)(x+2)}{2(\beta+1)(\gamma+1)^{x+3}}, \ x = 0, 1, 2, \ldots, \beta > 0, \gamma > 0.$$

Table 4. Discrete competitive models.

Distribution	Abbreviation	Reference
Discrete Gumbel	DG	[20]
Discrete inverse Weibull	DIW	[12]
Poisson-quasi-xgamma	PQX	[21]
Poisson	-	-
Geometric	-	-

5.1. Survival Times

The first data set consists of survival times in days for 72 guinea pigs. These data are taken from [22]. The flexibility of the BPL model is compared with other discrete flexible models, such as the DG, DIW, PQX, Poisson, and geometric models. The results of the fitted models along with their estimates together with the standard errors (SEs) are given in Table 5. This table demonstrates that the Poisson and geometric models, two of the researched models, may not be fitted to the relevant data set (based on their p-values), but we nevertheless use them for comparison since they are very common models to take into account. The BPL model, as can be observed, offers the highest p-value and the smallest AIC, BIC, and KS statistic values.

Table 5. AIC, BIC and p-values values for the survival times data.

Model	Parameters	Estimates (SE)	AIC	BIC	KS Value	p-Value
BPL	α	0.9900 (2.9821)	793.0159	797.5692	0.1299	0.176
	θ	0.0200 (0.0013)				
DG	β	4.2894 (0.7061)	800.2187	804.7720	0.14825	0.08443
	γ	0.9789 (0.0021)				
DIW	β	1.517024×10^{-41} (1.1371)	801.8879	806.4412	0.14357	0.1028
	γ	1.1214 (0.4120)				
Poisson	β	99.8194 (1.1774)	795.1784	797.9551	0.5697	2.2×10^{-16}
Geometric	β	0.0100 (0.0012)	808.1606	810.4372	0.2232	0.0015
PQL	β	1.527183×10^{-7} (0.0779)	798.0983	802.6516	0.1768	0.0222
	γ	3.005888×10^{-2} (0.0025)				

5.2. Final Examination Marks

The results of 48 slow space students' final mathematics exams from the Indian Institute of Technology in Kanpur in 2003 are included in the second data set (see [23]). The results of the fitted models given in Table 6.

The BPL model has the largest p-value, the smallest KS value, and the smallest AIC and BIC values, as seen in Tables 5 and 6. We can therefore conclude that the BPL model outperforms all other competitive models for the two real-life data sets.

Table 6. AIC, BIC and *p*-values values for the final examination marks.

Model	Parameters	Estimates (SE)	AIC	BIC	KS Value	*p*-Value
BPL	α	0.9950 (4.7501)	399.4703	403.2127	0.0976	0.7507
	θ	0.0774 (0.0114)				
DG	β	4.4664 (0.8884)	402.6350	406.3774	0.0987	0.7375
	γ	0.9224 (0.0089)				
DIW	β	2.750165×10^{-15} (0.4321)	406.3307	410.0731	0.1552	0.1978
	γ	1.3479 (0.5324)				
Poisson	β	25.8958 (0.7345)	795.1784	797.0496	0.3998	4.342×10^{-7}
Geometric	β	0.0386 (0.0055)	408.5140	410.3852	0.2501	0.0049
PQX	β	1.07574×10^{-8} (0.2323)	399.9926	403.7350	0.1093	0.6149
	γ	1.158624×10^{-1} (0.0183)				

6. Bernoulli–Poisson–Lindley Regression Model

We already mentioned that the BPL distribution is capable of modeling under-dispersed as well as over-dispersed data sets. However, over-dispersed data sets are of utmost significance. In order to describe such data sets, this section introduces a count regression model based on the BPL distribution.

6.1. Model Construction

Let Y be a random variable with the BPL distribution that indicates how many times an event has been counted.

Consider the following reparametrization:

$$\theta = \frac{\alpha + 1 - \mu + \sqrt{(\mu - \alpha - 1)^2 + 8(\mu - \alpha)}}{2(\mu - \alpha)}.$$

Then the pmf of the BPL distribution can be expressed in terms of the mean $E(Y) = \mu > 0$ as

$$P(y, \alpha, \mu) = \begin{cases} (1-\alpha)\left(\frac{\alpha+1-\mu+\sqrt{(\mu-\alpha-1)^2+8(\mu-\alpha)}}{2(\mu-\alpha)}\right)^2 \frac{\left(\frac{\alpha+1-\mu+\sqrt{(\mu-\alpha-1)^2+8(\mu-\alpha)}}{2(\mu-\alpha)}+2\right)}{\left(\frac{\alpha+1-\mu+\sqrt{(\mu-\alpha-1)^2+8(\mu-\alpha)}}{2(\mu-\alpha)}+1\right)^3}, & \text{if } y = 0 \\ \frac{\left(\frac{\alpha+1-\mu+\sqrt{(\mu-\alpha-1)^2+8(\mu-\alpha)}}{2(\mu-\alpha)}\right)^2}{\left(\frac{\alpha+1-\mu+\sqrt{(\mu-\alpha-1)^2+8(\mu-\alpha)}}{2(\mu-\alpha)}+1\right)^{y+3}} \left(\left[(1+\alpha\frac{\alpha+1-\mu+\sqrt{(\mu-\alpha-1)^2+8(\mu-\alpha)}}{2(\mu-\alpha)})\right.\right. \\ \left.\left. [y+\frac{\alpha+1-\mu+\sqrt{(\mu-\alpha-1)^2+8(\mu-\alpha)}}{2(\mu-\alpha)}+1]\right] + (1-\alpha)\right), & \text{if } y = 1, 2, 3, \ldots \end{cases} \quad (9)$$

with $0 < \alpha < 1$, $\mu > 0$ and $\mu - \alpha > 0$.

Assume that we have n observations of the response variable Y, which is also the response variable, with the i-th observation being a realization of a random variable Y_i for $i = 1, 2, \ldots, n$. In addition, assume that the mean of the response variable Y_i is linked to the covariates with a log link function given by

$$\mu_i = e^{x_i^T \gamma}, \quad i = 1, 2, \ldots, n \quad (10)$$

where $x_i^T = (1, x_{i1}, x_{i2}, x_{i3}, \ldots, x_{ik})^T$ is the covariate vector and $\gamma = (\gamma_0, \gamma_1, \ldots, \gamma_k)$ is the unknown regression coefficient vector. Substituting Equation (10) in Equation (9), a linear form for the pmf of Y_i provided that $\{X_i^T = x_i^T\}$ is realized and the BPL distribution with parameters α and μ_i, is obtained as

$$P(y_i, \alpha, e^{x_i^T \gamma}) = \begin{cases} (1-\alpha)\left(\dfrac{\alpha+1-e^{x_i^T\gamma}+\sqrt{(e^{x_i^T\gamma}-\alpha-1)^2+8(e^{x_i^T\gamma}-\alpha)}}{2(e^{x_i^T\gamma}-\alpha)}\right)^2 \\ \dfrac{\left(\dfrac{\alpha+1-e^{x_i^T\gamma}+\sqrt{(e^{x_i^T\gamma}-\alpha-1)^2+8(e^{x_i^T\gamma}-\alpha)}}{2(e^{x_i^T\gamma}-\alpha)}+2\right)}{\left(\dfrac{\alpha+1-e^{x_i^T\gamma}+\sqrt{(e^{x_i^T\gamma}-\alpha-1)^2+8(e^{x_i^T\gamma}-\alpha)}}{2(e^{x_i^T\gamma}-\alpha)}+1\right)^3}, & \text{if } y_i = 0 \\[2em] \dfrac{\left(\dfrac{\alpha+1-e^{x_i^T\gamma}+\sqrt{(e^{x_i^T\gamma}-\alpha-1)^2+8(e^{x_i^T\gamma}-\alpha)}}{2(e^{x_i^T\gamma}-\alpha)}\right)^2}{\left(\dfrac{\alpha+1-e^{x_i^T\gamma}+\sqrt{(e^{x_i^T\gamma}-\alpha-1)^2+8(e^{x_i^T\gamma}-\alpha)}}{2(e^{x_i^T\gamma}-\alpha)}+1\right)^{y_i+3}} \\ \left(\left(1+\alpha\dfrac{\alpha+1-e^{x_i^T\gamma}+\sqrt{(e^{x_i^T\gamma}-\alpha-1)^2+8(e^{x_i^T\gamma}-\alpha)}}{2(e^{x_i^T\gamma}-\alpha)}\right)\right. \\ \left.\left(y_i+\dfrac{\alpha+1-e^{x_i^T\gamma}+\sqrt{(e^{x_i^T\gamma}-\alpha-1)^2+8(e^{x_i^T\gamma}-\alpha)}}{2(e^{x_i^T\gamma}-\alpha)}+1\right)+(1-\alpha)\right), & \text{if } y_i = 1, 2, 3, \ldots \end{cases}$$

6.2. Estimation of the Model Parameters

The ML method is used to estimate the parameter α and the regression coefficient vector γ of the model. The logarithm of the likelihood function L of the BPL count regression model is given by

$$\log L = \sum_{i=1}^{y} \left\{ \log(1-\alpha) + 2\log\left(\frac{\alpha+1-e^{x_i^T\gamma}+\sqrt{(e^{x_i^T\gamma}-\alpha-1)^2+8(e^{x_i^T\gamma}-\alpha)}}{2(e^{x_i^T\gamma}-\alpha)}\right)^2 + \right.$$
$$\log\left(\left(\frac{\alpha+1-e^{x_i^T\gamma}+\sqrt{(e^{x_i^T\gamma}-\alpha-1)^2+8(e^{x_i^T\gamma}-\alpha)}}{2(e^{x_i^T\gamma}-\alpha)}\right)^2 + 2\right) -$$
$$\left. 3\log\left(\left(\frac{\alpha+1-e^{x_i^T\gamma}+\sqrt{(e^{x_i^T\gamma}-\alpha-1)^2+8(e^{x_i^T\gamma}-\alpha)}}{2(e^{x_i^T\gamma}-\alpha)}\right)^2 + 1\right) \right\} +$$
$$\sum_{i=1, x_i \ne 0}^{n-y} \left\{ 2\log\left(\frac{\alpha+1-e^{x_i^T\gamma}+\sqrt{(e^{x_i^T\gamma}-\alpha-1)^2+8(e^{x_i^T\gamma}-\alpha)}}{2(e^{x_i^T\gamma}-\alpha)}\right)^2 + \right.$$
$$\log\left(\left(1+\alpha\frac{\alpha+1-e^{x_i^T\gamma}+\sqrt{(e^{x_i^T\gamma}-\alpha-1)^2+8(e^{x_i^T\gamma}-\alpha)}}{2(e^{x_i^T\gamma}-\alpha)}\right)\right)$$
$$\left(y_i + \left(\frac{\alpha+1-e^{x_i^T\gamma}+\sqrt{(e^{x_i^T\gamma}-\alpha-1)^2+8(e^{x_i^T\gamma}-\alpha)}}{2(e^{x_i^T\gamma}-\alpha)}\right) + 1\right) +$$
$$\left. (1-\alpha)\right) - (y_i+3)\log\left(\left(\frac{\alpha+1-e^{x_i^T\gamma}+\sqrt{(e^{x_i^T\gamma}-\alpha-1)^2+8(e^{x_i^T\gamma}-\alpha)}}{2(e^{x_i^T\gamma}-\alpha)}\right) + 1\right)\right\}. \quad (11)$$

Now the unknown parameters α and γ are obtained by maximizing Equation (11).

6.3. Residual Analysis

This part introduces a residual to test the goodness-of-fit of the BPL model defined in Section 6.1 based on randomized quantile (RQ) residuals. Let $F(y, \mu)$ be the cdf of the BPL model in which the regression structures are assumed in the parameter as in Equation (10). The i-th RQ residual of the BPL regression model is

$$r_i^q = \Phi^{-1}(F(U_i, \hat{\mu}_i)), \quad i = 1, 2, \ldots, n,$$

where $\hat{\mu}_i = e^{x_i^T \hat{\gamma}}$, and $\Phi^{-1}(\cdot)$ represents the quantile function of the standard normal distribution. Furthermore, U_i is a random variable that follows the uniform $U\left(F(y_i - 1, \hat{\mu}_i), F(y_i, \hat{\mu}_i)\right)$ distribution. When the fitted model is correct, the RQ residuals are normally distributed with zero mean and unit variance.

6.4. Simulation of the Bernoulli–Poisson–Lindley Regression Model

This section provides a simulation exercise to assess how well the MLEs of the BPL regression model's parameters performed. We generate $N = 1000$ samples of sizes $n = 100, 200, 300$, and 500 for the parametric combinations ($\alpha = 0.25, \gamma_0 = 0.5, \gamma_1 = 0.4, \gamma_2 = 0.6$) and ($\alpha = 0.5, \gamma_0 = 0.3, \gamma_1 = 1.2, \gamma_2 = 2$) by using $\mu_i = \exp(\gamma_0 + \gamma_1 x_{i1} + \gamma_2 x_{i2})$. The independent variables x_{i1} and x_{i2} are generated from the standard uniform distribution, i.e., $U(0,1)$. On the basis of the estimates, biases, and MSEs, the simulation findings are discussed. The simulation results are listed in Table 7.

Table 7. Simulation results for the BPL regression model.

	$\alpha = 0.25, \gamma_0 = 0.5, \gamma_1 = 0.4, \gamma_2 = 0.6$					$\alpha = 0.5, \gamma_0 = 0.3, \gamma_1 = 1.2, \gamma_2 = 2$			
n	Parameters	Estimates	Bias	MSE	n	Parameters	Estimates	Bias	MSE
100	α	0.25781	0.00781	0.01867	100	α	0.51368	0.01368	0.01360
	γ_0	0.53025	0.03025	0.49531		γ_0	0.37353	0.07353	0.16408
	γ_1	0.49863	0.09863	0.26276		γ_1	1.19985	0.00015	0.37260
	γ_2	0.65218	0.05218	0.31935		γ_2	1.80780	0.19220	1.21552
200	α	0.25420	0.00420	0.00987	200	α	0.50673	0.00673	0.00525
	γ_0	0.53000	0.03000	0.55058		γ_0	0.35115	0.05115	0.11311
	γ_1	0.47112	0.07112	0.20901		γ_1	1.18296	0.01705	0.74723
	γ_2	0.63384	0.03384	0.24494		γ_2	1.93278	0.06722	1.10588
300	α	0.25214	0.00214	0.00223	300	α	0.50106	0.00106	0.00370
	γ_0	0.50183	0.00183	0.38789		γ_0	0.31464	0.01464	0.08764
	γ_1	0.44939	0.04939	0.16479		γ_1	1.20512	0.00512	0.52853
	γ_2	0.61069	0.01069	0.17588		γ_2	1.93557	0.06443	0.53403
500	α	0.25051	0.00051	0.00430	500	α	0.50121	0.00121	0.00215
	γ_0	0.50031	0.00031	0.00031		γ_0	0.30628	0.00628	0.07150
	γ_1	0.40352	0.01352	0.00141		γ_1	1.20053	0.00052	0.35168
	γ_2	0.60321	0.00321	0.16040		γ_2	1.96866	0.03134	0.36140

Table 7 shows that the bias and MSEs reduce as sample size rises, indicating the consistency property of the MLEs for estimating the regression parameters.

6.5. Applications

Two data sets are used here to assess the performance of the BPL regression model. Only the Poisson distribution is considered in both scenarios for comparison.

6.5.1. Titanic Survivors Data

The first data set used is the Titanic survivors data. These data, which come from the Titanic's survival record, show the proportion of survivors among all the passengers, broken down by age, sex, and class. They are available in the **CountsEPPM** package of the statistical programming language **R**. The aim of the study is to investigate the effects of *age* (adult) (x_{1i}), *sex* (male) (x_{2i}), and *classes* (2-nd class and 3-rd class) (x_{3i} and x_{4i}) on the number of survivors (y_i).

The summary statistics for the Titanic survivors data are shown in Table 8.

Table 8. Summary statistics for the Titanic survivors data set.

Variables	Min	Max	Median
survive	1	140	14
age adult	0	0.5	1
sex male	0	0.5	1
2-nd class	0	0	1
3-rd class	0	0	1

The results of the regression analysis applied to the Titanic survivors data are given in Table 9.

Table 9. Modeling results for the Titanic survivors data set.

Covariates	Poisson		BPL	
	Estimates	p-Values	Estimates	p-Values
γ_0	2.71128	<0.001	2.25802	<0.001
γ_1	2.04421	<0.001	2.03979	<0.001
γ_2	−0.59605	<0.001	−0.37823	0.01094
γ_3	−0.52602	<0.001	0.07812	0.03181
γ_4	−0.12805	0.02179	0.39305	<0.001
AIC		145.83530		111.45620
BIC		148.74480		114.85050

From this table, it is clear that the BPL regression model has a better fit than the Poisson regression model with the smallest AIC and BIC. In conclusion, all the covariates can explain the number of survivors.

The corresponding quantile–quantile (Q–Q) plots are shown in Figure 7. These graphs demonstrate that the BPL regression model is better than the Poisson regression model.

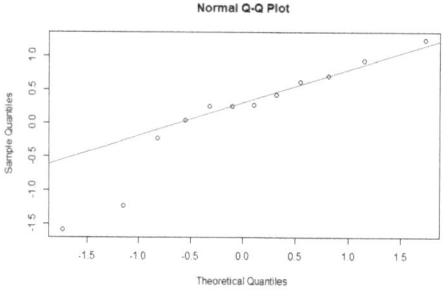

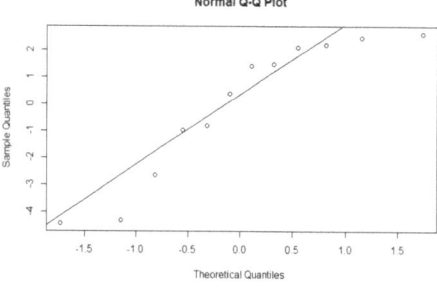

Figure 7. The Q–Q plots of the BPL and Poisson regression models, respectively.

6.5.2. Low Birth Weight Data

The second data set used here is the low birth weight data. It is taken from the **COUNT** package in the statistical programming language **R**. The BPL regression model is used to model the number of low-weight babies (*lowbw*) (y_i) by using the covariates, *cases* (x_{1i}), *race1* (x_{2i}) and *race2* (x_{3i}). The summary statistics for the low birth weight data are shown in Table 10.

Table 10. Summary statistics for the low birth weight data set.

Variables	Min	Max	Median
lowbw	12	60	16.5
cases	30	90	165
race1	0	0.5	1
race2	0	0	1

The results of the regression analysis applied to the low birth weight data are given in Table 11.

Table 11. Modeling results for the low birth weight data set.

Covariates	Poisson		BPL	
	Estimates	*p*-Values	Estimates	*p*-Values
γ_0	2.0679	<0.001	2.2041	0.0194
γ_1	0.0124	<0.001	0.0119	0.2390
γ_2	−0.3287	0.0690	−0.4641	0.8689
γ_3	0.2192	0.0505	0.1506	0.8273
AIC	61.9544		59.31121	
BIC	60.9132		58.06177	

According to this table, the BPL regression model offers a better fit than the Poisson regression model since it has lower AIC and BIC values. Additionally, the covariates have no statistically significant effect on the number of low-weight babies.

Figure 8 presents the Q–Q plots corresponding with the low birth weight data. Here also, these graphs demonstrate that the BPL regression model is better than the Poisson regression model.

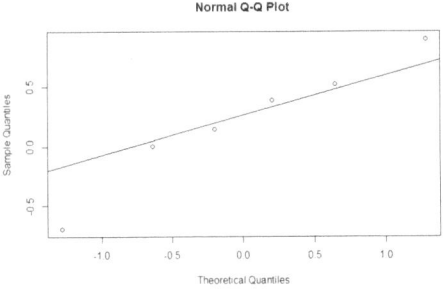

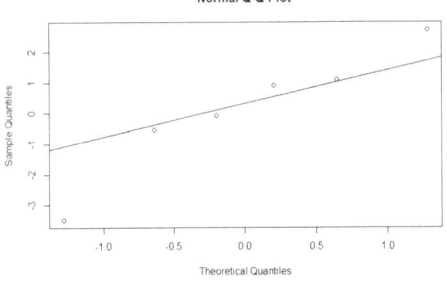

Figure 8. The Q–Q plots of the BPL and Poisson regression models, respectively.

7. Conclusions

This paper focused on a two-parameter discrete distribution generated from the sum of two independent random variables, one with the Bernoulli distribution and the other with the Poisson–Lindley distribution. We have naturally called it the Bernoulli–Poisson–Lindley distribution. This distribution has a number of advantages, including the absence of special functions in its pmf and cdf, as well as its utilization of only two parameters. Furthermore, the model's ability to exhibit under- or over-dispersion makes it well-suited for modeling purposes. With the aim of estimating the unknown parameter, the ML method was used, and a simulation exercise was conducted. Furthermore, its associated count regression model was developed and discussed from an inferential viewpoint. The regression model is applied to two real-life data sets, and it is observed that our model is competitive in modeling practical data. To assess the viability of the suggested paradigm, two real-world data sets are examined. Favorable results were obtained for the proposed modeling strategy in all cases. Thus, the BPL distribution will be productive in modeling count data, beyond the scope of this paper.

Author Contributions: Conceptualization, H.S.B., C.C., R.M., M.R.I., S.A. and N.Q.; methodology, H.S.B., C.C., R.M., M.R.I., S.A. and N.Q.; software, H.S.B., C.C., R.M., M.R.I., S.A. and N.Q.; validation, H.S.B., C.C., R.M., M.R.I., S.A. and N.Q.; formal analysis, H.S.B., C.C., R.M., M.R.I., S.A. and N.Q.; investigation, H.S.B., C.C., R.M., M.R.I., S.A. and N.Q.; writing—original draft preparation, H.S.B., C.C., R.M., M.R.I., S.A. and N.Q.; writing—review and editing, H.S.B., C.C., R.M., M.R.I., S.A. and N.Q.; visualization, H.S.B., C.C., R.M., M.R.I., S.A. and N.Q.; funding acquisition, N.Q. All authors have read and agreed to the published version of the manuscript.

Funding: This research received no external funding.

Data Availability Statement: The data used in this paper are well referenced.

Acknowledgments: The authors gratefully acknowledge Princess Nourah bint Abdulrahman University Researchers Supporting Project number (PNURSP2023R376), Princess Nourah bint Abdulrahman University, Riyadh, Saudi Arabia for the financial support for this project.

Conflicts of Interest: The authors declare no conflict of interest.

Appendix A

- The formula for a finite geometric series is as follows:

$$\sum_{i=0}^{n} r^i = \frac{1 - r^{n+1}}{1 - r},$$

where $r \in \mathbb{R}$ and n is a positive integer. When $|r| < 1$, by applying $n \to \infty$, we obtain the standard infinite geometric formula, which can be generalized for any non-negative integer k as follows:

$$\sum_{i=0}^{\infty} i(i-1)\ldots(i-k+1) r^{i-k} = \frac{k!}{(1-r)^{k+1}}.$$

- The R-code for the empirical study of BPL distribution is given below.

```
library(AdequacyModel)
data<-NULL

n<-length(data)
n
x<-mean(y)
x
TTT(y)
dbpl <- function(x,alpha,theta) {
```

```
ifelse (x==0,(((1-alpha)*(theta^2)*(theta+2))/((theta+1)^3)), \\
(((theta^2)*((1+alpha*theta)*(x+theta+1)+(1-alpha))/((theta+1)^(x+3)))))
}
dbpl(1,0.25,0.66)
pbpl <- function(q,alpha,theta){
(1-(1+theta*(3+q+theta+(q*alpha*theta)+ \\
(alpha*theta*(2+theta))))/((1+theta)^(q+3)))
}

z<-sort(y)
c1=c(0,-1)
a1=matrix(c(1,0,-1,0),byrow = TRUE,2)
a1

L<-function(par)
{alpha=par[1];theta=par[2]
res= - sum(log(dbpl(y,alpha,theta)));
return(res);
}
initial<-c()
est=constrOptim(initial,L,ci=c1,ui=a1,grad = NULL)
est
ks.test(y,"pbpl",initial)
```

References

1. Plan, E. Modeling and simulation of count data. In *CPT: Pharmacometrics & Systems Pharmacology*; ASCPT: Alexandria, VA, USA, 2014; Volume 3, pp. 1–12.
2. Miaou, S.P. The relationship between truck accidents and geometric design of road sections: Poisson versus negative binomial regressions. *Accid. Anal. Prev.* **1994**, *26*, 471–482. [CrossRef] [PubMed]
3. Sáez-Castillo, A.; Conde-Sánchez, A. A hyper-Poisson regression model for overdispersed and under-dispersed count data. *Comput. Stat. Data Anal.* **2013**, *61*, 148–157. [CrossRef]
4. Del Castillo, J.; Pérez-Casany, M. Weighted Poisson distributions for overdispersion and underdispersion situations. *Ann. Inst. Stat. Math.* **1998**, *50*, 567–585. [CrossRef]
5. del Castillo, J.; Pérez-Casany, M. Overdispersed and under-dispersed Poisson generalizations. *J. Stat. Plan. Inference* **2005**, *134*, 486–500. [CrossRef]
6. Greenwood, M.; Yule, G.U. An inquiry into the nature of frequency distributions representative of multiple happenings with particular reference to the occurrence of multiple attacks of disease or of repeated accidents. *J. R. Stat. Soc.* **1920**, *83*, 255–279. [CrossRef]
7. Nakagawa, T.; Osaki, S. The discrete Weibull distribution. *IEEE Trans. Reliab.* **1975**, *24*, 300–301. [CrossRef]
8. Stein, W.E.; Dattero, R. A new discrete Weibull distribution. *IEEE Trans. Reliab.* **1984**, *33*, 196–197. [CrossRef]
9. Khan, M.A.; Khalique, A.; Abouammoh, A. On estimating parameters in a discrete Weibull distribution. *IEEE Trans. Reliab.* **1989**, *38*, 348–350. [CrossRef]
10. Yang, Z. Maximum likelihood phylogenetic estimation from DNA sequences with variable rates over sites: Approximate methods. *J. Mol. Evol.* **1994**, *39*, 306–314. [CrossRef]
11. Krishna, H.; Pundir, P.S. Discrete Burr and discrete Pareto distributions. *Stat. Methodol.* **2009**, *6*, 177–188. [CrossRef]
12. Jazi, M.A.; Lai, C.D.; Alamatsaz, M.H. A discrete inverse Weibull distribution and estimation of its parameters. *Stat. Methodol.* **2010**, *7*, 121–132. [CrossRef]
13. Bakouch, H.S.; Jazi, M.A.; Nadarajah, S. A new discrete distribution. *Statistics* **2014**, *48*, 200–240. [CrossRef]
14. Dean, C.B.; Lundy, E.R. Overdispersion. In *Wiley StatsRef: Statistics Reference Online*; Wiley: Hoboken, NJ, USA, 2014; pp. 1–9.
15. Consul, P.; Famoye, F. Generalized Poisson regression model. *Commun. Stat.-Theory Methods* **1992**, *21*, 89–109. [CrossRef]
16. Sellers, K.F.; Shmueli, G. A flexible regression model for count data. *Ann. Appl. Stat.* **2010**, *4*, 943–961. [CrossRef]
17. Bonat, W.H.; Jørgensen, B.; Kokonendji, C.C.; Hinde, J.; Demétrio, C.G. Extended Poisson-Tweedie: Properties and regression models for count data. *Stat. Model.* **2018**, *18*, 24–49. [CrossRef]
18. Sankaran, M. 275. note: The discrete Poisson–Lindley distribution. *Biometrics* **1970**, *26*, 145–149. [CrossRef]
19. Bourguignon, M.; Gallardo, D.I.; Medeiros, R.M. A simple and useful regression model for under-dispersed count data based on Bernoulli–Poisson convolution. *Stat. Pap.* **2022**, *63*, 821–848. [CrossRef]

20. Chakraborty, S.; Chakravarty, D.; Mazucheli, J.; Bertoli, W. A discrete analog of Gumbel distribution: Properties, parameter estimation and applications. *J. Appl. Stat.* **2021**, *48*, 712–737. [CrossRef]
21. Altun, E.; Bhati, D.; Khan, N.M. A new approach to model the counts of earthquakes: INARPQX (1) process. *SN Appl. Sci.* **2021**, *3*, 274. [CrossRef]
22. Bjerkedal, T. Acquisition of Resistance in Guinea Pies infected with Different Doses of Virulent Tubercle Bacilli. *Am. J. Hyg.* **1960**, *72*, 130–148.
23. Gupta, R.D.; Kundu, D. A new class of weighted exponential distributions. *Statistics* **2009**, *43*, 621–634. [CrossRef]

Disclaimer/Publisher's Note: The statements, opinions and data contained in all publications are solely those of the individual author(s) and contributor(s) and not of MDPI and/or the editor(s). MDPI and/or the editor(s) disclaim responsibility for any injury to people or property resulting from any ideas, methods, instructions or products referred to in the content.

Article

Reliability Estimation of Inverse Weibull Distribution Based on Intuitionistic Fuzzy Lifetime Data

Xue Hu [1] and Haiping Ren [2,*]

[1] College of Science, Jiangxi University of Science and Technology, Ganzhou 341000, China; 6120210110@mail.jxust.edu.cn
[2] Teaching Department of Basic Subjects, Jiangxi University of Science and Technology, Nanchang 330013, China
* Correspondence: chinarhp@163.com or 9520060004@jxust.edu.cn; Tel.: +86-159-7901-4223

Abstract: As a commonly used model in reliability analysis, the inverse Weibull distribution (IWD) is widely applied in various scientific fields. This paper considers the reliability estimation of the IWD based on intuitionistic fuzzy lifetime data. Firstly, the related concepts of the fuzzy set theory are reviewed, and the concepts of the intuitionistic fuzzy conditional density, intuitionistic fuzzy likelihood function, and intuitionistic fuzzy conditional expectation are obtained by extension. In classical estimations, the maximum likelihood estimators of parameters and reliability are derived. Due to the nonlinearity, the EM algorithm is used to obtain the maximum likelihood estimates. In the Bayesian estimation, the gamma prior is selected, and the Bayesian estimation of the parameters and reliability is conducted under the symmetric entropy and the scale square error loss function, respectively. Since the integrals are complicated, the Lindley approximation is used to approximate the Bayesian estimates. Then, the performance of these estimators is evaluated by the Monte Carlo simulation. The simulation results show that the Bayesian estimation is more suitable than the maximum likelihood estimation for the reliability estimation. Finally, a set of real data is used to prove the effectiveness of these proposed methods. Through these methods, the reliability of the intuitive fuzzy life data is accurately estimated, which provides an important reference for the reliability analysis in the scientific field.

Keywords: Bayesian estimation; EM algorithm; intuitionistic fuzzy lifetime data; inverse Weibull distribution

MSC: 62F10; 62F15

1. Introduction

Reliability refers to the ability of a product to complete the specified tasks under the specified time and conditions. This is a theory based on product failure. Due to the existence of two parameters, the IWD is a very flexible life distribution that can be used to represent various failure characteristics. It has become one of the commonly used models in reliability analysis. Depending on the shape parameter, the risk function can be flexibly varied. Therefore, it is appropriate to use IWD for data fitting in many cases. Yilmaz and Kara [1] investigated the classical and Bayesian estimation methods for estimating the reliability of IWD. The classical approach involved obtaining the maximum likelihood estimation and the modified maximum likelihood estimation. Meanwhile, the Bayesian estimation method under symmetric and asymmetric loss functions was considered. The Bayes estimators were computed numerically using the Lindley approximation and MCMC algorithm. Chakrabarty and Chowdhury [2] analyzed two probability distributions formed by compounding the IWD with zero-truncated Poisson and geometric distributions, respectively. They derived some important statistical and reliability attributes for each distribution

and estimated the parameters of the distributions using the expectation–maximization algorithm and minimum distance estimation method. Cai et al. [3] investigated the statistical inference of the IWD with masked data in a series system under type-II censoring. They obtained Bayes estimators of parameters based on gamma priors, as well as multilevel Bayes estimators. Finally, they conducted a Monte Carlo simulation with different masking probabilities and effective sample sizes to compare the performances of various estimates. Bi and Gui [4] considered the stress-strength reliability estimation of an inverse Weibull lifetime model with identical shape parameters but different scale parameters. In terms of the classical estimation, maximum likelihood estimators and asymptotic distributions were obtained. As the estimators were in implicit forms, an approximate maximum likelihood estimator was proposed, and asymptotic confidence intervals were obtained. In terms of the Bayesian estimation, Bayes estimators were obtained by Gibbs sampling and the MH algorithm. The performance of each estimator was compared through Monte Carlo simulations. For an additional reliability analysis of the IWD, please refer to [5–9].

The key to reliability estimation lies in collecting lifetime data or transforming other reliability data collected into lifetime data. However, in the process of obtaining the data, there may be some degree of measurement errors, resulting in imprecise data collection. In 1965, Zadeh [10] introduced the fuzzy set theory, which offered a proper tool for handling inaccurate data. The importance of fuzzy sets lies in their ability to handle uncertainties and vagueness, making them valuable mathematical tools in fields, such as artificial intelligence, control theory, and decision analysis [11–17]. By using fuzzy sets, we can translate vague information from the real world into mathematical language, allowing for precise calculations and reasoning. In recent years, some scholars have extended the fuzzy set theory to reliability analysis. Hashim [18] considered the problem of the fuzzy reliability estimation for the Lomax distribution. The first step was to use the composite trapezoidal rule to estimate the fuzzy reliability based on its definition. The second step was the Bayesian estimation method, where a gamma prior was selected to estimate the fuzzy reliability under symmetric and asymmetric loss functions. Neamah and Ali [19] considered the parameter estimation for the Frechet distribution of fuzzy lifetime data. Maximum likelihood and Bayes estimators were obtained for both parameters and reliability. Through a comparison of the mean squared error and mean absolute percentage error, it was found that the performance of the Bayesian estimation was better than that of the maximum likelihood estimation. Abbas et al. [20] studied the Bayesian estimation of the parameters of the Rayleigh distribution for fuzzy lifetime data. As an explicit form of the Bayes estimator could not be obtained, Lindley and Tierney–Kadane approximations were used for the numerical computation. Monte Carlo simulations were conducted to evaluate their performance, and a set of examples were provided to illustrate the analysis.

However, fuzzy sets only use one attribute parameter (membership degree) to represent both support and opposition, and cannot represent a neutral state, i.e., neither supporting nor opposing. To address this, Atanassov [21] introduced the notion of the intuitionistic fuzzy set, which was an extension of Zadeh's fuzzy set. Compared with traditional fuzzy sets, intuitionistic fuzzy sets add a new non-membership parameter, which can more delicately characterize the ambiguity inherent in the objectively defined world. When dealing with decision-making problems, intuitionistic fuzzy sets can provide more information, making the decision results more accurate and reliable, and have a wider range of application prospects [22–26]. Zahra et al. [27] considered the parameter and reliability estimation of the Pareto distribution by setting the parameter as a generalized intuitionistic fuzzy number. First, an L-R-type intuitionistic fuzzy number was proposed, and its cut set was provided. Secondly, a series of generalized intuitionistic fuzzy reliability characteristics were defined and used to evaluate the reliability of series and parallel systems. Finally, generalized intuitionistic fuzzy reliability characteristics were provided for certain special parameters and cut-set cases. Ebrahimnejad and Jamkhaneh [28] considered the reliability estimation problem of the Rayleigh distribution by assuming the parameter as a generalized intuitionistic fuzzy number. Extending the fuzzy reliability concept, a series of generalized intuitionistic fuzzy reliability characteristics and their cut sets were provided, and a numerical example was provided to demonstrate the analysis.

There are many uncertainties in real-life phenomena, which are usually classified into three categories: randomness, fuzziness, and roughness. However, in many cases, multiple types of uncertainties are at play, making it impossible to solve these problems using only one uncertainty theory. Fuzzy stochastic phenomena, which are common in real life, are the result of the simultaneous interaction of randomness and fuzziness, and their study is of great significance. To better handle this phenomenon, the fuzzy stochastic theory has emerged, which is a theory combining the fuzzy set and probability theories. One of its important concepts is the fuzzy random variable proposed by Huibert [29]. Zahra et al. [30] extended the definitions of probability, conditional probability, and likelihood function to intuitionistic fuzzy observations, and considered the parameter and reliability function estimation problem of the two-parameter Weibull distribution based on intuitionistic fuzzy lifetime data. ML estimators were obtained using the Newton–Raphson and EM algorithms, and Bayes estimators were obtained using Lindley and Tierney–Kadane approximations. To demonstrate the applicability of the proposed estimation methods, a simulation dataset was analyzed.

In terms of the reliability estimation for the IWD, many scholars have conducted research; however, most of them are based on complete or censored samples, and these studies assume that the available data are precise. However, in real life, the available lifetime data may not be precise, which indicates the necessity of extending classical estimation methods to fuzzy numbers.

The main contribution of this paper is to provide a suitable estimation method for the parameters and reliability of IWD based on intuitionistic fuzzy lifetime data. For the classical estimation, we obtain MLEs for the parameters and reliability. Due to the nonlinearity of the likelihood equation, we provide the EM algorithm with specific iteration steps. For the Bayesian estimation, we obtain BEs of parameters and reliability under the SE loss and SSE loss functions. The approximate Bayesian estimates are obtained by the Lindley approximation. Based on several sets of different parameter values and a large number of simulation experiments, the simulation results show that the Bayesian estimation performs much better than the maximum likelihood estimation.

This paper considers the reliability estimation problem of the IWD based on intuitionistic fuzzy lifetime data. In Section 1, the article mainly introduces the research status of the reliability estimation of the IWD lifetime model, as well as the research background and significance of fuzzy sets and intuitionistic fuzzy sets. Section 2 reviews the concepts of fuzzy sets and intuitionistic fuzzy sets, and extends some important concepts of the probability theory to the fuzzy set theory. Section 3 performs the maximum likelihood estimators (MLEs) of IWD, and iteratively calculates them using the expectation–maximization (EM) algorithm. Section 4 performs the Bayes estimators (BEs) under the symmetric entropy (SE) loss function and scale squared error (SSE) loss function, and numerically calculates the results using the Lindley approximation. Section 5 evaluates the performance of each estimation method using the Monte Carlo simulation and illustrates it using the mean squared error (MSE). The feasibility of the proposed methods is verified by a real dataset in Section 6. Section 7 presents the conclusions, limitations, and future research.

2. Preliminary Knowledge

The probability density function (pdf), cumulative distribution function (cdf), and reliability function of IWD are defined, respectively, as:

$$y(t; \lambda, \eta) = \lambda \eta t^{-\eta-1} \exp(-\lambda t^{-\eta}), \ t > 0, \tag{1}$$

$$Y(t; \lambda, \eta) = \exp(-\lambda t^{-\eta}), \ t > 0, \tag{2}$$

$$R(t) = 1 - \exp(-\lambda t^{-\eta}), \ t > 0, \tag{3}$$

where $\lambda > 0$ is the scale parameter and $\eta > 0$ is the shape parameter. For convenience, denote IWD owing pdf (1) by $IW(\lambda, \eta)$. Figures 1 and 2 show the pdf and risk function under different values of the shape and scale parameters.

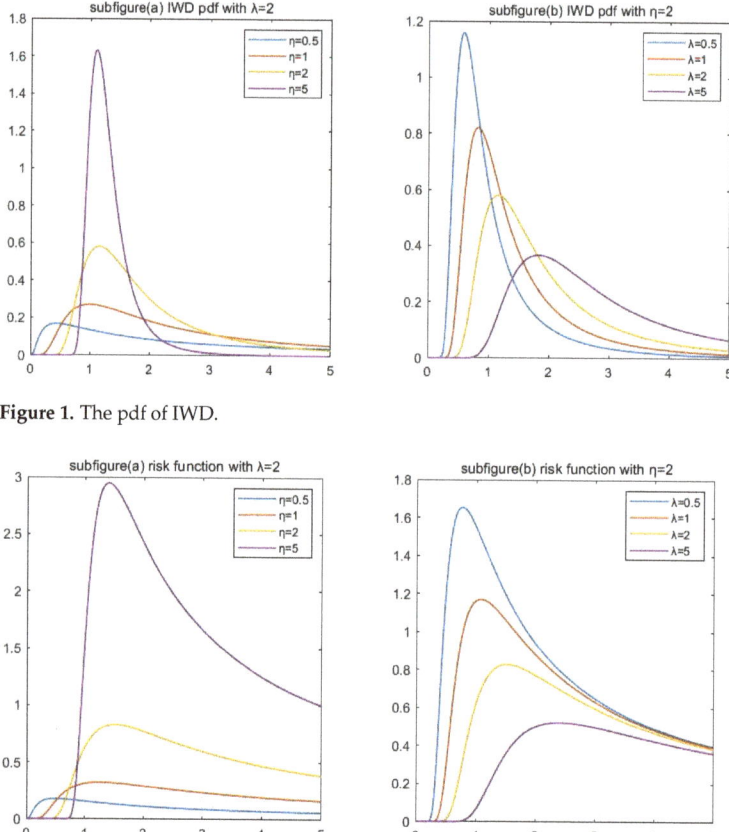

Figure 1. The pdf of IWD.

Figure 2. The risk function of IWD.

A fuzzy set is a set used to express the concept of fuzziness. Similar to the definition of the characteristic function of the classical set, the definition of fuzzy set can be obtained by extending its domain.

Definition 1 (Zadeh [10]). *Let $\mathbb{T}$ be a non-empty universal set. Fuzzy set $\widetilde{A}$ is defined as the form $\widetilde{A} = \{<t, \mu_{\widetilde{A}}(t)> | t \in \mathbb{T}\}$, where $\mu_{\widetilde{A}} : \mathbb{T} \to [0,1]$ is the degree of membership of t in $\widetilde{A}$.*

The intuitionistic fuzzy set (IFS) first proposed by Atanassov in 1986 contains two parameters, membership and non-membership degrees, which can more comprehensively describe the characteristics of things.

Definition 2 (Atanassov [21]). *Let $\mathbb{T}$ be a non-empty universal set. IFS $\widetilde{A}$ is defined as the form $\widetilde{A} = \{<t, \mu_{\widetilde{A}}(t), \nu_{\widetilde{A}}(t)> | t \in \mathbb{T}\}$, where $\mu_{\widetilde{A}} : \mathbb{T} \to [0,1]$ is the degree of membership of t in $\widetilde{A}$ and $\nu_{\widetilde{A}} : \mathbb{T} \to [0,1]$ is the degree of non-membership of t in $\widetilde{A}$. They satisfy $0 \leq \mu_{\widetilde{A}}(t) + \nu_{\widetilde{A}}(t) \leq 1$ for each t. When $\mathbb{T}$ has only one element, $\widetilde{A} = <\mu_{\widetilde{A}}, \nu_{\widetilde{A}}>$ is commonly referred to as a intuitionistic fuzzy number.*

Two special classes of intuitionistic fuzzy numbers are triangular intuitionistic fuzzy numbers (TriIFNs) and trapezoidal intuitionistic fuzzy numbers (TraIFNs), which serve as extensions of intuitionistic fuzzy numbers. In 2006, Shu et al. [31] proposed the definition of TriIFN and its application to fault tree analysis. Building on this work, Wang and Zhang [32] defined TraIFN in 2008. The membership and non-membership functions are:

$$\mu_{\tilde{A}}(t) = \begin{cases} \alpha \frac{t-a}{b-a} & t \in [a,b] \\ \alpha & t \in (b,c) \\ \alpha \frac{d-t}{d-c} & t \in [c,d] \\ 0 & \text{else} \end{cases} \quad (4)$$

$$\nu_{\tilde{A}}(t) = \begin{cases} \frac{b-t}{b-a} + \beta \frac{t-a}{b-a} & t \in [a,b] \\ \beta & t \in (b,c) \\ \frac{t-c}{d-c} + \beta \frac{d-t}{d-c} & t \in [c,d] \\ 1 & \text{else} \end{cases} \quad (5)$$

where α is the maximum membership degree and β is the minimum membership degree.

In this paper, we assume $\mathbb{T}$ be a set of real numbers, which is $\mathbb{T} = \mathbb{R}$. Additionally, we assumed that the IFSs discussed in this paper were TraIFNs.

To better investigate the estimation problem on the basis of intuitionistic fuzzy data, some concepts in the probability theory were extended to intuitionistic fuzzy random variables.

Definition 3. *Consider a probability space $(\mathbb{R}^n, \mathfrak{A}, \mathcal{P})$, the probability of an intuitionistic fuzzy observation $\tilde{x}$ in $\mathbb{R}^n$ is defined by*

$$P(\tilde{x}) = \int_{\mathbb{R}^n} \frac{1 - \nu_{\tilde{x}}(t) + \mu_{\tilde{x}}(t)}{2} d\mathcal{P} \quad (6)$$

Let the continuous random variable $T = (T_1, T_2, \ldots, T_n)$ obey the $IW(\lambda, \eta)$, and its intuitionistic fuzzy observations are denoted by $\tilde{x} = (\tilde{x}_1, \tilde{x}_2, \ldots, \tilde{x}_n)$. The conditional density of random variables in probability theory is introduced, and the intuitionistic fuzzy conditional density is given as below,

$$y(t|\tilde{x}) = \frac{s(t)y(t; \lambda, \eta)}{\int_{\mathbb{R}} s(t)y(t; \lambda, \eta)dt} \quad (7)$$

where $s(t) = \frac{1 - \nu_{\tilde{x}}(t) + \mu_{\tilde{x}}(t)}{2}$. In such a situation, the intuitionistic fuzzy likelihood function of $IW(\lambda, \eta)$ is:

$$h(\lambda, \eta|\tilde{x}) = \prod_{i=1}^{n} P(\tilde{x}_i|\lambda, \eta) = \prod_{i=1}^{n} \int_{\mathbb{R}} s_i(t)y(t; \lambda, \eta)dt, \quad (8)$$

where $s_i(t) = \frac{1 - \nu_{\tilde{x}_i}(t) + \mu_{\tilde{x}_i}(t)}{2}$.

Finally, intuitionistic fuzzy conditional expectation is introduced. Based on the intuitionistic fuzzy conditional density and intuitionistic fuzzy observation $\tilde{x} = (\tilde{x}_1, \tilde{x}_2, \ldots, \tilde{x}_n)$, the intuitionistic fuzzy conditional expectation of a random variable $T = (T_1, T_2, \ldots, T_n)$ is:

$$\begin{aligned} E(T|\tilde{x}) &= \int_{\mathbb{R}} t y(t|\tilde{x}) dt \\ &= \int_{\mathbb{R}} t \frac{s(t)y(t; \lambda, \eta)}{\int_{\mathbb{R}} s(t)y(t; \lambda, \eta)dt} dt \\ &= \int_{\mathbb{R}} t \frac{s(t)y(t; \lambda, \eta)}{h(\lambda, \eta|\tilde{x})} dt. \end{aligned} \quad (9)$$

3. Maximum Likelihood Estimation

The intuitionistic fuzzy likelihood function of $IW(\lambda, \eta)$ is shown in Equation (8). Thus, the intuitionistic fuzzy log-likelihood function is provided as:

$$H(\lambda, \eta | \tilde{x}) = \ln h(\lambda, \eta | \tilde{x}) = \sum_{i=1}^{n} \ln[\int_{\mathbb{R}} s_i(t) y(t; \lambda, \eta) dt]. \tag{10}$$

The MLEs $\hat{\lambda}_{ML}$ and $\hat{\eta}_{ML}$ are obtained by the below equations:

$$\begin{cases} \frac{\partial H(\lambda, \eta | \tilde{x})}{\partial \lambda} = 0 \\ \frac{\partial H(\lambda, \eta | \tilde{x})}{\partial \eta} = 0 \end{cases},$$

where $\frac{\partial H(\lambda, \eta | \tilde{x})}{\partial \lambda}$ and $\frac{\partial H(\lambda, \eta | \tilde{x})}{\partial \eta}$ are shown in Equations (11) and (12):

$$\frac{\partial H(\lambda, \eta | \tilde{x})}{\partial \lambda} = \sum_{i=1}^{n} \frac{1}{h(\lambda, \eta | \tilde{x}_i)} \int_{\mathbb{R}} s_i(t) \frac{\partial y(t; \lambda, \eta)}{\partial \lambda} dt, \tag{11}$$

$$\frac{\partial H(\lambda, \eta | \tilde{x})}{\partial \eta} = \sum_{i=1}^{n} \frac{1}{h(\lambda, \eta | \tilde{x}_i)} \int_{\mathbb{R}} s_i(t) \frac{\partial y(t; \lambda, \eta)}{\partial \eta} dt. \tag{12}$$

Here, $h(\lambda, \eta | \tilde{x}_i) = \int_0^{+\infty} s_i(t) y(t; \lambda, \eta) dt$, $\frac{\partial y(t;\lambda,\eta)}{\partial \lambda}$ and $\frac{\partial y(t;\lambda,\eta)}{\partial \eta}$ are shown in Equations (13) and (14):

$$\frac{\partial y(t; \lambda, \eta)}{\partial \lambda} = \frac{1}{\lambda} y(t; \lambda, \eta) - t^{-\eta} y(t; \lambda, \eta), \tag{13}$$

$$\frac{\partial y(t; \lambda, \eta)}{\partial \eta} = \frac{1}{\eta} y(t; \lambda, \eta) - y(t; \lambda, \eta) \ln t + \lambda t^{-\eta} y(t; \lambda, \eta) \ln t. \tag{14}$$

It is obvious that the abovementioned equations are nonlinear and difficult to solve. Then, we considered the EM algorithm.

The EM algorithm was first introduced by Dempster [33] in 1977, which is an algorithm used for ML estimations when there are missing observations. The algorithm involves two steps: E- and M-steps. The E-step is used to impute the missing part of the observed data, forming a pseudo-complete dataset. The M-step is used to maximize the likelihood function of the pseudo-complete dataset. Singh and Tripathi [34] considered the parameter estimation problem of the IWD based on a progressively type-I interval censored sample, using the EM algorithm to derive the MLEs. Kurniawan et al. [35] considered the MLEs of the shape parameter for the Weibull distribution based on type-II censored data, using the EM algorithm. Finally, an aircraft component lifetime data study was used as an example to illustrate the methods. For more references on the EM algorithm, please see [36–40].

The EM algorithm is also applicable to intuitionistic fuzzy data because the observed intuitionistic fuzzy data can also be considered as incomplete characterizations of the completed data. In order to better illustrate the iterative process of the EM algorithm, we first performed some processing on Equations (11) and (12).

Substitute Equation (13) into (11):

$$\begin{aligned} \frac{\partial H(\lambda, \eta | \tilde{x})}{\partial \lambda} &= \sum_{i=1}^{n} \frac{1}{h(\lambda, \eta | \tilde{x}_i)} \int_0^{+\infty} s_i(t) \frac{\partial y(t;\lambda,\eta)}{\partial \lambda} dt \\ &= \sum_{i=1}^{n} \frac{1}{h(\lambda, \eta | \tilde{x}_i)} \int_0^{+\infty} s_i(t) [\frac{1}{\lambda} y(t; \lambda, \eta) - t^{-\eta} y(t; \lambda, \eta)] dt \\ &= \sum_{i=1}^{n} \int_0^{+\infty} \frac{1}{\lambda} \frac{s_i(t) y(t;\lambda,\eta)}{h(\lambda, \eta | \tilde{x}_i)} dt - \sum_{i=1}^{n} \int_0^{+\infty} t^{-\eta} \frac{s_i(t) y(t;\lambda,\eta)}{h(\lambda, \eta | \tilde{x}_i)} dt \\ &= n\frac{1}{\lambda} - \sum_{i=1}^{n} E_{1i}. \end{aligned}$$

Let $\frac{\partial H(\lambda,\eta|\widetilde{x})}{\partial \lambda} = 0$,

$$\lambda = n(\sum_{i=1}^{n} E_{1i})^{-1}, \quad (15)$$

where

$$E_{1i} = E(T^{-\eta}|\widetilde{x}_i) = \int_0^{+\infty} t^{-\eta} \frac{s_i(t) y(t;\lambda,\eta)}{h(\lambda,\eta|\widetilde{x}_i)} dt.$$

Substitute Equation (14) into (12):

$$\begin{aligned}
\frac{\partial H(\lambda,\eta|\widetilde{x})}{\partial \eta} &= \sum_{i=1}^{n} \frac{1}{h(\lambda,\eta|\widetilde{x}_i)} \int_0^{+\infty} s_i(t) \frac{\partial y(t;\lambda,\eta)}{\partial \eta} dt \\
&= \sum_{i=1}^{n} \frac{1}{h(\lambda,\eta|\widetilde{x}_i)} \int_0^{+\infty} s_i(t) [\tfrac{1}{\eta} y(t;\lambda,\eta) - y(t;\lambda,\eta) \ln t + \lambda t^{-\eta} y(t;\lambda,\eta) \ln t] dt \\
&= n\tfrac{1}{\eta} - \sum_{i=1}^{n} E_{2i} + \lambda \sum_{i=1}^{n} E_{3i}
\end{aligned} \quad (16)$$

Let $\frac{\partial H(\lambda,\eta|\widetilde{x})}{\partial \eta} = 0$,

$$\eta = n(\sum_{i=1}^{n} E_{2i} - \lambda \sum_{i=1}^{n} E_{3i})^{-1}, \quad (17)$$

where

$$E_{2i} = E(\ln T|\widetilde{x}_i) = \int_0^{+\infty} \frac{s_i(t) y(t;\lambda,\eta)}{h(\lambda,\eta|\widetilde{x}_i)} (\ln t) dt,$$

and

$$E_{3i} = E(T^{-\eta} \ln T|\widetilde{x}_i) = \int_0^{+\infty} \frac{s_i(t) y(t;\lambda,\eta)}{h(\lambda,\eta|\widetilde{x}_i)} (t^{-\eta} \ln t) dt.$$

The iterative steps of using the EM algorithm to obtain MLEs are as follows:

Step 1. Let the initial value be $\theta^{(0)} = (\lambda^{(0)}, \eta^{(0)})$, and set $j = 0$. Give the accuracy $\varepsilon > 0$.

Step 2. At the $(j+1)$th iteration, compute the intuitionistic fuzzy conditional expectations below:

$$E_{1i} = \int_0^{+\infty} t^{-\eta} \frac{s_i(t) y(t;\lambda,\eta)}{h(\lambda,\eta|\widetilde{x}_i)} \Big|_{\theta^{(j+1)}=\theta^{(j)}} dt, \quad (18)$$

$$E_{2i} = \int_0^{+\infty} \frac{s_i(t) y(t;\lambda,\eta)}{h(\lambda,\eta|\widetilde{x}_i)} (\ln t) \Big|_{\theta^{(j+1)}=\theta^{(j)}} dt, \quad (19)$$

$$E_{3i} = \int_0^{+\infty} \frac{s_i(t) y(t;\lambda,\eta)}{h(\lambda,\eta|\widetilde{x}_i)} (t^{-\eta} \ln t) \Big|_{\theta^{(j+1)}=\theta^{(j)}} dt. \quad (20)$$

Step 3. Substitute Equation (18) into (15):

$$\lambda^{(j+1)} = n(\sum_{i=1}^{n} E_{1i})^{-1}. \quad (21)$$

Substitute Equations (19) and (20) into (17):

$$\eta^{(j+1)} = n(\sum_{i=1}^{n} E_{2i} - \lambda^{(j)} \sum_{i=1}^{n} E_{3i})^{-1}. \quad (22)$$

Step 4. If $|\theta^{(j+1)} - \theta^{(j)}| < \varepsilon$, the MLEs are obtained by $\hat{\lambda}_{ML} = \lambda^{(j)}$ and $\hat{\eta}_{ML} = \eta^{(j)}$. If not, then set $j = j+1$ and return to step 2.

According to the invariance of maximum likelihood estimation, the MLE $\hat{R}_{ML}(t)$ is derived by:

$$\hat{R}_{ML}(t) = 1 - \exp(-\hat{\lambda}_{ML} t^{-\hat{\eta}_{ML}}). \quad (23)$$

4. Bayesian Estimation

In the Bayesian statistical inference, the prior distribution plays a crucial role. It represents our prior knowledge or belief about the parameters and can help us estimate the posterior distribution more accurately [41]. Choosing an appropriate prior distribution is essential because it can affect the final inference results [42].

The gamma distribution is a flexible continuous probability distribution with many desirable properties, making it a common choice as the prior distribution for parameters in Bayesian statistics [43]. The parameters of the gamma distribution can be adjusted to accommodate different prior beliefs. Additionally, the gamma distribution has conjugacy, meaning that when used as a prior distribution, its product with the likelihood function remains a gamma distribution, making posterior distribution calculations simpler [44]. The pdf of the gamma distribution is ([44]):

$$\pi(\omega) = \frac{b^a}{\Gamma(a)} \omega^{a-1} e^{-b\omega}, \omega > 0, a, b > 0.$$

In this section, we assume that λ and η are random variables and independent of each other, where λ follows Gamma(c_1, d_1) and η follows Gamma(c_2, d_2). That is:

$$\pi_1(\lambda) \propto \lambda^{d_1-1} e^{-c_1 \lambda} \quad \lambda > 0,\ c_1 > 0,\ d_1 > 0, \tag{24}$$

$$\pi_2(\eta) \propto \eta^{d_2-1} e^{-c_2 \eta} \quad \eta > 0,\ c_2 > 0,\ d_2 > 0. \tag{25}$$

Thus, the joint prior distribution of λ and η is:

$$\pi(\lambda, \eta) = \pi_1(\lambda) \times \pi_2(\eta) \propto \lambda^{d_1-1} \eta^{d_2-1} e^{-c_1 \lambda - c_2 \eta}. \tag{26}$$

With reference to the Bayesian formulation, the posterior distribution of λ and η is

$$\begin{aligned}\pi(\lambda, \eta | \tilde{x}) &\propto h(\lambda, \eta | \tilde{x}) \times \pi(\lambda, \eta) \\ &\propto \lambda^{n(d_1-1)} \eta^{n(d_2-1)} e^{-c_1 n\lambda - c_2 n\eta} \prod_{i=1}^{n} \int_0^{+\infty} s_i(t) y(t; \lambda, \eta) dt\end{aligned} \tag{27}$$

According to the Equation (9), the posterior expectation of the function $g(\lambda, \eta)$ of λ and η is:

$$\begin{aligned}E[g(\lambda, \eta)|\tilde{x}] &= \int_0^{+\infty}\int_0^{+\infty} g(\lambda,\eta) \frac{\pi(\lambda,\eta|\tilde{x})}{\int_0^{+\infty}\int_0^{+\infty} \pi(\lambda,\eta|\tilde{x}) d\lambda d\eta} d\lambda d\eta \\ &= \int_0^{+\infty}\int_0^{+\infty} \frac{g(\lambda,\eta) \lambda^{n(d_1-1)} \eta^{n(d_2-1)} e^{-c_1 n\lambda - c_2 n\eta} \prod_{i=1}^{n}\int_0^{+\infty} s_i(t) y(t;\lambda,\eta)dt}{\int_0^{+\infty}\int_0^{+\infty} [\lambda^{n(d_1-1)} \eta^{n(d_2-1)} e^{-c_1 n\lambda - c_2 n\eta} \prod_{i=1}^{n}\int_0^{+\infty} s_i(t) y(t;\lambda,\eta)dt] d\lambda d\eta} d\lambda d\eta.\end{aligned} \tag{28}$$

The form of the posterior expectation is complex and not easily solved analytically. Therefore, the Lindley approximation is used to obtain the BEs.

With reference to the Lindley approximation, the posterior expectation can be written as:

$$E[g(\lambda, \eta)|\tilde{x}] = \frac{\int g(\lambda, \eta) e^{H(\lambda, \eta|\tilde{x}) + G(\lambda, \eta)} d(\lambda, \eta)}{\int e^{H(\lambda, \eta|\tilde{x}) + G(\lambda, \eta)} d(\lambda, \eta)}, \tag{29}$$

where $G(\lambda, \eta) = \ln \pi(\lambda, \eta)$. If the sample is large, Equation (29) can be formulated as:

$$E[g(\lambda, \eta)|\tilde{x}] = g(\hat{\lambda}_{ML}, \hat{\eta}_{ML}) + \frac{1}{2}(A + B + C + D), \tag{30}$$

$$A = (\hat{g}_{\lambda\lambda} + 2\hat{g}_\lambda \hat{G}_\lambda)\hat{\phi}_{\lambda\lambda} + (\hat{g}_{\eta\lambda} + 2\hat{g}_\eta \hat{G}_\lambda)\hat{\phi}_{\eta\lambda}, \tag{31}$$

$$B = (\hat{g}_{\lambda\eta} + 2\hat{g}_\lambda \hat{G}_\eta)\hat{\phi}_{\lambda\eta} + (\hat{g}_{\eta\eta} + 2\hat{g}_\eta \hat{G}_\eta)\hat{\phi}_{\eta\eta}, \tag{32}$$

$$C = (\hat{g}_\lambda \hat{\phi}_{\lambda\lambda} + \hat{g}_\eta \hat{\phi}_{\lambda\eta})(\hat{H}_{\lambda\lambda\lambda}\hat{\phi}_{\lambda\lambda} + \hat{H}_{\eta\lambda\lambda}\hat{\phi}_{\eta\lambda} + \hat{H}_{\lambda\eta\lambda}\hat{\phi}_{\lambda\eta} + \hat{H}_{\eta\eta\lambda}\hat{\phi}_{\eta\eta}), \tag{33}$$

$$D = (\hat{g}_\lambda \hat{\phi}_{\eta\lambda} + \hat{g}_\eta \hat{\phi}_{\eta\eta})(\hat{H}_{\lambda\lambda\eta}\hat{\phi}_{\lambda\lambda} + \hat{H}_{\eta\lambda\eta}\hat{\phi}_{\eta\lambda} + \hat{H}_{\lambda\eta\eta}\hat{\phi}_{\lambda\eta} + \hat{H}_{\eta\eta\eta}\hat{\phi}_{\eta\eta}), \tag{34}$$

where $\phi_{ij}(i,j = \lambda,\eta)$ is the element of the inverse matrix of $-H_{ij}$. The $\hat{g}_{\lambda\lambda}$ represents taking the second derivative of $g(\lambda,\eta)$ with respect to λ and placing $\hat{\lambda}_{ML}$ into it. In the same way, the rest can be shown as:

$$\begin{aligned}
H_{\lambda\lambda\lambda} &= \sum_{i=1}^{n}[2h^{-3}(\lambda,\eta|\tilde{x}_i)(\int_0^{+\infty}s_i(t)\tfrac{\partial y(t;\lambda,\eta)}{\partial \lambda}dt)^3 - h^{-1}(\lambda,\eta|\tilde{x}_i)\int_0^{+\infty}s_i(t)\tfrac{\partial^3 y(t;\lambda,\eta)}{\partial \lambda^3}dt] \\
&\quad - \sum_{i=1}^{n}[3h^{-2}(\lambda,\eta|\tilde{x}_i)\int_0^{+\infty}s_i(t)\tfrac{\partial y(t;\lambda,\eta)}{\partial \lambda}dt\int_0^{+\infty}s_i(t)\tfrac{\partial^2 y(t;\lambda,\eta)}{\partial \lambda^2}dt]
\end{aligned} \tag{35}$$

$$\begin{aligned}
H_{\lambda\lambda\eta} &= H_{\lambda\eta\lambda} = H_{\eta\lambda\lambda} \\
&= \sum_{i=1}^{n}[2h^{-3}(\lambda,\eta|\tilde{x}_i)\int_0^{+\infty}s_i(t)\tfrac{\partial y(t;\lambda,\eta)}{\partial \eta}dt(\int_0^{+\infty}s_i(t)\tfrac{\partial y(t;\lambda,\eta)}{\partial \lambda}dt)^2] \\
&\quad - \sum_{i=1}^{n}[2h^{-2}(\lambda,\eta|\tilde{x}_i)\int_0^{+\infty}s_i(t)\tfrac{\partial y(t;\lambda,\eta)}{\partial \lambda}dt\int_0^{+\infty}s_i(t)\tfrac{\partial^2 y(t;\lambda,\eta)}{\partial \lambda\partial \eta}dt] \\
&\quad - \sum_{i=1}^{n}[h^{-2}(\lambda,\eta|\tilde{x}_i)\int_0^{+\infty}s_i(t)\tfrac{\partial y(t;\lambda,\eta)}{\partial \eta}dt\int_0^{+\infty}s_i(t)\tfrac{\partial^2 y(t;\lambda,\eta)}{\partial \lambda^2}dt] \\
&\quad + \sum_{i=1}^{n}h^{-1}(\lambda,\eta|\tilde{x}_i)\int_0^{+\infty}s_i(t)\tfrac{\partial^3 y(t;\lambda,\eta)}{\partial \lambda^2\partial \eta}dt
\end{aligned} \tag{36}$$

$$\begin{aligned}
H_{\eta\eta\lambda} &= H_{\eta\lambda\eta} = H_{\lambda\eta\eta} \\
&= \sum_{i=1}^{n}[2h^{-3}(\lambda,\eta|\tilde{x}_i)\int_0^{+\infty}s_i(t)\tfrac{\partial y(t;\lambda,\eta)}{\partial \lambda}dt(\int_0^{+\infty}s_i(t)\tfrac{\partial y(t;\lambda,\eta)}{\partial \eta}dt)^2] \\
&\quad - \sum_{i=1}^{n}[2h^{-2}(\lambda,\eta|\tilde{x}_i)\int_0^{+\infty}s_i(t)\tfrac{\partial y(t;\lambda,\eta)}{\partial \eta}dt\int_0^{+\infty}s_i(t)\tfrac{\partial^2 y(t;\lambda,\eta)}{\partial \eta\partial \lambda}dt] \\
&\quad - \sum_{i=1}^{n}[h^{-2}(\lambda,\eta|\tilde{x}_i)\int_0^{+\infty}s_i(t)\tfrac{\partial y(t;\lambda,\eta)}{\partial \lambda}dt\int_0^{+\infty}s_i(t)\tfrac{\partial^2 y(t;\lambda,\eta)}{\partial \eta^2}dt] \\
&\quad + \sum_{i=1}^{n}[h^{-1}(\lambda,\eta|\tilde{x}_i)\int_0^{+\infty}s_i(t)\tfrac{\partial^3 y(t;\lambda,\eta)}{\partial \eta^2\partial \lambda}dt]
\end{aligned} \tag{37}$$

$$\begin{aligned}
H_{\eta\eta\eta} &= \sum_{i=1}^{n}[2h^{-3}(\lambda,\eta|\tilde{x}_i)(\int_0^{+\infty}s_i(t)\tfrac{\partial y(t;\lambda,\eta)}{\partial \eta}dt)^3 + h^{-1}(\lambda,\eta|\tilde{x}_i)\int_0^{+\infty}s_i(t)\tfrac{\partial^3 y(t;\lambda,\eta)}{\partial \eta^3}dt] \\
&\quad - \sum_{i=1}^{n}[3h^{-1}(\lambda,\eta|\tilde{x}_i)\int_0^{+\infty}s_i(t)\tfrac{\partial y(t;\lambda,\eta)}{\partial \eta}dt\int_0^{+\infty}s_i(t)\tfrac{\partial^2 y(t;\lambda,\eta)}{\partial \eta^2}dt]
\end{aligned} \tag{38}$$

$$G_\lambda = \frac{d_1 - 1}{\lambda} - c_1, \tag{39}$$

$$G_\eta = \frac{d_2 - 1}{\eta} - c_2. \tag{40}$$

The role of the loss function in the Bayesian statistical inference is crucial as it measures the discrepancy between model predictions and the true outcomes. In the Bayesian framework, we used the posterior distribution to represent uncertainty and used the loss function to choose the optimal decision or prediction. Different loss functions lead to different decisions or predictions; therefore, selecting an appropriate loss function is essential for the accuracy and reliability of the Bayesian inference.

Then, we studies the Bayesian estimation of the unknown parameters under the SE and SSE loss functions.

4.1. Bayesian Estimation under the SE Loss Function

The SE loss function is defined in Equation (41) [45]:

$$L_1(\theta, \hat{\theta}) = \frac{\hat{\theta}}{\theta} + \frac{\theta}{\hat{\theta}} - 2, \tag{41}$$

where $\hat{\theta}$ is the estimator of unknow parameter θ.

Lemma 1. *Suppose that $T = (T_1, T_2, \ldots, T_n)$ is a continuous random variable. For any prior distribution $\pi(\theta)$, the BE $\hat{\theta}_{SE}$ under SE loss function is:*

$$\hat{\theta}_{SE} = [\frac{E(\theta|T)}{E(\theta^{-1}|T)}]^{\frac{1}{2}}, \tag{42}$$

where $E(\theta|T)$ and $E(\theta^{-1}|T)$ are the posterior expectation.

Proof. The Bayesian risk of $\hat{\theta}_{SE}$ under SE loss function is:

$$R = E_\theta[E(L_1(\theta, \hat{\theta}_{SE})|T)].$$

Denote $r_1(\hat{\theta}_{SE}) = E(L_1(\theta, \hat{\theta}_{SE})|T)$, and

$$r_1(\hat{\theta}_{SE}) = \hat{\theta}_{SE}^{-1} E(\theta|T) + \hat{\theta}_{SE} E(\theta^{-1}|T) - 2.$$

The derivative of $r_1(\hat{\theta}_{SE})$ is:

$$r_1'(\hat{\theta}_{SE}) = -\hat{\theta}_{SE}^{-2} E(\theta|T) + E(\theta^{-1}|T).$$

Therefore, the BE $\hat{\theta}_{SE}$ under SE loss function is obtained by solving the equation $r_1'(\hat{\theta}_{SE}) = 0$. □

Referring to Lemma 1, the BEs $\hat{\lambda}_{SE}$, $\hat{\eta}_{SE}$ and $\hat{R}_{SE}(t)$ under SE loss function of $IW(\lambda, \eta)$ based on intuitionistic fuzzy lifetime data are obtained by:

$$\hat{\lambda}_{SE} = [\frac{E(\lambda|T)}{E(\lambda^{-1}|T)}]^{\frac{1}{2}}, \tag{43}$$

$$\hat{\eta}_{SE} = [\frac{E(\eta|T)}{E(\eta^{-1}|T)}]^{\frac{1}{2}}, \tag{44}$$

$$\hat{R}_{SE}(t) = [\frac{E(R(t)|T)}{E(R^{-1}(t)|T)}]^{\frac{1}{2}}. \tag{45}$$

Next, the steps to obtain the Lindley approximation for $\hat{\lambda}_{SE}$ are presented. The BEs $\hat{\eta}_{SE}$ and $\hat{R}_{SE}(t)$ are obtained by replacing $g(\lambda, \eta)$ in the following steps.

When $g(\lambda, \eta) = \lambda$, there are:

$$g_\lambda = 1, \; g_\eta = g_{\lambda\lambda} = g_{\lambda\eta} = g_{\eta\lambda} = g_{\eta\eta} = 0. \tag{46}$$

The posterior expectation $E(\lambda|T)$ can be written as:

$$\begin{aligned} E(\lambda|T) &= \hat{\lambda}_{ML} + \hat{G}_\lambda \hat{\phi}_{\lambda\lambda} + \hat{G}_\eta \hat{\phi}_{\eta\lambda} + \frac{1}{2}[\hat{\phi}_{\lambda\lambda}(\hat{H}_{\lambda\lambda\lambda}\hat{\phi}_{\lambda\lambda} + \hat{H}_{\lambda\eta\lambda}\hat{\phi}_{\lambda\eta} + \hat{H}_{\eta\lambda\lambda}\hat{\phi}_{\eta\lambda} + \hat{H}_{\eta\eta\lambda}\hat{\phi}_{\eta\eta}) \\ &+ \hat{\phi}_{\eta\lambda}(\hat{H}_{\lambda\lambda\eta}\hat{\phi}_{\lambda\lambda} + \hat{H}_{\lambda\eta\eta}\hat{\phi}_{\lambda\eta} + \hat{H}_{\eta\lambda\eta}\hat{\phi}_{\eta\lambda} + \hat{H}_{\eta\eta\eta}\hat{\phi}_{\eta\eta})] \end{aligned} \tag{47}$$

When $g(\lambda, \eta) = \lambda^{-1}$, there are:

$$g_\lambda = -\frac{1}{\lambda^2}, \; g_{\lambda\lambda} = \frac{2}{\lambda^3}, \; g_\eta = g_{\lambda\eta} = g_{\eta\lambda} = g_{\eta\eta} = 0. \tag{48}$$

The posterior expectation $E(\lambda^{-1}|T)$ can be written as:

$$\begin{aligned} E(\lambda|T) &= -\frac{1}{2}\hat{\lambda}_{ML}^{-2}[\hat{\phi}_{\lambda\lambda}(\hat{H}_{\lambda\lambda\lambda}\hat{\phi}_{\lambda\lambda} + \hat{H}_{\lambda\eta\lambda}\hat{\phi}_{\lambda\eta} + \hat{H}_{\eta\lambda\lambda}\hat{\phi}_{\eta\lambda} + \hat{H}_{\eta\eta\lambda}\hat{\phi}_{\eta\eta}) + \hat{\phi}_{\eta\lambda}(\hat{H}_{\lambda\lambda\eta}\hat{\phi}_{\lambda\lambda} + \hat{H}_{\lambda\eta\eta}\hat{\phi}_{\lambda\eta} \\ &+ \hat{H}_{\eta\lambda\eta}\hat{\phi}_{\eta\lambda} + \hat{H}_{\eta\eta\eta}\hat{\phi}_{\eta\eta})] + \hat{\lambda}_{ML}^{-1} + (\hat{\lambda}_{ML}^{-3} - \hat{\lambda}_{ML}^{-2}\hat{G}_\lambda)\hat{\phi}_{\lambda\lambda} - \hat{\lambda}_{ML}^{-2}\hat{G}_\eta\hat{\phi}_{\lambda\eta} \end{aligned} \tag{49}$$

BE $\hat{\lambda}_{SE}$ is obtained by substituting Equations (47) and (49) into (43).

4.2. Bayesian Estimation under the SSE Loss Function

The SSE loss function is defined in Equation (50) [46]:

$$L_2(\theta, \hat{\theta}) = \frac{(\theta - \hat{\theta})^2}{\theta^d}, \quad (50)$$

where d is a non-negative integer.

Lemma 2. *Suppose that $T = (T_1, T_2, \ldots, T_n)$ is a continuous random variable. For any prior distribution $\pi(\theta)$, the BE $\hat{\theta}_{SSE}$ under SSE loss function is:*

$$\hat{\theta}_{SSE} = \frac{E(\theta^{1-d}|T)}{E(\theta^{-d}|T)}, \quad (51)$$

where $E(\theta^{1-d}|T)$ and $E(\theta^{-d}|T)$ are the posterior expectations.

Proof. The Bayesian risk of $\hat{\theta}_{SSE}$ under the SSE loss function is:

$$R = E_\theta[E(L_2(\theta, \hat{\theta}_{SSE})|T)].$$

Denote $r_2(\hat{\theta}_{SSE}) = E(L_2(\theta, \hat{\theta}_{SSE})|T)$, and

$$r_2(\hat{\theta}_{SSE}) = E(\theta^{2-d}|T) - 2\hat{\theta}_{SSE} E(\theta^{1-d}|T) + \hat{\theta}_{SSE}^2 E(\theta^{-d}|T).$$

The derivative of $r_2(\hat{\theta}_{SSE})$ is:

$$r_2'(\hat{\theta}_{SSE}) = 2\hat{\theta}_{SSE} E(\theta^{-d}|T) - 2E(\theta^{1-d}|T).$$

Therefore, BE $\hat{\theta}_{SSE}$ under the SSE loss function is obtained by solving the equation $r_2'(\hat{\theta}_{SSE}) = 0$. □

According to Lemma 2, the BEs $\hat{\lambda}_{SSE}$, $\hat{\eta}_{SSE}$ and $\hat{R}_{SSE}(t)$ under the SSE loss function are presented in Equations (52)–(54):

$$\hat{\lambda}_{SSE} = \frac{E(\lambda^{1-d}|T)}{E(\lambda^{-d}|T)}, \quad (52)$$

$$\hat{\eta}_{SSE} = \frac{E(\eta^{1-d}|T)}{E(\eta^{-d}|T)}, \quad (53)$$

$$\hat{R}_{SSE}(t) = \frac{E(R^{1-d}(t)|T)}{E(R^{-d}(t)|T)}. \quad (54)$$

As in Section 4.1, the steps of the Lindley approximation of $\hat{\lambda}_{SSE}$ are provided. When $g(\lambda, \eta) = \lambda^{1-d}$, then:

$$g_\lambda = (1-d)\lambda^{-d}, \; g_{\lambda\lambda} = d(d-1)\lambda^{-d-1}, \; g_\eta = g_{\lambda\eta} = g_{\eta\lambda} = g_{\eta\eta} = 0. \quad (55)$$

The posterior expectation $E(\lambda^{1-d}|T)$ can be written as:

$$\begin{aligned} E(\lambda^{1-d}|T) =\; & \hat{\lambda}_{ML}^{1-d} + (1-d)\hat{\lambda}_{ML}^{-d}\hat{G}_\lambda\hat{\phi}_{\lambda\lambda} + (1-d)\hat{\lambda}_{ML}^{-d}\hat{G}_\eta\hat{\phi}_{\lambda\eta} + \tfrac{1}{2}[-d(d-1)\hat{\lambda}_{ML}^{-d-1}\hat{\phi}_{\lambda\lambda} \\ & + (1-d)\hat{\lambda}_{ML}^{-d}\hat{\phi}_{\lambda\lambda}(\hat{H}_{\lambda\lambda\lambda}\hat{\phi}_{\lambda\lambda} + \hat{H}_{\lambda\eta\lambda}\hat{\phi}_{\lambda\eta} + \hat{H}_{\eta\lambda\lambda}\hat{\phi}_{\eta\lambda} + \hat{H}_{\eta\eta\lambda}\hat{\phi}_{\eta\eta}) \\ & + (1-d)\hat{\lambda}_{ML}^{-d}\hat{\phi}_{\eta\lambda}(\hat{H}_{\lambda\lambda\eta}\hat{\phi}_{\lambda\lambda} + \hat{H}_{\lambda\eta\eta}\hat{\phi}_{\lambda\eta} + \hat{H}_{\eta\lambda\eta}\hat{\phi}_{\eta\lambda} + \hat{H}_{\eta\eta\eta}\hat{\phi}_{\eta\eta})] \end{aligned} \quad (56)$$

When $g(\lambda, \eta) = \lambda^{-d}$, then:

$$g_\lambda = -d\lambda^{-d-1}, \; g_{\lambda\lambda} = d(d+1)\lambda^{-d-2}, \; g_\eta = g_{\lambda\eta} = g_{\eta\lambda} = g_{\eta\eta} = 0. \quad (57)$$

The posterior expectation $E(\lambda^{-d}|T)$ can be written as:

$$\begin{aligned} E(\lambda^{1-d}|T) &= \hat{\lambda}_{ML}^{-d} - d\hat{\lambda}_{ML}^{-d-1}\hat{G}_\lambda\hat{\phi}_{\lambda\lambda} - d\hat{\lambda}_{ML}^{-d-1}\hat{G}_\eta\hat{\phi}_{\lambda\eta} + \tfrac{1}{2}[d(d+1)\hat{\lambda}_{ML}^{-d-1}\hat{\phi}_{\lambda\lambda} \\ &\quad -d\hat{\lambda}_{ML}^{-d-1}\hat{\phi}_{\lambda\lambda}(\hat{H}_{\lambda\lambda\lambda}\hat{\phi}_{\lambda\lambda} + \hat{H}_{\lambda\eta\lambda}\hat{\phi}_{\lambda\eta} + \hat{H}_{\eta\lambda\lambda}\hat{\phi}_{\eta\lambda} + \hat{H}_{\eta\eta\lambda}\hat{\phi}_{\eta\eta}) \\ &\quad -d\hat{\lambda}_{ML}^{-d-1}\hat{\phi}_{\eta\lambda}(\hat{H}_{\lambda\lambda\eta}\hat{\phi}_{\lambda\lambda} + \hat{H}_{\lambda\eta\eta}\hat{\phi}_{\lambda\eta} + \hat{H}_{\eta\lambda\eta}\hat{\phi}_{\eta\lambda} + \hat{H}_{\eta\eta\eta}\hat{\phi}_{\eta\eta})] \end{aligned} \quad (58)$$

BE $\hat{\lambda}_{SSE}$ under the SSE loss function is derived by submitting Equations (56) and (58) into (52).

5. Monte Carlo Simulation

In this section, the mean square error (MSE) was employed to compare the performance of these estimators, where m was the number of trials. We took different true values $(\lambda_{real}, \eta_{real})$ and n, and the number of trials was 1000. The hyper-parameters of the prior distribution were $(c_1, d_1) = (3, 2)$ and $(c_2, d_2) = (3, 2.5)$, and the parameter of the SSE loss function was $d = 4$. The simulation was conducted by MATLAB on a laptop, and the simulation results of each group took about 30 min. We used the average of reliability as the estimates. The MSEs of λ and η are shown in Table 1, and the MSEs and estimates of $R(t)$ with $t = 2$ are shown in Table 2.

Table 1. The MSEs of λ and η.

n	λ_{real}	η_{real}	MSE					
			$\hat{\lambda}_{ML}$	$\hat{\lambda}_{SE}$	$\hat{\lambda}_{SSE}$	$\hat{\eta}_{ML}$	$\hat{\eta}_{SE}$	$\hat{\eta}_{SSE}$
	5	1	0.6252	0.5126	0.2208	0.1247	0.0171	0.0056
20	8	4	0.8302	0.7005	0.4867	0.6479	0.2369	0.1875
	2	3	0.8011	0.6801	0.1644	0.8141	0.4975	0.1810
	5	1	0.4900	0.0584	0.0543	0.0458	0.0009	9.94×10^{-4}
50	8	4	0.6842	0.5550	0.4786	0.3718	0.0762	0.0530
	2	3	0.6195	0.0048	0.0053	0.5094	0.1396	0.0638
	5	1	0.1330	0.0143	0.0165	0.0358	0.0002	0.0003
100	8	4	0.2717	0.1148	0.1819	0.1138	0.0150	0.0154
	2	3	0.3339	0.0003	0.0013	0.1838	0.0218	0.0213
	5	1	0.0525	0.0034	0.0044	0.0217	4.64×10^{-5}	6.51×10^{-5}
200	8	4	0.0914	0.0562	0.0602	0.0454	0.0033	0.0040
	2	3	0.1020	0.0001	0.0004	0.0840	0.0039	0.0052
	5	1	0.0240	0.0016	0.0021	0.0214	2.12×10^{-5}	2.96×10^{-5}
300	8	4	0.0840	0.0253	0.0295	0.0096	0.0015	0.0019
	2	3	0.0863	5.31×10^{-5}	0.0002	0.0472	0.0017	0.0024
	5	1	0.0093	0.0009	0.0012	0.0184	1.24×10^{-5}	1.72×10^{-5}
400	8	4	0.0692	0.0142	0.0174	0.0016	8.25×10^{-4}	0.0011
	2	3	0.0691	2.21×10^{-5}	9.63×10^{-5}	0.0112	9.55×10^{-4}	0.0014
	5	1	0.0087	0.0006	0.0008	0.0168	7.89×10^{-6}	1.11×10^{-5}
500	8	4	0.0590	0.0092	0.0115	0.0008	5.50×10^{-4}	7.24×10^{-4}
	2	3	0.0489	1.27×10^{-5}	5.98×10^{-5}	0.0093	6.39×10^{-4}	9.28×10^{-4}

MSE of a parameter θ is defined as follows ([47]):

$$MSE(\theta) = \frac{1}{m}\sum_{i=1}^{m}(\hat{\theta}_i - \theta_{real})^2. \quad (59)$$

In order to perform simulations based on intuition fuzzy observations, we needed to transform the generated precise data into intuitive fuzzy data. According to the fuzzy representation proposed in the work of González et al. [48], each precise data x_i can be transformed into 0.6252 intuitive fuzzy data $\tilde{x}_i$, and its membership and non-membership functions are shown below:

$$\mu_{\tilde{x}_i}(t) = \begin{cases} \alpha_i \left(\frac{t-a_i}{x_i-a_i}\right)^{h_L(x_i)} & t \in [a_i, x_i] \\ \alpha_i \left(\frac{b_i-t}{b_i-x_i}\right)^{h_R(x_i)} & t \in [x_i, b_i] , \\ 0 & \text{else} \end{cases} \quad (60)$$

$$\nu_{\tilde{x}_i}(t) = \begin{cases} \left(\frac{x_i-t}{x_i-a_i}\right)^{h_L(x_i)} + \beta_i \left(\frac{t-a_i}{x_i-a_i}\right)^{h_L(x_i)} & t \in [a_i, x_i] \\ \left(\frac{t-x_i}{b_i-x_i}\right)^{h_R(x_i)} + \beta_i \left(\frac{b_i-t}{b_i-x_i}\right)^{h_R(x_i)} & t \in [x_i, b_i] . \\ 1 & \text{else} \end{cases} \quad (61)$$

such that:

(C1) $x_1, x_2, \ldots, x_n$ are random samples of observations that are exact and independently and identically distributed and obey IW(λ, η).

(C2) For any $i = 1, 2, \ldots, n$, a_i and b_i are chosen randomly with satisfying $a_i \leq x_i \leq b_i$

(C3) For any $i = 1, 2, \ldots, n$, the α_i and β_i are chosen randomly with satisfying $\alpha_i \in [0, 1]$, $\beta_i \in [0, 1]$, and $0 \leq \alpha_i + \beta_i \leq 1$.

(C4) $h_L(\cdot) : \mathbb{R} \to [0, 1]$, $h_R(\cdot) : \mathbb{R} \to [0, 1]$.

Table 2. MSEs and estimates of $R(t)$.

n	λ_{real}	η_{real}	$R(t)$	Estimates			MSE		
				$\hat{R}_{ML}(t)$	$\hat{R}_{SE}(t)$	$\hat{R}_{SSE}(t)$	$\hat{R}_{ML}(t)$	$\hat{R}_{SE}(t)$	$\hat{R}_{SSE}(t)$
20	5	1	0.9179	0.9500	0.8984	0.9286	0.0024	8.98×10^{-4}	3.21×10^{-3}
	8	4	0.3935	0.4089	0.3973	0.3465	0.0185	8.60×10^{-3}	2.80×10^{-3}
	2	3	0.2212	0.2826	0.3003	0.2798	0.0083	8.23×10^{-3}	1.82×10^{-2}
50	5	1	0.9179	0.9483	0.9122	0.9621	0.0011	6.48×10^{-5}	8.72×10^{-5}
	8	4	0.3935	0.3872	0.4086	0.3825	0.0048	8.11×10^{-4}	5.79×10^{-4}
	2	3	0.2212	0.1744	0.2604	0.2373	0.0044	5.80×10^{-3}	7.91×10^{-2}
100	5	1	0.9179	0.9262	0.9146	0.9143	0.0006	1.32×10^{-5}	2.04×10^{-5}
	8	4	0.3935	0.3891	0.4035	0.3885	0.0029	5.51×10^{-5}	2.55×10^{-5}
	2	3	0.2212	0.2819	0.2455	0.2312	0.0020	4.32×10^{-4}	3.43×10^{-4}
200	5	1	0.9179	0.9213	0.9164	0.9163	0.0002	2.69×10^{-6}	4.52×10^{-6}
	8	4	0.3935	0.3351	0.3933	0.3878	0.0012	8.66×10^{-6}	5.45×10^{-6}
	2	3	0.2212	0.1783	0.2331	0.2251	0.0013	5.95×10^{-5}	8.19×10^{-6}
300	5	1	0.9179	0.9399	0.9169	0.9168	0.0002	1.46×10^{-6}	2.23×10^{-6}
	8	4	0.3935	0.4096	0.3931	0.3901	0.0008	3.82×10^{-6}	2.18×10^{-6}
	2	3	0.2212	0.2580	0.2260	0.2235	0.0009	2.54×10^{-5}	3.78×10^{-6}
400	5	1	0.9179	0.9230	0.9172	0.9171	0.0001	1.25×10^{-6}	1.63×10^{-6}
	8	4	0.3935	0.3826	0.3945	0.3917	0.0008	2.05×10^{-6}	1.05×10^{-6}
	2	3	0.2212	0.1664	0.2252	0.2228	0.0007	1.38×10^{-5}	1.95×10^{-6}
500	5	1	0.9179	0.9393	0.9172	0.9171	0.0001	5.02×10^{-7}	7.84×10^{-7}
	8	4	0.3935	0.3737	0.3947	0.3921	0.0006	1.40×10^{-6}	6.87×10^{-7}
	2	3	0.2212	0.2048	0.2236	0.2217	0.0007	9.22×10^{-6}	1.38×10^{-6}

The simulation steps are shown below:

(i) Generate a set of data $x_1, x_2, \ldots, x_n$ from IW$(\lambda_{real}, \eta_{real})$ with $\lambda_{real} = (2, 3, 1.5, 5)$ and $\eta_{real} = (5, 4, 2, 1)$. Calculate the real reliability $R_{real}(t)$ with $t = 2$.

(ii) For convenience, let $h_L(\cdot) = h_R(\cdot) = 1$. The data $x_1, x_2, \ldots, x_n$ are transformed into TraIFNs according to Equations (60) and (61).

(iii) Calculate the MLEs by the EM algorithm and calculate the BEs by the Lindley approximation.

(iv) Repeat steps (i) to (iii) 1000 times and obtain 1000 estimates, respectively, and the MSE is calculated according to Equation (59).

From Tables 1 and 2, the following conclusions can be drawn.

(1) Whether parameters or reliability, the MSEs of MLEs and BEs decrease when the sample size increases. Thus, enlarging the sample size can appropriately enhance the accuracy of the estimation.

(2) In terms of the MSE, the performance of BEs under the SE and SSE loss functions is better than MLE. As for the reliability, the MSEs of BEs are much smaller than the MSEs of MLEs.

(3) From the simulation results of the different real values, the BEs of the parameters and corresponding reliability values both under the SE and SSE loss functions have different effects.

6. Real Dataset Analysis

In this section, we considered a real dataset proposed by Efron [49], as shown in Table 3. The dataset presents the survival times of 103 head and neck cancer patients treated with radiotherapy.

Table 3. Real dataset.

6.53	7	10.42	12.2	14.48	16.1	22.7	23.56	23.74	25.87
31.98	34	37	41.35	41.55	42	43	45.28	47.38	49.4
53.62	55.46	58.36	63	63.47	64	68.46	74.47	78.26	81
83	84	84	91	92	94	108	110	112	112
119	127	129	130	133	133	133	139	140	140
140	146	146	146	149	149	154	154	155	157
157	159	160	160	160	160	165	165	173	173
176	179	194	195	209	218	225	241	248	249
273	277	281	297	319	339	405	417	420	432
440	469	519	523	583	594	633	725	817	1101
1146	1417	1776							

According to the simulation results presented in Section 5, we took the Bayesian estimates of the parameters and reliability under the SE loss function to draw the cumulative distribution function plot. It can be seen in Figure 3 that the cdf of the IWD has a high degree of overlap with the empirical cdf. We can conclude that the IWD has a good fitting effect on this real dataset.

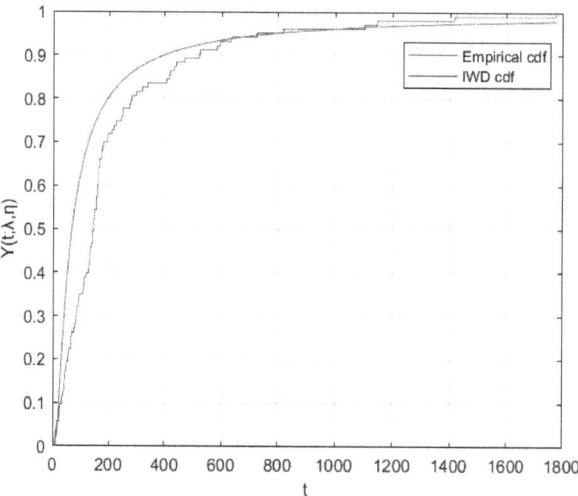

Figure 3. Empirical and IWD cdf values.

The real dataset was transformed into intuitional fuzzy data by Equations (60) and (61). All the estimates were calculated by MATLAB and are tabulated in Table 4.

Table 4. Real dataset estimates with $t = 49.4$.

$\hat{\lambda}$			$\hat{\eta}$			$\hat{R}(t)$		
MLE	SE	SSE	MLE	SE	SSE	MLE	SE	SSE
64.6171	67.7140	67.7630	0.8000	1.0886	1.0885	0.9423	0.6205	0.6170

7. Conclusions, Limitations, and Future Research

In a real-life scenario, the observed data may be less accurate due to uncontrollable factors, necessitating the use of fuzzy lifetime data for the reliability estimation of the IWD. While fuzzy sets are commonly used for this purpose, they only have one membership degree parameter, resulting in a less precise description of the objective world. In contrast, intuitionistic fuzzy sets can more accurately express uncertainty and fuzziness when dealing with fuzzy information, thereby improving the accuracy and efficiency of fuzzy reasoning. Therefore, this paper extended the probability to intuitionistic fuzzy sets and considered the parameters and reliability estimations for IWD based on intuitionistic fuzzy lifetime data. First, the MLEs were obtained through the EM algorithm. Then, BEs were obtained under the SE and SSE loss functions using the Lindley approximation. Finally, multiple sets of parameters were selected for the Monte Carlo simulation. Based on the simulation results, it was observed that by altering the true values of multiple sets of parameters, the mean square error under the Bayesian estimation was significantly smaller than that under the maximum likelihood estimation. This finding leads to the conclusion that the Bayesian estimation is a more effective approach for estimating parameters and reliability in an intuitionistic fuzzy environment.

Limited by the performance of the computer, we could not compare the performances of more methods during a limited time frame. In addition, there were many types of intuitionistic fuzzy numbers in addition to TraIFNs. We hope to discuss the statistical inference of lifetime distribution based on other types of intuitionistic fuzzy numbers in the future.

Author Contributions: Conceptualization, H.R. and X.H.; methodology, H.R.; software, X.H.; validation, H.R. and X.H.; writing—original draft preparation, X.H.; writing—review and editing, H.R.; funding acquisition, H.R. All authors have read and agreed to the published version of the manuscript.

Funding: This research was funded by the National Natural Science Foundation of China, grant number 71661012.

Data Availability Statement: Not applicable.

Conflicts of Interest: The authors declare no conflict of interest.

References

1. Yilmaz, A.; Kara, M. Reliability estimation and parameter estimation for inverse Weibull distribution under different loss functions. *Kuwait J. Sci.* **2022**, *49*, 1–24. [CrossRef]
2. Chakrabarty, J.B.; Chowdhury, S. Compounded inverse Weibull distributions: Properties, inference and applications. *Commun. Stat.-Simul. Comput.* **2019**, *48*, 2012–2033. [CrossRef]
3. Cai, J.; Shi, Y.M.; Zhang, Y.G. Robust Bayesian analysis for parallel system with masked data under inverse Weibull lifetime distribution. *Commun. Stat.-Theor. Methods* **2020**, *49*, 1422–1434. [CrossRef]
4. Bi, Q.X.; Gui, W.H. Bayesian and classical estimation of stress-strength reliability for inverse Weibull lifetime models. *Algorithms* **2017**, *10*, 71. [CrossRef]
5. Maurya, R.K.; Tripathi, Y.M.; Kayal, T. Reliability Estimation in a Multicomponent Stress-Strength Model Based on Inverse Weibull Distribution. *Sankhya B* **2022**, *84*, 364–401. [CrossRef]
6. Majd, A.; Amal, H. Estimation of the stress-strength reliability for the inverse Weibull distribution under adaptive type-II progressive hybrid censoring. *PLoS ONE* **2022**, *17*, 0277514–0277536.

7. Krishna, H.; Dube, M.; Garg, R. Estimation of stress strength reliability of inverse Weibull distribution under progressive first failure censoring. *Aust. J. Stat.* **2019**, *48*, 14–37. [CrossRef]
8. Yadav, A.S.; Singh, S.K.; Singh, U. Estimation of stress-strength reliability for inverse Weibull distribution under progressive type-II censoring scheme. *J. Ind. Prod. Eng.* **2018**, *35*, 48–55. [CrossRef]
9. Yusra, A.T.; Ehab, M.A.; Randa, R.; Ahmed, M.G.; El-Raouf, M.M.A.; Saima, K.K.; Eslam, H.; Bakr, M.E. Statistical inferences for the extended inverse Weibull distribution under progressive type-II censored sample with applications. *Alex. Eng. J.* **2022**, *65*, 493–502.
10. Zadeh, L.A. Probability measures of Fuzzy events. *J. Math. Anal. Appl.* **1968**, *23*, 421–427. [CrossRef]
11. Li, Z.; Wang, Z.; Song, Y.; Wen, C.F. Information structures in a fuzzy set-valued information system based on granular computing. *Int. J. Approx. Reason.* **2021**, *134*, 72–94. [CrossRef]
12. Dang, E.K.F.; Luk, R.; Allan, J. A principled approach using fuzzy set theory for passage-based document retrieval. *IEEE Trans. Fuzzy Syst.* **2021**, *29*, 1967–1977. [CrossRef]
13. Jiang, J.W.; Hu, Y.H.; Fang, Y.H.; Zhang, C.; Rui, X.S.; Wang, M. Fault diagnosis method of marine fans based on MTAD and fuzzy entropy. *China Mech. Eng.* **2022**, *33*, 1178–1188.
14. Pan, J.S. Research progress on deep learning-based image deblurring. *Comput. Sci.* **2021**, *48*, 9–13.
15. Xia, J.N.; Wang, D.J.; Wang, Y.Z.; Jin, Y.C.; Jiang, B. Prostate cancer diagnosis method based on structure adaptive fuzzy neural network. *Syst. Eng.-Theor. Pract.* **2018**, *38*, 1331–1342.
16. Taha, T.A.; Salman, A.N. Comparison Different Estimation Method for Reliability Function of Rayleigh Distribution Based on Fuzzy Lifetime Data. *Iraqi J. Sci.* **2022**, *63*, 1707–1719. [CrossRef]
17. Rudnei, D.D.C.; Elismar, R.O.; Filip, S. Fuzzy-set approach to invariant idempotent measures. *Fuzzy Sets Syst.* **2023**, *457*, 46–65.
18. Hashim, A.N. On the fuzzy reliability estimation for Lomax distribution. *AIP Conf. Proc.* **2019**, *2183*, 110002–110011.
19. Neamah, M.W.; Ali, B.K. Fuzzy reliability estimation for frechet distribution by using simulation. *Period. Eng. Nat. Sci.* **2020**, *8*, 632–646.
20. Abbas, P.; Gholam, A.P.; Mansour, S. Reliability estimation in Rayleigh distribution based on fuzzy lifetime data. *Int. J. Syst. Assur. Eng.* **2014**, *5*, 487–494.
21. Atanassov, K.T. Intuitionistic fuzzy sets. *Fuzzy Sets Syst.* **1986**, *20*, 87–96. [CrossRef]
22. Yazdi, M. Risk assessment based on novel intuitionistic fuzzy-hybrid-modified TOPSIS approach. *Saf. Sci.* **2018**, *110*, 438–448. [CrossRef]
23. Otay, R.; Ztayi, B.; Onar, S.E.; Kahraman, C. Multi-expert performance evaluation of healthcare institutions using an integrated intuitionistic fuzzy AHP&DEA methodology. *Knowl.-Based Syst.* **2018**, *133*, 90–106.
24. Xu, W.; Yu, Y.Y.; Zhang, Q.S. An evaluation method of comprehensive product quality for customer satisfaction based on intuitionistic fuzzy number. *Discret. Dyn. Nat. Soc.* **2018**, *2018*, 1–12. [CrossRef]
25. Gohain, B.; Chutia, R.; Dutta, P. Distance measure on intuitionistic fuzzy sets and its application in decision-making, pattern recognition, and clustering problems. *Int. J. Intell. Syst.* **2022**, *37*, 2458–2501. [CrossRef]
26. Xu, J.; Ma, Z.; Xu, Z. Novel intuitionistic fuzzy weighted geometric operators for intuitionistic fuzzy multi-attribute decision making. *J. Ind. Manag. Optim.* **2023**, *19*, 7196–7220. [CrossRef]
27. Zahra, R.; Ezzatallah, B.J.; Einolah, D. The reliability analysis based on the generalized intuitionistic fuzzy two-parameter Pareto distribution. *Soft Comput.* **2022**, *21*, 3095–3113.
28. Ebrahimnejad, A.; Jamkhaneh, E.B. System reliability using generalized intuitionistic fuzzy Rayleigh lifetime distribution. *Appl. Appl. Math.* **2018**, *13*, 97–113.
29. Huibert, K. Fuzzy random variables—I. definitions and theorems. *Inform. Sci.* **1978**, *15*, 1–29.
30. Zahra, R.; Ezzatallah, B.J.; Einolah, D. Parameters and reliability estimation for the Weibull distribution based on intuitionistic fuzzy lifetime data. *Complex Intell. Syst.* **2022**, *8*, 4881–4896.
31. Shu, M.H.; Cheng, C.H.; Chang, J.R. Using intuitionistic fuzzy sets for fault-tree analysis on printed circuit board assembly. *Microelectron. Reliab.* **2006**, *46*, 2139–2148. [CrossRef]
32. Wang, J.Q.; Zhang, Z. Programming method of multi-criteria decision-making based on intuitionistic fuzzy number with incomplete certain information. *Control Decis.* **2008**, *23*, 1145–1148.
33. Dempster, A.P. Maximum likelihood from incomplete data via the EM algorithm. *J. R. Stat. Soc.* **1977**, *39*, 1–38.
34. Singh, S.; Tripathi, Y.M. Estimating the parameters of an inverse Weibull distribution under progressive type-I interval censoring. *Stat. Pap.* **2018**, *59*, 21–56. [CrossRef]
35. Kurniawan, A.; Avicena, N.; Ana, E. Estimation of the shape parameter of Weibull distribution based on type II censored data using EM algorithm. *AIP Conf. Proc.* **2020**, *2264*, 030011–030020.
36. Barde, S.; Ko, Y.M.; Shin, H. General EM algorithm for fitting non-monotone hazard functions from truncated and censored observations. *Oper. Res. Lett.* **2022**, *50*, 476–483. [CrossRef]
37. Pal, S. A simplified stochastic EM algorithm for cure rate model with negative binomial competing risks: An application to breast cancer data. *Stat. Med.* **2021**, *40*, 6387–6409. [CrossRef]
38. Fu, E.; Heckman, N. Model-based curve registration via stochastic approximation EM algorithm. *Comput. Stat. Data An.* **2019**, *131*, 159–175. [CrossRef]

39. Wang, Z.G.; Liu, W.C. Stochastic reserving using policyholder information via EM algorithm. *Appl. Math. Model.* **2022**, *112*, 199–214. [CrossRef]
40. Lachos, V.H.; Prates, M.O.; Dey, D.K. Heckman selection-t model: Parameter estimation via the EM-algorithm. *J. Multivar. Anal.* **2021**, *184*, 104737–104755. [CrossRef]
41. Jia, X.; Cheng, Z.J.; Guo, B. Reliability evaluation for products based on entropy and Bayes theory. *Syst. Eng. Theory Pract.* **2020**, *40*, 1918–1926.
42. Li, D.W.; Wang, G.D.; Li, Y.Z. Qualification test risk analysis of binomial equipment based on Bayes theory. *J. Aerosp. Power* **2021**, *36*, 157–166.
43. Wang, C.Y.; Huang, X.J. Comparison of Bayesian estimation of the scale parameter for Log gamma distribution under Linex loss function and compound Linex loss function. *Math. Appl.* **2018**, *31*, 384–391.
44. Kundu, D.; Mitra, D. Bayesian inference of Weibull distribution based on left truncated and right censored data. *Comput. Stat. Data An.* **2016**, *99*, 38–50. [CrossRef]
45. Xu, B.; Wang, D.H.; Wang, R.T. Estimator of scale parameter in a subclass of the exponential family under symmetric entropy loss. *Northeast Math. J.* **2008**, *24*, 447–457.
46. Song, L.X.; Chen, Y.S.; Xu, J.M. Bayesian estimation of Poisson distribution parameter under scale squared error loss function. *J. Lanzhou Univ. Tech.* **2008**, *34*, 152–154.
47. Usta, I. Bayesian estimation for geometric process with the Weibull distribution. *Commun. Stat.-Simul. Comput.* **2022**, 1–27. [CrossRef]
48. González, R.G.; Colubi, A.; Ángeles, G.M. A fuzzy representation of random variables: An operational tool in exploratory analysis and hypothesis testing. *Comput. Stat. Data Anal.* **2006**, *51*, 163–176. [CrossRef]
49. Efron, B. Logistic regression, survival analysis, and the Kaplan-Meier curve. *J. Am. Stat. Assoc.* **1988**, *83*, 414–425. [CrossRef]

Disclaimer/Publisher's Note: The statements, opinions and data contained in all publications are solely those of the individual author(s) and contributor(s) and not of MDPI and/or the editor(s). MDPI and/or the editor(s) disclaim responsibility for any injury to people or property resulting from any ideas, methods, instructions or products referred to in the content.

Article

An Analytic Method to Determine the Optimal Time for the Induction Phase of Anesthesia

Mohamed A. Zaitri [1,2], Cristiana J. Silva [1,3,*] and Delfim F. M. Torres [1,4]

[1] Center for Research and Development in Mathematics and Applications (CIDMA), Department of Mathematics, University of Aveiro, 3810-193 Aveiro, Portugal; zaitri@ua.pt (M.A.Z.); delfim@ua.pt or delfim@unicv.cv (D.F.M.T.)
[2] Department of Mathematics, University of Djelfa, Djelfa 17000, Algeria
[3] Department of Mathematics, ISCTE—Instituto Universitário de Lisboa, 1649-026 Lisbon, Portugal
[4] Research Center in Exact Sciences (CICE), Faculty of Sciences and Technology (FCT), University of Cape Verde (Uni-CV), Praia 7943-010, Cape Verde
* Correspondence: cristiana.joao.silva@iscte-iul.pt

Abstract: We obtain an analytical solution for the time-optimal control problem in the induction phase of anesthesia. Our solution is shown to align numerically with the results obtained from the conventional shooting method. The induction phase of anesthesia relies on a pharmacokinetic/pharmacodynamic (PK/PD) model proposed by Bailey and Haddad in 2005 to regulate the infusion of propofol. In order to evaluate our approach and compare it with existing results in the literature, we examine a minimum-time problem for anesthetizing a patient. By applying the Pontryagin minimum principle, we introduce the shooting method as a means to solve the problem at hand. Additionally, we conducted numerical simulations using the MATLAB computing environment. We solve the time-optimal control problem using our newly proposed analytical method and discover that the optimal continuous infusion rate of the anesthetic and the minimum required time for transition from the awake state to an anesthetized state exhibit similarity between the two methods. However, the advantage of our new analytic method lies in its independence from unknown initial conditions for the adjoint variables.

Keywords: pharmacokinetic/pharmacodynamic model; optimal control theory; time-optimal control of the induction phase of anesthesia; shooting method; analytical method; numerical simulations

MSC: 49M05; 49N90; 92C45

Citation: Zaitri, M.A.; Silva, C.J.; Torres, D.F.M. An Analytic Method to Determine the Optimal Time for the Induction Phase of Anesthesia. *Axioms* **2023**, *12*, 867. https://doi.org/10.3390/axioms12090867

Academic Editor: Giuseppe Viglialoro

Received: 10 June 2023
Revised: 4 September 2023
Accepted: 6 September 2023
Published: 8 September 2023

Copyright: © 2023 by the authors. Licensee MDPI, Basel, Switzerland. This article is an open access article distributed under the terms and conditions of the Creative Commons Attribution (CC BY) license (https://creativecommons.org/licenses/by/4.0/).

1. Introduction

Based on Guedel's classification, the first stage of anesthesia is the induction phase, which begins with the initial administration of anesthesia and ends with loss of consciousness [1]. Millions of people safely receive several types of anesthesia while undergoing medical procedures: local anesthesia, regional anesthesia, general anesthesia, and sedation [2]. However, there may be some potential complications of anesthesia including anesthetic awareness, collapsed lung, malignant hyperthermia, nerve damage, and postoperative delirium. Certain factors make it riskier to receive anesthesia, including advanced age, diabetes, kidney disease, heart disease, high blood pressure, and smoking [3]. To avoid the risk, administering anesthesia should be carried out on a scientific basis, based on modern pharmacotherapy, which relies on both pharmacokinetic (PK) and pharmacodynamic (PD) information [4]. Pharmacokinetics is used to describe the absorption and distribution of anesthesia in body fluids, resulting from the administration of a certain anesthesia dose. Pharmacodynamics is the study of the effect resulting from anesthesia [5]. Multiple mathematical models were already presented to predict the dynamics of the pharmacokinetics/pharmacodynamics (PK/PD) models [6–9]. Some of these models were implemented following different methods [2,10,11].

The parameters of PK/PD models were fitted by Schnider et al. in [12]. In [6], the authors study pharmacokinetic models for propofol, comparing Schnider et al. and Marsh et al. models [13]. The authors of [6] conclude that Schnider's model should always be used in effect-site targeting mode, in which larger initial doses are administered but smaller than those obtained from Marsh's model. However, users of the Schnider model should be aware that in the morbidly obese, the lean body mass (LBM) equation can generate paradoxical values, resulting in excessive increases in maintenance infusion rates [12]. In [14], a new strategy is presented to develop a robust control of anesthesia for the maintenance phase, taking into account the saturation of the actuator. The authors of [15] address the problem of optimal control of the induction phase. For other related works, see [8,16] and references therein.

Here, we consider the problem proposed in [15], to transfer a patient from a state consciousness to unconsciousness. We apply the shooting method [17] using the Pontryagin minimum principle [18], correcting some inconsistencies found in [15] related with the stop criteria of the algorithm and the numerical computation of the equilibrium point. Secondly, we provide a new different analytical method to the time-optimal control problem for the induction phase of anesthesia. While the shooting method, popularized by Zabi et al. [15], is widely employed for solving such control problems and determining the minimum time, its reliance on Newton's method makes it sensitive to initial conditions. The shooting method's convergence is heavily dependent on the careful selection of initial values, particularly for the adjoint vectors. To overcome this limitation, we propose an alternative approach, which eliminates the need for initial value selection and convergence analysis. Our method offers a solution to the time-optimal control problem for the induction phase of anesthesia, free from the drawbacks associated with the shooting method. Furthermore, we propose that our method can be extended to other PK/PD models to determine optimal timings for drug administration. To compare the methods, we perform numerical simulations to compute the minimum time to anesthetize a man of 53 years, 77 kg, and 177 cm, as considered in [15]. We find the optimal continuous infusion rate of the anesthetic and the minimum time that needs to be chosen for treatment, showing that both the shooting method of [15] and the one proposed here coincide.

This paper is organized as follows. In Section 2, we recall the pharmacokinetic and pharmacodynamic model of Bailey and Haddad [19], the Schnider model [12], the bispectral index (BIS), and the equilibrium point [14]. Then, in Section 3, a time-optimal control problem for the induction phase of anesthesia is posed and solved both by the shooting and analytical methods. Finally, in Section 4, we compute the parameters of the model using the Schnider model [12], and we illustrate the results of the time-optimal control problem through numerical simulations. We conclude that the optimal continuous infusion rate for anesthesia and the minimum time that should be chosen for this treatment can be found by both shooting and analytical methods. The advantage of the new method proposed here is that it does not depend on the concrete initial conditions, while the shooting method is very sensitive to the choice of the initial conditions of the state and adjoint variables. We end with Section 5 of conclusions, pointing also some directions for future research.

2. The PK/PD Model

The pharmacokinetic/pharmacodynamic (PK/PD) model consists of four compartments: intravascular blood $(x_1(t))$, muscle $(x_2(t))$, fat $(x_3(t))$, and effect site $(x_4(t))$. The effect site compartment (brain) is introduced to account for the finite equilibration time between central compartment and central nervous system concentrations [19]. This model is used to describe the circulation of drugs in a patient's body, being expressed by a four-dimensional dynamical system as follows:

$$\begin{cases} \dot{x}_1(t) = -(a_{10} + a_{12} + a_{13})\, x_1(t) + a_{21}\, x_2(t) + a_{31}\, x_3(t) + u(t), \\ \dot{x}_2(t) = a_{12}\, x_1(t) - a_{21}\, x_2(t), \\ \dot{x}_3(t) = a_{13}\, x_1(t) - a_{31}\, x_3(t), \\ \dot{x}_4(t) = \frac{a_{e0}}{v_1}\, x_1(t) - a_{e0}\, x_4(t). \end{cases} \quad (1)$$

The state variables for system (1) are subject to the following initial conditions:

$$x(0) = (x_1(0), x_2(0), x_3(0), x_4(0)) = (0,0,0,0), \qquad (2)$$

where $x_1(t), x_2(t), x_3(t)$, and $x_4(t)$ represent, respectively, the masses of the propofol in the compartments of blood, muscle, fat, and effect site at time t. The control $u(t)$ is the continuous infusion rate of the anesthetic. The parameters a_{10} and a_{e0} represent, respectively, the rate of clearance from the central compartment and the effect site. The parameters $a_{12}, a_{13}, a_{21}, a_{31}$, and a_{e0}/v_1 are the transfer rates of the drug between compartments. A schematic diagram of the dynamical control system (1) is given in Figure 1.

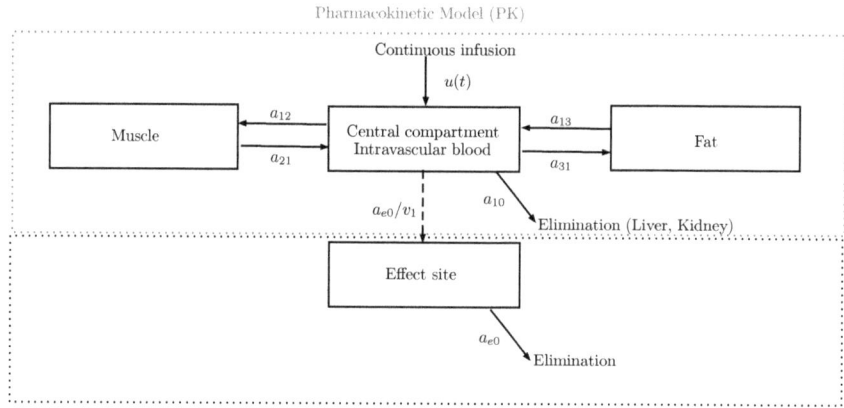

Figure 1. Schematic diagram of the PK/PD model with the effect site compartment of Bailey and Haddad [19].

2.1. Schnider's Model

Following Schnider et al. [12], the lean body mass (LBM) is calculated using the James formula, which performs satisfactorily in normal and moderately obese patients, but not so well for severely obese cases [20]. The James formula calculates LBM as follows:

$$\text{for Male, LBM} = 1.1 \times \text{weight} - 128 \times \left(\frac{\text{weight}}{\text{height}}\right)^2, \qquad (3)$$

$$\text{for Female, LBM} = 1.07 \times \text{weight} - 148 \times \left(\frac{\text{weight}}{\text{height}}\right)^2. \qquad (4)$$

The parameters of the PK/PD model (1) are then estimated according to Table 1.

Table 1. Parameter values for model (1) according to Schnider's model [12].

Parameter	Estimation
a_{10} (min^{-1})	$0.443 + 0.0107 \,(\text{weight} - 77) - 0.0159 \,(\text{LBM} - 59) + 0.0062 \,(\text{height} - 177)$
a_{12} (min^{-1})	$0.302 - 0.0056 \,(\text{age} - 53)$
a_{13} (min^{-1})	0.196
a_{21} (min^{-1})	$(1.29 - 0.024 \,(\text{age} - 53))/(18.9 - 0.391 \,(\text{age} - 53))$
a_{31} (min^{-1})	0.0035
a_{e0} (min^{-1})	0.456
v_1 (L)	4.27

2.2. The Bispectral Index (BIS)

The BIS is the depth of anesthesia indicator, which is a signal derived from the EEG analysis and directly related to the effect site concentration of $x_4(t)$. It quantifies the level of consciousness of a patient from 0 (no cerebral activity) to 100 (fully awake patient), and can be described empirically by a decreasing sigmoid function [19]:

$$BIS(x_4(t)) = BIS_0 \left(1 - \frac{x_4(t)^\gamma}{x_4(t)^\gamma + EC_{50}^\gamma} \right), \tag{5}$$

where BIS_0 is the BIS value of an awake patient typically set to 100, EC_{50} corresponds to the drug concentration associated with 50% of the maximum effect, and γ is a parameter modeling the degree of nonlinearity. According to [21], typical values for these parameters are $EC_{50} = 3.4$ mg/L and $\gamma = 3$.

2.3. The Equilibrium Point

Following [14], the equilibrium point is obtained by equating the right-hand side of (1) to zero,

$$\begin{cases} 0 = -(a_{10} + a_{12} + a_{13})x_1 + a_{21}x_2 + a_{31}x_3 + u, \\ 0 = a_{12}x_1 - a_{21}x_2, \\ 0 = a_{13}x_1 - a_{31}x_3, \\ 0 = \frac{a_{e0}}{v_1}x_1 - a_{e0}x_4, \end{cases} \tag{6}$$

with the condition

$$x_4 = EC_{50}. \tag{7}$$

It results that the equilibrium point $x_e = (x_{e1}, x_{e2}, x_{e3}, x_{e4})$ is given by

$$x_{e1} = v_1 EC_{50}, \quad x_{e2} = \frac{a_{12} v_1 EC_{50}}{a_{21}}, \quad x_{e3} = \frac{a_{13} v_1 EC_{50}}{a_{31}}, \quad x_{e4} = EC_{50}, \tag{8}$$

and the value of the continuous infusion rate for this equilibrium is

$$u_e = a_{10} v_1 EC_{50}. \tag{9}$$

The fast state is defined by

$$x_{eF}(t) = (x_1(t), x_4(t)). \tag{10}$$

The control of the fast dynamics is crucial because the BIS is a direct function of the concentration at the effect site.

3. Time-Optimal Control Problem

Let $x(t) = (x_1(t), x_2(t), x_3(t), x_4(t)) \in \mathbb{R}^4$. We can write the dynamical system (1) in a matrix form as follows:

$$\dot{x}(t) = A x(t) + B u(t), \tag{11}$$

where

$$A = \begin{pmatrix} -(a_{10} + a_{12} + a_{13}) & a_{21} & a_{31} & 0 \\ a_{12} & -a_{21} & 0 & 0 \\ a_{13} & 0 & -a_{31} & 0 \\ \frac{a_{e0}}{v_1} & 0 & 0 & -a_{e0} \end{pmatrix} \quad \text{and} \quad B = \begin{pmatrix} 1 \\ 0 \\ 0 \\ 0 \end{pmatrix}. \tag{12}$$

Here, the continuous infusion rate $u(t)$ is to be chosen so as to transfer the system (1) from the initial state (wake state) to the fast final state (anesthetized state) in the shortest possible time. Mathematically, we have the following time-optimal control problem [15]:

$$\begin{cases} \min J = \int_0^{t_f} dt, \\ \dot{x}(t) = A\,x(t) + B\,u(t), \quad x(0) = (0,0,0,0), \\ C\,x_{eF}(t_f) = x_{eF}, \\ 0 \leq u(t) \leq U_{max}, \quad t \in [0, t_f], \quad t_f \text{ is free,} \end{cases} \quad (13)$$

where t_f is the first instant of time that the desired state is reached, and C and x_{eF} are given by

$$C = \begin{pmatrix} 1 & 0 \\ 0 & 1 \end{pmatrix}, \quad x_{eF} = (x_{e1}, x_{e4}), \quad (14)$$

with

$$x_{eF}(t_f) = (x_1(t_f), x_2(t_f)). \quad (15)$$

3.1. Pontryagin Minimum Principle

According to the Pontryagin minimum principle (PMP) [18], if $\tilde{u} \in L^1$ is optimal for Problem (13) and the final time t_f is free, then there exists $\psi(t) = (\psi_1(t), \ldots, \psi_4(t))$, $t \in [0, t_f]$, $\psi \in AC([0, t_f]; \mathbb{R}^4)$, called the adjoint vector, such that

$$\begin{cases} \dot{x} = \dfrac{\partial H}{\partial \psi}, \\ \dot{\psi} = -\dfrac{\partial H}{\partial x}, \end{cases} \quad (16)$$

where the Hamiltonian H is defined by

$$H(t, x, u, \psi) = 1 + \psi^T (A\,x + B\,u). \quad (17)$$

Moreover, the minimality condition

$$H(t, \tilde{x}(t), \tilde{u}(t), \tilde{\psi}(t)) = \min_{0 \leq u \leq U_{max}} H(t, \tilde{x}(t), u, \tilde{\psi}(t)) \quad (18)$$

holds almost everywhere on $t \in [0, t_f]$.

Since the final time t_f is free, according to the transversality condition of PMP, we obtain:

$$H(t_f, x(t_f), u(t_f), \psi(t_f)) = 0. \quad (19)$$

Solving the minimality condition (18) on the interior of the set of admissible controls gives the necessary condition

$$\tilde{u}(t) = \begin{cases} 0 & \text{if } \tilde{\psi}_1(t) > 0, \\ U_{max} & \text{if } \tilde{\psi}_1(t) < 0, \end{cases} \quad (20)$$

where $\tilde{\psi}_1(t)$ is obtained from the adjoint system (16), that is, $\tilde{\psi}'(t) = -A^T \tilde{\psi}(t)$, and the transversality condition (19). This is discussed in Sections 3.2 and 3.3.

3.2. Shooting Method

The shooting method is a numerical technique used to solve boundary value problems, specifically in the realm of differential equations and optimal control. It transforms the problem into an initial value problem by estimating the unknown boundary conditions. Through iterative adjustments to these estimates, the boundary conditions are gradually satisfied. In [17], the authors propose an algorithm that addresses numerical solutions for parameterized optimal control problems. This algorithm incorporates multiple shooting and recursive quadratic programming, introducing a condensing algorithm for linearly constrained quadratic subproblems and high-rank update procedures. The algorithm's implementation leads to significant improvements in convergence behavior, computing time, and storage requirements. For more on numerical approaches to solve optimal control problems, we refer the reader to [22] and references therein.

Using (16), (17), (19), and (20), we consider the following problem:

$$\begin{cases} \dot{x}(t) = A\,x(t) + B \times \max(0, -U_{max}\,sign(\psi_1(t))), \\ \dot{\psi}(t) = -A^T\,\psi(t), \\ x(0) = (0,0,0,0),\ x_1(t_f) = x_{e1},\ x_4(t_f) = x_{e4}, \\ \psi(0) \text{ is free, } H(t_f, x(t_f), \max(0, -U_{max}\,sign(\psi_1(t_f))), \psi(t_f)) = 0. \end{cases} \quad (21)$$

Let $z(t) = (x(t), \psi(t))$. Then, we obtain the following two points' boundary value problem:

$$\begin{cases} \dot{z}(t) = A^* z(t) + B^*, \\ R(z(0), z(t_f)) = 0, \end{cases} \quad (22)$$

where $A^* \in M_{8 \times 8}(\mathbb{R})$ is the matrix given by

$$A^* = \begin{pmatrix} A & 0_{4\times4} \\ 0_{4\times4} & -A^T \end{pmatrix}, \quad (23)$$

$B^* \in \mathbb{R}^8$ is the vector given by

$$B^* = \begin{cases} (0,0,0,0,0,0,0,0) & \text{if } \psi_1(t) > 0, \\ (U_{max}, 0, 0, 0, 0, 0, 0, 0) & \text{if } \psi_1(t) < 0, \end{cases} \quad (24)$$

and $R(z(0), z(t_f))$ is given by (2), (15), and (19). We consider the following Cauchy problem:

$$\begin{cases} \dot{z}(t) = A^* z(t) + B^*, \\ z(0) = z_0. \end{cases} \quad (25)$$

If we define the shooting function $S : \mathbb{R}^4 \longrightarrow \mathbb{R}^3$ by

$$S(z_0) = R(t_f, z(t_f, z_0)), \quad (26)$$

where $z(t, z_0)$ is the solution of the Cauchy problem (25), then the two points' boundary value problem (21) is equivalent to

$$S(z_0) = 0. \quad (27)$$

To solve (27), we use Newton's method [23].

3.3. Analytical Method

We now propose a different method to choose the optimal control. If the pair (A, B) satisfies the Kalman condition and all eigenvalues of matrix $A \in n \times n$ are real, then any extremal control has at most $n - 1$ commutations on $\mathbb{R}^+$ (at most $n - 1$ switching times). We consider the following eight possible strategies:

Strategy 1 (zero switching times):

$$u(t) = U_{max},\ \forall t \in [0, t_f]. \quad (28)$$

Strategy 2 (zero switching times):
$$u(t) = 0, \forall t \in [0, t_f]. \tag{29}$$

Strategy 3 (one switching time):
$$u(t) = \begin{cases} U_{max} & \text{if } 0 \leq t < t_c, \\ 0 & \text{if } t_c < t \leq t_f, \end{cases} \tag{30}$$

where t_c is a switching time.

Strategy 4 (one switching time):
$$u(t) = \begin{cases} 0 & \text{if } 0 \leq t < t_c, \\ U_{max} & \text{if } t_c < t \leq t_f. \end{cases} \tag{31}$$

Strategy 5 (two switching times):
$$u(t) = \begin{cases} U_{max} & \text{if } 0 < t < t_{c1}, \\ 0 & \text{if } t_{c1} < t < t_{c2}. \\ U_{max} & \text{if } t_{c2} < t \leq t_f, \end{cases} \tag{32}$$

where t_{c1} and t_{c2} represent two switching times.

Strategy 6 (two switching times):
$$u(t) = \begin{cases} 0 & \text{if } 0 < t < t_{c1}, \\ U_{max} & \text{if } t_{c1} < t < t_{c2}. \\ 0 & \text{if } t_{c2} < t \leq t_f. \end{cases} \tag{33}$$

Strategy 7 (three switching times):
$$u(t) = \begin{cases} U_{max} & \text{if } 0 < t < t_{c1}, \\ 0 & \text{if } t_{c1} < t < t_{c2}. \\ U_{max} & \text{if } t_{c2} < t \leq t_{c3}. \\ 0 & \text{if } t_{c3} < t < t_f, \end{cases} \tag{34}$$

where t_{c1}, t_{c2}, and t_{c3} represent three switching times.

Strategy 8 (three switching times):
$$u(t) = \begin{cases} 0 & \text{if } 0 < t < t_{c1}, \\ U_{max} & \text{if } t_{c1} < t < t_{c2}. \\ 0 & \text{if } t_{c2} < t \leq t_{c3}. \\ U_{max} & \text{if } t_{c3} < t < t_f. \end{cases} \tag{35}$$

Let $x(t)$ be the trajectory associated with the control $u(t)$, given by the relation

$$x(t) = \exp(A\,t)\,x(0) + \int_0^t \exp(A(t-s))Bu(t)ds, \tag{36}$$

where $\exp(A)$ is the exponential matrix of A.

To calculate the switching times t_c, t_{c1}, t_{c2} and the final time t_f, we have to solve the following nonlinear equation:

$$\tilde{x}_{eF}(t_f) = (x_{e1}, x_{e4}). \tag{37}$$

We also solve (37) using the Newton method [23].

4. Numerical Example

In this section, we use the shooting and analytical methods to calculate the minimum time t_f to anesthetize a man of 53 years, 77 kg, and 177 cm.

The equilibrium point and the flow rate corresponding to a BIS of 50 are:

$$x_e = (14.518 \text{ mg}, 64.2371 \text{ mg}, 813.008 \text{ mg}, 3.4 \text{ mg}), \quad u_e = 6.0907 \text{ mg/min}. \tag{38}$$

Following the Schnider model, the matrix A of the dynamic system (11) is given by:

$$A = \begin{pmatrix} -0.9175 & 0.0683 & 0.0035 & 0 \\ 0.3020 & -0.0683 & 0 & 0 \\ 0.1960 & 0 & -0.0035 & 0 \\ 0.1068 & 0 & 0 & -0.4560 \end{pmatrix} \quad \text{and} \quad B = \begin{pmatrix} 1 \\ 0 \\ 0 \\ 0 \end{pmatrix}. \tag{39}$$

We are interested to solve the following minimum-time control problem:

$$\begin{cases} \min_{t_f} J = \int_0^{t_f} dt, \\ \dot{x}(t) = A x(t) + B u(t), \quad x(0) = (0, 0, 0, 0), \\ x_{e1}(t_f) = 14.518 \text{ mg}, \quad x_{e4}(t_f) = 3.4 \text{ mg}, \\ 0 \le u(t) \le 106.0907, \quad t \in [0, t_f], \quad t_f \text{ is free}. \end{cases} \tag{40}$$

4.1. Numerical Resolution by the Shooting Method

Let $z(t) = (x(t), \psi(t))$. We consider the following Cauchy problem:

$$\begin{cases} \dot{z}(t) = A^* z(t) + B^*, \\ z(0) = z_0 = (0, 0, 0, 0, \psi_{01}, \psi_{02}, \psi_{03}, \psi_{04}), \end{cases} \tag{41}$$

where

$$A^* = 10^{-4} \begin{pmatrix} -9175 & 683 & 35 & 0 & 0 & 0 & 0 & 0 \\ 3020 & -683 & 0 & 0 & 0 & 0 & 0 & 0 \\ 196 & 0 & -35 & 0 & 0 & 0 & 0 & 0 \\ 1068 & 0 & 0 & -456 & 0 & 0 & 0 & 0 \\ 0 & 0 & 0 & 0 & 9175 & -3020 & -196 & -1068 \\ 0 & 0 & 0 & 0 & -683 & 683 & 0 & 0 \\ 0 & 0 & 0 & 0 & -35 & 0 & 35 & 0 \\ 0 & 0 & 0 & 0 & 0 & 0 & 0 & 456 \end{pmatrix}, \tag{42}$$

$$B^* = \begin{pmatrix} \max(0, -106.0907 \, sign(\psi_1(t))) \\ 0 \\ 0 \\ 0 \\ 0 \\ 0 \\ 0 \\ 0 \end{pmatrix}. \tag{43}$$

The shooting function S is given by

$$S(z_0) = (S_1(z_0), S_2(z_0), S_3(z_0)), \qquad (44)$$

where

$$\begin{aligned} S_1(z_0) &= x_{e1}(t_f) - 14.518, \\ S_2(z_0) &= x_{e4}(t_f) - 3.4, \\ S_3(z_0) &= 1 + \psi^T(t_f)\Big(Ax(t_f) + B\max\big(0, -106.0907\,\text{sing}\,\psi_1(t_f)\big)\Big). \end{aligned}$$

All computations were performed with the MATLAB numeric computing environment, version R2020b, using the medium-order method and the function ode45 (Runge–Kutta method) in order to solve the nonstiff differential system (22). We have used the variable order method and the function ode113 (Adams–Bashforth–Moulton method) in order to solve the nonstiff differential system (25), and the function fsolve in order to solve equation $S(z_0) = 0$. Thus, we obtain that the minimum time is equal to

$$t_f = 1.8397\,\text{min}, \qquad (45)$$

with

$$\psi^T(0) = (-0.0076, 0.0031, -0.0393, -0.0374). \qquad (46)$$

4.2. Numerical Resolution by the Analytical Method

The pair (A, B) satisfies the Kalman condition, and the matrix A has four real eigenvalues. Then, the extremal control $u(t)$ has at most three commutations on $\mathbb{R}^+$. Therefore, let us test the eight strategies provided in Section 3.3.

Note that the anesthesiologist begins with a bolus injection to transfer the patient state from the consciousness state $x(0)$ to the unconsciousness state

$$x_{eF} = (14.518, 3.4),$$

that is,

$$u(0) = U_{max} = 106.0907\,\text{mg/min}. \qquad (47)$$

Thus, Strategies 2, 4, 6, and 8 are not feasible here. Therefore, in the sequel, we investigate Strategies 1, 3, 5, and 7 only.

Strategy 1: Let $u(t) = 106.0907\,\text{mg/min}$ for all $t \in [0, t_f]$. The trajectory $x(t)$, associated with this control $u(t)$, is given by the following relation:

$$x(t) = \int_0^t \exp(A(t-s))BU_{max}\,ds, \quad \forall t \in [0, t_f], \qquad (48)$$

where

$$\exp(A(t-s)) = VD(t-s)V^{-1} \qquad (49)$$

with

$$V = \begin{pmatrix} 0 & 0.9085 & 0.0720 & -0.0058 \\ 0 & -0.3141 & 0.9377 & -0.0266 \\ 0 & -0.1898 & -0.3395 & -0.9996 \\ 1 & -0.1997 & 0.0187 & -0.0014 \end{pmatrix} \qquad (50)$$

and
$$D(\tau) = \begin{pmatrix} \exp^{-0.4560\,\tau} & 0 & 0 & 0 \\ 0 & \exp^{-0.9419\,\tau} & 0 & 0 \\ 0 & 0 & \exp^{-0.0451\,\tau} & 0 \\ 0 & 0 & 0 & \exp^{-0.0024\,\tau} \end{pmatrix}. \tag{51}$$

System (37) takes the form
$$\begin{cases} x_1(t_f) = 14.518, \\ x_4(t_f) = 3.4, \end{cases} \tag{52}$$
and has no solutions. Thus, Strategy 1 is not feasible.

Strategy 3: Let $u(t)$, $t \in [0, t_f]$, be the control defined by
$$u(t) = \begin{cases} 106.0907\,\text{mg/min} & \text{if } 0 \le t < t_c, \\ 0 & \text{if } t_c < t \le t_f. \end{cases} \tag{53}$$

The trajectory $x(t)$ associated with this control $u(t)$ is given by
$$x(t) = \begin{cases} \int_0^t \exp(A(t-s))BU_{max}ds & \text{if } 0 \le t \le t_c, \\ \exp(A(t-t_c))\,x(t_c) & \text{if } t_c < t \le t_f, \end{cases} \tag{54}$$

where
$$\exp(A(t-t_c)) = VD(t-t_c)V^{-1}. \tag{55}$$

To calculate the switching time t_c and the final time t_f, we have to solve the nonlinear system (52) with the new condition
$$t_c < t_f. \tag{56}$$

Similarly to Section 4.1, all numerical computations were performed with MATLAB R2020b using the command `solve` to solve Equation (52). The obtained minimum time is equal to
$$t_f = 1.8397\,\text{min}, \tag{57}$$
with the switching time
$$t_c = 0.5467\,\text{min}. \tag{58}$$

Strategy 5: Let $u(t)$, $t \in [0, t_f]$, be the control defined by the relation
$$u(t) = \begin{cases} 106.0907\,\text{mg/min} & \text{if } 0 \le t < t_{c1}, \\ 0 & \text{if } t_{c1} < t < t_{c2}. \\ 106.0907\,\text{mg/min} & \text{if } t_{c2} < t \le t_f, \end{cases} \tag{59}$$

where t_{c1} and t_{c2} are the two switching times. The trajectory $x(t)$ associated with control (59) is given by
$$x(t) = \begin{cases} \int_0^t \exp(A(t-s))BU_{max}ds & \text{if } 0 \le t \le t_{c1}, \\ \exp(A(t-t_{c1}))\,x(t_{c1}) & \text{if } t_{c1} < t \le t_{c2}, \\ \exp(A(t-t_{c2}))\,x(t_{c2}) + \int_{t_{c2}}^t \exp(A(t-s))BU_{max}ds & \text{if } t_{c2} < t \le t_f. \end{cases} \tag{60}$$

To compute the two switching times t_{c1} and t_{c2} and the final time t_f, we have to solve the nonlinear system (52) with

$$0 \leq t_{c1} \leq t_{c2} \leq t_f. \tag{61}$$

It turns out that System (52) subject to Condition (61) has no solution. Thus, Strategy 5 is also not feasible.

Strategy 7: Let $u(t), t \in [0, t_f]$, be the control defined by the relation

$$u(t) = \begin{cases} 106.0907 \text{ mg/min} & \text{if } 0 \leq t < t_{c1}, \\ 0 & \text{if } t_{c1} < t < t_{c2}. \\ 106.0907 \text{ mg/min} & \text{if } t_{c2} < t \leq t_{c3}, \\ 0 \text{ mg/min} & \text{if } t_{c3} < t \leq t_f, \end{cases} \tag{62}$$

where t_{c1}, t_{c2}, and t_{c3} are the three switching times. The trajectory $x(t)$ associated with Control (62) is given by

$$x(t) = \begin{cases} \int_0^t \exp(A(t-s))BU_{max}ds & \text{if } 0 \leq t \leq t_{c1}, \\ \exp(A(t-t_{c1}))x(t_{c1}) & \text{if } t_{c1} < t \leq t_{c2}, \\ \exp(A(t-t_{c2}))x(t_{c2}) + \int_{t_{c2}}^t \exp(A(t-s))BU_{max}ds & \text{if } t_{c2} < t \leq t_{c3}, \\ \exp(A(t-t_{c3}))x(t_{c3}) & \text{if } t_{c3} < t \leq t_f. \end{cases} \tag{63}$$

To compute the three switching times t_{c1}, t_{c2}, and t_{c3} and the final time t_f, we have to solve the nonlinear system (52) with

$$0 \leq t_{c1} \leq t_{c2} \leq t_{c3} \leq t_f. \tag{64}$$

It turns out that System (52) subject to Condition (64) has no solution. Thus, Strategy 7 is also not feasible.

In Figures 2 and 3, we present the solutions of the linear system of differential Equation (40) under the optimal control $u(t)$ illustrated in Figure 4, where the black curve corresponds to the one obtained by the shooting method, as explained in Section 3.2, while the blue curve corresponds to our analytical method, in the sense of Section 3.3. In addition, for both figures, we show the controlled BIS Index, the trajectory of fast states corresponding to the optimal continuous infusion rate of the anesthetic $u(t)$, and the minimum time t_f required to transition System (40) from the initial (wake) state

$$x_0 = (0, 0, 0, 0)$$

to the fast final (anesthetized) state

$$x_{eF} = (14.518, 3.4)$$

in the shortest possible time. The minimum time t_f is equal to $t_f = 1.8397$ min by the shooting method (black curve in Figure 2), and it is equal to $t_f = 1.8397$ min by the analytical method (blue curve in Figure 3).

By using the shooting method, the black curve in Figure 4 shows that the optimal continuous infusion rate of the induction phase of anesthesia $u(t)$ is equal to 106.0907 mg/min until the switching time

$$t_c = 0.5467 \text{ min.}$$

Then, it is equal to 0 mg/min (stop-infusion) until the final time

$$t_f = 1.8397 \text{ min,}$$

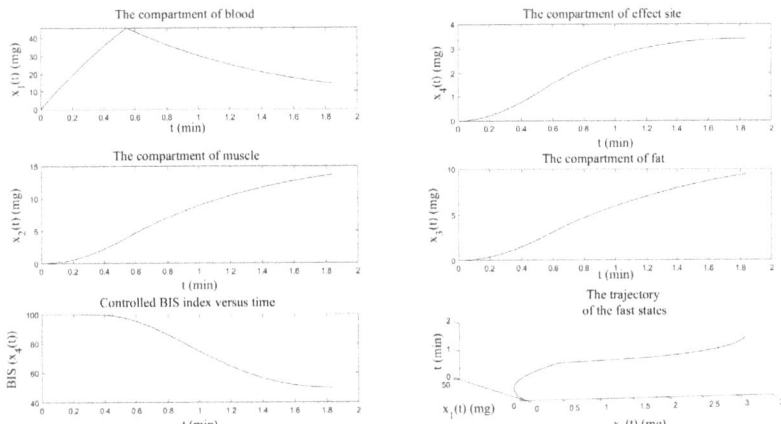

Figure 2. The state trajectory, controlled BIS index, and trajectory of the fast states corresponding to the optimal control $u(t)$ of Figure 4, using the shooting method.

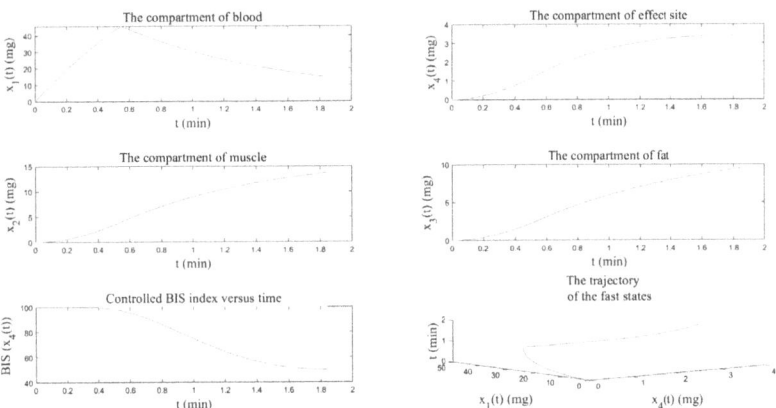

Figure 3. The state trajectory, controlled BIS index, and trajectory of the fast states corresponding to the optimal control $u(t)$ of Figure 4, using the analytical method.

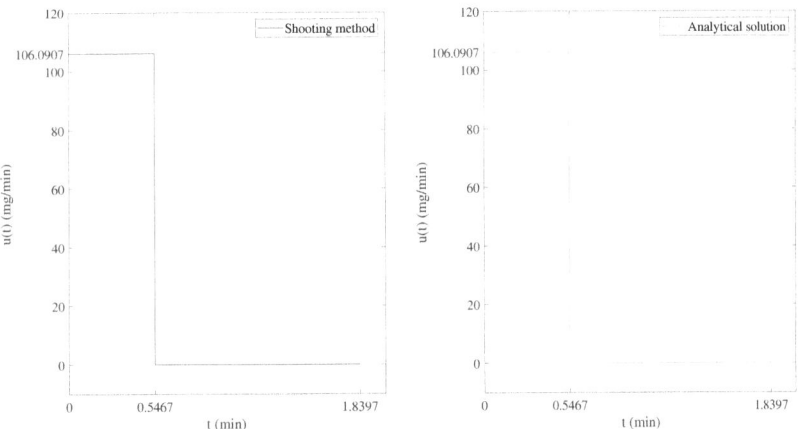

Figure 4. The optimal continuous infusion rate $u(t)$ of the induction phase of anesthesia, as obtained by the shooting and analytical methods.

By using the analytical method, the blue curve in Figure 4 shows that the optimal continuous infusion rate of the induction phase of anesthesia $u(t)$ is equal to 106.0907 mg/min until the switching time

$$t_c = 0.5467 \text{ min}.$$

Then, it is equal to 0 mg/min (stop-infusion) until the final time

$$t_f = 1.8397 \text{ min}.$$

We conclude that both methods work well and give similar results. However, in general, the shooting method does not always converge, depending on the initial conditions (46). To obtain such initial values is not an easy task since no theory is available to find them. For this reason, the proposed analytical method is logical, practical, and more suitable for real applications.

5. Conclusions

The approach proposed by the theory of optimal control is very effective. The shooting method was proposed by Zabi et al. [15], which is used to solve the time-optimal control problem and calculate the minimum time. However, this approach is based on Newton's method. The convergence of Newton's method depends on the initial conditions, being necessary to select an appropriate initial value so that the function is differentiable and the derivative does not vanish. This implies that the convergence of the shooting method is attached to the choice of the initial values. Therefore, the difficulty of the shooting method is to find the initial conditions of the adjoint vectors. Here, the aim was to propose a different approach, which we call "the analytical method", that allows to solve the time-optimal control problem for the induction phase of anesthesia without such drawbacks. Our method is guided by the selection of the optimal strategy, without the need to choose initial values and study the convergence. We claim that our method can also be applied to other PK/PD models, in order to find the optimal time for the drug administration.

In the context of PK/PD modeling, the challenges associated with uncertainties in plant model parameters and controller gains for achieving robust stability and controller non-fragility are significant [24]. These challenges arise from factors like inter-individual variability, measurement errors, and the dynamic nature of patient characteristics and drug response. Further investigation is needed to understand and develop effective strategies to mitigate the impact of these uncertainties in anesthesia-related PK/PD models. This research can lead to the development of robust and non-fragile control techniques that enhance the stability and performance of anesthesia delivery systems. By addressing these challenges, we can improve the precision and safety of drug administration during anesthesia procedures, ultimately benefiting patient outcomes and healthcare practices. In this direction, the recent results of [25] may be useful. Moreover, we plan to investigate PK/PD fractional-order models, which is a subject under strong current research [26]. This is under investigation and will be addressed elsewhere.

Author Contributions: Conceptualization, M.A.Z., C.J.S. and D.F.M.T.; methodology, M.A.Z., C.J.S. and D.F.M.T.; software, M.A.Z.; validation, C.J.S. and D.F.M.T.; formal analysis, M.A.Z., C.J.S. and D.F.M.T.; investigation, M.A.Z., C.J.S. and D.F.M.T.; writing—original draft preparation, M.A.Z., C.J.S. and D.F.M.T.; writing—review and editing, M.A.Z., C.J.S. and D.F.M.T.; visualization, M.A.Z.; supervision, C.J.S. and D.F.M.T.; funding acquisition, M.A.Z., C.J.S. and D.F.M.T. All authors have read and agreed to the published version of the manuscript.

Funding: This research was funded by the Portuguese Foundation for Science and Technology (FCT—Fundação para a Ciência e a Tecnologia) through the R&D Unit CIDMA, Grant Numbers UIDB/04106/2020 and UIDP/04106/2020, and within the project "Mathematical Modelling of Multi-scale Control Systems: Applications to Human Diseases" (CoSysM3), Reference 2022.03091.PTDC, financially supported by national funds (OE) through FCT/MCTES.

Institutional Review Board Statement: Not applicable.

Informed Consent Statement: Not applicable.

Data Availability Statement: No new data were created or analyzed in this study. Data sharing is not applicable to this article. The numerical simulations of Section 4 were implemented in MATLAB R2022a. The computer code is available from the authors upon request.

Acknowledgments: The authors are grateful to four anonymous referees for their constructive remarks and questions that helped to improve the paper.

Conflicts of Interest: The authors declare no conflict of interest. The funders had no role in the design of the study; in the collection, analyses, or interpretation of data; in the writing of the manuscript; or in the decision to publish the results.

References

1. Evers, A.S.; Maze, M.; Kharasch, E.D. *Anesthetic Pharmacology: Basic Principles and Clinical Practice*, 2nd ed.; Cambridge University Press: Cambridge, UK, 2011.
2. Singh, N.; Sidawy, A.N.; Dezee, K.; Neville, R.F.; Weiswasser, J.; Arora, S.; Aidinian, G.; Abularrage, C.; Adams, E.; Khuri, S.; Henderson, W.G. The effects of the type of anesthesia on outcomes of lower extremity infrainguinal bypass. *J. Vasc. Surg.* **2006**, *44*, 964–970. [CrossRef]
3. Merry, A.F.; Mitchell, S.J. Complications of anaesthesia. *Anaesthesia* **2018**, *73*, 7–11. [CrossRef]
4. Beck, C.L. Modeling and control of pharmacodynamics. *Eur. J. Control* **2015**, *24*, 33–49. [CrossRef]
5. Meibohm, B.; Derendorf, H. Basic concepts of pharmacokinetic/pharmacodynamic (PK/PD) modelling. *Int. J. Clin. Pharmacol. Ther.* **1997**, *35*, 401–413.
6. Absalom, A.R.; Mani, V.; Smet, T.D.; Struys, M.M.R.F. Pharmacokinetic models for propofol—Defining and illuminating the devil in the detail. *Br. J. Anaesth.* **2009**, *103*, 26–37. [CrossRef] [PubMed]
7. Enlund, M. TCI: Target Controlled Infusion, or Totally Confused Infusion? Call for an Optimised Population Based Pharmacokinetic Model for Propofol. *Upsala J. Med. Sci.* **2008**, *113*, 161–170. [CrossRef] [PubMed]
8. Oshin, T.A. Exploratory mathematical frameworks and design of control systems for the automation of propofol anesthesia. *Int. J. Dyn. Control* **2022**, *10*, 1858–1875. [CrossRef]
9. Wu, X.; Zhang, H.; Li, J. An analytical approach of one-compartmental pharmacokinetic models with sigmoidal Hill elimination. *Bull. Math. Biol.* **2022**, *84*, 117. [CrossRef]
10. Nanditha, C.K.; Rajan, M.P. An adaptive pharmacokinetic optimal control approach in chemotherapy for heterogeneous tumor. *J. Biol. Syst.* **2022**, *30*, 529–551. [CrossRef]
11. Wang, J.-J.; Dai, Z.; Zhang, W.; Shi, J.J. Operating room scheduling for non-operating room anesthesia with emergency uncertainty. *Ann. Oper. Res.* **2023**, *321*, 565–588. [CrossRef]
12. Schnider, T.W.; Minto, C.F.; Gambus, P.L.; Andresen, C.; Goodale, D.B.; Shafer, S.L.; Youngs, E.J. The influence of method of administration and covariates on the pharmacokinetics of propofol in adult volunteers. *Anesthesiology* **1998**, *88*, 1170–1182. [CrossRef]
13. Marsh, B.; White, M.; Morton, N.; Kenny, G.N. Pharmacokinetic model driven infusion of propofol in children. *Br. J. Anaesth.* **1991**, *67*, 41–48. [CrossRef] [PubMed]
14. Zabi, S.; Queinnec, I.; Tarbouriech, S.; Garcia, G.; Mazerolles, M. New approach for the control of anesthesia based on dynamics decoupling. *IFAC-PapersOnLine* **2015**, *48*, 511–516. [CrossRef]
15. Zabi, S.; Queinnec, I.; Garcia, G.; Mazerolles, M. Time-optimal control for the induction phase of anesthesia. *IFAC-PapersOnLine* **2017**, *50*, 12197–12202. [CrossRef]
16. Ilyas, M.; Khan, A.; Khan, M.A.; Xie, W.; Riaz, R.A.; Khan, Y. Observer design estimating the propofol concentration in PKPD model with feedback control of anesthesia administration. *Arch. Control Sci.* **2022**, *32*, 85–103. [CrossRef]
17. Bock, H.G.; Plitt, K.J. A Multiple shooting algorithm for direct solution of optimal control problems. *IFAC Proc. Vol.* **1984**, *17*, 1603–1608. [CrossRef]
18. Pontryagin, L.S.; Boltyanskii, V.G.; Gamkrelidze, R.V.; Mishchenko, E.F. *The Mathematical Theory of Optimal Processes*; Trirogoff, K.N., Neustadt, L.W., Ed.; Interscience Publishers John Wiley and Sons, Inc.: New York, NY, USA, 1962.
19. Bailey, J.M.; Haddad, W.M. Drug dosing control in clinical pharmacology. *IEEE Control Syst. Mag.* **2005**, *25*, 35–51. [CrossRef]
20. James, W.P.T. Research on obesity: A report of the DHSS/MRC Group. *Nutr. Bull.* **1977**, *4*, 187–190. [CrossRef]
21. Haddad, W.M.; Chellaboina, V.; Hui, Q. *Nonnegative and Compartmental Dynamical Systems*; Princeton Univ. Press: Princeton, NJ, USA, 2010.
22. Zaitri, M.A.; Bibi, M.O.; Bentobache, M. A hybrid direction algorithm for solving optimal control problems. *Cogent Math. Stat.* **2019**, *6*, 1612614. [CrossRef]
23. Deuflhard, P. *Newton Methods for Nonlinear Problems*; Springer Series in Computational Mathematics; Springer: Berlin, Germany, 2004; Volume 35.
24. Elsisi, M.; Soliman, M. Optimal design of robust resilient automatic voltage regulators. *ISA Trans.* **2021**, *108*, 257–268. [CrossRef]

25. Mohamed, M.A.E.; Mohamed, S.M.R.; Saied, E.M.M.; Elsisi, M.; Su, C.-L.; Hadi, H.A. Optimal energy management solutions using artificial intelligence techniques for photovoltaic empowered water desalination plants under cost function uncertainties. *IEEE Access* **2022**, *10*, 93646–93658. [CrossRef]
26. Morales-Delgado, V.F.; Taneco-Hernández, M.A.; Vargas-De-León, C.; Gómez-Aguilar, J.F. Exact solutions to fractional pharmacokinetic models using multivariate Mittag-Leffler functions. *Chaos Solitons Fractals* **2023**, *168*, 113164. [CrossRef]

Disclaimer/Publisher's Note: The statements, opinions and data contained in all publications are solely those of the individual author(s) and contributor(s) and not of MDPI and/or the editor(s). MDPI and/or the editor(s) disclaim responsibility for any injury to people or property resulting from any ideas, methods, instructions or products referred to in the content.

Article

Some Axioms and Identities of L-Moments from Logistic Distribution with Generalizations

Khalaf S. Sultan [1,*] and Nashmiah R. AL-Shamari [2]

[1] Department of Mathematics, Faculty of Science, Al-Azhar University, Nasr City 11884, Cairo, Egypt
[2] Department of Statistics and Operations Research, College of Science, King Saud University, P.O. Box 2455, Riyadh 11451, Saudi Arabia; naalshammari@ksu.edu.sa
* Correspondence: ksultan@azhar.edu.eg

Abstract: In this paper, we derive the L-moments for some distributions, such as logistic, generalized logistic, doubly truncated logistic, and doubly truncated generalized logistic distributions. We also establish some new axioms and identities, including recurrence relations satisfied by the L-moment from the underlying derivations. In addition, we establish some new general recurrence relations satisfied by the L-moment from any distribution.

Keywords: order statistics; L-moments; logistic distribution; generalized logistic distribution

MSC: 62G20; 62G32; 62E17

Citation: Sultan, K.S.; AL-Shamari, N.R. Some Axioms and Identities of L-Moments from Logistic Distribution with Generalizations. *Axioms* **2023**, *12*, 928. https://doi.org/10.3390/axioms12100928

Academic Editors: Nuno Bastos, Touria Karite and Amir Khan

Received: 26 August 2023
Revised: 22 September 2023
Accepted: 26 September 2023
Published: 28 September 2023

Copyright: © 2023 by the authors. Licensee MDPI, Basel, Switzerland. This article is an open access article distributed under the terms and conditions of the Creative Commons Attribution (CC BY) license (https://creativecommons.org/licenses/by/4.0/).

1. Introduction

Order statistics play an important role in the statistical inference of parametric and nonparametric statistics, estimation theory, and hypothesis testing. Order statistics have also found important applications, including life testing, reliability theory, characterization, statistical quality control, detection of outliers, analysis of censored data, goodness-of-fit tests, single image processing, and many other fields. Order statistics received attention from numerous researchers, among them Arnold et al. [1] and David and Nagaraja [2]. For a detailed discussion on the moments of order statistics, one can refer to [3].

Like other statistical moments, L-moments characterize the geometry of distributions, summarization, and description of theoretical probability distributions (observed data samples), estimation of parameters and quantiles of probability distributions, and hypotheses testing for probability distributions. L-moments are directly analogous to that and have similar interpretations as the moments. This makes L-moments conceptually accessible to many potential users.

Hosking [4] has defined the L-moments as based on linear combinations of differences in the expectations of order statistics, which are based on powers (exponents) of differences. They can be defined for any random variable whose mean exists. Hosking [5] concludes that "L-moments can provide good summary measures of distributional shape and may be preferable to moments for this purpose". Sillitto [6] has introduced population L-moments as alternatives to the classical population central moments determined by the population distribution. Greenwood et al. [7] have introduced probability weighted moments, which are an alternative statistical "moment" that, like the moments, characterize the geometry of distributions and are useful for parameter estimation. Karian and Dudewicz [8] have studied the method of L-moments in some of their examples, where the overall performance appears comparable to the overall performance of the percentile method, where the method of percentiles and the method of L-moments are related in the sense that they both are based on order statistics.

Sahu et al. [9] have described regionalization procedures for hydrological and climatological assessment of ungauged watersheds, where different techniques together with

L-moments are being utilized by many researchers and hydrologists for almost every extreme event, viz., extreme rainfall, low flow, flood, and drought. Domański et al. [10] have presented an application of L-moment statistics and the respective L-moment ratio diagrams to assess control performance, in particular, in terms of control system sustainability. In addition, the evolution in their performance over time is depicted visually. L-moment diagrams are common in extreme event analysis and are considered a very powerful tool in this field at the regional level. Anderson [11] has shown that the results of L-moments and L-moment ratios were less sensitive than traditional moments for the Barabási–Albert, Erdös–Rényi, and Watts–Strogratz network models when his research centered on finding the statistical moments, network measures, and statistical tests that are most sensitive to various node degradations for these three different network models. Fallahgoul et al. [12] have developed and applied a novel semiparametric estimation method based on L-moments. Unlike conventional moments, L-moments are linear in the data and therefore robust to outliers. Additionally, an extensive empirical analysis of portfolio choice under nonexpected utility demonstrated the effectiveness of the L-moment approach.

In this paper, we display the L-moments and the sample L-moments, some of their general properties, and how to use the sample L-moments to develop the method of L-moments for estimating the parameters that are described in Section 2. In Section 3, we establish general recurrence relations between L-moments for any distribution. Next, we derive the exact explicit expressions for L-moments of underlying distributions, namely, logistic distribution, generalized logistic distribution, doubly truncated logistic distribution, and doubly truncated generalized logistic distribution in Section 4. Then, in Section 5, we establish some recurrence relations by L-moments from specific distributions. Finally, we provide our conclusions in Section 6.

2. L-Moments

In this section, we present the definitions of the probability weight moments, L-moments, and L-moment ratios. Next, we establish some properties of L-moments and L-moment ratios.

2.1. Population of L-Moments

The probability weighted moments of a random variable X with a pdf $f(x)$, cdf $F(x)$, and quantile x_u are defined by the expectations as

$$M_{p,r,s} = E\big[X^p (F(X))^r (1-F(X))^s\big] = \int_0^1 x_u^p u^r (1-u)^s du,$$

where p, r, and s are integers. The most common probability weighted moment is

$$\beta_r = M_{1,r,0} = E\big[X(F(X))^r\big] = \int_0^1 x_u u^r du = \frac{1}{r+1} E[X_{r+1:r+1}] \quad \text{for } r = 0,1,2,\ldots, \quad (1)$$

where

$$\begin{aligned} E[X_{r:n}] &= \mu_{r:n} = \int_{-\infty}^{\infty} x f_{r:n}(x) dx \\ &= \int_{-\infty}^{\infty} x C_{r:n} [F(x)]^{r-1} [1-F(x)]^{n-r} f(x) dx, -\infty < x < \infty, \ C_{r:n} = \frac{n!}{(r-1)!(n-r)!}, \end{aligned} \quad (2)$$

gives the single moments for order statistics of $X_{r:n}$, $1 \leq r \leq n$, $n = 1,2,3,\ldots$ (see [1]).

Landwehr et al. [13–15] have considered the L-moments as beginning with the statistical needs for researchers of surface-water hydrology with an interest in floods and extreme rainfall hydrology. Historically, L-moments were developed from probability weighted moments. The core theory of L-moments for univariate applications was unified in the late 1980s to early 1990s. Hosking [16] has confirmed that probability weighted moments (or L-moments) are sometimes more popular than maximum likelihood because of their good performance for small samples. Additionally, L-moments can serve as a good choice for the starting values in the iterative numerical procedure required to obtain maximum likelihood estimates.

Hosking [4] has unified discussion and estimation of distributions using L-moments and used particular ratios of them as measures of skewness and kurtosis. They can be defined for any random variable whose mean exists. Hosking has also defined the theoretical L-moments from r^{th}-shifted Legendre polynomials:

$$\lambda_r = \int_0^1 x_u\, P^*_{r-1}(u)\, du \text{ for } r \geq 1, \tag{3}$$

where

$$P^*_{r-1}(u) = \sum_{k=0}^{r-1} p^*_{r-1,k} u^k, \tag{4}$$

$$p^*_{r-1,k} = (-1)^{r-1-k} \binom{r-1}{k}\binom{r-1+k}{k}. \tag{5}$$

is the shifted Legendre polynomial (see [17]) and x_u is a quantile function. The first few L-moments are

$$\lambda_1 = E[X] = \int_0^1 x_u\, du,$$
$$\lambda_2 = \int_0^1 x_u \times (2u-1)\, du,$$
$$\lambda_3 = \int_0^1 x_u \times (6u^2 - 6u + 1)\, du,$$
$$\lambda_4 = \int_0^1 x_u \times (20u^3 - 30u^2 + 12u - 1)\, du.$$

The L-moment ratios of X are the quantities

$$\tau_r = \lambda_r/\lambda_2 \text{ for } r = 3, 4, 5, \ldots,$$

satisfying $|\tau_r| < 1$. Note that $\tau_3 = \lambda_3/\lambda_2$ is called L-skewness and $\tau_4 = \lambda_4/\lambda_2$ is called L-kurtosis. The L-moments λ_1 and λ_2 and the L-moment ratios τ_3 and τ_4 are the most useful quantities for summarizing probability distributions. The most important property is that if X and Y are random variables with L-moments λ_r and λ_r^*, respectively, and suppose that $Y = aX + b$, then,

$$\lambda_1^* = a\lambda_1 + b,$$
$$\lambda_r^* = (sign\, a)^r |a| \lambda_r,\ r \geq 2,$$
$$\tau_r^* = (sign\, a)^r \tau_r,\ r \geq 3.$$

Hosking [5] concludes that "L-moments can provide good summary measures of distributional shape and may be preferable to moments for this purpose". Royston [18] and Vogel and Fennessey [19] have discussed the advantages of L-skewness and L-kurtosis over their classical counterparts.

The system of linear equations relating L-moments λ_r to probability weighted moments β_r can be obtained (see [20]) for $r \geq 0$ as follows:

$$\lambda_{r+1} = \sum_{m=0}^{r} p^*_{r,m} \beta_m. \tag{6}$$

The first four L-moments in terms of probability weighted moments are

$$\lambda_1 = \beta_0,$$
$$\lambda_2 = 2\beta_1 - \beta_0,$$
$$\lambda_3 = 6\beta_2 - 6\beta_1 + \beta_0,$$
$$\lambda_4 = 20\beta_3 - 30\beta_2 + 12\beta_1 - \beta_0.$$

Note that $\lambda_1 = E[X]$ is the L-location or the mean of the distribution, while λ_2 is a measure of the scale or dispersion of the random variable X, so λ_2 is the L-scale.

2.2. Sample L-Moments and Method of L-Moments

For any distribution with finite means, Hosking [4] defined the sample L-moments $\hat{\lambda}_r$ as follows:

$$\hat{\lambda}_r = \frac{1}{r\binom{n}{r}} \sum_{i=1}^{n} \left(\sum_{j=0}^{r-1} (-1)^j \binom{r-1}{j} \binom{i-1}{r-1-j} \binom{n-i}{j} \right) x_{i:n},$$

where $x_{1:n} \leq x_{2:n} \leq \ldots \leq x_{n:n}$ are the sample order statistics. We see that the statistic $\hat{\lambda}_1$ is the sample mean, the sample L-scale $\hat{\lambda}_2$ is half Gini's mean difference (see [21]), $\hat{\lambda}_3$ is used by Sillitto [6] as a measure of symmetry and by Locke and Spurrier [22] to test for symmetry, and $\hat{\lambda}_4$ is used by Hosking [4] as a measure of kurtosis. The rth sample L-moment ratios are the following quantities (see [23]):

$$\hat{\tau}_r = \hat{\lambda}_r / \hat{\lambda}_2, r = 3, 4, 5, \ldots.$$

Note that $\hat{\tau}_3 = \hat{\lambda}_3 / \hat{\lambda}_2$ is a measure of skewness, and $\hat{\tau}_4 = \hat{\lambda}_4 / \hat{\lambda}_2$ is a measure of kurtosis. These are, respectively, the sample L-skewness and sample L-kurtosis. The quantities $\hat{\lambda}_1, \hat{\lambda}_2, \hat{\tau}_3$, and $\hat{\tau}_4$ are useful summary statistics for a data sample. They can be used to identify the distribution from which a sample was drawn and applied to estimate parameters when fitting a distribution to a sample by equating the sample and population L-moments (see [24]).

From a random sample of size n, obtained from a probability distribution, the method of L-moments (LMOMs) is to equate the L-moments of the distribution to the sample L-moments such that $\lambda_r = \hat{\lambda}_r$ for the p number of unknown parameters is chosen for a distribution (see [25]).

3. General Relationships Based on L-Moments

The moments of order statistics have acquired considerable interest in recent years and, in fact, have been tabulated quite extensively for many distributions. Many authors have investigated and derived several recurrence relations because one could list the following four main reasons why these recurrence relations for the moments of order statistics are important:

1. They reduce the number of direct computations greatly;
2. They usefully express the higher order moments of order statistics in terms of the lower order moments and hence make the evaluation of higher order moments easy;
3. They are very useful in checking the computation of the moments of order statistics;
4. Results can be used for characterizing the distributions.

Now, for the same main reasons in the moments of order statistics, Hosking [26] has studied the recurrence relations between trimmed L-moments with different degrees of trimming, and he found the relation between trimmed L-moments and L-moments.

In order to establish new general recurrence relations between the L-moments, we need to review the most important lemmas that are necessary later in the theorem:

Lemma 1. *If*

$$P_n(x) = \frac{1}{2^n} \sum_{k=0}^{[n/2]} (-1)^k \binom{n}{k} \binom{2n-2k}{n} x^{n-2k},$$

where

$$\left[\frac{n}{2}\right] = \begin{cases} \frac{n}{2}, & n \text{ even,} \\ \frac{n-1}{2}, & n \text{ odd.} \end{cases}$$

is the Legendre polynomial (see [27]) of degree $n = 0, 1, 2, \ldots$ for $x \in [-1, 1]$ and $P_n^*(x)$ is the shifted Legendre polynomial of degree $n = 0, 1, 2, \ldots$. on the interval $[0, 1]$ in Equation (4), we then have

$$\frac{d}{dx} P_n^*(x) = 2 P_n'(2x - 1) \text{ where } P_n'(x) = \frac{d}{dx} P_n(x). \tag{7}$$

The shifted Legendre polynomial satisfies the following recurrence relations, $n = 0, 1, \ldots$,

$$P_{n+1}^*(x) = P_n^*(x) - \frac{2}{n+1}(1-x)\sum_{i=0}^{n}(2i+1)P_i^*(x), \tag{8}$$

and

$$P_{n+1}^*(x) = 2\sum_{i=0}^{n}(2i+1)\, q_{i+1}^*(x) - P_n^*(x). \tag{9}$$

where

$$q_{i+1}^*(x) = \int_0^x P_i^*(t)dt = \sum_{k=0}^{i} \frac{1}{k+1} p_{i,k}^* x^{k+1} \text{ for } i > 0,$$

is the integrated shifted Legendre polynomial.

Proof. To prove (7), by compensating x for $(2x - 1)$ in the differentiation of the Legendre polynomial

$$P_n'(x) = \frac{d}{dx} P_n(x) = \sum_{r=0}^{[(n-1)/2]} (2n - 4r - 1) P_{n-2r-1}(x),$$

(see [28]) and use $P_n^*(x) = P_n(2x - 1)$ (see [23]), we obtain

$$P_n'(2x - 1) = \frac{d}{dx} P_n(2x - 1) = \sum_{i=0}^{[(n-1)/2]} (2n - 4i - 1) P_{n-2i-1}^*(x). \tag{10}$$

By the comparison between the differentiation of shifted Legendre polynomials,

$$\frac{d}{dx} P_n^*(x) = 2\sum_{i=0}^{[(n-1)/2]} (2n - 4i - 1) P_{n-2i-1}^*(x),$$

(see [29–31]) and $P_n'(2x - 1)$ in (10), we can express the relationship (7).

To prove (8), we have the recursive formula for Legendre polynomials (see [28]) for $n = 0, 1, 2, \ldots$,

$$P_{n+1}(x) = P_n(x) - \frac{1}{n+1}(1-x)\sum_{i=0}^{n}(2i+1)P_i(x), \tag{11}$$

and then compensate x for $(2x - 1)$ in (11) and use $P_n^*(x) = P_n(2x - 1)$ (see [23]).

Now, for Equation (9), by bringing a recursive formula for Legendre polynomials (see [28]) for $n = 0, 1, 2, \ldots$, this relates the polynomials and their derivatives to each other as follows:

$$P_{n+1}'(x) = \sum_{i=0}^{n}(2i+1)P_i(x) - P_n'(x), \tag{12}$$

where we compensate x to $(2x - 1)$ in (12), use $P_n^*(x) = P_n(2x - 1)$ (see [23]) and (7); we have,

$$\frac{d}{dx} P_{n+1}^*(x) = 2\sum_{i=0}^{n}(2i+1)P_i^*(x) - \frac{d}{dx} P_n^*(x), \tag{13}$$

and afterward integrating both sides with respect to t from $t = 0$ to $t = x$ in (13). Hence,

$$P_{n+1}^*(x) - P_{n+1}^*(0) = 2\sum_{i=0}^{n}(2i+1)\int_0^x P_i^*(t)dt - (P_n^*(x) - P_n^*(0)), \tag{14}$$

and using that $P_n^*(0) = (-1)^n \forall n = 0, 1, 2 \ldots$ (see [23]). □

Theorem 1. Let X be a continuous random variable with cdf $u = F(x)$ and quantile function x_u; $0 \leq u \leq 1$. Then, L-moments λ_r satisfy the following recurrence relations:

$$\lambda_{r+2} = \frac{2r+1}{r+1}(2A_{r+1} - \lambda_{r+1}) - \frac{r}{r+1}\lambda_r, \; r = 0, 1, \ldots, \tag{15}$$

$$\lambda_{r+2} = \lambda_{r+1} - \frac{2}{r+1}\sum_{i=0}^{r}(2i+1)(\lambda_{i+1} - A_{i+1}), \; r = 0, 1, \ldots, \tag{16}$$

$$\lambda_{r+2} = 2(2r+1)B_{r+1} + \lambda_r, \; r = 1, 2, \ldots, \tag{17}$$

$$\lambda_{r+2} = 2\sum_{i=0}^{r}(2i+1) B_{i+1} - \lambda_{r+1}, \; r = 0, 1, \ldots, \tag{18}$$

where $A_{r+1} = \sum_{k=0}^{r} p_{r,k}^* \beta_{k+1}$, $B_{r+1} = \sum_{k=0}^{r} \frac{1}{k+1} p_{r,k}^* \beta_{k+1}$, and $p_{r,k}^*$ are in (5) and β_{k+1} is in (1).

Proof. For (15), we have a recurrence relation between shifted Legendre polynomials for $n = 0, 1, 2 \ldots,$ (see [29–31]):

$$P_{r+1}^*(u) = \frac{2r+1}{r+1}(2u-1)P_r^*(u) - \frac{r}{r+1}P_{r-1}^*(u), \; r = 0, 1, \ldots,$$

By multiplying both sides by x_u and integrating over u, we obtain

$$\lambda_{r+2} = \frac{2r+1}{r+1}\left[2\int_0^1 u P_r^*(u) x_u du - \lambda_{r+1}\right] - \frac{r}{r+1}\lambda_r. \tag{19}$$

Then,

$$\int_0^1 u P_r^*(u) x_u du = \int_0^1 u \left(\sum_{k=0}^{r} p_{r,k}^* u^k\right) x_u du = \sum_{k=0}^{r} p_{r,k}^* \int_0^1 u^{k+1} x_u du = \sum_{k=0}^{r} p_{r,k}^* \beta_{k+1} = A_{r+1}. \tag{20}$$

using (20) in (19), the proof is complete. For (16), the same technique as the method of proof for (15) is used, but begins by using (8).

Now, also for (17) and (18), they have the same technique as the method of proof, begun by using the recurrence relation between shifted Legendre polynomials for $n = 0, 1, 2 \ldots,$ (see [29–31]):

$$2(2n+1) q_{n+1}^*(x) = P_{n+1}^*(x) - P_{n-1}^*(x),$$

and (9), respectively, and multiplying both sides by x_u and integrating over u. □

All Equations (15)–(18) in Theorem 1 are equal to $\lambda_2, \lambda_3, \ldots,$ those given equations relating λ_r to β_r obtained by Zafirakou-Koulouris et al. [20] in (6).

4. L-Moments from the Logistic Distributions

In this section, we present some statistical distributions, like logistic, generalized logistic, doubly truncated logistic and doubly truncated generalized logistic with their first four implicit L-moments. Then, we derive the LMOMs for the unknown parameters from these distributions.

4.1. L-Moments of the Logistic Distribution

The pdf of a logistic distribution with the location parameter ζ (the mode, median, and mean) and scale parameter α is reported by Balakrishnan [32] and Walck [33]:

$$f(x) = \frac{1}{\alpha}\frac{e^{-(\frac{x-\zeta}{\alpha})}}{\left[1 + e^{-(\frac{x-\zeta}{\alpha})}\right]^2}, \; -\infty < x < \infty, \; -\infty < \zeta < \infty, \; \alpha > 0,$$

and the cdf is

$$F(x) = \frac{1}{1+e^{-(\frac{x-\zeta}{\alpha})}}, \quad -\infty < x < \infty, -\infty < \zeta < \infty, \alpha > 0.$$

For $0 < u < 1$, the quantile is

$$x_u = \zeta + \alpha \ln\left(\frac{u}{1-u}\right), \quad -\infty < \zeta < \infty, \alpha > 0.$$

The mean of the logistic distribution is $E[X] = \zeta$. The random variable of standard logistic Z can be obtained by putting $\zeta = 0$ and $\alpha = 1$.

The rth probability weighted moment in (1) can be obtained by (see [34])

$$\beta_r = \frac{\zeta}{r+1} + \frac{\alpha}{r+1}[\psi(r+1) + \gamma] = \frac{1}{r+1}[\zeta + \alpha[\psi(r+1) + \gamma]], r = 0, 1, 2, \ldots,$$

where $\gamma = -\psi(1) = 0.577216$ is Euler's constant and $\psi(\cdot)$ is the digamma function, which is defined as

$$\psi(r) = \frac{\Gamma'(r)}{\Gamma(r)} = \frac{d}{dr}\ln\Gamma(r), \quad r \neq 0, -1, -2, \ldots,$$

and $\Gamma(.)$ is a gamma function. Thus, the first four β_r can be computed as follows:

$$\beta_0 = \zeta, \; \beta_1 = \frac{\zeta+\alpha}{2}, \; \beta_2 = \frac{\zeta}{3} + \frac{\alpha}{2} \text{ and } \beta_3 = \frac{\zeta}{4} + \frac{11\alpha}{24},$$

where $\psi(1) = -\gamma$, $\psi(2) = 1 - \gamma$, $\psi(3) = \frac{3}{2} - \gamma$ and $\psi(4) = \frac{11}{6} - \gamma$. Then, the first four L-moments in (6) are given as (see [34])

$$\lambda_1 = \beta_0 = \zeta, \; \lambda_2 = 2\beta_1 - \beta_0 = \alpha, \; \lambda_3 = 6\beta_2 - 6\beta_1 + \beta_0 = 0, \; \tau_3 = \frac{\lambda_3}{\lambda_2} = 0,$$
$$\lambda_4 = 20\beta_3 - 30\beta_2 + 12\beta_1 - \beta_0 = \frac{\alpha}{6} \text{ and } \tau_4 = \frac{\lambda_4}{\lambda_2} = \frac{1}{6}. \quad (21)$$

The L-moment estimators for location parameter ζ and scale parameter α can be obtained from the first and second L-moments (λ_1, λ_2) in (21) as

$$\hat{\zeta} = \hat{\lambda}_1 \text{ and } \hat{\alpha} = \hat{\lambda}_2. \quad (22)$$

4.2. L-Moments of the Generalized Logistic Distribution

The generalized logistic distribution has three parameters and is thus fit to the mean, scale, and shape of a data set. The pdf and cdf of the generalized logistic distribution are given, respectively, for $-\infty < \zeta < \infty$ and $\alpha > 0$, as reported by Burr [35] and Asquith [25]:

$$f(x) = \frac{1}{\alpha} \frac{\left[1-\delta\left(\frac{x-\zeta}{\alpha}\right)\right]^{\frac{1}{\delta}-1}}{\left[1+\left[1-\delta\left(\frac{x-\zeta}{\alpha}\right)\right]^{1/\delta}\right]^2} \quad \begin{array}{l} ,-\infty < x \leq \zeta + \frac{\alpha}{\delta} \text{ if } 0 < \delta < 1, \\ ,\zeta + \frac{\alpha}{\delta} \leq x < \infty \text{ if } -1 < \delta < 0, \end{array}$$

and

$$F(x) = \frac{1}{1+\left[1-\delta\left(\frac{x-\zeta}{\alpha}\right)\right]^{1/\delta}} \quad \begin{array}{l} ,-\infty < x \leq \zeta + \frac{\alpha}{\delta} \text{ if } 0 < \delta < 1, \\ ,\zeta + \frac{\alpha}{\delta} \leq x < \infty \text{ if } -1 < \delta < 0. \end{array}$$

For $0 < u < 1$, the quantile is

$$x_u = \zeta + \frac{\alpha}{\delta}\left[1 - \left(\frac{1-u}{u}\right)^{\delta}\right], \quad -\infty < \zeta < \infty, \alpha > 0, \delta \neq 0.$$

The random variable of the standard generalized logistic Z can be obtained by putting $\zeta = 0$ and $\alpha = 1$. The first four moments, $k = 1, 2, 3, 4$ of the standard generalized logistic random variable are as follows (see [3]):

$$E\left[Z^k\right] = \frac{1}{\delta^k}\sum_{j=0}^{k}\binom{k}{j}(-1)^j\beta(1-j\delta, 1+j\delta), \quad |\delta| < \frac{1}{k}.$$

where $\beta(1-j\delta, j\delta+1)$ is the beta function and can be defined by the integral

$$\beta(a, b) = \int_0^1 t^{a-1}(1-t)^{b-1}dt, \; a, b > 0.$$

Now, we derive the first moment for the order statistics of the standard generalized logistic random variable.

Lemma 2. *The moments of order statistics in (2) of the standard generalized logistic random variable $Z_{j:n}$ are*

$$\mu_{j:n} = \frac{1}{\delta}\left(1 - \frac{\Gamma(j-\delta)\Gamma(n-j+1+\delta)}{\Gamma(j)\Gamma(n-j+1)}\right), \quad -1 < \delta < 1. \tag{23}$$

Proof. The jth moment of order statistics is

$$\mu_{j:n} = E[Z_{j:n}] = \int z f_{j:n}(z)dz = \frac{n!}{(j-1)!(n-j)!}\int z[F(z)]^{j-1}f(z)[1-F(z)]^{n-j}dz$$

$$= \frac{n!}{(j-1)!(n-j)!}\int_0^1 z_u u^{j-1}(1-u)^{n-j}du$$

$$= \frac{n!}{(j-1)!(n-j)!}\frac{1}{\delta}\int_0^1 \left(u^{j-1}(1-u)^{n-j} - u^{j-1-\delta}(1-u)^{n-j+\delta}\right)du$$

$$= \frac{n!}{(j-1)!(n-j)!}\frac{1}{\delta}(\beta(j, n-j+1) - \beta(j-\delta, n-j+\delta+1)),$$

after some simplification, we obtain the required result. □

Note that:
- By letting $n = j = 1$ in Lemma 2, we deduce the first moment established for a standard generalized logistic distribution.
- By letting the shape parameter $\delta \to 0$ in Lemma 2, we deduce the moment of order statistics of the standard logistic distribution (see [36]):

$$\mu_{r:n} = E[Z_{r:n}] = \psi(j) - \psi(n-j+1), \; j = 1, 2, \ldots, n. \tag{24}$$

Now, the rth, $r = 0, 1, 2, \ldots$, probability weighted moment in (1) for generalized logistic distribution can be stated as follows:

$$\beta_r = (\zeta + \alpha\mu_{r+1:r+1})/(1+r) = \frac{1}{r+1}\left(\zeta + \frac{\alpha}{\delta}\right) - \frac{\alpha}{\delta}\beta(r+1-\delta, \delta+1)$$

$$= \frac{1}{r+1}\left(\zeta + \frac{\alpha}{\delta}\right) - \frac{\alpha}{\delta}\beta(1-\delta, \delta+1)\frac{(1-\delta)^{(r)}}{\Gamma(r+2)}, \quad -1 < \delta < 1,$$

where

$$(1-\delta)^{(r)} = \frac{\Gamma(1-\delta+r)}{\Gamma(1-\delta)} = \prod_{i=1}^{r}(i-\delta),$$

are rising factorials.

Therefore, the L-moments in (6) are (see [25])

$$\lambda_1 = \left(\zeta + \frac{\alpha}{\delta}\right) - \frac{\alpha}{\delta}\beta(1-\delta, \delta+1), \; \lambda_2 = \alpha\beta(1-\delta, \delta+1), \; \lambda_3 = -\alpha\delta\beta(1-\delta, \delta+1), \; \tau_3 = -\delta,$$
$$\lambda_4 = \frac{1+5\delta^2}{6}\alpha\beta(1-\delta, \delta+1) \text{ and } \tau_4 = \frac{1+5\delta^2}{6}. \tag{25}$$

The L-moments estimators for location parameter ζ, scale parameter α, and shape parameter δ can be obtained from the first and second L-moments (λ_1, λ_2) and L-skewness τ_3 ($\tau_3 = \lambda_3/\lambda_2$ is a function of δ only) in (25), which are measures of location, scale, and skewness, respectively, as

$$\hat{\zeta} = \hat{\lambda}_1 - \frac{\hat{\alpha}}{\hat{\delta}}(1 - \beta(1-\hat{\delta},\hat{\delta}+1)), \quad \hat{\alpha} = \frac{\hat{\lambda}_2}{\beta(1-\hat{\delta},\hat{\delta}+1)} \quad \text{and} \quad \hat{\delta} = -\hat{\tau}_3. \tag{26}$$

4.3. L-Moments of the Doubly Truncated Logistic Distribution

The standard doubly truncated logistic distribution has been extended by Balakrishnan and Rao [3] with pdf:

$$f(z) = \frac{1}{P-Q}e^{-z}/(1+e^{-z})^2, \quad Q_1 \leq z \leq P_1,$$

and with cdf (see [32]):

$$F(z) = \frac{1}{P-Q}\left[\frac{1}{1+e^{-z}} - Q\right], \quad Q_1 \leq z \leq P_1,$$

where Q and $1 - P$ ($0 < Q < P < 1$) are given by

$$P = F(P_1) \text{ and } Q = F(Q_1),$$

where $F(\cdot)$ is given in the standard logistic distribution. Then,

$$Q_1 = \log\left(\frac{Q}{1-Q}\right) \text{ and } P_1 = \log\left(\frac{P}{1-P}\right).$$

The quantile is

$$z_u = \log\left[\frac{u(P-Q)+Q}{1-[u(P-Q)+Q]}\right], \quad 0 < u < 1.$$

The first moment of Z is given by

$$E[Z] = \frac{PP_1 - QQ_1 + \log\left[\frac{1-P}{1-Q}\right]}{P-Q}.$$

Note that by letting $Q \to 0$ and $P \to 1$, we deduce the first moment for the logistic distribution, which is equal to zero.

Next, we find the first four L-moments for the doubly truncated logistic distribution. In the following lemma, we derive the moment of order statistics of the random variable from a doubly truncated logistic distribution.

Lemma 3. *The moment of order statistics from the doubly truncated logistic distribution is given by, for* $j = 1, 2, \ldots, n$,

$$\begin{aligned}\mu_{j:n} &= \frac{n!}{(j-1)!(n-j)!}\sum_{i=0}^{n-j}\binom{n-j}{i}\frac{(-1)^i(-Q)^{i+j-1}}{(P-Q)^{i+j}}\left[PP_1 - QQ_1 + \log\left[\frac{1-P}{1-Q}\right]\right] \\ &+ \frac{n!}{(j-1)!(n-j)!}\sum_{i=0}^{n-j}\sum_{l=1}^{i+j-1}\binom{n-j}{i}\binom{i+j-1}{l}\frac{(-1)^i(-Q)^{i+j-1-l}}{(P-Q)^{i+j}(l+1)} \\ &\times \left[P^{l+1}P_1 - Q^{l+1}Q_1 + \log\left[\frac{1-P}{1-Q}\right] + \sum_{s=0}^{l-1}\frac{1}{s+1}(P^{s+1} - Q^{s+1})\right].\end{aligned} \tag{27}$$

Proof. The jth moment of order statistics is

$$\begin{aligned}
\mu_{j:n} &= E[Z_{j:n}] = \frac{n!}{(j-1)!(n-j)!} \int_{Q_1}^{P_1} z[F(z)]^{j-1} f(z) [1-F(z)]^{n-j} dz \\
&= \frac{n!}{(j-1)!(n-j)!} \int_{Q_1}^{P_1} z \left[\frac{1}{P-Q}\left[\frac{1}{1+e^{-z}} - Q\right]\right]^{j-1} \left[\frac{1}{P-Q} \frac{e^{-z}}{(1+e^{-z})^2}\right] \\
&\quad \times \left[1 - \left[\frac{1}{P-Q}\left[\frac{1}{1+e^{-z}} - Q\right]\right]\right]^{n-j} dz \\
&= \frac{n!}{(j-1)!(n-j)!} \sum_{i=0}^{n-j} \sum_{l=0}^{i+j-1} \binom{n-j}{i}\binom{i+j-1}{l} \frac{(-1)^i (-Q)^{i+j-1-l}}{(P-Q)^{i+j}} I_1,
\end{aligned} \quad (28)$$

where

$$I_1 = \int_Q^P \log\left(\frac{t}{1-t}\right) t^l dt = \frac{1}{l+1}\left[P^{l+1}\log\left(\frac{P}{1-P}\right) - Q^{l+1}\log\left(\frac{Q}{1-Q}\right) - \int_Q^P \frac{t^l}{1-t} dt\right], \quad (29)$$

substituting (29) into (28), we obtain

$$\begin{aligned}
\mu_{j:n} &= \frac{n!}{(j-1)!(n-j)!} \sum_{i=0}^{n-j} \binom{n-j}{i} \frac{(-1)^i(-Q)^{i+j-1}}{(P-Q)^{i+j}} \left[P\log\left(\frac{P}{1-P}\right) - Q\log\left(\frac{Q}{1-Q}\right) - I_2\right] \\
&\quad + \frac{n!}{(j-1)!(n-j)!} \sum_{i=0}^{n-j} \sum_{l=1}^{i+j-1} \binom{n-j}{i}\binom{i+j-1}{l} \frac{(-1)^i(-Q)^{i+j-1-l}}{(P-Q)^{i+j}(l+1)} \\
&\quad \times \left[P^{l+1}\log\left(\frac{P}{1-P}\right) - Q^{l+1}\log\left(\frac{Q}{1-Q}\right) - I_3\right],
\end{aligned} \quad (30)$$

where

$$I_2 = \int_Q^P \frac{1}{1-t} dt = -\log(1-t)\big|_{t=Q}^{t=P} = -\log(1-P) + \log(1-Q), \quad (31)$$

and

$$I_3 = \int_Q^P \frac{t^l}{1-t} dt = -\sum_{s=0}^{l-1} \int_Q^P t^s + \int_Q^P \frac{1}{1-t} dt = -\sum_{s=0}^{l-1} \frac{1}{s+1}\left(P^{s+1} - Q^{s+1}\right) - \log(1-P) + \log(1-Q). \quad (32)$$

Finally, by substituting (31) and (32) in (30) and doing some simplification, we obtain the required result. □

Note that:

- By letting $n = j = 1$ in Lemma 3, we deduce the first moment established for the doubly truncated logistic distribution.
- Furthermore, letting $Q \to 0$ and $P \to 1$ in Lemma 3 and using Proposition 1 as follows, we deduce the single moments order statistics for the logistic distribution established in (24).

Proposition 1. *Let $j = 1, 2, \ldots n$ and $n - j$ a non-negative integer. Then,*

$$\sum_{i=0}^{n-j} \binom{n-j}{i} (-1)^i \frac{1}{i+j} = \frac{(j-1)!(n-j)!}{n!},$$

$$\frac{n!}{(j-1)!(n-j)!} \sum_{i=0}^{n-j} \binom{n-j}{i} (-1)^i \frac{1}{i+j} \psi(i+j) = \psi(j) - \psi(n-j+1) - \gamma$$

where γ is Euler's constant.

Proof. For the first equation, we proceed by induction on n. As $n = 1$, it is $1 = 1$, and the proposition immediately follows. Assume now the proposition for n and observe that, since $\binom{n+1-j}{i} = \binom{n-j}{i} + \binom{n-j}{i-1}$, then for $n+1$ it holds:

$$\sum_{i=0}^{n-j+1} \binom{n-j+1}{i}(-1)^i \frac{1}{i+j} = \sum_{i=0}^{n-j} \binom{n-j}{i}(-1)^i \frac{1}{i+j} - \sum_{i=0}^{n-j} \binom{n-j}{i}(-1)^i \frac{1}{i+1+j}.$$

The hypothesis of induction yields

$$\sum_{i=0}^{n-j} \binom{n-j}{i}(-1)^i \frac{1}{i+j} = \frac{(j-1)!(n-j)!}{n!},$$

and

$$\sum_{i=0}^{n-j} \binom{n-j}{i}(-1)^i \frac{1}{i+1+j} = \frac{j!(n-j)!}{(n+1)!} = j\frac{(j-1)!(n-j)!}{(n+1)!}.$$

Therefore, the proposition is proved.

Now for the second equation, we proceed by induction on n. As $n = 1$, it is $\psi(1) = -\gamma$, and the proposition immediately follows. Assume now the proposition for n and observe that, since $\binom{n+1-j}{i} = \binom{n-j}{i} + \binom{n-j}{i-1}$, then for $n+1$ it holds:

$$\frac{(n+1)!}{(j-1)!(n-j+1)!} \sum_{i=0}^{n-j+1} \binom{n-j+1}{i}(-1)^i \frac{1}{i+j}\psi(i+j)$$
$$= \frac{(n+1)!}{(j-1)!(n-j+1)!} \sum_{i=0}^{n-j} \binom{n-j}{i}(-1)^i \frac{1}{i+j}\psi(i+j)$$
$$- \frac{(n+1)!}{(j-1)!(n-j+1)!} \sum_{i=0}^{n-j} \binom{n-j}{i}(-1)^i \frac{1}{i+1+j}\psi(i+1+j).$$

The hypothesis of induction yields

$$\frac{(n+1)!}{(j-1)!(n-j+1)!} \sum_{i=0}^{n-j} \binom{n-j}{i}(-1)^i \frac{1}{i+j}\psi(i+j) = \frac{n+1}{n-j+1}(\psi(j) - \psi(n-j+1) - \gamma),$$

and

$$\frac{(n+1)!}{(j-1)!(n-j+1)!} \sum_{i=0}^{n-j} \binom{n-j}{i}(-1)^i \frac{1}{i+1+j}\psi(i+1+j)$$
$$= \frac{1}{n-j+1} + \frac{j}{n-j+1}(\psi(j) - \psi(n-j+1) - \gamma), \left(\text{by using } \psi(1+j) = \psi(j) + \frac{1}{j}\right).$$

Therefore, we perform some simplification by using $1/(n-j+1) = \psi(n-j+2) - \psi(n-j+1)$, and obtain the required result. □

Lemma 4. *The L-moments for the doubly truncated logistic distribution are given by*

$$\lambda_1 = \frac{PP_1 - QQ_1 + \log\left[\frac{1-P}{1-Q}\right]}{P-Q}, \quad \lambda_2 = \frac{P - Q - PP_1Q + PQQ_1 - (-1+P+Q)\log\left[\frac{1-P}{1-Q}\right]}{(P-Q)^2},$$

$$\lambda_3 = \frac{1}{(P-Q)^3}\left(2(-1+Q)Q + P(2+Q^2(P_1-Q_1)) + P^2(-2+P_1Q - QQ_1)\right.$$
$$\left. + (2+(-3+P)P - 3Q + 4PQ + Q^2)\log\left[\frac{1-P}{1-Q}\right]\right), \tag{33}$$

$$\lambda_4 = \frac{1}{6(P-Q)^4}\left(Q(-30 + (45-16Q)Q) + P^3(16 - 6P_1Q + 6QQ_1)\right.$$
$$+ 6P(5 + Q^2(-7 - P_1Q + QQ_1)) + 3P^2(-15 + 2Q(7 - 3P_1Q + 3QQ_1))$$
$$\left. - 6(-1+P+Q)(5 + P^2 + (-5+Q)Q + P(-5+8Q))\log\left[\frac{1-P}{1-Q}\right]\right).$$

Proof. The rth, $r = 0, 1, 2, \ldots$, probability weighted moments are obtained easily by the Lemma 3 as

$$\begin{aligned}
\beta_r &= \int_{Q_1}^{P_1} z[F(z)]^r f(z) dz = \int_0^1 z_u u^r du = \frac{1}{1+r} \mu_{r+1:r+1}, \\
&= \frac{(-Q)^r}{(P-Q)^{r+1}} \left[PP_1 - QQ_1 + \log\left[\frac{1-P}{1-Q}\right] \right] \\
&\quad + \frac{1}{(P-Q)^{r+1}} \sum_{l=1}^r \binom{r}{l} \frac{(-Q)^{r-l}}{(l+1)} \left[P^{l+1} P_1 - Q^{l+1} Q_1 + \log\left[\frac{1-P}{1-Q}\right] + \sum_{s=0}^{l-1} \frac{1}{s+1} (P^{s+1} - Q^{s+1}) \right],
\end{aligned}$$

and by using (6), the proof is completed. □

The L-moment estimators for location parameter ζ and scale parameter α of the random variable of doubly truncated logistic $X = \alpha Z + \zeta$ can be obtained from the first and second L-moments (λ_1, λ_2) in (33) and using the linear transformation as

$$\hat{\zeta} = \hat{\lambda}_1^* - \hat{\alpha} \lambda_1 \text{ and } \hat{\alpha} = \frac{\hat{\lambda}_2^*}{\lambda_2}. \tag{34}$$

where $\hat{\lambda}_1^*$ and $\hat{\lambda}_2^*$ are the sample L-moments of X.

4.4. L-Moments of the Doubly Truncated Generalized Logistic Distribution

The doubly truncated standard generalized logistic pdf

$$f(z) = \frac{1}{P-Q} \frac{(1-\delta z)^{\frac{1}{\delta}-1}}{\left[1+(1-\delta z)^{1/\delta}\right]^2}, \quad \begin{array}{l} Q_1 < z < P_1 < \frac{1}{\delta} \text{ if } 0 < \delta < 1, \\ \frac{1}{\delta} < Q_1 < z < P_1 \text{ if } -1 < \delta < 0, \end{array}$$

with cdf

$$F(z) = \frac{1}{P-Q}\left[\frac{1}{1+(1-\delta z)^{1/\delta}} - Q\right], \quad \begin{array}{l} Q_1 < z < P_1 < \frac{1}{\delta} \text{ if } 0 < \delta < 1, \\ \frac{1}{\delta} < Q_1 < z < P_1 \text{ if } -1 < \delta < 0, \end{array}$$

where Q and $1 - P$ ($0 < Q < P < 1$) are given by

$$P = F(P_1) \text{ and } Q = F(Q_1),$$

where $F(\cdot)$ is given in the standard generalized logistic distribution. Then,

$$Q_1 = \frac{1}{\delta}\left[1 - \left(\frac{1-Q}{Q}\right)^\delta\right] \text{ and } P_1 = \frac{1}{\delta}\left[1 - \left(\frac{1-P}{P}\right)^\delta\right].$$

The quantile is

$$z_u = \frac{1}{\delta}\left[1 - \left[\frac{1-[u(P-Q)+Q]}{u(P-Q)+Q}\right]^\delta\right], \quad 0 < u < 1.$$

The kth, $k = 1, 2, 3, 4$, moment of Z is

$$E[Z^k] = \frac{\sum_{j=0}^k (-1)^j \binom{k}{j} [\beta(P; 1-j\delta, j\delta+1) - \beta(Q; 1-j\delta, j\delta+1)]}{\delta^k (P-Q)}, \quad |\delta| < \frac{1}{k}.$$

where $\beta(\cdot\,;\,1-j\delta,\,j\delta+1)$ is the lower incomplete beta function and can be defined by the variable limit integrals

$$\beta(x;\,a,\,b) = \int_0^x t^{a-1}(1-t)^{b-1}dt,\ 0 \leq x \leq 1,\ a,b > 0.$$

Note that by letting $Q \to 0$ and $P \to 1$, we deduce the moment for the generalized logistic distribution. Furthermore, by letting the shape parameter $\delta \to 0$, we deduce the mean of the standard doubly truncated logistic distribution.

Now, we are about to find the first four L-moments for the doubly truncated generalized logistic distribution. In the following lemma, we derive the first moment for the order statistic of the random variable from a doubly truncated generalized logistic distribution.

Lemma 5. *The moments of order statistics from the doubly truncated generalized logistic distribution are given by, for $j = 1, 2, \ldots, n$,*

$$\mu_{j:n} = \frac{1}{\delta}\left[1 - \frac{n!}{(j-1)!(n-j)!}\sum_{i=0}^{n-j}\sum_{l=0}^{i+j-1}\binom{n-j}{i}\binom{i+j-1}{l}\frac{(-1)^i(-Q)^{i+j-1-l}}{(P-Q)^{i+j}} \right. \tag{35}$$
$$\left. \times [\beta(P;1-\delta+l,1+\delta) - \beta(Q;1-\delta+l,1+\delta)]\right],\ |\delta| < 1.$$

Proof. The jth moment of order statistics

$$\mu_{j:n} = E[Z_{j:n}] = \frac{n!}{(j-1)!(n-j)!}\int_{Q_1}^{P_1} z[F(z)]^{j-1}f(z)[1-F(z)]^{n-j}dz \tag{36}$$
$$= \frac{n!}{(j-1)!(n-j)!}\int_0^1 z_u u^{j-1}(1-u)^{n-j}du = \frac{n!}{(j-1)!(n-j)!}\frac{1}{\delta}[I_1 - I_2],$$

where

$$I_1 = \int_0^1 u^{j-1}(1-u)^{n-j}du = \beta(j, n-j+1), \tag{37}$$

and

$$I_2 = \int_0^1 u^{j-1}(1-u)^{n-j}\left[\frac{1-[u(P-Q)+Q]}{[u(P-Q)+Q]}\right]^\delta du$$
$$= \sum_{i=0}^{n-j}\sum_{l=0}^{i+j-1}\binom{n-j}{i}\binom{i+j-1}{l}\frac{(-1)^i(-Q)^{i+j-1-l}}{(P-Q)^{i+j}} \tag{38}$$
$$\times [\beta(P;1-\delta+l,1+\delta) - \beta(Q;1-\delta+l,1+\delta)],\ |\delta| < 1.$$

Substituting (37) and (38) in (36), we obtain (35) and thus complete the proof. □

Note that:
- By letting $n = j = 1$ in Lemma 5, we deduce the first moment established for the doubly truncated generalized logistic distribution.
- Furthermore, by letting $Q \to 0$ and $P \to 1$ in Lemma 5 and using Proposition 2, we have the single moments order statistics established in (23) from the generalized logistic distribution.
- By letting the shape parameter $\delta \to 0$ in Lemma 5, we deduce the first moment for the order statistic of the random variable from the doubly truncated logistic distribution in Lemma 3.

Proposition 2. Let $j = 1, 2, \ldots n$ and $n - j$ a non-negative integer. Then,

$$\frac{n!}{(j-1)!(n-j)!} \sum_{i=0}^{n-j} \binom{n-j}{i} (-1)^i \beta(i+j-\delta, 1+\delta) = \frac{\Gamma(j-\delta)\Gamma(n-j+1+\delta)}{\Gamma(j)\Gamma(n-j+1)},$$

where $|\delta| < 1$.

Proof. We proceed by induction on n. As $n = 1$, it is $\beta(1-\delta, 1+\delta) = \Gamma(1-\delta)\Gamma(1+\delta)$, and the proposition immediately follows. Assume now the proposition for n and observe that, since $\binom{n+1-j}{i} = \binom{n-j}{i} + \binom{n-j}{i-1}$, then for $n+1$ it holds:

$$\frac{(n+1)!}{(j-1)!(n-j+1)!} \sum_{i=0}^{n-j+1} \binom{n-j+1}{i}(-1)^i \beta(i+j-\delta, 1+\delta)$$

$$= \frac{(n+1)!}{(j-1)!(n-j+1)!} \sum_{i=0}^{n-j} \binom{n-j}{i}(-1)^i \beta(i+j-\delta, 1+\delta)$$

$$- \frac{(n+1)!}{(j-1)!(n-j+1)!} \sum_{i=0}^{n-j} \binom{n-j}{i}(-1)^i \beta(i+1+j-\delta, 1+\delta).$$

The hypothesis of induction yields

$$\frac{(n+1)!}{(j-1)!(n-j+1)!} \sum_{i=0}^{n-j} \binom{n-j}{i}(-1)^i \beta(i+j-\delta, 1+\delta) = \frac{n+1}{n-j+1} \frac{\Gamma(j-\delta)\Gamma(n-j+1+\delta)}{\Gamma(j)\Gamma(n-j+1)},$$

and

$$\frac{(n+1)!}{(j-1)!(n-j+1)!} \sum_{i=0}^{n-j} \binom{n-j}{i}(-1)^i \beta(i+1+j-\delta, 1+\delta)$$

$$= \frac{j}{n-j+1} \frac{\Gamma(1+j-\delta)\Gamma(n-j+1+\delta)}{\Gamma(1+j)\Gamma(n-j+1)},$$

(by using $\Gamma(1+j-\delta) = (j-\delta)\Gamma(j-\delta)$ and $\Gamma(1+j) = j\Gamma(j)$)

$$= \frac{j-\delta}{n-j+1} \frac{\Gamma(j-\delta)\Gamma(n-j+1+\delta)}{\Gamma(j)\Gamma(n-j+1)},$$

therefore, we perform some simplification by using

$$(n-j+1+\delta)\Gamma(n-j+1+\delta)/(n-j+1)\Gamma(n-j+1) = \Gamma(n-j+2+\delta)/\Gamma(n-j+2),$$

and we obtain the required result. □

Lemma 6. The first four L-moments for doubly truncated generalized logistic distribution are

$$\lambda_1 = \frac{1}{(P-Q)\delta}[(P-Q) - (\beta(P; 1-\delta, 1+\delta) - \beta(Q; 1-\delta, 1+\delta))],$$

$$\lambda_2 = \frac{1}{(P-Q)^2\delta}[(P+Q)(\beta(P; 1-\delta, 1+\delta) - \beta(Q; 1-\delta, 1+\delta))$$
$$- 2(\beta(P; 2-\delta, 1+\delta) - \beta(Q; 2-\delta, 1+\delta))],$$

$$\lambda_3 = \frac{1}{(P-Q)^3\delta}[-(P^2+4PQ+Q^2)(\beta(P; 1-\delta, 1+\delta) - \beta(Q; 1-\delta, 1+\delta))$$
$$+ 6(P+Q)(\beta(P; 2-\delta, 1+\delta) - \beta(Q; 2-\delta, 1+\delta))$$
$$- 6(\beta(P; 3-\delta, 1+\delta) - \beta(Q; 3-\delta, 1+\delta))],$$

$$\lambda_4 = \frac{1}{(P-Q)^4\delta}[(P^3+9P^2Q+9PQ^2+Q^3)(\beta(P; 1-\delta, 1+\delta) - \beta(Q; 1-\delta, 1+\delta))$$
$$- 12(P^2+3PQ+Q^2)(\beta(P; 2-\delta, 1+\delta) - \beta(Q; 2-\delta, 1+\delta))$$
$$+ 30(P+Q)(\beta(P; 3-\delta, 1+\delta) - \beta(Q; 3-\delta, 1+\delta))$$
$$- 20(\beta(P; 4-\delta, 1+\delta) - \beta(Q; 4-\delta, 1+\delta))].$$

(39)

and using the above L-moments, we can obtain τ_3 and τ_4.

Proof. By applying Lemma 5, β_r becomes:

$$\beta_r = \int_{Q_1}^{P_1} z[F(z)]^r f(z)dz = \int_0^1 z_u u^r du = \frac{1}{1+r}\mu_{r+1:r+1}$$

$$= \frac{1}{\delta}\left(\frac{1}{r+1} - \frac{\sum_{l=0}^{r}\binom{r}{l}(-Q)^{r-l}(\beta(P;1-\delta+l,1+\delta)-\beta(Q;1-\delta+l,1+\delta))}{(P-Q)^{r+1}}\right), \; |\delta|<1.$$

Since β_r is given as

$$\beta_0 = \frac{1}{\delta}\left[1 - \frac{1}{P-Q}(\beta(P;1-\delta,1+\delta)-\beta(Q;1-\delta,1+\delta))\right],$$

$$\beta_1 = \frac{1}{\delta}\left[\frac{1}{2} - \frac{1}{(P-Q)^2}(-Q[\beta(P;1-\delta,1+\delta)-\beta(Q;1-\delta,1+\delta)]\right.$$
$$\left.+[\beta(P;2-\delta,1+\delta)-\beta(Q;2-\delta,1+\delta)])\right],$$

$$\beta_2 = \frac{1}{\delta}\left[\frac{1}{3} - \frac{1}{(P-Q)^3}\left(Q^2[\beta(P;1-\delta,1+\delta)-\beta(Q;1-\delta,1+\delta)]\right.\right.$$
$$-2Q[\beta(P;2-\delta,1+\delta)-\beta(Q;2-\delta,1+\delta)]$$
$$\left.\left.+[\beta(P;3-\delta,1+\delta)-\beta(Q;3-\delta,1+\delta)])\right],$$

$$\beta_3 = \frac{1}{\delta}\left[\frac{1}{4} - \frac{1}{(P-Q)^4}(-Q^3[\beta(P;1-\delta,1+\delta)-\beta(Q;1-\delta,1+\delta)]\right.$$
$$+3Q^2[\beta(P;2-\delta,1+\delta)-\beta(Q;2-\delta,1+\delta)]$$
$$-3Q[\beta(P;3-\delta,1+\delta)-\beta(Q;3-\delta,1+\delta)]$$
$$\left.+[\beta(P;4-\delta,1+\delta)-\beta(Q;4-\delta,1+\delta)])\right].$$

and by using (6), the proof is completed. □

If we denote λ_r in (39) by $\lambda_r(\delta)$, then the L-moments estimators for location parameter ζ, scale parameter α, and shape parameter δ of the random variable of doubly truncated generalized logistic $X = \alpha Z + \zeta$ can be obtained from the first and second L-moments $(\lambda_1(\delta), \lambda_2(\delta))$ and L-skewness $\tau_3(\delta)(\tau_3(\delta) = \lambda_3(\delta)/\lambda_2(\delta))$ in (39) and using the linear transformation, which are measures of location, scale, and skewness, respectively, as solved numerically in the three systems of the nonlinear equations:

$$\hat{\zeta} = \hat{\lambda}_1^* - \hat{\alpha}\lambda_1(\hat{\delta}), \hat{\alpha} = \frac{\hat{\lambda}_2^*}{\lambda_2(\hat{\delta})}, \text{ and } \hat{\tau}_3^* = \tau_3(\hat{\delta}). \tag{40}$$

where $\hat{\lambda}_1^*$ and $\hat{\lambda}_2^*$ are the sample L-moments of X and $\hat{\tau}_3^*$ is the sample L-moment ratios.

5. Particular Relationships Based on L-Moments

In this section, we establish some particular recurrence relations between the L-moments satisfying for logistic, generalized logistic, doubly truncated logistic, and doubly truncated generalized logistic distributions that enables computation and allows for evaluation of all the L-moments $\lambda_r(r \geq 2)$, starting from λ_1 in a simple recurrent manner, where the calculation of L-moments in the traditional way of greater degrees depends on special functions that need more mathematical calculations and special programs.

The following lemma is important throughout the results in this section.

Lemma 7. *For $r = 0,1,2,3,\ldots$, the relation between the L-moments in (3) and moments of order statistics in (2) are*

$$\mu_{r+1:r+1} = (r+1)\sum_{i=0}^{r} c_{r,i}\lambda_{i+1}, \tag{41}$$

and

$$\mu_{1:r+1} = (r+1)\sum_{i=0}^{r}(-1)^i c_{r,i}\lambda_{i+1}, \tag{42}$$

where the coefficients $c_{r,i}$ are given as

$$c_{r,i} = (2i+1)\int_0^1 u^r P_i^*(u)\, du = (2i+1)\sum_{k=0}^{i} p_{i,k}^* \frac{1}{r+k+1}, i = 0,1,2,\ldots, \quad (43)$$

and $p_{r,k}^*$ is given in (5).

Proof. The function u^r, which is sequence integrable on $[0,1]$, may be expressed in terms of $P_i^*(u)$ as (see [37])

$$u^r = \sum_{i=0}^{r} c_{r,i} P_i^*(u), 0 \leq u \leq 1.$$

Multiplying both sides by x_u and integrating over u, we obtain

$$\int_0^1 x_u u^r\, du = \sum_{i=0}^{r} c_{r,i} \int_0^1 x_u P_i^*(u)\, du,$$

then (41) is proved.

The function $(1-u)^r$, which is sequence integrable on $[0,1]$, may be expressed in terms of $P_i^*(1-u)$ as (see [37])

$$(1-u)^r = \sum_{i=0}^{r} c_{r,i} P_i^*(1-u), \; 0 \leq 1-u \leq 1,$$

by using the property of a shifted Legendre polynomial function from Hetyei [38]:

$$(-1)^i P_i^*(-u) = P_i^*(u+1),$$

then,

$$P_i^*(1-u) = P_i^*(-u+1) = (-1)^i P_i^*(u).$$

So, we have

$$(1-u)^r = \sum_{i=0}^{r} (-1)^i c_{r,i} P_i^*(u).$$

Again, multiplying both sides by x_u and integrating over u, we obtain

$$\int_0^1 x_u(1-u)^r\, du = \sum_{i=0}^{r} (-1)^i c_{r,i} \int_0^1 x_u P_i^*(u)\, du,$$

then (42) is proved. □

5.1. Relations for Logistic Distribution

In this subsection, we establish recurrence relations satisfied by L-moments from a logistic distribution.

Lemma 8. *For $r = 1, 2, \ldots$, then the L-moments from standard logistic distribution satisfy*

$$\lambda_{r+1} = \frac{1}{(r+1)(-1)^r c_{r,r}} \left[\sum_{i=0}^{r-1}(-1)^i(-(r+1)c_{r,i} + rc_{r-1,i})\lambda_{i+1} - \frac{1}{r} \right]. \quad (44)$$

where λ_1 and $c_{.,.}$ are given in (21) and (43), respectively.

Proof. The recurrence relation of order statistics from standard logistic distribution follows (see [3]):

$$\mu_{1:r+1} = \mu_{1:r} - \frac{1}{r}, r \geq 1,$$

Substituting from (42), we have

$$(r+1)\sum_{i=0}^{r}(-1)^i c_{r,i}\lambda_{i+1} = r\sum_{i=0}^{r-1}(-1)^i c_{r-1,i}\lambda_{i+1} - \frac{1}{r}.$$

Therefore,

$$\begin{aligned}(r+1)(-1)^r c_{r,r}\lambda_{r+1} &= -(r+1)\sum_{i=0}^{r-1}(-1)^i c_{r,i}\lambda_{i+1} + r\sum_{i=0}^{r-1}(-1)^i c_{r-1,i}\lambda_{i+1} - \frac{1}{r} \\ &= \sum_{i=0}^{r-1}(-1)^i(-(r+1)c_{r,i}+rc_{r-1,i})\lambda_{i+1} - \frac{1}{r},\end{aligned}$$

by simplifying the resulting expression, we obtain the relation. □

5.2. Relations for Generalized Logistic Distribution

In this subsection, we establish recurrence relations satisfied by L-moments from a generalized logistic distribution.

Lemma 9. *For $r = 1, 2, \ldots$, then the L-moments from standard generalized logistic distribution satisfy*

$$\lambda_{r+1} = \frac{1}{(r+1)(-1)^r c_{r,r}}\left[\sum_{i=0}^{r-1}(-1)^i(-(r+1)c_{r,i}+(r+\delta)c_{r-1,i})\lambda_{i+1} - \frac{1}{r}\right]. \quad (45)$$

where λ_1 and $c_{.,.}$ are given in (25) and (43), respectively.

Proof. The recurrence relation for the single moments of order statistics follows (see [3]):

$$\mu_{1:r+1} = \left(1+\frac{\delta}{r}\right)\mu_{1:n} - \frac{1}{r}, \; r \geq 1,$$

Substituting from (42), we have

$$(r+1)\sum_{i=0}^{r}(-1)^i c_{r,i}\lambda_{i+1} = \left(1+\frac{\delta}{r}\right)r\sum_{i=0}^{r-1}(-1)^i c_{r-1,i}\lambda_{i+1} - \frac{1}{r}.$$

Therefore,

$$\begin{aligned}(r+1)(-1)^r c_{r,r}\lambda_{r+1} &= -(r+1)\sum_{i=0}^{r-1}(-1)^i c_{r,i}\lambda_{i+1} + \left(1+\frac{\delta}{r}\right)r\sum_{i=0}^{r-1}(-1)^i c_{r-1,i}\lambda_{i+1} - \frac{1}{r} \\ &= \sum_{i=0}^{r-1}(-1)^i(-(r+1)c_{r,i}+(r+\delta)c_{r-1,i})\lambda_{i+1} - \frac{1}{r},\end{aligned}$$

by simplifying the resulting expression, we obtain the relation. □

Letting the shape parameter $\delta \to 0$ in Lemma 9, we deduce the recurrence relation for L-moments from the standard logistic distribution in Lemma 8.

5.3. Relations for Doubly Truncated Logistic Distribution

Recurrence relations for doubly truncated logistic distribution are given by Lemma 10 in this subsection.

Lemma 10.

$$\lambda_2 = (1-B)\lambda_1 - AP_1 - D_1 \quad (46)$$

and for $r \geq 2$,

$$\begin{aligned}\lambda_{r+1} &= \frac{1}{(r+1)(-1)^r c_{r,r}}\left[\sum_{i=0}^{r-2}(-1)^i[-(r+1)c_{r,i}+rBc_{r-1,i}+(r-1)Ac_{r-2,i}]\lambda_{i+1}\right. \\ &\quad \left.+(-1)^{r-1}[-(r+1)c_{r,r-1}+rBc_{r-1,r-1}]\lambda_r + D_r\right],\end{aligned} \quad (47)$$

where λ_1 and $c_{.,.}$ are given in (33) and (43), respectively, and

$$A = \frac{P_2}{P-Q}, \quad B = \frac{(2P-1)}{P-Q}, \text{ and } D_m = -\frac{1}{P-Q}\left(Q_1 Q_2 + \frac{1}{m}\right) \text{ for } m \geq 1. \quad (48)$$

Proof. First, before beginning the proof, denote that

$$P_2 = P(1-P)/(P-Q) \text{ and } Q_2 = Q(1-Q)/(P-Q),$$

and we simplify the following recurrence relations (see [3]):

$$\mu_{1:2} = Q_1 + \frac{1}{P-Q}[P_2(P_1-Q_1) + (2P-1)(\mu_{1:1}-Q_1) - 1],$$

for $n \geq 2$,

$$\mu_{1:n+1} = Q_1 + \frac{1}{P-Q}\left[P_2(\mu_{1:n-1}-Q_1) + (2P-1)(\mu_{1:n}-Q_1) - \frac{1}{n}\right].$$

Note that by letting $Q \to 0$ and $P \to 1$, we have the recurrence relation for the single moments of the standard logistic distribution, so that we can rewrite them as

$$\mu_{1:2} = AP_1 + B\mu_{1:1} + D_1, \quad (49)$$

and for $n \geq 2$:

$$\mu_{1:n+1} = A\mu_{1:n-1} + B\mu_{1:n} + D_n, \quad (50)$$

where A, B, and D_m are given in (48).

Now, to prove (46), we have (49), which gives

$$\mu_{1:1} = \lambda_1, \quad (51)$$

and $\mu_{1:2}$ can be found as follows by using (42):

$$\mu_{1:2} = 2\sum_{i=0}^{1}(-1)^i c_{1,i}\lambda_{i+1} = \lambda_1 - \lambda_2, \quad (52)$$

So, by substituting (51) and (52) into (49), it reduces to

$$\lambda_1 - \lambda_2 = AP_1 + B\lambda_1 + D_1.$$

By ordering this equation, we obtain the relation in (46).

Now, the second equation in the lemma can be proved by using (50), where we can find $\mu_{1:r-1}$, $\mu_{1:r}$ and $\mu_{1:r+1}$ by using (42), as follows:

$$\mu_{1:r-1} = (r-1)\sum_{i=0}^{r-2}(-1)^i c_{r-2,i}\lambda_{i+1}, \quad (53)$$

$$\mu_{1:r} = r\sum_{i=0}^{r-1}(-1)^i c_{r-1,i}\lambda_{i+1} = r(-1)^{r-1}c_{r-1,r-1}\lambda_r + r\sum_{i=0}^{r-2}(-1)^i c_{r-1,i}\lambda_{i+1}, \quad (54)$$

$$\begin{aligned}\mu_{1:r+1} &= (r+1)\sum_{i=0}^{r}(-1)^i c_{r,i}\lambda_{i+1} \\ &= (r+1)(-1)^r c_{r,r}\lambda_{r+1} + (r+1)(-1)^{r-1}c_{r,r-1}\lambda_r + (r+1)\sum_{i=0}^{r-2}(-1)^i c_{r,i}\lambda_{i+1}.\end{aligned} \quad (55)$$

Upon substituting (53), (54), and (55) in (50) and simplifying the resulting expression, we obtain the relation given in (47). □

Note that by letting $Q \to 0$ and $P \to 1$ in Lemma 10, we obtain the simple recurrence relations between L-moments of logistic distribution in Lemma 8.

5.4. Relations for Doubly Truncated Generalized Logistic Distribution

In this subsection, we establish the recurrence relation for single moment order statistics from the standard doubly truncated generalized logistic distribution in Lemma 11. Then, recurrence relations for the doubly truncated generalized logistic distribution between the L-moments are given by Lemma 12.

Lemma 11. For $n \geq 2$,
$$\mu_{1:n+1} = A\mu_{1:n-1} + B_n\mu_{1:n} + D_n, \tag{56}$$

and
$$\mu_{1:2} = AP_1 + B_1\mu_{1:1} + D_1, \tag{57}$$

where
$$A = \frac{P_2}{P-Q}, \; B_m = \frac{1}{P-Q}\left[(2P-1) + \frac{\delta}{m}\right], \text{ and } D_m = -\frac{1}{P-Q}\left(Q_1Q_2 + \frac{1}{m}\right) \text{ for } m \geq 1. \tag{58}$$

Proof. For $n \geq 1$, denoting that
$$P_2 = P(1-P)/(P-Q) \text{ and } Q_2 = Q(1-Q)/(P-Q),$$

let us consider the characterizing differential equation for the doubly truncated generalized logistic population as follows:
$$\begin{aligned}(1-\delta z)f(z) &= (1-2Q)F(z) - (P-Q)[F(z)]^2 + Q_2 \\ &= (1-P-Q)F(z) + (P-Q)F(z)[1-F(z)] + Q_2,\end{aligned}$$

and
$$f_{1:n}(z) = nf(z)[1-F(z)]^{n-1}, Q_1 < z < P_1,$$

then,
$$\begin{aligned}1 - \delta\mu_{1:n} &= n\bigg[(1-P-Q)\int_{Q_1}^{P_1} F(z)[1-F(z)]^{n-1}dz + (P-Q)\int_{Q_1}^{P_1} F(z)[1-F(z)]^n dz \\ &\quad + Q_2\int_{Q_1}^{P_1} [1-F(z)]^{n-1}dz\bigg],\end{aligned} \tag{59}$$

By integrating by parts, treating 1 for integration, and the rest of the integrands for differentiation, we obtain
$$1 - \delta\mu_{1:n} = n[(1-P-Q)(\mu_{1:n-1} - \mu_{1:n}) + (P-Q)(\mu_{1:n} - \mu_{1:n+1}) + Q_2(\mu_{1:n-1} - Q_1)], \tag{60}$$

The relation in (56) follows simply by rewriting (60).
Relation (57) is obtained by setting $n = 1$ in (59) and simplifying. □

Note that:
- By letting the shape parameter $\delta \to 0$ in Lemma 11, we deduce the recurrence relations established in (49) and (50) for the single moments of order statistics from the doubly truncated logistic distribution.
- By letting $Q \to 0$ and $P \to 1$, we deduce the recurrence relations for the generalized logistic distribution, established in the proof of Lemma 9.

Lemma 12.
$$\lambda_2 = (1 - B_1)\lambda_1 - AP_1 - D_1, \tag{61}$$

and for $r \geq 2$,

$$\begin{aligned}\lambda_{r+1} &= \tfrac{1}{(r+1)(-1)^r c_{r,r}} \Big[\sum_{i=0}^{r-2}(-1)^i[-(r+1)c_{r,i}+rB_rc_{r-1,i}+(r-1)Ac_{r-2,i}]\lambda_{i+1} \\ &\quad + (-1)^{r-1}[-(r+1)c_{r,r-1}+rB_rc_{r-1,r-1}]\lambda_r + D_r\Big],\end{aligned} \qquad (62)$$

where λ_1 and $c_{.,.}$ are given in (39) and (43), respectively, and A, B_r, and D_r are given in (58).

Proof. This lemma has the same proof method that we used in Lemma 10, but by taking (56) and (57) to prove (61) and (62), respectively. □

Note that:

- By letting $Q \to 0$ and $P \to 1$ in Lemma 12, we have the recurrence relations between L-moments established in Lemma 9 from generalized logistic distribution.
- By letting the shape parameter $\delta \to 0$ in Lemma 12, we obtain the recurrence relations between L-moments of the doubly truncated logistic distribution in Lemma 10.

The results in Lemmas 8–12 can be applied in different fields that have actual data sets from the logistics and generalized logistics distributions. These include network analysis (see [11]), statistical inference, (see [39,40]), and rainfall modeling (see [41]).

6. Conclusions

In this paper, the L-moments are derived for some distributions, such as logistic, generalized logistic, doubly truncated logistic, and doubly truncated generalized logistic. Methods of estimation by L-moment are used to obtain the unknown parameters for logistic, generalized logistic, doubly truncated logistic, and doubly truncated generalized logistic distributions. Finally, some new recurrence relations based on L-moment are established and used for calculating the higher moments, where sometimes calculating the moments of order statistics for certain distributions may not be explicit, so recurrence relations are used to calculate higher order moments using lower order moments to reduce the risk of approximation in numerical calculations, which is very helpful. In the future, theoretical results can be utilized in several directions, such as the process of estimating unknown values using the modified moments method, and to some applications for linear moments, especially in electrical engineering, architecture, natural sciences and network analysis.

Author Contributions: Conceptualization, K.S.S. and N.R.A.-S.; methodology, K.S.S. and N.R.A.-S.; software, K.S.S. and N.R.A.-S.; validation, K.S.S. and N.R.A.-S.; formal analysis, K.S.S. and N.R.A.-S.; investigation, K.S.S. and N.R.A.-S.; resources, K.S.S. and N.R.A.-S.; writing—original draft preparation, N.R.A.-S.; writing—review and editing, K.S.S. and N.R.A.-S.; visualization, K.S.S. and N.R.A.-S.; supervision, K.S.S. All authors have read and agreed to the published version of the manuscript.

Funding: This research was funded by the authors.

Data Availability Statement: No new data were created or analyzed in this study. Data sharing is not applicable to this article.

Acknowledgments: The authors would like to thank the referees for their helpful comments, which improved the presentation of the paper.

Conflicts of Interest: The authors declare no conflict of interest.

References

1. Arnold, B.C.; Balakrishnan, N.; Nagaraja, H.N. *A First Course in Order Statistics*; Wiley: New York, NY, USA, 1992.
2. David, H.; Nagaraja, H.N. *Order Statistics*, 3rd ed.; Wiley: New York, NY, USA, 2003.
3. Balakrishnan, N.; Rao, C.R. (Eds.) *Handbook of Statistics: Order Statistics: Theory and Methods*, 1st ed.; Elsevier Science (North-Holland): Amsterdam, The Netherlands, 1998; Volume 16.
4. Hosking, J.R.M. L-Moments: Analysis and estimation of distributions using linear combinations of order statistics. *J. R. Stat. Soc. Ser. B Methodol.* **1990**, 52, 105–124. [CrossRef]

5. Hosking, J.R.M. Moments or L moments? An example comparing two measures of distributional shape. *Am. Stat.* **1992**, *46*, 186–189. [CrossRef]
6. Sillitto, G.P. Derivation of approximants to the inverse distribution function of a continuous univariate population from the order statistics of a sample. *Biometrika* **1969**, *56*, 641–650. [CrossRef]
7. Greenwood, J.A.; Landwehr, J.M.; Matalas, N.C.; Wallis, J.R. Probability weighted moments: Definition and relation to parameters of several distributions expressible in inverse form. *Water Resour. Res.* **1979**, *15*, 1049–1054. [CrossRef]
8. Karian, Z.A.; Dudewicz, E.J. Comparison of GLD fitting methods: Superiority of percentile fits to moments in L^2 norm. *J. Iran. Stat. Soc.* **2003**, *2*, 171–187.
9. Sahu, R.T.; Verma, M.K.; Ahmad, I. Regional Frequency Analysis Using L-Moment Methodology-A Review. In *Recent Trends in Civil Engineering (Lecture Notes in Civil Engineering)*; Pathak, K.K., Bandara, J.M.S.J., Agrawal, R., Eds.; Springer: Singapore, 2021; Volume 77, pp. 811–832.
10. Domański, P.D.; Jankowski, R.; Dziuba, K.; Góra, R. Assessing Control Sustainability Using L-Moment Ratio Diagrams. *Electronics* **2023**, *12*, 2377. [CrossRef]
11. Anderson, T.S. Statistical L-moment and L-moment Ratio Estimation and their Applicability in Network Analysis. Ph.D. Thesis, Air Force Institute of Technology, Air University, OH, USA, 2019.
12. Fallahgoul, H.; Mancini, L.; Stoyanov, S.V. *An L-Moment Approach for Portfolio Choice under Non-Expected Utility*; Working Paper 18–65; Swiss Finance Institute Research Paper: Geneva, Switzerland, 2023.
13. Landwehr, J.M.; Matalas, N.C.; Wallis, J.R. Estimation of parameters and quantiles of Wakeby distributions. *Water Resour. Res.* **1979**, *15*, 1362–1379.
14. Landwehr, J.M.; Matalas, N.C.; Wallis, J.R. Probability weighted moments compared with some traditional techniques in estimating Gumbel parameters and quantiles. *Water Resour. Res.* **1979**, *15*, 1055–1064. [CrossRef]
15. Landwehr, J.M.; Matalas, N.C.; Wallis, J.R. Quantile estimation with more or less floodlike distributions. *Water Resour. Res.* **1980**, *16*, 547–555. [CrossRef]
16. Hosking, J.R.M. Maximum-likelihood estimation of the parameters of the generalized extreme-value distribution. *Appl. Stat.* **1985**, *34*, 301–310. [CrossRef]
17. Hosking, J.R.M. *Some Theoretical Results Concerning L-Moments*; Research Report RC14492; T. J. Watson Research Center (IBM Research Division): Yorktown Heights, NY, USA, 1989.
18. Royston, P. Which measures of skewness and kurtosis are best? *Stat. Med.* **1992**, *11*, 333–343. [CrossRef]
19. Vogel, R.M.; Fennessey, N.M. L moment diagrams should replace product moment diagrams. *Water Resour. Res.* **1993**, *29*, 1745–1752. [CrossRef]
20. Zafirakou-Koulouris, A.; Vogel, R.M.; Craig, S.M.; Habermeier, J. L-moment diagrams for censored observations. *Water Resour. Res.* **1998**, *34*, 1241–1249. [CrossRef]
21. Elamir, E.A.; Seheult, A.H. Control charts based on linear combinations of order statistics. *J. Appl. Stat.* **2001**, *28*, 457–468. [CrossRef]
22. Locke, C.; Spurrier, J. The use of U-statistics for testing normality against non-symmetric alternatives. *Biometrika* **1976**, *63*, 143–147. [CrossRef]
23. Hosking, J.R.M. *Fortran Routines for Use with the Method of L-Moments*, 3rd ed.; Research Report RC20525; T. J. Watson Research Center (IBM Research Division): Yorktown Heights, NY, USA, 1996.
24. Hosking, J.R.M. The four-parameter kappa distribution. *IBM J. Res. Dev.* **1994**, *38*, 251–258. [CrossRef]
25. Asquith, W.H. Univariate Distributional Analysis with L-Moment Statistics Using R. Ph.D. Thesis, Texas Tech University, Lubbock, TX, USA, 2011.
26. Hosking, J.R.M. Some theory and practical uses of trimmed L-moments. *J. Stat. Plan. Inference* **2007**, *137*, 3024–3039. [CrossRef]
27. Koepp, W. *Hypergeometric Summation: An Algorithmic Approach to Summation and Special Functions Identities*; Vieweg: Braunschweig, Germany, 1998.
28. Abramowitz, M.; Stegun, I.A. *Handbook of Mathematical Functions*; Dover: New York, NY, USA, 1972.
29. Sadov, S. Coupling of the Legendre Polynomials with Kernels $|x-y|^\alpha$ and $\ln|x-y|$. Available online: http://arxiv.org/abs/math/0310063v1 (accessed on 3 January 2023).
30. Obsieger, B. *Numerical Methods III—Approximation of Functions*; University-Books.eu; University of Rijeka: Rijeka, Croatia, 2011.
31. Cher, C.-T. Identification of linear Distributed systems by using Legendre polynomials. *J. Lee-Ming Inst. Technol.* **1985**, *3*, 285–295.
32. Balakrishnan, N. *Handbook of the Logistic Distribution*; Marcel Dekker: New York, NY, USA, 1992.
33. Walck, C. *Handbook on Statistical Distributions for Experimentalists*; Report number SUF-PFY/96-01; University of Stockholm: Stockholm, Sweden, 2007.
34. Hamdan, M.S. The Properties of L-moments Compared to Conventional Moments. Master's Thesis, The Islamic University of Gaza, Gaza, Palestine, 2009.
35. Burr, I.W. Cumulative frequency functions. *Ann. Math. Stat.* **1942**, *13*, 215–232. [CrossRef]
36. Gupta, S.S.; Balakrishnan, N. *Logistic Order Statistics and Their Properties*; Defense Technical Information Center: Fort Belvoir, VA, USA, 1990.
37. Sweilam, N.H.; Khader, M.M.; Mahdy, A.M.S. Computational methods for fractional differential equations generated by optimization problem. *J. Fract. Calc. Appl.* **2012**, *3*, 1–12.

38. Hetyei, G. Shifted Jacobi Polynomials and Delannoy Number. Available online: http://arxiv.org/abs/0909.5512?context=math.CO (accessed on 17 April 2023).
39. Usman, S.; Ishfaq, A.; Ibrahim, M.A.; Nursel, K.; Muhammad, H. Variance estimation based on L-moments and auxiliary information. *Math. Popul. Stud.* **2022**, *29*, 31–46.
40. Usman, S.; Ishfaq, A.; Ibrahim, M.A.; Nadia, H.; Muhammad, H. A novel family of variance estimators based on L-moments and calibration approach under stratified random sampling. *Commun. Stat.-Simul. Comput.* **2023**, *52*, 3782–3795.
41. Nain, M.; Hooda, B.K. Regional Frequency Analysis of Maximum Monthly Rainfall in Haryana State of India Using L-Moments. *J. Reliab. Stat. Stud.* **2021**, *14*, 33–56. [CrossRef]

Disclaimer/Publisher's Note: The statements, opinions and data contained in all publications are solely those of the individual author(s) and contributor(s) and not of MDPI and/or the editor(s). MDPI and/or the editor(s) disclaim responsibility for any injury to people or property resulting from any ideas, methods, instructions or products referred to in the content.

Article

A Nonclassical Stefan Problem with Nonlinear Thermal Parameters of General Order and Heat Source Term

Ammar Khanfer [1,*], Lazhar Bougoffa [2] and Smail Bougouffa [3]

1. Department of Mathematics and Sciences, Prince Sultan University, Riyadh 11586, Saudi Arabia
2. Department of Mathematics, Faculty of Science, Imam Mohammad Ibn Saud Islamic University (IMSIU), Riyadh 11623, Saudi Arabia; lbbougoffa@imamu.edu.sa
2. Department of Physics, Faculty of Science, Imam Mohammad Ibn Saud Islamic University (IMSIU), Riyadh 11623, Saudi Arabia; sbougouffa@imamu.edu.sa
* Correspondence: akhanfer@psu.edu.sa

Abstract: The analytic solution for a general form of the Stefan problem with nonlinear temperature-dependent thermal parameters and a heat source the term is obtained. We prove the existence and uniqueness of the solution to the problem in the absence of a heat source ($\beta = 0$), and in the presence of a heat source $\beta(x) = \exp(-x^2)$. Then, we establish lower and upper bounds for the solutions of the homogeneous equation and the nonhomogeneous equation, for different values of δ_i and γ_i. It was found that the lower bounds exhibit an excellent alignment with the numerical solutions of the homogeneous and nonhomogeneous equations, so the lower bounds can serve as approximate analytic solutions to the problem. This is a generalization to the open problem proposed by Cho and Sunderland in 1974 and also generalizes the problem proposed by Oliver and Sunderland in 1987, in addition to the problems investigated recently.

Keywords: Stefan problem; nonlinear thermal parameters; modified error function; lower- and upper-bound solutions

MSC: 80A22; 35R35; 35R37; 35R45

1. Introduction

Moving (or free) boundary problems deal with modeling the processes with a phase-change phenomenon that occurs naturally and industrially, such as the diffusion of oxygen, ice melting, or the vaporization of liquids. In these types of problems, when the phase change occurs, the boundary starts to move, from which the name of these problems comes. To model these moving boundaries, a Stefan condition is needed to describe that moving boundary, and consequently, these problems are usually referred to as "Stefan problems" [1,2]. These problems have a deep connection with heat transfer theory since they tend to model phase-change problems due to melting or liquidation processes. The scientific studies concerning these problems have significantly increased in the last two decades due to the high importance and demands of describing and analyzing many industrial and physical processes, see, for example, [3–16]. The classical Stefan problems deal with constant thermal parameters (thermal conductivity and specific heat) for the substances, but due to the recent developments in technology and science, researchers realized that models that described temperature-dependent parameters would be more realistic. In 1978, Cho and Sunderland [1] investigated the nonlinear problem:

$$\left((1 + \delta y)\frac{dy}{dx}\right)' + 2x\frac{dy}{dx} = 0,\ 0 < x < \infty,\ y(0) = y(\infty) = 1 \qquad (1)$$

with a linear thermal conductivity, and they obtained a numerical solution, which was defined as the modified error function φ_δ, where δ is the thermal coefficient of the thermal conductivity $1 + \delta y$, and y represents the temperature distribution. They also proposed the problem

$$\frac{d}{dx}\left[(1+\delta y + \gamma y^2)^n \frac{dy}{dx}\right] + 2x\frac{dy}{dx} = 0, \quad x > 0, \ y(0) = 0, \ y(\infty) = 1 \quad (2)$$

as a generalization of (1).

Oliver and Sunderland [2] investigated a model similar to (1) where thermal conductivity and specific heat are linear functions of temperature. No existence and uniqueness theorems were established in the preceding two articles, which has motivated subsequent researchers [3–9] to establish the existence and uniqueness theorems for the solutions to such problems. In particular, the authors in [3] proved the existence and uniqueness of the modified error function for small values of $\delta > 0$. The general case $\delta > -1$ was investigated and established in [4]. In [5], the authors investigated problem (2), with a nonlinear thermal conductivity of the form $(1 + \delta y + \gamma y^2)^n$, where $\delta > -1$ and $\gamma > -1$. Existence and uniqueness theorems for the solution were obtained, and the solution was obtained in the following form:

$$\varphi_{\delta,\gamma} = C \int_0^x \frac{1}{\Psi(\eta)} \exp\left(-2 \int_0^\eta \frac{\xi}{\Psi(\xi)} d\xi\right) d\eta. \quad (3)$$

This solution was called: "the modified error function of two parameters", because it can be viewed as a generalization to the modified error function obtained by [1,3], when $\gamma = 0$, and to the classical error function when $\delta = \gamma = 0$. As shown in [5], the solution $\varphi_{\delta,\gamma}$ shares some properties with the classical error function.

The present paper aims to investigate the problem

$$\frac{d}{dx}\left[(1+\delta_1 y + \gamma_1 y^2)^n \frac{dy}{dx}\right] + 2x(1+\delta_2 y + \gamma_2 y^2)^m \frac{dy}{dx} = \beta(x), \ 0 < x < \infty \quad (4)$$

together with the following two sets of conditions:

$$y(0) = 0, \ y(\infty) = 1, \quad (5)$$

and

$$y(0) = 1, \ y(\infty) = 0, \quad (6)$$

where $\delta_i > -1$, $i = 1, 2$ are constants that influence the nonlinearity of the problem, $\gamma_i \geq 0$ describes the impact of temperature-dependent thermal parameters and $n, m \geq 1$ determines the degree of nonlinearity in the problem and influences the behavior of the material and the characteristics of the phase transition. The term $\beta(x)$ is an external heat source that represents a source or sink term.

This new problem presents a Stefan problem characterized by the nonlinear thermal conductivity of the form $(1 + \delta_1 y + \gamma_1 y^2)^n$ and a nonlinear specific heat of the form $(1 + \delta_2 y + \gamma_2 y^2)^m$. In principle, the thermal conductivity and specific heat of a material are connected with the internal energy of the molecule, and so to link specific heat to temperature is a more natural and realistic form of modeling. Recent studies have shown that the thermal properties of substances show nonlinearity behavior concerning temperature. This leads to several important applications to nonlinear heat conduction problems, such as nonlinear optical crystals [17–19], Lazer welding experiments [20], friction stir welding [21], and the resistance spot welding process, which is important for the automotive industry [22]. The authors in [21] formulated a three-dimensional thermal diffusion equation to model friction stir welding, which involves complex heat transfer and moving heat courses since thermal conduction becomes a transient process. The authors used the thermal conductivity and specific heat defined as a cubic function of temperature and they observed a good agreement between the experimental results and the models. In [22], the authors constructed a three-dimensional electromechanical model, where the thermal parameters were determined for high-speed thermography. Furthermore, in [23], the author derived a nonlinear differential equation of thermal conductivity phenomenologically, which is important in self-organization processes. In addition, the temperature evolution dynamics were analyzed in the nonstationary case, and consequently, the thermal conductivity was given as a square function and a cubic of the function of thermal conductivity. In [24], the authors developed a procedure for regenerators with the temperature-dependent specific heat of the fluid, and they observed that a constant specific heat model is not adequate except for special cases. In [25], the authors assumed the specific heat capacity of a carbonaceous substance to be a polynomial of degree 4. Also, other research assumed the nonlinear specific heat for an Earth mineralogical model [26], for coal [27,28], for liver tissue [29], and for steroid thermal models [30]. It is for this reason that representing thermal parameters as nonlinear functions of temperature become of vital importance to physical and industrial applications and has caused a great deal of interest in recent research.

The nonhomogeneous term $\beta \in \mathbb{C}^1(\mathbb{R}^+)$ represents the so-called volumetric heating source. As proposed by E.P. Scott [31], this type of source term is important in studying freeze-drying processes using microwave energy technology to speed up the process. Scott proposed the following form for the source term: $\beta(\eta) = \frac{K}{t} e^{-(\eta+d)^2}$, where the similarity $\eta = \frac{x}{2a\sqrt{t}}$, K and d are physical parameters, and t is a temporal variable that refers to the time required to track the progression of the absorption. This function reflects the rapid decrease in the heating effect with distance and time. As noted in [31], this function helps understand the absorption between dried and frozen regions and facilitates the analytical solution of the problem. Several papers have investigated the solution of the Stefan problem for heat sources with constant thermal parameters [32–35] and temperature-dependent thermal parameters [36–39]. The existence of solutions has been established, and explicit solutions have been obtained for particular cases.

The purpose of this paper is two-fold: the first goal is to establish an existence and uniqueness theorem for Pr. (4)–(5) with no source term, i.e., $\beta = 0$. Then, an analytic solution to the problem is provided in addition to lower and upper bounds. It can be seen that the solution obtained here reduces to $\varphi_{\delta,\gamma}$ when $\delta_2 = \gamma_2 = 0$. This implies that Pr. (4)–(5) generalize all the problems proposed by the preceding papers [1–5], and the solution generalizes the error function $\varphi_{\delta,\gamma}$. The second goal is to provide an analytic solution in addition to lower and upper bounds to Pr. (4)–(5) and Pr. (4)–(6) when $\beta(x) = e^{-kx^2}$, $k > 0$, which was adopted in [39]. The paper is organized as follows: In Section 2, we present a preliminary analysis of the homogeneous problem. In Section 3, we obtain the lower and upper bounds of the solution for Pr. (4)–(5) when $\beta(x) = 0$. In Section 4, the existence of the solution is established. In Section 5, we also establish the lower and upper bounds of the solution for Pr. (4)–(6) with $\beta(x) = e^{-kx^2}$, $k > 0$. In Section 6, we explore various numerical results and we conclude with useful remarks.

2. Analytic Treatment

First of all, we give a generalization to (Theorem 2 in [3]). Note that the following theorem is an important tool in the proof of the lower and upper bounds of the solution to Pr. (4)–(5).

Theorem 1. *The solution y of Pr. (4)–(5) when $\beta(x) = 0$ can be expressed by*

$$y = C \int_0^x \frac{1}{\Psi_1(\eta)} \exp\left(-2 \int_0^\eta \frac{\xi \Psi_2(\xi)}{\Psi_1(\xi)} d\xi\right) d\eta, \quad 0 \leq x < \infty, \tag{7}$$

where $\Psi_1(x) = (1 + \delta_1 y + \gamma_1 y^2)^n$, $\Psi_2(x) = (1 + \delta_2 y + \gamma_2 y^2)^m$ and

$$C = \left[\int_0^\infty \frac{1}{\Psi_1(x)} \exp\left(-2 \int_0^x \frac{\xi \Psi_2(\xi)}{\Psi_1(\xi)} d\xi\right) dx\right]^{-1}. \tag{8}$$

Proof. Rewrite Equation (4) as

$$\frac{d}{dx}\left[\Psi_1(x)\frac{dy}{dx}\right] + 2x\frac{\Psi_2(x)}{\Psi_1(x)}\left[\Psi_1(x)\frac{dy}{dx}\right] = 0. \qquad (9)$$

Setting $\Phi(x) = \Psi_1(x)\frac{dy}{dx}$ gives

$$\frac{d\Phi(x)}{dx} + 2x\frac{\Psi_2(x)}{\Psi_1(x)}\Phi(x) = 0. \qquad (10)$$

Solving Equation (10) in $\Phi(x)$, we obtain

$$\Phi(x) = C\exp\left(-2\int_0^x \frac{\eta\Psi_2(\eta)}{\Psi_1(\eta)}d\eta\right), \qquad (11)$$

where C is an unknown constant. Hence,

$$y' = \frac{C}{\Psi_1(x)}\exp\left(-2\int_0^x \frac{\eta\Psi_2(\eta)}{\Psi_1(\eta)}d\eta\right). \qquad (12)$$

Now, integrating (12) from 0 to x, taking into account that $y(0) = 0$, we obtain (7). The constant C can be determined by using the second boundary condition $y(\infty) = 1$ to obtain (8). □

Remark 1. *When $\gamma_i = 0$, $i = 1, 2$, $\delta_2 = 0$ and $n = m = 1$, this reduces to (Theorem 2 in [1]).*

3. Lower and Upper Bounds of the Solution y

Now, we establish lower and upper bounds of the solution y for different values of $\delta_i > -1$ and $\gamma_i \geq 0$, $i = 1, 2$. Please note that all bounds involve the error function. Another remark that we shall need is

Remark 2. *Since $0 \leq y \leq 1$ [1,2], we can assert for $\gamma_i \geq 0$, $i = 1, 2$ that*

- *If $\delta_i \geq 0$, then $0 \leq \delta_i y \leq \delta_i$. So $1 \leq 1 + \delta_i y + \gamma_i y^2 \leq 1 + \delta_i + \gamma_i$;*
- *If $-1 < \delta_i < 0$, then $\delta_i \leq \delta_i y \leq 0$. So $\delta_i + 1 \leq 1 + \delta_i y + \gamma_i y^2 \leq 1 + \gamma_i$;*
- *If $\delta_1 \geq 0$ and $-1 < \delta_2 < 0$, then $1 \leq 1 + \delta_1 y + \gamma_1 y^2 \leq 1 + \delta_1 + \gamma_1$ and $\delta_2 + 1 \leq 1 + \delta_2 y + \gamma_2 y^2 \leq 1 + \gamma_2$;*
- *If $-1 < \delta_1 < 0$ and $\delta_2 \geq 0$, then $\delta_1 + 1 \leq 1 + \delta_1 y + \gamma_1 y^2 \leq 1 + \gamma_1$ and $1 \leq 1 + \delta_2 y + \gamma_2 y^2 \leq 1 + \delta_2 + \gamma_2$.*

In view of these, we have $1 + \delta_i y + \gamma_i y^2 > 0$, $i = 1, 2$ for $\gamma_i > 0$ and $\delta_i > -1$.

We are now ready to give a theorem on the lower and upper bounds of the solution y.

Theorem 2. *If $y \in \mathbb{C}^2[0, \infty)$ is a solution of Pr. (4)–(5) when $\beta(x) = 0$, then there are upper and lower bounds of the solution $y(x)$ such that*

$$y_1(x) \leq y \leq y_2(x) \text{ for } \delta_i \geq 0, \ i = 1, 2, \ 0 \leq x < +\infty, \qquad (13)$$

$$y_3(x) \leq y \leq y_4(x) \text{ for } -1 < \delta_i < 0, \ i = 1, 2, \ 0 \leq x < +\infty, \qquad (14)$$

$$y_5(x) \leq y \leq y_6(x) \text{ for } \delta_1 > 0, \ -1 < \delta_2 < 0, \ 0 \leq x < +\infty, \qquad (15)$$

$$y_7(x) \leq y \leq y_8(x) \text{ for } -1 < \delta_1 < 0, \ \delta_2 > 0, \ 0 \leq x < +\infty, \qquad (16)$$

where

$$\begin{cases} y_1 &= \dfrac{C\sqrt{\pi}}{2(\gamma_1+\delta_1+1)^n\sqrt{(\gamma_2+\delta_2+1)^m}} erf\left(\sqrt{(\gamma_2+\delta_2+1)^m}x\right), \ 0\le x<\infty,\\[4pt]
y_2 &= \dfrac{C\sqrt{(\gamma_1+\delta_1+1)^n\pi}}{2} erf\left(\dfrac{x}{\sqrt{(\gamma_1+\delta_1+1)^n}}\right), \ 0\le x<\infty,\\[4pt]
y_3 &= \dfrac{C\sqrt{\pi(\delta_1+1)^n}}{2(\gamma_1+1)^n\sqrt{(\gamma_2+1)^m}} erf\left(\dfrac{\sqrt{(\gamma_2+1)^m}}{\sqrt{(\delta_1+1)^n}}x\right), \ 0\le x<\infty,\\[4pt]
y_4 &= \dfrac{C\sqrt{\pi(\gamma_1+1)^n}}{2(\delta_1+1)^n\sqrt{(\delta_2+1)^m}} erf\left(\dfrac{\sqrt{(\delta_2+1)^m}}{\sqrt{(\gamma_1+1)^n}}x\right), \ 0\le x<\infty,\\[4pt]
y_5 &= \dfrac{C\sqrt{\pi}}{2(\gamma_1+\delta_1+1)^n\sqrt{(\gamma_2+1)^m}} erf\left(\sqrt{(\gamma_2+1)^m}x\right), \ 0\le x<\infty,\\[4pt]
y_6 &= \dfrac{C\sqrt{(\gamma_1+\delta_1+1)^n\pi}}{2\sqrt{(\delta_2+1)^m}} erf\left(\dfrac{\sqrt{(\delta_2+1)^m}}{\sqrt{(\gamma_1+\delta_1+1)^n}}x\right), \ 0\le x<\infty,\\[4pt]
y_7 &= \dfrac{C\sqrt{(\delta_1+1)^n\pi}}{2(\gamma_1+1)^n\sqrt{(\gamma_2+\delta_2+1)^m}} erf\left(\dfrac{\sqrt{(\gamma_2+\delta_2+1)^m}}{\sqrt{(\delta_1+1)^n}}x\right), \ 0\le x<\infty,\\[4pt]
y_8 &= \dfrac{C\sqrt{(\gamma_1+1)^n\pi}}{2(\delta_1+1)^n} erf\left(\dfrac{x}{\sqrt{(\gamma_1+1)^n}}\right), \ 0\le x<\infty,
\end{cases} \quad (17)$$

where

$$\dfrac{2}{\sqrt{(\gamma_1+\delta_1+1)^n\pi}} \le C \le \dfrac{2(\gamma_1+\delta_1+1)^n\sqrt{(\gamma_2+\delta_2+1)^m}}{\sqrt{\pi}} \ \text{for } \delta_i\ge 0,\ i=1,2, \quad (18)$$

$$\dfrac{2(\delta_1+1)^n\sqrt{(\gamma_2+1)^m}}{\sqrt{\pi(\gamma_1+1)^n}} \le C \le \dfrac{2(\gamma_1+1)^n\sqrt{(\gamma_2+1)^m}}{\sqrt{\pi(\delta_1+1)^n}} \ \text{for } -1<\delta_i<0,\ i=1,2, \quad (19)$$

$$\dfrac{2\sqrt{(\delta_2+1)^m}}{\sqrt{(\gamma_1+\delta_1+1)^n\pi}} \le C \le \dfrac{2(\gamma_1+\delta_1+1)^n\sqrt{(\gamma_2+1)^m}}{\sqrt{\pi}} \ \text{for } \delta_1>0,\ -1<\delta_2<0, \quad (20)$$

$$\dfrac{2(\delta_1+1)^n}{\sqrt{(\gamma_1+1)^n\pi}} \le C \le \dfrac{2(\gamma_1+1)^n\sqrt{(\gamma_2+\delta_2+1)^m}}{\sqrt{(\delta_1+1)^n\pi}} \ \text{for } -1<\delta_1<0,\ \delta_2>0. \quad (21)$$

Proof. The proof of this theorem requires the use of the inequalities that appear in Remark 2. A simple computation leads to

$$\dfrac{1}{(\gamma_1+\delta_1+1)^n} \le \dfrac{1}{\Psi_1} \le 1 \ \text{and } 1\le \Psi_2 \le (\gamma_2+\delta_2+1)^m,\ \text{for } \delta_i\ge 0,\ i=1,2, \quad (22)$$

$$\dfrac{1}{(\gamma_1+1)^n} \le \dfrac{1}{\Psi_1} \le \dfrac{1}{(\delta_1+1)^n} \ \text{and } (\delta_2+1)^m \le \Psi_2 \le (\gamma_2+1)^m,\ \text{for } -1<\delta_i<0,\ i=1,2, \quad (23)$$

$$\dfrac{1}{(\gamma_1+\delta_1+1)^n} \le \dfrac{1}{\Psi_1} \le 1 \ \text{and } (\delta_2+1)^m \le \Psi_2 \le (\gamma_2+1)^m,\ \text{for } \delta_1\ge 0,\ 1<\delta_2<0, \quad (24)$$

and

$$\dfrac{1}{(\gamma_1+1)^n} \le \dfrac{1}{\Psi_1} \le \dfrac{1}{(\delta_1+1)^n} \ \text{and } 1\le \Psi_2 \le (\gamma_2+\delta_2+1)^m \ \text{for } -1<\delta_1<0,\ \delta_2\ge 0. \quad (25)$$

Substituting (22)–(25) into (7), we obtain

$$\dfrac{C}{(\gamma_1+\delta_1+1)^n}\int_0^x e^{-(\gamma_2+\delta_2+1)^m\xi^2}d\xi \le y \le C\int_0^x e^{-\frac{\xi^2}{(\gamma_1+\delta_1+1)^n}}d\xi \ \text{for } \delta_i\ge 0,\ i=1,2, \quad (26)$$

$$\frac{C}{(\gamma_1+1)^n}\int_0^x e^{-\frac{(\gamma_2+1)^m}{(\delta_1+1)^n}\xi^2}d\xi \leq y \leq \frac{C}{(\delta_1+1)^n}\int_0^x e^{-\frac{(\delta_2+1)^m}{(\gamma_1+1)^n}\xi^2}d\xi \text{ for } -1<\delta_i<0,\ i=1,2, \qquad (27)$$

$$\frac{C}{(\gamma_1+\delta_1+1)^n}\int_0^x e^{-(\gamma_2+1)^m\xi^2}d\xi \leq y \leq C\int_0^x e^{-\frac{(\gamma_2+1)^m}{(\gamma_1+\delta_1+1)^n}\xi^2}d\xi \text{ for } \delta_1\geq 0,\ -1<\delta_2<0, \qquad (28)$$

and

$$\frac{C}{(\gamma_1+1)^n}\int_0^x e^{-\frac{(\gamma_2+\delta_2+1)^m}{(\delta_1+1)^n}\xi^2}d\xi \leq y \leq \frac{C}{(\delta_1+1)^n}\int_0^x e^{-\frac{\xi^2}{(\gamma_1+1)^n}}d\xi \text{ for } -1<\delta_1<0,\ \delta_2\geq 0, \qquad (29)$$

which gives the desired inequalities.
Substituting (22)–(25) into (8), we obtain (18)–(21) and the proof is complete. □

Similarly, we also have the following estimations for the derivative y'.

Theorem 3. *For Pr. (4)–(5) when $\beta(x)=0$, there are upper and lower bounds of y' such that we have*

$$z_1(x) \leq y' \leq z_2(x) \text{ for } \delta_i \geq 0,\ i=1,2,\ 0\leq x<+\infty, \qquad (30)$$

$$z_3(x) \leq y' \leq z_4(x) \text{ for } -1<\delta_i<0,\ i=1,2,\ 0\leq x<+\infty, \qquad (31)$$

$$z_5(x) \leq y' \leq z_6(x) \text{ for } \delta_1 \geq 0,\ -1<\delta_2<0,\ 0\leq x<+\infty, \qquad (32)$$

$$z_7(x) \leq y' \leq z_8(x) \text{ for } -1<\delta_1<0,\ \delta_2\geq 0,\ 0\leq x<+\infty, \qquad (33)$$

where

$$\begin{cases}
z_1 &= \frac{C}{(\gamma_1+\delta_1+1)^n}e^{-(\gamma_2+\delta_2+1)^m x^2},\ 0\leq x<\infty,\\
z_2 &= Ce^{-\frac{x^2}{(\gamma_1+\delta_1+1)^n}},\ 0<x<\infty,\\
z_3 &= \frac{C}{(\gamma_1+1)^n}e^{-\frac{(\gamma_2+1)^m}{(\delta_1+1)^n}x^2},\ 0\leq x<\infty,\\
z_4 &= \frac{C}{(\delta_1+1)^n}e^{-\frac{(\delta_2+1)^m}{(\gamma_1+1)^n}x^2},\ 0\leq x<\infty,\\
z_5 &= \frac{C}{(\gamma_1+\delta_1+1)^n}e^{-(\gamma_2+1)^m x^2},\ 0<x<\infty,\\
z_6 &= Ce^{-\frac{(\gamma_2+1)^m}{(\gamma_1+\delta_1+1)^n}x^2},\ 0<x<\infty,\\
z_7 &= \frac{C}{(\gamma_1+1)^n}e^{-\frac{(\gamma_2+\delta_2+1)^m}{(\delta_1+1)^n}x^2},\ 0\leq x<\infty,\\
z_8 &= \frac{C}{(\delta_1+1)^n}e^{-\frac{x^2}{(\gamma_1+1)^n}},\ 0<x<\infty.
\end{cases} \qquad (34)$$

Proof. Theorem 3 follows immediately by incorporating (22)–(25) into (12) as in the proof of Theorem 2. □

4. Existence and Uniqueness of the Solution

In this section, the following theorem (Theorem 3, see [40]) is an important tool in the proof of our result.

Theorem 4. *(Theorem 3 in [40]) For the given boundary value problem*

$$\begin{cases} v'' = h(x,v,v'),\ 0 < x < \infty, \\ -\alpha v(0) + \beta v'(0) = r,\ v(\infty) = 0, \end{cases} \quad (35)$$

where $\alpha > 0, \beta \geq 0$ and r is a given constant. If $h(x,v,p)$ is continuous and satisfies the following conditions:

1. *There is a constant $M \geq 0$ such that $vh(x,v,0) \geq 0$ for $|v| > M$;*
2. *There are functions $A(x,v) > 0$ and $B(x,v) > 0$, which are bounded when v varies in a bounded set and if $|h(x,v,p)| \leq A(x,v)p^2 + B(x,v)$;*
3. *There is a continuous function φ such that $\varphi(x) \to 0$ as $x \to \infty$ and $|v(x)| \leq \varphi(x)$ for $0 \leq x < \infty$.*

Then, this boundary value problem has at least one solution in $\mathbb{C}^2[0,\infty)$.

Also, our main result makes use of the following fundamental lemma:

Lemma 1.
1. *Pr. (4)–(5) with $\beta(x) = 0$ can be converted into the nonlinear boundary value problem*

$$\begin{cases} u'' + f(x,u,u') = 0,\ 0 < x < \infty, \\ u(0) = \frac{\delta_1}{2\gamma_1},\ u(\infty) = 1 + \frac{\delta_1}{2\gamma_1}, \end{cases} \quad (36)$$

where

$$f(x,u,u') = 2\gamma_1 n \frac{u}{\gamma_1 u^2 + \alpha_1}(u')^2 + 2x \frac{\left(\gamma_2(u+\sigma)^2 + \alpha_2\right)^m}{(\gamma_1 u^2 + \alpha_1)^n} u', \quad (37)$$

$u = y + \frac{\delta_1}{2\gamma_1},\ \alpha_i = 1 - \frac{\delta_i^2}{4\gamma_i},\ i = 1,2$ and $\sigma = \frac{\delta_2}{2\gamma_2} - \frac{\delta_1}{2\gamma_1}$.
Further,

$$\frac{\delta_1}{2\gamma_1} \leq u(x) \leq 1 + \frac{\delta_1}{2\gamma_1},\ 0 \leq x < \infty. \quad (38)$$

2. *Pr. (4)–(5) with $\beta(x) = 0$ can also be converted into*

$$\begin{cases} v'' = g(x,v,v'),\ 0 < x < \infty, \\ v(0) = -1,\ v(\infty) = 0, \end{cases} \quad (39)$$

where $g(x,v,v')$ is continuous and defined on $[0,\infty) \times [-1,0] \times \mathbb{R}$ by

$$g(x,v,v') = -2\gamma_1 n \frac{(v+1+\frac{\delta_1}{2\gamma_1})}{\gamma_1(v+1+\frac{\delta_1}{2\gamma_1})^2 + \alpha_1}(v')^2 - 2x \frac{\left(\gamma_2(v+1+\frac{\delta_2}{2\gamma_2})^2 + \alpha_2\right)^m}{(\gamma_1(v+1+\frac{\delta_1}{2\gamma_1})^2 + \alpha_1)^n} v', \quad (40)$$

where $v = u - 1 - \frac{\delta_1}{2\gamma_1}$.

3. *For the given BVP (39), there are functions $A(x,v), B(x,v) > 0$, which are bounded when v varies in a bounded set $[-1,0]$ such that*

$$|g(x,v,p)| \leq A(x,v)p^2 + B(x,v). \quad (41)$$

Proof. 1. By writing the nonlinear terms $1 + \delta_i y + \gamma_i y^2, i = 1,2$ of Pr. (4) in the form

$$1 + \delta_i y + \gamma_i y^2 = \gamma_i(y^2 + \frac{\delta_i}{\gamma_i} y + \frac{1}{\gamma_i}) = \gamma_i(y + \frac{\delta_i}{2\gamma_i})^2 + 1 - \frac{\delta_i^2}{4\gamma_i},\ \gamma_i > 0, i = 1,2, \quad (42)$$

the nonlinear differential equation of Pr. (4) becomes

$$\frac{d}{dx}\left[\left(\gamma_1(y+\frac{\delta_1}{2\gamma_1})^2+\alpha_1\right)^n\frac{dy}{dx}\right]+2x\left(\gamma_2(y+\frac{\delta_2}{2\gamma_2})^2+\alpha_2\right)^m\frac{dy}{dx}=0, \quad (43)$$

where $\alpha_i = 1 - \frac{\delta_i^2}{4\gamma_i}$, $i = 1, 2$. Thus,

$$\frac{d}{dx}\left[\left(\gamma_1(y+\frac{\delta_1}{2\gamma_1})^2+\alpha_1\right)^n\frac{d}{dx}(y+\frac{\delta_1}{2\gamma_1})\right]+2x\left(\gamma_2(y+\frac{\delta_2}{2\gamma_2})^2+\alpha_2\right)^m\frac{d}{dx}(y+\frac{\delta_1}{2\gamma_1})=0. \quad (44)$$

Using the change of variable

$$u = y + \frac{\delta_1}{2\gamma_1}. \quad (45)$$

Equation (44) becomes

$$\frac{d}{dx}\left[\left(\gamma_1 u^2+\alpha_1\right)^n\frac{du}{dx}\right]+2x\left(\gamma_2\left(u+\frac{\delta_2}{2\gamma_2}-\frac{\delta_1}{2\gamma_1}\right)^2+\alpha_2\right)^m\frac{du}{dx}=0, 0<x<\infty. \quad (46)$$

Hence,

$$\frac{d}{dx}\left[\left(\gamma_1 u^2+\alpha_1\right)^n\frac{du}{dx}\right]+2x\left(\gamma_2(u+\sigma)^2+\alpha_2\right)^m\frac{du}{dx}=0, 0<x<\infty, \quad (47)$$

where $\sigma = \frac{\delta_2}{2\gamma_2} - \frac{\delta_1}{2\gamma_1}$. Therefore,

$$\left(\gamma_1 u^2+\alpha_1\right)^n\frac{d^2u}{dx^2}+n\left(\gamma_1 u^2+\alpha_1\right)^{n-1}\left(2\gamma_1 u\left(\frac{du}{dx}\right)^2\right)+2x\left[\gamma_2(u+\sigma)^2+\alpha_2\right]^m\frac{du}{dx}=0. \quad (48)$$

Consequently,

$$\frac{d^2u}{dx^2}+2\gamma_1 n\frac{u}{\gamma_1 u^2+\alpha_1}\left(\frac{du}{dx}\right)^2+2x\frac{\left(\gamma_2(u+\sigma)^2+\alpha_2\right)^m}{\left(\gamma_1 u^2+\alpha_1\right)^n}\frac{du}{dx}=0. \quad (49)$$

2. The second part of this lemma follows from the first one.
3. Since $v'(x) = u'(x) = y'(x)$, from the upper bounds of $y'(x)$, we have

$$v'(x) \leq Ce^{-\frac{x^2}{(\gamma_1+\delta_1+1)^n}} \text{ for } \delta_i \geq 0, \, 0 \leq x < \infty, \quad (50)$$

$$v'(x) \leq \frac{C}{(\delta_1+1)^n}e^{-\frac{(\delta_2+1)^m}{(\gamma_1+1)^n}x^2} \text{ for } -1 < \delta_i < 0, \, 0 \leq x < \infty, \quad (51)$$

$$v'(x) \leq Ce^{-\frac{(\gamma_2+1)^m}{(\gamma_1+\delta_1+1)^n}x^2} \text{ for } \delta_1 \geq 0, -1 < \delta_2 < 0, \, 0 \leq x < \infty \quad (52)$$

and

$$v'(x) \leq \frac{C}{(\delta_1+1)^n}e^{-\frac{x^2}{(\gamma_1+1)^n}} \text{ for } -1 < \delta_1 < 0, \delta_2 \geq 0, \, 0 \leq x < \infty. \quad (53)$$

Thus,

$$|g(x,v,v')| \leq 2\gamma_1 n \frac{(v+1+\frac{\delta_1}{2\gamma_1})}{\gamma_1(v+1+\frac{\delta_1}{2\gamma_1})^2+\alpha_1}(v')^2 \\ +2xCe^{-\frac{x^2}{(\gamma_1+\delta_1+1)^n}} \frac{[\gamma_2(v+1+\frac{\delta_2}{2\gamma_2})^2+\alpha_2]^m}{\gamma_1(v+1+\frac{\delta_1}{2\gamma_1})^2+\alpha_1]^n}, \qquad (54)$$

where $\delta_i \geq 0$, $i = 1,2$,

$$|g(x,v,v')| \leq 2\gamma_1 n \frac{(v+1+\frac{\delta_1}{2\gamma_1})}{\gamma_1(v+1+\frac{\delta_1}{2\gamma_1})^2+\alpha_1}(v')^2 \\ +2x\frac{C}{(\delta_1+1)^n}e^{-\frac{(\delta_2+1)^m}{(\gamma_1+1)^n}x^2} \frac{[\gamma_2(v+1+\frac{\delta_2}{2\gamma_2})^2+\alpha_2]^m}{[\gamma_1(v+1+\frac{\delta_1}{2\gamma_1})^2+\alpha_1]^n} \qquad (55)$$

for $-1 < \delta_i < 0$,

$$|g(x,v,v')| \leq 2\gamma_1 n \frac{(v+1+\frac{\delta_1}{2\gamma_1})}{\gamma_1(v+1+\frac{\delta_1}{2\gamma_1})^2+\alpha_1}(v')^2 \\ +2xCe^{-\frac{(\gamma_2+1)^m}{(\gamma_1+\delta_1+1)^n}x^2} \frac{[\gamma_2(v+1+\frac{\delta_2}{2\gamma_2})^2+\alpha_2]^m}{[\gamma_1(v+1+\frac{\delta_1}{2\gamma_1})^2+\alpha_1]^n} \qquad (56)$$

for $\delta_1 \geq 0$, $-1 < \delta_2 < 0$ and

$$|g(x,v,v')| \leq 2\gamma_1 n \frac{(v+1+\frac{\delta_1}{2\gamma_1})}{\gamma_1(v+1+\frac{\delta_1}{2\gamma_1})^2+\alpha_1}(v')^2 \\ +2x\frac{C}{(\delta_1+1)^n}e^{-\frac{x^2}{(\gamma_1+1)^n}} \frac{[\gamma_2(v+1+\frac{\delta_2}{2\gamma_2})^2+\alpha_2]^m}{[\gamma_1(v+1+\frac{\delta_1}{2\gamma_1})^2+\alpha_1]^n} \qquad (57)$$

for $\delta_2 \geq 0$ and $-1 < \delta_1 < 0$.
Hence, for $\delta_i \geq 0$, we have

$$A(x,v) = 2\gamma_1 n \frac{(v+1+\frac{\delta_1}{2\gamma_1})}{\gamma_1(v+1+\frac{\delta_1}{2\gamma_1})^2+\alpha_1} \qquad (58)$$

and

$$B(x,v) = 2xCe^{-\frac{x^2}{(\gamma_1+\delta_1+1)^n}} \frac{[\gamma_2\left(v+1+\frac{\delta_2}{2\gamma_2}\right)^2+\alpha_2]^m}{[\gamma_1(v+1+\frac{\delta_1}{2\gamma_1})^2+\alpha_1]^n}. \qquad (59)$$

For $-1 < \delta_i < 0$, we have

$$A(x,v) = 2\gamma_1 n \frac{(v+1+\frac{\delta_1}{2\gamma_1})}{\gamma_1(v+1+\frac{\delta_1}{2\gamma_1})^2+\alpha_1} \qquad (60)$$

and

$$B(x,v) = 2x\frac{C}{(\delta_1+1)^n}e^{-\frac{(\delta_2+1)^m}{(\gamma_1+1)^n}x^2} \frac{[\gamma_2(v+1+\frac{\delta_2}{2\gamma_2})^2+\alpha_2]^m}{[\gamma_1(v+1+\frac{\delta_1}{2\gamma_1})^2+\alpha_1]^n}. \qquad (61)$$

For $\delta_1 \geq 0$ and $-1 < \delta_2 < 0$, we have

$$A(x,v) = 2\gamma_1 n \frac{(v+1+\frac{\delta_1}{2\gamma_1})}{\gamma_1(v+1+\frac{\delta_1}{2\gamma_1})^2+\alpha_1} \qquad (62)$$

and

$$B(x,v) = 2xCe^{-\frac{(\gamma_2+1)^m}{(\gamma_1+\delta_1+1)^n}x^2} \frac{[\gamma_2(v+1+\frac{\delta_2}{2\gamma_2})^2 + \alpha_2]^m}{[\gamma_1(v+1+\frac{\delta_1}{2\gamma_1})^2 + \alpha_1]^n}. \tag{63}$$

For $-1 < \delta_1 < 0$ and $\delta_2 \geq 0$, we have

$$A(x,v) = 2\gamma_1 n \frac{(v+1+\frac{\delta_1}{2\gamma_1})}{\gamma_1(v+1+\frac{\delta_1}{2\gamma_1})^2 + \alpha_1} \tag{64}$$

and

$$B(x,v) = 2x \frac{C}{(\delta_1+1)^n} e^{-\frac{x^2}{(\gamma_1+1)^m}} \frac{[\gamma_2(v+1+\frac{\delta_2}{2\gamma_2})^2 + \alpha_2]^m}{[\gamma_1(v+1+\frac{\delta_1}{2\gamma_1})^2 + \alpha_1]^n}. \tag{65}$$

When v varies in a bounded set $[-1,0]$, we have

$$|A(x,v)| \leq 2\gamma n + n\delta_1, \ |B(x,v)| \leq 2C[\gamma_2(1+\frac{\delta_2}{2\gamma_2})^2 + \alpha_2]^m, \ \delta_i \geq 0 \tag{66}$$

$$|A(x,v)| \leq 2\gamma n + n\delta_1, \ |B(x,v)| \leq 2C\frac{[\gamma_2(1+\frac{\delta_2}{2\gamma_2})^2 + \alpha_2]^m}{(\gamma_1+1)^n}, \ -1 < \delta_i < 0 \tag{67}$$

$$|A(x,v)| \leq 2\gamma n + n\delta_1, \ |B(x,v)| \leq 2C[\gamma_2(1+\frac{\delta_2}{2\gamma_2})^2 + \alpha_2]^m, \ \delta_1 \geq 0, \ -1 < \delta_2 < 0, \tag{68}$$

$$|A(x,v)| \leq 2\gamma n + n\delta_1, \ |B(x,v)| \leq 2C\frac{[\gamma_2\left(1+\frac{\delta_2}{2\gamma_2}\right)^2 + \alpha_2]^m}{(\gamma_1+1)^n}, \ -1 < \delta_1 < 0, \delta_2 \geq 0. \tag{69}$$

□

Thus, we are now ready for the existence theorem.

Theorem 5. *Pr. (39) has at least one solution v in $\mathbb{C}^2[0,\infty)$.*

Proof. By Lemma 1, the function $g(x,v,v')$ defined by (40) satisfies the first condition of Theorem 4 (Theorem 3 in [40]). To see this, note for $v' = 0$, there exists a constant $M \geq 0$ when v varies in a bounded set $[-1,0]$ such that $vg(x,v,0) = 0$ for $|v| \geq M$. Furthermore, the second condition of Theorem 4 (Theorem 3 in [40]) holds, that is, $|g(x,v,p)| \leq A(x,v)p^2 + B(x,v)$, where $A(x,v) > 0$ and $B(x,v) > 0$ are two bounded functions for different values of $\delta_i > -1$ and $\gamma_i \geq 0$, $i = 1,2$ (see (66)–(69)). It remains, therefore, only to prove the third condition of Theorem 4 (Theorem 3 in [40]), that is, there is a continuous function $\varphi(x)$ such that $\varphi(x) \to 0$ as $x \to \infty$ and $|v(x)| \leq \varphi(x)$ for $0 \leq x < \infty$. Indeed, from the upper bounds of $y(x)$, if we choose, for example,

$$C = \frac{2}{\sqrt{(\gamma_1+\delta_1+1)^n\pi}} \text{ for } \delta_i \geq 0, \tag{70}$$

$$C = \frac{2\sqrt{(\delta_1+1)^n}\sqrt{(\gamma_2+1)^m}}{\sqrt{\pi}} \text{ for } -1 < \delta_i < 0 \ i=1,2, \tag{71}$$

$$C = \frac{2\sqrt{(\gamma_2+1)^m}}{\sqrt{(\gamma_1+\delta_1+1)^n\pi}} \text{ for } \delta_1 > 0, \ -1 < \delta_2 < 0, \tag{72}$$

$$C = \frac{2(\delta_1+1)^n}{\sqrt{(\gamma_1+1)^n\pi}} \quad \text{for } -1 < \delta_1 < 0, \, \delta_2 > 0 \tag{73}$$

and in view of $v(x) = y - 1$, we obtain

$$\begin{cases} v(x) \leq \varphi(x) = -1 + \operatorname{erf}\left(\frac{x}{\sqrt{(\gamma_1+\delta_1+1)^n}}\right), & \delta_i \geq 0, \, 0 \leq x < \infty, \\ v(x) \leq \varphi(x) = -1 + \operatorname{erf}\left(\frac{\sqrt{(\delta_2+1)^m}}{\sqrt{(\gamma_1+1)^n}}x\right), & -1 < \delta_i < 0, \, 0 \leq x < \infty, \\ v(x) \leq \varphi(x) = -1 + \operatorname{erf}\left(\frac{\sqrt{(\gamma_2+1)^m}}{\sqrt{(\gamma_1+\delta_1+1)^n}}x\right), & \delta_1 > 0, \, -1 < \delta_2 < 0, \, 0 \leq x < \infty, \\ v(x) \leq \varphi(x) = -1 + \operatorname{erf}\left(\frac{x}{\sqrt{(\gamma_1+1)^n}}\right), & \delta_1 > 0, \, -1 < \delta_2 < 0, \, 0 \leq x < \infty. \end{cases} \tag{74}$$

This means that there exists a continuous function $\varphi(x)$ such that $v(x) \leq \varphi(x)$, where

$$\varphi(x) \to 0 \text{ as } x \to \infty \text{ for } \delta_i \geq 0, \, -1 < \delta_i < 0, \, i = 1, 2, \, 0 \leq x < \infty. \tag{75}$$

Therefore, the function $g(x, v, v')$ satisfies the conditions of Theorem 4 (Theorem 3 in [40]). Consequently, Pr. (39) has at least one solution $v(x)$. □

Uniqueness of the Solution

Theorem 6. *If $g(x, v, p)$ is monotone increasing in v for each fixed $x \in [0, \infty)$ and $p \in \mathbb{R}$. Then, the boundary problem Pr. (39) has at most one solution v in $\mathbb{C}^2[0, \infty)$.*

Proof. In proving the uniqueness of the solution, we make use of the following important result [40]:
If $g(x, v, v')$ is monotone increasing in v, then the boundary value on a finite interval

$$\begin{cases} v'' = g(x, v, v'), \, 0 < x < b, \\ v(0) = \sigma_1, \, v(b) = \sigma_2 \end{cases} \tag{76}$$

has at most one solution.
The rest of the proof is similar to the proof of the uniqueness of the solution of our result (see Pr. (2) in [5]). □

5. The General Problem: Nonhomogeneous Equation

Now, we investigate the general problem.

5.1. Pr. (4)–(5) with $\beta(x) = e^{-kx^2}$, $k > 0$

For the general problem

$$\begin{cases} \frac{d}{dx}\left[(1+\delta_1 y + \gamma_1 y^2)^n \frac{dy}{dx}\right] + 2x(1+\delta_2 y + \gamma_2 y^2)^m \frac{dy}{dx} = \beta(x), \, 0 < x < \infty, \\ y(0) = 0, \, y(\infty) = 1, \end{cases} \tag{77}$$

where $\beta(x) = e^{-kx^2}$, $k > 0$, we have

Theorem 7. *The solution y of Pr. (77) can be expressed by*

$$y = \int_0^x \frac{1}{\Psi_1(\eta)} \exp\left(-2\int_0^\eta \frac{\xi\Psi_2(\xi)}{\Psi_1(\xi)}d\xi\right) \left[\int_0^\eta \beta(\xi)\exp\left(2\int_0^\xi \frac{t\Psi_2(t)}{\Psi_1(t)}dt\right)d\xi\right]d\eta$$
$$+ D\int_0^x \frac{1}{\Psi_1(\eta)} \exp\left(-2\int_0^\eta \frac{\xi\Psi_2(\xi)}{\Psi_1(\xi)}d\xi\right)d\eta, \tag{78}$$

where

$$D = \frac{1 - \int_0^\infty \frac{1}{\Psi_1(x)} \exp\left(-2\int_0^x \frac{\zeta \Psi_2(\zeta)}{\Psi_1(\zeta)} d\zeta\right) \left[\int_0^x \beta(\zeta) \exp\left(2\int_0^\zeta \frac{t\Psi_2(t)}{\Psi_1(t)} dt\right) d\zeta\right] dx}{\int_0^\infty \frac{1}{\Psi_1(x)} \exp\left(-2\int_0^x \frac{\zeta \Psi_2(\zeta)}{\Psi_1(\zeta)} d\zeta\right) dx}. \quad (79)$$

Proof. Proceeding as in the proof of Theorem 1, we have

$$\frac{d\Phi(x)}{dx} + 2x\frac{\Psi_2(x)}{\Psi_1(x)}\Phi(x) = \beta(x). \quad (80)$$

Solving Equation (80) in $\Phi(x)$, we obtain

$$\begin{aligned}\Phi(x) &= \exp\left(-2\int_0^x \frac{\zeta\Psi_2(\zeta)}{\Psi_1(\zeta)} d\zeta\right)\left[\int_0^x \beta(\zeta) \exp\left(2\int_0^\zeta \frac{t\Psi_2(t)}{\Psi_1(t)} dt\right) d\zeta\right] \\ &\quad + D\exp\left(-2\int_0^x \frac{\eta \Psi_2(\eta)}{\Psi_1(\eta)} d\eta\right),\end{aligned} \quad (81)$$

where D is a constant of the integral. Hence,

$$\begin{aligned}y' &= \frac{1}{\Psi_1(x)}\exp\left(-2\int_0^x \frac{\zeta\Psi_2(\zeta)}{\Psi_1(\zeta)} d\zeta\right)\left[\int_0^x \beta(\zeta) \exp\left(2\int_0^\zeta \frac{t\Psi_2(t)}{\Psi_1(t)} dt\right) d\zeta\right] \\ &\quad + \frac{D}{\Psi_1(x)}\exp\left(-2\int_0^x \frac{\eta \Psi_2(\eta)}{\Psi_1(\eta)} d\eta\right).\end{aligned} \quad (82)$$

Integrating (82) from 0 to x and taking into account that $y(0) = 0$, we obtain (78). The constant D can be determined using the second boundary condition $y(\infty) = 1$ to obtain (79). □

For the lower and upper bounds of the solution y of Pr. (77) for different values of $\delta_i > -1$ and $\gamma_i \geq 0$, $i = 1, 2$, the following theorem follows immediately by incorporating the inequalities (22)–(25) into (78) as in the proof of Theorem 2.

Theorem 8. *If $y \in \mathbb{C}^2[0, \infty)$ is a solution of Pr. (77), then there are upper and lower bounds of the solution $y(x)$ such that*

$$w_1(x) \leq y \leq w_2(x) \text{ for } \delta_i \geq 0, \ i = 1, 2, \ 0 \leq x < +\infty, \quad (83)$$

$$w_3(x) \leq y \leq w_4(x) \text{ for } -1 < \delta_i < 0, \ i = 1, 2, \ 0 \leq x < +\infty, \quad (84)$$

$$w_5(x) \leq y \leq w_6(x) \text{ for } \delta_1 > 0, \ -1 < \delta_2 < 0, \ 0 \leq x < +\infty, \quad (85)$$

$$w_7(x) \leq y \leq w_8(x) \text{ for } -1 < \delta_1 < 0, \ \delta_2 > 0, \ 0 \leq x < +\infty, \quad (86)$$

where

$$\begin{cases}
w_1 &= \dfrac{D\sqrt{\pi}}{2(\gamma_1+\delta_1+1)^n\sqrt{(\gamma_2+\delta_2+1)^m}}\,\mathrm{erf}\!\left(\sqrt{(\gamma_2+\delta_2+1)^m}\,x\right) \\
&\quad + \dfrac{\sqrt{\pi}}{2(\gamma_1+\delta_1+1)^n\sqrt{k-\frac{1}{(\gamma_1+\delta_1+1)^n}}}\int_0^x e^{-(\gamma_2+\delta_2+1)^m\eta^2}\,\mathrm{erf}\!\left(\sqrt{k-\tfrac{1}{(\gamma_1+\delta_1+1)^n}}\,\eta\right)d\eta,\ k>\tfrac{1}{(\gamma_1+\delta_1+1)^n}, \\[4pt]
w_2 &= \dfrac{D\sqrt{(\gamma_1+\delta_1+1)^n\pi}}{2}\,\mathrm{erf}\!\left(\dfrac{x}{\sqrt{(\gamma_1+\delta_1+1)^n}}\right) \\
&\quad + \dfrac{\sqrt{\pi}}{2\sqrt{k-(\gamma_2+\delta_2+1)^m}}\int_0^x e^{-\frac{1}{(\gamma_1+\delta_1+1)^n}x^2}\,\mathrm{erf}\!\left(\sqrt{k-(\gamma_2+\delta_2+1)^m}\,\eta\right)d\eta,\ k>(\gamma_2+\delta_2+1)^m, \\[4pt]
w_3 &= \dfrac{D\sqrt{\pi(\delta_1+1)^n}}{2(\gamma_1+1)^n\sqrt{(\gamma_2+1)^m}}\,\mathrm{erf}\!\left(\dfrac{\sqrt{(\gamma_2+1)^m}}{\sqrt{(\delta_1+1)^n}}\,x\right) \\
&\quad + \dfrac{\sqrt{\pi}}{2(\gamma_1+1)^n\sqrt{k-\frac{(\delta_2+1)^m}{(\gamma_1+1)^n}}}\int_0^x e^{-\frac{(\gamma_2+1)^m}{(\delta_1+1)^n}\eta^2}\,\mathrm{erf}\!\left(\sqrt{k-\tfrac{(\delta_2+1)^m}{(\gamma_1+1)^n}}\,\eta\right)d\eta,\ k>\tfrac{(\delta_2+1)^m}{(\gamma_1+1)^n}, \\[4pt]
w_4 &= \dfrac{D\sqrt{\pi(\gamma_1+1)^n}}{2(\delta_1+1)^n\sqrt{(\delta_2+1)^m}}\,\mathrm{erf}\!\left(\dfrac{\sqrt{(\delta_2+1)^m}}{\sqrt{(\gamma_1+1)^n}}\,x\right) \\
&\quad + \dfrac{\sqrt{\pi}}{2(\delta_1+1)^n\sqrt{k-\frac{(\gamma_2+1)^m}{(\delta_1+1)^n}}}\int_0^x e^{-\frac{(\delta_2+1)^m}{(\gamma_1+1)^n}\eta^2}\,\mathrm{erf}\!\left(\sqrt{k-\tfrac{(\gamma_2+1)^m}{(\delta_1+1)^n}}\,\eta\right)d\eta,\ k>\tfrac{(\gamma_2+1)^m}{(\delta_1+1)^n}, \\[4pt]
w_5 &= \dfrac{D\sqrt{\pi}}{2(\gamma_1+\delta_1+1)^n\sqrt{(\gamma_2+1)^m}}\,\mathrm{erf}\!\left(\sqrt{(\gamma_2+1)^m}\,x\right) \\
&\quad + \dfrac{\sqrt{\pi}}{2(\gamma_1+\delta_1+1)^n\sqrt{k-\frac{(\delta_2+1)^m}{(\gamma_1+\delta_1+1)^n}}}\int_0^x e^{-(\gamma_2+1)^m\eta^2}\,\mathrm{erf}\!\left(\sqrt{k-\tfrac{(\delta_2+1)^m}{(\gamma_1+\delta_1+1)^n}}\,\eta\right)d\eta,\ k>\tfrac{(\delta_2+1)^m}{(\gamma_1+\delta_1+1)^n}, \\[4pt]
w_6 &= \dfrac{D\sqrt{(\gamma_1+\delta_1+1)^n\pi}}{2\sqrt{(\delta_2+1)^m}}\,\mathrm{erf}\!\left(\dfrac{\sqrt{(\delta_2+1)^m}}{\sqrt{(\gamma_1+\delta_1+1)^n}}\,x\right) \\
&\quad + \dfrac{\sqrt{\pi}}{2\sqrt{k-(\gamma_2+1)^m}}\int_0^x e^{-\frac{(\delta_2+1)^m}{(\gamma_1+\delta_1+1)^n}\eta^2}\,\mathrm{erf}\!\left(\sqrt{k-(\delta_2+1)^m}\,\eta\right)d\eta,\ k>(\delta_2+1)^m, \\[4pt]
w_7 &= \dfrac{D\sqrt{(\delta_1+1)^n\pi}}{2(\gamma_1+1)^n\sqrt{(\gamma_2+\delta_2+1)^m}}\,\mathrm{erf}\!\left(\dfrac{\sqrt{(\gamma_2+\delta_2+1)^m}}{\sqrt{(\delta_1+1)^n}}\,x\right) \\
&\quad + \dfrac{\sqrt{\pi}}{2(\gamma_1+1)^n\sqrt{k-\frac{1}{(\gamma_1+1)^n}}}\int_0^x e^{-\frac{(\gamma_2+\delta_2+1)^m}{(\delta_1+1)^n}\eta^2}\,\mathrm{erf}\!\left(\sqrt{k-\tfrac{1}{(\gamma_1+1)^n}}\,\eta\right)d\eta,\ k>\tfrac{1}{(\gamma_1+1)^n}, \\[4pt]
w_8 &= \dfrac{D\sqrt{(\gamma_1+1)^n\pi}}{2(\delta_1+1)^n}\,\mathrm{erf}\!\left(\dfrac{x}{\sqrt{(\gamma_1+1)^n}}\right) \\
&\quad + \dfrac{\sqrt{\pi}}{2(\delta_1+1)^n\sqrt{k-\frac{(\gamma_2+\delta_2+1)^m}{(\delta_1+1)^n}}}\int_0^x e^{-\frac{1}{(\gamma_1+1)^n}\eta^2}\,\mathrm{erf}\!\left(\sqrt{k-\tfrac{(\gamma_2+\delta_2+1)^m}{(\delta_1+1)^n}}\,\eta\right)d\eta,\ k>\tfrac{(\gamma_2+\delta_2+1)^m}{(\delta_1+1)^n}.
\end{cases}$$

Further, the constant D satisfies

$$D_1 = \left[1 - \dfrac{\sqrt{\pi}}{2\sqrt{k-(\gamma_2+\delta_2+1)^m}}\int_0^\infty e^{-\frac{1}{(\gamma_1+\delta_1+1)^n}x^2}\,\mathrm{erf}\!\left(\sqrt{k-(\gamma_2+\delta_2+1)^m}\,\eta\right)d\eta\right] \\ \times \dfrac{2}{\sqrt{(\gamma_1+\delta_1+1)^n\pi}}, \tag{87}$$

$$D_2 = \left[1 - \dfrac{\sqrt{\pi}}{2(\gamma_1+\delta_1+1)^n\sqrt{k-\frac{1}{(\gamma_1+\delta_1+1)^n}}}\int_0^\infty e^{-(\gamma_2+\delta_2+1)^m\eta^2}\,\mathrm{erf}\!\left(\sqrt{k-\tfrac{1}{(\gamma_1+\delta_1+1)^n}}\,\eta\right)d\eta\right] \\ \times \dfrac{2}{\sqrt{\pi}}(\gamma_1+\delta_1+1)^n\sqrt{(\gamma_2+\delta_2+1)^m}, \tag{88}$$

$$D_3 = \left[1 - \frac{\sqrt{\pi}}{2(\gamma_1+1)^n\sqrt{k-\frac{(\delta_2+1)^m}{(\gamma_1+1)^n}}} \int_0^\infty e^{-\frac{(\gamma_2+1)^m}{(\delta_1+1)^n}\eta^2} \operatorname{erf}\left(\sqrt{k-\frac{(\delta_2+1)^m}{(\gamma_1+1)^n}}\eta\right)d\eta\right]$$
$$\times \frac{2(\gamma_1+1)^n\sqrt{(\gamma_2+1)^m}}{\sqrt{(\gamma_1+\delta_1+1)^n\pi}}, \tag{89}$$

$$D_4 = \left[1 - \frac{\sqrt{\pi}}{2(\delta_1+1)^n\sqrt{k-\frac{(\gamma_2+1)^m}{(\delta_1+1)^n}}} \int_0^\infty e^{-\frac{(\delta_2+1)^m}{(\gamma_1+1)^n}\eta^2} \operatorname{erf}\left(\sqrt{k-\frac{(\gamma_2+1)^m}{(\delta_1+1)^n}}\eta\right)d\eta\right]$$
$$\times \frac{2(\delta_1+1)^n\sqrt{(\delta_2+1)^m}}{\sqrt{\pi(\gamma_1+1)^n}}, \tag{90}$$

$$D_5 = \left[1 - \frac{\sqrt{\pi}}{2\sqrt{k-(\gamma_2+1)^m}} \int_0^x e^{-\frac{(\delta_2+1)^m}{(\gamma_1+\delta_1+1)^n}\eta^2} \operatorname{erf}\left(\sqrt{k-(\delta_2+1)^m}\eta\right)d\eta\right]$$
$$\times \frac{2\sqrt{(\delta_2+1)^m}}{\sqrt{(\gamma_1+\delta_1+1)^n\pi}}, \tag{91}$$

$$D_6 = \left[1 - \frac{\sqrt{\pi}}{2(\gamma_1+\delta_1+1)^n\sqrt{k-\frac{(\delta_2+1)^m}{(\gamma_1+\delta_1+1)^n}}} \int_0^\infty e^{-(\gamma_2+1)^m\eta^2} \operatorname{erf}\left(\sqrt{k-\frac{(\delta_2+1)^m}{(\gamma_1+\delta_1+1)^n}}\eta\right)d\eta\right]$$
$$\times \frac{2}{\sqrt{\pi}}(\gamma_1+\delta_1+1)^n\sqrt{(\gamma_2+1)^m}, \tag{92}$$

$$D_7 = \left[1 - \frac{\sqrt{\pi}}{2(\delta_1+1)^n\sqrt{k-\frac{(\gamma_2+\delta_2+1)^m}{(\delta_1+1)^n}}} \int_0^x e^{-\frac{1}{(\gamma_1+1)^n}\eta^2} \operatorname{erf}\left(\sqrt{k-\frac{(\gamma_2+\delta_2+1)^m}{(\delta_1+1)^n}}\eta\right)d\eta\right]$$
$$\times \frac{2(\delta_1+1)^n}{\sqrt{(\gamma_1+1)^n\pi}}, \tag{93}$$

and

$$D_8 = \left[1 - \frac{\sqrt{\pi}}{2(\gamma_1+1)^n\sqrt{k-\frac{1}{(\gamma_1+1)^n}}} \int_0^x e^{-\frac{(\gamma_2+\delta_2+1)^m}{(\delta_1+1)^n}\eta^2} \operatorname{erf}\left(\sqrt{k-\frac{1}{(\gamma_1+1)^n}}\eta\right)d\eta\right]$$
$$\times \frac{2(\gamma_1+1)^n\sqrt{(\gamma_2+\delta_2+1)^m}}{\sqrt{(\delta_1+1)^n\pi}}. \tag{94}$$

5.2. *Pr. (4) – (6) with* $\beta(x) = e^{-kx^2}$, $k > 0$

$$\begin{cases} \frac{d}{dx}\left[(1+\delta_1 y+\gamma_1 y^2)^n \frac{dy}{dx}\right] + 2x(1+\delta_2 y+\gamma_2 y^2)^m \frac{dy}{dx} = \beta(x), \ 0 < x < \infty, \\ y(0) = 1, \ y(\infty) = 0, \end{cases} \tag{95}$$

where $\beta(x) = e^{-kx^2}$, $k > 0$,

Theorem 9. *The solution y of Pr. (95) can be expressed by*

$$y = 1 + \int_0^x \frac{1}{\Psi_1(\eta)} \exp\left(-2\int_0^\eta \frac{\xi\Psi_2(\xi)}{\Psi_1(\xi)}d\xi\right)\left[\int_0^\eta \beta(\xi)\exp\left(2\int_0^\xi \frac{t\Psi_2(t)}{\Psi_1(t)}dt\right)d\xi\right]d\eta$$
$$+ E\int_0^x \frac{1}{\Psi_1(\eta)}\exp\left(-2\int_0^\eta \frac{\xi\Psi_2(\xi)}{\Psi_1(\xi)}d\xi\right)d\eta, \tag{96}$$

where

$$E = -\frac{1 + \int_0^\infty \frac{1}{\Psi_1(x)} \exp\left(-2\int_0^x \frac{\zeta \Psi_2(\zeta)}{\Psi_1(\zeta)} d\zeta\right) \left[\int_0^x \beta(\zeta) \exp\left(2\int_0^\zeta \frac{t\Psi_2(t)}{\Psi_1(t)} dt\right) d\zeta\right] dx}{\int_0^\infty \frac{1}{\Psi_1(x)} \exp\left(-2\int_0^x \frac{\zeta \Psi_2(\zeta)}{\Psi_1(\zeta)} d\zeta\right) dx}. \quad (97)$$

Similarly, for the lower and upper bounds of the solution y of Pr. (95) for different values of $\delta_i > -1$ and $\gamma_i \geq 0$, $i = 1, 2$, the following theorem follows immediately by incorporating the inequalities (22)–(25) into (96).

Theorem 10. *If $y \in \mathbb{C}^2[0, \infty)$ is a solution of Pr. (95), then there are upper and lower bounds of the solution $y(x)$ such that*

$$v_1(x) \leq y \leq v_2(x) \text{ for } \delta_i \geq 0, \, i = 1, 2, \, 0 \leq x < +\infty, \quad (98)$$

$$v_3(x) \leq y \leq v_4(x) \text{ for } -1 < \delta_i < 0, \, i = 1, 2, \, 0 \leq x < +\infty, \quad (99)$$

$$v_5(x) \leq y \leq v_6(x) \text{ for } \delta_1 > 0, \, -1 < \delta_2 < 0, \, 0 \leq x < +\infty, \quad (100)$$

$$v_7(x) \leq y \leq v_8(x) \text{ for } -1 < \delta_1 < 0, \, \delta_2 > 0, \, 0 \leq x < +\infty, \quad (101)$$

where

$$\begin{cases}
v_1 = 1 + \frac{E\sqrt{(\gamma_1+\delta_1+1)^n \pi}}{2} \operatorname{erf}\left(\frac{x}{\sqrt{(\gamma_1+\delta_1+1)^n}}\right) \\
\quad + \frac{\sqrt{\pi}}{2(\gamma_1+\delta_1+1)^n \sqrt{k - \frac{1}{(\gamma_1+\delta_1+1)^n}}} \int_0^x e^{-(\gamma_2+\delta_2+1)^m \eta^2} \operatorname{erf}\left(\sqrt{k - \frac{1}{(\gamma_1+\delta_1+1)^n}} \eta\right) d\eta, \, k > \frac{1}{(\gamma_1+\delta_1+1)^n}, \\
v_2 = 1 + \frac{E\sqrt{\pi}}{2(\gamma_1+\delta_1+1)^n \sqrt{(\gamma_2+\delta_2+1)^m}} \operatorname{erf}\left(\sqrt{(\gamma_2+\delta_2+1)^m} x\right) \\
\quad + \frac{\sqrt{\pi}}{2\sqrt{k-(\gamma_2+\delta_2+1)^m}} \int_0^x e^{-\frac{1}{(\gamma_1+\delta_1+1)^n} x^2} \operatorname{erf}\left(\sqrt{k - (\gamma_2+\delta_2+1)^m} \eta\right) d\eta, \, k > (\gamma_2+\delta_2+1)^m, \\
v_3 = 1 + \frac{E\sqrt{\pi(\gamma_1+1)^n}}{2(\delta_1+1)^n \sqrt{(\delta_2+1)^m}} \operatorname{erf}\left(\frac{\sqrt{(\delta_2+1)^m}}{\sqrt{(\gamma_1+1)^n}} x\right) \\
\quad + \frac{\sqrt{\pi}}{2(\gamma_1+1)^n \sqrt{k - \frac{(\delta_2+1)^m}{(\gamma_1+1)^n}}} \int_0^x e^{-\frac{(\gamma_2+1)^m}{(\delta_1+1)^n} \eta^2} \operatorname{erf}\left(\sqrt{k - \frac{(\delta_2+1)^m}{(\gamma_1+1)^n}} \eta\right) d\eta, \, k > \frac{(\delta_2+1)^m}{(\gamma_1+1)^n}, \\
v_4 = 1 + \frac{E\sqrt{\pi(\delta_1+1)^n}}{2(\gamma_1+1)^n \sqrt{(\gamma_2+1)^m}} \operatorname{erf}\left(\frac{\sqrt{(\gamma_2+1)^m}}{\sqrt{(\delta_1+1)^n}} x\right) \\
\quad + \frac{\sqrt{\pi}}{2(\delta_1+1)^n \sqrt{k - \frac{(\gamma_2+1)^m}{(\delta_1+1)^n}}} \int_0^x e^{-\frac{(\delta_2+1)^m}{(\gamma_1+1)^n} \eta^2} \operatorname{erf}\left(\sqrt{k - \frac{(\gamma_2+1)^m}{(\delta_1+1)^n}} \eta\right) d\eta, \, k > \frac{(\gamma_2+1)^m}{(\delta_1+1)^n}, \\
v_5 = 1 + \frac{E\sqrt{(\gamma_1+\delta_1+1)^n \pi}}{2\sqrt{(\delta_2+1)^m}} \operatorname{erf}\left(\frac{\sqrt{(\delta_2+1)^m}}{\sqrt{(\gamma_1+\delta_1+1)^n}} x\right) \\
\quad + \frac{\sqrt{\pi}}{2(\gamma_1+\delta_1+1)^n \sqrt{k - \frac{(\delta_2+1)^m}{(\gamma_1+\delta_1+1)^n}}} \int_0^x e^{-(\gamma_2+1)^m \eta^2} \operatorname{erf}\left(\sqrt{k - \frac{(\delta_2+1)^m}{(\gamma_1+\delta_1+1)^n}} \eta\right) d\eta, \, k > \frac{(\delta_2+1)^m}{(\gamma_1+\delta_1+1)^n}, \\
v_6 = 1 + \frac{E\sqrt{\pi}}{2(\gamma_1+\delta_1+1)^n \sqrt{(\gamma_2+1)^m}} \operatorname{erf}\left(\sqrt{(\gamma_2+1)^m} x\right) \\
\quad + \frac{\sqrt{\pi}}{2\sqrt{k-(\gamma_2+1)^m}} \int_0^x e^{-\frac{(\delta_2+1)^m}{(\gamma_1+\delta_1+1)^n} \eta^2} \operatorname{erf}\left(\sqrt{k - (\delta_2+1)^m} \eta\right) d\eta, \, k > (\delta_2+1)^m, \\
v_7 = 1 + \frac{E\sqrt{(\gamma_1+1)^n \pi}}{2(\delta_1+1)^n} \operatorname{erf}\left(\frac{x}{\sqrt{(\gamma_1+1)^n}}\right) \\
\quad + \frac{\sqrt{\pi}}{2(\gamma_1+1)^n \sqrt{k - \frac{1}{(\gamma_1+1)^n}}} \int_0^x e^{-\frac{(\gamma_2+\delta_2+1)^m}{(\delta_1+1)^n} \eta^2} \operatorname{erf}\left(\sqrt{k - \frac{1}{(\gamma_1+1)^n}} \eta\right) d\eta, \, k > \frac{1}{(\gamma_1+1)^n}, \\
v_8 = 1 + \frac{E\sqrt{(\delta_1+1)^n \pi}}{2(\gamma_1+1)^n \sqrt{(\gamma_2+\delta_2+1)^m}} \operatorname{erf}\left(\frac{\sqrt{(\gamma_2+\delta_2+1)^m}}{\sqrt{(\delta_1+1)^n}} x\right) \\
\quad + \frac{\sqrt{\pi}}{2(\delta_1+1)^n \sqrt{k - \frac{(\gamma_2+\delta_2+1)^m}{(\delta_1+1)^n}}} \int_0^x e^{-\frac{1}{(\gamma_1+1)^n} \eta^2} \operatorname{erf}\left(\sqrt{k - \frac{(\gamma_2+\delta_2+1)^m}{(\delta_1+1)^n}} \eta\right) d\eta, \, k > \frac{(\gamma_2+\delta_2+1)^m}{(\delta_1+1)^n}.
\end{cases}$$

Further, the constant D satisfies

$$E_1 \leq E \leq E_2 \text{ for } \delta_i \geq 0, \, i = 1, 2, \tag{102}$$

$$E_3 \leq E \leq E_4 \text{ for } -1 < \delta_i < 0, \, i = 1, 2, \tag{103}$$

$$E_5 \leq E \leq E_6 \text{ for } \delta_1 > 0, \, -1 < \delta_2 < 0, \tag{104}$$

$$E_7 \leq E \leq E_8 \text{ for } -1 < \delta_1 < 0, \, \delta_2 > 0, \tag{105}$$

where

$$E_1 = -\left[1 + \frac{\sqrt{\pi}}{2\sqrt{k - (\gamma_2 + \delta_2 + 1)^m}} \int_0^\infty e^{-\frac{1}{(\gamma_1 + \delta_1 + 1)^n} x^2} \operatorname{erf}\left(\sqrt{k - (\gamma_2 + \delta_2 + 1)^m} \eta\right) d\eta\right]$$
$$\times \frac{2}{\sqrt{\pi}} (\gamma_1 + \delta_1 + 1)^n \sqrt{(\gamma_2 + \delta_2 + 1)^m}, \tag{106}$$

$$E_2 = -\left[1 + \frac{\sqrt{\pi}}{2(\gamma_1 + \delta_1 + 1)^n \sqrt{k - \frac{1}{(\gamma_1+\delta_1+1)^n}}} \int_0^\infty e^{-(\gamma_2+\delta_2+1)^m \eta^2} \operatorname{erf}\left(\sqrt{k - \frac{1}{(\gamma_1 + \delta_1 + 1)^n}} \eta\right) d\eta\right]$$
$$\times \frac{2}{\sqrt{(\gamma_1 + \delta_1 + 1)^n \pi}}, \tag{107}$$

$$E_3 = -\left[1 + \frac{\sqrt{\pi}}{2(\gamma_1 + 1)^n \sqrt{k - \frac{(\delta_2+1)^m}{(\gamma_1+1)^n}}} \int_0^\infty e^{-\frac{(\gamma_2+1)^m}{(\delta_1+1)^n} \eta^2} \operatorname{erf}\left(\sqrt{k - \frac{(\delta_2 + 1)^m}{(\gamma_1 + 1)^n}} \eta\right) d\eta\right]$$
$$\times \frac{2(\delta_1 + 1)^n \sqrt{(\delta_2 + 1)^m}}{\sqrt{\pi (\gamma_1 + 1)^n}}, \tag{108}$$

$$E_4 = -\left[1 + \frac{\sqrt{\pi}}{2(\delta_1 + 1)^n \sqrt{k - \frac{(\gamma_2+1)^m}{(\delta_1+1)^n}}} \int_0^\infty e^{-\frac{(\delta_2+1)^m}{(\gamma_1+1)^n} \eta^2} \operatorname{erf}\left(\sqrt{k - \frac{(\gamma_2 + 1)^m}{(\delta_1 + 1)^n}} \eta\right) d\eta\right]$$
$$\times \frac{2(\gamma_1 + 1)^n \sqrt{(\gamma_2 + 1)^m}}{\sqrt{(\gamma_1 + \delta_1 + 1)^n \pi}}, \tag{109}$$

$$E_5 = -\left[1 + \frac{\sqrt{\pi}}{2\sqrt{k - (\gamma_2 + 1)^m}} \int_0^x e^{-\frac{(\delta_2+1)^m}{(\gamma_1+\delta_1+1)^n} \eta^2} \operatorname{erf}\left(\sqrt{k - (\delta_2 + 1)^m} \eta\right) d\eta\right]$$
$$\times \frac{2}{\sqrt{\pi}} (\gamma_1 + \delta_1 + 1)^n \sqrt{(\gamma_2 + 1)^m}, \tag{110}$$

$$E_6 = -\left[1 + \frac{\sqrt{\pi}}{2(\gamma_1 + \delta_1 + 1)^n \sqrt{k - \frac{(\delta_2+1)^m}{(\gamma_1+\delta_1+1)^n}}} \int_0^\infty e^{-(\gamma_2+1)^m \eta^2} \operatorname{erf}\left(\sqrt{k - \frac{(\delta_2 + 1)^m}{(\gamma_1 + \delta_1 + 1)^n}} \eta\right) d\eta\right]$$
$$\times \frac{2\sqrt{(\delta_2 + 1)^m}}{\sqrt{(\gamma_1 + \delta_1 + 1)^n \pi}}, \tag{111}$$

$$E_7 = -\left[1 + \frac{\sqrt{\pi}}{2(\delta_1 + 1)^n \sqrt{k - \frac{(\gamma_2+\delta_2+1)^m}{(\delta_1+1)^n}}} \int_0^x e^{-\frac{1}{(\gamma_1+1)^n} \eta^2} \operatorname{erf}\left(\sqrt{k - \frac{(\gamma_2 + \delta_2 + 1)^m}{(\delta_1 + 1)^n}} \eta\right) d\eta\right]$$
$$\times \frac{2(\gamma_1 + 1)^n \sqrt{(\gamma_2 + \delta_2 + 1)^m}}{\sqrt{(\delta_1 + 1)^n \pi}} \tag{112}$$

and

$$E_8 = -\left[1 + \frac{\sqrt{\pi}}{2(\gamma_1+1)^n \sqrt{k - \frac{1}{(\gamma_1+1)^n}}} \int_0^x e^{-\frac{(\gamma_2+\delta_2+1)^m}{(\delta_1+1)^n}\eta^2} \operatorname{erf}\left(\sqrt{k - \frac{1}{(\gamma_1+1)^n}}\eta\right) d\eta\right]$$
$$\times \frac{2(\delta_1+1)^n}{\sqrt{(\gamma_1+1)^n \pi}}. \tag{113}$$

6. Numerical Results

6.1. Homogeneous Case

We used the capabilities of the robust Maple software for the rigorous numerical validation and developed an intuitively navigable program, featuring straightforward statements tailored to address boundary value problems (BVPs.).

Our program, based on the Maple software, possesses the capability to identify the nature of the problem at hand and autonomously select the most appropriate algorithm for its resolution.

In particular, we implemented the mid-defer method, an advanced midpoint technique that incorporates enhancement schemes. Among these enhancement schemes, the Richardson extrapolation method emerged as the fastest choice [41–43], while deferred corrections excelled in handling complex problems due to their lower memory usage. Furthermore, this method exhibited proficiency in addressing end-point singularities, a challenge that the trapezoidal scheme often struggles with.

The utilization of the continuation method is of paramount importance in minimizing global error while determining the optimal number of maximum mesh points. This numerical technique has been rigorously tested and proven effective in previous studies [44,45].

In Figure 1, we depict a comparative analysis involving the numerical solution and the lower solution for the first scenario and different values of $(n = 1, m = 2)$ and $(n = 2, m = 1)$, where $\delta_i \geq 0$, plotted against the independent variable x. This evaluation was conducted for a specific set of parameters: $\delta_1 = 0.1; \delta_2 = 0.5; \gamma_1 = 0.5; \gamma_2 = 1$, and the constant C was specifically assigned a value of $C = 4$ for both cases.

The lower bound, which was chosen to conform to the condition $C_1 \leq C \leq C_2$ in this particular case, exhibited a remarkable alignment with the numerical solution.

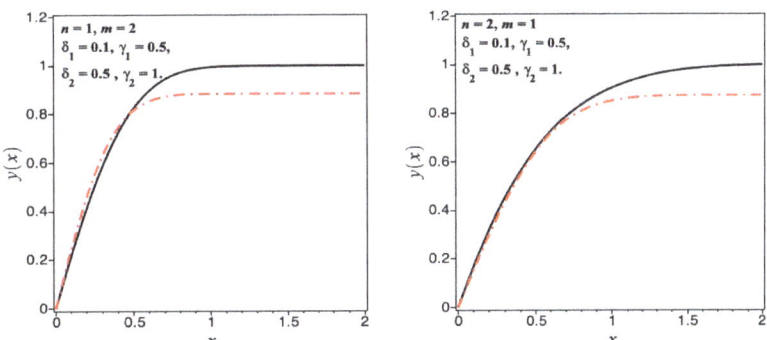

Figure 1. The numerical solution and the lower bound of Pr. (4)–(5) for a specific parameter set, namely, $\delta_1 = 0.1; \delta_2 = 0.5; \gamma_1 = 0.5; \gamma_2 = 1$, and with the constant C set to $C = 4$. Left panel $n = 1, m = 2$. Right panel $n = 2, m = 1$. The solid line corresponds to the numerical solution and the dash-dotted line corresponds to the lower bound.

Figure 2 illustrates a comparative analysis involving the numerical solution and the lower solution $y_3(x)$ for two distinct scenarios: one with $(n = 1, m = 2)$ and another with $(n = 2, m = 1)$, all under the constraint that $-1 < \delta_i < 0$. The plotted data are presented against the independent variable x.

This investigation utilized a specific parameter set: $\delta_1 = -0.1, \delta_2 = -0.5, \gamma_1 = 0.5, \gamma_2 = 1$. In both cases, a constant value of C was employed, with C taking the values 2.6 and 3.2, respectively. It is noteworthy to highlight that the lower bound $y_3(x)$ was in good accordance with the numerical solution for small values of the independent variable, i.e., $x \leq 1$ when the constant C was thoughtfully chosen to adhere to the condition $C_3 \leq C \leq C_4$ within this context. However, for larger values of $x \geq 1$, the numerical results indicate a rapid convergence of the solution in the first case.

We additionally present a plot of the lower bound, denoted by

$$y_1(x) = \frac{C\sqrt{\pi}}{2(\gamma_1 + \delta_1 + 1)^n \sqrt{(\gamma_2 + \delta_2 + 1)^m}} \operatorname{erf}\left(\sqrt{(\gamma_2 + \delta_2 + 1)^m} x\right),$$

(indicated by the dashed blue line), which was carefully selected with an appropriate constant value, C, ensuring that $y_1(\infty) \simeq 1$. The selected lower bound, i.e., $y_1(x)$ to satisfy the condition $y_1(\infty) \simeq 1$ in this context, displayed a striking agreement with the numerical solution in the second case and can be considered as a good approximation.

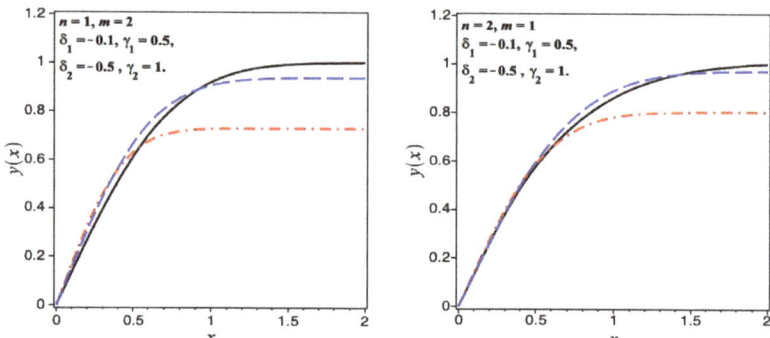

Figure 2. The numerical solution and the lower bound of Pr. (4)–(5) for a specific parameter set, namely, $\delta_1 = -0.1; \delta_2 = -0.5; \gamma_1 = 0.5; \gamma_2 = 1$. Left panel $n = 1, m = 2$, and $C = 2.6$. Right panel $n = 2, m = 1$, and $C = 3.2$. The solid line corresponds to the numerical solution and the dash-dotted line corresponds to the lower bound. The dashed blue line represents the lower bound $y_1(x)$ with $C \approx 2.222$, which can be chosen from $y_1(\infty) \simeq 1$.

Figure 3 presents a comparative examination involving the numerical solution and lower solution $y_5(x)$ for two distinctive scenarios: one characterized by $(n = 1, m = 2)$ and the other by $(n = 2, m = 1)$. These scenarios were subject to specific constraints: $-1 < \delta_2 < 0$ and $\delta_1 > 0$. The plotted data are displayed as a function of the independent variable x.

We employed a parameter configuration for this analysis: $\delta_1 = 0.1; \delta_2 = -0.5; \gamma_1 = 0.5; \gamma_2 = 1$. Notably, both cases were governed by constant values of $C = 2.5$ and $C = 3.5$, respectively.

It is worth emphasizing that the lower boundary, carefully chosen to adhere to the condition $C_5 \leq C \leq C_6$ in this context, exhibited a remarkable alignment with the numerical solution for small values of the independent variable $x \lesssim 1$.

We include a graph showing the lower bound, denoted by $y_1(x)$ (represented by the dashed blue line). This approximate solution was carefully chosen with a constant value, C, to ensure that $y_1(\infty) \simeq 1$. It is worth noting that the chosen approximate solution, i.e., $y_1(x)$, satisfies the condition $y_1(\infty) \simeq 1$ in this context, and it showed an excellent agreement with the numerical solution in the third case.

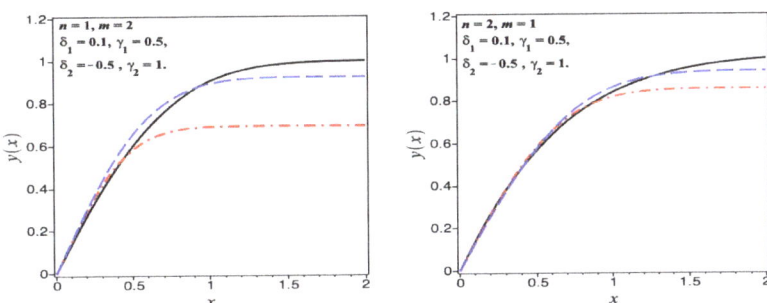

Figure 3. The numerical solution and the lower bound of Pr. (4)–(5) for a specific parameter set, namely, $\delta_1 = 0.1; \delta_2 = -0.5; \gamma_1 = 0.5; \gamma_2 = 1$. Left panel $n = 1, m = 2$, and $C = 2.5$. Right panel $n = 2, m = 1$, and $C = 3.5$. The solid line corresponds to the numerical solution and the dash-dotted line corresponds to the lower bound. The dashed blue line represents the lower bound $y_1(x)$, which can be chosen from $y_1(\infty) \simeq 1$.

Figure 4 shows a comparative analysis involving the numerical solution and lower solution $y_7(x)$ for two distinct scenarios: one characterized by $(n = 1, m = 2)$ and the other by $(n = 2, m = 1)$. These scenarios were subject to specific constraints: $\delta_2 > 0$ and $-1 < \delta_1 < 0$. The data plotted are represented as a function of the independent variable x.

In this analysis, we utilized a parameter setup characterized by $\delta_1 = 0.1; \delta_2 = -0.5; \gamma_1 = 0.5; \gamma_2 = 1$. It is important to note that the first case had a constant of $C = 3.7$, while the second case had $C = 3.9$.

It is noteworthy that the lower bound, thoughtfully chosen to satisfy the condition $C_7 \leq C \leq C_8$ in this context, exhibited a remarkable alignment with the numerical solution for small values of $x \lesssim 1$.

We, again, include a graph that clearly shows the lower bound, denoted by $y_1(x)$, which is represented by the dashed blue line. This approximate solution was meticulously chosen with a constant value, C, to ensure that $y_1(\infty) \simeq 1$. It is crucial to note that the selected approximate solution, i.e., $y_1(x)$, satisfied the condition $y_1(\infty) \simeq 1$ in this context, and it exhibited an outstanding agreement with the numerical solution in the fourth case.

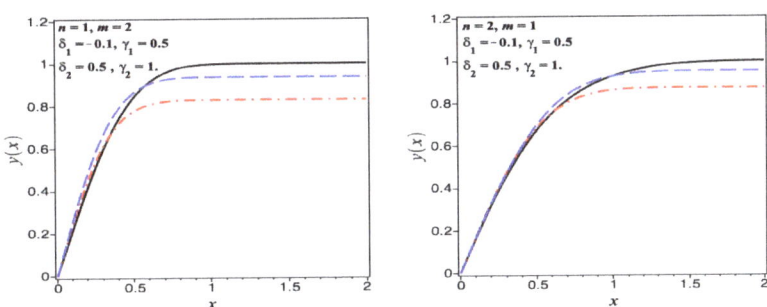

Figure 4. The numerical solution and the lower bound of Pr. (4)–(5) for a specific parameter set, namely, $\delta_1 = -0.1; \delta_2 = 0.5; \gamma_1 = 0.5; \gamma_2 = 1$ and $C = 3.7$. Left panel $n = 1, m = 2$ and $C = 3.7$. Right panel $n = 2, m = 1$, and $C = 3.9$. The solid line corresponds to the numerical solution and the dash-dotted line corresponds to the lower bound. The dashed blue line represents the lower bound $y_1(x)$, which can be chosen from $y_1(\infty) \simeq 1$.

Based on the previous results, an interesting observation can be made regarding the numerical and approximated solutions. For small values of the independent variable $x \lesssim 1$, the numerical solution and the approximated solution, obtained using the lower bound with a carefully chosen constant C, exhibited perfect agreement. However, for large values

($x \gg 1$), a slight deviation between the solutions was noticeable. Nevertheless, it is worth noting that the numerical solutions converged rapidly to unity. Furthermore, the first lower-bound solution $y_1(x)$ aligned well with the numerical solution when the constant C was suitably chosen such that $y_1(\infty) \simeq 1$. This approximated solution can be considered the best approximation and called the limit superior to the lower bounds.

6.2. Nonhomogeneous Case

Now, we consider the nonhomogeneous Pr. (4)–(5) in the fourth case with the source term $\beta(x) = e^{-kx^2}$, where $k > 0$. We restricted our exploration to two cases, i.e., $\delta_i > 0$ and $-1 < \delta_i < 0$.

Figure 5 shows a comparative analysis involving the numerical solution and lower solution $y_7(x)$ for two distinct scenarios: one characterized by ($n = 1, m = 2$) and the other by ($n = 2, m = 1$). These scenarios were subject to specific constraints: $\delta_2 > 0$ and $\delta_1 > 0$. The data plotted are represented as a function of the independent variable x.

In this analysis, we utilized a parameter setup characterized by $\delta_1 = 0.1; \delta_2 = 0.5; \gamma_1 = 0.5; \gamma_2 = 1$. It is important to note that both cases had a constant of $D = 3.9$, and $k = 6.5$ such that $k \geqslant \sup(k_1, k_2)$, where $k_1 = \frac{1}{(\gamma_1+\delta_1+1)^n}$ and $k_2 = (\gamma_2 + \delta_2 + 1)^m$.

For $x \lesssim 1$, the numerical solution aligned remarkably well with the lower bound $w_1(x)$, where D was chosen to satisfy $D_1 \leq D \leq D_2$.

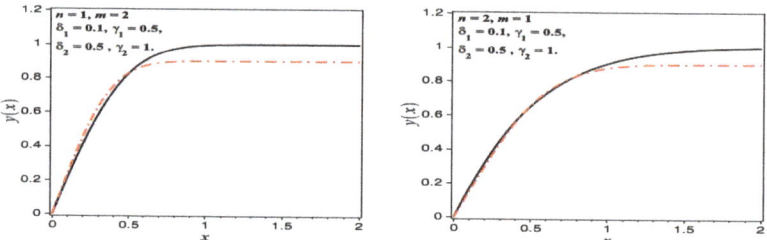

Figure 5. The numerical solution and the lower bound of Pr. (4)–(5) and $\beta(x) = e^{-kx^2}$ for a specific parameter set, namely, $\delta_1 = 0.1; \delta_2 = 0.5; \gamma_1 = 0.5; \gamma_2 = 1$. Left panel $n = 1, m = 2$. Right panel $n = 2, m = 1$. The constants D and k were chosen to be $D = 3.9$ and $k = 6.25$ for both cases. The solid line corresponds to the numerical solution and the dash-dotted line corresponds to the lower bound $w_1(x)$.

Figure 6 displays a comparison between the numerical solution and the lower solution $w_3(x)$ for two different situations. One scenario is characterized by ($n = 1, m = 2$) while the other is characterized by ($n = 2, m = 1$). Both scenarios had specific constraints: $-1 < \delta_2 < 0$ and $-1 < \delta_1 < 0$. The data plotted are a function of the independent variable x.

In our analysis, we used the following parameter setup: $\delta_1 = -0.1, \delta_2 = -0.5, \gamma_1 = 0.5$, and $\gamma_2 = 1$. It is worth noting that both cases had a constant of $D = 1.9$ and $D = 3.9$, respectively. The constant k was chosen to be $k = 6.5$ such that $k \geqslant \sup(k_3, k_4)$, where $k_3 = \frac{(\delta_2+1)^m}{(\gamma_1+1)^n}$ and $k_2 = \frac{(\gamma_2+1)^m}{(\delta_1+1)^n}$. When $x \lesssim 1$, the numerical solution was in good agreement with the lower bound $w_3(x)$. We chose D to satisfy $D_3 \leq D \leq D_4$. To make things clearer, we include a graph that shows the lower bound, represented by the dashed blue line and denoted as

$$w_1(x) = \frac{D\sqrt{\pi}}{2(\gamma_1+\delta_1+1)^n \sqrt{(\gamma_2+\delta_2+1)^m}} \mathrm{erf}\left(\sqrt{(\gamma_2+\delta_2+1)^m}\, x\right)$$

$$+ \frac{\sqrt{\pi}}{2(\gamma_1+\delta_1+1)^n \sqrt{k - \frac{1}{(\gamma_1+\delta_1+1)^n}}} \int_0^x e^{-(\gamma_2+\delta_2+1)^m \eta^2} \mathrm{erf}\left(\sqrt{k - \frac{1}{(\gamma_1+\delta_1+1)^n}}\,\eta\right) d\eta,$$

with $k > \frac{1}{(\gamma_1+\delta_1+1)^n}$.

We carefully selected this approximate solution to ensure that $w_1(\infty) \simeq 1$, using a constant value of D. It is important to note that the chosen solution, $w_1(x)$, closely matched the numerical solution.

Finally, we explore the nonhomogeneous problem (4)–(6), in addition to the source term $\beta(x) = e^{-kx^2}$, where $k > 0$. We limited our analysis to two cases, i.e., $\delta_i > 0$ and $-1 < \delta_i < 0$.

Figure 7 displays a comparison between the numerical solution and the lower solution $v_1(x), v_3(x)$ for two different situations, respectively. The first scenario was characterized by $\delta_i > 0$, while the second was characterized by $-1 < \delta_i < 0$. Both scenarios had specific constants: $n = 1, m = 2$. The data plotted are a function of the independent variable x. The dashed blue line in the right panel represents the good approximation of the solution $v_1(x)$ such that $v_1(x) \approx 1$.

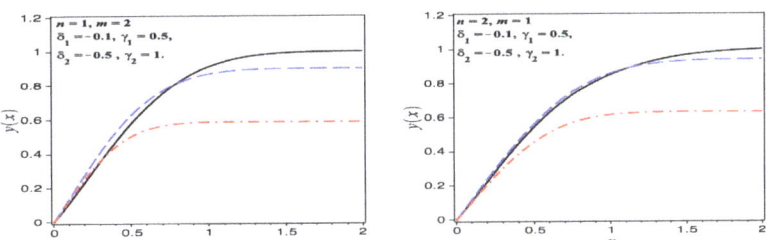

Figure 6. The numerical solution and the lower bound for boundary problem (4) with boundary conditions (5) and $\beta(x) = e^{-kx^2}$ for a specific parameter set, namely, $\delta_1 = 0.1; \delta_2 = 0.5; \gamma_1 = 0.5; \gamma_2 = 1$. Left panel $n = 1, m = 2$ and $D = 1.9$. Right panel $n = 2, m = 1$ and $D = 3.9$. The constant k was chosen to be $k = 6.25$ for both cases. The solid line corresponds to the numerical solution and the dash-dotted line corresponds to the lower bound $w_3(x)$. The dashed blue line represents the approximate solution $w_1(x)$ with the suitable choice of the constant D such that $w_1(x) \approx 1$. The dashed blue line represents the lower bound $w_1(x)$ with $w_1(\infty) \simeq 1$.

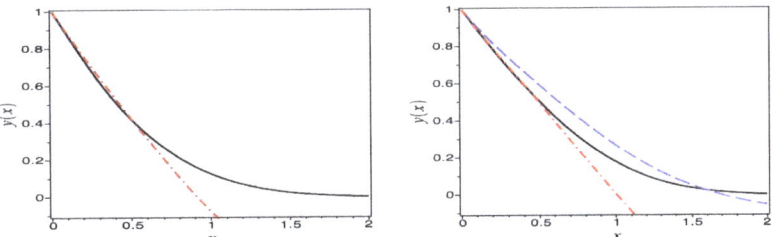

Figure 7. The numerical solution and the lower bound for boundary problem (4) with boundary conditions (6) and $\beta(x) = e^{-kx^2}$ for a specific parameter set, namely, $\delta_1 = 0.1; \delta_2 = 0.5; \gamma_1 = 0.5; \gamma_2 = 1$ (left panel) and $\delta_1 = -0.1; \delta_2 = -0.5; \gamma_1 = 0.5; \gamma_2 = 1$ (right panel). In both cases $n = 1, m = 2$. The constants E and k were chosen to be $E = -1$. and $k = 6.25$ for both cases. The solid line corresponds to the numerical solution and the dash-dotted line corresponds to the corresponding lower bound $v_1(x), v_3(x)$, respectively. The dashed blue line in the right panel represents the good approximation that is chosen as $v_1(x)$ such that $n_1(x) \approx 1$.

Throughout the previous instances, solely the lower bounds exhibited a notable approximation to the numerical solution. We omitted the upper bounds due to their lack of this advantageous alignment. This outcome aligned with our expectations as the upper bounds were characterized by functions displaying exponential growth.

However, justifying the selection of initial constants (C and D) in approximate solutions for homogeneous and nonhomogeneous equations to ensure their alignment with numerical solutions can be approached using various methods. Initially, confirming that the initial or boundary conditions specified in the approximate solutions correspond with those utilized in the numerical solutions is essential. Subsequently, adjusting the constants C and D is necessary to meet these conditions. Additionally, conducting an error analysis between the analytical solution (using initial constants C and D) and the numerical solution is crucial. The aim here is to minimize the error by adjusting the values of C and D, striving for the closest agreement between both solutions. Moreover, verifying that the assumptions and constraints utilized in deriving the approximate solutions are consistent with those inherent in the numerical method is vital. Adjusting C and D accordingly helps maintain coherence between the models. These aspects were all considered in our analysis and the selection of constants adhered to these principles.

7. Conclusions

The Stefan problem with nonlinear thermal conductivity and specific heat properties was thoroughly explored. This study employed lower- and upper-bound techniques to establish the existence and uniqueness of the theorem, addressing both homogeneous and nonhomogeneous scenarios. Additionally, a detailed numerical analysis was conducted, yielding a highly accurate approximation solution. Moreover, the alignment between the lower bound and the numerical solution, achieved through a suitable selection of the constant, confirms the validity of the chosen bounding techniques. This agreement not only validates the reliability of these techniques in delineating the system's response but also offers valuable insights into the behavior of the solution to the problem. Additionally, it acts as a confirmation of the efficacy of the employed analytical methods. Such methodologies pave the path for the investigation of analogous challenges in forthcoming research endeavors. Understanding and interpreting solutions to the nonclassical Stefan problem holds paramount significance in material design, thermal management, and process optimization—making it an essential aspect across the scientific, engineering, and technological domains.

Author Contributions: Conceptualization, A.K., L.B. and S.B.; methodology, A.K., L.B. and S.B.; software, S.B.; validation, A.K., L.B. and S.B.; formal analysis, A.K., L.B. and S.B.; investigation, A.K., L.B. and S.B.; writing original draft preparation, A.K., L.B. and S.B.; writing review and editing, A.K., L.B. and S.B. All authors have read and agreed to the published version of the manuscript.

Funding: This work was supported and funded by the Deanship of Scientific Research at Imam Mohammad Ibn Saud Islamic University (IMSIU) (grant number IMSIU-RG23018).

Institutional Review Board Statement: Not applicable.

Informed Consent Statement: Not applicable.

Data Availability Statement: This paper focuses on theoretical analysis and does not involve experiments and data.

Acknowledgments: The authors would like to thank the support of the Deanship of Scientific Research at Imam Mohammad Ibn Saud Islamic University (IMSIU) (grant number IMSIU-RG23018).

Conflicts of Interest: The authors declare no conflict of interest.

References

1. Cho, S.H.; Sunderland, J.E. Phase Change Problems With Temperature-Dependent Thermal Conductivity. *J. Heat Transf.* **1974**, *96*, 214–217. [CrossRef]
2. Oliver, D.; Sunderland, J. A phase change problem with temperature-dependent thermal conductivity and specific heat. *Int. J. Heat Mass Transf.* **1987**, *30*, 2657–2661. [CrossRef]
3. Ceretani, A.N.; Salva, N.N.; Tarzia, D.A. Existence and uniqueness of the modified error function. *Appl. Math. Lett.* **2017**, *70*, 14–17. [CrossRef]
4. Bougouffa, S.; Khanfer, A.; Bougoffa, L. On the approximation of the modified error function. *Math. Methods Appl. Sci.* **2022**, *46*, 11657–11665. [CrossRef]

5. Khanfer, A.; Bougoffa, L. A Stefan problem with nonlinear thermal conductivity. *Math. Methods Appl. Sci.* **2022**, *46*, 4602–4611. [CrossRef]
6. Briozzo, A.C.; Tarzia, D.A. Existence, Uniqueness and an Explicit Solution for a One-Phase Stefan Problem for a Non-classical Heat Equation, Free Boundary Problems. *Int. Ser. Numer. Math.* **2006**, *154*, 117–124.
7. Bougoffa, L. A note on the existence and uniqueness solutions of the modified error function. *Math. Methods Appl. Sci.* **2018**, *41*, 5526–5534. [CrossRef]
8. Bougoffa, L.; Rach, R.; Mennouni, A. On the existence, uniqueness, and new analytic approximate solution of the modified error function in two-phase Stefan problems. *Math. Methods Appl. Sci.* **2021**, *44*, 10948–10956. [CrossRef]
9. Zhou, Y.; Xia, L.-J. Exact solution for Stefan problem with general power-type latent heat using Kummer function. *Int. J. Heat Mass Transf.* **2015**, *84*, 114–118. [CrossRef]
10. Kumar, A.; Singh, A.K.; Rajeev A moving boundary problem with variable specific heat and thermal conductivity. *J. King Saud Univ.-Sci.* **2020**, *32*, 384–389. [CrossRef]
11. Chen, X.; Lou, B.; Zhou, M.; Giletti, T. Long time behavior of solutions of a reaction-diffusion equation on unbounded intervals with Robin boundary conditions. *Ann. Inst. H. Poincare Anal. non lin.* **2016**, *33*, 67–92. [CrossRef]
12. Ribera, H.; Myers, T.G. A mathematical model for nanoparticle melting with size-dependent latent heat and melt temperature. Microfluid. *Nanofluidics* **2016**, *20*, 147. [CrossRef]
13. Font, F.; Myers, T.G.; Mitchell, S.L. A mathematical model for nanoparticle melting with density change. *Microfluid. Nanofluid.* **2015**, *18*, 233–243. [CrossRef]
14. Briozzo, A.C.; Natale, M.F. One-phase Stefan problem with temperature-dependent thermal conductivity and a boundary condition of Robin type. *J. Appl. Anal.* **2015**, *21*, 89–97. [CrossRef]
15. Bougoffa, L.; Khanfer, A. On the solutions of a phase change problem with temperature-dependent thermal conductivity and specific heat. *Results Phys.* **2020**, *19*, 103646. [CrossRef]
16. Voller, V.; Swenson, J.; Paola, C. An analytical solution for a Stefan problem with variable latent heat. *Int. J. Heat Mass Transf.* **2004**, *47*, 5387–5390. [CrossRef]
17. Beasley, J.D. Thermal conductivities of some novel nonlinear optical materials. *Appl. Opt.* **1994**, *33*, 1000–1003. [CrossRef]
18. Aggarwal, R.L.; Fan, T.Y. Thermal diffusivity, specific heat, thermal conductivity, coefficient of thermal expansion, and refractive-index change with temperature in $AgGaSe_2$. *Appl. Opt.* **2005**, *44*, 2673–2677. [CrossRef]
19. Henager, C.H.; Pawlewicz, W.T. Thermal conductivities of thin, sputtered optical films. *Appl. Opt.* **1993**, *32*, 91. [CrossRef]
20. de Azevedo, A.M.; dos Santos Magalhães, E.; da Silva, R.G.D. A comparison between nonlinear and constant thermal properties approaches to estimate the temperature in LASER welding simulation. *Case Stud. Therm. Eng.* **2022**, *35*, 102135. [CrossRef]
21. Xiao, Y.; Wu, H. An explicit coupled method of FEM and meshless particle method for simulating transient heat transfer process of friction stir welding. *Math. Probl Eng.* **2020**, *2020*, 2574127. [CrossRef]
22. Brizes, E.; Jaskowiak, J.; Abke, T.; Ghassemi-Armaki, H.; Ramirez, A.J. Evaluation of heat transfer within numerical models of resistance spot welding using high-speed thermography. *J. Mater. Process. Technol.* **1985**, *297*, 117276. [CrossRef]
23. Gladkov, S.O.; Bogdanova, S.B. On the theory of nonlinear thermal conductivity. *Tech. Phys.* **2016**, *61*, 157–164. [CrossRef]
24. Sahoo, R.; Sarangi, S. Effect of temperature-dependent specific heat of the working fluid on the performance of cryogenic regenerators. *Cryogenics* **1985**, *25*, 583–590. [CrossRef]
25. Tomeczek, J.; Palugniok, H. Specific heat capacity and enthalpy of coal pyrolysis at elevated temperatures. *Fuel* **1996**, *75*, 1089–1093. [CrossRef]
26. Saxena, S.K. Earth mineralogical model: Gibbs free energy minimization computation in the system MgO-FeO-SiO_2. *Geochim. Cosmochim. Acta* **1996**, *60*, 2379–2395. [CrossRef]
27. Merrick, D. Mathematical models of the thermal decomposition of coal: 2. Specific heats and heats of reaction. *Fuel* **1983**, *62*, 540–546. [CrossRef]
28. Hanrot, F.; Ablitzer, D.; Houzelot, J.; Dirand, M. Experimental measurement of the true specific heat capacity of coal and semicoke during carbonization. *Fuel* **1994**, *73*, 305–309. [CrossRef]
29. Haemmerich, D.; dos Santos, I.; Schutt, D.J.; Webster, J.G.; Mahvi, D.M. In vitro measurements of temperature-dependent specific heat of liver tissue. *Med. Eng. Phys.* **2006**, *28*, 194–197. [CrossRef]
30. Ghosh, A.; McSween, H.Y. Temperature dependence of specific heat capacity and its effect on asteroid thermal models. *Mefeorifrcs Planet. Sci.* **1999**, *34*, 121–127. [CrossRef]
31. Scott, E.P. An Analytical Solution and Sensitivity Study of Sublimation-Dehydration Within a Porous Medium With Volumetric Heating. *J. Heat Transf.* **1994**, *116*, 686–693. [CrossRef]
32. Menaldi, J.L.; Tarzia, D.A. Generalized Lamé–Clapeyron solution for a one-phase source Stefan problem. *Comput. Appl. Math.* **1993**, *12*, 123–142.
33. Briozzo, A.C.; Natale, M.F.; Tarzia, D.A. Explicit solutions for a two-phase unidimensional Lamé–Clapeyron–Stefan problem with source terms in both phases. *J. Math. Anal. Appl.* **2007**, *329*, 145–162. [CrossRef]
34. Briozzo, A.C.; Tarzia, D.A. A Stefan problem for a non-classical heat equation with a convective condition. *Appl. Math. Comput.* **2010**, *217*, 4051–4060. [CrossRef]
35. Briozzo, A.C.; Tarzia, D.A. Exact Solutions for Nonclassical Stefan Problems. *Int. J. Differ. Equ.* **2010**, *2010*, 868059. [CrossRef]

36. Briozzo, A.C.; Natale, M.F. Two Stefan problems for a non-classical heat equation with nonlinear thermal coefficients. *Differ. Integral Equ.* **2014**, *27*, 1187–1202. [CrossRef]
37. Briozzo, A.C.; Natale, M.F. Non-classical Stefan problem with nonlinear thermal coefficients and a Robin boundary condition. *Nonlinear Anal. Real World Appl.* **2019**, *49*, 159–168. [CrossRef]
38. Bollati, J.; Natale, M.F.; Semitiel, J.A.; Tarzia, D.A. Exact solution for non-classical one-phase Stefan problem with variable thermal coefficients and two different heat source terms. *Comput. Appl. Math.* **2022**, *41*, 375. [CrossRef]
39. Bougoffa, L.; Bougouffa, S.; Khanfer, A. An Analysis of the One-Phase Stefan Problem with Variable Thermal Coefficients of Order p. *Axioms* **2023**, *12*, 497. [CrossRef]
40. Willett, D. Uniqueness for second order nonlinear boundary value problems with applications to almost periodic solutions. *Ann. Mat. Pura Appl.* **1969**, *81*, 77–92. [CrossRef]
41. Quarteroni, A.; Sacco, R.; Saleri, F. *Numerical Mathematics*; Springer Science & Business Media: Berlin/Heidelberg, Germany, 2007.
42. Hamming, R. *Numerical Methods for Scientists and Engineers*; Courier Corporation: Chelmsford, MA, USA, 1987.
43. Ascher, U.; Petzold, L. *Computer Methods for Ordinary Differential Equations and Differential-Algebraic Equations*; SIAM: Philadelphia, PA, USA, 1998.
44. Bougoffa, L.; Bougouffa, S.; Khanfer, A. Generalized Thomas-Fermi equation: existence, uniqueness, and analytic approximation solutions. *AIMS Math.* **2023**, *8*, 10529–10546. [CrossRef]
45. Khanfer, A.; Bougoffa, L.; Bougouffa, S. Analytic Approximate Solution of the Extended Blasius Equation with Temperature-Dependent Viscosity. *J. Nonlinear Math. Phys.* **2023**, *30*, 287–302. [CrossRef]

Disclaimer/Publisher's Note: The statements, opinions and data contained in all publications are solely those of the individual author(s) and contributor(s) and not of MDPI and/or the editor(s). MDPI and/or the editor(s) disclaim responsibility for any injury to people or property resulting from any ideas, methods, instructions or products referred to in the content.

MDPI AG
Grosspeteranlage 5
4052 Basel
Switzerland
Tel.: +41 61 683 77 34

Axioms Editorial Office
E-mail: axioms@mdpi.com
www.mdpi.com/journal/axioms

Disclaimer/Publisher's Note: The statements, opinions and data contained in all publications are solely those of the individual author(s) and contributor(s) and not of MDPI and/or the editor(s). MDPI and/or the editor(s) disclaim responsibility for any injury to people or property resulting from any ideas, methods, instructions or products referred to in the content.